Hernando
de Soto

Books by David Ewing Duncan

Pedaling the Ends of the Earth (1985)
From Cape to Cairo: An African Odyssey (1989)
Residents: The Perils and Promise of Educating Young Doctors (1996)

Hernando de Soto

A Savage Quest in the Americas

David Ewing Duncan

Crown Publishers, Inc.

New York

Published by Crown Publishers, Inc., 201 East 50th Street, New York, New York 10022.
Member of the Crown Publishing Group.

Random House, Inc. New York, Toronto, London, Sydney, Auckland

CROWN is a trademark of Crown Publishers, Inc.

Printed in the United States of America

Design by Lenny Henderson

Library of Congress Cataloging-in-Publication Data

Duncan, David Ewing.
    Hernando de Soto : a savage quest in the Americas / by David Ewing Duncan.
      p. cm.
    Includes bibliographical references and index.
    1. Soto, Hernando de, ca. 1500–1542. 2. Explorers—America—Biography.
3. Explorers—Spain—Biography. 4. Southern States—Discovery and exploration—Spanish.
I. Title.
    E125.S7D86 1995
    970.01´6´092—dc20
    [B]   95-663
                                              CIP

ISBN 0-517-58222-8

10 9 8 7 6 5 4 3 2

In Memoriam

To *Evelyn Duncan Brown*

who taught me a reverence for history,
and for matters of the soul

CONTENTS

ILLUSTRATIONS

A NOTE ON REFERENCES

Sources are located in the bibliography. Reference notes can be found at the end of the narrative, located by page numbers and an identifying phrase quoted from the text. A "^" mark in the text refers to an informational note.

Ved de cuán poco valor
son las cosas tras que andamos
y corremos;
que, en este mundo traidor,
aun primero que muramos
las perdemos
de ellas deshace le edad,
de ellas casos desastrodos
que acaecen,
de ellas, por su calidad,
en los más altos estados
desfallecen.

See of how little value
are the things we run after
and pursue;
for in this deceptive world,
even before we die
we lose them:
Some are decayed by age,
some by disasters
that occur,
some, by their very nature,
in their finest moment
fade away.

—JORGE MANRIQUE, 1492

Hernando de Soto's Life and Travels, 1500–42

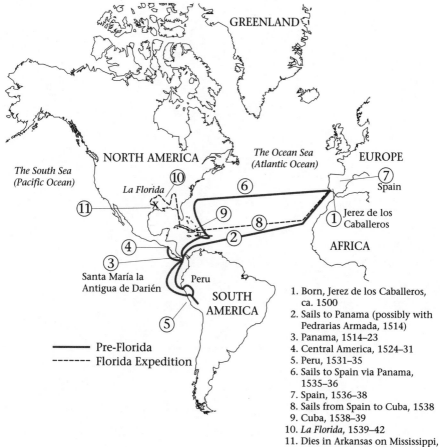

GREENLAND

NORTH AMERICA

The Ocean Sea
(Atlantic Ocean)

EUROPE

The South Sea
(Pacific Ocean)

⑩

La Florida

⑥

Spain

⑦

⑪

X

⑨

⑧

① Jerez de los
Caballeros

②

④

③

AFRICA

Santa María la
Antigua de Darién

Peru

SOUTH
AMERICA

⑤

———— Pre-Florida

------- Florida Expedition

1. Born, Jerez de los Caballeros,
   ca. 1500
2. Sails to Panama (possibly with
   Pedrarias Armada, 1514)
3. Panama, 1514–23
4. Central America, 1524–31
5. Peru, 1531–35
6. Sails to Spain via Panama,
   1535–36
7. Spain, 1536–38
8. Sails from Spain to Cuba, 1538
9. Cuba, 1538–39
10. *La Florida*, 1539–42
11. Dies in Arkansas on Mississippi,
    May 21, 1542

FOREWORD:

Heroes, Demons, and Conundrums

NORTH AMERICANS HAVE LONG neglected Hernando de Soto, a strange fate for the first European to penetrate deeply into the interior of our continent. From 1539 to 1543, his army of six hundred men^ traveled four thousand miles, twice the distance covered by Lewis and Clark some 265 years later. On the way, Soto explored the Old South when it was truly old—when this was a land of canopied forests, savannas, cypress swamps, and abundant game. The major inhabitants were a mysterious and advanced civilization few people have heard of, whom we now call, for want of a better name, Mississippians.

Yet most Americans know Hernando de Soto only as a shadowy figure in a Spanish *cabasset* helmet, or as the namesake of a mid-century line of automobiles famous for sweeping fins and heavy metal.^ We know even less about the Mississippians, whose civilization Soto helped destroy in an apocalypse so thorough that archaeologists only recently have begun to understand the strange mounds and ruined cities they left behind.

This biography is about a man who tried to conquer North America, who began life as the son of an impoverished Spanish squire, and went on to become spectacularly wealthy and famous as a major conqueror in Central America and Peru—only to gamble everything on the chance that he might find a second Inca Empire. He failed, but not for lack of trying. Experienced and ruthless, brilliant and obsessed, this twenty-five-year veteran of the Spanish *conquista* spent over one thousand days scouring the southeastern United States for treasure, canvassing an astonishing four hundred thousand square miles of territory, and plunging into ten future U.S. states, chasing his golden empire. Had it existed in the ancient South, he almost certainly would have found and conquered it. The fact it did not was simply the bad luck of a lifelong gambler who rolled his dice in this country he called *La Florida,* and came up empty.

✛   ✛   ✛

Hernando de Soto's reputation over the years has tended toward extremes. Europeans and most historians in America, particularly non-Hispanics, have

Hernando de Soto's Route
in *La Florida* (The Hudson Route)

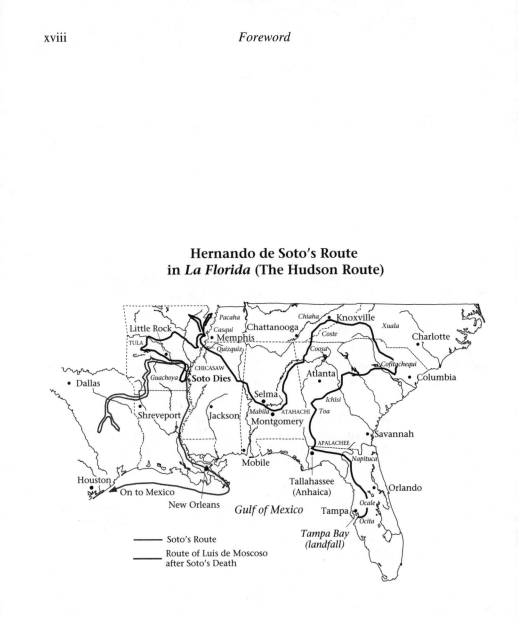

long dismissed him as a minor figure, insisting his explorations were inconclusive, since they seemed to have little impact on the eventual colonization of North America by France and Britain. Sharply contrasting this view is Soto's standing in the Deep South, where he remains today a cult figure venerated as Dixie's first white hero, one of those "knights in the army of God to bring Christianity to the savages," according to a children's history of Soto penned as recently as 1989. Southerners have attached Soto's name to towns, lakes, creeks, counties, islands, and parks; to car dealerships, schools, barbershops, and at least one newspaper; to T-shirts, visors, plastic souvenir helmets, bumper stickers, and neoprene soft-drink holders. Every year, towns and cities hold De Soto parades, De Soto barbecues, and De Soto costume pageants. In Bradenton, Florida, not far from the marshy beach in Tampa Bay where Soto may have landed in 1539, the local Hernando de Soto Historical Society each spring names a "Hernando de Soto"—the year I visited, he was an air-conditioning contractor from Tampa Bay—and crowns a Miss De Soto. They hold the ceremony in the local De Soto Mall.

Yet neither characterization of Hernando de Soto—of obscure explorer or saint—is correct. To say his expedition meant nothing ignores the great impact of his failure. Had Soto been a different man, more interested in colonizing than plundering, Spain's imperial red and gold would have been flying permanently over Dixie *two centuries* before the Fleur-de-lis and the Union Jack. Soto the Obscure also ignores his *entrada*'s* disastrous impact on the Indians.^ Indeed, though the Mississippians eventually drove out Soto's Spaniards, and killed over half his men,^ the price of victory was the collapse of their civilization, caused in part by Soto's systematic looting of their villages, towns, and cities; the kidnapping, discrediting, and murder of Mississippian leaders; and the deaths of tens of thousands killed in warfare, from being worked to death as slaves and porters, from starvation when Soto's army plundered food supplies, and from contracting Old World diseases to which they had no immunity.^

Soto as saint is laughable, though this hardly has stopped De Soto mythmakers from insisting he was more humane than his fellow conquistadors, and more interested in settlement and saving souls than in conquest or gold. In Panama, the real Hernando de Soto tortured *caciques*† for gold. In Nicaragua, he captured and worked slaves to death by the thousands, and earned substantial profits from selling and shipping them to other Spanish colonies. In Peru,

---

* *Entrada* literally means an "entrance," or "beginning"; it also can mean an assault or onslaught. In reference to the *conquista* it usually refers to the first expedition and conquest of a country.

†*Cacique* is a Taino (Caribbean Indian) word for "chief" that the Spanish used to describe virtually every native leader, from the simplest headman in a hunter-gatherer society to the emperor of the Incas.

Soto led an organized rape of Inca sacred virgins at Cajas, and nearly skewered alive an Inca general during interrogations at Cajamarca. And in *La Florida* and elsewhere, he routinely hacked off Indians' hands and noses, cleaved them to pieces with heavy swords, ran them through with lances, and turned loose war dogs to tear them to pieces.^

But dismissing Hernando de Soto as some sort of psychopathic killer—which some have done—misses the point. Soto's towering obsession was not to kill. It wasn't even to acquire gold. What Soto craved, more than anything, was *success*. This was his religion, his mantra, and his fate. But Soto's willingness to invent his own rules to further his aspirations, particularly within the context of his time, should shock no one. Nor should the fact that this conquistador's tactics to win big at all costs were as senseless, wasteful, and shortsighted then as they have been in our own century. The agelessness of Soto's conquistador mentality—of the person whose aspirations justify any cruelty or act of destruction, who becomes so addicted to his quest he cannot stop, who winds up either self-destructing, or being destroyed by others—is one of my major interests in writing this book.

✛   ✛   ✛

Assembling a biography of Hernando de Soto presents numerous challenges, not the least of which is untangling the real Hernando de Soto from the man of legend. For starters, I want to restore this man's proper name, which is not the strangely anglicized *De* Soto, but simply Soto. This is what he called himself, and what his contemporaries knew him by. Next, we must throw out wholesale nearly two centuries of feverish pseudoscholarship by fawning authors, poets, historians, and sycophants, who have churned out, by my count, no fewer than thirteen full-length biographies, five novels, three epic poems, and countless monographs, stories, local histories, and tracts, most of them written during the nineteenth and early twentieth centuries, and nearly all useless in terms of accuracy and scholarship.^

In recent years mythmaking, thankfully, has given way to a growing body of more serious work as anthropologists and historians have picked apart the heroic *De* Soto, digging deeper for the real man, not only by studying his expedition chronicles and archival records more critically, but also by comparing and augmenting the historic record with a growing mass of archaeological material about Soto, the sixteenth-century Spanish presence in North America, and the native peoples of this era. This more sober approach bore fruit as early as 1939, when anthropologist John Swanton edited and largely wrote the first large-scale, scholarly work attempting to treat Soto objectively. Published amidst the hoopla of the Soto Quadricentennial, commemorating the four hundredth anniversary of Soto's expedition, Swanton wisely ignored the mostly

The Swanton Route

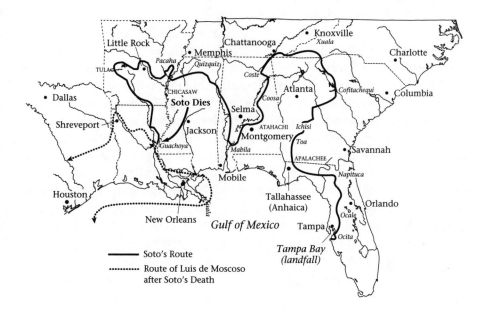

laudatory appraisal of that time to write a classic in Soto scholarship: *Final Report of the United States De Soto Expedition Commission*—391 pages of tightly packed print, paid for with a modest grant from the U.S. Congress. A make-work project for anthropologists during the Great Depression, Swanton's tour de force compiles and analyzes virtually every fact then known about Soto's Florida expedition, and provides an exhaustive attempt to trace Soto's route through *La Florida*. Recent discoveries have augmented or superseded much of Swanton's information. Yet his *Report*—though hardly final, as Swanton himself admitted—remains a major source for this and any other study of Hernando de Soto.

Swanton's report is also notable because it was the last major Soto study to concentrate on the man and his expedition, as much as the Indians he met. Since Swanton, there has been a sea change in Soto studies, from an emphasis on what he did to a sometimes feverish effort among anthropologists, historians, and ethnologists to solve one of the great mysteries of American history— the truth about the Mississippians. Recently, their dedication and hard work has begun to pay off as pieces of the puzzle begin to come together. This fresh material provides the basis for my descriptions of the people Soto encountered in ancient North America. Yet questions about the Mississippians remain as basic as: Where did they come from? How many were they? Who were their gods? Why did they build the magnificent mounds scattered across the Southeast and north-central plains of North America? Why did they die out so quickly? Inevitably, attempts to answer these queries lead back to Hernando de Soto, since his chroniclers offer the only detailed written record of this vanished civilization.

Another conundrum is to reconstruct the life of a man who lived almost five centuries ago, and spent the first half of his life in virtual obscurity. We don't even know what Soto looked like, despite dozens of images painted, etched, and drawn over the centuries, including a massive portrait in the rotunda of the United States Capitol. All these, however, are flights of fancy, since no image exists of Soto rendered by anyone who saw him. Written descriptions are also surprisingly scarce, the only eyewitness account coming from Pedro Pizarro, who knew him in Peru. But he tells us mostly what we already know, that Soto was "dexterous and cunning in Indian warfare, valiant and strong, and affable with the soldiers." Pizarro adds he was "a small man," which is, incredibly, the only authentic physical description of Hernando de Soto we have, despite thousands of pages written about him.

Soto complicates matters further because he left few of the private records, journals, and letters that contemporary biographers crave. This is partly explained by the era in which he lived, when modern notions of preserving and recording personal details were only dimly conceived, particularly for a figure not born into the spotlight of a royal or high noble family. Soto also was a man of action. This means most of our information comes not from the man himself, but from those who knew him, who cannot always be trusted, given the usual biases that color chronicles and histories of all eras. Worse still are recollections written long after the events they describe, which depend on memory, or those written by chroniclers who knew only *of* Soto, but never met him. But this is not to say these records have no value, as Barbara Tuchman once noted in comments about medieval chroniclers. "I realize it is unfashionable among medievalists today to rely on the chroniclers," she wrote in *A Distant Mirror,* "but for a sense of the period and its attitudes I find them indispensable. Furthermore, their form is narrative and so is mine." I would add that the chroniclers I draw from are not entirely bereft of useful facts, particularly when their information can be verified by other sources—including archaeological digs, and less consciously prejudicial archives and documents.

This is not to say Hernando de Soto left no written records of his own, though these can be counted on the fingers of one hand. In fact, his output is sparse enough that we cannot be entirely sure he wrote these documents himself, and did not dictate them to one of his secretaries. As a *hidalgo,* or gentleman squire, he should have learned the rudiments of reading and writing. But we have no absolute proof he was literate.^ All we know for sure is that he could sign his name. His signature appears on numerous documents as severe and slightly crimped, except for a wide, flamboyant *H,* and two decorative swirls before and after.

A conqueror as prolific and successful as Hernando de Soto, however, inevitably leaves in his wake a crush of official documentation, most of it stored in archives—official reports, shipping manifests, sales receipts, trial records, and letters. The most important legal document comes from a bitter and costly suit filed by Soto's longtime business partner, Hernán Ponce de León, against Soto's wife, Isabel de Bobadilla, shortly after the outside world learned of Soto's death. Consisting of some four thousand mostly unpublished, handscribed pages, the suit, which lasted from 1546 to 1550, contains a treasure trove of Soto material, ranging from his will and his wife's dowry to detailed testimony by over one hundred people who knew Soto and worked with him in all stages of his career, from his youth in Panama to his final days in *La Florida.* Because it remains mostly in manuscript form and is very difficult to read and decipher, the suit as a whole has seldom been tapped by Sotoists— until now.

Despite this wealth of documentation, holes remain where nothing was written down about certain events, or key records over the course of nearly five centuries were misplaced, lost in shipwrecks, eaten by worms, burned in fires, and destroyed in earthquakes. The biggest gap is in Soto's early years. Because

he was a descendant of minor nobility, we know the bare outline of his genealogy—the names of his parents and family, the region of his birth, and the
names of his most illustrious ancestors. Yet virtually no details exist to illumi-
nate his youth and family, and to explain the roots of his obsessions, successes,
and ultimate failure. This is why my first chapters tend to describe Soto in
terms of broad historic trends, personalized here and there by retrospective ex-
trapolations of his later actions and personality.

As Soto grows into adulthood and fame, documentation increases, and Soto
as an individual slowly emerges. Thus the records of his teenage years in
Panama are spotty, becoming more profuse as he rises to the rank of captain at
the age of twenty and, in 1524, becomes a battalion commander in the conquest
of Nicaragua. By the late 1520s, when he is one of the most influential men in
Central America, the name Hernando de Soto appears on hundreds of pages of
trials, hearings, town-council meetings, and letters—enough to establish
Soto's whereabouts and activities almost month by month. In Peru, the documentation becomes even more prolific as Soto becomes a major figure in one
of the biggest stories of that distant century—the conquest of the Incas. In
Florida, he *is* the story. Yet small gaps remain throughout, necessitating an an-
noying proliferation of "probablies" and "most likelies" in this text. I expect
more empty spaces to be filled in by future archaeological and archival finds.
But I suspect the record will never be complete.

The most important sources for the *La Florida* expedition are four eyewitness accounts written by *entrada* survivors, two of which exist in their entirety,
a third that is transcribed by someone else, and a fourth that is the fragment of
a longer document, now lost.^

The most lengthy and detailed of the eyewitness accounts was penned by an
anonymous Portuguese officer in Soto's army who calls himself the Gentleman of Elvas, Elvas being a Portuguese city located a few miles east of the
Spanish border near Badajoz, capital of Soto's home region of southern Extremadura. First published in Portuguese in 1557,^ and later in Spanish,
Elvas's *True Relation of the Toils and Hardships Suffered by Governor Hernando de Soto and Certain Portuguese Gentlemen During the Discovery of the
Province of Florida* was a minor best-seller during the centuries after its initial
publication, with two printings in Portuguese, and translations into Dutch,
French, and English, the foreign interest coming as these emerging powers
searched for clues to guide them in their own colonizing efforts. Most scholars
agree that this man, whoever he was, is usually dependable for basic information, despite the fact he probably wrote his *relación* by memory several years
after the expedition. There are, however, numerous lapses in his veracity,

where he gets his facts mixed up, or seems to omit major episodes related by other chroniclers. Elvas also has pretensions here and there of writing an Iberian romance, inserting, for instance, long, flowery speeches supposedly delivered by Soto, Indian kings, and others that have far more in common with a bad chivalric novel than real life.

The other extant chronicle was written by the king's royal agent on the expedition, Luis Hernández de Biedma. He penned a terse, no-nonsense narrative presented to the king in 1544 as the official *entrada* report. Biedma's meticulous rendering, which reads like a legal deposition, is disappointing only because it is regrettably succinct, touching only briefly on most key events.

The third eyewitness chronicle was written by Rodrigo Ranjel, Soto's private secretary.^ Apparently, he kept a daily journal of the expedition, now lost. Fortunately, the sixteenth-century historian Gonzalo Fernández de Oviedo y Valdés saw a copy of the original, and incorporated its descriptions and stories into his massive *General and Natural History of the Indies.* This is perhaps the most reliable of the chronicles in terms of factual information about the route and what the expedition encountered, though it is flawed by the fact that Oviedo, who knew Soto in Panama as a young man, frequently interjects his own opinions into Ranjel's account. Among other things, he accuses Soto of being a braggart, smooth talker, liar, and butcher of Indians—all of which are true, though one is frequently left wondering where Ranjel begins and Oviedo leaves off.

The fourth and final chronicle was written by one of the priests accompanying Soto, Fray Sebastián de Cañete, whose work remained lost and unknown until a one-page fragment was discovered in 1982 by Florida archivist Eugene Lyons. Though tantalizingly short, this heavily damaged manuscript page not only offers fresh details and observations about the Mississippians, but also reveals an intelligent and highly observant man in Cañete, whose full manuscript will be, one hopes, someday recovered.

Yet another major source for the *La Florida* expedition is *The Florida of the Inca,* by Garcilaso de la Vega, published in 1605. The *mestizo* son of a Spanish captain in Peru and an Inca princess, Garcilaso wrote what is often called a Soto "chronicle," though it is really a historical biography written shortly after its subject's death, based on interviews with elderly expedition survivors, and on unpublished notes and memoirs, now lost. A skilled romantic writer, Garcilaso's narrative gives us by far the most dramatic—and lengthy—account of the *entrada,* though this is achieved, in many cases, by embellishment and outright fiction. *The Florida of the Inca* contains some useful information, but is skewed by the author's deep nostalgia for the supposed glories of the *conquista,* and his ardent desire to promote further exploration and conquest in *La Florida.*

A final challenge in preparing this text has been how to handle perhaps the greatest controversy of all about Hernando de Soto—where, exactly, he marched his army through the southeastern United States. For over a century, Soto scholars and admirers in the Old South and beyond have been obsessed with finding the *entrada*'s precise route, stymied by the fact that the chroniclers offer only vague information in terms of geography and distances covered. In the absence of definitive evidence, local town and county governments in the South have bickered for years over where to erect monuments and to hold commemorative fêtes, while academics feud endlessly about such questions as where Soto made his landfall in Florida in 1539 (was it Tampa Bay, Charlotte Harbor, or San Carlos Bay?), and where, exactly, he first set eyes on the Mississippi (was it Sunflower Landing, near Rena Lara, Mississippi; Friar's Point a few miles to the north; or Walls, Mississippi, near the Tennessee border?). Some of these debates can get ridiculous, as everyone strains to draw conclusions based on too little evidence, and to read between the lines of chronicles that simply do not provide enough conclusive information.

Incredibly, only one site in North America can be linked to Soto beyond a shadow of a doubt. This is the army's 1539–40 winter camp, discovered in 1986 in downtown Tallahassee by archaeologist Calvin Jones. He found enough Spanish beads, nails, coins, crossbow quarrels, bits of chain mail, and pottery of the correct date to convince even his most vociferous critics that Hernando de Soto actually laid his head to rest on a patch of ground some three-quarters of a mile from the Florida state capitol building, on what is now the lawn of an office complex. As for the rest of Soto's journey, the chronicles offer up enough circumstantial evidence—a river here, a mountain there—to reconstruct a general route, which can be matched to known topographical and archaeological sites to make a hypothetical "fit," though hard evidence at even the most likely spots cannot be one hundred percent confirmed.

Over the course of two years, I personally retraced the "Hudson Route,"^ named for Georgia anthropologist Charles Hudson, who has spent over a decade attempting to reconstruct a viable Soto route, working in concert with dozens of anthropologists, geologists, historians, and local experts. I believe Hudson's controversial route tugs too hard in some places to make a "fit," though none of his critics—mostly academics whose theories Hudson has superseded or called into doubt, or local city boosters who find their towns left out of Hudson's updated route—can offer a better-argued and comprehensive alternative.

Since the mid-sixteenth century, the topography of Soto's route has been altered so dramatically it barely resembles what he and his men saw four and half centuries ago. Yet with some persistence, and a lot of poking around on backroads, it is possible to recapture at least a feeling for what Soto and his men experienced. Over the past five years, as I rummaged around the South, I was frequently rewarded by finding small, out-of-the-way pockets of preserved wilderness where I could briefly put myself in the place of Hernando de Soto and his men as I tramped barefoot through oozing swamps in Florida and Georgia, sidestepped alligators in the St. Mark's wilderness area near Tallahassee, hiked up steep and buggy mountain trails in the Appalachian Mountains, and nearly capsized in a small boat as I crossed the Mississippi.

In all, I traveled some fifteen thousand miles in ten states and five countries researching this book, retracing Soto's marches and travels and visiting important sites and research facilities in the U.S., Spain, Mexico, Panama, and Nicaragua. I drew the line, however, at getting shot at or killed, which forced me to cancel my plans to retrace Pizarro and Soto's route of conquest through Peru. The Shining Path guerrillas, who then controlled much of the territory along Pizarro's route, took no prisoners.

David Ewing Duncan
Baltimore, Maryland

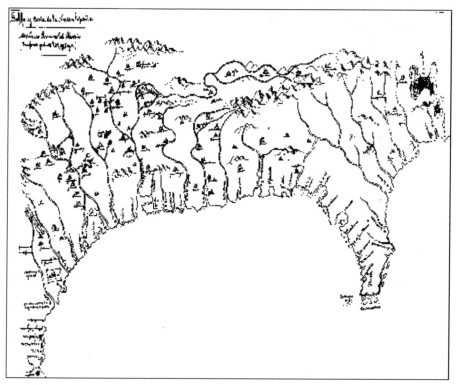

The Soto Map

A Note on Names

IN THIS TEXT, I do my best to stay true to what a character called himself or herself, though I am not entirely consistent. For instance, I call Vasco Núñez de Balboa both Vasco Núñez, which is what he called himself, and Balboa, the anglicized version. In a few cases, I have adopted the common, if technically incorrect, version. For instance, I almost never refer to Gonzalo Fernández de Oviedo y Valdés as Fernández de Oviedo y Valdés, but as the much more widely used (even in Spain) Oviedo. The one name I insist on restoring to its original form in all instances is Hernando de Soto, whom I always refer to as Soto, not *de* Soto, or *De* Soto.

A Note on Money

SPANISH CURRENCY IN SOTO'S era was based on the *maravedí*, equal to .01 grams of fine gold. Below are the relative values of currencies frequently mentioned in the text:

1 gold peso (also called a *castellano*) ..450 *maravedíes*
1 ducat .... 375 *maravedíes*
1.2 ducats .... 1 gold peso

Silver was sometimes measured in pesos, though more frequently weighed out in *marcos* (marks) of silver, which equaled roughly a half pound.

Because precious-metal prices in our era change almost daily, I hesitate to equate Spanish currencies with today's rates (mid-1995). Yet even an instantly out-of-date rate will provide some basis for comparison:

Maravedí .... $ .15
Gold peso (*castellano*) 66.74
Ducat 55.61
Silver mark (fine silver) 48.05

These amounts give some idea of the plunder Soto amassed in Peru, some 130,000 to 200,000 gold pesos, or eight and a half to thirteen million dollars. The value of this currency, however, is meaningless without some idea of the purchasing power during Soto's lifetime. Kathleen Romoli, in *Balboa of Darién,* listed the price of several items in the Hispanic world taken from documents in the first two decades of the sixteenth century:

Maravedíes

Colonial governor's salary (annual)...............366,000*

Military captain's salary, colonies 48,000

Ordinary seaman's salary (plus food) 7,300

Bushel of wheat...294

Wine, low grade, gallon 8

Wine, good quality, gallon....................................38

Crash linen, yard 38

Silk velvet, yard 850

Mule, medium quality 8,000

Stallion 30,000

Slave (African)...12,000

Passage, Spain-Hispanolia (with food) 3,000

Passage, deluxe 5,500

Caravel, to purchase, 250 *toneladas* ....750,000†

Rent, small house, annual.....................................3,600

Rent, "elegant residence," annual 75,000

Soto's salary as governor of Cuba and La Florida was 750,000 maravedíes to be paid out of his own colonial coffers.

†This is based on a selling price of 3,000 *maravedíes* per *tonelada.* Note: A *tonelada* was not a measure of displacement, but of how many casks, or *toneladas,* of wine would fit into the hull of a vessel.

PROLOGUE

Soto "Discovers" the Mississippi

*May 8, 1541: Near Walls, Mississippi^*

BIVOUACKED ON A LOW bluff five miles east of the Mississippi, Hernando de Soto's starving band of would-be conquerors slept fitfully. For eight days, they had been lost in a wilderness dense with towering loblolly pines, oaks, maples, and sweet-scented magnolias, slowly running out of food, and desperate to find a native town with enough maize and beans to feed hundreds of men and servants. All night long, exhausted slaves stoked bonfires for warmth and security against bears and panthers as soldiers, artisans, priests, cooks, porters, and concubines huddled round the flames, the Spaniards' once-magnificent clothing reduced to rags, their neat campaign tents and wool blankets replaced by buckskin and piles of dried grass. Death lingered over the sprawling camp—the sharp odor of decay from nearby marshes, the moaning of Spaniards wounded in recent battles, the gaunt expressions of conquistadors and slaves alike who knew they must find food soon, or perish.

Sentries on four-hour shifts stood in Spanish pairs around the camp, armed with what was left of the troop's once-splendid arsenal—pikes, swords, crossbows, arquebus rifles, and scattered bits of armor. Mounted guards, also in pairs, reconnoitered the forests beyond the perimeter on lean, hungry horses, scanning the murk and gloom for Indian sharpshooters—*guerrillas* (fighters) waiting in ambush to shoot arrows tipped in razor-sharp flint and mica. Deadly accurate, these silent missiles already had killed dozens of Spaniards, striking them down without warning as they ate dinner, slept, and trudged wearily through endless wilderness, bogs, and cane brakes. Since landing at Tampa Bay two years earlier, 1 in 5 of Soto's original 650 men had died—some from arrows, others from starvation, exhaustion, snake bites, and disease.

Within a few hours, Hernando de Soto would arrive at the Mississippi River, an event long celebrated by European Americans as a defining moment in our

Soto's Camp Above the Mississippi,
March 7–8, 1541

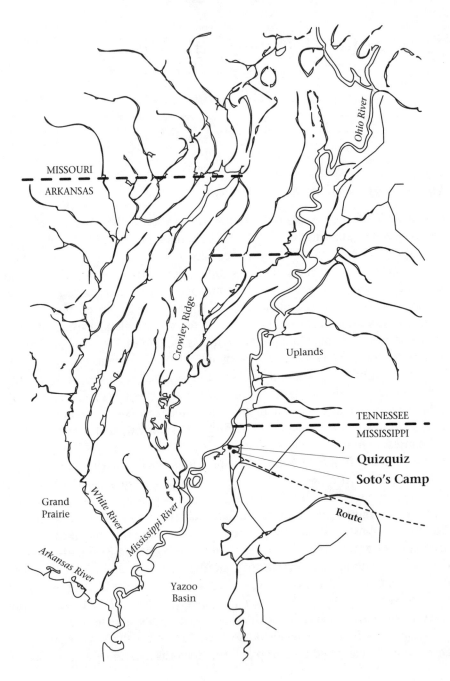

history. Countless paintings and etchings hang in courthouses, museums, and town halls across the United States depicting Soto at this auspicious moment, usually as a well-fed conquistador dressed in glittering armor, and beaming in triumph on the banks of the great river. The product of late-nineteenth-century artists with overactive imaginations, these heroic images evoke a mythic Hernando de Soto whose *entrada* represented everything Americans worshiped in that giddy era—progress, can-do thinking, and the triumph of European civilization. Never mind that most of these devotees were English-speaking Protestant settlers and their descendants, and that the real Soto was a Spanish-speaking Catholic conqueror. And never mind that the Mississippi was "discovered" for Europe not by Soto, but unnamed Spanish mariners as early as 1510^—a fact that may still shock latter-day admirers, particularly those who live along his route in the Old South, where the Soto legend is still very much alive.

The real Hernando de Soto was probably feeling somewhat less than triumphant on that long-ago day in May. Dressed like his men in a motley blend of animal skins, furs, and armor, his face emaciated by hunger and creased by the strain of command, he undoubtedly saw this mile-wide strip of roiling water not as the highway for settlement and commerce it later became, but as a monumental nuisance—for the very practical reason that he had to cross it. This meant boats would have to be built, and hundreds of men and horses ferried across without drowning. It also meant a delay of days, perhaps weeks; an intolerable respite for a man who had already traveled sixteen hundred miles through seven future U.S. states, and had come up empty in terms of treasure and great empires to conquer. Desperate to keep moving in search of the golden city he was sure existed in the unexplored interior, the last thing he needed was this inconvenient swath of mud and water.

✛　✛　✛

The forty-one-year-old conquistador camped above the Mississippi that morning in 1541 was one of the toughest, most ruthless, most able conquistadors in the Indies. A man of thunder and passion, of towering ambition and brutal resolve, he epitomized everything epic, petty, grand, and horrific about the *conquista*. Born into poverty and obscurity in a backwater province of Castile, he had left home at fourteen for early colonial Panama, where he not only flourished, but became a teenage sensation, at one point saving an entire Spanish army from obliteration by a native Panamanian troop, and going on to become a flamboyant leading figure in far-flung conquests from the Carolinas to Peru. A brilliant cavalryman and fighter, Hernando de Soto dazzled and terrified peers and enemies alike, proving again and again his mastery of the *conquista*'s most potent weapon: the sudden, lightning-quick lunge forward, exemplified by the swift thrust deep into enemy territory, and the unexpected charge in the midst of battle. For twenty-six years, he had lived on the cutting edge of a rapidly moving frontier, an outrider who reveled in danger and action; a consummate gambler whose career had been a series of spectacular risks and, until now, victories.

He was a colossal paradox of a man in an age of contradictions: grim and engaging, fascinating and contemptible, pious and hypocritical, prudent and reckless, at once enterprising, destructive, arrogant, bold, and savage. Medieval in his certainty and disregard for human life, he was Renaissance in his tactics and individualism, and modern in his megalomaniac worship of himself. Ultimately, though, Hernando de Soto was his own invention—an *American,* an offspring of two hemispheres conceived in violence, vitality, and an insatiable lust to move forward. His was a new era born out of the bloody coupling of two worlds, where old rules were suddenly rendered moot, fortunes could be won and lost in an instant, cruelty and expediency reigned, and everything seemed possible.

He had a gift for inspiring his men to perform extraordinary feats, whether it was a forced march in Peru, where his outriders once covered 250 miles in just five days, or a plea to stick with him in *La Florida.* Yet he was not above lying. Several times in *La Florida,* he goaded on his army with claims of easy marches ahead and rumors of gold he knew were false. He also could be hot-tempered, ordering severe punishments for minor offenses, though he usually cooled down quickly enough to countermand excessive sentences. He had a reputation for surrounding himself with the boldest and most able of young officers—men nearly as volatile and talented as himself—but he hated to be contradicted. More than once, this led to fiascoes when Soto failed to heed their counsel. As a subordinate himself, in the days before he became supreme commander of his own expedition, Soto was a troublemaker constantly scheming to improve his position. His skills as a senior officer and a warrior meant he was always in demand, though the commander who engaged the cocky young captain did so at his own peril.

To the Indians he conquered, Hernando de Soto must have seemed an apocalyptic figure, a terrifying and utterly alien being who appeared from beyond the edge of their world to offer impossible ultimatums, backed up by an infernal killing machine. But this does not mean Hernando de Soto should be dismissed simply as a bloodthirsty barbarian, greedy for gold and glory. If treasure and fame had been his only motivation, he would never have set foot in *La Florida.* Already, he was fabulously wealthy from plundering Nicaragua and Peru. He also was cheered in Seville when he arrived home in 1536, hailed as a "hero" of the Inca conquest, and heaped with honors by the Spanish emperor,^ Charles V. For Soto, however, this was not enough. Ambitious to a fault, and addicted to action, he could not stop until he had scored a triumph equal to or better than the giants of the *conquista*—Francisco Pizarro and Hernán Cortés. Yet one wonders if Soto could have quit even if he had found his empire of gold in North America. For neither Pizarro nor Cortés, both still alive in May 1541, was retiring gracefully. Within weeks of Soto arriving at the Mississippi, on June 26, 1541, Francisco Pizarro, now sixty-three, would be assassinated in Lima by rival partisans. And the fifty-six-year-old Cortés, who had frittered away his wealth and health on fruitless *entradas,* was pursuing endless lawsuits against his rivals. Soon enough, it would become clear that Soto, too, suffered from Pizarro's and Cortés's disability, common to conquistadors and gamblers of all ages—he did not know when to stop.

✛   ✛   ✛

By May 1541, Soto's men were painfully aware that *La Florida* was no Peru, even as Soto clung stubbornly to his quest. If the often hyperbolic Garcilaso can be believed, one of Soto's senior officers, the royal treasurer Juan Gaitan, had become so disenchanted the previous autumn he attempted a half-baked mutiny, though it was quickly squelched after Soto assured his men they soon would "find some land so rich that it might sate his greed," hinting he had knowledge of "great secrets" concerning gold in the interior. (Garcilaso tells a marvelous but unsubstantiated story about Soto learning of the coup in time to stop it by disguising himself and circulating among his men in the camp, like Shakespeare's Henry V on the eve of Agincourt, a play coincidentally written about the same time Garcilaso's book was published.)^

Of course, the great irony about Hernando de Soto is that he already had discovered North America's Eldorado, and didn't know it. From the moment he arrived on the Florida coast in 1539, and had begun marching through the natural opulence of the future United States, it had been all around him—in the rich piedmont forests of north Florida and Georgia; the fertile up-country meadows and hardwood forests of the Carolinas; the high meadows of the Appalachians, where Soto's exhausted horses "grew fat because of the luxuriance of the land"; the "level, dry and fertile" land of northwestern Georgia and central Alabama, "greatly abounding in maize"; and now in the muddy alluvial lowlands spreading out on either side of the Mississippi.

This was a country where nature itself was the greatest treasure—where the game was so plentiful and fearless that French explorers later killed deer and bear with swords; where the forests teemed with panther, cougar, beaver, muskrat, opossum, turkeys, partridges, and, in the fall and springtime, waterfowl so numerous that William Bartram, an eighteenth-century explorer and naturalist, said they were "like a Vast Dark thunderstorm" when they flew overhead; where fish, mollusks, and crayfish filled great rivers and lakes;

where oaks and pines towered up to 120 feet high, rising above woodland thickets smelling sweetly in the spring of magnolia and dogwood blossoms; and where cypresses grew thick along rivers and swamps, with "cone-like buttresses" on the bottom and great canopies of branches, leaves, and vines up above.

This is not to say Soto's men shared his disdain for this organic treasure. Nearly all of them had grown up in rural Spain close to the soil, and knew the value of good land. Which is why several times they implored their governor-general to stop and establish a colony where they could build plantations, and enslave the local inhabitants as laborers. But Soto, intent on his quest, and always obstinate when crossed, repeatedly refused, earning him in death the scorn of critics such as the sixteenth-century historian Gonzalo Fernández de Oviedo, who chastised him for failing to colonize North America, and for being single-mindedly obsessed with gathering loot and glory. Soto, writes Oviedo, "never halted or settled anywhere; saying that [his aim] was neither to populate nor to conquer, but rather to disturb and devastate the land."

✛   ✛   ✛

Neither treasure nor colonies mattered that damp morning of May 8, 1541. With the *entrada* starving, Soto's overriding concern was to find food, a task he plunged into with his usual zeal. He probably joined the vanguard himself as the sun rose over the great river valley. Crashing through thickets of pine and brush, he and his men began descending a low bluff, probably above Lake Cormorant, Mississippi, not far from the modern town of Walls.^ Here Soto and his outriders would have seen through breaks in the vegetation the valley spread out below—the great, muddy slash of water off in the distance, and, miraculously, several dozen native houses below on a shallow lake surrounded by fields of newly planted maize, squash, pumpkins, beans, and sweet potatoes.

Normally, a Mississippian enclave of this size would have known the Spaniards were coming days ahead of their arrival. But Soto was approaching from an uninhabited wilderness perhaps a sixth the size of modern Mississippi, a natural buffer these Indians apparently felt no need to patrol with their usual frontier sentries. Called Quizquiz by the Spaniards, this *pueblo* was home to several hundred Indians completely ignorant of the maelstrom about to strike. If typically Mississippian, the town would have been a neat, sprawling cluster of whitewashed adobe dwellings topped by tall, sloping roofs of woven cane and straw, and interspersed with cooking houses, plazas, saunalike hothouses, and temples. The most striking feature was a flat-topped earthen pyramid three or four meters high, and topped by a large building that would have been decorated with shells and statues, and painted in bright pigments—the palace of the ruling *cacique,* situated at one end of a broad central plaza. Destroyed by bulldozers during a farm expansion in the 1950s,^ this mound in 1541 was probably surrounded by *barbacoas,* small huts on stilts containing corn and furs paid in tribute by neighboring villages the *cacique* controlled, or that he was storing to send on as his own tribute to a more powerful king called Aquixo,^ who lived across the river, and dominated all the smaller principalities in the region.^ These *barbacoas,* and others in villages closer to the Great River, held the maize that the starving Spaniards would demand as they swept down on the startled people of Quizquiz, before heading off to the Mississippi a mile and a half away.

Soto must have felt a tremendous relief as he sighted the valley, spurred his horse, and rushed down the bluff toward Quizquiz, knowing his *entrada* had once again been saved by luck, and by his iron-willed determination. But it would be a brief victory. For very soon, he would cross the Mississippi and enter an even greater wilderness in Arkansas, composed not only of wood, leaves, and water, but of his own gathering horror as the reality of his failure became evident even to him.

A year later, Hernando de Soto would die not far from this spot, an exhausted, ruined man whose life had gone full circle, ending in obscurity and poverty, just as it had begun some forty-two years earlier, in a small town in Extremadura, far across the Ocean Sea.

Book I
Youth

Soto Is Born

WE START BY IMAGINING a wiry, muscular boy of perhaps eleven, riding a lean Andalusian stallion fast across a low, rugged range of mountains in south-central Spain—a hot, desolate place of rocks, gnarled oaks, sheep, goats, deer, rabbits, snakes, and the occasional mountain lion. Abruptly, the boy draws his sword and hacks viciously at a nearby sapling, neatly slicing off a branch. Turning again, he makes another cut, and another, slashing at the tree and shouting as loudly as he can a battle paean to St. James, a mythical hero of the Moorish wars and patron saint to Spanish warriors. *"Santiago! Cierra España!"* Soto screams. "St. James! Close in, Spain!"^

Unfortunately, this conjured depiction of Hernando de Soto at eleven is all we have, given the lack of records to tell us what he was really doing as a boy. Nor do we know much about his birth, upbringing, family life, dreams, fears, favorite foods, best friends, length of hair, and other pertinent or impertinent details about the fourteen or so years he spent in Spain, from birth to early manhood—fully a third of his lifetime. However, because he was born the son of a Spanish *hidalgo*—a cross between a medieval knight and a country squire—and because of his later wealth and fame, enough information was jotted down here and there to construct a bare-bones outline of Soto's birth and childhood, and to trace back the modestly illustrious lineage of his family.

Soto himself told us when he was born, though he shared his century's nonchalance about dates, giving two different years at different times. In 1535, just after resigning as the first military governor of Cuzco, he testified in a legal document that he was "thirty-five years old, more or less." A year later, in Spain, he described himself as "about forty." This suggests he was born in either 1496 or 1500, or sometime in between. I lean toward the later date, since a birth in the range of 1499 or 1500 makes him roughly fourteen years old when he left home for the Indies, the typical age when a boy became a man in

3

sixteenth-century Spain, and when basic decisions were made by his family about his future.^ Particularly if he were, like Soto, a second-born son, who would not inherit any of his father's meager property; his family could not afford to keep him any longer than necessary. Another reason I advocate the later date is Soto's reputation as a fast learner, and the abundant evidence of his meteoric rise once he bursts into the history books as a young Captain of the Horse in Panama. As early as 1518–19 he emerges fully formed as a mounted fighter, literally dashing about and savagely hacking off the limbs (and heads, noses, and arms) of real people—namely, the Indians of Central America. A final piece of evidence for a birth in or near 1500 is a line written by Soto's sixteenth-century biographer, Garcilaso de la Vega. He firmly states that Soto was forty-two years old when he died on May 21, 1542—a contention that, if true, supports a birth year sometime around 1500.^

Soto's birthplace has likewise been confused by contradictory claims, though in this case the matter is more easily resolved.^ Soto was not born in Villanueva de Barcarrota, a tiny *pueblo* eleven miles from Jerez de los Caballeros, as Garcilaso de la Vega claims, with no proof whatsoever.^ Nor is it likely he was born in Badajoz, capital of southern Extremadura and the hometown of Soto's mother, as others have insisted. In the absence of an actual birth certificate or other definitive documentation,^ the available evidence overwhelmingly suggests Hernando de Soto was a *natural,* or native, of Jerez de los Caballeros, a fortified market town with a population of some eight thousand people in the early sixteenth century,^ situated seventy miles north-northwest of Seville. Soto himself affirmed that Jerez, his father's hometown, was his place of origin.^ So did several friends of his family.^ And if this is not enough, we have the word of at least three *La Florida* expedition survivors, including Gonzalo Vázquez, himself a native of Villanueva de Barcarrota. "Soto," Vázquez says emphatically, "was a native of Jerez, situated four leagues from this village of Barcarrota."

As for Soto's family, we know little more than the names of his parents and siblings, and the genealogy of the House of Soto.^ The bloodline was founded by a certain Méndez Sorred, a Burgos squire and captain under Alfonso IV, king of León in the early tenth century,^ about whom nothing more is known. Undoubtedly he gained the rank of *hidalgo* by performing some signal service for the Crown, perhaps during a raid or battle against the Moors, or some other enemy.

After Méndez Sorred, Soto's ancestors spread out from León into Castile, Andalusia, and Extremadura, all the while serving as middle-level captains and commanders to kings, occasionally rising to the status of a high noble—a *caballero* or a *grandee.* Soto's most famous ancestor was Pedro Ruiz de Soto, a Knight of Santiago who served as King Ferdinand III's captain general in the

Spain in the Early Sixteenth Century

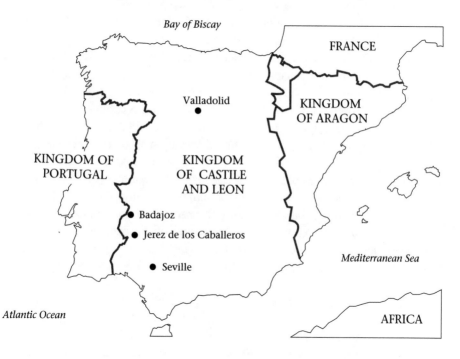

Bay of Biscay

FRANCE

Valladolid

KINGDOM
OF ARAGON

KINGDOM OF
PORTUGAL

KINGDOM
OF CASTILE
AND LEON

Badajoz

Jerez de los Caballeros

Mediterranean Sea

Seville

Atlantic Ocean

AFRICA

mid-thirteenth century. He led the campaign that captured Seville from the
Moors, a legendary victory the young Hernando undoubtedly grew up hearing
about repeatedly from storytellers in his family. Otherwise, the Soto clan appears to have been of middling importance, one of thousands of small-time,
petty elites who had accomplished very little in the centuries after their pro-
genitor's elevation.

This seems to be the case with Soto's father, Francisco Méndez de Soto. Apparently, he inherited the Soto flair for not drawing attention to himself, at least in
terms of written records. Everything we know about Francisco is summed up in
the comments of a longtime friend of the Soto family, who described him in 1538
as a *"hidalgo* and son of *hidalgos"* with "a commonly known reputation . . . and
has no blood of Jews, no Conversos, no Moors, no peasants." This was merely the
formulaic legal definition of a *hidalgo* at the time, however, and tells us nothing
about the man who fathered the would-be conqueror of North America.

It seems likely that Francisco was not rich, his family's modest *hidalgo*
wealth having long ago succumbed to the harsh climate and infertility of the
region. The youthful Soto is said to have arrived in Panama not with the slaves,
horses, and wardrobe of a wealthy and prominent *hidalgo,* but penniless, bringing with him, according to someone who later met him, "nothing else his own
except for a sword and shield."[^] This observation is suspect because it was
written by a Soto chronicler in *La Florida* who did not know Soto in Panama,
though the notion that Soto's family was less than prominent is further backed
by a near-complete dearth of archival material mentioning the Méndez de
Sotos in Jerez de los Caballeros during the early sixteenth century.[^] Had they
been well-off, records of contracts, sales, and other legal documents would
have been deposited in the archives. The apparent invisibility of Soto's father
in the record books means he was either dead when Soto was a boy, or lived a
life of mediocrity.

Slightly more is known about Soto's mother, Leonor Arias Tinoco—including the fact that the Tinocos were more prominent in Badajoz than the
Sotos were in Jerez. For centuries, they were considered an important *hidalgo*
family among the class who served as lawyers, administrators, and military officers in the provincial capital. We also know the names of Leonor's parents—
Hernán Gutiérrez de Cardeñosa and Juana González Tinoco—whose stature in
Badajoz was such that when Soto needed character witnesses to vouch for him
many years later, when he sought to join the Knights of Santiago, he went to
Badajoz, not Jerez, to ask prominent friends of his mother's family to testify
on his behalf. One of these witnesses says he saw the marriage of Soto's parents in Badajoz in the 1490s.[^] Several others verified that Leonor Arias Tinoco
was descended from a "line of noble *hidalgos* in the city of Badajoz."[^]

Soto had at least three siblings, including an older brother, Juan Méndez de
Soto, heir to the family properties, such as they were. Nothing, however, is

heard from this brother until 1537, when he received an undisclosed monetary grant from King Charles I, possibly arranged by his then-famous little brother as compensation for money the Crown borrowed from Soto after he returned from Peru with his thousand pounds of gold.^ Two years later, in 1539, we hear again of Juan Méndez when Soto in his will designates him an executor of his estate.^ In 1543, Juan Méndez de Soto was elected a *regidor* member of the town council in Jerez,^ a position he may also have obtained because of his association with his brother. Soto's other known siblings were sisters—Catalina de Soto, whose young son, Pedro de Soto, accompanied Soto to Cuba; and María de Soto, who married the prefect of Badajoz, Don Alonso Enríquez.^

After leaving home at the age of fourteen in 1514, Soto spent no more than a few weeks in Jerez de los Caballeros during the remainder of his life. Yet his strong attachment to hometown and family—a common trait among conquistadors of this period—was proven in 1539, when Soto ordered in his will that two thousand ducats be spent constructing a lavish chapel and tomb in Jerez's church of San Miguel. His body, according to his instructions, was to be laid to rest inside an ornate sepulcher, with his mother and father buried beside him. Writing with an obvious relish that this son of middling *hidalgos* was to be laid out like a great noble, he directed his executors to place his body in the center of the chapel "in such a manner that the foot of the sepulcher adjoins the footstone of the altar; and thereon I order to be placed a tomb covered over by a fine black broadcloth, in the middle of which be put a red cross of the Commandery of the Order of the Knights of Santiago, that shall be for use on weekdays, and another pall of black velvet, with the same cross in the midst, with four escutcheons of brocade, bearing my arms; which escutcheons I wish and order to be likewise placed on the chapel, altarpiece, and railing, and vestments in such a manner to the patron and executors shall appear most becoming."

Soto's executors were unable to follow these lavish instructions. This is because when he died, Soto was far away from Jerez de los Caballeros, bivouacked on the banks of the Mississippi River, and claiming to be a god to the local Indians. This forced his men to secretly stuff their governor's corpse into a hollow log (or in a blanket, depending on whose version one believes) and dump it during the night in the swirling, muddy waters of the great river, to avoid an awkward situation should the Indians discover this "god" had died. Soto's parents' remains, which briefly stood a chance of being preserved in grandiose style, are now lost, the bones long ago having turned to dust and dissolved into the bare, hardscrabble earth of Extremadura.

✛   ✛   ✛

These are the facts as we know them about Soto's early life, his hometown and family—a sparse outline that hardly begins to assuage our curiosity about that black-haired boy riding fast across the mountains of Extremadura. Yet even if we will never know more specifics, we still can learn a great deal about Soto by delving into the culture and society that shaped him as a boy.

First and foremost, the young Hernando was influenced by his region, Extremadura. Called the Cradle of the Conquistadors^ in tourist brochures, this desolate province in southwest Spain produced not only Soto, but Hernán Cortés, Vasco Núñez de Balboa, Francisco Pizarro and his brothers, and many, many others. Fully one in six of all Spaniards who sailed to the Indies in the sixteenth century came from Extremadura, including nearly half of Soto's six hundred to seven hundred men in *La Florida*.^

One need only stand on Jerez de los Caballeros' battlements, perched high on a mountain crag above the city, to understand why they left. For miles around, you see only rocky hills and brown, parched fields and pastures, stony canyons, and slopes of twisted scrub oak and cork trees. It is a place where sudden floods in the spring and winter erode away entire fields, houses, hamlets, sheep, and the occasional human being, and where extremes in temperatures between summer and winter bring to mind the old Spanish quip: "nine months' winter, and three months' hell." Though hauntingly beautiful in its immense silence and desolation, it is hard to imagine anyone prospering here, even now. Indeed, it is hardly surprising Extremadura produced such tough, no-nonsense men and women four and a half centuries ago, who not only survived when they traveled to America, but thrived amidst the hardships of the *conquista*. Even today, *extremeños* are a hardscrabble people—small, wiry, practical, and tenacious, representing the same extremes of Spanish poverty and vitality they did in Soto's era.

Survival of the fittest in Soto's world began at birth. Half of all children born in Renaissance Europe died before the age of five, most often within minutes or hours of leaving the womb.^ Millions more died of disease—cholera, typhoid, dysentery, diphtheria, measles, mumps, smallpox, and plague—aided and sometimes caused by the filth and cramped conditions Soto and every other child in Europe grew up in during the sixteenth century. Indeed, Jerez de los Caballeros was not the pleasant town of whitewashed houses and scrubbed-clean streets one sees today, but a barely tolerable place where eight thousand people squeezed inside a walled area less than a tenth of one square mile.^ Here Soto and the citizens of Jerez lived amidst a maze of narrow streets reeking of garbage and excrement, where one sometimes had to step carefully to avoid sewage running down troughs in the lanes and alleys, left open in part so that edible refuse could be thrown in and eaten by dogs, chickens, and goats. Houses likewise were tiny and cramped, with all but the very rich living in small, cavelike town houses where bedrooms were barely big enough for beds, and dining rooms were not much larger—leading most people to spend their time in small gardens, or in one of the city's three open public plazas, the largest one facing the church of San Miguel, Soto's own parish church.^

Why the people of Jerez tolerated such extreme discomfort was simple. It was far more dangerous outside the city walls. In Soto's day, the countryside of Spain and most of Europe was virtually lawless, a place where uninhabited thickets and forests predominated over pastures and cultivated fields, and bandits, renegade bands of soldiers, and wild animals made even daylight travel hazardous.^ During the era of Soto's birth and early life, King Ferdinand and Queen Isabel were making significant inroads toward mitigating this rural anarchy. Yet nearly every person in Spain remained instinctively fearful of the countryside, making sure they were safely inside their city walls by nightfall. This meant peasants ventured out to work their fields only during daylight hours, and wealthier people left their towns and cities only when properly armed, or accompanied by a guard. The rest of the time, the Sotos, like most *hidalgos,* stayed in town, sleeping in their tiny town house inside Jerez's cocoon of stone and mortar, hiring an overseer and perhaps armed watchmen to guard and manage their pastures, wineries, olive groves, or whatever else they owned, properties that Francisco Méndez de Soto and his sons would have visited only a few times a year.

This also was a time of frequent drought and famine, which struck Spain and Europe with appalling regularity, and sometimes killed hundreds of thousands as they spread across a continent then populated by some eighty million people. Those who survived were either lucky, or over the centuries had built up a genetic fortitude for enduring starvation and disease that at least begins to explain how men such as Soto endured so much in the Americas. Twice during Hernando de Soto's boyhood, in the winters of 1502–3 and 1506–7, spring and summer droughts led to devastating famines in southern Spain, where witnesses describe thousands dead and refugees wandering "down the roads carrying their children, dead of hunger, on their backs."^ During the 1507 famine, widespread hunger was also accompanied in Andalusia—and possibly as far north as Jerez de los Caballeros—by a fresh outbreak of bubonic plague, which swept through the squalid streets of Seville, killing fifteen hundred people in one parish alone, during a single week in May.^ In the early sixteenth century, Seville was the largest city in Spain, numbering about thirty-five thousand people.^

✛　　✛　　✛

One can easily overstate the miseries of sixteenth-century life. For Extremeños in Soto's day had moments of pleasure and even happiness, particularly when they put aside their work and indulged in frequently held entertainments and ceremonies—weddings, religious festivals, tournaments, bullfights, and funerals. Jerez, as a regional trading center, also attracted a steady flow of wandering troubadours and musicians, appearing on market days each week to sing songs, lead dances, tell stories, play flutes and drums, and strum the *vihuela,* an instrument halfway between a lute and a guitar. It's easy to picture the youthful Soto wandering around the cluttered Jerez market, wearing a sword and a dark cloak, and strutting with his *hidalgo* friends as they stop off to hear a rendition of a *cantares de gesta,* an epic poem-song, sung by a brightly clad *trovador* on a makeshift platform. While stirring and often beautiful, these bloody and violent stories, glorifying combat, plundering, camaraderie, and faith in God, undoubtedly fired the imagination of the young Soto, who would later become famous as both a fighter and a dreamer as he eagerly sought out golden cities and great empires to conquer and rule.

Imagine the scene: a crowded, smoky square in Jerez, smelling of dung and perspiration, where Soto and his friends are standing below a tiny stage, listening to a storyteller recite lines from *El Poema de Mio Cid. "La seña sacan fuera, de Valencia dieron salto,"* the *trovador* shouts with great dramatic emphasis, leaning toward the audience, and speaking low to draw them into his story. "They left Valencia with their standard carried in front."

"Quatro mill menos treínta con Mio Cid van a cabo," he continues, theatrically raising his voice, *"a los cinquaenta mill van los ferir de grado!"*—"Four thousand all but thirty forming the Cid's company, going eagerly to the attack of fifty thousand Moors!"

"Mio Cid enpleó la lanca, al espada metió mano," he continues, strutting onstage like a knight heading off to battle, *"atantos mata de moros que non fueron contados, por el cobdo ayuso la sangre destellando"*—"The Cid first used his lance and then wielded his sword, killing countless Moors while the blood dripped down to his elbow."

He then goes on, reciting the poem in verse:

"Toda esta ganancia en su mano á rrastado.
Los cinquaenta mill por cuenta fuero[n] notados,
non escaparon más de ciento e quatro.
Mesnadas de Mio Cid rrobado an el campo,
entre oro e plata fallaron tres mill marcos,
las otras ganancias non avía rrecabdo.
Alegre era Mio Cid e todos sos vassallos
que Dios les ovo merced que vencieron el campo."

"All that booty fell to the Cid,
and of the fifty thousand Moors they counted
not more than one hundred and four as having escaped.
The Cid's vassals plundered the field
and found three thousand gold and silver marks
and enormous quantities of other spoils.
The Cid and his vassals were overjoyed
that by God's favor they had won the day."

Other forms of storytelling were less gruesome. For instance, there were *vil-lancios,* or songbooks, that celebrated love, beauty, and daily life—subjects in which the young Soto probably had less interest than the epics, though the *vil-lancios* could become quite lewd in their overt sexual references. The original oral renditions Soto would have heard in Jerez have been long forgotten, though musicians of the day wrote down sanitized versions for retelling at the royal court. One of these songs, the *Song of the Sybil Cassandra,* was first per-formed at the court of Ferdinand and Isabel in 1513, when Soto was twelve or thirteen—a polished version of a *villancio* already well-known in the Spanish countryside, which may have been performed in Jerez when Soto was a boy.

For this song, the *trovador* would have been accompanied by a drum and flute as he started his performance by seeking out a beautiful young woman in the audience. He sings to her:

"How charming the girl is!
How lovely and beautiful!"

The woman blushes, which makes the crowd laugh as the *trovador* searches the throng for a knight or a gentleman, easily recognizable by his rich cloak, jewelry, and sword.

"Tell me, knight,
you who carry arms,
if the horse or the arms or the war
are as beautiful."

The woman and the crowd again react as the singer points out a shepherd in town for market day:

"Tell me, shepherd,
you who guard the flocks,
if the flocks or the valleys or the mountains
are as beautiful."

And on it went, verse after verse, getting cruder and more lively as the music and lyrics grew louder, and the audience drank wine and danced to flute and drums.

Nothing the *trovadors* could offer, however, matched the greatest solace and diversion of all in Soto's day—the church. Providing not only hope for the miserable, and justification for the rich, this all-pervasive entity also alleviated the monotony of medieval life with an astonishing variety of saintly cults, prayers, admonitions, sacraments, festivals, ritualized tortures, heretic burnings, and the daily Mass.^

It is impossible to know how much the church influenced the young Hernando de Soto. Yet if his later life is any indication, he was not overly devout, following the protocol of the day when he mentions God in his letters and reports, and claims to be fulfilling the Crown's orders to evangelize the Indians. Indeed, though he brought at least eight priests with him to *La Florida,* and possibly twelve, they seldom appear in the narratives, and seemed to have little, if any, influence over Soto or the expedition. This is not to say that Soto himself never discussed religion with the Indians, because he frequently did. But it was always in the context of power, and of Soto's attempts to manipulate, the Spanish God typically being mentioned in the same breath as demands to succumb to Spanish steel.

Soto's Machiavellian improbity about Christian ideals, however, does not mean the Spanish religion made no deep impression. For in sixteenth-century Spain, the church was more than a set of ideas, or even a way of life. It was an all-embracing entity that excited great fervor among a people who had been fighting a war for centuries to defend the Christian faith, and had just won a shattering victory over the Moors at Granada in 1492—capping off a reconquest of Iberia begun in the eighth century. In fact, little in Soto's youth would have mattered more than this great triumph of a nation that passionately believed they were the chosen people of God, and that He had made them not only invincible against their enemies, but had bequeathed to them the cunning, martial skills, and courage to seize the day—and whatever booty was available—whether it be in America, Italy, Africa, or France. This passion for the Spanish God—who was more a god of war to Soto and his ilk than one of love or humanity—is why the crowds at religious festivals worked themselves up into a frenzy that frightened cooler heads and visiting dignitaries, and why few countries could match sixteenth-century Spain's ferocity and violence in worshiping and defending their version of God, a deity as paradoxical as Spain itself—composed of fire and blood, love and hate, life and death, and, most of all, an intensity of purpose that drove men like Soto across the Ocean Sea to conquer half a hemisphere in the space of a single generation.

✛   ✛   ✛

The final ingredient in young Soto's upbringing was his formal education, another blank that can only be hinted at around the edges. Because he was frequently called a "good *hidalgo,*" a "man of truth," and a "man of worth," we can assume he acquired the basic skills and learning expected of his class. This included at least a functional knowledge of reading and writing, and a rudimentary introduction to subjects ranging from Latin and theology to mathematics, which *hidalgos* learned from members of their family, priests in local churches, and, in wealthier villages, from *maestros* hired by the town council.^

Book learning, however, was only a small part of a young *hidalgo*'s education. Given Soto's later reputation as an expert horseman and fighter, he obviously devoted much more time as a boy to mastering the skills of a knight and warrior, and to learning the basics of how to wage battles and to maintain horses, weapons, and a fighting edge. I imagine him being a serious, determined boy who woke up each day before dawn to start a full day of training with swords and lances, in his free time leading other boys in hunting expeditions, or in games of mock warfare, the future governor-general of *La Florida* already showing a capacity for command. On special occasions, he and his friends would have competed as youths in tournaments, demonstrating their skills in children's competitions while older knights jousted, dueled, fought on horseback with bulls and other animals, and played a dangerous game of mock combat called *juego de cañas.*

Soto's education as a *hidalgo,* however, was more than practicing ripostes, thrusts, and skirmishes, or the fundamentals of scholarship. For more than anything, *hidalguía* was an attitude, a system of beliefs and practices developed over the centuries by a warrior caste created to fight the far-flung *reconquista* against the Moors. Originally, they formed an elite of independent, highly mobile citizen-knights on call at all times, their ongoing mission being to defend their local territory, and to join the king in offensive thrusts. In exchange, *hidalgos* were legally exempted from paying taxes, provided with their small estates and, sometimes, with vassals. They also were given permission to take on the trappings of nobility—that is, to bear a coat of arms, wear the plumes and headgear of a noble, attend the fêtes and tournaments of the aristocracy, and to wear fine clothes otherwise banned by the church's sumptuary laws.

Not surprisingly, these barely noble gentlemen clung to their prerogatives with the determination of any group relegated to the lowest rung of an elite society. This in part explains why the *hidalgos*—and why Soto—developed reputations for exceptional haughtiness and pretentiousness, holding fast to a strict code of conduct that not only forbade performing manual labor (*el deshonor de trabajo,* "the dishonor of work"), but also any dealings in commerce, even if it meant starving their families. To be a *hidalgo* meant never to leave home without a weapon, preferably the most ornate and flashy Toledo blade available; to answer any insult with a grim challenge of a duel to the death, and a clash of swords; and to uphold certain chivalric values summed up in the term "point of honor"—courage, loyalty to comrades, the sanctity of one's word, cruelty toward enemies, and a deep respect for family, country, and one's own name. The name *hidalgo* literally means "son of someone"—an indicator of why Soto and his class had no greater aspiration than to be elevated to a status of high nobility, and to receive titles, land, and recognition.

By Soto's day, however, this citizen-warrior caste organized to reclaim and guard frontiers within Spain was giving way to the professional soldier fighting foreign wars, and would soon become superfluous. Yet the country remained saturated with petty *hidalgos* whose sons inherited the family name, privileges, and a horror of *el deshonor de trabajo,* but little more. Just a generation after Soto's death, the *hidalgo* would be reduced to absurdity by Miguel de Cervantes, whose Don Quixote is the epitome of the impoverished, vainglorious *hidalgo,* a farcical remnant of an anachronistic fighting class whose "stallion" is a broken-down nag with "cracked hoofs and . . . blemishes," and whose "helmet" is half steel and half pasteboard. Yet Quixote's fantastic aspirations were every bit as real to him as Soto's ambitions in America. Indeed, in Soto's time, before the Spanish became jaded by wealth and the inevitable disillusionment of an empire past its formative stages, war and conquest remained a glorious occupation. With Granada fresh in every Spaniard's mind, and ongoing campaigns in Italy, North Africa, and the Americas, organized violence remained vital to the life of every aspiring young *hidalgo.* It offered a chance at plunder, to restore the family fortune, and to alleviate the boredom of being a frontier warrior without a frontier to defend.

But most of all, the foreign wars, and particularly America, offered a final coda to the Middle Ages, the Golden Age of the *hidalgo.* Poised on the edge of change not only in Spain, but in the rest of Europe, where the medieval knight was fast being replaced by Renaissance infantry armed with rifles and waves of lightly armored cavalry, these young men could still imagine themselves as El Cid—in this case, riding off to America to make their fortunes and kill Indians (i.e., Moors). Yet Soto was not an exclusively medieval creation. Nor are the ideals of the *hidalgo* entirely an anachronism even today, when pride, a sense of entitlement, and the yearning for glory can be as volatile a mixture as it has ever been. Indeed, one has to keep in mind that these medieval figures dashing about in the jungles of ancient America, donned in armor and quoting El Cid, were among the most adept of their era at utilizing the new high technology of the Renaissance—the weapons, ships, instruments, know-how, and spirit of the fledgling modern age.

✢ 2 ✢

Across the Ocean Sea

SOMETIME IN HIS EARLY teens, Hernando de Soto packed up a few belongings and left home. Hoisting a small satchel onto his back, and strapping on a sword, buckler, and polished boots, he swaggered down the narrow, fetid streets of Jerez, past the familiar plaza and church of San Miguel, and out a plain stone gate. Chances are the young Hernando was not traveling alone, but in the company of a local captain or noble responding to a recruitment call from the king or one of his generals. If so, Soto departed Jerez with a band of other young *hidalgos,* eventually joining Castile's main north-south highway, and the endless procession of oxcarts, royal messengers, criminals, nobles riding in ornate coaches, military units on the march, and sheriffs transporting criminals. Everyone seemed headed either away from or to the center of the world for these people—the great city of Seville.

Unfortunately, we have no record of when, and how, Soto left home. All we know for sure is that Hernando de Soto at some point departed his hometown and traveled to Seville, then Spain's only legal debarkation port for the Indies. From there, he sailed to the Americas, where there is no trace of him until he appears in Panama in 1517, participating in an expedition to Colombia.

Most Soto scholars speculate Soto left Extremadura for Seville in 1513 or 1514, where he joined the great armada to Panama commanded by Pedrarias Dávila as one of two thousand colonists.^ I am inclined to go along with this tradition, though the proof is hardly conclusive. Soto just as easily could have sailed on one of many ships bringing in fresh colonists and supplies between 1514 and 1517, though the overwhelming majority of settlers going to Panama during this period sailed with Pedrarias.

What paltry evidence exists about Soto's crossing and arrival in Panama is contained in a few vague statements made by men who knew him, and were asked years later in legal proceedings a perfunctory question about how long

Soto had lived in the Americas. Most placed him in Panama midway between 1513 and 1519.^ Once, in 1535, Soto himself said he had resided in the Indies "twenty years, more or less,"^ speaking with his usual nonchalance about time and dates. This takes him back to 1515, "more or less," and at least within range of Pedrarias's arrival date.^

The Seville glimpsed by the wide-eyed Soto as he approached from the hills to the north would have been, to our modern eyes, a small river town on a mud plain, surrounded by thick stone walls. As he drew closer, Soto saw emerging in the dust a great heap of ramparts, roofs, and steeples, the largest heap of all being the then recently completed Seville Cathedral. Coming closer still, he would have seen the domes and towers of the city's other churches and shrines rising above knots of red tile and thatched-roof houses, punctuated by bustling, wide-open plazas, narrow streets, and courtyards. Soaring above it all was the slim, exotic Giralda Tower, a twelfth-century Moorish relic that was then one of the tallest man-made objects in Europe, rising about two hundred feet above the city.^

Like other great sixteenth-century cities in Europe, Soto's Seville was a place of stark contrasts—of grandiose palaces pressed up against extraordinary squalor; opulently dressed nobles with their retinues stepping carefully to avoid ragged beggars; the cool gardens of the Alcázar, planted like an oasis amidst hot-baked plazas; the busy markets filled with sharp odors of dung, refuse, and spices; the babble of voices and activity surrounding the Casa de Contratación, headquarters of the monopoly controlling trade with the Indies; and, finally, the quays along the river, where Hernando de Soto would set sail for America.

Nothing better illustrates what the quays looked like in the sixteenth century than a magnificent painting that hangs in Madrid's Museo de América, attributed to Alonso Sánchez Coello, one of Philip II's official court *artistas*.^ Titled *Vista of Seville from Triana,* Sánchez Coello's painting depicts the city as if he were sitting on a godlike perch above the east bank of the river. He captures Seville at the height of a frenzied day, with the river and docks in the foreground, and the city brooding in the background, nearly lost in the murky shadows of swirling gray-and-black storm clouds. Only the Giralda Tower is illuminated, shimmering amidst the gloom as it is struck by a powerful ray of sunlight.^

In the painting, the river is crowded with ships of every size and description—flat-keeled, square-rigged galleons headed for the Mediterranean, where the waters are relatively calm; swift, multimasted caravels built with high gunwales and sharp keels for sailing the more rugged seas of the Atlantic; ferries taking people, horses, goats, and donkeys to and fro across the river; and several half-assembled vessels in dry dock. Some ships are festooned in bright

Seville

Antonio Sánchez Coello, c. 1560

banners, celebrating an arrival or debarkation, their decks outfitted in colorful flags and bunting. Tiny figures on board man oars, steer wheels, and hoist or trim the sails. Passengers stand by on decks, the wealthy dressed in rich cloaks and shining helmets.

On shore, the artist painted numerous set scenes—two *hidalgos* dueling with swords as their somber, black-clad seconds look on; a small crowd watching a guitarist perform as they await a ship's arrival; two nobles in bright cloths sitting at a sumptuous table, eating their last decent meal before debarking on a long voyage; caravans of oxcarts carrying hay and produce toward the city; a group of priests carrying a large cross as they pass a yard filled with ship's tackle and stacks of timber; and a captain behind a table signing up recruits for a voyage to the Indies, West Africa, or just about anywhere.

It is easy to imagine the young Soto standing in one of these scenes, watching solemnly as the *hidalgos* duel, studying the ships as they come and go, or gazing at a retinue of gaudily dressed nobles walking past. I wonder if he was on hand at the quays in 1514, when the first pineapples arrived in Europe at Seville, brought over from the Indies; or when word arrived about a recent New World discovery, a find that would mean a great deal to him a quarter century later. Indeed, in May 1513, the former governor of Puerto Rico, Juan Ponce de León, had visited what he thought was an island north of Cuba,^ and named it *La Florida,* after Easter Sunday, called the Feast of *Pascua Florida* in Spain. According to his report, Juan Ponce had skirted the shore of this new country, probably from the modern Daytona Beach to as far west as Pensacola Bay, stopping here and there to claim beaches for the king, and to snatch slaves to sell in Cuba. The natives, he said, were unusually ferocious, and the land low, marshy, and unpromising. But he excited the attention (and imagination) of at least one official at King Ferdinand's court, the Italian advisor and historian Peter Martyr, who claimed Juan Ponce heard a rumor about a magic spring in Florida that was supposed to make old men young again.^

+   +   +

Most of the recruits for the Pedrarias venture arrived in Seville in late summer 1513, when Soto, if he was there, joined thousands of other would-be colonists lured by dubious reports of gold and an easy life in Panama. Mustering outside the Casa de Contratación, they stood in long lines in front of tables manned by the *entrada*'s senior officers and notaries. These officials interviewed each man, asking his name, age, and military experience, accepting or rejecting candidates based on their health, attitude, and, as often as not, the size of their gratuity. Among the throng that summer were several young men who would later become closely linked with Soto, including his future business partner, Hernán Ponce de León, a *hidalgo* from Talavera de la Reina, near

Toledo; Gabriel de Rojas, who would, like Soto, make a name for himself in Nicaragua and Peru as a "pacifier"^ of Indians; and Alonso Martín, a steady, plebeian conquistador and platoon captain who served alongside Soto in numerous expeditions.^

The massing of would-be colonists, however, was premature. Ordered by the king to assemble in anticipation of an October 1513 sailing date, these summer recruits found themselves waiting impatiently as October came and went, and winter descended on Andalusia. Ostensibly, the delay was logistical, the organizers discovering as the weeks wore on how difficult it was to outfit one of the most ambitious colonizing efforts yet attempted by the Spanish Crown. But the real reason for the creeping pace lay with the king and his advisors. For Ferdinand II, the aging Catholic King—who with his late wife, Isabel, had smashed the Moors at Granada, launched Columbus's explorations, established the infamous Spanish Inquisition, expelled the Jews, and laid the foundations for Spain's ascendancy—was intent on creating nothing less than the ideal colony, based on his own notions of common sense, Catholic-Christian values, and the need to turn a profit. A consummate Renaissance politician and strategist,^ a man as practical and ruthless as he was visionary, Ferdinand saw the Pedrarias effort as an opportunity not only to extend the nascent Spanish Empire, but also to try his hand one last time at what would become the great paradox facing colonial planners for the next five centuries—how to conquer and establish a high-minded, yet lucrative, colony with as little violence as possible, and at minimal cost to the government, with an equal emphasis on native exploitation, fair treatment, cash flow, and conversion to Christianity. The fact that these ideals were contradictory, and nearly always ended up with natives killed, in revolt, or in misery, failed to dissuade Ferdinand and other empire builders from insisting it all would work.

This was not the king's first attempt at carving out a new colony. In the twenty years since Columbus's first voyage in 1492, he and Isabel had sponsored two major efforts across the Ocean Sea. Columbus led the first in 1493, transporting twelve hundred settlers to found Santo Domingo, Spain's (and Europe's) first permanent settlement in the Western Hemisphere. The second departed Seville in 1502 under Nicolás de Ovando. He conveyed twenty-five hundred more colonists to Santo Domingo, which then became a base to conquer and settle Puerto Rico, Cuba, and the mainland, then called Tierra Firme. Both *entradas* had been near-disasters, each losing hundreds of settlers to hunger, disease, Indian hostilities, and an inability to adapt to the steamy, unfamiliar climate. Even for those who survived, the profits were mostly disappointing as Spaniards panned island streams for small traces of gold, raised hogs and cattle, and, when all else failed, scoured Hispaniola and nearby islands for slaves. This, in turn, had decimated the Indians of the central

Caribbean. By 1514, hundreds of thousands had already died in a carnage of warfare, forced labor, disease, and suicidal despair.^

To say the least, the Indies so far had not lived up to Columbus's early claims of a "Paradise" rich in gold and populated by docile people only too happy to serve. Indeed, when most people in Europe thought about America—if they did at all—it was as an impoverished, unhealthy cluster of islands and a shadowy mainland inhabited by hostile primitives, a place that had yielded little of value, and was proving a first-rate nuisance for ships trying to sail to Asia. Only a few diehards continued to think of the Americas as a land of opportunity, or a place to save souls. One of these happened to be the king, however, though his enthusiasm was as much a matter of imperial strategy as idealism. For he knew that if Spain failed to stake out its claims in the Americas, it would mean giving up this territory to a rival power.^

Yet even Ferdinand was having a difficult time selling America—until, unexpectedly, he received a series of highly optimistic letters in 1511 and 1512 from a fledgling Spanish colony in Panama, written by a *hidalgo* previously unknown to the court, by the name of Vasco Núñez de Balboa. This Vasco Núñez claimed to be the leader of three hundred survivors from two privately financed expeditions dispatched from Hispaniola in 1509—both of which had come close to self-destructing because of poor planning and harsh conditions in Tierra Firme. In fact, before the arrival of Balboa's letters in 1511, Ferdinand and the court had not heard from either expedition for so long many feared they had been swallowed up by the enormity of the new continent.

They nearly had been. Within months of their arrival at the swampy, steamy coast of Tierra Firme, where both groups attempted to found rival settlements on opposites sides of the Gulf of Urabá, over seven hundred men had died from hunger, hostile Indians, and the incompetence of their leaders. These were two prominent citizens of Hispaniola, Alonso de Hojeda and Diego de Nicuesa, both of whom had disappeared by 1511—Hojeda by abandoning his men and fleeing in disgrace to Spain,^ and Nicuesa by setting out on an expedition into the Darién jungle, and failing to return.^ Into this leadership void had emerged this man Balboa, who not only combined the two struggling colonies into one, and negotiated peace with the local Indians, but also had managed to get the colony up and running, eventually establishing a rough-hewn but reasonably comfortable life for its inhabitants.

Balboa's positive reports electrified the court with confident claims that Darién was the prize in the Americas everyone had been looking for. The land, he wrote, was fertile, inhabited by peaceful Indians, and pleasant once one became acclimated. At least fifty streams in the Darién region bore substantial traces of gold, he insisted, with "large lumps in great abundance." Certain Indian tribes, said Balboa, had so much gold in the form of jewelry, shields, and figurines that they kept it "in *barbacoas* [cribs] like maize." Even more entic-ing to the king was Balboa's news that a "Southern Sea" existed just a few days' march south of Santa María. This information, he wrote, came from "trusted" native informers who assured him that "on the south side" of a nar-row isthmus the Indians were fabulously wealthy in gold and pearls, and that they lived beside a sea that was "very good to navigate in canoes, being always pacific"—a comment that may be the source of this (not always calm) ocean's name. All he needed, Balboa told the king, was a thousand men, weapons, and Crown support, and he would secure vast riches, and conquer "a great part of the world."

In short, like Columbus, Balboa greatly exaggerated his claims of gold, though here the comparison ends between the dreamy, incredulous Admiral of the Ocean Sea and the swarthy, down-to-earth Balboa. Other than spurious claims of gold, which he clearly offered as a calculated attempt to attract the attention of the king, most everything else Balboa wrote in these letters rings true, particularly his pragmatic advice for what it would take to establish a thriv-ing colony. In one letter, for instance, he suggests that Ferdinand limit the num-ber of colonists to one thousand, insisting that these men be recruited "from the island of Hispaniola, for those who might come direct from Castile would not be fit for much until they were accustomed to the country." He also recom-mends, not surprisingly, that he, Vasco Núñez de Balboa, should be named gov-ernor of Darién—an immodest, if practical, request that might have prevented the tragedies about to occur in Tierra Firme, had the king acquiesced.

Ferdinand received most of Balboa's letters on a battlefield in northern Spain, where he was busy conquering Navarre, one of the last small, indepen-dent kingdoms in Iberia. The war kept him occupied during the final five months of 1512, after which he returned to Valladolid and plunged into orga-nizing his new colony, spurred on not only by Balboa's letters, but also by dis-turbing reports that a Portuguese fleet had been sighted in the Caribbean, and that several French corsairs had been spied off the Atlantic seaboard of North America. Reacting in an uncharacteristic fit of anxiety, the normally patient Ferdinand ordered, in May 1513, that the great armada be prepared "without losing a single day," warning his court and everyone involved in the expedi-tion that "it would be a great loss"^ if another power beat them to Balboa's sup-posedly golden country.

For a sixty-one-year-old man who would be dead in three years, the king plunged into the project with astonishing energy, issuing a barrage of orders, edicts, and decrees encompassing virtually every detail of the enterprise. He began in July by changing the nondescript name Tierra Firme to the more al-luring Castilla del Oro—"Golden Castile"—quickly moving on to consider questions ranging from how many hammocks the settlers would require to whether he approved of an idea to outfit the colony's soldiers in armor made of tortoiseshell. (He said no, though this armor later proved effective against poison arrows.) In one edict, the king laid out his ideas for the design of future settlements, specifying that they be organized in a grid, with a central plaza surrounded by the main church and public buildings. This later became the blueprint for thousands of towns and cities built in Latin America over the next five centuries.^ In the same edict, he issued rules forbidding a wide range of "offenses," giving Pedrarias license to "go beyond the [usual] laws of these kingdoms" in prosecuting perpetrators—the belief being, as with most Utopian ventures, that the supposed moral shortcomings afflicting the bad "Old" World could be washed away in this "New" World simply by decreeing they did not exist.

But most of Ferdinand's thinking that summer, when he was not approving supply lists and initialing petitions from would-be colonists, was devoted to the Indian Question. With continuing reports of abuse and genocide coming out of Hispaniola and other colonies, this vexing issue—of how to balance exploitation with Christian values—was again being loudly debated among intellectuals at the court. A crucial moment came when a Dominican priest from Santo Domingo, Fray Antonio de Montesino, burst into the king's private apartments one day in 1512 and began shouting out a harangue against the cruelty and greed he had witnessed on Hispaniola. He ended his tirade by asking, "Is this what Your Highness commands?" Ferdinand, shocked by hearing what he must have known was true, but had never heard put so bluntly, answered, "No, by God, nor ever so commanded in my life!"^

Ferdinand reacted to Montesino's outburst, and other urgent appeals to stop the abuses, by issuing a flurry of documents during 1512 and 1513, designed to reform his Indian policies and to control the colonists' often wanton abuse of natives—at least on paper. Because these policies remained in effect throughout Soto's career, it is worth taking a brief look at them, even if they were ignored almost completely by Soto and virtually all conquistadors and colonists far away across the sea.

The three most important Indian edicts prepared on the eve of the Pedrarias armada were, first, the so-called Laws of Burgos,^ a list of regulations enacted by a council held in this northern Spanish city, mandating the good treatment of Indians and ordering a surprising array of modern-sounding regulations ranging from required pregnancy leaves for female laborers to maximum hours an Indian could be worked in a mine. Next came the king's detailed *Instrucciónes* given to Pedrarias, in which Ferdinand commanded the new governor to set an example by behaving humanely toward the Indians, and to punish offenders severely. But by far the most remarkable of the three was the infamous *El Requerimiento*^—"The Requirement"—a document conquistadors were "required" to read to any new Indians they encountered, this being the official explanation of not only who the Spanish were, but also a brief history of the world as seen by Ferdinand and his advisors. This began with the Creation story in Genesis, the birth and life of Jesus, the nature of the church and papacy, and ended with two stark choices offered to the Indians—submit to Spanish rule, or die by Spanish steel.

These documents comprise a stack of paper perhaps one inch high, containing paragraph after paragraph of high-minded rhetoric about fairness and Christian brotherhood. None of this, however, mattered more than a few critical passages read out in jungles across America by Soto and other heavily armed conquistadors to newly encountered Indian peoples. These lines come at the end of a statement several pages long (and theoretically translated by an interpreter, though it was often delivered in Spanish or Latin), when the conquistador finally says to his audience of presumably very patient and attentive Indians: "Therefore, I entreat and require you to understand well what I have told you . . . that you recognize the Church as mistress and superior of the world universe, and the Supreme Pontiff called Pope in her name, and the King and Queen our lords in her place as overlords . . . If you thus do . . . Their Highnesses, and I in their name, will receive you with all love and charity, and will leave you your wives, sons, and property, freely and without servitude."

But—and this is a very big "but"—should the Indians fail to abide by this baffling document, the conquistador in question was to say: "[W]ith God's help I will powerfully invade you, and make war on you in every region and manner of which I might be capable, and I will subject you to the yoke and obedience of the Church and of Their Highnesses, and I will seize your persons and those of your wives and children and will make them slaves, and as such I will sell them and dispose of them as His Highness might command; and I will seize your goods and do you all hurt and harm which I can . . . And I declare that the deaths and damage which might grow out of it will be your fault, and not that of His Highness, nor mine, nor of these *caballeros* who accompany me."

Apologists for Ferdinand long have defended him as a true reformer who intended the "make war on you" lines in the *Requerimiento* to be used only in extreme cases. Others insist Ferdinand was a Machiavellian monster and hypocrite who talked about fairness and humanity, but looked the other way when his conquistadors behaved with cruelty—so long as they brought home gold and riches, and planted the Spanish flag.

Both positions miss the critical point about King Ferdinand and most other Spaniards of his day, including Soto. They believed their nation had a divine calling to conquer and dominate the Indies, and to convert the natives and spread the Hispanic culture. How, exactly, this was to be accomplished, and what it meant in terms of morality, was something for Ferdinand's clerics and intellectuals to debate, and councils to address in high-minded documents. Ultimately, however, this talk and paper mattered very little, success being the only true standard a conqueror—or a king—lives by.

This does not mean that Ferdinand approved of the savage tactics used on Hispaniola, and about to be unleashed by Pedrarias in Panama. He consistently opposed them, devoting considerable time and energy to developing and pushing for reform. Yet if this behavior appears paradoxical to us, it apparently did not to Ferdinand, who genuinely seemed to believe that conquest could be compatible with benevolence, and greed with common sense. He was not the last armchair imperialist to think so.

The other great matter for Ferdinand to decide that summer of 1513 was who would govern his new colony. Apparently, he agonized over this decision, waiting until late July to announce the appointment of Pedro Arias de Avila, a native of Segovia and a recent hero of the Algerian campaigns, naming him "Our Captain and Governor of Castilla del Oro." The king, we are told, considered other candidates, including Vasco Núñez de Balboa. But in the end he was persuaded to choose Pedrarias by his chief colonial advisor, Bishop Juan Rodríguez de Fonseca, for reasons that have baffled historians ever since.

To begin with, Pedrarias was nearly seventy years old, fair-skinned, with green eyes, red hair, and an advanced kidney disease. He also had, as far as we know, no experience in the Indies or in any governing capacity, was little known at court, and had spent his entire career as a lackluster minor captain, until a single courageous act defending a citadel in the recent Algerian campaign, which won him a royal commendation and the nickname Lion of Bugía. His other major qualification, besides being one of Fonseca's men, was his pedigree, which was thick with close associations to the Crown, including a paternal grandfather who served as *contador,* treasurer, and power behind the throne of King Enrique IV,* Queen Isabel's brother and predecessor. Pedrarias's wife's aunt also had been one of Queen Isabel's closest friends and advisors. For Pedrarias himself, however, the historic record is mostly a blank before 1509,^ and his spirited defense at Bugía, which gives us little to go on in trying to understand this man who would soon turn Ferdinand's grand plans into a travesty, and who would play such a critical role in Soto's education.

✛   ✛   ✛

Originally, Ferdinand planned to dispatch eight hundred colonists to Panama, sailing in nine Crown vessels, at a cost of five million *maravedíes.* But by the time the armada was ready to sail on January 15, 1514, three months late according to the king's original schedule, the expedition had become such a cause célèbre that its personnel had increased beyond any semblance of reason, to well over two thousand settlers sailing in eighteen vessels, costing twenty million

---

*Enrique IV reigned from 1454 to 1474, and was deposed for incompetence.

maravedíes—most of it paid for with high-interest loans from the same Italian bankers in Seville who financed Columbus's expeditions, and later would help finance at least a small portion of Soto's venture in *La Florida*.^

This lavish funding paid not only for the ships, tackle, and crew for the voyage, but a mountain of supplies that included 375,000 pounds of flour, 300,000 pounds of biscuit, 69,000 gallons of oil and wine, "kits" of armor and weapons for several hundred soldiers, tools for planting and carpentry, five hundred young fruit trees, sixteen bushels of three-month wheat, seeds for planting, tents, pharmaceutical supplies, fifty beds for a new hospital, bells and crosses for a new church, and heaps of chains and fetters for securing slaves, in case they faltered in vigorously endorsing the *Requerimiento*.^ No expense was spared, to the point that Ferdinand's treasury, already under a severe strain from his many wars, never fully recovered—and was heavily in debt when he died two years later.

Individual colonists also expended fortunes large and small on paying for their passage and personal equipment. The wealthiest brought along slaves, horses, and, most important of all, the finest clothing money could buy for an *entrada* that was as much a social event for well-heeled Spaniards as a serious attempt at settlement and conquest. No one indulged in luxurious, flashy apparel more than Pedrarias Dávila. Known in his youth as The Gallant because of his ostentatious ways, he obtained a royal exemption from the church's sumptuary laws. He also convinced the king to spend a large sum on the fleet's going-away party, hiring bands, organizing fireworks and fiestas, and buying huge flags and banners made of silk and cotton to festoon the masts and gunwales of his ships.

Even before it set sail, the expedition to Darién was turning into a disaster of wildly unrealistic expectations, poor planning, and, ultimately, deadly miscalculations. This became painfully evident the very morning the armada was to sail, and the festivities began with a farewell Mass at the cathedral, leading to a grand parade through the narrow streets of Seville to the river. Witnesses describe the colonists as "very well dressed, none owning less than a jacket of silk and many one of brocade," and "the most splendid people who ever left Spain." The people of Seville, undoubtedly overjoyed to be free from the burden of supporting two thousand extra people, lined the streets, cheering and waving. Unfortunately, the parade fell flat when it reached the docks. For here the shipmasters discovered something they should have known—that there was simply not enough room aboard the vessels for everyone in this resplendent company.

Six weeks later, on February 26, Carnival Sunday, the throng again mustered at the cathedral and marched to the quays, where additional ships and cutbacks on personnel meant that everyone was finally accommodated in the fleet,

which now numbered twenty-one vessels—sixteen Crown caravels and large
naos, one *burchón,* and four or five chartered ships. On this occasion, Pedrarias
and his settlers made it down the wide, meandering Río Guadalquivir as far as
the small port of Sanlúcar, on the coast, before bad luck struck again. This time
it came in the form of a late-winter storm lashing in off the sea. Blasting into
the fleet as it pulled clear of the river's sandbar, the storm forced the ships
to return to shore in disarray, with several nearly colliding, two running
aground, and most damaged by the wind. For two days, the bulk of the fleet
was forced to ride out the storm at anchor off the coast, with the exhausted and
seasick passengers finally coming ashore at Sanlúcar on the third day, when
the storm abated.

For another six weeks, the colonists were compelled to stay in this small
coastal village while the ships were repaired. It was a miserable respite, with
no place to bed down, and little food available to feed such a horde. Several
hundred would-be colonists quit and went home in disgust. This gave the new
governor a chance to sign up even more recruits from those left behind in
Seville, and to puff up the rolls with as many bribe-paying passengers as he
could squeeze into the ships. Oviedo, who was there, said the number of
colonists grew again in Sanlúcar, once more swelling to over two thousand.
Historian Kathleen Romoli, who perused archival records in Seville, suggests
the number was as high as three thousand,^ dispatched to a colony whose acting governor had requested one thousand men, whom he explicitly warned
should be only well-seasoned veterans with years of prior experience living in
the Indies.

The armada finally set sail on April 11, 1514, successful at last on their third
try.^ Once clear of the Iberian coastline, which Hernando de Soto would not
see again for twenty-two years, the ships made for the Canary Islands, following the same route Soto's armada would take in 1538. On the island of Gomera
they picked up fresh meat, vegetables, wine, and extra horses, departing on
May 9 for the open sea. Heading south by southwest, they sailed the same route
as Columbus on his second voyage, riding trade winds away from the coast of
Africa to the island of Dominica, some three hundred miles north of
Venezuela, halfway around the crescent arc of the Caribbean's Leeward and
Windward chains.

Almost certainly, this was Soto's first voyage by sea—if he was, in fact,
present in the armada—an exhilarating moment for a teenager from Jerez de
los Caballeros as he breathed in the smells of the sea and watched its endless
sweep in all directions. Chances are Soto, as a page or a simple soldier, would
have been sequestered belowdecks for most of the voyage, out of the way except for brief sojourns topside to catch some air. In the hold, he probably slept
on whatever floor space was available, crammed in with dozens of other men,

bales of supplies, crates, jars, barrels, goats, chickens, and, because mounts were a page's responsibility, horses. (Horses were given far more space than most human passengers; they traveled in cloth slings that kept them upright and secure against rough seas and spells of kicking.)

The fleet sighted land at Dominica Island on June 2. For the settlers, unaccustomed to crossing an ocean, the appearance of this Caribbean island's rugged hills on the horizon must have been a tremendous relief. Sighting any speck of shoreline, particularly one familiar to the pilots, was a time for rejoicing, praying, and solemnly singing hymns. But because this island was rumored to be a haven of cannibals and ferocious "Caribes," Pedrarias held the Mass celebrating their safe arrival on board the ships, instead of on the beach, which was the usual practice.

For four days, the fleet stayed anchored off Dominica taking on fresh water, pumping dry the ships' hulls, and making minor repairs. It was during this hiatus that Pedrarias Dávila gave his earliest indication of how he planned to administer his new colony. The incident occurred when several Spaniards went ashore against the governor's orders, got drunk, and disappeared just as the fleet was preparing to sail. Pedrarias, in a rage, sent a unit of halberdiers to fetch them. When one of the escapees, a servant named San Martín, drunkenly insisted on staying on the island, Pedrarias ordered him hung from the nearest tree.

This summary execution, without a trial or last rites, dampened the festive mood of the colonists. For in Spain, even murderers and other vicious criminals were not hung without a chance to commend their souls to heaven. If this was how their governor behaved less than a month away from Spain, what could they expect from the man whom they would soon be calling *El Furor Domini*, "the Scourge of God"?

✣ 3 ✣

The Scourge of God

THE FLEET'S NEXT WATER stop was at the Gulf of Santa Marta on the north coast of Colombia, where Pedrarias and one thousand men—including, perhaps, Hernando de Soto—engaged in operations that foreshadowed the slaughter to come in Panama. For three days, they harassed local Indians—burning huts, plundering gold trinkets, capturing slaves, and twice fighting pitched battles that quickly devolved into massacres. One Indian captured was a "princess" found hiding in a thicket by an African slave belonging to the young Gonzalo Fernández de Oviedo, the future historian, who had come along as a minor official in the Pedrarias government. He says this young girl was "sixteen or seventeen years old, pretty, and as fair-skinned as a Castilian; she was quite naked, but held herself with such grave pride that she gave an impression of dignity." Later, Oviedo would criticize Soto and others of gross mistreatment of the Indians, though in this case his behavior is hardly better. Spiriting away this "princess" from Santa Marta, he reports she died soon after arriving in Darién—he says of "heartbreak" at being separated from her people.

Nearly two weeks after departing Santa Marta, on June 26, most of the armada finally dropped anchor in the Gulf of Urabá, off the Darién region of Panama. If anyone was on hand to greet them, there is no record. The settlement itself stood inland three or four miles, on a height above the fetid coastal swamps, and out of sight of the beach. Nor do we know the colonists' reaction as they crowded onto the decks to stare at what amounted to a nondescript stretch of sand bordered by canebrakes and palms, and topped off by the Serranía de Darién, its six-thousand-foot peaks undoubtedly obscured by wisps of fog. Sold on the notion this was a paradise on earth, or at least a reasonable facsimile of temperate Spain, most of Pedrarias's settlers must have been stunned by what they saw. Where, they asked, was the great capital of Castilla del Oro? Where were the docks, houses, and ships? Where was the treasury packed with gold?

Even more distressing was the intense, superheated humidity settling over the ships. On a map, the Gulf of Urabá looks like a long finger of water wedged between the northwest coast of South America and the narrow Isthmus of Panama. Trapped between two mountain ranges, with low, steamy swamps on either side, and the murky Atrato River disgorging mud and water to the south, Urabá draws heat and sogginess like a sponge. For those used to a drier and more temperate climate, sudden immersion without a proper acclimation can be miserable. Stomachs become nauseous, fingers swell, and heads pound. And if the heat were not enough, the settlers that first night discovered another prominent feature of Urabá ecology—the mosquito. Swarms of them must have feasted happily on the sweat, filth, and blood of so many people crammed aboard two dozen wooden vessels, awaiting orders to disembark.^

✛   ✛   ✛

When Pedrarias Dávila arrived in Panama that hot, sticky summer in 1514, the Spanish were aware of some twenty thousand miles of coastline in the Americas, appearing on maps as a shadowy line running from Newfoundland south almost to the Río de la Plate in Argentina. Why, then, did they chose Urabá for Europe's first mainland colony? Almost no one who came here during the *conquista* liked it. Chroniclers called it an "evil" place, where "sickly vapors" rose from malodorous swamps, and few natives lived. Even today, the site of Santa María is considered unhealthy. It remains lightly populated, a haven for contraband runners in skiffs and native *barcos* (dugout canoes) who eke out a living fishing, or trading cocaine from Colombia for air conditioners and televisions smuggled in from Panama.

None of this mattered to the Spaniards for one simple reason. In 1514, they were convinced that Darién was overflowing with gold.

This mistaken notion originated with Christopher Columbus. In 1502, he discovered and reconnoitered the coast of Central America on his fourth and final expedition, announcing upon his return that there was "a vast quantity of gold" in the interior of the isthmus. He never saw much of the stuff himself, however, his information having come from Indians he met on the coast. Rumors were also enough to excite the explorer and mapmaker Juan de la Cosa. He landed on the coast of Urabá in 1504 and plundered ninety-one hundred pesos worth of gold kettledrums, earrings, pendants, and small idols^ from tribes living on the eastern shore, claiming this was proof of vast riches in this country. But like most gold in Panama, this tiny cache almost certainly originated hundreds of miles away, deep in the interior of Colombia and Peru, having been brought to Panama by traders over the course of several centuries. Yet another explorer, Rodrigo de Bastidas, also explored the coast of Colombia east of Urabá in 1500–1501, and returned to Hispaniola with more gold trinkets, and more claims of boundless riches.^

Thus we have three prominent explorers bringing home hardly enough treasure to fill a hatbox, yet insisting that Colombia and Panama were saturated with precious metals. And what better place to exploit these riches than the Gulf of Urabá, poised in the geographic center of these supposedly golden shores? Lost in the enthusiasm, however, was the fact this loot was obtained at tremendous cost. Nearly everyone on the Columbus, Bastidas, and Cosa expeditions died. The Great Mariner's *entrada* was plagued by fever, Indian attacks, devastating storms, and an infestation of termites that eventually wrecked his ships and left him stranded. Cosa, too, was shipwrecked and grounded in Urabá for eighteen months, where he lost half his one hundred men to poison arrows, starvation, and the deadly climate. And if this were not enough, there was the more recent example of the Nicuesa and Hojeda fiascoes, where over seven hundred men had died, with hardly any gold collected. So far, the only positive development in this wretched country was the astonishing success of Vasco Núñez de Balboa and his five hundred men. Surviving the climate, they also had organized, by 1514, a reasonably comfortable, if austere, colony at Santa María la Antigua de Darién, on Urabá's western shore.

Founded in 1510 by the remnants of the Nicuesa and Hojeda expeditions, Balboa and his senior officers chose the site for Santa María because it was one of the few tracts of dry ground near a freshwater stream, within walking distance of the sea. It also was as far away as possible from the hostile Urabá Indians living across the gulf. Incensed by Juan de la Cosa and his men looting and raping during their months of shipwreck, Urabá's warriors had henceforth attacked any Spaniards daring to approach their province, firing at them the most potent and fearful aboriginal weapon in the Indies—small arrows dipped in the venom of jungle snakes and frogs, and concoctions brewed from highly toxic herbs.^

Balboa's Spaniards did not build their settlement from scratch, however. In the usual *conquista* fashion, they had seized an existing town belonging to a *cacique* named Darién, whose Cuevas did not fight with arrows, poison or otherwise. They also proved much more amenable to Spanish domination, in part because Balboa and his men were so emaciated at first by hunger and privation they were forced to treat the natives decently, in exchange for food and servants—a novel idea that benefited both Spaniards and Cuevas. Indeed, by 1514 it had become Balboa's official policy, and was largely responsible for the modest measure of prosperity for both peoples.

✛   ✛   ✛

The first inkling that life was about to change radically for the Darién settlers and their Indian vassals came when a messenger from His Magnificence, the Lord Governor Pedrarias, marched down a trail through the low-lying swamps and canebrakes and reached the outskirts of the settlement. According to the sixteenth-century historian and priest Bartolomé de las Casas,^ the messenger asked the first people he met—who must have been startled to see a resplendently dressed Spanish *criado* suddenly emerging out of the jungle—to take him to Balboa.

" 'Where is Vasco Núñez de Balboa?' queried the messenger.

" 'There he is,' someone said, pointing to a man dressed in a cotton blouse over a linen shirt and wearing hemp sandals and coarse breeches, who was looking on and helping his slaves at thatching a house." The messenger was taken aback by such a plainly dressed man. "He could not believe that was Vasco Núñez," says Las Casas, "whose exploits and riches were so famous in Castile that he had expected to see him seated on a majestic throne." Indeed, this scene of Pedrarias's flashy *criado* meeting the down-to-earth Balboa has become a seminal episode in histories of the early *conquista,* which typically begin their lengthy sections on the coming enmity between Pedrarias and Balboa by setting up their protagonist, Vasco Núñez, as the practical, no-nonsense man performing a chore that is unexceptional, but essential to the survival of the colony, against the tyrannical and vain Pedrarias, more interested in appearances than in practicalities.

In 1514, Vascó Nuñez de Balboa—a man who would have a tremendous impact on young Soto—was about forty years old. "Handsome of face and figure, very tall and well built, clean-limbed and strong," he was famous for his fair skin and bright red hair and beard. Born and raised in Soto's hometown of Jerez de los Caballeros—apparently in Soto's own parish of San Miguel^—Balboa had departed Spain in 1500 to explore the coast of Colombia with Rodrigo de Bastidas. Eventually, he ended up on Hispaniola, where he bought a plantation and tried to settle down. His efforts to raise hogs, however, not only led to mounting debts, but also to a fervent desire to flee the tedium of settled life. In 1510, hounded by creditors and legally unable to depart the island without first paying off his loans, Balboa escaped by hiding out in a barrel as a stowaway aboard a ship headed for Panama to reinforce Hojeda's faltering expedition.

As it turned out, Balboa's talent was not in raising swine, but in crisis management. This quickly became evident as Balboa the stowaway emerged from obscurity that autumn to save the survivors of Hojeda's and Nicuesa's expeditions, who gratefully elected him their *caudillo* (a leader or chief), summarily deposing senior expedition officers who were legally entitled to govern. By December 1510, the king had named Balboa acting captain and governor of Darién. The appointment, however, was temporary. Apparently, the king wanted to name his own man, and did not entirely trust this upstart *caudillo* chosen outside the usual chain of command.

Ironically, Balboa was much closer in temperament and ability to Ferdinand's ideal governor than was Pedrarias Dávila, as spelled out in the king's 1513 *Instrucciónes* and other documents. Firm, energetic, and cunning, Balboa shared the king's belief in ruling through a shrewd mix of benevolence and cruelty, reward and punishment. He also took care to prevent his men from overworking native laborers, giving the Indians time to grow their own crops and attend to their families. But this hardly justifies the admiration of most historians and biographers over the centuries, who laud Balboa as a great humanitarian, depicting him as a charming rogue with a talent for governing, a man beloved by both Spaniards and Indians.^ Balboa himself admitted his policies were based more on expediency than any moral imperative, and on his belief that a well-treated Indian was more profitable than one mistreated.^ Indeed, Vasco Núñez could be as iron-willed and ruthless as any highly ambitious man during this period, treating any Indian that crossed him with cruelty and contempt^—or any Spaniard, as officials of the Nicuesa and Hojeda *entradas* discovered when they opposed his elevation to *caudillo*. This included Diego de Nicuesa, the lost governor, who abruptly emerged from the jungle one day in the spring of 1511 to reclaim his position as legal head of the colony—only to be seized by Balboa and placed on a leaky, worm-rotted ship with his followers. Forced to set sail toward the open sea, neither ship nor passengers were heard from again.^

Balboa was not always this obvious when dealing with threats to his aspirations. In 1512, he put down a rebellion over gold shares by resorting not to the usual arrests and punishments, but by leaving town, ostensibly on a hunt. This prompted the rebels to storm the treasury, and then to begin fighting over who got what—as Balboa knew they would. In the end, after several colonists were killed and Santa María was reduced to chaos, even the malcontents begged Balboa to return and restore order. He did, and was cheered by all in Santa María's makeshift plaza.

But Balboa's greatest achievement in Santa María was his carefully wrought network of alliances with some two dozen Cueva *caciques* in the region surrounding Darién, affiliations that not only made life less tense in Darién, but also made possible his recent trek to "discover" the South Sea (the Pacific) with a mere 190 men. Even the usually critical Alonso Zuazo, a young Crown lawyer in Panama, writes admiringly of Balboa's Indian policy. "Vasco Núñez had labored with very good skill to make peace with many *caciques* and principal lords of the Indians," he tells us, "by which he kept in peace about thirty *caciques* with all their Indians, and did so by not taking from them more than they were willing to give, aiding them in their wars they had with one another, and thereby Vasco Núñez became so well liked that he could go in security through a hundred leagues of Tierra Firme. In all parts the Indians willingly gave him much gold and also their sisters and daughters to take with him to be married or used as he wished."

✛   ✛   ✛

Pedrarias's messenger did not dawdle in Santa María. Rushing back down the jungle trail to the fleet, he delivered the startling news to the colonists—that Vasco Núñez had been to the South Sea. The excited messenger breathlessly announced it was close by, adding that it was just a nine- or ten-day march across a narrow isthmus, over the mountains they all could see in the distance. And Vasco Núñez, the messenger said, had made the trip the previous September with only 190 men.

Pedrarias's initial response is unrecorded, though he must have been furious. One of his chief enticements to come here was the hope of making this discovery himself, and enjoying the eternal fame as the man who opened up the long-sought passage to the far sea, and thus to the Orient. Now, in a single stroke, this Balboa had elevated himself from usurper to hero, from a rival of little consequence to a potential enemy whose fame would protect him should he prove a nuisance. The old man also knew that word of Balboa's feat must have arrived by now at the court of the Catholic King, since Balboa's ship bearing the account of his discovery was crossing east at the same time Pedrarias's armada crossed west. This meant Ferdinand was probably already concocting a sumptuous reward for Vasco Núñez de Balboa that could only undermine Pedrarias's own position.

For Pedrarias Dávila, however, the Balboa situation was mostly a worry for the future. More immediate was the need to organize a suitably magnificent entrance into his new colony—both to encourage his dispirited followers and to impress Balboa, should the acting governor attempt to militarily contest Pedrarias's authority. (This was highly unlikely, but not entirely impossible.) Ordering the fighting men among his two to three thousand settlers to arm themselves, he saw to it they were "ranged in very good order." Likewise, he ordered the colonists to arrange themselves according to protocol, with the *hidalgos* and armed footmen in front protecting the governor, his family, and the bishop. Next came the other officials, lesser nobility, and so forth, down to the lowly blacksmiths, bootmakers, housemaids, stableboys, whores, porters, and slaves, who took up the rear. Soto, if he was there, probably marched as a page or squire, following in the company of his patron.

Stepping along the trail with his comrades, swaggering in the heat and singing a marching song, Soto first passed through stands of canebrakes beyond the beach, getting his first glimpse of an environment he soon would know all too well as he heard parrots screeching overhead, circling loudly in chaotic flocks. He would have seen pelicans, ducks, and cormorants skittering through the rushes, and possibly an alligator sunning himself near shallow pools along the path. As the grand procession approached the higher ground leading up to Santa María, he would have seen the brakes give way to palms, mangroves, cedars, and, perhaps, a towering ceiba or *espave*, with its massive trunks bare of branches until eighty or ninety feet up in the air.

Reaching the cleared fields around the settlement, they were met by the five hundred *vecinos* (citizens) of Santa María, who presented their own spectacle as they marched forth unarmed in their faded, simple clothing, their faces sun-

burned and leathery, their frames hard and lean. Historian Kathleen Romoli
has suggested that Pedrarias's hatred for Balboa may have begun at this very
moment, "when Vasco Núñez stood tall and easy before him, his bronzed face
schooled to seemly deference, his manner at once respectful and confident," as
opposed to Pedrarias, who "was nearing seventy . . . had a chronic kidney ail-
ment . . . [and] had just covered three miles of rough trail in a *tenue* singularly
unadapted to exertion in the tropics." Romoli concludes: "[S]omething had
gone wrong with his studied pageant; the effect of the shabby, competent *vecinos* on his overmarshalled, overarmed forces" being "like that of a skillful
understatement on a paragraph of bombast."

The next big disappointment for Pedrarias and his people was Santa María
la Antigua de Darién itself. Expecting a bustling, substantial city, the settlers
instead found themselves in a sprawling cluster of about one hundred native-
style huts "with walls of canes tied with *lianas* [vines] . . . plastered over with
earth," and roofs "covered with straw or long grass," the whole town arranged
around a dusty, makeshift plaza. Beyond the town, they could see terraced
fields carved into a ridge, haphazardly planted in Indian fashion with maize,
beans, sweet potatoes, melons, and pineapples, a crop adequate for Balboa's
five hundred men and some fifteen hundred native servants and laborers, but
hardly enough to support thousands more—as the more astute among the
colonists must have realized even then.

That first night, Balboa made room in his own home for Pedrarias and his
wife, Isabel de Bobadilla y Peñalosa.* A few days later the governor returned
the favor by turning out his host and appropriating most of the former acting
governor's property. Meanwhile, Pedrarias assigned quarters to officials and
nobles in the homes of Balboa's chief men, while common soldiers seized Indian homes in the Cueva town, forcing many of the natives out into the bush.
The remaining colonists probably slept on the ground, wrapping themselves in
their expensive cloaks until tents and other supplies could be unloaded from
the ships. Among them, Soto undoubtedly spent his first night in Darién sleeping under the stars—assuming that he slept at all.

✦   ✦   ✦

Pedrarias Dávila's governorship began with pretensions of being a pageant
out of a romance, but quickly became a farce, then a tragedy. For neither the
king, Bishop Fonseca, Pedrarias, nor the settlers seem to have considered that
the sudden arrival of two to three thousand raw recruits might stretch the resources of a colony where several hundred people had already died from the
harsh climate and paucity of food.^

---

*This Isabel de Bobadilla is the mother of the Isabel de Bobadilla whom Soto later married.

At first, the newcomers avoided starvation by eating from the ship's provisions, leaving the still-precarious homegrown food supply to the original settlers and Indians. After a month, however, the king's orders allowed Pedrarias to cease free distribution, and to charge a "fair price" for the royal stores. True to form, the governor, Royal Agent Juan de Tavira, and other officials took this decree to mean they could lock up the provisions and charge exorbitant rates few people could afford.

The effect was immediate and disastrous. Within days, Santa María's meager resources were exhausted, and hunger set in, soon aggravated by the appearance of a strange and lethal malady the settlers called *modorra*. This may have been typhoid or, some have suggested, bubonic plague.^

One can surmise the horror of those among Pedrarias's splendid company suddenly finding themselves without sustenance, walking the makeshift streets of Santa María with no place to sleep and nothing to eat, a situation that quickly grew into a near hysteria as even the rich were forced to sell their brocades and gold rings for what little native grain was on hand. Meanwhile, the governor and his cronies locked up the remainder of the ship's stores in a warehouse near the harbor, and ordered a heavily armed guard to keep everyone but paying customers away.

By midsummer, Oviedo tells us "fifteen or twenty" settlers were dying "every day . . . [of] exhaustion and illness," with Alonso Zuazo claiming twelve or thirteen hundred died by summer's end—fully "two thirds"^ of the colonists. Las Casas dryly notes: "Hunger became so acute that many gentlemen, who had mortgaged their inheritance in Castile, were dying with the cry, 'Give me bread,' while others exchanged garments of crimson silk for a pound of corn bread." Pedrarias himself became feverish and ill and threatened to abandon Darién, staying on only because the bishop of Santa María, Juan de Quevedo, and others suggested the king might hold him responsible for the plague and famine should he suddenly reappear in Spain.

In the early days of the crisis, Pedrarias and his well-fed clique reacted by doing nothing. Then, after a freak fire burned down the shack containing the king's provisions, leaving even him and his cronies without food, the old governor panicked, responding to the gathering disaster with a hastily arranged strategy of dispatching fighting men to fan out in all directions in search of food—which they were ordered to steal from the Indians, along with whatever gold they found. This remedy, however, merely added to the catastrophe as the poorly disciplined soldiers, sent off to strip bare the surrounding countryside, unleashed a bloodbath of looting, killing, slave taking, and destruction, attacking Balboa's native friends and foes indiscriminately, and utterly ignoring Ferdinand's *Requerimiento* and other finely crafted documents. Overnight, this wanton destruction transformed the region from a state of peaceful coexistence to one of terror, kidnappings, skirmishes, and chaos, adding to the colony's woes the peril of Indian attacks.

Initially, the Spaniards' incompetence and inexperience caused them to suffer casualties perhaps as high, per capita, as their native victims. Soon enough, however, the conquerors caught on to their bloody business.^

Oviedo describes one particularly savage *entrada* to the northwest of Darién, led by Pedrarias's second-in-command, Juan de Ayora. "On this journey," writes Oviedo, "Juan de Ayora not only failed to read the *Requerimiento* and give the warnings he was supposed to give the Indians before making war on them, but he attacked them at night and tortured the *caciques* and *principales* to get gold from them, roasting some on grills, having some eaten alive by dogs, hanging some, and devising new forms of torture for others; they also enslaved the men and seized their wives and daughters wherever they went, and these Indians they divided up among themselves."

The victims of this slaughter called themselves the Cueva. Because they became extinct within a half century of Pedrarias's arrival, no one knows what they looked like. Probably, they were short and big-boned, with round faces and skin the color of rosewood like the present-day Cuna of eastern Panama, whose race descends from pre-Columbian tribes from Urabá and the Atrato basin. According to Oviedo and other eyewitnesses, the Cueva were generally a peaceful people, spending most of their time raising maize and vegetables, conducting minor raids against nearby tribes, and hunting. Organized into loose chiefdoms composed of several towns and villages, they were ruled by a high chieftain, or *queví*—a hereditary king who extracted tribute from vassal enclaves, and whose subjects considered him a semidivine descendant of the sun.^

Most Cuevas wore very little. Across their chests and backs, and up and down their arms and legs, they etched elaborate tattoos patterned in circles and diamonds, and shaped like snakes, birds, and lizards. The women, says chronicler Pascual de Andagoya, wore cotton mantles from the waist down, and the men wore brightly colored seashells over their "private parts . . . secured round the loins by cords." On special occasions the *quevíes* and their principal men also covered themselves with body paint, elaborate feather capes, headdresses, and gold ornaments.^ As for housing, Cuevas lived in large, rectangular huts made out of wood planks, woven reeds, and thatch roofing, and arranged in small clusters around central plazas, or in farmsteads erected near fields of maize, beans, and vegetables. Chiefs lived in more elaborate palaces called *bohíos,* some measuring as large as 150 paces long by 80 wide, and containing dozens of rooms. In these massive huts, surrounded by stone walls and scrupulously clean and tidy grounds, Cueva kings such as Comogre—Balboa's first and most important ally on his trip to the South Sea—held court, dispensed law, collected and stored tribute from vassal villages, and displayed in a special "Hall of the Ancestors" the mummified remains of their progenitors, hanging from the ceiling by cotton cords.^

As it turned out, Comogre's kingdom was an early victim of Pedrarias's slash-and-burn *entradas*. According to Zuazo, Captain Juan de Ayora marched on Comogre's magnificent *bohío* with some four hundred men and joined the *queví*'s baptized son, Ponquiaco—the old king had recently died—in a friendly feast. The Spaniards then demanded the young king produce gold, which he did, though not enough to satisfy Ayora.^ Refusing to believe the Indians had no more precious metals, he ordered the young king's principal men torn to shreds by Spanish war dogs. Ponquiaco himself was burned at the stake.

Oviedo labels these first years in Darién a *montería infernal*—a "hellish hunting"—as the captains and soldiers of Pedrarias turned what began as a desperate expediency into a thriving business. Zuazo describes his fellow Castilians as maintaining themselves "like birds of prey" in a land that quickly became "lost and desolate." Within a decade the Cueva culture was near extinction, with its leaders murdered, religious beliefs discredited and violently suppressed, villages wrecked and abandoned, families and friends dispersed or killed, homes, fields, and towns burned, and thousands forced to work themselves to death.

✛ ✛ ✛

Hernando de Soto must have participated in some of these early bloody *cabalgados*—raids for plunder—though once again we are frustrated by having no record of his comings and goings. Thankfully, the silence ends late in 1517, when we can, at last, place Hernando de Soto in Darién on a specific expedition, one typical for this period. Soto himself provides the information, speaking as a witness in a hearing in 1535, in Lima, where he was asked by an old friend, Alonso Martín de Don Benito, to verify certain facts about the latter's career in the Indies. During the hearing, the magistrate asks Soto if he can confirm that Alonso Martín "was with the Factor of His Majesty,* Juan de Tavira, who was sent by Captain Pedrarias Dávila in the fleet that made for the Río Grande, conquering for him more than five or six leagues." According to the trial's scribe, "the said Captain Hernando de Soto . . . said he knows about the contents of the question . . . because he saw it happen, and . . . helped discover the place in this question"—the "place" being the Atrato River basin in Colombia, then called El Río Grande, and the date being autumn 1517.

We have no details about Soto's role in this disastrous expedition.^ Most likely, he was a common soldier, one of 160 *hombres* who set off in a "fleet"

*A royal factor, or agent, represented the king's business interests, and regulated commerce moving in and out of a colony.

of three brigantines and seven *barco* canoes from Santa María, in search of yet another legendary kingdom of gold, called Dabaibe.^

Little is known about Juan de Tavira, other than his family had connections with Ferdinand's daughter, the queen of Portugal, who helped this young *hidalgo* secure a position in the king's court. This led to his appointment in 1513 as Ferdinand's factor in Castilla del Oro. A quiet, unassuming man, Tavira nonetheless had managed in the three years since the armada's arrival to amass a sizable fortune from embezzling funds and overcharging for his royally mandated services as the keeper of the king's stores in Santa María—gains he was now using to finance his expedition to the Atrato.^

The little fleet departed the beach below Santa María at the end of September 1517, with Tavira's flagship brigantine* in the lead, festooned with his own herald, and the purple-and-gold arms of the Castilian monarchy. From Santa María, they first paddled south twenty or thirty miles before reaching the Atrato Delta, which Balboa says was composed of "ten arms, six of which carried no less water than the Guadalquivir of Andalusia." An enormous waterway edged by dense forests and "great swamps and many lagoons," Balboa reports it was "a river of great current and not easy to navigate, even in Indian canoes." Tavira, however, seems to have had little trouble as he and his men paddled for several days upriver, apparently without sighting so much as a single Indian or settlement to break up the gloomy, steamy, endless marshes. Finally, after traveling some sixty miles, they came to a tributary called El Río Sucio,† which Balboa had told them marked the border of Dabaibe territory. Up until this point, Tavira had been following in the wake of Vasco Núñez's Atrato expeditions in 1512 and 1515, though he would soon pass beyond the point on the Sucio where Balboa's group in 1515 was forced to turn back, having been soundly thrashed by a contingent of Dabaibe warriors, and facing starvation as food became scarce. This time, however, the Indians inexplicably—and suspiciously—left Tavira's Spaniards alone as they proceeded cautiously up the dark, muddy waters of the Sucio, expecting an attack at any moment.

Every Spaniard in the tiny fleet knew how vulnerable they were on this river—not only to ambush, but to Indian snipers, whose poison-tipped missiles could at any moment come whizzing silently from behind a tree or bush on the shore to strike without warning, sinking into a man's neck or some other unprotected patch of skin. They also knew the slightest prick by the smallest

---

*A brigantine during this period referred to a small, usually open boat with a single sail, both with and without oars.

†This literally translates into "The Dirty River." Balboa, however, called it by the more elegant name of El Río Negro.

splinter from these arrows would cause convulsions and excruciating pain, and death within hours.^

Arrows, poison or otherwise, were not the only Indian weaponry the Spanish feared.^ For even with their substantial edge in technology, the Spanish knew from experience how formidable the Indians could be in close combat with their heavy clubs and maces, fashioned by the Indians out of stone and hardwood, the heads beautifully carved into shapes of jaguars, boars, snakes, spheres, and diamonds. Indians also carried wooden swords and throwing sticks sharpened and toughened by fire.

Set against this Bronze and Stone Age weaponry was the latest in Renaissance military know-how, then the finest and deadliest in the world, particularly in the hands of conquistadors such as Hernando de Soto.

The most versatile weapon wielded by the men in Tavira's vessels was the sword, which came in two variations—the saber, a single- or doubled-edged cutting blade, often curved, and a smaller rapier for thrusting. No other weapon—except, perhaps, the lance held by a charging cavalryman—was more deadly to unarmored Indians than these hard, light, flexible, and razor-sharp blades of metal.

Less important, but certainly impressive, were the arquebus muskets carried by Tavira's men—crude, cannonlike predecessors of the much more effective flintlock musket, which would not be invented for another century. The arquebus had less of an impact in terms of killing than is generally realized. Weighing as much as fifty pounds, it had to be supported on a foldable pole when fired, and was not only highly inaccurate, but frequently did not even fire in the tropics, given the sensitivity of Renaissance-era gunpowder to moist environments. In 1513, Balboa told the king that arquebuses were useful mainly as noisemakers to frighten Indians.

The Spaniards also carried crossbows, though they too were cumbersome for the quick hit-and-run tactics of the Indians. Designed to propel an arrow with enough force to penetrate European armor, and to travel great distances with speed and accuracy, a crossbow was a time-consuming weapon to load and fire, requiring up to several minutes to crank taut a bowstring with a complex series of pulleys and levers. At best, a crossbowman might get off one or two arrows in a brief Indian skirmish, though this weapon could still be useful in a pitched battle if several crossbowmen worked as a unit to fire continuous volleys.

All of Tavira's men wore some sort of armor—which, in the early sixteenth century, ranged from crude, shapeless steel shirts and skirts to dazzlingly etched and ornamented full suits. Most conquistadors did not wear anything approaching full armor on *entradas.* It was simply too hot. Nor did Indian weaponry require the thick steel hide necessary in a European field of war. According to historian John Hemming, Spanish conquistadors typically wore mail shirts "which weighed between fourteen and thirty pounds. These varied according to the size of their links, but most could withstand a normal thrust . . . Other conquistadors abandoned even chain mail in favor of padded cloth armor called *escaupil*," which "normally consisted of canvas stuffed with cotton. Spanish soldiers also defended themselves with small shields, generally oval bucklers of wood or iron covered in leather." Helmets ranged from those that fully enclosed the head to the lighter, open-faced *morrión*, with its sharp crest and wide brim.

This armor was not as uncomfortable as one might think. By Soto's day, advancements in metallurgy and design in Europe and elsewhere had produced astonishingly light and flexible suits of metal, as I discovered when I tried one on in Florida while retracing Hernando de Soto's route. Though oppressively hot and constricting, particularly during the early-summer months in Tampa Bay, the full suit of armor I wore seemed much lighter than its forty pounds, the weight being evenly distributed.

Weaponry was not always the most decisive factor in Spanish-Indian warfare, however, as Juan de Tavira was about to discover. Time and again the Indians used their knowledge of local topography to outmaneuver and outwit the Castilians, luring them into canyons and up steep hills where their horses were ineffective and their armor cumbersome, or attacking them by surprise when they were crossing a stream, or were sleeping. This is exactly what happened when Tavira and his men were suddenly assailed without warning by a riverborne force of Dabaibe warriors. They came from upriver, striking as the would-be invaders struggled in a section of white water. According to Las Casas, who tells this story, the natives descended on Tavira's fleet in "three large canoes," killing one Spaniard and wounding several others before the men of Santa María could drive them off with their swords, lances, and crossbows.^ After this brief skirmish, Tavira moved even more cautiously as he headed up the river, deeper into unexplored territory.

Few records exist about what this branch of the Atrato looked like in 1517, other than it got its brown color from the runoff of autumn rains, and it was surrounded by banks high enough for Tavira to order a squad to march onshore as sentinels against future attacks.^ For several days the Spaniards trekked onward this way, probably paddling far enough up the river to glimpse the heavily wooded foothills of the Cordillera Occidental far off to the east. This makes them the first Europeans to set eyes on the Andes—if the clouds of the rainy season did not block the view of the great range that would figure so prominently in Soto's later career.

The next disaster to befall the Tavira expedition was not an attack by the Indians, but "heavy forest rains." This was the end of the wet season in the Atrato

River basin, a particularly bad time to be forcing one's way through a region where over four hundred inches of rain falls each year, almost all of it during the summer and early fall. By late autumn, when the expedition was approaching the Andes foothills, the ground would have been fully saturated and the river poised to flood at any moment.

The Indian rowers must have been the first to sound the alarm that the river was suddenly rising, and the current, which they were paddling against, was picking up speed. Tavira, being a competent, if uninspiring, commander, quickly ordered the ships to rescue the soldiers marching by land, saving them from certain drowning. But he was not up to coping with what happened next as the rain continued to fall in heavy, dense sheets, and the river came rushing in full fury against the tiny armada. Apparently, in the mad scramble to keep control of the large, open vessels, and to stay together in the raging waters, Tavira's own canoe got snagged on a half-submerged tree and flipped, throwing Spaniards, Indians, tackle, sails, food, and other equipment into the muddy river. Las Casas says Tavira himself drowned because he could not swim, though he just as easily could have been trapped under the boat, tangled in rigging, or pulled under by the currents. Many others drowned with him, some weighted down by weapons, mail, and heavy jerkins. Most of the other vessels managed to stay upright, but only after the men tossed everything they could overboard.^

This debacle meant the expedition was finished, the imperative of the survivors now being to escape back to Santa María with their lives. This wasn't easy as they coasted down the flooded river, lacking food, and attacked repeatedly by Indians who badly "knocked [them] about," according to Soto's friend, Alonso Martín. Several more Spaniards died in these conflagrations. Martín himself was wounded by an arrow that struck him in the shoulder. "Stripped of everything we had," he says, "we retreated, desperate to reach the [town of] Pedrarias Dávila." To lead them home the men chose a dour, thirty-nine-year-old veteran of the *conquista* by the name of Francisco Pizarro, the first time we know of that Soto served under the man who would later become his commander and adversary in Peru.

In the end, the total take in plunder for this expensive fiasco was a laughable fifty-two pesos of gold^—hardly a stellar showing for Soto, or for anybody associated with the Tavira expedition, though this failure did contain a silver lining for the Indians of northeastern Colombia. For almost another century they were spared further intrusions by Spaniards, now thoroughly weary of the harsh climate^ and the Indians' deadly arrows.

✦ ✦ ✦

Other than the Tavira expedition, Soto's participation in the Darién *"montería infernal"* is largely a blank. The only evidence we have that he indulged in the atrocities is a single documented instance of the young Hernando tortur-

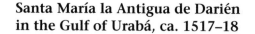

Santa María la Antigua de Darién
in the Gulf of Urabá, ca. 1517–18

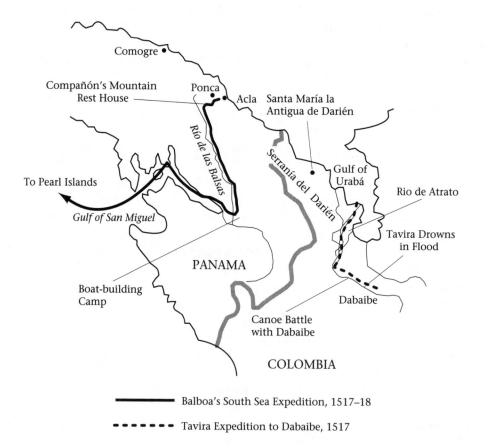

ing a Cueva native. This occurred during a raid on an unnamed Indian village, where an eyewitness says he saw "Captain Soto" burning a *"cacique* in a *barbacoa,** because he did not give enough gold, and because he refused to tell him where his father was buried [with more gold]."^ Beyond this, we have only Oviedo's general assessment of Hernando de Soto in Panama, where he informs us Soto was "instructed in the school of Pedrarias Dávila, in the dissipation and devastation of the Indians of Castilla del Oro," and "was very occupied in the hunt to kill Indians."

Oviedo provides no specific examples, mentioning Soto only in passing as he reports on the misdeeds of older and more prominent members of the Pedrarias "school." Listing thirty-nine "diabolical" captains by name, he provides a short history of each man. This includes many of Soto's close associates, and suggests the sort of company he kept in his formative years. Besides Balboa and Pedrarias, Oviedo names Soto's future business partner, Hernán Ponce de León, whom Oviedo ambiguously describes as being "better than these others in his treatment of the Indians"; Soto's close associate Francisco Compañón, "a man of spirit, and kindred to the above-mentioned in blood, and in other things alike in wickedness, although a better talker and better bred"; Francisco Pizarro, whose assassination several years later in Peru was, according to Oviedo, "perfect justice" for his crimes; and Martín Estete, a future Soto ally and sometime rival in the frenetic politics of Nicaragua, whom Oviedo calls a great butcher of Indians.

No other chronicler so much as mentions Hernando de Soto in Darién—undoubtedly because he was simply too young and insignificant. Yet we know he was there, at least from 1517 onward, a young man anxious to please his peers and enhance his position, which in this case meant terrorizing Indians, hacking them to pieces, and burning them alive.

It was during his years in the "school of Pedrarias" that Soto first learned the brutal mechanics of conquest in the Indies—the basics of how to organize an *entrada* designed not to colonize or settle a place, but to comb it efficiently and ruthlessly for slaves and treasure. He also learned how to equip an expedition; to organize a marching column of vanguard, outriders, native porters, servants, and rear guard; to select the best men for his captains and scouts; to keep his soldiers, horses, and war dogs healthy by living off food plundered from Indians; to gather intelligence properly on his intended victims; and to act pragmatically in almost any situation. But even more important was Soto's continuing education in the mores of his era, and of a culture in which men like these never doubted their right to lay waste to entire nations and peoples in the

---

*A *barbacoa* was a grill used by the Indians to cook meat and to torture human beings over a fire. The Spanish probably learned the technique from the Indians.

name of profit, conquest, salvation, and glory. Indeed, Pedrarias's conquest by pillage and violence is essentially the story of El Cid, and of knight-errantry throughout Europe, the point being that the wise man served in equal measure the king, God, his *compañeros,* and his own ambitions.

We will never know how many Indians died in Panama during Soto's teenage years. Oviedo says two million expired from 1514 to 1526 in all of Panama, a number that seems impossibly high, and is not supported by the admittedly sparse archaeological record. On the other hand, eyewitness accounts all claim that Panama in 1514 was mostly under cultivation or cleared for hunting, and that a sizable population lived in the interior of Darién.^ Moreover, Oviedo was not sitting back in Spain guessing at Indian populations. He knew Panama intimately during these years, having traveled its length and breadth countless times.

Other chroniclers not only agree the country was heavily populated when the Spanish arrived, but also that by the early 1520s it had already been so decimated from disease, plundering, and abuse that the *vecinos* of Santa María were compelled to import slaves to Darién from more distant regions. By then, however, Pedrarias had abandoned Santa María la Antigua de Darién, after ravaging it so thoroughly that even today this region remains virtually uninhabited, a vast jungle that ecologists prize as a rich swath of supposedly "undisturbed" rain forest, not realizing that its "natural" state before the Europeans came was to be cleared and covered with crops, Indian roads, villages, savanna-like hunting grounds burned to eliminate trees, and the cities and *bohíos* of the long-extinct Cueva people.

And what, in the end, did the Spanish gain in propagating this *montería infernal* in Darién? Ironically, in this land named *oro,* where Balboa claimed one could draw out gold from the rivers by the basketful, and where Columbus and others insisted precious metals existed in great quantities, the Spaniards found little naturally occurring gold. During the period 1511 to 1526,^ miners recovered only about 115,000 gold pesos—less than Soto's personal fortune when he returned from Peru in 1536. The colonists had more luck stealing gold from Indians, plundering a grand total of 527,331 gold pesos over a period of fifteen years.^ This means that if Oviedo's two million dead is correct, the Spanish in Panama earned, in today's currency, roughly sixteen dollars per Indian killed, or some $32 million for the entire Cueva race.

✛ 4 ✛

Balboa Is Dead

PEDRARIAS DÁVILA TREATED HIS own people with nearly as much contempt as he did the Indians. A cold-blooded, spiteful man, contemporaries depict him as so thoroughly evil it is difficult to find a single honest compliment or mitigating trait. Yet somehow he managed to hang on in Castilla del Oro for over a decade, despite a chorus of invective directed by his enemies to colonial officials in Seville, and to the royal court in Valladolid.

No one understood the depravities of Pedrarias Dávila better than Vasco Núñez de Balboa, the chief object of the venal governor's rage for half a decade in Darién. It is a testament to Balboa's own abilities that he survived Pedrarias's wrath as long as he did.

Pedrarias set the tone for their enmity almost immediately when he confiscated Balboa's house and property, enraged and jealous because Balboa had discovered the South Sea, a prize Pedrarias had coveted for himself. The governor also subjected Vasco Núñez to a long, bruising *residencia*. Usually a routine legal examination of an outgoing governor's administration, Pedrarias in this instance ordered his predecessor held under house arrest during the six months of the inquiry, while the governor and his cronies concocted one scurrilous charge after another, accusing Vasco Núñez of everything from blasphemy to treason. In one fiery letter to the king, he even suggested that Diego de Nicuesa—the bungling governor Balboa dispatched to sea in a fatally leaky vessel—had discovered the South Sea, not Balboa.^ Ultimately, the colony's chief justice, Gaspar de Espinosa, cleared Vasco Núñez of all charges, but not before it was clear to all that the new governor was not overly fond of his predecessor.

Balboa responded as best he could, though his options were limited. He fired off letters of his own to the king, insisting that Pedrarias lacked "any knack or talent for the business of the *gobernación*," and that he was "a man

ruled by all envy and covetousness in the world." Beseeching the king to hold
a *residencia* for Pedrarias, he repeatedly nominated himself as a suitable replacement as governor. Beyond this, Balboa undoubtedly made sure that the
old governor understood his own support ran deep among the settlers, particularly those loyalists he had governed before the armada arrived.

Pedrarias's hatred of Vasco Núñez de Balboa was not entirely unreasonable.
Any new governor would have felt put out being upstaged by such a dashing,
successful antagonist. Then came a ship in March 1515 carrying fresh edicts
from the king, who heaped so many honors and titles on Balboa that even the
most benevolent governor would have felt imperiled, even betrayed. First off,
Ferdinand named Balboa "Adelantado of the coast of the South Sea,"^ an honorific that literally means "one who advances forward." He also appointed him
governor of Coiba and Panama, the area to the south and west of Castilla del
Oro, where Vasco Núñez had explored during his recent discovery. But most
unpalatable of all for Pedrarias was the king commanding him to "favor" Balboa and to "look after him as someone who has also served us." The only good
news for Pedrarias was the king's order leaving him in overall command of all
Spanish colonies in the region, including Balboa's new *gobernación,* a measure Ferdinand apparently added in an effort to impose order and a clear chain
of command. If this was the intent, it backfired. For despite these edicts, Pedrarias still could manage a smile, having been given exactly the loophole he
needed to thwart his adversary, who would have to come to him for approval
of virtually everything pertaining to his new colony.

Pedrarias's position became even stronger when a second ship arrived that
autumn announcing that Ferdinand was ill and dying. For the old governor
knew that without the king's steady hand, the affairs of the empire would begin
to drift, particularly around the edges. This meant that when Balboa came to
him asking permission to move men and gather supplies to settle his new *gobernación,* Pedrarias could deny his requests with impunity—which he did
throughout the closing weeks of 1515. Uncowed, Balboa made preparations
for an *entrada* anyway, an effort made easier by the timely arrival in November of a boatload of volunteers joining him from Hispaniola. This so infuriated
Pedrarias he decided to ignore the substantial support for Balboa in the colony
and order Balboa arrested, put in chains, and again charged with treason.

This was too much for Vasco Núñez's followers, who threatened to storm
the prison. Pedrarias, however, moved too quickly for Balboa's unorganized
supporters to act, moving his prisoner to the patio of his own mansion—where,
under heavy guard, he incarcerated the adelantado of the South Sea in a cage
like an animal. Here Balboa remained for several weeks as Pedrarias tried to
contain what loomed as a full-scale insurrection. As the crisis deepened, however, even a man as stubborn as Pedrarias realized that he had gone too far—

particularly after his formidable wife, Isabel de Bobadilla, insisted he not only back down, but offer a gesture of reconciliation.^ Thus one day late in 1515 or early 1516 Pedrarias stunned the colony again by not only releasing Vasco Núñez de Balboa from his cage, but also by announcing that he and his rival had made peace, sealing the deal with the surprise announcement that Balboa was to be betrothed to one of Pedrarias's five daughters, the teenaged María de Bobadilla, then back in Spain.^ The colonists greeted this announcement first with astonishment, and then relief, though at least some must have realized that a quarrel as bitter as this could never be fully resolved, and that it was just a matter of time before these two elemental forces would clash again.

For Soto and other young would-be conquerors in Darién, the twists and turns of this bitter conflict offered a vivid education in two starkly contrasting styles of governing and leadership—the charming fighter and can-do organizer versus the dour, petty yet thorough tyrant; the plain-spoken and plain-dressed man of the people versus the autocrat who earned respect through terror and cunning, attracting his following by appealing to their greed. This is not to say, however, that the Balboa-Pedrarias rivalry was strictly a case of good versus evil. Both men aspired to the same ends—conquest of the Indians, and profit and power for themselves—and both were ruthless when it suited their interests. Where they differed was in tactics and attitudes, with Balboa ruling by the expediency of common sense, and Pedrarias by expediency alone. Believing his avarice could best be satisfied by being reasonable, Balboa took the long-term approach to colonization, advocating policies that produced steady, predictable wealth by preserving a colony's resources in land and Indians. In contrast, Pedrarias preferred the strip-mine approach to getting rich, unleashing whatever force and terror necessary to maximize profits in the shortest time possible.

Which potential mentor Soto supported is unknown. More than most colonists, however, Soto had reason to support Vasco Núñez, who apparently grew up near the Sotos in the same parish in Jerez de los Caballeros.^ Soto also would have been strongly attracted to the charismatic Balboa, a man of action and inspiration to an aspiring young conquistador. On the other hand, it is just as likely that Soto hedged his romantic and regional impulses to avoid overly offending Pedrarias, the power broker in Darién, and the man any apprentice conqueror had to impress—and obey—if he wanted to advance in the colony.

Whatever Soto's loyalties during the Balboa-Pedrarias feud, it is clear that later in life his attachments were seldom ironclad, but remained in a constant state of reappraisal, based on who might best serve his ambitions for the moment. This predilection for shifting loyalties—which Soto undoubtedly learned amidst the heated politics of Darién—explains why we find him in the fall of 1517 riding in a *barco* with Juan de Tavira, a Pedrarias crony, but later that same year spot him hurrying off to meet up with Balboa's group headed for the South Sea.

✛   ✛   ✛

Soto was late joining Balboa's South Sea expedition, presumably catching up with it shortly after he returned (and recuperated) from his watery ordeal on the Río Sucio. This was almost a year after Vasco Núñez had departed Santa María with eighty men, later augmented by one hundred more, to begin carving out his new domain on the southern shore of Panama. Balboa's project was made possible by his recent rapprochement with Pedrarias, whom he now addressed as "Father." Yet the old ogre still could not help himself from being stingy with his son-in-law, continuing to make it difficult for him to acquire supplies and men, and giving him an impossibly short time of eighteen months to settle his colony.

Showing his usual pragmatism, Balboa had not moved immediately to the other sea. For several months, he had been building and organizing Acla, a settlement on the Caribbean side, eighty miles west of Santa María. Selected for its protected harbor and its location below the mountain passes leading south, Acla was ideal as a base of operations, and a link with the outside world for Balboa's *gobernación* on the Pacific side.^ Delay in Acla also gave Balboa a chance to see if Pedrarias would stick to his conciliation, something he needed to be reasonably sure of before moving to the South Sea coast. There he would be heavily dependent in the first few months on supplies—and goodwill— from Darién. Furthermore, Balboa may have lingered in Acla hoping to hear from Spain, where he was convinced that Ferdinand's eventual successor would remove Pedrarias, and name someone more to his liking.

By late autumn 1517, when Soto returned from the Tavira debacle, Acla was already a small but reasonably prosperous community, "settled in the same manner as that of Darién," according to one eyewitness, who said the town was composed of several dozen *bohíos* and a church arranged around a central square, and flanked by terraced foothills growing maize, beans, yams, pineapples, and spices. By late November, the earliest Soto could have arrived, Vasco Núñez was finished with his city and preparing to launch the second stage of his colonial strategy—a project to cut timber in the hills above Acla to be transported across the isthmus to the Gulf of San Miguel, where he planned to have carpenters build four brigantines. With these, the Governor of the South Sea hoped to explore the gulf, and to investigate rumors of a mysterious country called Birú, where he was told the people "eat and drink out of golden vessels, and gold is as cheap as iron is with you." This was an early reference to Peru, which Balboa, had he lived, might have discovered years before Francisco Pizarro.

Again, Soto's role in this expedition is unknown. But there is evidence that it was during this *entrada* Soto formed his first pact of brotherhood with Francisco Compañón and Hernán Ponce de León, launching what would later become one of the most successful partnerships in the early *conquista*. The information comes from a 1535 document signed by Soto and Ponce in Cuzco (and reaffirmed in Havana in 1539)^ where both men verify it had been "eighteen or nineteen years" since their "company and brotherhood was founded" between the two of them and Compañón, who died in 1528. This seems to take us back to the years 1513–19,^ perhaps during the Balboa expedition. Indeed, all three men were present in Acla during this period—Compañón as Balboa's second-in-command,^ a steady, competent cavalryman who would seldom be away from Soto's side for the next decade; and Hernán Ponce, a quiet, highly efficient young man who arrived in Acla sometime in August 1517, after serving as a captain in Gaspar de Espinosa's 1516–17 conquest of western Panama.*^

One imagines the three young men swearing solemn oaths of brotherhood one night in Panama, pledging to share everything in a pact similar to the more formal contract Soto and Ponce later signed in Cuzco. In it, they promised to divide equally "anything we acquire through our work and industry and earnings in any manner such as worked gold and silver and ships and bergantines and all rents . . . any earnings of mines, Indians of *encomiendas*† in countries and islands and the mainland and Negro and white and Indian slaves and ransoms of Indians and rewards and salaries of offices . . . and plots of land and clothes of cloth and silk and finery," and on and on. Of course, this would have been a laughably ambitious list for the three young conquistadors in 1518, whose joint assets probably totaled next to nothing—though not for long.

Later, in Nicaragua, Soto would become the most prominent and notorious of the three partners. Now, however, this distinction belonged to Francisco Compañón, whose bold, decisive actions during the boat-building project read like a chapter out of Soto's life story—a similarity that may explain their mutual attraction.

We first hear about Compañón early in 1517, when Balboa ordered him to scout out a suitable base of operations across the isthmus, and to organize a *bohío* halfway across "to rest the men that were to carry on their backs the timbers, the anchors, and the riggings, and to keep provisions, and necessaries for their defense." Balboa next put Compañón in charge of "conveying the timber"

---

*The other possible date for Soto launching his partnership is 1520, when the three *compañeros* were together in Natá, in western Panama.
†An *encomienda* is a grant of land allotted to the care of a conquistador, usually after a conquest, who collects tribute from its Indian inhabitants, and can demand the use of native labor in his mines and fields.

to this mountain way station, halfway between Acla and the spot on the Chucunaque River where he planned to build the boats and float them into the South Sea.

By all accounts, this was a painstaking, horrific operation, probably designed more to further delay the move south than to serve any useful purpose. Loading their Indian laborers down with long, unwieldy planks weighing over a hundred pounds apiece, Balboa and Compañón forced hundreds of natives to walk in chain gangs until they dropped dead from exhaustion—all for a boat-building project in which wood from the south coast would have worked just as well.^ According to Las Casas, at least five hundred Indians died, and possibly "in excess of 2,000,"^ a carnage he blames not only on Balboa—whose capacity for cruelty is proven here beyond doubt—but also on Compañón, whom he vilifies in his *historia* as a "chief executioner"^ of the Indians. Soto, of course, is too insignificant to mention. Yet he was there, participating in a project that reveals a great deal about Spanish attitudes, and their assumption that it was normal to work hundreds of human beings to death purposely, valuing them as worth no more than a few days of hard labor before they expired and had to be replaced. That Soto shared this attitude becomes abundantly clear later in *La Florida,* where several times he overworked native porters, caring about their demise only because it meant he would have to locate more backs and shoulders to carry his supplies.

For once, however, the Indians were not entirely alone in their suffering. This was because Vasco Núñez, probably realizing his native porters were going to die long before all his planks were transported over the mountains, ordered the Spaniards themselves to join in the operation, with Balboa grabbing the first plank, hoisting it onto his back, and carrying it across. Normally, such a mundane task would have been anathema for Spaniards raised to abhor manual labor, though somehow the charismatic Vasco Núñez convinced his men to pitch in anyway. Years later, Soto's friend, Alonso Martín de Don Benito, even bragged about carrying on his back the first iron anchor to be used on the South Sea, something Soto may have witnessed, and perhaps helped with.^

As spring turned to summer, the hardships of this bloody portage across the isthmus became merely the first of several calamities bedeviling the boat-building project. For starters, once the wood was delivered, Balboa found himself with only enough to build two brigantines, not four. Next came the stunning revelation that the timber was honeycombed with worms and rot from "sea water," and therefore useless. Then, just as Balboa was rallying his men to cut fresh planks on the South Sea, the Chucunaque River abruptly flooded, washing away not only the newly cut wood, but also the *entrada*'s camp and provisions. According to the seventeenth-century historian Antonio de Herrera Tordesillas, the rising water "carried away a part of the camp, and buried another part in mud, the flood rising two fathoms [twelve feet] above it, the men having no other way to save themselves but by climbing the trees, where they were hardly safe."

For Soto, this potentially deadly inundation was the Tavira fiasco all over again, though this time the men were stranded in the middle of a flooded valley with nothing to eat and no boats to make their escape, a situation that drove even the optimistic Balboa to "despair," and to consider abandoning his project. "Vasco Núñez was himself forced to feed on roots," reports Las Casas, "whence may be concluded how his men lived, not to mention the Indians." It was in the midst of this crisis that Compañón volunteered to take a small squadron and comb the surrounding country for food, with Herrera telling us he and his men "made a bridge of two large timbers bound together, effected by some that could swim." This allowed them to cross out of the camp, where Compañón and his contingent marched through "water up to their middles in passing, and some up to their breasts." Finally reaching dry land, Herrera tells us "Francisco Compañón" and his group soon "returned with provisions loaded on many Indians," thus saving the *entrada*.

It didn't take long for Balboa to recover his composure, rebuild his camp, and cut new timbers. By the summer of 1518, he had launched two brigantines, and was sailing with a hundred men down the Chucunaque, which feeds into the Tuira River, and then into the Gulf of San Miguel. According to Pascual de Andagoya, who was there, "Vasco Núñez, having built the ships, came to the Gulf . . . and landed in a populous district called Pequeo," to the south of the Tuira, "where he remained for two months, seizing Indians and sending them to Acla for more cordage or pitch." Herrera adds that once the ships were entirely seaworthy, Balboa "embarked with as many Spaniards as the ships could carry, and sailed to the greatest of the Pearl Islands,"* a chain of lovely, mountainous isles in the gulf. Here, continues Andagoya, "while the Brigantines carried over the rest of his men, [Balboa] endeavored to bring together all of the provisions that could be found on the island, so as well as to conquer the inhabitants and seize their food, as to have enough for himself while he stayed there." From these islands, Balboa launched several more expeditions in the brigantines, most of them aimed at the Panamanian coast to the east near the modern border with Colombia. Here "the Indians told him there was much gold" to the south, "an indication," says Herrera, "of the prodigious wealth of Peru." Almost certainly, Soto participated in all or some of these missions.

✛   ✛   ✛

Balboa's explorations continued until late in 1518, when the fledgling colony on the South Sea received word that the new king, Charles I, had finally named a replacement for Pedrarias Dávila. Reportedly, this new governor was

---

*This is the Isla del Rey.

to arrive early in the next year.^ This was a fateful moment for Vasco Núñez de Balboa, who decided to send a few trusted aides back to Acla and Santa María to ascertain quietly if these reports were true—a delicate task given his father-in-law's suspicious nature.

Balboa's men found the old man already furious about the news from Spain, and convinced his new son-in-law would seize the opportunity. Finding out about the messengers, he promptly arrested them, claiming they were spies—a belief encouraged by one of Balboa's men, Andrés Garabito, who fanned the flames of the old man's paranoia by turning coat and insisting Vasco Núñez was indeed a traitor. (This "confession" probably saved him from the executioner's block.) Vowing to destroy his nemesis once and for all, Pedrarias issued a command for Balboa to return immediately to the northern coast, though he wrote the order "in a pleasant, fatherly manner to the Adelantado, asking him to come to Acla."

The deception worked. Balboa, according to Oviedo, "as an obedient son, immediately came there to see the governor and find out what orders he wanted to give him, believing not unreasonably that he was still in his favor. But when he arrived," Oviedo continues, "Pedrarias had him arrested," the officer being his one-time friend, the dour Francisco Pizarro. The charge, as before, was treason.

This time, Pedrarias incarcerated Balboa in Acla, far away from his supporters in Santa María and the Pearl Islands. This left the governor free to levy a host of spurious charges, including claims that Vasco Núñez had committed "excesses, violence, and abuses . . . against the Indians," and that he was hatching conspiracies against Pedrarias. This was followed by a swift and perfunctory trial in which the outcome was never in doubt. For this time Chief Justice Gaspar de Espinosa—now firmly in Pedrarias's camp—found Balboa and four of his supporters guilty on all charges, including some Espinosa had dismissed four years earlier for lack of evidence.

Pedrarias did not publicly attend the execution, possibly out of embarrassment for what he knew was a travesty—or because he feared an insurrection even in the lightly populated Acla settlement. Oviedo, however, claims the old man watched the proceedings surreptitiously, "peering through the reed wall of a house that was ten or twelve paces from where the men were beheaded, one after the other, like sheep." Oviedo then adds a grisly detail demonstrating Pedrarias Dávila's determination to debase the memory of the popular Balboa once and for all, telling us that the governor ordered "a pole . . . placed in the ground," where "the Adelantado's head was left . . . for many days."

Meanwhile, Francisco Compañón, Hernando de Soto, and the others in Balboa's South Sea expedition waited anxiously at their camp on the Pearl Islands, knowing nothing of their leader's fate until long after it was over. No one recorded how Soto and the others reacted when they heard the news, though Balboa's death must have been a bitter blow. It also must have sent a strong message to young Soto about the raw uses of power in this wild country, which ultimately depended not on loyalty, position, charm, or even intelligence, but on who was most willing to act decisively on his own behalf—and who, in the end, was most ruthless.

✛ 5 ✛

The Southern Sea

BY 1519, WHEN VASCO Núñez de Balboa was executed, Santa María la Antigua de Darién had become, despite its noxious reputation, a prosperous *pueblo* for its Spanish *vecinos*—comfortable, predictable, and, with the tragic demise of the Cuevas, dull. When not out marauding, each of the six hundred or so Spaniards living there could now "sleep safe in a downy bed, be well served at a table, [and] sit in a comfortable chair; he could deal at shops which carried goods from Spain," and enjoy his "children, white or brown, who grew up in his house."^ Oviedo says he lived there in a two-story wooden house that cost him fifteen hundred *castellanos,* fully equipped with "garrets and windows" and "spacious rooms" that were "so comfortable that I could receive a great noble and put him up quite comfortably."

Soto, however, spent little time in Santa María during this period. Indeed, from the moment we can locate him heading off to the Atrato River in the fall of 1517, the pattern of his adult life is already evident—his resistance to living in settled places, his preference for the frontier, his need to be forever marching on. Probably, he maintained a housing arrangement in Santa María, perhaps sharing a hut with other young conquistadors. He may also have owned a slave or two, and a modest share in a mine or plantation, though most likely Soto in Darién remained short on assets and long on aspirations.

Soto's lack of attachment to Santa María was just as well, since the pace of conquest in Castilla del Oro by the time of Balboa's death was quickly moving beyond this small, misplaced settlement on the Urabá. The city had never made much sense as the colony's capital. It had no harbor, a swampy climate, and was poorly situated as an Atlantic terminus for a trans-isthmus highway. More importantly, its resources in gold and slaves had by now run so low that Pedrarias's captains were having to move far afield to find fresh supplies.^

No one was happier to see Santa María marginalized than Pedrarias Dávila.

Since his arrival, he had loathed this hot, steamy settlement, so closely associated with his rival, Vasco Núñez de Balboa. Now, with the news that a new
governor was coming, armed with full authority to prosecute El Furor Domini
for his crimes, Pedrarias's hatred of his capital took on a fresh urgency, compelling him by late spring to march his *vecinos* across the isthmus on Compañón's road to the Gulf of San Miguel. Here he appropriated Balboa's boats
and sailed first to the Pearl Islands, where he picked up Balboa's "people who
had remained in the South Sea"—including, presumably, Francisco Compañón, Hernán Ponce de León, and Hernando de Soto—and then to a small
coastal hamlet called Panamá, meaning "a place abounding in fish"^ in the
local tongue. First visited by Antonio Tello de Guzmán in 1515, and later by
Gaspar de Espinosa in 1517, Panama in the early sixteenth century hardly
seemed destined to become one of Central America's most important and glittering capitals. Originally, Espinosa described it as a makeshift fishing camp
consisting of "three houses and a woman,"^ situated on a marshy *punta* (point)
beside a small river. Even the Indians considered it unhealthy, a spot where humidity still hugs the ground in a dense gauze for weeks at a time, the soil is
salty and poor, and the "harbor" is little more than a shallow inlet.

Panama City, however, had one critical advantage that to this day remains
its only asset—its location at the narrowest and flattest point on the isthmus,
only thirty-three miles from the Caribbean. This is why it was an important city
during the Spanish era, and why a half-million people today—a fifth of
Panama's total population—live there in glass towers, sprawling villas, squalid
barrios, and shantytowns, and why many of them still are tied directly or indirectly to servicing either the Panama Canal itself, or the shipping and trade that
goes through it.

On August 15, 1519, Pedrarias held a ceremony officially designating
Panama City the new capital of Castilla del Oro. The entire population of the new
city turned out, standing in their finest clothes and armor on the beach beside the
tiny Río Gallinero. As usual, the wizened old man was probably wrapped in a
fortune in clothes—sweat-soaked silks and burnished armor, and perhaps a
sweeping cape made of satin, a wide-brimmed hat, and polished boots set off by
spurs of gold or silver. Behind him stood the standard of Castile and León, with
its golden castles and purple lions, the religious banners of the church, and Pedrarias's own family crest and herald hanging limp in the dampness.

Eyewitness Pascual de Andagoya says four hundred Spaniards gathered that
day to sign on as founding *vecinos* of the city,^ and to receive a grant of land
complete with an allotment of local Indians. These *encomiendas* allowed each
vecino to extract tribute and labor from natives under his control. Theoretically, this was in exchange for teaching them about the church and making sure
they had enough food and were well cared for. In practice the *encomienda* sys-

tem frequently degenerated into a brutal form of slave labor responsible for directly and indirectly killing hundreds of thousands, if not millions, of Indians in the Spanish colonies. This was before *encomiendas* were outlawed by King Charles I in 1550. However, because in Panama "the captains had carried off great numbers of Indians," says Andagoya, "and as the land was of small extent from one sea to the other, there were very few Indians at the time that the land was divided, and the governor could give only ninety Indians in *repartimiento,** or fifty, or forty."^

Pedrarias proved to be an adept city builder. He organized Panama City along a neat east-west, north-south grid, with wide streets and a large *plaza mayor* near the sea, dominated by the two most important structures in the colony, representing God and mammon—the cathedral and, behind it, just above the piers of the harbor, the stone Casa Reales, or Royal Customs House. This is where gold, slaves, and trade goods were stored, taxed, and regulated.^ Beyond the city, Pedrarias dispatched teams of *naborías* (indentured native servants) to finish a project originally envisioned by Vasco Núñez de Balboa— to carve out of the jungle a highway to connect the two seas. Within a few months, laborers pushing north from Panama City would complete the first paved European road in the Americas,^ running thirty-five miles across the isthmus to another town founded by Pedrarias, Nombre de Dios, slated to become the new Atlantic terminus for a highway destined to open up new worlds for men such as Soto to conquer and exploit.

✛   ✛   ✛

Neither Hernando de Soto's nor his two partners' names appear on the lists of Panamanian *vecinos* and *encomenderos,* for the simple reason they were not in Panama at the time. Restless as ever, the three *compañeros* had departed on July 21 with Gaspar de Espinosa, chief justice and alcalde of the colony, and 150 other *hombres* on a mission to organize food supplies for the new city in the agricultural region of Parita, one hundred miles to the west. This was the same region that Espinosa had plundered during his first campaign in Coiba in 1516–17—with Hernán Ponce as one of his captains^—netting 55,300 pesos of gold and some two thousand slaves, one of the largest single hauls of booty so far in the brief history of Tierra Firme. Soto's specific role in this second Espinosa *entrada* is unknown, though he was considered prominent enough to sign as a witness in the official *relación* of the expedition.^ This means he was almost certainly a captain, though a junior one, perhaps a temporary field commander assigned by Espinosa to lead a platoon of outriders to loot a village, hunt down a fleeing *cacique,* or scout ahead on reconnaissance.

---

*An *encomienda*, when it was granted, was called a *repartimiento*, or "division."

Soto set sail with Espinosa's army in the same boats he had helped build on the Tuira River with Balboa a few months earlier, the *Santa María de Buena Esperanza* and the *San Cristóbal*.^ Their destination was Natá—a flat, lush region of alluvial soil rich in maize and vegetables that to this day remains the breadbasket of Panama, and would soon become, in 1520, the home base for Hernando de Soto and his partners, until they left for Nicaragua.

Natá was then the homeland of the Coiban people, close cousins to the Cueva in terms of language and customs, the major difference being the Coibans' greater proclivity for waging war—for fielding armies supposedly numbering in the thousands, fighting in highly disciplined battalions, and showing extraordinary bravery in the face of Spanish steel.^ In 1515, their greatest king, Paris, had routed a Spanish force under Gonzalo de Badajoz.^ A year later, Espinosa's much-larger force was held in check during a ferocious six-hour battle, breaking through to defeat the Coibans only after repeated charges of the invaders' handful of horses. Even the usually terse Espinosa had been impressed by the Parisians and their *cacique*-general, whom he described as brilliantly attired in "many disks and armor of gold . . . over a garment of cotton."

According to Espinosa, the current expedition arrived by ship in late July 1519 at the village of Pocrí, near the eastern tip of the Azuero Peninsula. There the chief justice loaded a vessel with maize and sent it back to Panama, where the lack of a ready local food supply had been causing some distress among the colonists. Traveling north by land and sea to the Río Escoria (now the Santa María), they marched toward Paris's capital. The objective, as always, was to collect slaves, food, and pledges of fealty from Paris and other *caciques* in the Natá region, and generally to plunder the country for whatever gold they had neglected to steal in 1516–17.

Stopping at the first village in his path, ruled by the *cacique* Susa, Espinosa quickly established his *modus operandi* by demanding slaves, treasure, and submission. This prompted this *cacique* to flee in terror to the mountains. Which, in turn, triggered a series of set strategies by Espinosa to bring him in, starting with gifts and conciliatory messages, and escalating into a bloody rampage as the *cacique* refused to surrender, and the chief justice ordered his men to hunt down and capture Susa. In the end, Espinosa's men not only flushed out the hapless Susa, bringing him to Espinosa in chains, but also seized hundreds of Susa's subjects, and some thirty-three thousand gold pesos' worth of gold jewelry, armor, and trinkets, most of it found buried "among the dead" in tombs.

Espinosa's next target was the former capital of Paris (later called Asiento Viejo, or "Old Town"), which the chief justice's forces had largely destroyed in 1517, though the surrounding area remained heavily populated. We pick up what happened next in the official report of Espinosa's campaign, in a section Soto signed onto as a witness. "[Espinosa] came up with the said men to Asiento Viejo of the said *cacique* [of Paris]," writes Espinosa's scribe, "and he remained . . . a league behind, and there he [captured and] separated out the Indians, the women, young boys and children; and there [Espinosa] held a meeting with the principle men, and told them about the *Requerimiento,* as commanded by Their Highnesses, and asked them to tell these things to the *cacique,* and they told Espinosa that the old *cacique* [Paris] was dead, and Espinosa said many words of love, telling them he wanted them to become vassals of the king, that he would then give back their women and sons." He then gave the Indians the usual choice—acquiesce or die—saying that if the new *cacique,* Paris's young son Queco, would give himself up and obey the *Requerimiento,* "they would be well-treated, like the other *caciques* of Comogre, and Chepo, and Pacora."* Failure to comply, however, would result in the *cacique* and all his people being "punished and destroyed."

Espinosa followed the delivery of his ultimatum by returning with the captive members of Queco's family to his ships on the coast, where the chief justice set up camp and waited for the young *cacique* to turn himself in. Queco, suspecting the Spaniards really wanted to kill him in revenge for his father's military prowess, responded from his hiding place by sending worked gold pieces worth two hundred pesos, and a desperate plea for Espinosa to go away. According to Espinosa's *relación,* "the *cacique"* told him "he dared not come; that he did not want war with the Christians, only peace, nor did he want gold, only to eat, and this *cacique* had experienced war before with the Christians, before his father died," and he was "young" and had "much fear of the Christians."

After receiving this anguished message, the chief justice saw no point in sending soldiers out to comb the hills for this terrified young man, who he suspected would surrender soon enough on his own. Thus Espinosa, a patient, deliberate man, simply waited, sending out messages reiterating his "words of love," and firmly repeating his demands.

Queco stayed away for two more days, sending back Espinosa's messengers with more gifts of worked gold, and pleas to go away. On the third day, he finally bowed to the inevitable, and surrendered with ten of his *principales.* Queco arrived on the morning of August 3, 1519, dressed in a Castilian outfit given to his brother as a gift from Espinosa, carrying with him "several pieces of armor and plates made of gold, from which 162 pesos were obtained, as well as some iguanas and venison." That same day, Espinosa sat down with the

*This promise would hardly have been reassuring, had the Parisians heard of these distant places, and of their fate.

young king to go over the legal details of his acquiescence, and "to reassure the *cacique* and relieve him of his fear, because he was trembling all over."

The *relación* then dutifully reports that Queco listened to the *Requerimiento,* read "one, two, three, and more times," and that he agreed that he and his people would become "the vassals, servants, and *churigras*"* of the king, and that they would "make houses, plant fields, and build roads for the Christians." In a final blow to the young *cacique*'s dignity, and that of his people, Espinosa's men— who were literally tearing apart every village and hamlet in the area in a frenzied search for treasure and hidden tombs—stumbled on a spectacular find, the hidden tomb of Queco's father, the late *cacique* Paris, who in death had been garbed as resplendently as he had been in life. "The body," writes historian Carl Sauer, "was encased in three shrouds, the finest innermost, and was decked with gold ornaments from the helmeted head to gold bands about the legs."

This rich prize, added to the thirty-three thousand pesos of gold looted in Susa, became the first plunder we know of that Hernando de Soto may have shared. Probably, he got no more than one hundred gold pesos, a typical take for a cavalryman and field captain in this period, given the size of the total booty, and the number of conquistadors in Espinosa's group.^ But whatever his share, to the teenage Soto it must have seemed a fortune—probably more than his family back in Jerez made in an entire year from their modest properties. And when combined with the shares of Ponce and Compañón, his partners, it must have seemed a truly extraordinary sum—the first significant contribution to what would become, a decade and a half later, one of the great fortunes in early American history.

+ + +

Previously, I have suggested two major role models during these Panama years for Hernando de Soto—Pedrarias Dávila and Vasco Núñez de Balboa. Now we must add a third—Gaspar de Espinosa. Not only did he assign Soto to his first known command as a field captain, he also was the most systematic and efficient *entrada* leader Soto had yet served under. Indeed, this nononsense style of conquest closely resembled the mature Soto's own methods of finely balancing friendship and cruelty, patience and sudden, unremitting violence in dealing with Indian leaders. Bartolomé de las Casas describes Espinosa in terms that sound much like Oviedo's description of Soto in Florida two decades later. "The Lawyer Espinosa," says Las Casas, systematically killed Indians by "setting some to the dogs," ordering others hung, "[and] others to have their noses hacked off."^

Espinosa and Soto were quite different in temperament, however, Espinosa

*Laborers.

being the cool, dispassionate conqueror-lawyer, and Soto the hotheaded, reckless warrior. Yet both shared an uncommon mastery of classic *conquista* strategies against the Indians. Moreover, Soto's style was always more methodical
and calculated than most in the school of Pedrarias. For as we shall see, he
would make a name for himself not only as a virtuoso of the quick charge, but
also as a master negotiator frequently called up in Nicaragua and Peru to par-
lay with Indians.

✛   ✛   ✛

Espinosa's 1519 *entrada* returned to Panama City in October, after securing
the fealty of several more *caciques,* and organizing food shipments from the
Parita region to the capital. Soto, however, did not stay in Pedrarias's new city
for long. In 1520, he departed again for the Parita region, accompanying Espinosa's third and final campaign in western Panama.^ This time, the chief justice headed north into the mountains above the flatlands around Natá. He
planned not only to extend Spanish authority in the area, but also to chase down
a rumor of copious amounts of gold hidden in a region ruled by the *cacique* Urraca. It was on this expedition that Soto suddenly became more than a name in
an obscure archival document, and burst forth on the pages of at least one *conquista* history in an incident where he not only proved himself a daunting
fighter, but also managed to save Espinosa and his entire army from almost
certain annihilation during an ambush deep in the interior.

The expedition began in Panama City, with Espinosa dividing his army into
two sections. The main group traveled by ship under his own command, while
a smaller contingent of one hundred men trekked overland. Led by Captain
Francisco Pizarro, this smaller unit was further divided into a main army and a
vanguard, the latter commanded by Soto—a position he would repeatedly hold
for much of his career, most notably in Peru. Bartolomé de las Casas tells the
story of what happened several days out from Panama City, when Soto was
leading his vanguard of thirty men—composed of a handful of horsemen and
the rest on foot—across the wild, open foothills of the Tabasará Mountains,
some fifteen or twenty miles north of the Gulf of Parita.

Apparently, he was reconnoitering this rugged country—which looks remarkably like the hills around his hometown of Jerez, with the same rocky,
desolate beauty—when suddenly he heard the "shouts and noise of battle" up
ahead. Knowing that Espinosa's main force might be in the area, he gave the
order for his men to rush forward. Las Casas says Soto then rode up a height
overlooking a valley, where he saw, to his horror, that hundreds of Urraca's Indians—perhaps a thousand—had pinned down Espinosa's forces. Trapped in a
gully, Herrera says "the Spaniards could make no use of their horses, which was
a great disadvantage, because the Indians lacked neither courage nor strength."

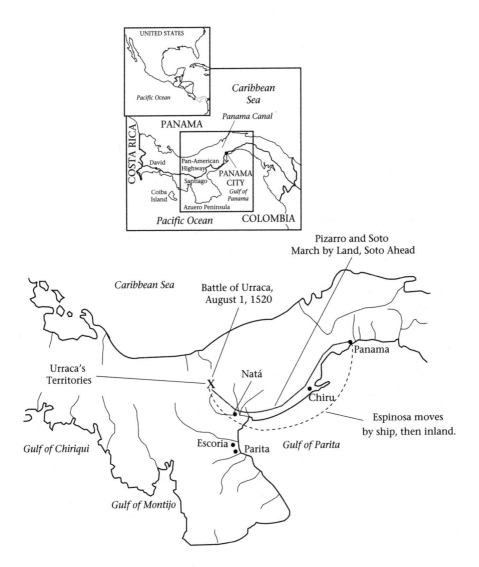

Urraca Campaign, 1520

Soto had several choices. The safest and most prudent was to ride hard back to Pizarro and summon the entire overland force as reinforcements. But Soto, making the sort of snap decision for which he later became famous, chose instead the most dramatic, reckless option available. Herrera tells us he led his tiny force to bring "unexpected succor" to Espinosa's forces, attacking directly into the rear of an army that outnumbered him by as much as thirty to one—a move foolhardy enough that it should have ended the young captain's career before it got started. Skill and luck prevailed, however, as somehow Soto caused enough confusion to force the Indians to pull back momentarily from their assault. Apparently, they believed themselves to be under attack by a much larger contingent of Spaniards. This gave Espinosa's men time to erupt out of the valley and face down Urraca with their own horses, though the native army, once they realized their error, quickly reengaged the Spaniards in country still too rugged for the effective use of cavalry. Forcing them to retreat, the Indians harassed them "with great vigor" as Espinosa's army "withdrew with no small dread to the ships."

Soto's brazen charge was not the only foolhardy action he undertook during the Espinosa expedition. After being driven out of the mountains by Urraca, the chief justice sailed a few miles down the coast to Natá itself, where he deposited Soto and fifty other men. Under the command of Francisco Compañón, they had orders to build a town and a garrison to oversee food shipments to the capital.^ Yet no sooner had Espinosa departed with the main army, and the Spaniards had begun to build their first *bohíos,* than the irrepressible Urraca swept down from the mountains to attack the tiny settlement.^

The fighting was fierce as Urraca and his army, engaging in one of the few long-distance offensives mounted against the Spaniards by the Panamanian Indians, pressed in so hard amidst the trees and hills surrounding Natá that Compañón's men were forced to retreat into their town, behind whatever makeshift palisades they had erected. This led to an Indian siege as Urraca and his tattooed, heavily armed warriors formed a circle of native troops around what must have looked like a frontier fort from an old Hollywood Western, a structure made out of rough-hewn timbers planted in the ground. But instead of cowboys, there would have been crossbowmen and Renaissance gunners in helmets and armor manning platforms just below and inside the tops of the walls, underneath the standard of Castile and León.

Compañón, was hardly content to wait out this siege and do nothing, knowing he was hopelessly outnumbered and at a great disadvantage, holed up in a small fort where supplies of ammunition and food were minimal. "Understanding the many men Urraca brought about them," writes Las Casas, "Captain Francisco Compañón sent out in a fury Hernando de Soto," followed by another conquistador, Pedro Miguel, the two of them mounted and charging into the massed Coiban warriors, where the force of their rushing horses briefly opened a breach in Urraca's siege, wide enough to "free many men."

Once clear of Urraca's warriors, Soto and his small group rode hard to Panama City, covering one hundred miles in just two days to warn Pedrarias. The governor quickly dispatched Soto's friend, Hernán Ponce de León—then known primarily as a ship's pilot—to take a brigantine "with forty men" to relieve Compañón's beleaguered garrison, and to bring in fresh food and supplies. They "arrived in time," says Las Casas, to use their horses to cut through the siege and strengthen Compañón's small troop, which held out a few more days until Pedrarias himself arrived with a larger force of 140 men. Even then, Urraca fought the Spaniards for five full days before ordering his warriors to retreat into the interior, battered but still very much intact. For the next eleven years, this remarkable *cacique* continued to harass the Spaniards from hideouts in the mountains, living the life of a fugitive and leading a band of guerrilla fighters until he died, still a free man, in 1531.^

After the battle for Natá, Pedrarias stayed in Natá to divide the lands and remaining Indians in the Parita region, naming sixty Spanish conquistadors to be *vecinos* of Natá—including Hernando de Soto, Hernán Ponce de León, and Francisco Compañón, who was named commandant and lieutenant governor of this new Spanish municipality.^ For the next three years, Soto and his *compañeros* would live here in this pleasant, fertile valley at the base of the Tabasará Mountains, accumulating gold and Indian laborers, and building the foundation for their future prosperity in Nicaragua and Peru.

Book II
Consolidation

❖ 6 ❖

The Invasion of Nicaragua

ONE DAY EARLY IN 1520, with Soto off in Coiba on his bloody *entrada* with Espinosa, messengers arrived in Panama City to announce a startling discovery. "They call it *Mexica,*"^ the criers shouted to *vecinos* gathered on the new plaza in the baking sun, listening in amazement to descriptions of exotic cities, caches of gold, and the dramatic story of an unknown *hidalgo* named Cortés. Further details about the conquest came in snatches over the next year or two—about Cortés's march across Mexico in the autumn of 1519; his arrival at the Aztec capital of Tenochtitlán in November; his meeting with the emperor Montezuma, whom he brazenly kidnapped in classic *conquista* style; and the battles, victories, near defeats, and honors heaped upon this upstart *hidalgo* whose audacity, ruthlessness, and come-from-nowhere rise to wealth and fame would inspire a generation of conquistadors, including Hernando de Soto.

Few in Panama, however, felt admiration for Cortés. The overriding emotion on the *plaza mayor* that day was one of intense jealously that they had not found Montezuma first. The only consolation for the choleric old governor and his colonists was their potent belief that if one great empire existed in the Indies, others must be waiting to be discovered and conquered.

This conviction was powerfully reinforced on June 5, 1523, when another explorer appeared off the beach at Panama in three leaking, worm-eaten brigantines,^ packed with a hundred exhausted men, and 112,000 pesos of gold.^ His name was Gil González Dávila, and he, too, had astonishing news for the crowd gathered on Panama City's humid plaza—the discovery of a country he claimed was as rich as Mexico, where the people lived in cities filled with pyramids and palaces, and were ruled by powerful kings. He named this territory after one of its most prominent sovereigns, Nic-atl-nahuac, which he mispronounced Nicaragua.

González Dávila's success was unexpected. Four years earlier, this longtime *vecino* of Hispaniola, with powerful connections at the court in Spain, had arrived in Acla on a dual royal mission—to investigate certain discrepancies in the colony's tax payments to the Crown, and then to organize an expedition to explore west along the uncharted Pacific coast of Central America. The king's hope was to settle once and for all whether this coastline was connected to the Orient. Predictably, Pedrarias had stonewalled both the tax investigation and González Dávila's efforts to secure ships, supplies, and men for an *entrada*. When the young courtier finally assembled his "armada," it was hardly the resplendent force the Crown had envisioned to explore the South Sea and parley with the Great Khan of China. Composed of four poorly constructed brigantines, 115 ill-equipped men, four hundred porters and servants, and only four horses, González Dávila's shabby fleet seemed destined for disaster when it departed the Pearl Islands on January 21, 1522.

Just three or four days out, González Dávila's makeshift brigantines began taking on water, the hulls so "badly damaged by shipworm" that the men barely made it back to shore. They landed some two hundred miles west of Panama City, in Chiriqui, where González Dávila left his ships to be beached and repaired before continuing onward by land. Apparently, he hoped to march on foot all the way to the Great Khan's court. Instead, he barely made it through Costa Rica. There his men spent several weeks tramping through dense, cane-choked swamps swelled by winter rains, finally emerging onto dry ground in the Nicoya region, near the modern border between Costa Rica and Nicaragua. There the Spaniards found themselves in a pleasant country covered with maize fields and sophisticated villages obviously belonging to an advanced civilization. González Dávila also found his brigantines at anchor in the emerald green waters of a broad gulf, patched up and loaded with fresh provisions and supplies from Panama.

From Nicoya, González Dávila began a slow trek to the northwest. Following a wide Indian highway, he vowed to his men "not to turn back until I found someone who could stop me by force of arms." Along this road, kings and *caciques* in broad plazas edged by step pyramids, temples, and palaces entertained the Spaniards, as González Dávila used his courtier's tongue to impress and entertain his hosts so much that they willingly gave him gold, and allowed his priests to baptize thirty-two thousand Indians—or so he claimed.

González Dávila had little choice but to use words, given his small, ragtag army. This situation amply was demonstrated when a *cacique* named Diriangen grew weary of the stranger's rhetoric and, suspecting the worst of the Spaniards, attacked with three thousand warriors near modern Managua. The assault came unexpectedly when Diriangen pretended to be bringing his people to be baptized. He might even have destroyed the Spaniards if González Dávila, a cool-headed commander and *conquista* veteran, had not rallied his men and dispatched his three remaining horses to cut a hole through Dirian-gen's infantry. The roar and flame of the Spaniards' guns^ further confused the Indians long enough for the Spaniards to escape and retreat to the coast, where they hastily boarded their ships.^

Giving up on the Orient, Gil González Dávila returned with his treasure to Panama. There his troubles continued when Pedrarias tried to arrest him and confiscate his gold. Somehow, González Dávila managed to get to Nombre de Dios, where he bought a ship and fled at full sail as the governor's constable approached to take him prisoner.

But this was not the last the Panamanians, or Soto, would see of Gil González Dávila. Arriving home in Santo Domingo, he would stay just long enough to spend his fortune outfitting a fresh expedition to conquer the king-doms of Nic-atl-nahuac. This time he hoped to avoid El Furor Domini by land-ing on the Caribbean side of Central America, and marching overland to seize the great valley on the Pacific side. Pedrarias, however, had other ideas— which ultimately would pit Soto against González Dávila in a tiny hamlet named Toreba, where the courtier and the young frontiersman would fight a battle over who would rule this section of Central America.

✢   ✢   ✢

For Hernando de Soto, the period of Cortés's and González Dávila's tri-umphs was one of consolidation in an obscure corner of Castilla del Oro. Cash-ing in on his martial successes in the Urraca wars, he lived for some forty months—between August 1519 and late 1523—in the tiny frontier *pueblo* of Natá. There he accumulated the wealth and aura he would need to transform himself—with the help of his older and more experienced partners, Hernán Ponce de León and Francisco Compañón—from a mere *soldado* into a senior captain and conquistador.^

Today, Natá is a quiet *pueblo* surrounding a small, grassy plaza shaded by hardwoods and scattered palms. Edged on three sides by small shops with cool, dark porches, the most prominent structure is an ancient mud-brick church, which runs along the fourth side—a thatch-and-tin-topped *bohío* with a dirt floor and worn adobe facade. In front of the church stands a small bronze bust of Gaspar de Espinosa, looking more the lawyer than the conqueror, with a thin face, thin lips, and high collar.^ Behind the church, the Río Chico flows quickly, a cold mountain stream running down from the Tabasará Mountains.

In Soto's day, Natá would have had a more makeshift, frontier feeling to it, with half-finished houses being assembled by *encomienda* Indians, an early and more-primitive thatch church than the one in Natá today, and a crude mar-ket selling food, horses, cattle, goats, chickens, and a few precious Spanish goods ferried over from Panama City. Slaves were also sold here, hawked by

traders prancing up and down the square displaying their human wares, and
shouting out prices.

Our only source for life in Natá during these early days is Bartolomé de las
Casas, who inexplicably singles out this insignificant *pueblo* to condemn once
more *conquista* excesses, providing in the process a spare (if hyperbolic) account of what happened here during Soto's stay—beginning with Pedrarias's
allotments after Urraca's siege was broken.

"Pedrarias," writes Las Casas, "to reward the Spaniards who worked so
much there, decided to make a village for them near the *cacique* known as
Natá; and because the Spaniards in the Indies, especially those who walk in
those evil ways, care very little about cultivating and working to improve the
land, and would rather eat someone else's food without working for it, at the
cost of the Indians' lives and souls, Pedrarias made *repartimientos* of the villages to give them *encomiendas*," ordering each man "to settle [his land] and
to take up a certain number of Indians in their villages in these provinces, subjugated by violence and war and what the Spaniards call pacification, and out
of fear the Indians came to serve them . . . making the houses and farms for the
Spaniards, hunting, fishing and performing all of the other work to sustain a
settlement of fifty or sixty Spanish *vecinos*, a work force larger than what
would be required to sustain a village of two thousand in Castile, because they
wanted to be served like sons of counts and dukes in luxury, and not only
served, but adored.

"They established these intolerable duties," Las Casas continues, pouring
on the invective, "though the Indians were unused to them, and when some
came to work late, others became sick, and others ran away, the Spaniards
called it a revolt. They then sent Diego Albítez*^ to go after the Indians, and
he took some and killed them and captured others to punish severely, and in
this way they forced them to come and serve their *encomiendas* and tyrannical ways."

The "revolt" Las Casas describes was probably not a single event, but a general state of upheaval, rebellion, bloodshed, and thuggery that persisted
throughout Soto's forty months in Natá, when Indians lived in terror for their
lives, and the Spanish, outnumbered hundreds to one, lived in constant fear of
being overwhelmed by their desperate vassals. Once again, Hernando de Soto
was almost certainly in the middle of this reign of terror, serving as a platoon
captain under Diego Albítez in large sorties, and on his own commanding
smaller parties to hunt down supposed rebels and capture slaves, two activities
he became renowned for in Nicaragua and Peru.

*Diego Albítez was Compañón's uncle, and a senior captain in the colony known for his brutality in deal-
ing with the Indians.

Not all Coibans succumbed to Spanish intimidation. Up in the mountains of the Tabasará, some thirty or forty miles from Natá, the redoubtable Urraca and a small troop of Coiban rebels continued to elude Albítez, Soto, and other "pacifiers," exploiting the advantages offered by the rugged up-country of jungle and volcanic outcrops. Pursuing his own policy of terror against the Spaniards, Urraca promulgated one of the first sustained guerrilla wars in Latin America, attacking Spanish villages and ranches, and brutally cutting down any Spaniard foolish enough to travel alone. Eventually, Pedrarias replaced Albítez with Compañón, though he too failed to reign in Urraca, who pressed his resistance for another decade, killing "many Spaniards" before finally dying of natural causes.

Despite Urraca's resistance, the Coibans eventually suffered the same fate as the Arawak in the Caribbean and the Cuevans of Darién, succumbing within a few years to the strip-mine approach of conquest favored by Pedrarias and his men. Just a half century later, historians and eyewitnesses describe the Cuevans as being virtually extinct, with one geographer noting in the 1570s that only three or four hundred Indians remained in the entire central region of the isthmus—this in a place where thousands, perhaps tens of thousands were thriving a generation earlier.^

In sum, Soto and his partners' time in Natá was brief and bloody, but highly profitable; a period in which they built up a solid base of wealth and influence, while acquiring a taste for the independence, risks, and possibilities of frontier life far away from the colony's central government—and from its intrusive governor. By the summer of 1523, when González Dávila arrived from Nicaragua, and talk in Panama's hot plazas turned to gold and conquest in the north, the twenty-something Soto was no longer a nobody in Panamanian society. He was a rising captain already locally famous for his fighting acumen and ruthlessness, a young man eagerly sought after by the senior captains and officials of the colony as they contemplated a military operation far larger and more costly than the invasion of western Panama four years earlier.

✦ ✦ ✦

By royal decree, González Dávila held the concession to conquer Nicaragua. By the fall of 1523, however, several rivals were also organizing expeditions to invade Nicaragua, and other territories in Central America. These included not only Pedrarias Dávila in Panama, but also two captains of Hernán Cortés's, sent out in late 1523 and early 1524 by the conqueror of Mexico on probing expeditions south of Mexico City. The first of these was Pedro de Alvarado, marching southeast near the Pacific coast with five hundred men, headed toward Guatemala and El Salvador. Cristóbal de Olid, the second, led another five hundred men across the Yucatán toward Honduras. Later, Hernán

Cortés himself would become yet another entrant into the competition when that October he led a large force out of his base near Tenochtitlán (Mexico City) toward Honduras—ostensibly to punish Olid, who by then had mutinied and was trying to set up his own government, but also with the intention of seizing Central America for himself.

. Pedrarias's effort began in late summer 1523, when the governor and a core group of investors formed a *compañia* to invade Nicaragua. According to the *Contrato de Compañia,* signed on September 22, 1523, the major investors included the governor, two colonial officials, a prominent lawyer, a wealthy ship owner named Juan Téllez, and Téllez's heretofore obscure young kinsman, Francisco Hernández de Córdoba, captain of the governor's guard, and the man chosen to command the invasion force.^ Hernando de Soto's name does not appear on this contract, though the fact he was to serve as a battalion leader in the invasion means he and his partners were almost certainly involved as major participants from the start.

Soto's senior role in the expedition was probably purchased with a generous contribution by the partners, linked to the role Natá and its plantations would play in supplying Córdoba's *entrada* with food, horses, and other agricultural supplies. *Compañia* organizers also would have been attracted by the young Soto's skills as a fighter—and by his reputation as the sort of brash, ambitious young man they considered ideal for this highly risky enterprise. For not only was Córdoba invading the territory of a people whose warriors had already driven out one Spanish army, he also was likely to confront rival Spanish troops armed not with stone maces and wooden clubs, but with Renaissance blades and lances. This explains why this invasion force was composed almost exclusively of young captains, with little fame or reputation, commanding troops equally young and obscure, while more senior Panamanian captains—those who already had earned a measure of local fame, and of wealth and ease with their *encomiendas*—opted to stay in Panama to await the outcome of the campaign.

Hernán Ponce, the business manager of the partnership, probably negotiated the terms of Soto's participation; he and the royal treasurer Alonso de la Puente may also have paid some of the expenses incurred in outfitting the young captain, since they are later listed as the recipients of Soto's share of Nicaraguan booty. (Another explanation is that Soto was not around to collect his share personally.) Neither Ponce nor Compañón participated in Córdoba's initial invasion.^ Apparently, both stayed in Natá to look after the affairs of the partnership while Soto was away, waiting until at least midway through 1524 to head north.

With the financial arrangements concluded, Córdoba's next move was to raise an army. With only five or six hundred Spaniards living in Castilla del

Oro at the time, and Pedrarias's long-standing reluctance to detach any significant force, this was no easy task. Only the promise of Aztec-like piles of gold convinced El Furor Domini to dispatch 229 men—a small, but, as it turned out, adequate number to defeat the native armies of the Great Valley. Córdoba's recruits marched in three divisions, with Córdoba commanding one hundred men,* Captain Francisco de la Puente commanding sixty-one, and Soto commanding seventy-six. They took only seventeen horses, distributed more or less equally among the three captains—seven for Córdoba, six for Soto, and five for Puente.^

Little is known about Soto's seventy-six men, other than their names, though a handful became prominent enough later on to provide some personal details. These include Soto's two lieutenants in the Nicaragua campaign— Rodrigo Lozano, a cavalryman who remained a staunch Soto ally all the way to Cuzco in Peru; and Sebastián de Benalcázar, who soon became a rival and sometime enemy in the heated politics of the Nicaraguan colony, and later tried to one-up Soto by leading his own small troop to reinforce Pizarro in Peru. Other notables included one of Pedrarias's sons, Diego Arias Dávila, a young ne'er-do-well who inherited neither his father's abilities as a fighter, nor as a political operative; Francisco de Fuentes, a longtime Soto friend and ally who rode in Soto's Peruvian vanguard with Rodrigo Lozano; and Pedro Díaz, a silversmith later given the enviable job of weighing out the gold and silver of the Inca's ransom at Cajamarca.^

✛　✛　✛

The country Francisco Hernández de Córdoba planned to invade comprises one of the most fertile valleys in Latin America, a wide corridor of rich, black soil, dark blue lakes, and a string of smoldering volcanoes stretching 250 miles along a major fault line just inside the Pacific coast. Few landscapes in Latin America impressed the Spaniards more—the dramatic sweep of abrupt, steaming cones, some five or six thousand feet high; the deep lagoons filling collapsed *volcánes;* and an inland sea the size of the Chesapeake Bay, which some of the Indians called Cocibolca, and the Spanish renamed El Mar Dulce, "the Fresh Water Sea."

Las Casas, during a visit in the late 1520s, called Nicaragua "a Paradise of God." Oviedo called it "the most beautiful and satisfying country . . . to be found in the Indies." Pascual de Andagoya was particularly impressed by the volcanoes, writing that the pyrotechnics atop one near modern-day Managua were visible "for three leagues around." He adds that "the Indians, to appease the fire so that it may not come and destroy them, bring a virgin there, at cer-

*Including twenty men who formed his personal guard.

tain times of the year, to offer her up, and they throw her in. They are then joyful, for they believe that they are saved."

But Córdoba and his invaders cared little about the violent beauty of the *bocas del infiernos,* the "mouths of hell," or the freshness of the water. They were after only one thing—gold—which they had convinced themselves would exceed even Cortés's haul in Mexico.

The reality would be far less spectacular, though Spanish aspirations to conquer a second Aztec Empire were not entirely misdirected. Originating in Mexico, the culture the Spaniards were about to crush may have been distant "country" cousins of the Aztecs and other Mexican peoples. Six centuries earlier, their ancestors had emigrated from the Chiapas region of southern Mexico, and from points farther north, traveling south in a great exodus to escape oppression by the Olmec. Ending up in the Great Valley after years of wandering, they seized it from a people called the Corobici, about whom nothing more is known, though presumably the Mexicans destroyed this people as thoroughly as the Spaniards were about to obliterate them. Isolated in their lush valley, these Mexican emigrants had flourished, organizing over the centuries a system of small, incessantly warring city-states ruled by kings. In their capitals, they built crude but recognizable versions of Mexican-style pyramids, plazas, temples, and palaces. By the time of Córdoba's invasion, perhaps 500,000 Indians inhabited the valley, including several newly established colonies built by Mexican trader-settlers from as far away as Tenochtitlán.^

Like the Aztecs, the peoples known as Pipil, Chorotega, Maribio, and Nicarao blended a high degree of elegance and complexity in matters of dress, trade, architecture, and politics with an extraordinarily violent religion—as Córdoba, Soto, and the others could plainly see as they marched up the Great Valley. Entering city after city, they encountered not only well-disciplined warriors, but idols glaring down from temples and causeways; frightening visages of jaguars, eagles, and snakes drenched in blood from human sacrifices. These were the gods of Nicaragua—Tamagastad and Cipattonal, bloodthirsty creators of human beings, earth, the moon, and the stars; Bizteot, god of hunger; and dozens more.^

Nicaraguan leaders could also be open-minded and sophisticated, traits that emerge with great clarity in González Dávila's narrative of his 1522–23 expedition. Almost unique in the chronicles of the *conquista,* this record describes the journey of an unusually well-bred conquistador whose feeble army forced him to explore not by destroying, but by visiting the courts of *caciques* to talk and observe. Thus we have a scene in González Dávila's *relación* where he is reading the *Requerimiento* to King Nic-atl-nahuac at a feast held in the Spaniard's honor, not as an ultimatum, but as a set of ideas to be discussed at supper. Who was this king of the Spaniards? How could Jesus' mother be a virgin? What caused the night and coldness? And, more to the point at hand, why did "the Christians so love gold?" Apparently, the slick courtier gave convincing answers, since after González Dávila had "spoken with him over two or three days about matters of God, [Nic-alt-nuhuac] made up his mind to become a Christian, along with all his Indians and wives, and in one day 9,017 of them were baptized, both young and old, and they did this so willingly."

Not all the kings of Nicaragua reacted with such decorum. Within days of the feast with Nic-atl-nahuac, González Dávila was beating a hasty retreat to his brigantines on the coast, fleeing from the *cacique* Diriangen and his army, who apparently did not appreciate the courtier's conversational skills.^

+   +   +

Late in 1523, Francisco Hernández de Córdoba and his 230-man army, accompanied by several hundred servants, boarded ships for the Costa Rican coast just south of Nicaragua. They landed at an Indian village named Urutina, across the Gulf of Nicoya from where a year earlier González Dávila had rested his men before exploring the Great Valley. According to a report written by Pedrarias and sent to the king—based on lost dispatches sent by Córdoba^—the Spaniards first established a garrison in Urutina, before heading north. What happened next, however, is a mystery. In one of the more regrettable gaps in early *conquista* history, there is no real record of Córdoba's invasion of Nicaragua—no soldier's chronicles, eyewitness historian's account, letters home, or official *relación*. The only firsthand source of information we know about was Córdoba's missing dispatches to Pedrarias, which the old governor incorporated into his 1525 report to the king, a mostly worthless document that is little more than a list of provinces captured and natural resources to be exploited—so many Indians here, so much game there, a mine here, rich cropland there. Yet it is possible to reconstruct at least a broad outline of what happened.

Córdoba probably encountered armed resistance from the moment he left Urutina,^ given what we know about the Nicaraguans' almost ceaseless warfare among themselves, and the fact that the valley was not going to react as peacefully to a second visit by armored Spaniards. Córdoba would have marched in the usual *conquista* formation, assigning himself to lead the main army. Most likely, given Soto's reputation as a talented and fast-thinking outrider in the Urraca wars, Córdoba placed him in command of the lead battalion. This means Captain Francisco de la Puente probably commanded the rear guard, assigned to keep open communication lines with the Spanish base at Nicoya. If this battle configuration is correct, Hernando de Soto was the first officer in the invasionary force to encounter the peoples of Nicaragua—just as he was often the first to arrive at the cities, valleys, and rivers of Peru and *La Florida*.

As Soto stormed across the Great Valley, entering each new kingdom in turn, he first would have found himself on a dirt road snaking through wild, overgrown bands of forest and scrub that served as a buffer between two neighboring polities. Next, he would have entered partially burned and cleared land used for hunting, which soon gave way to farmsteads, small villages, and expansive fields of maize, beans, sweet potatoes, pineapple, papaya, avocado, and "cash" crops of cotton, cacao, tobacco, and *yaat,* the latter being dried coca beans used to relieve pain. Finally, Soto would have reached the chief city of the kingdom, where he and the army probably fought a decisive battle, crushing their native counterparts before marching down narrow streets lined by the city's *bohíos,* constructed of whitewashed adobe and thatch. Eventually, these streets led the invaders into the city's central plaza, edged by small earthen and stone pyramids, and large *bohío* temples and palaces.

The common people Soto passed along the way dressed in deerskin sandals and finely woven cotton cloth, the women donning toga-like gowns that hung from their shoulders to their knees, and the men wearing short cotton skirts and loincloths. Nobles, priests, and the highly revered warrior class covered their bodies with tattoos and wore elaborate gold jewelry, feather headdresses, and animal skins denoting rank and, for soldiers, success in battle.^

The powerful armies of Nicoya, Nicaragua, and Diriangen apparently succumbed quickly to the Spanish onslaught, though not without a fight. According to González Dávila, the largest city-states were capable of fielding armies of several thousand men used to fighting in ordered ranks and battle formations, and armed with a formidable arsenal of clubs, stone-topped maces, slings, javelins, small bows and arrows, and swords carved out of wood and stone. The Nicaraguans also used armor, the rank and file dressing themselves in quilted cotton jerkins and heavy wooden helmets, and kings and generals wearing breast, arm, and leg plates made of gold.

Given this formidable array of weaponry, it is surprising the highly disciplined armies of Nicaragua collapsed so quickly—apparently in a matter of weeks—something of a record among the more-advanced peoples in the Indies. For even though the Spaniards possessed a powerful technological edge, most organized native armies were able to maintain an effective fighting force for up to several months before succumbing, with the Peruvians, Mexicans, Mayans, and scattered other nations putting up a considerable—and, for the Spanish, quite bloody—resistance for years and even decades once the threat to their existence was fully understood. The Aztecs, for instance, nearly smashed Cortés during the Night of Sorrows, when they drove the invaders out of Tenochtitlán, while the Incas kept up an organized fight against the Spaniards for over forty years after Pizarro executed Atahualpa, the Inca emperor, and seized Peru.

The explanation in the Great Valley, however, lies not so much with gaps in technology, but with the Nicaraguan style of warfare. Over the centuries, it had evolved into an almost ceremonial exercise fought less to conquer or kill an enemy than to score minor victories on matters of territorial disputes and, even more important, to capture prisoners, the major source of victims destined for the sacrificial blade. Nicaraguans conducted war according to a set of rules that began with elaborate ceremonies to prepare for battle—offering gifts and inviting one another to feasts—and then progressed to skirmishes fought more to get close enough to one's opponent to knock him senseless or otherwise grab him and haul him away than to kill him. This mode of fighting explains why González Dávila's one hundred poorly armed men escaped Diriangen's surprise attack without a single man killed (one man was captured), and why Córdoba lost few, if any, men during his invasion.

Yet the Indians still were capable of fighting with great ferocity and cunning, as indicated by a grisly story Oviedo tells about what happened when Córdoba's army approached the chief city of the Maribios. "When the Indians saw the daring and vigor of the Spaniards," Oviedo writes, "they devised a new stratagem of war . . . And for this . . . [the Indian soldiers] killed many old Indians, male and female, their parents and neighbors, and they flayed them, afterwards they killed them, and they ate the meat and they kept the skins, and the live Indians wore them outside, with only the eyes removed, thinking, it is said, with this innovation, that the sight would scare away the Christians and frighten their horses. So when the Christians left their camp, the Indians refused to engage them in battle: before they had formed their forward line those Indians cloaked in their disguises, and with their bow and arrows they started the battle in a spirited fashion with many terrifying shouts. The Christians marveled greatly at their audacity, and even felt some fear under the circumstances, but falling into place they commenced to attack the enemy and wound and kill those that had lined themselves with the flayed skins of the dead."

By late spring 1524, with the conquest of the Great Valley complete, Francisco Hernández de Córdoba began a task he apparently relished far more than warfare—the building of cities and a nascent colonial government. In March or April, he founded Granada, built near the Indian city of Jalteba, "on a little bay" in Lake Nicaragua "which there bends its crescent into the land so as to afford a comparative shelter from the constant and often severe northeast winds." At the same time, he settled León,* naming Soto as one of its thirty-three founding *vecinos,* and designating it as the capital of the new colony. Situated north of Granada on the banks of Lake Managua, it was close to both the fertile Chinandega Plain to the northwest, where thousands of Indians lived

---

*Which city was founded first remains a matter of dispute in Nicaragua.

and farmed, and to the new port city of La Posesión, the future base of Soto and
Ponce's lucrative shipping business.

Córdoba had grand ideas for his new cities. In his lost dispatches sent to Pedrarias, he laid out detailed plans for plazas, public buildings, and churches,
though his first priority in mid-1524 was to erect defenses—against both rebel
Indian attacks and the expected appearance of rival Spanish captains. For even
as the first buildings in León and Granada were being raised, Córdoba heard
from Indian informants that Pedro de Alvarado was headed south into modern
El Salvador. He may also have heard about Cristóbal de Olid in Honduras,
though so far he had heard nothing about González Dávila.

Córdoba reacted to these reports by ordering his men and slaves to build
stockades and organize defenses, and by dispatching reconnaissance parties
north into the mountains in the interior of Central America, and south into Lake
Nicaragua. Soto participated in at least one of these early expeditions, exploring the great lake with his lieutenant, Sebastián de Benalcázar, and Ruy Díaz,
the first alcalde of Granada. Pedrarias says Córdoba ordered a brigantine from
Panama disassembled and hauled overland to Granada, which Soto reassem-
bled and sailed to "many populated islands" before locating a waterway running east, toward the North Sea and the Spanish Caribbean. But the river they
discovered, the San Juan, was not navigable.^

One platoon Córdoba sent out that summer was led by Gabriel de Rojas,
Soto's colleague from the Balboa boat-building expedition. His assignment
was to explore the Indian highway heading north out of León, leading a troop
of perhaps thirty men through the rugged foothills of the Segovia Mountains,
and on north through the valleys and volcanic hills of central Honduras. On the
way, Rojas not only discovered veins of gold in the Segovias, which Soto and
his partners would later mine, but also "by chance encountered Gil González
Dávila," says Oviedo, then marching south from his newly established base on
the Caribbean coast of Honduras.

González Dávila was not pleased to see one of Pedrarias's captains in his
domain. According to Oviedo, he angrily told Rojas that "he had no business
in that land, nor had Pedrarias, and that he should return at once to Francisco
Hernández; and he also said that although Captain Rojas could personally have
as much [booty] as he wanted there, he could not allow him or anyone else, as
captains of Pedrarias, to travel through that land." Rojas, whose force was far
too small to challenge González Dávila's army, dutifully returned to Córdoba
to deliver González Dávila's message, enriching himself at the expense of Indians along the way.

Back in León, Córdoba received more bad news soon after Rojas returned,
when he heard that Pedro de Alvarado was moving ever farther south toward
the Indian province of Nequepio, in modern El Salvador—a city-state barely

one hundred and fifty miles northwest of León. His response to this crisis was to dispatch his best outrider—Hernando de Soto—to deal with these twin perils, sending him off with seventy or eighty men to locate and confront both Alvarado and González Dávila with the news that Nicaragua was already taken. In doing so, Francisco Hernández de Córdoba fired the first salvo in what I'll call the War of the Captains, launching a deep thrust into disputed territory on a mission spearheaded by a young firebrand whose success or failure would determine the future not only of Córdoba's fledgling colony, but of the entire region.

✣ 7 ✣

War of the Captains

DURING THE FIRST THREE decades of the *conquista,* power and position in the Indies emanated from Spain, where aptitude often gave way to connections and pedigree. Then came Hernán Cortés in 1519, and his triumph against the Aztecs. Accomplished after a brazen act of insubordination against his governor, Diego de Velázquez of Cuba, who had specifically ordered his unruly captain not to launch an invasion, Cortés not only snatched a fabulous prize but also shattered the already precarious chain of command established in the Indies after 1493 by Ferdinand. In its place arose a period of near anarchy on the mainland, where captains, governors, and *caudillo* strongmen rose and fell according to who had the quickest sword arm and was most ruthless.

By the early 1520s, the cutting edge of the *conquista* more than ever was held by a new breed of young, brash fighting men, trained not on the battlefields of Italy and Granada, nor in the political intrigues of the court, but in the Indies. Audacious, haughty, and talented, these avaricious children of conquest rose up like whirlwinds during the summer of 1524, headed in a mad scramble for an unexplored region of the Americas rumored to contain gold and rich cities.

Originally, Soto's mission was to head due north to ferret out Gil González Dávila. However, when Pedrarias's men received the alarming news that Pedro de Alvarado seemed to be headed toward the northern approaches of the Great Valley, with an army numbering nearly five hundred men, Córdoba ordered his young captain to march as quickly as possible toward Alvarado's last reported position.

Soto departed León early that summer, 1524, leading some eighty men up the Pacific side along the route of the modern Pan American highway. Moving with his usual dispatch, Soto double-time marched through Nicaragua, around the Gulf of Fonseca, and into the region the Spaniards then called Malaca*—

*Also Malalaca.

today's northern El Salvador and southern Honduras. "From this city of León," Pedrarias wrote in a letter to the king about the expedition, "they went exploring and pacifying up to the great city of Nequepio that they say is Malaca[n], where Alvarado had arrived with his men of Cortés."

Fortunately for Soto, however, the expected encounter with Alvarado and his formidable army never took place.^ For even as the young captain cautiously approached Nequepio, he received word that the Mexican army was pulling back to Guatemala,^ where Alvarado had just been named governor by the king.

With Pedro de Alvarado abruptly removed from the scene, Soto set off to find and drive away Gil González Dávila. Plunging into the rugged Comayagua Mountains north of El Salvador, he followed a circuitous route through steamy jungle valleys and over rocky, fern-choked passes, moving again with the remarkable speed that would become his trademark in Peru and *La Florida.* Covering close to two hundred miles in a matter of days, Soto arrived in the Ulúa River valley of central Honduras.^ Here he discovered a wide Indian track on the valley floor, flanked by fields of maize growing under volcanic ridges two to three thousand feet high. This was the heartland of the Lenca, a rustic people who wore Mayan-style cotton gowns and worshiped idols of beautifully carved animals.^ But this time Soto's quest did not involve the local Indians. Marching fast toward a Lenca *pueblo* called Toreba, he was chasing Spanish prey.

Had circumstances been different, Soto might have found a great deal to admire in Gil González Dávila. A highly ambitious man in his forties, this courtier turned conquistador was as ruthless as anyone in the *conquista.* He also could be unusually pragmatic about the business of conquest and colonization. In 1518, as a senior official on Hispaniola, he wrote a surprisingly trenchant report to the young Charles I blaming the depopulation of the Arawak Indians not only on mistreatment, but on what he called "ruinous" colonial policies that not only decimated native lifestyles, diet, and "the will to live," but also was slowly destroying the colony's economy. Endorsing an end to the *encomienda* system, he correctly predicted that future prosperity in the Caribbean lay not with get-rich-quick schemes, but with the more stable economies of sugar cane, cattle, and horses. Then came González Dávila's remarkable *entrada* into Nicaragua, where he overcame floods, leaking ships, and an attack by thousands of natives to carry off a fortune in gold. But Hernando de Soto and González Dávila were not destined to become friends, even if the young captain from Jerez de los Caballeros was briefly deceived into thinking so.

Every period chronicler recounts what happened as these two small Spanish troops converged, launching the War of the Captains. It began with Soto

The War of the Captains, 1523–27

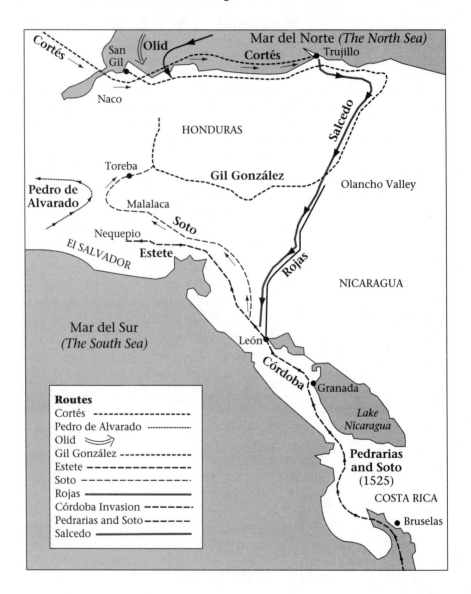

approaching Toreba not with stealth, but by cutting a wide and noisy swath through Lenca territory,^ since he assumed he had the superior force. González Dávila, being a more prudent man, moved with far less fanfare, knowing Soto's whereabouts long before Soto knew his.^

This boisterous progression was nearly Soto's undoing. Indeed, González Dávila was able to sneak up and launch a surprise attack as Soto and his army slept one night in the *bohíos* of Toreba. According to Pedrarias's dispatch, he attacked "in four regiments." This means González Dávila mimicked the Indian tactic of striking from the four cardinal points—a strategy guaranteed to cause maximum confusion, particularly when an inferior force wanted to appear larger than they were.^ At first, the tactic worked, as the attackers stormed into camp, catching Soto and his men in their bedclothes. Yet Soto's mastery of battlefield stratagems, and his uncanny ability to rally his men even as they faced almost sure defeat, turned the tide as Soto's forces slowly drove back those of González Dávila. Finally, says Pedrarias, González Dávila "cried out in a great voice: Señor captain! Peace, peace in the name of the king!" To which Soto should have responded with a slash of his sword, and victory. Instead, he foolishly responded, "Yes, peace, peace in the name of the Emperor!"

This was to be his undoing. For González Dávila, the glib courtier, then proceeded to sweet-talk the young *hombre de frontera*—"man of the frontier"—to the point that Soto not only made no moves against his enemy, but also "did not set a guard on his camp," though "the one force was very close to the other." Herrera adds that Soto's own captains warned him to beware of Gil González Dávila's "cunning." But Soto, showing the same stubborn faith in himself that at times so frustrated his men in *La Florida,* did not listen, even as González Dávila secretly sent for reinforcements, and planned to launch a second surprise attack in the dead of the night.

This time, it worked, as the conquistadors from Hispaniola overwhelmed the Panamanians sleeping in their huts. Taking Soto "prisoner, and securing his arms," they also snatched Soto's gold plundered from various Indians "as if Soto and his men were his enemies," says Pedrarias—"130,000 pesos of gold from the lower country and certain [other] spoils." Andagoya adds that "of the troops who came out to resist" on Soto's side, "two men were killed with two arquebuses."

For Soto, the defeat was humiliating, though he ultimately prevailed. As Herrera reports: Gil González Dávila had "disarmed Soto and his people . . . [but] did not feel that he was safe, fearing Francisco Hernández [de Córdoba], so he released those he had taken . . . and returned to Puerto de Caballos," his base on the north coast of Honduras. Oviedo also insists González Dávila returned Soto's gold, though he may have taken some of it for himself^—a more likely outcome for a man who must have felt bitterly cheated of his prize.

Despite Hernando de Soto's embarrassment at Toreba, it did not affect his standing with Córdoba, who greeted the news of Soto's success, and the retreat of González Dávila and Alvarado, with great relief. On September 19, when Francisco Hernández assembled the conquerors of Nicaragua in the hot, makeshift plaza of León to divide shares of plunder from the invasion, Soto was given "1,000 pesos of good gold" for "his person and a horse and a negro"—a full division commander's allotment from a total of 35,724 pesos of gold.^ Córdoba also gave Soto his first substantial *encomienda* of land and Indians, and named the twenty-four-year-old *capitán* the alcalde of León,*^ one of the most senior posts in the new colony.

✛   ✛   ✛

As Córdoba's captains "pacified" the last remaining pockets of native resistance in the Great Valley, and the stone-and-thatch cities of León and Granada rose beside the inland lakes, the War of the Captains reached a second and even more confusing stage as Gil González Dávila retreated to his base on the Honduran coast, and a fresh wave of interlopers made their appearance.

First came Cortés's captain, Cristóbal de Olid, who not only founded a rival colony near González Dávila's base on the Caribbean coast, but soon mutinied against Cortés's authority, setting himself up as a self-declared *caudillo* of the region.^ Next came a Crown attorney named Pedro Moreno, sent to the Honduran coast as a representative of the Royal *Audiencia* on Hispaniola—the highest court in the Indies—whose magistrates in May 1525 staked a claim to most of Central America because Christopher Columbus, when he first discovered this coast in 1502, was sailing under their authority. The *Audiencia*'s claim extended from the settlements founded by Olid and González Dávila to the Great Valley of Nicaragua, which the magistrates hoped to bring under the authority of their council by "inviting" Córdoba "to quit his obedience to Pedrarias, and to give it to the Judges of the Royal *Audiencia* on Hispaniola."

We know very little about Francisco Hernández de Córdoba. Judging by his actions, he was a cautious man who lacked the audacity and volatility of someone like Soto. He also seemed far more interested in building churches and public buildings^ than in the intrigues he was about to be swept into. Yet even the most reticent commander in Córdoba's position, having just finished a highly successful conquest, and surrounded by a mostly grateful army, would have been tempted by the *Audiencia*'s offer. For here was a land essentially un-

---

*An alcalde was nominated by the governor, and approved by the city council. Two were elected each year. Alcaldes were responsible for the city's day-to-day executive functions. In some cases, the king also appointed a royal alcalde mayor, who acted as his representative in running the day-to-day affairs of the colony. Royal alcaldes could be removed only by order of the king.

claimed that he now controlled, a place considerably richer than Panama, where the climate was healthy, the scenery breathtaking, the soil fertile, and the Indians plentiful. Yet still, Francisco Hernández hesitated, remembering Balboa's fate when he crossed Pedrarias Dávila.

Thus we are left with a five-century-old mystery. Did Francisco Hernández de Córdoba intend to rebel against Pedrarias Dávila, as his enemies claimed, or was he framed by rivals who wanted him out of the way, including his once loyal captain, Hernando de Soto? The answer may lie in what Córdoba wrote in his response to Pedro Moreno and the *Audiencia,* which he dispatched overland with his trusted captain, Gabriel de Rojas, in the summer of 1525—a missive now lost. In it, did Córdoba agree to the *Audiencia*'s request that he switch his allegiance to them? Or did he reply more cautiously, perhaps indicating he was interested, but not prepared to break with Pedrarias? The only thing we know for sure is that the pragmatic Córdoba asked the Honduran authorities for access to the Caribbean coast, so the Nicaraguans could organize an overland route to the Caribbean independent of Panama.^

Unfortunately for Córdoba, by the time Gabriel de Rojas trekked across the mountains with the lieutenant governor's letter, the situation on the Honduran coast had again reversed itself. Pedro Moreno had been rejected by the settlers there in favor of another would-be conqueror of the region suddenly arriving on the scene—Hernán Cortés. Having marched overland from Mexico to put down Cristóbal de Olid's insurrection,^ Cortés had recently arrived, only to discover that Olid was dead, having been murdered in his own home. The killer was none other than Gil González Dávila. Captured earlier by Olid, and kept under arrest in the usurper's own house, González Dávila had killed him with a table knife one night at supper.^

Having firmly established his authority in Honduras by the time Rojas arrived, Cortés met him and read the letters from Córdoba to the *Audiencia.* Pleased to see that Córdoba was at least exploring the possibility of breaking away from Pedrarias, and anxious to plunge into the scramble for Honduras and Nicaragua, Cortés dispatched, via Rojas, presents and letters of his own to León. He offered to assist Córdoba in setting up his northern port at Cortés's new settlement of Trujillo. He also hinted that the young lieutenant governor might want to consider siding with him, though for the time being he suggested sticking with Pedrarias.^

The arrival of Cortés's presents and epistles in León, coming early in the fall of 1525, was the beginning of the end for Córdoba. For no sooner had Rojas returned than a sizable faction of *vecinos* decided to oppose any move linking Nicaragua with Cortés in Trujillo, or Moreno in Santo Domingo. The leader of these dissenters, according to Oviedo, was the alcalde of León, Hernando de Soto.

What happened next is also unclear. Depending on whom one believes, Córdoba either conspired to rebel by inviting Cortés to march on the Great Valley, or he was framed by Soto and his followers, who hoped to remove Córdoba in order to advance their own ambitions. Andagoya, who was there, insists that Córdoba meant to rebel, and was open about his plans.^ Oviedo, on the other hand, suggests Córdoba was only guilty of sending some vague letters to Pedro Moreno. Insisting he personally investigated the Córdoba affair when he toured Nicaragua in 1527, Oviedo writes that he "heard . . . many others in León [blame] Hernández' death on Captains Francisco Compañón and Hernando de Soto and on others who were jealous of him, accusing them of having stirred up Pedrarias' anger against him." The Nicaraguan historian Carlos Melendez adds that Soto and Compañón turned against Hernández de Córdoba because they saw "major opportunities to accede to a possible leadership in Nicaragua, with the elimination of Hernández." It is just as likely that Córdoba was simply indecisive, which makes his motives seem muddled—and gave Soto and his clique their opening. Indeed, Andagoya says Córdoba did not do what most captains would have done—brazenly seize power by dispatching his supporters to capture or kill his opponents. Instead, he assembled the *vecinos* of León and Granada late in 1525 in the *plaza mayor* to collectively sign a letter to the *Audiencia* in Santo Domingo and to the king requesting that Nicaragua be proclaimed a colony. Some chroniclers insist he also declared his intention to break away from Pedrarias at this meeting; others say he asked only for recognition for an independent colony.

Most of the 150 Spaniards, pleased with Córdoba's handling of the conquest, and their share of the booty, agreed to sign. A small but vocal minority did not—led by Hernando de Soto, who apparently delivered a blistering speech accusing Córdoba and his followers of disloyalty to Pedrarias. This reveals a new dimension to Soto's character—that of the charismatic schemer, of the political operator who does not hesitate to betray a commander, even one who has given him wealth and honors. Soto, however, was unable to sway the majority that day on the hot, steamy plaza. Yet his strong opposition finally forced Córdoba to act decisively. "Fearing these captains and their followers," writes Andagoya, "he seized upon Soto, and put him into the fortress at Granada." But not for long. "Francisco Compañón, however, with nine of his friends, marched to Granada, and took Soto out of prison."

Again, the chronicles are tantalizingly spare on details. How was Soto captured? How did Compañón break him out? Did he bribe the guards? Storm the fortress? Scale the walls? However it was done, the break was well planned, with Compañón and nine accomplices arriving from León "well armed and mounted," and carrying armor, weapons, and a spare horse for Soto. "The whole party then took the field," says Andagoya.

Again, Córdoba reacted quickly. Assembling a posse of sixty men in León, he rode hard to cover the fifty miles between the two cities, catching up with Soto outside Granada. The fugitives, however, did not try to run away. Instead, Soto turned on his mount and brazenly shouted out a taunt to the lieutenant governor, threatening to charge in and hack him to pieces if his men attempted an attack.

This threat was not only audacious, but shrewd, revealing that Soto knew well his opponent's essentially unwarlike temperament. Indeed, it was at this point that Córdoba, facing the haughty young fighter, lost his nerve, and his insurrection began to unravel. Taking Soto's threat seriously, and believing the young captain was capable of destroying him even with the odds six to one in his favor, the lieutenant governor called off the attack, fearing Soto "would try to kill him."

Córdoba was humiliated, but remained secure enough among his loyalists that Soto decided to flee Nicaragua with his ten coconspirators to inform Pedrarias of his captain general's supposed defection. Trekking overland from Granada, because Córdoba controlled the ports, they headed south, following in reverse Gil González Dávila's disastrous 1522 march from Chiriqui, in western Panama. These Spaniards, however, were traveling in the dry season. Therefore, they avoided the devastating floods that nearly drowned González Dávila and his army. Soto and his followers probably hugged the shore during their eight-hundred-mile trek, cutting inland only where the coastal marshes turned to quick mud and became impenetrable. At some point Andagoya says they "abandoned their horses," either because the animals were a hindrance in the swamps, or because they were unable to feed them. The horses also made stealth more difficult as the renegades moved through potentially hostile Indian territory, stealing food from small, scattered villages of a primitive people known as the Rana.

Carlos Melendez thinks Córdoba's revolt occurred in late November or December 1525,^ meaning that Soto and his men probably departed Granada at the beginning of December. We know they arrived in Natá by late January 1526.^ This means Soto's jungle trek probably took seven to eight weeks, with an average march of fifteen or sixteen miles a day. This was a remarkable feat, given the terrain and hardship endured by the men. It should be kept in mind when considering distances covered when Soto traveled through *La Florida*.

The journey of the ten ended when they stumbled unexpectedly on a new Spanish settlement called Fonseca in western Panama, governed by Captain Benito Hurtado.* "Here they were refreshed," says Andagoya, "and this

*This name comes from Andagoya. This man may be the Bartolomé Hurtado who served as a captain to Balboa in Panama.

Soto's Trek After Córdoba's Rebellion, 1525–26

captain gave them a canoe, in which they came as far as Natá." This is where Soto dispatched his first urgent message to Pedrarias in Panama City about Córdoba's insurrection—before he collapsed in exhaustion in the partners' house on Natá's city square.^

Pedrarias was predictably enraged,^ particularly when Soto presented details—real or trumped-up—about Córdoba's betrayal. It took the old man only four weeks to assemble a small army to go after his lieutenant governor, a troop Soto expected to command. But the eighty-four-year-old governor, wanting to reassert his authority in person, and perhaps suspicious of Soto's aspirations, decided to head up the campaign himself, with a bitterly disappointed Soto at his side as captain general.^

Departing Panama in early March, Pedrarias, Soto, and their small army^ landed first on Chira Island, in the Gulf of Nicoya, where they waited several days as dozens of defectors from Córdoba's supporters arrived from Granada and León. Prominent among them was Martín Estete, the alcalde of Granada Diego de Molina, and the captains Diego Albítez and Gonzalo de Badajoz.^

By now, whatever revolt Francisco Hernández de Córdoba had planned was doomed. In León and Granada his support had withered to only a few cronies. In Santo Domingo, the *Audiencia* had long since abandoned him. Even Cortés, who had briefly shown an interest in marching his troops from Trujillo to León, deserted Córdoba and left Honduras on April 25, returning to Mexico to deal with an insurrection of his own.^

The collapse of Francisco Hernández de Córdoba's "rebellion" meant Soto's march from Chira to León was little more than a police action. In short order, Córdoba and his clique surrendered to the governor without a fight. Claiming he had never intended to revolt, Córdoba begged Pedrarias for mercy. But the old governor was not the compassionate sort. Declared guilty after a quick trial in early June, Pedrarias Dávila ordered the *vecinos* of León to assemble in the *plaza mayor*. Here, under the smoky fires of the nearby Momotombo volcano, the somber colonists watched as Pedrarias's executioner raised his blade and chopped down hard, severing the head of yet another man who had the audacity to cross El Furor Domini.^

✦ ✦ ✦

With the situation in Central America growing more confusing by the week, King Charles attempted to rein in his warring captains. Diverting his attention momentarily from his many European entanglements and wars, he issued missives late in 1525 to his restive subjects in the Americas. First, he forbade any Spaniard from drawing his sword against another—an edict that may have been prompted by the conflagration between Gil González Dávila and Hernando de Soto.^ Then he attempted to reassert the Crown's authority over disputed territories by appointing a lackluster *caballero* from Córdoba, Pedro de los Ríos, to replace Pedrarias Dávila as governor of Castilla del Oro, and a prominent *vecino* of Santo Domingo, Diego López de Salcedo, to serve as the first governor of Honduras.

But the Crown, as usual, was too far away to be effective. Charles's initiatives helped clarify to some extent who was in charge, but failed to delineate borders and lines of authority, only adding to the existing mayhem by introducing new competitors into the scramble for Central America.

Pedrarias's reaction to the king's new edicts was to stay as far away as possible from Panama, where he knew the incoming governor would want to hold an official review of Pedrarias's regime—a *residencia*—almost certain to expose the outgoing governor's many crimes. This prompted Pedrarias to stay put in León, an outcome bitterly resented by Soto and his clique, since his presence dashed their own hopes to rule Nicaragua. Possibly, Soto's falling out with his old mentor dates from this time.

Thus the octogenarian governor plunged into the business of running yet another nascent, rough-hewn colony displaying his usual energy and pique. He further aggrandized Córdoba's cities, lavished *encomiendas* on his friends, and launched fresh expeditions to ruthlessly scour the country for gold and slaves.^ Also aware of Salcedo's appointment in Honduras, and trying to capitalize on the weakness of the small colony left behind by Cortés in Trujillo, Pedrarias dispatched bands of marauders to seize as much of Honduras as possible before its new governor arrived, including, he hoped, a suitable harbor to link up Nicaragua with the Spanish Caribbean—something Córdoba had also tried to do, for the same reason of wanting to avoid having to make contact with the outside world through Panama.

Pedrarias, however, could not simply expropriate Honduras, lacking the men and resources to crush both the Lenca, whose warriors were now holed up in the jungles and mountains, preparing to contest Spanish incursions furiously, and Hernán Cortés's men, now under the command of Hernando de Saavedra. The situation became even more complicated when small traces of gold were discovered in two valleys to the north of León—in the Nueva Segovia Mountains, some eighty miles from the Nicaraguan capital, and in the fertile Valley of Olancho, forty miles north of Segovia, in present-day Honduras. Indeed, when Pedrarias rushed a platoon of men under Gabriel de Rojas to claim the Segovian mines and build a settlement called Santa María de Buena Esperanza, Saavedra sent his own expedition to build a fort and village named Cáceres in the Valley of Olancho. This in turn prompted Pedrarias to order a rival settlement raised in Olancho, Hermosa, and to explore the Honduran coast with an eye toward building his port city.^

Inevitably, the two sides clashed, with the *vecinos* of Cáceres and Hermosa launching raids and sparring incessantly across the rugged landscape of Olancho's scrub oaks, cactus, yuccas, fields of maize, and hundreds of small, open pits where wretched Indian slaves dug for gold nuggets with small stone knives. Little is known about this obscure conflict in Olancho, other than the two settlements were so intent on pursuing their rivalry that something wholly unexpected happened—the Indians, most of them former warriors dragooned in from either the Honduran coast or the Great Valley, revolted. Taking the feuding settlers completely by surprise, the Indians crept into Hermosa one night and murdered several Spaniards in their sleep, including the commandant, Benito Hurtado, the man who recently had given Soto canoes in western Panama. That same night, another band of slaves massacred some of Saavedra's men in their *pueblo,* including their leader, Juan de Grijalva, an early explorer of the Yucatán.^

These bloody assaults launched an all-out native rebellion that quickly overwhelmed the settlers, with Pedrarias's men in Hermosa so hard-pressed they abandoned their town to make a mad dash to Cáceres, where their recent enemies welcomed them inside their palisades. By now, the desperate Spaniards numbered only about forty men, the Indians having killed at least two dozen,^ with the rest huddled behind makeshift walls, fast running out of provisions and ammunition. Somehow, the miners managed to get a message out to the nearest Spanish town at the Segovia mines, forty miles to the south, where Francisco Compañón had taken over from Gabriel de Rojas as commandant.

A report written later by Francisco de Castañeda, royal alcalde of Nicaragua after 1527, describes what happened next. "The Captain Compañón [and with him, perhaps, his *compañero* Hernando de Soto] came in relief to this said *pueblo* of the mines and with his men left the city to the Indians. They routed the Indians and captured many without any risk to the Christians nor other danger, except that there was one horse that the Indians killed belonging to Captain Compañón." In other words, the settlers barely escaped with their lives with the timely intervention of Compañón, who was so hard-pressed he lost a horse—then considered far more valuable than a man—as the Spaniards fled Olancho, abandoning the settlement and mines to the victorious Indians.

About this same time, Pedro de los Ríos arrived in Panama to claim his *gobernación,* dropping anchor at Nombre de Dios on July 30, 1526. Armed with the authority to prosecute Pedrarias, Ríos's first act was to seize the former governor's property, and hold it as a security against his return to Panama to face his *residencia.* Unwilling to forfeit those plantations, houses, and *encomiendas*, Pedrarias departed Nicaragua sometime that fall, leaving behind Martín Estete as lieutenant governor of León and acting governor. He also assigned Gabriel de Rojas to be lieutenant governor of Granada, Gonzalo de

Badajoz as lieutenant in Bruselas, and Francisco Compañón as lieutenant of Buena Esperanza, the Spaniards' chief settlement in the Segovia mines.

Soto's absence from this list is conspicuous—particularly since a few months earlier he had served as captain general of Pedrarias's forces against Córdoba. Possibly, he was absent at the time "pacifying" one of the many rebellions in Nicaragua, though more likely the two had a falling-out, either over Soto's disappointment at Pedrarias taking overall command of the Córdoba campaign himself, or the old man's stubborn insistence on staying to govern a colony Soto wanted for himself. For his part, Pedrarias by now seems to have concluded that his highly able, but overly ambitious, captain from Jerez de los Caballeros was not to be trusted—either because the young man made his aspirations far too apparent, or because the old man may have heard the rumors about Soto embellishing Córdoba's revolutionary intentions. Whatever the reason, Soto's distancing himself from his mentor became plain for all to see in late 1526, when he gave Ríos, the new governor, far more than the customary welcoming gift expected out of a prosperous *vecino,* sending to Panama a gold necklace valued at 104 pesos.^ Worth a small fortune (it was close to the annual salary of a royal captain), it suggests not only Soto's obvious attempts to flatter Pedrarias's enemy, but also how wealthy Soto and his partners had become in the two years since the invasion.

When Pedrarias finally departed León, boasting he would be back, few Spaniards in Nicaragua believed him. They knew better than anyone the severity of his crimes. Most expected, at best, that El Furor Domini would be chastised by the Crown, pardoned, and sent home to retire on his estates in Castile. Despite his age, however, Pedrarias remained too pertinacious to be pushed aside without a fight. Always a master manipulator, he had been at work for some time to ensure a favorable outcome of his trial; first by dispatching to the royal court in Spain his influential wife, Isabel de Bobadilla, to intervene on his behalf at court; and, second, by insuring that most of his enemies were safely out of the way in Nicaragua, and unavailable to testify against him.^

+   +   +

Shortly after Pedrarias's departure from León, the new governor of Honduras, Diego López de Salcedo, cast anchor off Trujillo, his small fleet packed with supplies, horses, and some 150 men recruited in Hispaniola.^ His arrival, however, did not go smoothly. At first, Cortés's men, under Saavedra, refused Salcedo permission to land. They relented only when he showed them that the *cédulas* he carried were issued not by the hated *Audiencia* in Santo Domingo, but by the king himself.

Seeing the squalid, dusty little capital he was about to take over, Salcedo might have wished he *had* been turned away. Trujillo sat on a stunningly beautiful bay of turquoise water, though the town itself comprised little more than the usual cluster of dingy plank-and-thatch huts surrounding a balmy, sun-baked plaza, half overgrown with weeds. Perhaps thirty Spaniards and several hundred native servants lived in and around the town, barely sustained by a countryside lacking both fertile land and nearby Indians to use as laborers.

In the highlands, other colonists were exploiting more promising locales in the valley of Naco, near the modern border with Guatemala, and in the region surrounding the Mayan city of Chacujal farther in the interior, to the west of Trujillo. But these frontier settlements remained undermanned and precarious. Indeed, the prospects of this new *gobernación* seemed poor. Unless, of course, Salcedo could expand his domain to incorporate the rich valleys to the south—Olancho, then under control of the rebellious Indians, and the Great Valley itself, now bereft of Pedrarias Dávila, and only loosely connected to distant Panama.

Unlike Córdoba, Salcedo was a blunt man of action. He waited only as long as it took to organize an expedition before heading out, ostensibly to "pacify" the rebels of Olancho, though no one in the region doubted his true intentions lay farther to the south. Leading a force of 150 men, most of them mounted, Salcedo stormed down the mountain highways of Honduras during February and March 1527, viciously attacking and killing Indian rebels, capturing slaves, and executing large numbers of natives by hanging, fire, and torture. Cruel even by the standards of the *conquista,* Salcedo's slaughter seems motivated by an appetite for butchery rather than for "pacification," since he not only failed to restore Spanish authority in the area, but also managed to infuriate previously peaceful Indian polities all along his route, transforming the isolated Olancho revolt into a rebellion stretching from Trujillo to the Great Valley.^ Overrunning Spanish *haciendas* and outlying settlements, the enraged Indians enacted their revenge by killing as many Europeans as possible, and driving the rest into the fortified cities of León and Granada. Indeed, Salcedo may even have intended this to happen. For when he finally arrived in León, the hard-pressed city council had little choice but to recognize him as their new governor, desperately hoping that his 150-man army would provide the edge needed to fend off the rebellion.

From the start, Soto, Compañón, and Ponce were among Salcedo's more enthusiastic supporters—perhaps because they hoped the confusion surrounding Salcedo's arrival would further their own aspirations. Proof of the partners' support came soon after Salcedo's arrival, when he put Soto in charge of an army sent to crush the rebellion to the north, rather than sending one of his own captains. But Soto's cooperation came with a price. According to Oviedo, he and his partners were amply rewarded for their support, with Salcedo granting them generous *encomiendas* when Salcedo redistributed Indians to himself and his cronies. The partners received "many good *caciques* and Indians to serve them," writes Oviedo, "and, with the favor of the governor, they collected much property." At some point, Salcedo also named Soto the Captain of the Governor's Guard^—roughly the equivalent of a chief of staff, defense minister, and security chief rolled into one.

Little is known about Soto's punitive expedition against the Indians in the valleys to the north, other than it took several weeks, and, in the end, the Spaniards considered it successful. One eyewitness, Bartolomé de Celada, summed up the campaign by saying Soto "set off to punish some of the *caciques* and native Lords of the land, and to pacify them. This was done by the captain in the service of God and of His Majesty." In other words, Soto once again showed his talent for "handling" Indians—that is, for running them down, capturing them, hanging them, and torturing them. But Soto did not rely on savagery alone. Having learned his lessons well in Panama from Espinosa, Pedrarias, and Balboa, he adeptly mixed violence, terror, and torture with parleys, verbal threats, and "treaties" that forced insurgent *caciques* and rebel leaders to swear obedience in exchange for their lives. As witness Celada declares, Soto during this expedition showed great skill not only in "punishing" Indians, but also in organizing all stages of Indian "pacification."

✛　　✛　　✛

In the spring of 1527, when Soto returned from his successful campaign, the colony under Diego López de Salcedo was at peace for the first time since its founding, though only for a moment. For no sooner had the usurper settled into Córdoba's mansion in León than a ship arrived carrying Pedro de los Ríos, the new governor of Panama, coming to claim Nicaragua for the *gobernación* of Castilla del Oro. But Ríos, an unimaginative bureaucrat, and somewhat out of touch with reality, neglected to bring an army. Apparently, he expected the rough, independent-minded frontiersmen of Nicaragua simply to obey his authority. But Pedro de los Ríos was no Pedrarias Dávila. Within days of his arrival, this lackluster courtier was spurned by the *vecinos,* and ordered by Salcedo to depart Nicaragua, or face a fine of ten thousand pesos.^

This Salcedo victory was short-lived. Within weeks of Ríos's hasty departure, a royal *cédula* dated May 17 arrived in León, informing the *vecinos* that the king had at last settled the issue of who was to rule in the Great Valley. He did not choose Diego López de Salcedo, naming instead Pedrarias Dávila, of all people, to be the first legal governor of the newly designated colony of Nicaragua—pending a positive outcome in his trial and *residencia* in Panama. (This *cédula* was apparently arranged by Pedrarias's wife, working behind the scenes in Valladolid.)^

In another *cédula* issued that fall, the Crown also appointed royal officials to administer the colony, including the usual complement of treasurer, factor (also called veedor, or royal agent), and contador (accountant); a bishop of León; and, for the first time in the region, an independent royal alcalde mayor.^ This latter position, which brought with it an unusually high degree of autonomy vis-à-vis the governor, suggests that King Charles thought it prudent—as did his grandfather, King Ferdinand—to choose a powerful subordinate to keep Pedrarias in check. The man tapped for this formidable assignment, a former royal alcalde of Grand Canary Island, was already well known at court for his iron will, intelligence, and ability to promote his own interests steadfastly. Shrewd and ruthless as anyone in the Americas, Francisco de Castañeda was soon to become a close political ally of Soto and Ponce's in the coming intrigues against Pedrarias Dávila.

Had Diego López de Salcedo been a popular leader in León, he might have stood a chance of keeping his job. But Salcedo was deeply loathed by many Nicaraguans for his heavy-handed tactics, particularly his arbitrary seizure and redistribution of *encomiendas,* most notably to himself at the expense of others. By some estimates, his personal holdings totaled some thirty-five thousand Indians, compared to about nine thousand owned by Pedrarias at the peak of his tenure.^ As it was, Salcedo must have followed the details of Pedrarias's trial with the interest of a condemned man. His fervent hope was that the spiteful old man would be found guilty, leading the king to change his mind and appoint him governor. Salcedo also prayed Pedrarias would finally succumb to his ailments and die, something his enemies had wished on him for years.

But this was not to be. Though the king clearly disapproved of Pedrarias's indiscretions—on November 29, 1527, Charles signed a *cédula* reprimanding Pedrarias for the illegal invasion of Nicaragua and cruelty to the Indians—the Crown grudgingly determined (with Pedrarias's wife nudging in the background) that he was the only man capable of bringing order to Nicaragua. This sentiment became law on March 27, 1528, when Governor Ríos, almost certainly under instructions from the Crown, acquitted Pedrarias of all charges, and confirmed him as governor of Nicaragua.^ In Spain, Pedrarias's wife also secured for her husband a generous annual salary of fifteen hundred ducats, and title to two thousand Indians in *encomienda.*^

At this point, Salcedo should have exited gracefully, saving face by claiming a disputed valley or two along the Nicaragua-Honduran border as he headed back to Trujillo. Instead, the now renegade governor dug in, sending the unscrupulous Andrés Garabito, betrayer of Balboa and Córdoba and friend of Soto, on a pointless mission to destroy the city of Bruselas, in the Gulf of Nicoya^—the most likely debarkation point for Pedrarias when he returned to Nicaragua.

This attempt at a scorched-earth defense was rendered moot in early April, when the *vecinos* of León decided they had had enough of Diego López de Salcedo and threw him in prison. This came about, according to Oviedo, during a palace coup engineered by the Captain of the Governor's Guard, Hernando de Soto, who once again betrayed a superior who had provided him with wealth and honors. Soto's coconspirator was Martín Estete, who, several months after Salcedo's appearance in León, suddenly decided to do his duty as Pedrarias's lieutenant governor and arrest the interloper from Honduras.

Oviedo, who delights in describing Soto's less-than-noble machinations, writes that "Hernando de Soto, captain of the guard of Diego López de Salcedo . . . with his group, and the lieutenant Martín Estete and others revolted, stirring up this colony and the major part of the city of León. And they placed Salcedo in such a pressing situation that this sheep had to buy his own life . . ." This last bit indicates Soto and Estete not only arrested Salcedo, but also humiliated him by demanding a ransom to spare his life. This ransom included, says Oviedo, "the best buildings" in León—perhaps Salcedo's palace, or houses owned by the deposed *caudillo.*

By March, Pedrarias was back in León. The newly appointed governor, now approaching ninety, undoubtedly held a grand fiesta and ceremony celebrating his acquittal and accession to the *gobernación* of Nicaragua. Everyone attended—except Diego López de Salcedo, who listened to the party from a cell in León's fortress, high on a knoll above Lake Managua. And there he would continue to sit for nearly a year, lucky to have kept his head, but nonetheless forced by the spiteful Pedrarias to endure a captivity so severe he died soon after his release, early in 1529—and after paying a fine of one thousand pesos.^

With Salcedo's death, this phase of the War of the Captains in Central America ended, though it has been the tragic misfortune of this region to endure a seemingly endless plague of Sotos, Córdobas, Salcedos, and Dávilas—governors, dictators, *caudillos,* captains, and filibusters whose aspirations have made life miserable for millions in Nicaragua and Central America over the past five centuries. But this does not mean that all the young captains in 1529 were satisfied with the outcome of the War of the Captains. Several of them, including Hernando de Soto, not only remained hungry for more, but also possessed the means and the determination to take advantage of whatever opportunities came along.

✤ 8 ✤

Lord of Tosta

IN THE SPRING OF 1528, after the fall of Diego López de Salcedo, Hernando de Soto was twenty-eight years old. I imagine him strutting about the dusty streets of León, dressed in a flashy cape and a sword glittering with inlaid swirls of gold and silver. Already prosperous and influential in his small world, Soto by now was known throughout Tierra Firme for his fighting prowess, drive, and *apasionado*. For the next four years in Nicaragua, he would further consolidate his wealth and power, building up with his *compañeros* what was fast becoming one of the great business empires in Central America, with *encomiendas* among "the best in this land, with many Indians"; sizable "mining estates" in the Nueva Segovia Mountains; a shipping business that included one of the largest vessels then operating in the Pacific;^ and a slaving operation that for half a decade helped keep markets throughout the empire filled with fresh supplies of Indians. Oviedo says that by 1527, the three *compañeros* were known in Tierra Firme simply as "the captains." He describes them as being "[p]artners in their plantations, and all three *hidalgos* and fine persons; and with the help of their business and ingenuity* in Nicaragua . . . [they acquired] many good caciques and Indians to serve them, and . . . they collected much property."

By far, the most lucrative source of revenue—and power—for the *compañeros* were the Indians they owned and held in *encomienda,* and those they captured, bought, and sold. Over the course of Soto's eight years in Nicaragua, the partners had under their control at any given time perhaps one or two thousand Indian vassals^ paying tribute and working their land and mines—laborers, farmers, armed auxiliaries, servants, and *peónes* living on the *compañeros'* estates. These provided the partners with a steady income, though the real

---

*The Spanish word used here, which I translate as "ingenuity," is *maña*. It also means "guile" or "trick."

money in Indian flesh came from hunting down natives during supposed "pacifications"—snatching them from their homes, locking them up in neck-irons, branding them in the face, and marching them to León. The survivors were sold locally, shipped to Panama, or sent off to work the mines.

Technically, the wanton capture and sale of slaves was illegal in the Spanish Indies, though by the late 1520s the *Requerimiento* and other carefully wrought edicts written in Ferdinand's day, which allowed slavery only in cases where Indians violently resisted Spanish hegemony, were universally scorned and ignored. This was particularly true in Nicaragua, where gold supplies were soon exhausted, leaving only one other source of ready profit—the trade in human beings. Naturally, slavers remained secretive about the details of their operations, leaving us few written records to peruse. In the case of Soto and Ponce, however, we have enough to piece together a rough sketch. This is because Pedrarias—an important slave trader himself—so distrusted *los capitáns*^ in the period of 1529–30 that he felt compelled to record the details of their transactions, lest he be cheated or taken advantage of.^ In turn, Soto and Ponce's ally and business partner, Royal Alcalde Francisco Castañeda, kept records to keep Pedrarias and other rivals in check.

The first of the partners' documented slave fleets departed Nicaragua in March 1529, when five vessels set sail under the command of Hernán Ponce, whose flagship, the *San Geronimo,* was a galleon owned by the partners, and was capable of carrying some 450 slaves. Specifics about this fleet's cargo are unknown, though a report written by Castañeda says the *"piezas"*—literally "pieces," or slaves—realized "great profits" when sold in Panama.

A second shipment sailed in early summer 1529, when Ponce and Soto loaded slaves aboard a vessel named *Santiago,* owned by Francisco Pizarro and commanded by his master pilot, Bartolomé Ruiz, who had sailed to Nicaragua to recruit volunteers for the conquest of Peru. Like most maritime captains of this era, Ruiz also ran a profitable and illicit business on the side transporting slaves, which Soto and Ponce gladly supplied.^

Yet another slave fleet departed that October, when Ponce again took command of the *San Geronimo* and at least one other vessel owned all or in part by the partners, *La Concepción.* Documented in meticulous detail,^ this fleet transported exactly 385 Indians to Panama—154 *piezas* "branded with the mark of the king,"^ meaning they were freshly enslaved; 178 Indians listed as *esclavos,* meaning they had already served at least one master; and 11 *naborías* originally belonging to Indian *caciques* and nobles, who kept slaves before and after the Spanish conquest. One of the Spanish passengers, Royal Factor Alonso Pérez de Valer, also brought along 42 slaves of his own, some of which he intended to sell. Based on the going rates for slaves—which ranged from two or three pesos for most Indians, and up to ten or twelve pesos for a beau-

tiful woman or an exceptionally strong man, and occasionally much more^—
Ponce's 1529 haul of 385 slaves fetched between one thousand and as much as
four thousand pesos.^* This was in an era when a single peso bought a year's
supply of grain and wine for an entire family in Spain, and an ordinary seaman
on *San Geronimo* earned an annual salary of sixteen or seventeen pesos.^

The partners' slaving operation also included the procurement phase, where
Soto's expertise as a master Indian "pacifier" was turned to great advantage as
he marauded about in the countryside raiding villages—burning huts, looting,
and running down and capturing as many natives as possible. Records from
this period describe Soto leading armed expeditions in regions ranging from
the Olancho valley in Honduras to El Salvador, and from Lake Nicaragua to
the Cosiguina Peninsula in northwestern Nicaragua—the latter being a place
he "pacified" as many as three times.^ How many slaves Soto seized on individual *entradas* is not recorded. Based on other documented "pacifications,"
it's likely he captured as many as several hundred natives in a single expedition, though the numbers must have declined as supplies became exhausted.^

During the late 1520s, Soto's *compañia* was also known for its sizable share
in the mines of Gracias a Dios in the Sierra de Nueva Segovia, where Francisco
Compañón served as commandant until his death in 1527 or 1528, after which
Ponce took over. First discovered in 1524, Gracias a Dios was located in a re-
mote, mountainous region of dense bush, pines, and hardwood forests, home
to a rustic people called the Sumu before the European era, and a haven for
rebels, guerrillas, and smugglers in the centuries since. In Soto's time, the
Spaniards–or, rather, their Indian slaves—prospected several dozen individual
veins of gold at Gracias a Dios, buried just under the topsoil along streams,
rivulets, and steep mountain downspouts. Accessible only during the winter
dry season, when streams are reduced to trickles, these veins were so small and
widely dispersed that to produce even minute amounts of gold required tedious
and backbreaking labor in the intense heat and humidity, scratching out shallow surface pits, and sifting dirt and rock for tiny nuggets.^

At first, the Spaniards probably forced the local Sumu Indians to work the
mines, supplemented soon after by natives marched up in chain gangs from the
Great Valley—mostly *encomienda* Indians illegally diverted from their villages,^ in addition to a small number of African slaves. Within months after arriving, most of these Indians died, succumbing to an inhospitable region where
little agriculture existed to feed them. Apparently, the Spanish overseers provided virtually no shelter or clothing for lowlanders used to a temperate climate, who did not fare well in a mountain region where temperatures swing
from blistering hot in the summer to near freezing during the rainy season.

---

*See "A Note on Money," page xxix.

Worse still was the brutal work itself—the grueling labor, digging, sifting, and hauling that Bartolomé de las Casas says went on "night and day without rest and without ceasing." Thousands expired in these mines where the Soto-Ponce-Compañón company held a majority interest,^ though the Segovian mines during Soto's years yielded only fifty-two thousand pesos of gold,^ equal to a few dollars a head in Indians killed amidst the blood, dust, and terror of a mine ironically named "By the Grace of God."^

No amount of gold, however, could prevent the death of Francisco Compañón in late 1527 or 1528, when a *figo y enfermedades*—a "fever and sickness"—abruptly struck the mines, killing so many Indians and Spaniards that the survivors fled for their lives.^ Escape from the pestilence brought even more misery as "many perished"^ trying to traverse roads washed out by the rainy season, and to cross rivers in high flood.^

The death of Francisco Compañón was a deep personal loss to Hernando de Soto. For years, the two of them had been inseparable, through the years with Balboa on the South Sea, the Urraca Wars, Natá, the Córdoba affair, and the success of the *compañia*. Soto's affection and loyalty to Francisco Compañón are proved by a paragraph in Soto's will. Drawn up more than a decade after his friend's death, Soto orders his executors to say "twenty masses of *requiem* . . . for the soul of the Captain Compañón," a tribute he gave to no one else.^

✛   ✛   ✛

For the natives of Nicaragua and surrounding areas, the decade of Hernando de Soto's ascendancy was the time of their apocalypse. In an astonishingly short period, the proud Indian city-states of the Chorotegans, Nicaraos, and Maribios in Nicaragua were obliterated, their cultures destroyed, and their peoples implacably pushed toward extinction that would be all but complete by the end of the century.

Before the conquest of Nicaragua, Bartolomé de las Casas suggests that over a million Indians lived in the Great Valley, a number he says had dwindled to perhaps 200,000 by 1537. Even if exaggerated, this suggests a spectacular decline.^ Las Casas, who visited the Great Valley in the mid-1520s, blames this sudden depopulation on the familiar combination of warfare, forced labor, disease, and suicidal despair. The scope of the killing, however, staggered even his considerable imagination as he reported "murders and robberies" on a scale so vast "it is not possible for pen to relate. Upon the slightest pretext, the soldiers massacred the inhabitants without regard to age, sex or condition. They exacted from them certain measures of corn, and certain numbers of slaves, and if these were not rendered, hesitated not to kill the delinquents."

Profit was not the sole motivation behind the slaughter. Fear also played its role—the murderous paranoia of a small, heavily armed group of conquerors intent upon controlling a large, restive population. Oviedo tells a grisly story in his *Historia General* suggesting the extent of Spanish savagery as they attempted to mitigate the often-violent desperation of the Indians. It happened in 1528, when the royal treasurer, Alonso de Peralta, departed León with three men to visit "the villages and Indians belonging to him," only to be massacred on the way by his "own vassals" in a desolate area beyond the city. When word of the killings reached Pedrarias, he immediately dispatched soldiers to punish and terrorize the region where Peralta's natives lived, and "to bring in some of the malefactors," including "seventeen or eighteen *caciques*." Then, without any attempt to separate the guilty from the innocent, Pedrarias ordered the entire group of eighteen executed by *apperrear,* a Spanish verb that literally means "to be thrown to the dogs"—that is, ripped apart by mastiffs, hounds, and other specially trained dogs originally bred for warfare and fighting in Europe.

Yet numbers of Indians slain by the sword—or ripped to shreds by dogs—paled beside the suffering and carnage inflicted by the slave trade. Las Casas claims Soto and his fellow slavers shipped out to other colonies some 500,000 Nicaraguan Indians between 1524 and 1549, a count almost certainly too high for slaves actually exported from the shores of Nicaragua.^ But if one includes the total Indians *captured*—many of whom died during the brutal marches to market, or in the dark holds of slaving ships such as the *San Geronimo*—the count must have reached at least into the tens of thousands, and possibly as high as 100,000, or more.^

Disease in Nicaragua also inflicted its familiar and ghastly devastation on the Indian population, with death tolls reaching as high as one-third to one-half in some areas.^ The only recorded epidemic in Nicaragua during the 1520s was the plague that killed Francisco Compañón at Gracias a Dios—which also struck down several thousand Indians. Other plagues undoubtedly went unrecorded as Old World pathogens from measles to smallpox raged up and down the isthmus during this period.^

As if warfare, slavery, and disease were not enough, Las Casas further blames the Nicaraguan holocaust on the continuing Spanish practice of redistributing Indians like chattel, with little regard for food supplies, housing, family, and lifestyle requirements. "The Governor once arbitrarily changed the distribution of Indians," Las Casas reports, "conveying most of them to his favorites, to the exclusion of those with whom he was displeased. The result of this was a great scarcity of food; and the Spaniards, seizing on the provisions of the Indians, caused a great distress, and induced a disorder which destroyed upwards of thirty thousand people." Again, this number sounds high, though whether the proper count is thirty thousand, ten thousand, or one thousand, the bishop's point is clear—great numbers of Indians died in Nicaragua as a result of petty whims and political favoritism.

Another way to look at this redistribution is to focus on a single transaction of human goods, choosing one of the thousands of exchanges and sales recorded during the 1520s in Nicaragua. This one occurred in 1529, when Soto bought a *cacique* and, perhaps, some of his people, from a certain Francisco de Munana in a sale that included Indians from all over Honduras and Nicaragua—Chorotegans living near León, Lencans from Honduras, and one Maribio boy from the Chinandega area. "Francisco de Munana declared that he brought forty Indians," records an official document dated February 28, 1529, belonging to "two [*caciques*] of Agateyte and two of Olocoton, and one of Juana Gasta [belonging to] the said Soto, and another of Tesputeca, that came with his grandchildren, and a small boy of the Maribios." On the day of the sale, there would have been a huddle of some forty Indians, dressed in bits and pieces of native and Spanish garb, roped or chained together and standing in the corner of the plaza in León as Francisco de Munana negotiates with Soto and other *vecinos.* Standing nearby is an old man, his body covered with the tattoos of a king and warrior of Tesputeca, his face worn and tired. Near him sits his grandchildren, perhaps three or four children born into what was turning out to be the final days of the old man's people. Sitting with them is a young boy of the Maribios, an entirely different people whose language is only roughly akin to that spoken by the old man and his grandchildren. What was his story? Where were his parents and people? What was he doing there alone with an old grandfather from another tribe? And what happened to the parents of the grandchildren?

✛   ✛   ✛

Of course, life for the *vecinos* of Nicaragua in the 1520s was not just one long tirade of bloody raids, rebellions, "pacifications," and political intrigue. For most Spaniards, ordinary daily life was actually far more relaxed, slow, and, for long stretches, uneventful.

When not out "pacifying," Soto lived in a comfortable town house in León, outfitted with all the luxuries available in this distant outpost. Situated just off the *plaza mayor,* Soto's dwelling—sometimes described by eyewitnesses as a *hacienda,* and at other times a *casa,* or house—was one of fourteen permanent structures in the Spanish town, constructed out of stone, *tapia* (mud brick), and thatch. Other stone-and-*tapia* buildings in León included the main cathedral, on the east side of the plaza; the governor's house on the north side; the Casa de la Fundación, or smelting house, to the south; and the homes of other prominent *vecinos.* A second cluster of buildings stood a half mile south of the plaza—the church of Our Lady of Mercy, surrounded by two or three private homes.

In the late 1520s, the entire city of León covered no more than one or two square miles, with the silent, overgrown fields one sees today then occupied by broad dirt streets lined by plank-and-thatch structures—the homes and shops of the European population. And rising above the city, between the plaza and the cool blue waters of Lake Managua, was a steep knoll topped by the fortress of León. Made of stone and timber, it commanded a broad view of the surrounding country, including Indian villages to the north where natives serving the Spanish city lived.

Today, in partially excavated ruins of Old León, archaeologists have identified a rectangular structure about the size of a three-car garage as the "Casa de Hernando de Soto." Evidence that this is in fact Soto's house comes from an archival document dated June 1530, in which the town crier of León is described as delivering a public proclamation outside "the major church of this city at the corner of the house of the captains Hernando de Soto and Hernán Ponce de León"^—a prominent location befitting Soto and Ponce's importance in the colony.

Little remains today of Soto's home. Heavily damaged by the earthquake that destroyed the city in 1610, the structure was buried under dirt, ash, and foliage for centuries. Excavated in the 1960s, the ruined stone walls today stand knee-high amidst piles of scattered bricks and broken pottery. When Soto was alive, his house would have looked similar to the modern adobe structures located in today's nearby village of León Viejo—a brick-and-mortar building plastered with clay, whitewashed with pigments from ground shells, and thatched with reeds collected in marshes around the lake. The house was probably larger than the ruins indicate, with attached rooms made of planks that long ago rotted into dust, and outbuildings for storing supplies, servants' dwellings, and, perhaps, a *bohío* reserved for Soto's concubine of the moment. (Sometime during these Nicaraguan years, Soto acquired a Spanish mistress named Juana Hernández, who may have been the mother of a daughter he later recognized in his will as María de Soto).^ Near the servants' quarters would have been barns for the horses and other animals, and vegetable gardens and fruit trees for Soto's kitchen. Surrounding the entire compound Soto built a mud-daub wall with a high gate,^ a common feature of Spanish and Mediterranean homes that remains in Latin American cities even today.

By 1528, Soto and Ponce were already important players in one of two major factions vying for political and economic dominance in León. The first was led by Pedrarias Dávila; and the second by Francisco de Castañeda, the new royal alcalde. A dynamic and shrewd man of about forty, Castañeda was able to operate with considerable autonomy as the colony's chief magistrate, because his appointment came directly from the king.

Almost from the moment Pedrarias returned from his *residencia* in Panama,

Soto and Ponce sided with Castañeda. Indeed, his astuteness and vitality in advancing his own interests fit in perfectly with the aims of *los capitáns*. Witnesses later recalled that as early as 1528 the captains were frequently seen eating in the house of the royal alcalde, adding that Castañeda and "the Captains Hernán Ponce and Soto . . . were very great friends," and that Ponce and and Soto "favored" the alcalde "during the differences he had with . . . the Lord Pedrarias Dávila." In 1530, Pedrarias himself, during a city-council meeting, noted with annoyance that "Hernando de Soto and Hernán Ponce de León" could not be trusted because "they are friends and allies of the alcalde mayor," and did his bidding. Other eyewitnesses said that the alcalde and the captains collaborated not only in politics and commerce, but in corruption—selling illegal slaves, embezzling royal taxes, bribing officials, and rigging elections in city-council meetings.

One typically brazen example of the Soto-Ponce-Castañeda clique's dirty dealings was when Ponce and Castañeda siphoned off a large cache of royal funds from the colony's Casa de la Fundación in 1531. An eyewitness, the scribe Diego Sánchez, later testified that "Hernán Ponce de León . . . [and] the Licenciado Castañeda serving as accountant for His Majesty sent Rojel de Loria to take out a ledger from the books of the accountant's office of Your Majesty and put in another . . . and this witness wants to resolve that he heard . . . that Hernán Ponce amended and added and subtracted from the ledgers of the Royal Treasurer . . ." In another case, a prominent *vecino* named Juan de Quiñones remembered that Castañeda once illegally "gave away many estates and *repartimientos* [to Soto and Ponce] . . . and he also received from the Captains Hernán Ponce and Hernando de Soto [in exchange] two or three greyhounds and certain orange orchards and other small things."^

Politically, the alliance of the royal alcalde and the captains sought to check the governor's influence on everything from naming appointees to colonial offices to who received what *encomienda*. Their chief weapon was the alcalde's position as chief justice of the colony, with authority over lawsuits and contracts. Later, when Royal Treasurer Diego de la Tovilla joined the clique, the alliance also gained an edge in controlling much of the royal commerce in the colony, including registration of property and gold, and collection of taxes. Armed with these powers, Castañeda tried to undermine the governor's power and authority by manipulating property disputes, holding up gold disbursements in the royal countinghouse, and constantly harassing Pedrarias supporters on technicalities and false charges.

El Furor Domini, finally faced with an equally formidable and underhanded opponent, fought back hard by using his powers as chief executive, in charge of issuing permits and licenses, appointing captains and officials, and running the day-to-day business of the colony. A longtime master at manipulating these levers of office, Pedrarias frustrated Castañeda's faction by appointing his own cronies to key positions, ignoring rulings from the alcalde and his partisans, blocking permits for everything from selling slaves to acquiring weapons, and, at one point, monopolizing the colony's skilled shipbuilders so that Soto and Ponce could not expand their fleet.^

Not surprisingly, the result of this political struggle was often a standoff, punctuated by public name-calling, petty recriminations, heated hearings called to verbally attack one another, and, as always, angry epistles directed to the king. In one particularly rancorous hearing, called on September 17, 1529, to investigate "the causes of the enmity between the Alcalde Mayor and the Governor," supporters of Castañeda alleged that Pedrarias was hatching a plot to rid the colony of the alcalde and other royal appointees, and that he had secretly offered rewards of one thousand and two thousand pesos for anyone who could "find a legal way to force" Castañeda out of office. Other witnesses, including Hernán Ponce de León, charged that Pedrarias had once tried to arrest Castañeda, who escaped capture by "receiving a timely warning." In his remarks at this hearing, Soto accused the governor of arbitrarily arresting his rivals and enemies for personal reasons, "according to his passing fancy."

Pedrarias answered these accusations at a subsequent meeting of the city council, where he charged Castañeda with "deliberately acting disrespectfully to this government, resulting in much scandal to His Majesty." He also wrote to the king, claiming that Castañeda was incompetent, a liar, and a thief. Castañeda retorted by telling the king that the governor had instigated rebellions and mismanaged royal funds, and that he was too old and sick to govern. Pedrarias, he said, was paralyzed and almost always carried on a litter or seated in a chair.^

Despite this internecine strife, León in the late 1520s remained a small, isolated frontier capital, where even bitter political foes still frequented one another's dinner tables, and were seen walking and conversing together in the plaza. The fact that opposing partisans never turned to violence in this violent era indicates that combatants on both sides found the situation made for an edgy but reasonably profitable and satisfying *modus vivendi*. Reading through the dense archival records of this period, one gets the feeling that Soto and the others thrived on the intrigue and competition, treating politics as they treated the games of gambling to which they were all addicted—a high-stakes game governed by certain unspoken rules agreed to by everyone, where a player might lose a fortune today, but never seemed to lose so much that he could not play again tomorrow. Perhaps this explains why Castañeda's and Pedrarias's supporters could viciously attack one another in meetings in the afternoon, and then retire in the evening to the house of the governor or the alcalde for dinner, cards, and wine; and why witnesses often mention Soto strolling in the plaza and chatting not only with Ponce and Castañeda, but also with his former mentor, Pedrarias.^

Soto's deep involvement in the politics and commerce of Nicaragua reveals again a man whose talents reached far beyond the battlefield. Though he obviously preferred carving out his destiny with a sword, his years in León prove he also was capable of sitting in interminably boring council meetings and giving endless testimony in hearings, if he thought it would further his ambitions. The mass of pertinent archival data from this period reveals a young man whose peers not only considered him a major political player, but one who showed a grasp of governance beyond what most historians allow him.^

✦ ✦ ✦

In the late 1520s, Soto spent most of his time in León or away on "pacifications," though he also made inspection tours of the partnership's *encomiendas* and estates in the countryside. The largest of these was at Tosta,* situated thirty miles northwest of León, on the fertile plains of Chinandega, and convenient to both the capital and the port at La Posesión.^ I am unable to pinpoint Tosta's exact location, though it was almost certainly located within a few miles of the modern town of El Viejo, capital of the once-powerful Nicarao city-state of Tezoatega. Possibly, it stood on the banks of the Río Telica, which appears on some old maps as Río Tosta. The Telica River, however, was in Maribio country, while Tosta is referred to as a Nicarao town allied with Tezoatega.^

Witnesses describe the partners' *hacienda* at Tosta as a complex of *"bohíos"*—large wood-plank and thatch houses—and *"estancia"* ranch houses that might have referred to more European-style dwellings—perhaps with gauze windows, plaster walls in the interior, and wooden floors. At least one of the structures at Tosta contained a large *cámara,* or hall, where the estate's hired hands dined, gambled, and otherwise entertained themselves, and perhaps held feasts when Soto and Ponce were in attendance. Surrounding this main building would have been individual *bohíos* apportioned out to the partnership's servants, retainers, and private militia, and the usual gardens, stables, groves, and outbuildings, arranged as a large compound around an Indian plaza seized during the invasion. Nearby, the natives that served the *hacienda* as servants, gardeners, cooks, laborers, and Indian police lived in smaller *bohíos.* Other native vassals lived farther afield on farmsteads and small pueblos scattered across an *encomienda* that may have totaled several hundred acres of villages, crops, forests, and scrub.

Piecing together details of life on a country estate in Soto's day is a difficult business, though in this case the task is easier because of a crime committed at

---

*Tosta is either the name of a province, its capital, or both.

Tosta on February 24, 1530—the murder of one Soto retainer by another during a game of cards.

According to testimony from eyewitnesses, the incident occurred when four Soto ranch hands were gambling late one night in the main *cámara* at Tosta. These were Pedro de Torres, an overseer; Francisco de Torres, a Soto retainer unrelated to Pedro; Gómez González, a tribute collector; and Alonso de Galiano, also a Soto aide. Another man present in the hall but not playing was Juan Pérez de Tudela, a neighbor who either owned his own small *encomienda*, or worked as a senior retainer for someone else, possibly Soto.

Gómez González, one of the card players, testified that on the night of the murder, Francisco de Torres was dealing cards during a game called *agujetes* when Pedro de Torres accused him of cheating, demanding he return a sum of money. When Francisco refused, Pedro cursed him and "got up from where he was sitting and walked into the room of the said Francisco de Torres," a small chamber off the main hall, "to get his money." Francisco responded by bolting from his seat, knocking over the table, and scattering the cards. Grabbing "a lance against the said Pedro de Torres," Francisco was stopped from charging only because Gómez González disarmed him.

After this dustup, the witnesses say "Francisco de Torres entered into his chamber and the others returned to where they were seated during the card game." Francisco returned a few minutes later, however, this time armed "with a sword in his hand and an upside down shield on his arm." Rushing forward "before they had a chance to stop him," Francisco attacked Pedro, stabbing him "two or three times in his upper arm" before Pedro could grab a weapon to defend himself. (Weapons were always close at hand on the Spanish frontier.) The ensuing sword duel ended when Pedro deflected a powerful slash by Francisco, whose blade reportedly slid off Pedro's sword and cut his own arm, severing it at the elbow. All agreed this wound had been inflicted by "Francisco de Torres . . . himself by his own hand."

Three days later, Francisco died, from loss of blood and probably infection. Before he expired, he testified to the authorities that his wound was indeed self-inflicted, and that Pedro de Torres was blameless.

Meanwhile, as Francisco lay dying, Pedro de Torres fled Tosta for the church of Our Lady of Mercy in León, where he took sanctuary for nearly a month as the authorities interviewed witnesses and gathered evidence. This included testimony from Ponce and Soto, who insisted Pedro de Torres was "a good man," "well respected," and incapable of committing murder. Still, Pedro had technically killed Francisco—which clearly meant that a trial should be held. Indeed, preparations were being made for a hearing when, in early April, Francisco de Castañeda abruptly pardoned Pedro de Torres, who was set free.

The case file provides no explanation for the pardon, though several years later the royal scribe who recorded the depositions during the investigation claimed Pedro de Torres was, in fact, guilty of murder, but was not prosecuted by Francisco de Castañeda as a favor to Ponce and Soto. "It was public knowledge," says the scribe, that Soto and Castañeda had "taken Pedro de Torres by the hand who had killed another named Francisco de Torres . . . the Licenciado Castañeda did not convict Pedro de Torres to corporal punishment because he was a servant of the captains Hernán Ponce and Soto and he favored them because they were very great friends of his and he was favored by them in the differences between the Licenciado Castañeda and the Señor Pedrarias de Avila."

Of course, the corruption in early Spanish colonies—and in other nation's distant outposts—is hardly uncommon in large, unwieldy empires. So are local rivalries. It also was not unheard of for certain players in those distant rivalries to become so ambitious that they quickly outgrew the possibilities offered by a small frontier colony. For, even as the litany of murder, embezzlement, and bickering played itself out in León, and the possibilities for easy profits in slaves and gold diminished, Soto and many others were eyeing opportunities far afield—particularly one far to the south, where a discovery even more spectacular than Cortés stumbling on the Aztecs was just getting under way.

✤ 9 ✤

Conspirator

IN EARLY 1527, SOMETIME before Soto began plotting to overthrow Diego López de Salcedo in León, a chance encounter occurred far to the south. Coasting Ecuador, two small Spanish vessels stumbled on a sophisticated oceangoing raft constructed out of reeds and planks, and manned by small Indians dressed in intricately woven costumes and elaborate jewelry. "They were carrying many pieces of silver and gold as personal ornaments," one of Pizarro's men later wrote, "including crowns and diadems, belts and bracelets . . . tweezers and rattles and strings and clusters of beads and rubies; [and] mirrors decorated with silver . . . They were carrying many wool and cotton mantles and Moorish tunics . . . worked with different types of ornate embroidery, in figures of birds, animals, fish, and trees." When the Spaniards approached the raft, called a *balsa,** eleven of the twenty people aboard the native vessel promptly jumped overboard. The others, behaving with more aplomb and, as it turned out, less wisdom, were taken prisoner. Six were later set free on the coast, but three others were held as captives to be taught Spanish and trained as interpreters for a future invasion of their country.^

The Spanish ships were commanded by Bartolomé Ruiz, the talented and shrewd master pilot sent out to scout the coast of South America by his captain general, Francisco Pizarro, Soto's former commander in Panama. Then encamped with his main army on the swampy San Juan River in Colombia, Pizarro was desperately in need of the good news his pilot was rushing to deliver. Indeed, up to that moment, this would-be conqueror's second attempt to find the legendary "Birú" was failing miserably, having been bogged down for months on the pestilent, mosquito-ridden coast of Colombia. Already several men had died of disease, exhaustion, and malnutrition.

Balsa means anything that's light, or floats.

One can imagine the elation in Pizarro's squalid camp when Ruiz returned with his three captives and the splendid cargo of the *balsa* raft. For just when his expedition seemed on the verge of disaster, this twenty-five-year veteran of the Indies suddenly knew his moment had come at last.

A few months later, early in 1528, Pizarro and Ruiz confirmed the latter's discovery of a new and wondrous society by sighting their first Inca city, Tumbez, just south of the border between modern Peru and Ecuador. Here Pizarro and his small band of adventurers beheld a city possibly as large as Seville, with neat, well-ordered streets, paved roads, public buildings constructed out of stone, and an elaborate network of terraced gardens rising on hills above and behind the rooftops. Inca rafts made out of thick reeds plowed the nearby Río Tumbez* and the Gulf of Guayaquil, their occupants undoubtedly staring with amazement at the sudden appearance of a caravel, with its steep wooden hull, broad sails marked with crimson crosses, and bearded men dressed in metal suits. For several days, Pizarro's emissaries visited the city, behaving peacefully throughout their stay as they gathered intelligence, and enough gold and finely wrought objects to convince even the staunchest critic that Birú was for real.

Returning to Panama, an exuberant Pizarro immediately set sail for Spain, where he dazzled the king, then holding court at Toledo, with Peruvian treasures and stories about the Incas that must have sounded to late-Renaissance ears like a fantasy kingdom out of *Amadis of Gaul* and other popular romance novels of the day. But claims of fairy-tale kingdoms had been coming true with some regularity since the discovery of the Aztecs in Mexico ten years earlier. In fact, Pizarro's visit coincided with the triumphant arrival at King Charles's court of Hernán Cortés, who came loaded down with his own grandiose display of booty, and tales of Aztec wonders. The meeting of these two conquerors, whose combined exploits would eventually expand Charles's domains to ten times their original size, caused such a sensation at court that the king, in a fit of uncharacteristic excitement, granted Pizarro unheard-of honors for an illiterate former swineherd, authorizing him not only to invade Peru, and to serve as the governor and captain general of the enterprise, but also to join the prestigious Order of Santiago. Later, after the conquest, the king elevated Pizarro to a marquis.^

+   +   +

When news of Pizarro's discovery of the Peruvian frontier reached Nicaragua in 1528, Soto and other leaders in the colony were preoccupied by their coup against Salcedo, and the subsequent return of Pedrarias from his *res-*

---

*The modern name for this river is Río Puyango.

idencia in Panama. By early 1529, however, Captains Soto and Ponce, and the newly arrived Francisco de Castañeda, were already showing interest in Peru, starting construction of two jointly owned vessels at La Posesión in which they eventually hoped to convey troops to join Pizarro.

Their plans were quickly frustrated by the newly reinstated governor, Pedrarias Dávila. Having just sold out his own investment in the Pizarro project for one thousand pesos, the irascible old man decided that no one else under his suzerainty could become involved with Peru. Petty to the last, he spent the three years until his death in 1531 repulsing all efforts by Castañeda, Soto, Ponce, and a sizable number of *vecinos* to depart Nicaragua for Peru. Claiming this was for the good of the colony, he correctly argued that the venture would empty Nicaragua of its best men, though his real reason was the jealous rage of an old man who knew he was, at last, too old and enfeebled to make another big play.

The conflict over Peru between Pedrarias and the Castañeda-Soto-Ponce clique began in earnest in June 1529, when Bartolomé Ruiz and another Pizarro lieutenant, Nicolás de Ribera, arrived unexpectedly at La Posesión looking for recruits—and, as mentioned earlier, for slaves to ship to Panama. Pedrarias reacted immediately by banning all commerce with the ship, called the *Santiago*—forbidding the transport not only of would-be recruits, but of all other "cargo," including slaves. But this hardly stopped Ruiz and Ribera from making contact with Soto and Ponce, and regaling them with stories about the riches of Peru during a series of "secret talks" held between Pizarro's men and the partners "to get Ponce to go to Panama . . . so they could make an agreement"—talks possibly held in the *cámara* at Tosta where Francisco de Torres was murdered, located conveniently a few miles inland from the port. Perhaps it was here that the two sides agreed to an informal pact that would become the basis for the contract they would sign later in Panama, offering Soto's ships and services, and a troop of Nicaraguan *soldados,* in exchange for a senior role for Soto in the conquest, and the pick of the best Peruvian *encomiendas* for both partners.

As a gesture affirming their deal, Soto and Ponce organized a smuggling operation to fill the holds of the *Santiago* with thirty or forty Spanish recruits, most of them debtors forbidden by law to leave the colony—and with as many as three hundred slaves.^ The conspirators, however, could not for long keep secret an operation of this size. Indeed, after fifteen days at anchor, Pedrarias ordered the contador of the port, Hernando de Guzmán, and a constable, Luis Daza, to board and inspect the *Santiago*. But Ruiz was alerted in advance. He prevented Pedrarias's men from coming aboard by seizing all available transport craft in the port, beaching them on an island at the mouth of the harbor. This included skiffs from Soto and Ponce's galleon the *San Geronimo*.

Onshore, a frustrated Constable Daza detained Soto and Ponce, then in the harbor, while Guzmán rode off to fetch reinforcements for what looked like a possible violent confrontation with the *Santiago*. But by the time Guzmán returned with a small force, Ruiz had loaded up a skiff with men armed with "lances, crossbows, and arquebuses" to challenge any attempt to board his vessel. To underscore his determination, Ruiz fired shots from his ship's cannon warning off any armed effort from the shore. He then raised his sails and departed La Posesión with his illicit cargo. As for Soto and Ponce, they were soon released, pending the outcome of a hearing called by Pedrarias.

It is yet another measure of the partners' influence that despite testimony implicating them, they were never seriously considered offenders in this hearing, and received no direct punishment from Pedrarias. But the governor did retaliate in other ways, stepping up his efforts to block construction of Soto and Ponce's new ships, and virtually shutting down the partners' slaving operations by refusing to grant Soto and Ponce permission to ship slaves in the *San Geronimo*.

This ban did not last long, however. Because Soto and Ponce owned the largest ship in the colony, and controlled a sizable share of the slave trade, no one involved in the business could afford to have the *San Geronimo* idle for long. Thus on August 19, 1529, the governor issued a permit allowing Ponce to transship a load of slaves to Castilla del Oro—but only after Soto agreed to remain in Nicaragua, and after Ponce, as captain of the fleet, swore in an elaborate oath taken at León's church of Our Lady of Mercy that he would ship only those slaves and Spaniards approved by the governor, and that he would return to Nicaragua, upon pain of death.

Ponce departed La Posesión on October 15, carrying the 402 slaves and *naborías* mentioned earlier. Ponce also took along a passenger, Royal Factor Alonso Pérez de Valer, whose mission is unclear. He may have been sent as a secret emissary of Pedrarias to ask Governor Pedro de los Ríos's help in ridding Nicaragua of Francisco de Castañeda. Ponce also carried the trial records of the Ruiz affair, to be delivered to Governor Ríos in Panama.

Of course, once in Panama, Ponce seized this chance to continue negotiations with Pizarro's lieutenants—and, early in 1530, with Don Francisco Pizarro himself when he arrived from Spain. With these meetings come the first mention of Hernando de Soto in the Peruvian chronicles, a passage written by Pizarro's cousin, Pedro Pizarro, who accompanied his suddenly famous relative to Panama from Spain along with Francisco Pizarro's three half brothers, Hernando, Juan, and Gonzalo. Later Pedro Pizarro wrote a highly partisan *relación* of the invasion.

"Hernán Ponce de León came from Nicaragua with two ships* loaded with

---

*One of these ships was the *San Geronimo,* the other is unidentified.

slaves to sell in Panama," writes Pedro Pizarro, "his and his companion's Hernando de Soto. Then Hernando Pizarro visited Hernán Ponce, bargaining with him for the two ships he brought, to transfer the men to [Peru], because the major necessity they had at that time was ships. Hernán Ponce came there often, getting many agreements to his advantage and for his partner Soto, so Hernando Pizarro and his brother Francisco Pizarro obliged him for the ships and then, if the land was good, to his partner Hernando de Soto he promised to make lieutenant governor of the principal city and its people,* and to the said Hernán Ponce they would give a *repartimiento* of Indians, the best in the kingdom."^

In other words, Ponce, a master negotiator, understood that the Pizarros were desperate for ships, and forced the brothers to make numerous promises, some of which they would keep, and others they would not as the conquest of Peru proceeded.

✛   ✛   ✛

When Ponce returned to Nicaragua with news of the contract, the partners became even bolder in signing up recruits and organizing their illicit expedition. Several eyewitnesses say they saw Soto and Ponce "meeting with and attracting in public and in secret men to accompany them to Peru." Scores of men signed up, and others eagerly invested horses, weapons, and gold. None of this enthusiasm, however, budged the governor as he and his supporters accused Soto, Ponce, and Castañeda of neglecting their mines and *encomiendas,* and conspiring to ruin the colony.

The political struggle over the Peruvian question climaxed in December 1530, as Francisco Pizarro and about two hundred men prepared to depart Panama for Peru, and the partners became desperate enough to risk a head-on clash with the old governor. They did this by staging a clumsy effort to stack the city council in their favor, hoping to override Pedrarias's ban on leaving the colony for Peru. Castañeda's strategy depended on a royal edict issued two years earlier that ordered colonial councils to seat more royally appointed officials—something most governors, used to seating their own people, had largely ignored. The alcalde's idea was to create a pro-Castañeda majority on the council by forcing Pedrarias to accept new royal officials, and to dismiss locally appointed council members. But Pedrarias predictably balked, ordering the existing council to elect enough of his supporters to preserve his majority. During this same stormy council meeting, Castañeda also made an unsuccessful attempt to have Soto and Ponce elected as co-alcaldes in León for 1531.

*Ponce and Soto claimed that the Pizarros agreed to name Soto lieutenant general of the army—i.e., second in command—not just lieutenant governor of Peru's major city.

Pedrarias killed this effort, too, by refusing to accept the council's nomination of the two captains, whom he loudly condemned as unfit for office, aiming his always-venomous wrath against Soto, his onetime protégé. In a long and bitter tirade, the old man insisted that Soto and Ponce could not be trusted to run the city because they were "henchmen" of Castañeda, a "man who is notoriously scandalous and brings constant harm to this country." Pedrarias also blasted the partners for planning to depart Nicaragua for Peru—and, in a parting blow against Soto, claimed "in the year Hernando de Soto was elected alcalde of this city [in 1525] he looked down on serving this high office of Your Majesty, and he did not serve in the said office or hold council meetings before the year passed."

This last accusation was backed up in this meeting by Sebastián de Benalcázar, Soto's former friend and subcaptain during the invasion of Nicaragua. More recently, he had become a stanch Pedrarias partisan, insisting on this occasion that when "Soto was alcalde of this city" in 1525, he "had not wanted to serve in this office . . . and that he did not care that he insulted the office of alcalde and the name of His Majesty and of the Lord Governor." Moreover, said Benalcázar, "because he was [Soto's] friend" he had, at the time, "tried to persuade Hernando de Soto . . . to come out and serve his office on some occasions but that he never did . . . nor did he understand magisterial duties because he knew little of the judiciary and he was a passionate man and had trouble paying attention."^

Supporters of Soto, Ponce, and Castañeda countered that the captains were "good and responsible men." But their voices were all but drowned out in what became a political disaster for the partners. Indeed, in the wake of this fiasco, Castañeda and his followers were left without any immediate options. This must have greatly frustrated Soto, a man of action who in the past had been known to lash out when he didn't get his way. Perhaps this explains why we find Castañeda ordering him a few days later to lead yet another expedition north to "pacify" the Cosiguina region—a wholly unnecessary *entrada* that seems at least in part a pretext by the royal alcalde to get the hotheaded Soto out of León, in case his temper got the better of him, and he tried something foolish.^

Thus 1531 began with Soto away in Cosiguina, and he and his friends smarting from a political defeat at the hands of a ninety-year-old man born half a century before Columbus first sailed to the Indies, and whose remarkable longevity had long frustrated his many enemies and detractors. By now, Pedrarias's continued survival had become legendary. Some were even convinced the old man had a pact with the devil, and would never die. The superstitious in Nicaragua supposedly believed Pedrarias had, in fact, expired some years earlier in Spain, but had come back to life, startling the mourners at his funeral by sitting up in his coffin and announcing that he wanted something to eat. Every year afterward, it was said, on the anniversary of his "death," the governor spent the entire day in his coffin, a ritual that allowed him to live another year.^

But not even El Furor Domini could go on forever. On March 6, 1531, nine weeks after his victory in the city council, this old man who had governed in Tierra Firme for almost two decades, whose record of cruelty and pettiness remains virtually unequaled in the bloody annals of American history, finally died—this time permanently.

Soto, however, was not there to see it. He returned from Cosiguina just three days later, leading yet another miserable chain gang of slaves from a region that by now was thoroughly "pacified." His reaction to the news of Pedrarias's death is not known, though he must have been elated. At last, he was free to depart a country where possibilities for quick profit and fame were quickly running out, to head out to a new frontier far to the south, where he would stake everything on another quest of blood and steel.

Isla de la Puná

GLITTERING AND IMPERIOUS IN his ornate armor, donned for the oblig-atory farewell ceremony, Hernando de Soto watched the shore of Nicaragua fade off the bow as he stood on the deck of the *San Geronimo,* flagship of his slave fleet turned armada.^ His complement that day consisted of two or three vessels containing some one hundred Spaniards, twenty or thirty sailors, forty or fifty horses,^ and several hundred servants, slaves, and armed Indian auxil-iaries, the latter looking strangely out of place with their tattoos, feathers, and war clubs. Soto also brought along his mistress, the same Juana Hernández who probably bore Soto's illegitimate daughter, María.^

Little is known about the armada's preparations. Soto and Hernán Ponce probably divided the duties along their familiar pattern, with Ponce handling the details of equipment, horses, finance, and shipping, and Soto the selection and training of men, officers, and Indian troops. Unlike other *entradas* launched by the partners during the 1520s, this one was larger in terms of men and material, and logistically more complex, given the great distance to be traveled by ship—some fifteen hundred miles—and the fact that Soto and Ponce knew nothing about the climate and terrain of Peru, or the nature of the enemy.

Apparently, the project was well financed. Most of the money came from Soto and Ponce themselves, and the rest from wealthy *vecino* investors^ like Francisco de Castañeda, who helped pay for the construction of the partners' new ship in Puerto Realejo.^ Other investors contributed gold, horses, food, and weapons in exchange for a future share in Peruvian plunder, while recruits "paid freight charges to the owners of the ships,"^ according to the Peruvian chronicler Pedro Pizarro. He adds that many of them sold all their property and *encomiendas,* in typical *conquista* style, to pay expenses, with the wealthiest lavishing money on retinues of servants, fine clothes, spacious campaign tents, and horses.^ The less well off scrimped to purchase the bare essentials of a sword, buckler, shield, helmet, and coat of mail.

Just after Pedrarias Dávila's timely death in March 1531, the partners received an additional financial boost from Francisco Pizarro himself. Already on his way to Peru, Pizarro transshipped to Ponce and Soto some three thousand pesos of gold, culled from the plunder seized in the early days of the expedition and sent to "encourage" the Nicaraguans "on seeing them . . . to come to these parts."^ The enticement, of course, worked. "As soon as the wealth which the ship brought was seen, Hernando de Soto . . . armed his Indians, and assembled as many as one hundred [Spanish] men," all of them anxious to sail to a country rumored to be far richer than Mexico—a rumor that, for once, would turn out to be true.

Most of the Spaniards who crowded the decks of the vessels that day were illiterate peasants in their mid-twenties, who had lived in the Indies for five years or less.^ The majority, however, had some limited experience in Indian warfare, having participated in minor missions to put down local Indian insurrections, or in gangs sent out to collect Indian tribute. A few had served as cavalrymen and hired thugs with Soto and other senior captains on large-scale "pacifications" and punitive expeditions in the hinterlands of Nicaragua. From these came the core of Soto's partisans and officers in Peru—a young company of ruthless but talented outriders hungry for blood and glory, and ardently devoted to a man they admired not only for his fighting prowess and his energy, but also for his unwavering confidence that he—and, by extension, they—could do anything.^

Other than Soto, the only senior captain in Nicaragua to take a chance on Peru in 1531 was Sebastián de Benalcázar. He was the Pedrarias crony who recently had lambasted Soto in the León council for planning to rob the colony of *vecinos* to take to Peru, a project he said would "destroy this country." Obviously, these sentiments had not been entirely heartfelt, for within weeks of Pedrarias's death, Benalcázar was scrambling as hard as Soto to organize his own small *entrada* to meet up with Pizarro. He left in two ships just before Soto, in early autumn 1531.^ Benalcázar, however, lacked Soto's charisma and skills as a commander—not to mention his financial clout—and was able to recruit only some thirty men, most of whom promptly joined up with Soto's clique after they arrived in Peru.

✛   ✛   ✛

If Soto and his men had known what awaited them far to the south, on Puná island near the modern border between Peru and Ecuador, they would not have felt so enthusiastic. Indeed, even as Soto's ships plowed through the water headed toward Peru, Pizarro's army was in a pitiable condition. Sick, wounded, and exhausted from a year of setbacks during a long march from Ecuador, they were currently under seige by fierce and well-organized Puná islanders, who had not taken kindly to having their villages seized, and their food and women stolen. Too emaciated to break the siege, the Spaniards were slowly starving as provisions ran low, and they continued to be bloodied in skirmishes with the natives.

Later, when Soto's troops paddled ashore in their *barcos,* they would hear from Pizarro's men the woeful story of what had happened over the past year, as they marched south to Puná from their debarkation point in Ecuador. They would recount a nightmare journey that began even before Pizarro touched down in Ecuador, when a strange storm with powerful northerly winds and currents forced them to put ashore some 250 miles north of Tumbez.*^ Here, Pizarro's men said, the army had experienced its only good luck so far when they discovered a populated region called Coaque, and found hidden in the huts an unexpected cache of gold and jewels worth some fifteen thousand pesos, abandoned by the inhabitants as they "fled in terror to the neighboring forests." This loot was the source of the three thousand pesos dispatched to Soto in Nicaragua.^

The excitement of this find quickly faded as Pizarro's *entrada* reeled from disaster after disaster on the road to Tumbez. While still in Coaque, numerous Spaniards contracted an agonizing malady they called *berrugas,* which Pedro Pizarro described as "so bad and tormenting that it caused many men to be wearied and worn by pain just as if they had tumors, and even great sores came out all over the body, and some were as big as eggs, and they corrupted the skin, and much puss and blood ran out of them." Others contracted a measleslike rash accompanied by high fevers, where "the whole body swelled up." "Few . . . escaped having them," Pizarro adds, reporting that some died. Others had to be carried in litters as the *berrugas* lingered on for weeks and even months.

As the army had painfully marched toward Peru, the country had shifted from tropical scrub, where the troops could find minimal food and water, to a desert that one historian later described as desolate and "checkered by strips of sandy waste," where great dunes "drifted about in the winds, blinding the soldiers, and affording only treacherous footing for man and beast. The glare was intense; and the rays of a vertical sun beat fiercely on the iron mail and thick quilted doublets of cotton." This coastal desert, denied moisture by a high-pressure system permanently hovering between the Andes and the sea, remains today one of the driest and most desolate regions on earth, receiving less rain than the Sahara Desert. By pure chance they came across a few wells and rivers, carrying the runoff from the distant Andes, enabling them to struggle

*This was probably an El Niño.

on. Reaching the Gulf of Guayaquil, they had left the mainland in small, native boats for Puná, confident they could subdue the local inhabitants, steal their food, and get some rest before marching on Tumbez, across the gulf to the southeast.

Suffering was hardly a novel experience for Francisco Pizarro. Since long before Soto arrived in the Indies, this veteran conquistador had been enduring everything from deadly floods and poisoned arrows to starvation, most recently in his dogged seven-year pursuit of Peru. Already, it had cost the lives of over two hundred men, most of them dying from lack of food, exhaustion, and disease.

During his first attempt to find and conquer Peru in a "fleet" consisting of one tiny caravel, Pizarro in 1524 had lost eighty men exploring the jungle coast of Colombia, where he had found little evidence of gold or sophisticated cultures, encountering mostly hunger, Indian attacks, and swarms of mosquitoes.^ Similar hardships on Pizarro's second voyage, in 1527–28, caused another one hundred men to die. The rest became so disaffected that the survivors sailed back to Panama, marooning Pizarro and thirteen loyalists on the desolate island of Gallo. They were not rescued until Bartolomé Ruiz returned with his astonishing news about the Inca raft.

By now, Francisco Pizarro, the man who would dominate Soto's life for the next half decade, was one of the oldest active conquistadors in the Indies. Well into his fifties, this taciturn former swineherd from Extremadura had been hacking through jungles and plundering small-time *caciques* before most of his youthful Peruvian troops had been born. Typecast for most of his life as the grimly efficient stopgap, Pizarro before Peru had served almost exclusively as an unimaginative second- or third-in-command who could always be depended on to at least return home alive. Indeed, Pizarro was a man driven less by the burning, reckless ambition of a Hernando de Soto or Hernán Cortés, and more by the sheer momentum and obsessive restlessness of a man who began life as the bastard son of a prominent *hidalgo* from Trujillo, and ever since had been on the move, vacillating from one frontier to the next, forever trying, and hereto failing, to break out of what seemed a case of terminal mediocrity.

From the moment the young Francisco Pizarro arrived on Hispaniola from Spain in 1502, he had been mostly content to follow the center of the *conquista* as it shifted from Hispaniola to Darién, and then from Darién to Panama City, where, in 1519, Pedrarias awarded him a large enough *encomienda* to suggest a certain success, but nothing spectacular. Then, in 1523, Pizarro made a crucial decision. Instead of following the majority heading north toward Nicaragua and Mexico, he headed south toward the country the Indians called Birú, taking up the quest first proposed by his one-time commander, Vasco

Núñez de Balboa. This was a natural course for Pizarro, whose long association with South Sea ventures began when he accompanied Balboa on his 1513
"discovery" of the Pacific Ocean. It was during this expedition that the
Spaniards first heard rumors from local Indians about "a country where you
may obtain your fill of gold . . . where the people eat out of vessels of gold, and
have large cities and wealth unbounded."

Francisco was not the only Pizarro waiting for Soto to make his landfall on
the shore of Puná. With him were his three half brothers from Trujillo—Hernando, Juan, and Gonzalo—who would later earn the sobriquet the Brothers of
Doom. For as Soto was about to find out, this formidable foursome had few
equals in haughtiness, single-minded devotion to their own self-interest, and
pathological distrust of everyone but themselves—characteristics that would
lead them over the next several years to ravage an empire and incite two bloody
civil wars. Eventually, two of them would die violently, with swords in their
hands; a third would be executed by order of the king for treason; and the
fourth would serve two decades in a Spanish prison, also by order of the king,
for gross insubordination.

The oldest and most self-impressed of Pizarro's three half brothers was Hernando,^ then slightly older than Soto, being in his early thirties. A large, bearlike man who possessed enormous physical strength, Hernando Pizarro was
the sole legitimate son of the brothers' *hidalgo* father, the late Gonzalo Pizarro,
a one-time royal captain and hero of King Ferdinand's campaigns in Granada
and Navarre. Because he was the head of the Pizarro family and the only senior officer with any European military experience—he claimed to have served
in the Navarre campaign with his father—Hernando Pizarro had come to Peru
with a status among his brothers almost equal to his illegitimate half brother,
who welcomed a polished and literate ally he could trust. Juan Pizarro, then
twenty-two or twenty-three years old, was easily the most outgoing and popular Pizarro among the troops.^ Frequently, he rode with Soto and his hotshot
outriders in the vanguard of the army, both because he was an accomplished
horseman and because his brothers wanted to keep an eye on Soto. Gonzalo,
the third Pizarro, was a teenager in 1531, and played an insignificant role in the
initial conquest, though he later earned considerable notoriety as the pernicious
and cruel leader of a short-lived Peruvian rebellion against the crown.^

✛   ✛   ✛

When Soto's lookouts finally located Pizarro's base on Puná on December
1, the men on board the *San Geronimo* and *La Concepción* cheered, prayed,
and sang "Te Deum." After two weeks aboard tiny vessels crowded with un-

washed men, horses, and the general filth of a long voyage, they were anxious to disembark and see with their own eyes the golden country for which many had sacrificed their comfortable *encomiendas* and businesses in Nicaragua.

What they found instead was Pizarro's 180 miserable Spaniards, ill with *berrugas* and pinned down by hostile Indians.

The newcomers were stunned. "Francisco Pizarro and those who were with him received much pleasure and contentment," wrote Pedro Pizarro of Soto's arrival, "although those who had come [did not feel the same way], because as they had left the Paradise . . . which Nicaragua was and had found an island in revolt and lacking in food and the greater part of the troops sick and neither gold nor silver . . . some and all wished to return whence they had come, and the captain [Soto] shamefully did not prevent [the talk], nor did the [principal] soldiers, not being able to do so."

Far more distressing for Soto was the discovery that Francisco Pizarro had named his brother Hernando to the post of lieutenant general, or second-in-command, despite the agreement worked out between Ponce and the Pizarros in Panama. Sixteenth-century historian Pedro Cieza de León notes that when Soto was informed he had not been "given the duties of general, because Hernando Pizarro held it already," the captain from Nicaragua "was not pleased." Later, the Pizarros claimed they had agreed only to name Soto lieutenant of the chief city of Peru, and not lieutenant general of the army,^ a discrepancy that turned Soto sour on the Pizarros from the start, and quickly set him scheming to enhance his own position—probing weaknesses and testing his own strength and standing within an army he almost certainly felt he deserved to lead, instead of the bungling Pizarro and his overbearing brothers, whose leadership skills up to this point were something less than inspiring.

✣ II ✣

Empire of the Four Quarters

WITH SOTO'S ARRIVAL AT Puná, Francisco Pizarro's band of *cabalgada* raiders and conquerors now totaled just under 300 Spaniards—150 to 200 footmen, and perhaps 100 horsemen. These included the usual complement of experienced conquistadors, greenhorns fresh from Iberia, sailors, petty criminals, plebeians, and *hidalgos*. There was a swordsmith, six tailors, a cooper, two horseshoer-veterinarians, a stonemason, a Greek artillery expert, and a free "negro" herald who later received a five-eighths share of gold at Cajamarca.^ Slightly larger than Córdoba's 224-man army in Nicaragua, and smaller than the 500 soldiers Cortés commanded against the Aztecs, Pizarro's army had one advantage that these others had not, particularly in a campaign over enormous distances—a larger-than-average cavalry. Córdoba had only seventeen horse, and Cortés sixteen. With five times as many mounts, Pizarro possessed a far greater flexibility in terms of reconnaissance, quick thrusts, and emergency deployments as the Spaniards raced across an empire twenty-five hundred miles long and up to five hundred miles wide. He also had one of the best cavalry officers in the Americas to lead his horsemen—Hernando de Soto.

But even with this edge in horseflesh, Pizarro's situation on Puná in December 1531 hardly seemed the stuff of epic conquest. Here was a motley band of half-starved, ailing adventurers preparing to invade the largest and most powerful empire in the Western Hemisphere, a country five times the size of Spain, with six million inhabitants and one or two hundred thousand men under arms. Sophisticated and, in some areas of science and technology, ahead of Renaissance Europe, the Inca Empire embraced advanced cultures that stretched back four millenniums—to the time of ancient Sumer, the early Middle Kingdom of Egypt, and the Yangtze River culture in China.

But the Spaniards knew none of this. Their information about the Inca Empire came mostly from rumors and brief excursions to minor coastal cities, where they heard about the existence of larger Inca centers high in the Andes, but they knew nothing about what the empire was really like, or such vital facts as the size and fighting prowess of the native army, the terrain, and the availability of food. What they did know suggested they would face overwhelming odds against man and nature, though this hardly mattered to the Castilians, who soon after Soto's arrival staged the obligatory ceremony claiming the unexplored and unconquered Peru for Spain, giving it the name New Castile.

As the army prepared to depart Puná late in 1531, Hernando de Soto was still furious over Hernando Pizarro's elevation to lieutenant general. This did not stop him, however, from quickly seizing the initiative and establishing himself as Pizarro's most-reliable captain in the field. When the army finally departed Puná early in 1532,^ Soto appears in most chronicles leading the first party to cross the gulf, while the two senior Pizarros stayed back with the ships and the army. This became a frequent pattern during the invasion of Peru—the energetic Soto leading the first waves of exploration and fighting, heading up his crack vanguard of cavalry, while Hernando Pizarro took charge of the main army, and the governor-general assumed overall command.

Soto departed Puná for the mainland with fifteen men, traveling forty miles across the choppy Strait of Jambeli on rafts provided by Quillemesa, the *cacique* of Tumbez, with whom Pizarro had formed an alliance during the trouble with the Puná Islanders.^ Soto expected a routine crossing to friendly territory. This is evident by his laxness in keeping the *balsas* together during the day-long voyage, an oversight he would soon regret as his men approached the beach widely separated—and, it turned out, vulnerable to a surprise attack.

For once, Soto was not the very first to arrive. If he had been, his life story might have ended here with a sudden assault by native soldiers, and a long, excruciating death by torture. Instead, this fate befell three young soldiers who beat their captain to the mainland. According to Pedro Cieza de León, the men were attacked by Tumbez fighters as they came ashore. Hiding in the nearby bush, the natives burst onto the beach, overwhelmed the men, and dragged them into a nearby forest. "These wretches," writes Cieza, "they went [ashore] without suspecting anything, and they cried out as the Indians with great cruelty removed their eyes . . . then the barbarians hacked off their penises and, having kettles put over great fires, they put them inside and finished them off, killing them in great torment."

Accounts differ slightly about what happened next as other rafts in Soto's party came ashore. According to Cieza, Soto was near enough the three captured men to attempt a rescue, but was turned back by a ferocious native assault. Another period historian, Agustín de Zárate, writes that Soto landed some distance down the beach and knew nothing about his men's fate until being warned away.^ Moments later, Soto himself was attacked, though he managed to fend off the natives until reinforcements arrived the next morning. Whatever really happened, the Spaniards were thoroughly duped by Quillemesa, whose surprise offensive extended beyond the shore and out into the gulf, where Tumbez soldiers in *balsas* attacked bands of Spaniards bivouacking for the night on small islands between Puná and the coast.^

As Soto spent that night trapped on the beach, surrounded by hostile Tumbez soldiers, we get a rare glimpse of him being circumspect. According to Cieza, Soto was "frustrated and even shamed that the men had come to be killed, and that he had come with so few Spaniards." Yet one wonders if this sensitivity toward his men came from the genuine grief of a commander responsible for the deaths of three men, or from the embarrassment of a man with a reputation as a master Indian fighter, who has just botched his very first assignment.^

None of the chroniclers mentions what caused Quillemesa to turn from friend to foe, though one can guess it was for the usual reasons involving Spanish demands and thievery. In any event, his success was short-lived. Forced to evacuate his position on the beach, he fled Tumbez itself when Pizarro's main army landed and drove him into the rugged country northeast of the city. There Quillemesa holed up with a small army, hoping the Spaniards would quickly move inland toward richer prizes. But he underestimated Spanish fury. "Pizarro wanted to avenge the deaths of the Christians," writes Cieza, "and soon sent out some of his captains into the land to pillage, capturing whatever Indians they could find. They killed many" while also gathering up "sheep [llamas] to eat, and stealing anything else they could find."

This drove Quillemesa even farther into the mountains, leading Pizarro to pull back and settle into the familiar *conquista* tactic of first trying to coerce the *cacique* to surrender on his own. When Quillemesa refused the "daily embassies to the Lord of that city," which demanded he "yield to the Emperor's service," Pizarro dispatched sixty or seventy men under his most-experienced Indian "pacifier," Hernando de Soto.

It was a difficult mission. Not only was Quillemesa lodged deep in the steep foothills of the Andes, but also his hideout was situated across the Tumbez River, then in full flood.

According to Cieza, "Soto set out and crossed the river; he killed some Indians and captured more, even though all of them put together were few because this was a swampy quagmire. As those from Tumbez saw the boldness of the Spaniards they took it to mean they wanted war, so they . . . asked for forgiveness for what had happened and offered peace without conditions." Pedro Pizarro adds that Quillemesa's decision to surrender was greatly influenced by the Spaniards' horses and Soto's riding skill. "As . . . Soto was going in search of Quillemesa," Pizarro writes, "it happened that while the cavalry was going up a very sharp slope, Quillemesa saw them from a mountain where he was hidden, and Quillemesa said to some chiefs whom he had with him: '[I]f these Christians go up the mountains with their horses I cannot escape. It would be a good thing for us to go out to them in peace.' He then dispatched an Indian to Soto to say that if they would pardon him, he would come to them in peace. When Soto gave him assurances, [Quillemesa] came in with his chiefs and Indians." In Zárate's version, Soto's campaign was less benign. Setting out on rafts with Pizarro and other senior officers across the Tumbez, this historian says, Soto and his men "set upon the enemy's camp, and made a marvelous spoil among them which endured with fire and sword the space of fifteen days, in revenge of the three Spaniards which the Indians had so traitorously massacred." Only then, says Zárate, did the *cacique* give up.

After Quillemesa's capture, the army remained in Tumbez for nearly a month while Pizarro rested his men, and Soto and Hernando Pizarro conducted reconnaissance missions to "mark the land and gather information about . . . the Inca."

This was hardly a period of calm for Pizarro, however, as his bad luck continued. For the city he had been so desperate to reach for over a year, which he was sure would prove to his dispirited army that their quest was real, had changed dramatically in the four years since his visit in 1528. Once prosperous, the city was now in ruins, having been decimated first by plague, and then by a series of local wars triggered by a bloody four-year civil war just finished between two rival Inca factions in the south and north of the empire. One of Pizarro's notaries described the disgust of the army when "they arrived in Tumbez, discovering that this place was depopulated and without people; for that which was good now seemed bad, and there was no good place, and everything was ruined . . . And the men were very confused, because for all this time they had been told of the great grandeur and riches of this city, and they thought of all the toil they had endured to come here." Cieza adds that "many of the Spaniards muttered about the land and the lack of faith that they had in what lay ahead. They were very disappointed. There were some who asked for permission to return to Nicaragua or Panama," which Pizarro refused.

Chief among these grumblers was Hernando de Soto, whom Pizarro tried to mollify by naming him military governor of Tumbez.^ This may also have been an attempt to fulfill the Pizarros' version of the Ponce contract, though

Pizarro's Route of Conquest in Peru, 1531–34

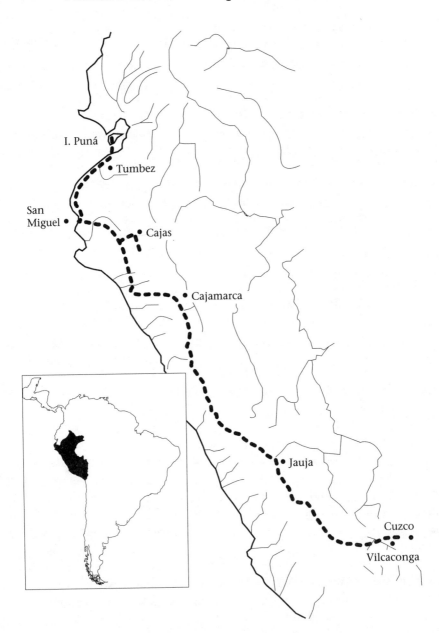

Soto was hardly impressed with the governorship of a ruined, depopulated city. Soto's dissatisfaction was so great that Pedro Pizarro reports he attempted a "half-hearted rebellion against the governor" during this period. While off searching for Quillemesa, he writes, Soto "and the men who were with him . . . [pretended] to go to a certain province in the direction of Quito," apparently in violation of orders. What Soto meant to accomplish with this "rebellion" is unclear. Nor is it certain that Pedro Pizarro isn't exaggerating what may have been a minor infraction. Certainly, it indicates Soto remained unhappy enough with events in Peru that he was falling back into his Nicaragua role as the scheming subordinate trying to enhance his own position. Still, it's hard to believe that Soto was actually contemplating mutiny. More likely, he was responding to the Pizarro brothers' heavy-handed attempts during this period to push aside other senior captains from their inner circle, including Sebastián de Benalcázar and two other captains recruited in Panama—Juan de Salcedo and Cristóbal de Mena.

Whatever happened in the mountains outside of Tumbez, Soto during this period was intent on convincing the Pizarros they could not easily shove him aside—if for no other reason than that he retained a considerable influence among not only the Nicaraguan recruits, but also a portion of Pizarro's original army.^ In fact, the tone of the pro-Pizarro chronicles during this period, which cast Soto as a reckless, if talented, outrider constantly at odds with Pizarro's intentions, suggests that Soto may have enjoyed a considerable following, particularly among those disaffected by Pizarro's leadership. Evidence that the Pizarros took him seriously comes in Pedro Pizarro's comment after the supposed "rebellion," that "thenceforth, whenever Soto went anywhere he [Pizarro] sent with him his two brothers Juan Pizarro and Gonzalo Pizarro." This emphasizes not only Pizarro's distrust of Soto, but also an acknowledgment of Soto's sway in the army.

✛   ✛   ✛

Pizarro departed Tumbez on May 16, convincing his reluctant troops to forge ahead by talking up fresh Indian rumors about golden cities in the interior, high up in the mountains, which in the coming days would loom ahead like a wall of haze as insubstantial as many in the army considered Pizarro's claims of riches. Before leaving, the governor-general divided up the duties of his senior staff, confirming his brother Hernando as lieutenant general and captain of the cavalry; himself as captain of the infantry, in charge of "150 men on foot"; and his brothers Gonzalo and Juan as sergeant major of the camp and commissar, respectively.^ As for Soto, Pizarro officially designated him captain of the vanguard, "with 64 men," a position technically subordinate to the lieutenant general, though in this case it was not really the snub Soto perceived

it to be. For the vanguard in this far-flung invasion would become the most critical unit in the army. This was where the intelligence would be gathered, most
of the action would occur, and where Pizarro needed his most able and quick-
minded field commander.

Before heading inland, Pizarro, again following standard *conquista* procedure, decided it would be prudent to establish a base on the coast where he
could leave his ships, keep open lines of communication with Panama, and
have ready a defensible city to fall back on if forced to make a hasty retreat.^
Tumbez was to have been this city. But the destruction inflicted by plague and
civil war now meant this was impossible, since there was no longer a native
population large enough, or enough crops under irrigation, to feed and maintain a Spanish settlement. Thus Pizarro departed Tumbez following the shoreline south, in search of a suitable port.

For several days, the army marched with the sea to their right and a desolate, rocky desert to their left, eventually reaching a region known as Chimor,
home to one of the oldest civilizations in not only the Western Hemisphere,
but the world as well. According to archaeologists, the rulers of Chimor were
building elaborate stone cities and conquering up and down the Peruvian coast
some four millenniums before Pizarro and his band of raiders showed up. This
makes the first Chimorans contemporaries with the Old Kingdom Egyptians
who built the Sphinx and pyramids at Giza. By the sixteenth century, however,
when Pizarro passed through, Chimor had long ago fallen into a steep decline,
with most of its cities abandoned and in ruins. One still can see the shattered
walls half-buried amidst the yellow-white sands of northwestern Peru, stretching in patterns of squares and rectangles across entire hillsides.

Chimor was not entirely extinct when Pizarro came through. As the
Spaniards marched first along the coast, and then later turned inland near
present-day Talara, they passed through Chimor cities still modestly thriving,
kept alive in this mostly dry, infertile country by a network of wide, meandering rivers that still flood once a year as the rainy season high in the mountains
runs off to the sea, carrying with it rich deposits of sediment to settle along the
banks.

Before leaving the coast, Pizarro arrived at a small Chimor city called Paita.
Situated on the coast beside a crescent-shaped bay, it was a small but well-fed
enclave, untouched by the civil war, and inhabited by Indians so docile they allowed the Spaniards to seize their houses, food, and port without a fight, and
agreed with minimal coercion to become their servants, porters, and laborers.
For three months, Pizarro lingered in Paita, which he renamed San Miguel.
This allowed ample time for his men to rest and recover from their travails, and

for Pizarro to show a heretofore unsuspected interest in urban planning. He personally drew up plans for the plaza, port facilities, and public buildings. He also organized a garrison of forty men to stay and guard the city, composed mostly of those too ill to march, or too dubious about the *entrada*'s prospects to risk their lives any further.

+ + +

Francisco Pizarro departed San Miguel with two hundred men on a hot, clear day in September, marching due east toward the mountains—and, he hoped, the empire of his ambitions. First, however, they had to pass through yet another wasteland, the Desert of Sechura, which Pedro de Cieza describes as an "intensely dry, stony, or sandy waste, where nothing is seen but a tree with a few leaves and no fruit." Once again, Pizarro's men nearly died of thirst, being saved only by the fortuitous appearance of a wide highway a few days out. This took them first to the broad and fertile Piura River valley, and then on to a string of small, well-watered cities tucked up under the towering wall of the Andes—the ancient enclaves of Serrán, Olmos, Motupe, and, farther south, Saña, where Pizarro and his men would later rest before plunging into the mountains.

During the march, Pizarro assumed a posture of nonbelligerency toward the Chimor people and other Peruvians he encountered, with his men under strict orders to fight only if attacked. The idea was to put the local Indians at their ease while Pizarro and his officers assessed the situation, and tried to determine the size, strength, and technology of the armies that might oppose them. Again, this was classic *conquista* strategy, particularly for a tiny band of *conquistadors* confronting what some in the army already suspected might be a formidable Indian army.

Pizarro's strategy had the unintended effect of attracting large crowds of Peruvians in the populated river valleys, who lined the highway to stare at the bizarre strangers. What they saw must have astonished them—a troop of late-medieval-European warriors dressed in metal, singing loudly in cadence as they marched, and riding animals one Indian described as "large and noisy deer."

The army would have marched through these crowds in its usual order, with Hernando de Soto and his vanguard in the lead, riding under stiff banners and wearing their capes, shirts of mail, flared cotton trousers, tall black boots, and helmets glimmering in the hot sun—an ensemble of rich, dark hues looking ominous and somber against the Peruvians in their colorful tunics and pointed caps, woven in pinwheels of fibers dyed in reds, oranges, yellows, blues, greens, and purples. After Soto came the retinue of Governor Pizarro, dressed as always in his plain infantryman's armor and carrying a royal standard backed by an embroidered image of a knight in full regalia,^ followed by ranks of footmen with long, sharp-tipped pikes resting against their shoulders, and sheathed swords swaying as they marched. These in turn would have been followed by two or three hundred Indian auxiliaries from Nicaragua and the Peruvian coast, dressed in cotton tunics and feathers, and carrying their clubs and javelins. Behind them came long trains of native porters carrying everything from iron kettles and boxes of beads and other trinkets to European campaign tents and cannon balls. Last of all came the rear guard, undoubtedly followed by small clusters of local children laughing and pointing, thoroughly enjoying the festive air of this strange parade.

Pizarro's feigned peacefulness—and the carnival-like atmosphere of the Spanish march—worked even better than the governor had hoped to dupe the Peruvians into concluding the Spaniards were no threat to the empire. For not everyone in the frolicking crowds was there to gawk with amazement. Hidden among the onlookers were spies sent by the Inca Atahualpa,* whose absolute authority encompassed not only Chimor, but countries well beyond it—and who, at this moment, was receiving regular reports from messengers about the arrival of the strangers, and their odd dress, weapons, animals, and behavior.

This was not the first time Atahualpa and the Incas had heard about these pale foreigners. Five years earlier, in Atahualpa's home city of Quito, he almost certainly was present or nearby when his father, Huayna Capac, was first told about strangers from beyond the sea arriving at Tumbez. "One day Huayna Capac was taking his ease at his palaces," writes the priest Bernabé Cobo, when "awed and frightened messengers reported that strange people never before seen had landed on the beach at Tumbez . . . they were white, they had beards and fierce looks . . . they traveled by sea in great wooden houses . . . where they slept by night . . . and by day they went ashore; and by gestures they had asked to see the lord of the land.

"The Inca was stunned upon hearing these things," continues Cobo, "and fell into such apprehension and melancholy that he went alone into his chambers and did not come out until nearly night." Later, when he was told the strangers had departed in their floating houses, the Inca Huayna Capac was greatly relieved, though Cabo says he warned his court that should these strangers return, it might mean the end of their empire.

For Huayna Capac himself, the end came earlier than he anticipated. Just a few months after Pizarro's departure, this great Inca conqueror—who had added parts of Ecuador and about a third of modern Peru to the empire during a thirty-four-year reign—died from the most insidious, if unplanned, weapon

---

*The word *Inca*, as used by the Spanish to describe the natives of Peru, was both the name of the people ("the Inca people") and a title roughly equivalent to "emperor" given to the ruler of the Incas (the "Inca Atahualpa").

of the *conquista*—disease. According to legend, Huayna Capac was stricken when a subject *cacique* brought him a small casket, filled with moths and butterflies. When the Inca took off the lid, the insects flew out, spreading the disease. Whatever really happened, the plague ended up striking down not only Huayna Capac, but as many as 200,000 Inca, including the heir to the throne, Crown Prince Ninan Cuyuchi.^ It was this catastrophe that led to the Inca civil war between two of Huayna Capac's surviving sons—Atahualpa and his half brother Huascar.

Five years after Huayna Capac's untimely death, it was now Atahualpa's turn to deal with the strangers, which he did by dismissing his father's warning about the danger posed by the invaders. Later, the Inca admitted to Pizarro that his emissaries had told him the exact opposite of what Huayna Capac had heard—that the strangers "were not fighting men and that the horses were unsaddled at night." They also told him the Spaniards were laughably few in number, compared to the Inca's vast armies of highly disciplined soldiers. One of the emissaries, a local *cacique* named Marcavilca, boasted to the Inca that "if he were given two hundred Indians he could tie them all up." This led Atahualpa to largely ignore the Spaniards as they penetrated ever deeper into his empire, with the Inca later telling Pizarro that he had planned to capture the Spaniards eventually and kill some, while enslaving the others—when he found the time.

One can hardly fault the native crowds that autumn^ if they did not take the Spaniards seriously. After all, they were used to watching the Inca's resplendent troops march past not by the dozens, but by the tens of thousands. Nor, apparently, could anyone in the Inca leadership imagine that this tiny army was planning to conquer the Inca Empire. Most thought they were, at worst, a band of marauders here to rob and plunder, and then go home. It was this inability to comprehend the true intentions of Pizarro, Soto, and company that time and again would work to the Spaniards' advantage—and ultimately would work to fulfill the dire prophecy of the Inca Huayna Capac concerning these strange foreigners.

✢   ✢   ✢

In 1532, the empire this small band of Spaniards planned to conquer was barely a hundred years old. Called Tahuantinsuyu by its own people—"the four quarters of the earth"^—Inca hegemony had begun almost by accident in the mid-1400s, when a nearby city-state tried to conquer the Valley of Cuzco, but was instead defeated by Cuzco's first emperor, Pachacuti. Nor did the Incas stop with this local victory. Indeed, this previously rustic people, who for centuries had been more interested in tending llamas than in conquest, literally erupted out of their valley. Led by Pachacuti, who turned out to be a brilliant general and strategist, their armies raged across the high valleys that run up and down the central spine of the Andes, snatching up in the space of twenty-five years virtually every city, kingdom, and empire in central Peru, from modern Huánuco in the north to Lake Titicaca, 650 miles to the south.

Pachacuti's burst of conquering energy continued with his son, Tupa Inca, an even more successful general-king, whose feats are comparable to Alexander the Great's in their breadth and audacity. In only thirty years Tupa conquered much of his known world, marching as far south as Constitución in Chile, and north all the way to Quito in Ecuador. In all, he carved out an empire some twenty-five hundred miles long—equal to the distance from New York City to the Great Salt Lake in Utah.

But even with Tupa's death in 1493—the same year Columbus returned to Spain from his first voyage of discovery—the Incas were not finished. Tupa's son, Huayna Capac, completed nearly a century of Inca conquest by pushing his father's borders up to the edges of the Amazon jungles below the Andes' eastern slope, and north beyond the present-day border of Colombia. By the time Huayna Capac died of plague, the domains of the Tahuantinsuyu stretched from modern Cali, in southwestern Colombia, to the Río Maule in southern Chile, and from Tumbez to Santa Cruz in Bolivia—a world empire second in size at that time only to the Ottomans', then at their zenith in Asia, Europe, and Africa.

Historians sometimes call the Incas the Romans of the Americas.^ This sounds suspiciously Eurocentric, though in this case the comparison rings more true than not. Like the early Latin tribes who inhabited the Tiber River valley, the Incas were originally a peripheral culture living within the sphere of more ancient and highly advanced peoples such as the Chimor. They shared with them certain basic tenets of religion, commerce, agriculture, and government, though the more urbane and sophisticated in ancient Peru probably considered them unrefined, provincial folk, never imagining they would one day be masters of their known world. The other similarity between the Romans and Incas was their sudden and unsurpassed talent not only in warfare, but in building and establishing an imperial structure of government designed to last for centuries—though in the Incas' case, this was cut short by Pizarro. The cornerstone of this organization was a system of highways and administrative centers that connected the empire's far-flung cities with an astonishing ten thousand miles of pavement, augmented by bridges, houses for maintenance crews, fortresses, barracks for army units on the move (fully stocked with provisions), Inca administrative posts and colonies, and a detailed program for maintaining it all. Most impressive of all was the Incas' skill in masonry—in the construction of roadways, and in the laying of stone foundations for public buildings, made from massive blocks of rock weighing several tons, but cut by Inca stonemasons so precisely that they fit together perfectly, using no visible mortar.

Much has been written about the Inca style of government—its communal system of agriculture and land-ownership; its highly efficient welfare system that reportedly insured basic food and housing from cradle to grave; and its strong government support for scientists, who made significant advances in such areas as brain surgery, astronomy, mathematics, irrigation, and horticulture.* The facts, however, hardly support the notion that the Incas represented some sort of pre-Columbian socialist utopia, as some have claimed, where the common man was king, and the Inca and his *principales* served everyone's needs in some ancient, far-flung version of Lenin's "vanguard of the people." Indeed, the Incas invented their highly centralized system not out of altruism, but as conquerors aiming to assimilate the vanquished, and to perpetuate an elite headed by a sovereign who forced his subjects to follow a sometimes brutal code of conformity; proscribing what clothes people could wear, what language they could speak, what work they could do, and which gods they could worship. Failure to obey often resulted in a swift and bloody retribution by the Inca army. In fact, Soto would soon see evidence of the Inca Empire's darker side when he reconnoitered in the mountains above the Desert of Sechura, and passed under limbs of trees strung up with hundreds of anti-Atahualpa partisans mutilated and crucified in the recent civil war.

The war had begun soon after the Inca Huayna Capac and his heir died of plague, throwing the imperial succession into disarray as Atahualpa and his brother both claimed the *llautu* crown of the Tahuantinsuyu.

Huascar, son of Huayna Capac and his official consort, had the more legitimate claim, being the eldest male member of the traditional royal family in Cuzco. Atahualpa, however, was apparently a favorite of the late emperor, who had depended on him as one of his most able generals. Huayna Capac also had preferred Atahualpa's city of Quito—and Atahualpa's mother, a princess of the Quito royal house—to his consort and the Inca culture in Cuzco, a city he seldom visited.

The fighting had started when Atahualpa, in Quito, declared himself inde-

*This makes it all the more incredible that the cultures of ancient Peru never invented the wheel, except for use on toys.

pendent of Cuzco, and Huascar sent an army to bring him to heel—which not only failed to reconquer the north for the empire, but was eventually crushed by the more-experienced troops from Quito. But not before the bloody conflagration had raged across the empire for some four years, killing tens of thousands, and devastating cities and entire regions—including Tumbez. The war finally ended when one of Atahualpa's generals, Quizquiz, captured Huascar late in 1531, entered Cuzco, and massacred virtually the entire royal Inca family, on orders from Atahualpa. Huascar himself was imprisoned, pending the arrival of the triumphant Atahualpa, then traveling from Quito to Cuzco with an army of as many as eighty thousand soldiers.

✛   ✛   ✛

As they marched toward the mountains, the Spaniards began to hear more details about the civil war, and to see for themselves more evidence of the devastation wrought by the fighting. Yet Pizarro was still operating mostly on hearsay and rumors. He lacked solid reconnaissance about not only the political situation in the empire, but also the empire itself—its size, the sophistication of its chief cities up in the mountains, and, of course, the availability of gold, which down on the desert remained a scarce commodity. This type of probing mission was ideal for his captain of the vanguard, Hernando de Soto, whom Pizarro dispatched "with horse and foot" sometime in October 1532 from the desert town of Serrán, tucked under the shadow of peaks rising abruptly from near sea level to over twelve thousand feet.

Charging toward the wall of rock ahead, Soto's destination was an Inca administrative city called Cajas, fifty miles—and some eight thousand vertical feet—away, where Indian informers told the Spaniards that Atahualpa himself was at that moment resting on his way to Cuzco.

This was another dangerous mission for Soto—riding deep into a potentially hostile enemy's territory high in the sierras, where Indian sources claimed Atahualpa had assembled a detachment to ambush the Spaniards should they come that way. Later, Atahualpa himself admitted he almost did order an ambush, but decided instead to delay dealing with the strangers, whom he still considered a minor matter as he focused on crushing what remained of Huascar's loyalists, and on his triumphant entry into Cuzco.

By the time Soto arrived in Cajas, Atahualpa's army had already left, though he found ample evidence the Inca had been there. According to eyewitness Cristóbal de Mena, "this village was in considerable ruin from the fighting which Atahualpa had carried on . . . in the hills were the bodies of many Indians hanging from the trees, because they had not consented to surrender, for all these villages were in the first place under Cuzco and acknowledged him as master and paid tribute to him." Later, the city's leader would complain bitterly to Soto that Atahualpa's forces "had brought ruin to them and killed many people, [and] that of the ten or twelve thousand Indians which he used to have he had left no more than 3,000."

Even with the destruction, Soto was greatly impressed by Cajas, a grand city of large temples, storehouses, and palaces built out of massive stones and topped with elaborately ornamented towers like church steeples, and decorated with statuary, carvings, and paintings. And then there was the main Inca Highway, which Spaniards saw here for the first time. Mena says Soto and all of them stood in awe of this extraordinary feat of engineering, approaching it one day on their horses where it ran through the middle of the city, a tightly packed surface of bricks stretching thirty feet wide, and edged by drainage channels to handle prodigious downpours during the rainy season.

It's worth pausing for a moment to comment further on this great highway, which Soto would be racing up and down over the next three years. According to Pedro Cieza de León, who traveled the length and breadth of its ten-thousand-mile network in the mid-sixteenth century, there was no road "as great as this . . . in the memory of man . . . Laid through deep valleys and over high mountains, through snow banks and quagmires, through live rock and along raging rivers; in some places smooth and paved; in others tunneled through cliffs, skirting gorges, linking snow peaks with stairways and rest stops; everywhere swept clean and litter free." He adds that the roads were lined with frequent rest stations for royal couriers and "depots of provisions for the troops" as they conquered and patrolled across the empire. In fact, these roads were ideal conduits for armies on the move, though the Inca, like Adolf Hitler with his autobahns in Germany, failed to realize they might one day be turned against them, affording an invader not only easy access inward, but large storehouses of food, clothes, and weapons.

After investigating the great highway, Soto moved in force into Cajas and "sent for the headman of this village," whom he informed with his usual haughtiness that they were now subjects of the Spanish king, and that "they should be at peace with the Christians . . . and should have no fear of Atahualpa."

"The *cacique*," Mena says, was so pleased by these words that he "opened a house" for the Spaniards, "[one] of those which was closed and under the guard by Atahualpa and took out of it four or five women and gave them to the captain to serve the Christians in preparing food on the march. As for gold, he said he had none because Atahualpa had taken it all. Still he gave [Soto] four or five *tejuelos* [large tiles] of unrefined gold."

"While this was going on," Mena continues, "a captain from Atahualpa arrived. The *cacique* [of Cajas] became greatly frightened and arose to his feet, for he did not dare remain seated in his presence. But Hernando de Soto made him sit down near him. This captain brought a gift for the Christians from

Atahualpa. It was of skinned ducks; which meant that they would skin the Christians in that manner, and besides he brought small models of two very strong fortresses made of earthenware, saying that there were others ahead like these."

Soto's sojourn in Cajas was not all business. Despite the war, the city still retained enough of its opulence and wealth for the Spaniards to partake of its pleasures, including the richly varied Inca menu of maize, potatoes, exotic fruits, *chicha* (maize) beer—and, undoubtedly, the choicest and most comfortable apartments. But he did not stop there. In a notorious incident recorded by a young eyewitness named Diego de Trujillo, Soto also partook of more carnal pleasures—namely, the beautiful virgin nuns of Cajas's Temple of the Sun.

Soto and his men were under strict orders from Pizarro to restrain themselves from raping and pillaging. However, the temptation of five hundred young women selected for their beauty, and cloistered right off the main Cajas plaza, apparently proved too much. Trujillo describes what happened to the virgins in a simple soldier's terms. He says "the women were brought out on to the square, and there were over five hundred of them, [and] Captain [Soto] gave many of them to the Spaniards." In other words, Soto and his men stormed into the virgins' cloisters, forced the women outside at the point of a sword, and then divided them up.

As this organized rape proceeded, however, the Spaniards were interrupted by Inca officials in Cajas, who heard the fracas in the plaza and rushed over to find out what was happening. What they saw outraged them—their sacred nuns being manhandled by these foreigners. Gathering the citizens of Cajas into a mob, they grabbed whatever weapons they could find and tried to stop Soto and his men, who responded not only by defending themselves, but unleashing a brief but bloody slaughter that Cieza says "killed many Indians." Trujillo adds that he saw one man, Juan Jiménez, slice an Inca "into many pieces," apparently in retaliation for a flesh wound delivered by this Indian, probably with a club or wooden dagger.

After the conflagration, the Inca's infuriated envoy confronted Soto and shouted, "How dare you do this when Atahualpa is only twenty leagues from here. Not a man of you will remain alive!"

It's a sign of Soto's arrogance that this threat meant nothing to him. Nor did this great city make him so much as pause to consider the folly of a few dozen men trying to conquer an empire of such power and majesty. But for Hernando de Soto, Cajas and the civilization that built this place was not something to fear, but a welcome indication of fantastic riches to be had if a man was strong enough, and willing to risk everything.

Book III

Fame

✢ 12 ✢

Cajamarca

FROM CAJAS, SOTO TOOK his tiny troop and rode a few miles down the wide, paved highway to an even larger and more impressive Inca city, Huancabamba, before marching back down the steep mountains to rejoin Pizarro and the army. Traveling with him was the Inca ambassador he had met in Cajas, who wanted to parley with the governor.

They arrived a few days later at Saña, on the Chancay River, when Soto was able to confirm at last for the old conquistador that the rumors he had been chasing all these years were true. With their own eyes, the army could see the splendor of the Inca ambassador, carried in an ornate litter by brilliantly attired servants and bodyguards. Greeted warmly by Pizarro, the ambassador presented gifts of llamas and gold for the strangers. In exchange, Mena tells us, the governor "gave him a very fine shirt and two glass cups for his master and told him to tell [Atahualpa] that he was his friend and that he would be very pleased to see him."

The envoy, who was as much spy as ambassador, responded cordially that if it pleased them, he was empowered by the Inca to invite the Spaniards to meet Atahualpa in the interior. Explaining that the emperor was then marching south toward Cuzco, the ambassador suggested that Pizarro cross over the mountains to the east and join his master in a small town famous for its hot springs, where Atahualpa was then resting. The town was called Cajamarca, he said, which must have sounded like just another Indian enclave to the Spaniards, though it soon would become famous throughout the Western world as a place of empires lost and won.

A few days later, the army turned due east from Saña, leaving behind a garrison of eighty men on the desert to guard lines of communication with San Miguel. This left an invasionary force stripped down to a scant 168 men—106 foot and 62 cavalry.^

Pizarro decided to take the most direct route to Cajamarca. This meant turning off the main highway he had been following and passing through a region Hernando Pizarro describes as "very rugged, and obstructed by very difficult passes"—a desolate region of steep, rocky ridges, narrow trails, and the occasional grazing llama—and, towering above everything like a dream done in white, the lofty, snow-clad peaks of the Andes.

At first, finding guides and willing informants in this wilderness proved difficult, because of the great fear that locals had of Atahualpa. This soon gave way to the greater terror of Spanish torture as Hernando Pizarro and Soto coerced Indians to serve as guides, and to divulge the location of any Inca troops along their route. The unspecified torture, however, did not produce reassuring information as Indians told them "they had heard that Atahualpa was waiting for the Governor in the mountains to give him battle." The Spaniards, of course, plunged ahead anyway into the mountains, many of them undoubtedly wondering if they were marching to their deaths.

Historian John Hemming, who personally retraced Pizarro's route to Cajamarca in the 1960s, says "the Spaniards probably marched up an Inca trail ascending the Chancay stream past the town of Chongoyape. From the sands of the coastal desert they would have passed through plantations of sugar and cotton. As they climbed through the Andean foothills the valley narrowed into a canyon whose sides would have been covered in fields and terraces. At the source of the Chancay Pizarro's force probably swung south along the watershed of the Andes, crossing treeless savanna at some 13,500 feet." According to Hernando Pizarro, "the road was so bad that, in truth, if they had been waiting for us . . . they could very easily have stopped us; for, even by exerting all our skill, we could not have taken the horses by the roads."^

Incredibly, though, the Inca did nothing to impede the Spaniards' progress, though Pizarro and his men felt a crushing apprehension as they passed fortresses intentionally left unmanned. To their further dismay, the Inca began dispatching porters bearing food and more gifts—as if Atahualpa was toying with them, and enticing them forward into a trap.

The harrowing march finally ended on November 15 when, after five days in the mountains, Pizarro topped the hills above Cajamarca and looked down on "a beautiful fertile valley, only a few miles wide but remarkably flat—a very rare distinction in the vertical world of the Andes, where most rivers rush through precipitous canyons, and the only flat ground is on the high, infertile savannas.

"Modern Cajamarca," continues Hemming, "is a charming red-roofed Spanish town, with fine colonial monasteries and a lovely cathedral." Pizarro's

Spaniards, however, saw little charm in the valley laid out below them. For near the small Inca town was arrayed the largest army any of them had ever seen, numbering at least forty thousand men, and possibly as many as eighty thousand.^ Not even Hernando Pizarro, who says he served with King Ferdinand at Navarre, in northern Spain, had ever seen an army so vast.

And this was only an escort for Atahualpa! The main army, as the Spanish would soon discover, was to the south, split up into occupying forces in Cuzco, Jauja, and other key locations.^

"The Indians' camp looked like a very beautiful city," wrote Juan Ruiz de Arce, another soldier-chronicler. "So many tents were visible that we were truly filled with great apprehension. We never thought that Indians could maintain such a proud estate nor have so many tents in such good order. Nothing like this had been seen in the Indies up to then. It filled all us Spaniards with fear and confusion. But it was not appropriate to show any fear, far less to turn back. For had they sensed any weakness in us, the very Indians we were bringing with us would have killed us."

Given this impossible state of affairs, there was really only one thing the Spaniards could do—march into the valley with all the pomp, circumstance, and haughtiness they could muster. Thus Pizarro ordered his men to unfurl every flag and banner, take out their flutes, drums, and trumpets, and strap on every weapon and ornament. Organizing his 168 Renaissance warriors into three divisions, one probably led by Hernando de Soto,^ Pizarro then commanded his trumpeter, Pedro de Alconchel, to sound the order to move out.

Guides sent by Atahualpa led the resplendent little army down a steep trail at the northwest edge of the valley, and onward to Cajamarca. Situated on the west side of the valley, the city stood three or four miles from Atahualpa and his army, bivouacked in their thousands up and down the valley's eastern slopes.

Passing through Cajamarca's thick stone gate, the Spaniards found the city emptied of people, with only four or five hundred of its usual two thousand inhabitants remaining to act as servants for the Inca's guests. With considerable apprehension, the Spaniards marched through the city streets, past a temple to the sun, a convent of holy virgins, and onto a large, triangular-shaped plaza lined on three sides "by long buildings each of which had a series of doors on to the open space." As they filed into the plaza, they expected an ambush in what was essentially a stone enclosure. Instead, the Inca sent over "presents of many cooked ewes [llamas] and corn bread and pitchers of *chicha*," which the nervous Spaniards gave to their porters, fearing it might be poisoned.

With the sun now dropping, Pizarro thought he had better dispatch a small party to offer greetings to the Inca—and to size him up. Pizarro chose Soto for this delicate mission, once again confirming Soto's reputation as an envoy and negotiator, a man as skilled at the arts of persuasion and diplomacy as he was with a sword. He also must have been considered a keen observer, since a critical part of this mission was to gather intelligence about Atahualpa, his army, and his court.

✢   ✢   ✢

To reach Atahualpa, Soto and a select group of outsiders rode down a paved road that ran the length of the valley, eventually entering into the midst of the massive Inca army. Standing at attention in battle dress outside their tents, the native soldiers watched in disciplined silence as the anxious Spaniards rode past in "full armor, magnificently mounted, with plumed helmets and jingling bells." Atahualpa himself was residing in a small palace just beyond a small river. There Soto left his men. Taking a single interpreter, he rode on through "a squadron of infantry, and came to the lodging of Atahualpa."

The emperor Soto was about to meet was roughly his own age, "thirty years old, good looking, somewhat stout, with a fine face, handsome and fierce, the eyes bloodshot. He spoke with great dignity, like a great lord," and had a reputation for being ruthless, intelligent, and greatly feared by his subjects.

From his later comments, we know that Atahualpa had been following the progress of the Spaniards at least since Puná, and possibly since Pizarro's landfall in Ecuador, on the outer edge of the empire. Yet the emperor still lacked two vital pieces of information. First, none of his informants had seen the Spaniards fight more than a light skirmish. So he had no idea how they measured up as soldiers. Nor did he know, exactly, why the Spaniards were there. For it never occurred to the sovereign of this vast empire, victorious in war and surrounded by an overwhelming army, that 168 strangers might be contemplating an invasion.

When Soto arrived at the gate to the Inca's palace, he found Atahualpa seated in a courtyard outside a small palace, surrounded by the brilliantly clad nobles, servants, and aides of his court. A retinue of female servants sat "at his feet;" a ceremonial guard of four hundred men stood around him, armed with glittering weapons.^

The Inca's throne was not one of the massive, imposing seats favored by European monarchs, but "a small stool, very low to the ground," as if to say his person was awe-inspiring enough. Likewise, his crown, called a *llautu*, was a simple circlet of colorful cords hung with a tassel of "very fine scarlet wool, cut very even, and cleverly held towards the middle by small golden bugles. The wool was corded, but below the bugles it was unwound and this was the part that fell onto the forehead . . . This tassel fell to the eyebrows, an inch thick, and covered his entire forehead."

I picture Soto sitting tall on his horse, resplendent in his Renaissance finery as he sought to impress the emperor with his polished armor, plumes, weapons, and fierce demeanor.

The effort fell flat, however, as the Inca greeted this dazzling and puffed-up warrior from across the sea by staring at the ground and ignoring him.

An awkward silence ensued, broken when Soto prodded his mount forward "so close" to the Inca "that the horse's nostrils stirred the fringe that the Inca had placed on his forehead." The Inca "never moved," says Mena, though apparently the novelty of this large beast exhaling hot, damp breath into his face impressed him enough that he ordered one of his retinue to accept a large gold ring Soto took "from his finger . . . as a token of peace and friendship on behalf of the Christians." Encouraged by this brief stirring of interest, Soto sat up even higher in the saddle, looked at the faces of the courtiers assembled, and delivered a set speech that included greetings from Pizarro and a brief explanation of who he was and where he came from.

Still Atahualpa "gave no answer, nor did he even raise his eyes to look at the Captain." Instead, a *cacique* nearby answered for him, telling Soto that Atahualpa was in the midst of a religious ceremony and fasting, and that he was to tell the governor that the Inca would visit Cajamarca the next day.

About this time, Hernando Pizarro arrived at the Inca's palace, dispatched by his brother with a small force to reinforce Soto, should he need help. Told that this was the brother of the Spanish leader, the Inca finally looked up and began to speak. What he said, however, startled the captains. For instead of the usual pleasantries and boasts of peaceful intentions, the Inca presented them with a list of infractions they had committed since arriving in Peru, including looting, raping, and stealing food. He also told Soto and Hernando Pizarro that a *cacique* from the San Miguel area on the coast had told him the Spaniards were "bad people and not good for war, and that he himself had killed" some of the strangers, "both men and horses."

If the Inca's harsh words caused Soto or Pizarro any anxiety, they did not dare show it. Both men understood that the Inca was testing them for signs of fear and weakness. Indeed, Pizarro answered as arrogantly as possible "that those [Indians] of San Miguel were like women," and that "one [cavalryman] was enough for the whole of them." He added that the Inca need only see how the Spaniards fought to appreciate their skill as warriors. He then offered to help Atahualpa "conquer" his enemies. The Inca replied that "four marches from that spot, there were some very rebellious Indians who would not submit to him."

"I said that the Governor would send ten horsemen," wrote Hernando in his account, "who would suffice for the whole country, and that his Indians were unnecessary, except to search for those who concealed themselves."

Atahualpa was apparently amused by this boasting, for he now looked the men in the eye and ordered his women retainers to bring a special blend of *chicha* maize beer, drunk only by high Inca nobles, served on this occasion in "cups of gold."

As they drank, Atahualpa, now warming up to his guests, admired the Spaniards' mounts, "closely examining the horses, which undoubtedly seemed good to him." This gave Soto an idea. Always something of a show-off, he decided to give a little demonstration of Spanish martial skills, asking the Inca's permission to send for a mount among those he had left outside the gate, a "little horse that had been trained to rear up." According to the chronicler Miguel de Estete, Soto then "maneuvered it there for a while with good grace," running a vigorous drill of charges, tight turns, curvets, and skirmishes. "The nag was spirited and made much foam at its mouth," which left the heretofore stone-faced Inca "amazed . . . at seeing the agility with which it wheeled.

"But the common people," continues Estete, "showed even greater admiration and there was much whispering. One squadron of troops drew back when they saw the horse coming towards them. Those who did this paid for it that night with their lives, for Atahualpa ordered them to be killed because they had shown fear."

As night approached, the two Spaniards asked if they might return to their camp. At first, Atahualpa insisted one of them stay, but finally relented, apparently still believing these strangers posed no threat. He then repeated his intention to accept Governor Pizarro's invitation to visit Cajamarca the next day.

When Soto and Pizarro returned to the camp, what they had to report about the Inca and his enormous force hardly assuaged the near panic gripping the tiny army. That evening, the senior leaders convened in Pizarro's newly acquired apartment off the main Cajamarca plaza to assess the situation. "We took many views and opinions among ourselves," recalled Hernando Pizarro, "about what should be done. All were full of fear, for we were so few and were so deep in the land where we could not be reinforced . . . All assembled in the Governor's quarters to debate what should be done the following day . . . Few slept, and we kept watch in the square, from which the camp fires of the Indian army could be seen. It was a fearful sight. Most of them were on a hillside and close to one another: it looked like a brilliantly star-studded sky."

Mena adds that among the Spaniards that evening "There was no distinction between great and small, or between foot-soldiers and horsemen. Everyone performed sentry rounds fully armed that night. So also did the good old Governor, who went about encouraging the men. On that day all were knights."

The Spaniards' situation seemed hopeless. Here were 168 men trapped deep inside an enormous, highly advanced empire, whose army carried primitive weapons, but easily matched the Spaniards in terms of resolve and discipline, and vastly outnumbered them. Nor did Pizarro's men know "how these Indians fought or what spirit they had," though the destruction wreaked by the Inca's troops in the recent civil war left no one in doubt about their ferocity.

But these were not the sort of men to give up. After much discussion, they decided that their only recourse was to fall back once again on a tried-and-true stratagem of the *conquista*—lure the *cacique* into a trap and capture him.

Their plan was breathtakingly simple. They would conceal themselves in the buildings surrounding the plaza, invite Atahualpa to supper when he visited them the next day, and launch an overwhelming assault before his army had time to react.

Of course, this was an audacious long shot even for gamblers as foolhardy as Pizarro, Soto, and the other Spanish leaders. Once the tactic was decided, however, the Spaniards plunged into preparations, with Pizarro staying outwardly cool, encouraging his men to keep busy as he dispersed them around the plaza, hiding them "in three large houses" that seemed perfect for staging an ambush, each enclosed on all sides by heavy stone walls, and each "which had more than 200 windows and twenty doors."

The idea was to wait until the Inca was inside the plaza, where Pizarro would then send out the expedition's priest, Father Vicente de Valverde, to invite him to dinner—a ploy to trick Atahualpa into separating himself from his guard. If this failed—and Pizarro suspected it would—Father Vicente was ordered to wave to an artilleryman situated on the roof of a nearby building, who would shoot off his small cannon to signal the attack.*

✦   ✦   ✦

The following day, November 16, 1532, Atahualpa waited until late afternoon to begin the four-mile journey to Cajamarca. This forced the Spaniards to wait for what seemed an eternity, huddled and tense in their hiding places. Once under way, the Inca and his entourage moved very slowly as thousands of troops and retainers paraded with him. They were carrying no weapons, however, apparently because Atahualpa did not want to offend or frighten their guests.^

---

*Soto, Hernando Pizarro, and Sebastián de Benalcázar each commanded a division of cavalry;^ Francisco Pizarro commanded a mixed division of horsemen and infantry specifically assigned to capture the Inca.^

"All the Indians wore large gold and silver discs like crowns on their heads," wrote Mena, who stood on the roof of Cajamarca's fortress with the other captains and senior staff, anxiously eyeing the approaching horde of Indians. "First came a squadron of Indians dressed in a livery of different colors, like a chessboard. They advanced, removing the straws from the ground, and sweeping the road" for the emperor to pass. Atahualpa himself was dressed in a mountain of ornate robes and gold jewelry, carried on a litter decorated with plates of silver and gold, and "lined with plumes of macaw's feathers, of many colors."

Meanwhile, inside their dark rooms, the frightened Spaniards, getting the word that the Inca was approaching, quietly took Mass, "commending ourselves to God, begging him to keep us in his hand." For some, however, God was little comfort. As Pedro Pizarro later recalled, "I saw many Spaniards urinate without noticing it out of pure terror."

After several more delays, the Inca and his host finally entered the stone gate of the city and arrived inside the plaza, deploying themselves in the large space with great aplomb, according to their rank, with Atahualpa sitting regally on his golden litter held aloft on nobles' shoulders.

Picture the scene as the powerful emperor of the Incas waits impatiently inside the large, triangular plaza. High above him, the sun is setting behind snow-capped peaks. As the air begins to cool, the brilliant company strains to see if any of the strangers will appear. Thinking the Spaniards had fled in fear,^ Atahualpa turns and asks one of his aides to find out "where the Christians were," not having a clue that "all were concealed." Suddenly, a door opens on one end of the plaza. A strange, bearded man in a long, simple black cassock emerges carrying "a cross in one hand and a bible in the other," accompanied only by a translator. Walking boldly up to the Inca, this man begins to shout out what sounds like a speech. The interpreter, a young Inca boy, relays the message—an invitation to join Pizarro for dinner. The Inca refuses, saying "he would advance no further" until the governor himself appeared. This leaves everything hanging in the balance.

According to Pizarro's plan, this refusal was supposed to trigger the attack, with Father Vicente signaling to Pedro de Candía up on the roof to fire his cannon. But Vicente decided instead to stop and deliver a sermon to the Emperor of the Four Quarters, lecturing him about the basic tenets of Christianity and the history of the world, according to the Bible. He then delivered a short version of the *Requerimiento*—including the incredible demand that Atahualpa recognize the king of Spain and the pope in Rome as his new masters.^

It took only a few minutes of this talk to infuriate the Inca, who angrily asked to see the Bible that Vicente had been waving at him, knowing it was some sort of religious relic important to the Spaniards. "The priest gave it to him," says Mena, "thinking he would like to kiss it." Instead, the impatient Inca "took it and threw it over his retinue." Only then did Father Vicente finally turn to Pedro de Candía and, according to Cristóbal de Mena, shout, "Come out! Come out, Christians, and attend to these unfriendly dogs who do not care for the things of God. That *cacique* has thrown on the ground the book of our sacred law.'

"In this moment," Mena continues, "a signal was given to the artillerymen to fire into the midst of [the Incas] and they let go two salvos," which echoed in great booms across the plaza. The Incas, who had never heard this thundering noise before, at first looked around in confusion as several men lay in bloody heaps, struck point-blank by the cannon. Then came the shrill blast of a trumpet and the sudden shout of 168 men screaming a battle paean as they flung open the doors of the surrounding buildings and lunged outside into the late-afternoon sunlight, smashing directly into the crowds of unarmed Incas.

According to Pedro Pizarro, "the Indians were thrown into confusion and panicked. The Spaniards fell upon them and began to kill." Nor were the Incas even able to defend themselves, since they carried only a few ceremonial weapons.

The slaughter must have been horrific, with the Spaniards cutting, jabbing, and hacking in all directions, and the Incas "so filled with fear," according to eyewitness Juan Ruiz de Arce, "that they climbed on top of one another—to such an extent that they formed mounds and suffocated one another."

As Inca blood filled the plaza, Pizarro launched the second phase of the attack—the kidnapping of the Inca. According to Pizarro's private secretary, Francisco de Jerez, "the Governor took out his sword and dagger, and, with the Spaniards who were with him, entered amongst the Indians most valiantly; and, with only four men who were able to follow him, he came to the litter where Atahualpa was, and fearlessly seized him by the arm, crying out Santiago . . . not being able to pull him out of the litter because he was raised so high. Then the Spaniards made such a slaughter amongst those who carried the litter that they fell to the ground, and, if the governor had not protected Atahualpa, that proud man would there have paid for all the cruelties he had committed."^ Pizarro, in defending Atahualpa from his own men's swords, received a minor cut on the hand from a Castilian's blade—the only Spanish casualty that day.

Pedro Cataño, one of Soto's most loyal outriders, who dictated a brief memoir later in life that is bordering on worshipful of Soto, claims that he and Soto were closely involved with the actual capture of the Inca. During the early confusion of the attack, Cataño recalls in his third-person narrative, recorded by a scribe, that "the Captain Hernando de Soto came out with three others on horseback, the witness [Cataño] being one of the men with this group, because they were friends, and in this way they came out and went for the litter among the Indians, and . . . fighting as they went, they joined the secret armies [commanded by Pizarro] and in this way they seized the *cacique* . . ."

After snatching his prize, Pizarro hustled the stunned Inca into the Temple of the Sun at the edge of town, where he was placed under heavy guard. At first, the Inca was sure the Spaniards would kill him. But Pizarro assured him he would not, and topped off the evening by once again inviting the emperor to supper.

The killing raged on until long after darkness fell over the valley. At one point, the press of Incas desperate to escape toppled a wall and opened a breach into the valley. Incas poured out and tried to run for their lives, but the cavalry pursued them, with the Spaniards shouting, "Do not let any escape!" and "Spear them!' " Soto himself led a squadron of twenty-two men in this grisly operation, with the Spaniards "continuing to lance Indians in the fields"—including troops from Atahualpa's main army that had come to see what was happening. Late that night the massacre finally ended with a peal of the Spanish army's trumpeters sounding the recall.

Most chroniclers put the death count from this slaughter at eight thousand, while Atahualpa, who had access to a more reliable count, said seven thousand died.^ This means that each Spaniard at Cajamarca killed an average of some forty unarmed Indians during this bloodletting, with lead horsemen such as Soto killing considerably more. Most of the Incas killed that afternoon were no ordinary soldiers, however. They were the elite of Atahualpa's government—his nobles, governors, generals, priests, and advisors—those most responsible for running the imperial government, whose sudden death en masse dealt a devastating blow for an empire that had already lost thousands of its ruling class in the recent civil war.

✢   ✢   ✢

What was served that night for supper is not recorded, though several chroniclers describe the euphoric mood of the usually taciturn governor, and the self-congratulatory speechifying the Inca was forced to endure. "The Governor," writes Cristóbal de Mena, "was very pleased over the victory which God our Lord had given us and he asked the *cacique* why he was sad"—as if losing seven thousand men and being captured were not reason enough—"and [the Governor] told him not to be sorrowful because . . . in all the lands through which we had come there were very great men and all these had been made friends and subjects of the Emperor for war and peace and that he should not be frightened at having been taken prisoner by us.^

"[Atahualpa] answered half smiling that he was not sad about that, but because he had expected to make the Governor a prisoner and that the reverse had come true and for this reason he was sad."

Another eyewitness, Miguel de Estete, says the Inca "told of his great intentions: what was to have been done with the Spaniards and the horses . . . He had decided to take and breed the horses and mares, which were the thing he admired most; and to sacrifice some of the Spaniards to the sun and castrate others for service in his household and in guarding his women." When asked why he allowed himself to be duped by riding into this trap, he replied: "I was deceived by my Captains, who told me to think lightly of the Spaniards." Atahualpa knew as well as anyone, however, that the real reason he had been captured was because he had grossly misjudged these strangers, toying with them and allowing them to come to Cajamarca when he might easily have destroyed them on several occasions.

Yet who could have imagined that 168 men, even armed with steel and horses, posed a serious threat to a monarch encamped in the midst of at least forty thousand soldiers? Nor did it cross the Inca's mind that the strangers would attack first against such odds, launching a surprise assault even before the two leaders met.

This hardly means the outcome was as inevitable as Pizarro claimed. Out of earshot from Atahualpa, the Spaniards exclaimed that they could not believe their phenomenal good luck. Even the usually terse and haughty secretary of Pizarro, Francisco de Jerez, could hardly believe it as he writes: "The Governor, with great joy, said: 'I give thanks to God our Lord, and we all, gentlemen, ought to give thanks for the great miracle we have wrought this day.' "

But neither the Spaniards nor the Inca that night fully grasped the situation, that the world's second-largest empire had just been dealt a near-fatal blow by a handful of fighters who just a few hours earlier had been urinating in their pants out of sheer terror, convinced they were going to die.

Now the question was, what would they do with their victory?

✣ 13 ✣

13,000 Pounds of Gold

THE MORNING AFTER ATAHUALPA'S capture, Hernando de Soto woke up early for another round of marauding. As the sun at 13,500 feet dissolved the mists and chill of the night, he strapped on his armor, sword, and helmet and assembled his outriders in the plaza of Cajamarca, still soaked in blood. Thousands of corpses littered the ground—Inca nobles, priests, *caciques,* and servants lying in great heaps, their splendid clothes torn and stained as "Spaniards in the camp made Indian prisoners remove the dead from the square."

Thundering out of the city's gate, Soto probably did not yet realize his life had been transformed forever by what had happened in the past few hours—from that of a successful but obscure frontiersman to a soon-to-be sensation throughout the Hispanic world. In the coming weeks, as word spread to the colonies and then to Europe about the kidnapping of the Inca, the exploits of the flamboyant Hernando de Soto would be told again and again, first by messengers, storytellers, and *trovadores,* then by chroniclers, historians, poets, and novelists—about how Soto became the first European to journey into the Andes, and was the first to meet the Inca Atahualpa, whom he audaciously entertained with a display of Castilian horsemanship before leading one of the units of cavalry in the attack at Cajamarca.

On that cool November morning, however, fame was far from Soto's mind. Tense and on guard as he sat up high in his Moorish saddle, he was off on yet another risky mission—taking thirty men to check on Atahualpa's forty-thousand-man infantry, still encamped four miles to the east. Earlier that morning, Pizarro had forced Atahualpa to issue orders to his army to surrender. The Spaniards, however, had no idea if the Inca had actually complied, or if the fighters would give up if their emperor ordered them to. Riding warily in standard battle formation—a tight, flying-wing arrangement, with Soto in the middle of two flanks splayed out behind him in the shape of a *V*—the platoon first reached the Inca's sentries posted on the highway, and then the first rows of tents. Here they were met by tens of thousands of stunned soldiers, reeling from the realization that their great victory in the civil war had just been transformed by an unimaginable disaster. Riding slowly up the lines of tents, Soto solemnly acknowledged signals of acquiescence by Inca unit commanders, captains, and senior officers, who flashed him the sign of the cross with their fingers, a signal devised by Pizarro, and passed on by order of Atahualpa.^

Two days earlier, these same troops had heckled Soto and his outriders as they passed by on their way to meet the Inca, "saying they were sorry for us because we were going to get killed." But no one was making fun now as the Spaniards quickly finished the formalities of surrender, and ordered the Incas to turn over their weapons. Later, Pizarro ordered the troops to disband and "go to their homes," though hundreds of *caciques* and senior leaders stayed on, it being protocol for them to remain with the Inca's court, even under these conditions. Pizarro allowed the Inca himself to set up a sizable household inside his heavily guarded rooms, so that he could continue to administer the empire, and to live amidst the luxuries and ceremony he was accustomed to.

Meanwhile, once Soto finished with the formalities of the surrender, he and his men began looting. Still wary about a possible attack, he kept his men in good order, leading them first to the Inca's palace by the hot springs—a small fairy-tale structure plastered bright red with bitumen, crowned in rosewood,^ and surrounded by a sea of resplendent tents. Made of spun wool dyed in reds, oranges, greens, and purples, this sprawling city of color belonged to the scores of nobles, *caciques,* senior military officers, and court officials who always traveled with the Inca, most of whom now lay dead inside the walls of Cajamarca. The Spaniards wasted no time. Gathering up a train of Inca servants to use as porters, Soto and his outriders ransacked the palace and the richest tents, seizing "monstrous effigies, large and small dishes, pitchers, jugs, basins and large drinking vessels." In just two or three hours, they gathered loot worth a staggering eighty thousand pesos—one-sixth the entire kitty of the Nicaraguan conquest, and nearly a fifth of the total stolen during the sixteen years the Spaniards were active in Darién. By noon, they were back in Cajamarca, where the men crowded around the outriders to stare at the incredible haul in disbelief, knowing that each one of them was now richer than most had dreamed possible.

The euphoria wore off quickly, however, as the reality of their situation sank in. For even though they held Atahualpa prisoner, and had disbanded his army in Cajamarca, the Spaniards' position deep in Inca territory remained precarious. Most troubling was the fact that large Inca armies remained in the field to the south and north, under the command of seasoned generals whose forces outnumbered the invaders at least five hundred to one. The Inca assured Pizarro that his men would not dare attack unless he commanded them to, a claim they could only pray was true.

As for Atahualpa, his own shock and horror soon gave way to the realization that his life would be spared, at least for now—which got him thinking about a plan to extricate himself. Indeed, as the Sun King watched his captors come and go, and the avaricious enthusiasm that greeted Soto's return from looting the royal palace, it didn't take him long to understand that these strangers had an unnatural attraction to the precious metals his people called "the sweat of the sun" and the "tears of the moon." This gave him the idea to propose one of history's most audacious ransoms.

His plan was to offer the Spaniards so much "sweat" and "tears" they would be overwhelmed, and gladly release him and go away—a scheme he set into motion by asking Pizarro to meet him in one of his rooms. Here, to the astonishment of the crusty old conquistador, the Emperor of the Four Quarters took a piece of chalk and dramatically drew a line as high as he could reach on the wall, promising to fill the entire space with treasure up to this mark—once with gold and twice with silver.

Of course, the thought of ransom had crossed the Spaniards' minds. But not even in their wildest fantasies would they have even considered asking for such a treasure, equal to the greatest fortunes in Spain. So stunned was Pizarro that he immediately ordered his secretary, Francisco de Jerez, to write down the deal on paper for Atahualpa's mark before he changed his mind. The governor then assembled Soto and other senior staff to witness the formal pledge.

According to Jerez's account, the room in question "measured 22 feet long by 17 feet wide," which Atahualpa promised to fill "to a white line half way up its height"—which was over eight feet high. "[U]p to this level," says Jerez, the Inca agreed to "fill the room with various objects of gold—jars, pots, tiles and other pieces. He would also give the entire chamber filled twice over with silver. And he would complete this within two months." Pizarro, in turn, promised to restore Atahualpa "to his former liberty, provided he did no treason," and that he return in exile to Quito, "the land that his father had left to him."

✢   ✢   ✢

Once again, the Spaniards could not believe their luck. For not only did this ransom mean they would be wealthy men, it also meant that Atahualpa would see to it they were not harmed—as long as he believed he would be released. This gave the Spaniards an unexpected hiatus to assess their situation, and to send out word to San Miguel and the world about their feat. Pizarro also had a chance to summon desperately needed reinforcements from Panama, where his partner, Diego de Almagro, was raising an army of fresh recruits. Meanwhile, the governor allowed Atahualpa to administer the empire from his rooms in Cajamarca—to receive envoys, issue orders, and consult with advisors. This arrangement not only kept the empire functioning, but at peace. "We have him prisoner in our power," wrote Gaspar de Gárate, a young soldier who sent a letter home to his father in Spain, "and with him prisoner, a man can go by himself 500 leagues without getting killed, instead they give you whatever you need and carry you on their shoulders in a litter."

Freed for the moment from the fear of imminent attack, the Spaniards also found time to sample the offerings of Cajamarca, and to learn more about the empire they hoped to conquer. Deprived of even minimal comforts these past months, Pizarro's men helped themselves to whatever they could find. Most took on large retinues of servants and concubines, and spent the warm days and frigid nights gorging themselves on *chicha* beer, maize cakes, cocoa, and the odd tubers the Indians called *papas*—which ranged from our familiar potato to other potatoes that taste like chocolate and pine nuts. To keep his men occupied and sharp, Pizarro also arranged for the usual games of combat and strategy, holding tournaments and jousts, and playing endless games of dice, cards, and chess. Once, a bored Atahualpa even helped sponsor a wrestling match, pitting a famed Inca wrestler named Tucuycuyuche against the Spanish champion, Alonso Díaz. The Inca champion, however, lost after a grueling duel, in yet another setback for Inca pride.

Another diversion for the Spaniards, including Soto, was the Inca himself. His habits, intellect, and almost Castilian arrogance greatly impressed his captors. According to Jerez, Atahualpa "reasoned well, and when the Spaniards understood what he said, they knew him to be a wise man. He was cheerful; but, when he spoke to his subjects, he was very haughty, and showed no sign of pleasure."

The conquistadors also watched with fascination the daily rituals of a man considered semidivine by his people; who ate only from the finest vessels, wore no garment twice, spoke directly to only the highest born, and received visitors sitting behind a transparent screen held up by female retainers. According to Pedro Pizarro, every item he touched was burned—"reduced to ashes and thrown into the air," including "the clothes he had discarded, the bones of meat or birds he had eaten, [and] the cores of the ears of corn he had held in his hands." He did not even "spit on the ground when he expectorated," adds Ruiz de Arce. "A woman held out her hand and he spat into it."

How much Soto saw of the Inca is unknown, though Garcilaso de la Vega, the half-Inca who wrote both a biography of Soto's Florida expedition and a detailed history of his own people, hints he commanded Atahualpa's guard. If true, this means Soto got to know the Inca well, spending countless hours with him talking and playing chess, which the Inca is said to have learned and become adept at.^

Most diverting of all during this lull in the conquest, however, was the gold that began arriving in late November, strapped to long trains of llamas— "vases, jars, and pots of gold, and much silver." Jerez reports that great fortunes of treasure arrived every day; "on some days twenty thousand, on others thirty thousand, on others still fifty thousand or sixty thousand pesos of gold arrived. The Governor ordered it all to be put in the house where Atahualpa had his guards, until he had accomplished what he had promised." At one point, some of Pizarro's overanxious men began crushing gold objects in the ransom chamber so it would hold more. "Why do you do that?" a frustrated Atahualpa asked. "I will give you so much gold that you will be satiated with it!"

Life in Cajamarca, however, became more tense as time wore on, and rumors began to come in claiming Inca troops were massing to attack—all of which Atahualpa hotly denied, insisting "that throughout the land there was no one who would move without his permission."

Pizarro had little choice but to believe him, though he felt it prudent to dispatch troops to investigate the more persistent rumors—and, to keep his increasingly nervous men busy, to look for gold. One of these patrols left in early January, when Hernando Pizarro took twenty cavalry and some infantry to investigate a report that one of Atahualpa's generals, Chalcuchima, was massing soldiers fifty miles to the south. When this turned out to be false, Hernando decided to ride even farther south to plunder the temple of Pachacámac, an ancient pyramidal complex near present-day Lima. Another sortie left in mid-February, when Pizarro dispatched three men to Cuzco with orders to speed up the collection there of the Inca's treasure. Riding with great ceremony on noble litters provided by Atahualpa, a minor captain named Martín Bueno and two other footmen, Pedro de Moguer and Juan de Zárate, journeyed south 650 miles to the Inca capital, becoming the first Europeans to set eyes on what the Peruvians called the navel of the world.^

Apparently, Soto stayed in Cajamarca during these months. But he was hardly idle. Shortly after the Inca's capture, Pizarro appointed him military governor of Cajamarca, in charge of the daily chores of administering the military government in the city—organizing supplies, supervising the legal system, paying officials, deciding disputes, and performing other executive duties. Because we hear none of the usual stories about Soto dashing off on sorties or reconnaissance, we can assume that for once he concentrated on his administrative obligations. Of course, he had a strong incentive. For one of his responsibilities was overseeing the collection of Atahualpa's ransom, as well as guarding the Inca himself—if Garcilaso is correct. The Spaniards' precarious situation also kept the work interesting in Cajamarca, as Pizarro pointedly kept his best field captain close at hand in case of an attack.^

Soto is mentioned only once during this period by an eyewitness chronicler—as a participant in the brutal interrogation and torture of Chalcuchima, Atahualpa's commander in chief. The incident occurred in April 1533, after this great Inca general was tricked into leaving the protection of his army in Jauja to travel to Cajamarca. Hernando Pizarro engineered this deception, forging an order from Atahualpa summoning his general to visit him, and then promptly seizing him the moment he arrived at Cajamarca.

Chalcuchima's loss to the already-disheartened native resistance was devastating. As the most senior commander in Peru, and the most successful and respected of the late Inca Huayna Capac's generals, he was one of the few Indian leaders capable of organizing a united resistance in Atahualpa's absence. When the Inca found out Chalcuchima had been taken, Mena says he "was deeply distressed . . . but since he was very astute he pretended that it pleased him."

The Spaniards wasted no time in interrogating the old general. Presumably, he knew military secrets of immediate value, which would have prompted the usual beatings and proddings with hot irons. Yet Mena reports that military concerns played a minor role in the initial interrogations. Convinced that Chalcuchima had plundered great quantities of loot when Atahualpa's troops captured Cuzco and other cities in the civil war, the general's tormentors, led by Soto and Hernando Pizarro, initially wanted to know only one thing—how much treasure the Quito army had taken, and where it was hidden. Chalcuchima answered "that he had no gold," insisting that his armies had not dared loot Cuzco, a sacred city that Atahualpa had planned to claim as his capital.

But Soto and the others came from a culture where loot was the by-product of any military action, and did not believe him. Soto "took him aside and threatened to burn him unless he told the truth," says Mena. But he "gave the same answer as before. They then erected a stake and tied him to it, and brought much firewood and straw, saying that they would set fire to him unless he told the truth. He asked to call his lord. [Atahualpa] came with the Governor and spoke to his captain, who was tied up." Chalcuchima explained his situation to his sovereign, who told him to say nothing, telling him this was a ploy to intimidate him, "for they would not dare to burn him. They then asked him for the gold once more and he would not tell about it. But as soon as they set a little fire to him, he asked that his lord be taken away from him, for he was signaling him with his eyes not to tell the truth. Atahualpa was therefore removed."

Chalcuchima eventually did talk, though only about military matters. He told Soto as the fire smoldered under him "that on the *cacique's* orders he had come on three or four occasions with a large force against the Christians. But, as the Christians knew, his ruler Atahualpa had himself ordered him to withdraw for fear that the Christians would kill him . . ."

Apparently, this information satisfied Soto and the others, for Chalcuchima was taken down off the charred pole and carried "to the house of Hernando Pizarro," his body covered with blisters and open wounds. In Pizarro's *casa* the Spaniards "kept a close guard on him. Such a guard was necessary, for the greater part of the army obeyed the orders of this captain even more than they did those of their lord the *cacique* Atahualpa himself . . . And although he was half burned, many Indians came to serve him because they were his servants." Hernando Pizarro adds that Chalcuchima came to him "with his legs and arms burned and his tendons shriveled; and I cured him in my lodging."^

Hernando de Soto's role in Chalcuchima's torture should dispel any lingering notion that Soto was morally superior to his peers. To underscore this point, Raúl Porras Barrenechea wrote a short essay in 1937 sarcastically titled *Soto el bueno,* "Soto the Good," where he uses the Chalcuchima story to lambaste certain "purple Anglo-Saxon biographies and histories" that "praise the magnanimity of Soto with the Indians in contrast to the cruel criminality of Pizarro." He compiles a devastating list of Soto's cruelties, starting in Panama and Nicaragua, and taking us through to Peru. He also could have cited incidents in *La Florida* where Soto sliced off hands and noses to punish petty infractions, and routinely ordered Indians hacked to death, burned, and torn to shreds by war dogs. "The true Soto," concludes Porras Barrenechea, "was neither better nor worse than other conquistadors, but in no way can we call him a paradigm of blessedness and meekness."

+   +   +

Originally, Atahualpa promised to fill his roomfuls of gold and silver in just two months. But he quickly discovered that not even his near-absolute authority could deliver such a quantity in this short a time. It turned out to be a laborious process that involved sending envoys repeatedly to Cuzco and other cities with orders to collect all the gold they could, most of it being widely dispersed in palaces, households, and temples in the form of statues, cups, plates, jewelry, and tiles attached to buildings. Transporting such an enormous quantity of gold hundreds of miles was also not easy, as huge trains of llamas labored for weeks to carry the heavy objects across the empire.

Not that Pizarro was complaining over the delay. For he was having his own problems getting word to Panama, and waiting for Diego de Almagro to organize his armada, sail to Peru, and then march up to Cajamarca. As the two months came and went, and the summer months in South America turned to fall in February and March, neither the roomful of gold nor Diego de Almagro and his reinforcements had appeared in the small city high up in the mountains.

By coincidence, when Almagro and the gold finally did come, they arrived at roughly the same time, with Almagro marching into town on April 14, and several hundred llamas arriving soon after, carrying a sizable portion of gold and silver for the ransom.

Almagro's army, however, was not what Pizarro expected. Indeed, his partner had only been able to recruit 153 men—hardly the great army Pizarro had hoped to take against the vast hordes of Inca fighters. Even so, these men nearly doubled Pizarro's troop, which now numbered, with the addition of men coming up from garrisons on the coast, some 350 men. Almagro also brought 50 horses to bolster the all-important cavalry.

One can imagine the excitement in the Spanish camp as the governor rode out to meet the reinforcements as they marched over the pass in the northwest corner of the valley, the small troop bedecked in the usual flags and finery. Outside the gates of the city, Pizarro and his equally resplendent troops stand waiting, arranged in crisp ranks below the high peaks, their own banners waving in the thin mountain air. When they meet, the two old partners exchange greetings, and ride slowly back into the plaza, where solemn Masses and ceremonies soon give way to festivities as the veterans of Cajamarca regale the newcomers with the incredible story of the Inca's capture, and their own personal contributions on that momentous day—already being embellished, no doubt, with each telling.

One man in Cajamarca greeted the arrival of 153 more Spanish conquistadors not with relief, but with anger—mostly directed at himself for being so gullible. This was, of course, the Inca Atahualpa, who only now grasped the reality of his situation—that his captors were not simply a group of marauders seeking plunder, but invaders.

Within days of Almagro's arrival, the last great trains of Inca gold and silver arrived in Cajamarca, where each item was carried into the ransom room and added to the growing pile of glittering cups, earrings, pendants, disks, and statuary, a hoard of art and finery fashioned by countless artists over the centuries—and about to be melted down that spring into small bars of metal carefully weighed and stamped with the royal seal of Castile.

The beauty and craftsmanship lost to the furnaces of Cajamarca can only be guessed at from the few artifacts that remain today, and from descriptions written down by the awestruck Spaniards. They tell of delicately pressed gold leaves fashioned into highly realistic stalks of maize, hibiscus blossoms, palms, and trees ripe with fruit; of elaborate depictions of animals in gold and silver, ranging from renderings of tiny shrews to life-size deer with antlers; of golden statues of Inca deities; of men and women making love; of children; and of toy-size boats, llamas, people, houses, and tiny litters.^

On May 3, as the heap of treasure reached ever closer to the Inca's chalk line, Pizarro ordered his goldsmiths to fire up their smelters. Ten days later, the three envoys to Cuzco arrived just ahead of the largest llama train of gold yet, stripped from Cuzco's temples and palaces. These included solid-gold panels removed from the walls of the city's great Temple of the Sun, called the Coricancha, and two massive, beautifully wrought fountains of gold, one worth nineteen thousand pesos, the other twelve thousand pesos.^

Melting down such a quantity of treasure was an enormous operation, though one suspects the *entrada*'s goldsmith, Pedro de Pineda, relished it as he supervised a gang of Indian smiths working nine forges day and night, melting down an average of sixty thousand pesos a day.^ "Over eleven tons of gold objects were fed into the fires," reported Pizarro's secretary, "to produce 13,400 pounds of 22½ carat good gold; the silver objects yielded some 26,000 pounds of good silver." When the fires finally cooled, the treasure totaled 1,326,539 pesos of gold and 51,610 marks of silver.^ At today's prices,* this equals $88.5 million in gold and $2.5 million in silver, for a total ransom of $91 million.

As always, a fifth of the loot was reserved for the crown. The rest was divided into shares determined by a committee of *repartidores*^—distributors— that included Hernando de Soto and one of Soto's partisans, Miguel de Estete. (Another Soto man, Pedro Díaz, was the silversmith in charge of weighing the treasure.) Francisco Pizarro, Hernando Pizarro, and Gonzalo de Pineda rounded out this five-man committee.

With input from the king's appointed royal officers,^ the distributors met in the governor's quarters late in May to argue out who would get what amount of gold, with the most important decisions being what would constitute standard shares for a horseman, and for a footman. They finally settled on shares of 90 pounds of gold and 180 of silver for cavalrymen—which included a share for each man's horse—and roughly half this amount for footmen, with the leaders and investors receiving considerably more.

Soto's place on the committee, however, was not enough to win him the second-largest share, after the governor—which he certainly deserved, given his pivotal role in not only the capture of the Inca, but also in taking the lead in

*1995.

nearly every major step along the path to Cajamarca. Instead, second place went to the man who already had robbed Soto of his position as lieutenant general, Hernando Pizarro. He received 31,080 pesos of gold and 1,267 marks of silver^—almost twice Soto's third-largest share of 17,740 pesos of gold and 724 marks of silver. The governor got far more than either of the Hernandos— a total of 57,220 pesos of gold and 2,350 marks of silver.

By any measure, Soto's share was a staggering amount of loot, though he probably interpreted his poor third-place showing as a snub, if a mild one. Indeed, Pizarro at this time seems to have been carefully balancing his distrust of the ambitious Soto with a realization that even with Almagro's arrival, Hernando de Soto remained his most effective captain in the field. Nor did the governor want to alienate a man who still commanded the loyalty of several dozen Nicaraguans, including the most-talented horsemen in the army.

Significantly, Soto's share exceeded those of Juan and Gonzalo Pizarro, who received the fourth- and fifth-largest shares. He also received more than other senior captains, including Sebastián de Benalcázar, Juan Cortés, Pedro de Candía, Gonzalo de Pineda, Luis Hernández Bueno, and Juan de Salcedo, each of whom the committee awarded just under ten thousand pesos of gold.^

✢   ✢   ✢

With the treasure melted, counted, and distributed, the final business to be concluded in Cajamarca was the fate of Atahualpa. The Spaniards were divided about what to do with their captive. Some wanted him killed, convinced that he would undermine Spanish authority if kept alive. Others wanted him sent into exile in Panama or Spain. Still others thought they should hold on to him as a hostage during the march to Cuzco. Nearly everyone, however, agreed on one point—that it would be suicidal to free the Inca, or to remain in Cajamarca once he realized the Spaniards were reneging on their promise.

Still ensconced in his luxurious prison, the Inca himself watched the process of smelting and distributing the gold with mounting alarm, realizing the Spaniards were making no moves to release him. Fearing they would kill him, he issued a desperate order in early July to his general in the north, Rumiñavi, to march on Cajamarca. He quickly reversed himself, however, knowing the Spaniards would kill him for sure the moment his army drew close to the valley.

As each day passed after the distribution of gold and silver, fresh rumors came in about Inca troops massing, raising Spanish anxieties to near hysteria. One evening, a group of Indian informers appeared at the gates to warn Pizarro that Atahualpa had ordered General Rumiñavi to attack. "All these men . . . are very close to here," said the breathless Indians, talking excitedly to Pizarro, who had rushed out of his apartments after dinner to meet them on the plaza. "They will come by night and will attack this camp," they said, "setting fire to it on all sides. The first person they will endeavor to kill will be you, and they will release their lord Atahualpa from his prison." According to Jerez, who reports this incident, the informers estimated the size of Rumiñavi's army at "two hundred thousand natives," clearly an exaggeration of a force that probably numbered more like twenty or thirty thousand.

Pizarro immediately put his army on alert. He ordered mounted patrols of 50 men dispatched every six hours, and 150 more to remain under arms and ready to fight on a moment's notice. Jerez recalled that "during all these nights the Governor and his captains did not sleep: they were inspecting the watches and arranging what was necessary. During the watches when it was the men's turn to sleep they did not remove their arms, and the horses remained saddled."^

After debriefing the informers and issuing his orders, Pizarro confronted Atahualpa about Rumiñavi. " 'What treason is this you have prepared for me?' " he asked. " 'For me who have treated you with honor, like a brother, and have trusted in your words!' " Atahualpa denied everything, saying, " 'Are you laughing at me? You are always making jokes when you speak to me. What am I, and all my people, that we should trouble such valiant men as you are? Do not talk such nonsense to me.' He said all this," added Jerez, "without betraying a sign of anxiety; but he laughed the better to conceal his evil design, and practiced many other arts such as would suggest themselves to a quick-witted man . . . The Governor ordered a chain to be brought," concludes Jerez, "which was fastened around the neck of Atahualpa."

Faced with what seemed like an imminent assault, Pizarro's senior staff became even more bitterly divided over the Inca emperor's fate. Atahualpa's defenders, including Soto and others who had come to know and respect him during his captivity, argued that it would be an injustice to kill the leader of a great empire without more proof, particularly since he had just made them all wealthy men by fulfilling his side of the agreement. Those favoring execution—led by Diego de Almagro and his lieutenants, who had not shared in the Inca's ransom, and were eager to get on with the conquest so they could gather plunder of their own—charged that Atahualpa had reneged on his pledge not to mass troops. The hot-tempered Almagro said that the Inca would be a constant problem as long as he remained alive, adding that the tiny Spanish force lacked the men to guard him and conduct an effective conquest.

The decision over the Inca's fate was Pizarro's, and his alone. Yet to this day historians argue over the governor's true disposition in this matter. This is because most accounts of the Inca's final days were penned several years after the fact, during the political struggles of the late 1530s, when pro- and anti-Pizarro factions wrote their recollections more with an eye toward portraying their side in a positive light than with relating the truth. Therefore, different accounts disagree on almost every major point, except for two central facts— first, that the governor, faced with a rancorous senior staff, decided to dispatch Hernando de Soto and his outriders to investigate the Rumiñavi rumor;^ and, second, that while Soto was away, Pizarro abruptly executed Atahualpa for treason, only to discover when Soto returned that the rumor was false, and there were no Inca troops headed their way. Beyond this, we have Pizarro sympathizers insisting that their man did not really want to kill Atahualpa, and that he was forced to by Diego de Almagro—who in the late 1530s happened to be Pizarro's chief political rival in Peru. On the other hand, we have Almagroists telling us Pizarro wanted the Inca executed.

This finger-pointing began when the outside world reacted to the execution with horror, as virtually everyone condemned the killing of a great monarch with no proof he had committed any crime. To this day, Pizarro's reputation remains marred by this senseless act, which his followers and associates— many of whom were defending their own support of the execution at Cajamarca—tried mightily to defend in their versions of history.

These include Francisco de Jerez, the Governor's personal secretary, who claims the decision to execute the Inca was made hastily during a card game one evening shortly after Soto left to investigate the Rumiñavi rumor. According to Jerez's story, Pizarro was gambling with friends when Diego de Almagro burst into the room dragging a Nicaraguan Indian scout who insisted he had just seen a horde of Peruvian soldiers three leagues from Cajamarca, gathering for an attack. "Is your Lordship going to allow us to die?" Jerez says Almagro shouted, to which Pizarro's fellow gamblers and cronies responded by loudly calling for the Inca to die—a demand quickly taken up by most of the army as the rumor spread. Thus Pizarro was forced to take action, says Jerez, who adds that the governor was so saddened by the thought of executing the Inca that he was reduced to tears. But what could he do, asks Jerez, hinting that to have denied his army's demand might have resulted in dire consequences, perhaps even mutiny.

Eyewitnesses and historians less enamored of Pizarro tell an entirely different story. They claim that the governor sided from the start with Almagro, and duped Soto and other Atahualpa defenders into leaving Cajamarca to stop them from interfering with the execution. Pascual de Andagoya, for one, accuses Pizarro of deceit, saying he "made Indian sorcerers who bore ill-will against Atahualpa declare that he had an army ready to kill them. Atahualpa replied that it was a lie . . . and that they should send someone out on the plain where it was said that the army was [allegedly massing] to verify the story. Captain

Soto was sent out for this purpose with some companions. But Pizarro and his councilors, as was prearranged, killed Atahualpa before Soto's return." Juan Ruiz de Arce, who rode with Soto to investigate the rumor, also accused Pizarro of "practicing deception on the conquistadors."

Though we will probably never know the truth about Francisco Pizarro's intentions, the timing of Atahualpa's swift trial and execution, occurring almost immediately after Soto's departure, seems highly suspicious, particularly since the governor could easily have waited until Soto returned with his report a few days later.

Once the decision was made, Pizarro moved swiftly. Rushing through a sham trial, he charged the Inca with everything from conspiring to attack the Spaniards to practicing polygamy because he had more than one wife, finding him guilty of all charges in late July.

Originally, the non-Christian Atahualpa was sentenced to burn at the stake. This was commuted at the last minute to death by garroting when the Sun King—who proved less inclined to suffering than many of his aides, including Chalcuchima—agreed to convert to Christianity. On July 26, Father Vicente performed the conversion ceremony and baptismal.^ Shortly thereafter, the executioner strung a damp leather thong around the Inca's neck, which contracted as it dried in the arid mountain air, slowly and painfully strangling to death the last emperor of the original Inca Empire.

A few days after Atahualpa's garroting, Soto and his men returned to Cajamarca with the news that the Rumiñavi rumor was false—that there was no Inca army massing to the north, and, therefore, no basis on which to execute Atahualpa.

Not surprisingly, this information cast a pallor over the city as Pizarro, Almagro, and the others responsible for Atahualpa's summary death began to realize they had made a terrible blunder. For not only had they directly violated the *Requerimiento* by killing a nonbelligerent *cacique,* which was common enough during the *conquista,* but they also had made the mistake of executing a *"cacique"* who happened to rule one of the world's largest empires.

According to witnesses, the governor at least pretended to be stunned by this news, "showing much emotion," with "his eyes wet with tears," though one wonders if this show of contriteness (and yet more tears) had more to do with Pizarro's fear that his reputation might be sullied than a genuine remorse for killing an innocent man. Pedro Pizarro adds that his uncle, the governor, "sorrowed deeply for having killed him; and Soto was even more grieved for, said he, and he was right, it would have been much better to send him to Spain, and [he said] that he would [gladly] have taken on the duty himself of setting him upon the sea."^

Indeed, Hernando de Soto was the most senior of Pizarro's critics in Caja-marca, though he was hardly alone, as some biographers have suggested. At least a dozen others went on record opposing the execution. Most were Soto's men, though also prominent in their own right. These included Miguel de Estete, Francisco de Fuentes, Luis Maza, and Pedro Cataño. Some of Almagro's followers likewise registered their disapproval, including a certain Luis de Moscoso, a young *hidalgo* from Badajoz who later became Soto's second-in-command in *La Florida,* and later still served as acting governor in Florida after Soto's death.^

Outside of Peru, Soto's criticism was echoed across the Spanish world and beyond. In Panama, Gaspar de Espinosa's reaction was typical when he wrote the king saying: "[T]hey killed the *cacique* because they claim he had made a great assembly of men to attack our Spaniards. Because of this the governor was persuaded—almost forced—to do it, with great pleas and demands put to him by Your Majesty's officials . . . In my opinion [the Inca's] guilt should have been very clearly established and proved, and there should have been no possible alternative whatsoever, before it became necessary to kill a man who had fallen into their hands and who had done no harm to any Spaniard or other person." Espinosa blamed the execution on greed, a subject on which he was as expert as any in the Indies. King Charles himself condemned Pizarro's act, saying that he was "displeased by the death of Atahualpa,"^ not only because it was done quickly and without sufficient evidence, but also because it set a bad precedent to have an upstart such as Francisco Pizarro kill a monarch of the Inca's stature. European kings of the sixteenth century were adamant about this point of royal prerogative—that only kings could order kings killed.

As for Soto's moral uprightness on this occasion, one should note that he had reasons other than chivalry to oppose Atahualpa's execution. This is not to say his affection for the Inca was less than genuine. Apparently, the two men enjoyed each other's company, and this may have been motivation enough for Soto to protect the Inca. However, as James Lockhart has suggested: "Atahualpa alive and free would represent a threat to . . . the Pizarros, but for Soto, already in the process of being pushed out, such a fluid and insecure situation might bring with it great opportunities." Garcilaso de la Vega offers yet another intriguing clue to Soto's attachment to the Inca. In his 1605 biography of Soto, he claims that Atahualpa in captivity showered gifts on Soto, because he "took a fancy to him, he being the first Spaniard whom he had seen and spoken to." While this sounds suspiciously like one of Garcilaso's flights of romance, it hints that perhaps the Inca sought to influence Soto with gifts of gold, and that greed may have played a role in Soto's spirited defense.

Whatever Soto's motivation, it's clear he understood far better than Pizarro that executing Atahualpa without cause was pushing beyond the boundaries of what was acceptable behavior, even by the lax standards of the *conquista.*

✢ I4 ✢

The Dash South

SOON AFTER ATAHUALPA'S EXECUTION, Pizarro dispatched a column of Spaniards to San Miguel on the coast. Accompanied by long lines of native porters, they marched slowly across the rugged mountains and harsh deserts, retracing the route taken by the army to Cajamarca seven months earlier. Riding up front was the enormous, bearlike Hernando Pizarro, returning to Spain along with the governor's secretary, Francisco de Jerez, and Captain Cristóbal de Mena. Their mission was to sail home and tell the world what had happened at Cajamarca, to take the king his taxes—a fifth of the total Inca's ransom— and to defend the governor against the growing outrage over Atahualpa's execution.

In San Miguel, the party boarded the *La Concepción,* owned by Ponce and Soto,^ and sailed to Panama and then on to Seville, where they arrived at the quays on the Río Guadalquivir as heroes.* From Seville, they hurried on to visit the king, who gave Jerez and Mena permission to publish the first eyewitness accounts of the Peruvian invasion^—*relaciónes* that not only became instant best-sellers, but also thrust into the limelight the leading figures of the conquest, including one of the most prominent names in the narratives—*el capitán* Hernando de Soto. (Soto comes out in a particularly favorable light in Mena's account, since Mena had a falling-out with the Pizarros; other accounts, including a long letter from Espinosa published in 1534, also praise Soto's role.) This hardly means Hernando de Soto became a household name in Spain, though the general buzz throughout the country about Peru paved the way for Soto's triumphant return home in 1536, and set in motion the fame he would later trade on for the concession to conquer *La Florida.*

*Mena arrived on December 5, 1533, and Hernando Pizarro on January 9, 1534.

+   +   +

Back in Peru, in the aftermath of Atahualpa's execution, both Indians and Spaniards took a moment to consider their respective situations. For the Incas, their god-king's death at the hands of these avaricious foreigners was a devastating blow, but not necessarily fatal. The Peruvians still fielded over a hundred thousand native soldiers, commanded by two of Atahualpa's most able generals—Rumiñavi in the north, and Quizquiz to the south. General Chalcuchima's army—now led by Chalcuchima's second-in-command, Yucra-Hualpa—also remained intact at Jauja, roughly halfway between Cajamarca and Cuzco.

In the short term, the death of Atahualpa was far more troublesome to the Spaniards, who suddenly found themselves more vulnerable to attack than ever without the standoff they had enjoyed during the Inca's incarceration. For eight months, Atahualpa had kept the empire at peace, his armies at bay, and gold flowing into Spanish coffers. Now that he was gone, the most pressing need for Pizarro was to seize the initiative and try to control the succession to the Inca throne by quickly naming a new emperor sympathetic to the Spaniards, before the Incas themselves in either Quito or Cuzco—or both—named a candidate beyond Pizarro's control.

Thus Pizarro moved quickly, taking advantage of the shock wave that momentarily paralyzed the empire when Atahualpa was killed. Within a week of the execution, Pedro Sancho, another of Pizarro's secretaries, tells us that the governor ordered "the immediate assembling in the chief plaza of that city all *caciques* and principal lords who were then living there in company with the dead [ruler]—there were many . . . and from distant lands, and [Pizarro's] intention was to give them another lord who should govern in the name of [His Majesty]." Pizarro's choice was a younger brother of the slain Huascar named Tupac Huallpa. Having escaped the slaughter of his family ordered by Atahualpa, he owed his life to the Spaniards, who had protected him from Atahualpa's assassins.^ Pizarro hoped this would make him beholden to the invaders, though the main impetus for choosing Tupac Huallpa was because he came from the south in the recent war. Indeed, Pizarro understood Incan politics well enough to understand that choosing a southerner would make him and the Spaniards heroes and liberators in the eyes of the Cuzco faction—whose territories he was about to invade. Moreover, it would reinvigorate southern passions against Atahualpa's troops from Quito, whom most in the south considered a foreign army of occupation—when, in fact, they were the Incas' last hope against their true enemy.

The day after the assembled *caciques* overwhelmingly approved Tupac Huallpa as Inca, he was crowned with "the appropriate ceremonies . . . and each [chief] came up to offer him a white plume as a token of vassalage, for this had been the ancient custom among them ever since the country had been conquered by the Incas. After this they sang and danced, and held a great feast."

Later, Pizarro organized a ceremony of his own. Dressing up in his most impressive silks and armor, and accompanied by Soto and other *hidalgos* bedecked in their Renaissance finery, he read to the assembled *caciques* the *Requerimiento,* little changed from King Ferdinand's time. The Indians listened solemnly and then agreed to submit to the Spanish king and God, each signaling his submission by taking a royal standard and raising it above his head three times, to the sound of trumpets. "They then went to embrace the Governor who received them with great delight at their prompt submission," says Pedro Sancho. "When it was all over the Inca and the chiefs held great festivities. There were daily celebrations and entertainments with games and parties which were generally held in the Governor's house."

+   +   +

Pizarro finally departed Cajamarca on August 11, 1533, headed for Cuzco, 750 miles to the south across a breathtaking topography of mountains, high ridges, and deep-cut valleys. The army was in high spirits, buoyed by the coronation ceremony and the enthusiasm of their Cuzco "allies." Yet the governor remained cautious, fearing an attack by one of the Quito armies. Pedro Sancho says they marched in battle formation, "always using great vigilance in learning of the affairs of the land, and always having both a vanguard and a rear guard." Most likely, Soto and Diego de Almagro—also known as a formidable horseman and outrider—rotated the command of the vanguard, which apparently rode only a short distance ahead to the keep the army intact in case of ambush. In this sort of tight marching formation Pizarro would have deployed horsemen in small squads to patrol ahead, behind, and on either side of the column. Tupac Huallpa also supplied him with native scouts and informers, and with messengers sent ahead to prepare food and lodging.

One of the great mysteries of the Spanish invasion of Peru is why the Quitoans once again failed to take advantage of their overwhelming numbers to attack at any of several strategic passes and river valleys. Apparently, they preferred to have the Spaniards come to them in their strongholds far to the south. This meant Pizarro and his 350 men were able to move fast and unhindered across the rugged topography of the central Andes, following the Pacific side of the great divide that runs alongside the Huaylas River. Marching unimpeded along wide paved and graded highways, they were greeted—with the young Inca in tow—as liberators, with local "*caciques* and lords . . . providing all that they needed."

On August 31, the army crossed its first major Inca bridge, spanning the

Santa River near the town of Huaylas. Miguel de Estete describes how the Incas built these magnificent structures. "At a point where the rivers were narrowest and most terrifying," he writes, "and their waters most compressed, they make a great stone foundation on either bank. Thick wooden beams are laid across this stonework, and they fasten across the river cables of a thick osier, made like anchor ropes except that these cables are each some three *palmos* [three and a half feet] thick. When half a dozen of these have been joined and laid across the river, to the width of a cart, they are interwoven with strong hemp and reinforced with sticks. When this is done, they place edges on either side like the sideboards of an oxcart . . . And so it lies suspended in mid-air, far above the water."^

After crossing the Santa River and resting in Huaylas, Pizarro climbed into a high valley between the bare rock ridges of the Cordillera Negra to the west, and the snowy peaks of the Cordillera Blanca to the east, the latter topped off by Mount Huascarán, the tallest mountain in Peru at 22,200 feet. Now marching above the tree line, the army passed the heads of several major rivers, where it became so bitterly cold at night that snow fell. Some of the men became dizzy and nauseous, suffering from *soroche,* the Quechua name for high-altitude sickness.

By now, more than a month into the march, the euphoria of the final days in Cajamarca had again given way to a palpable tension. For not only had the Quitoans not attacked as expected, but many also suspected once again that the Indians were drawing them into a trap. Anxieties grew daily as Pizarro's column passed through towns and villages entirely emptied of people, but fully stocked with food and supplies. This eerie stillness in the high, thin air, coupled with a topography that daily provided excellent sites for ambushes, soon made the men nervous enough that Pizarro decided he must take action.^

As always, this meant making a bold lunge forward—in this case, splitting off a troop of cavalry to plunge ahead and try to surprise the Quito army before they could organize their own offensive. The governor himself, though he was a poor horseman, led seventy-five mounts, accompanied by Soto, Almagro, and Juan Pizarro,^ with the treasurer Alonso Riquelme left behind in command of the main army. He guarded the prisoner Chalcuchima, the heaps of Cajamarca gold, and the *entrada*'s heavy baggage. With "three or four light horsemen" going ahead to look for Inca scouts and sentries, Pizarro's troop moved with the urgency of men driven by mounting fear, crossing a rugged pass where informers had claimed the Incas planned a surprise attack. Sancho describes the pass as being "so full of difficulties that it would be [nearly] impossible to go up it, because there was a bad road of stone down into the gully where all the riders had to dismount, after which it was necessary to go up the heights by a slope about a league long, the greater part of which was steep and difficult forest."

Near dark that same day, they reached the village of Tarma, a compact and indefensible little town tightly wedged between two steep hills. Pizarro stopped only long enough to feed the horses, and to stock up on food, before climbing back up onto a mountain height above the city to make camp. This was a tension-filled overnight spent "always on the alert and having the horses saddled." It also was extremely cold as "the men were without [proper] food and even without any comfort because there was neither firewood nor water, nor had they [in their haste] brought their tents with them to shelter them, because of which they all nearly died of cold on account of the fact that it rained much early in the night and then snowed so that the arms and clothes were drenched." And if this were not bad enough, the men knew that before dawn the next morning they would march on Jauja, headquarters of General Yucra-Hualpa's army.

Early the next day, as the first light glowed silver-blue on the horizon, the Spaniards rose, patted down their freezing mounts, and headed south toward Jauja. With his breath steaming in the cold, Pizarro issued orders dividing his men into three squadrons led by himself, Soto, and Almagro. "In this order they journeyed to Porsi," writes Sancho, "a league from Jauja," where they were greeted by a grisly sight—over four thousand rotting corpses hanging from trees, another carnage committed by Atahualpa's troops during the civil war, and yet another alarming reminder of the Quito army's ferocity.

But the Spaniards kept moving, passing by pre-Inca ruins scattered across the hills, until they came to a steep ridge overlooking the broad, flat Jauja Valley. At the far end they could see the city and, for the first time in the eighteen months since leaving the Isle of Puná, their enemy—numbering some ten to twenty thousand.^

The Spaniards immediately steeled themselves for battle, though as they descended into the valley along a steep path, they found themselves engulfed not by hostile soldiers, but by local Indians who had suffered greatly under the occupying Quito army, and greeted them as liberators. Meanwhile, down below, the enemy saw the Spaniards and deployed to meet them in the first major engagement since the invaders had arrived at Tumbez.

The Quito army, however, was caught largely unprepared, being unfamiliar with how quickly one can cover great distances on a horse. Pizarro was also extraordinarily lucky, arriving when the Quitoans were not dug in, but moving out of Jauja to a more defensible position across a small river—the first step toward heading south to join forces with Quizquiz's army in Cuzco. Startled to find a troop of Spanish horsemen suddenly bearing down on them, the

Quitoans reacted first by deploying six hundred men to race on foot across the river, with orders to burn down Jauja's thatch-topped storehouses, arranged in neat rows on a rise above the city. This was to prevent the Spaniards from capturing and using them to feed their army. But Pizarro's men, again relying on the swiftness of their horses, charged across the valley to stop the arsonists after they had torched only a few buildings. Almagro's platoon, which was closest to the storehouses, crashed at full charge into these men, cutting them down with lances and swords as they splashed through the shallow river. Hardly pausing, they kept advancing, a few minutes later reaching the rear of the main Quito army as it struggled to move up into the hills.

At this point, both armies were largely ignorant about how the other fought. Of course, the Spaniards possessed their overwhelming edge in technology, pitting their swords, steel-tipped lances, horses, and armor against the Incas' wood and stone clubs, maces, javelins, and highly accurate slings for tossing stones.

The Indians of Peru possessed two formidable advantages of their own—their great numbers, and the discipline of their professional soldiers, whose lines would hold time and again despite savage attacks by Spanish cavalry. Yet the Quito army and their leaders still remained ignorant of why the Spaniards were there, and what motivated them. Even after Atahualpa's execution, neither they nor the Incas of Cuzco could yet comprehend that three or four hundred men were contemplating the conquest of this great empire. This meant the Quitoans repeatedly reacted to Spanish offensives without a coherent plan, their leaders unable to decide whether the strangers meant to attack, offer a show of force, or parley.

The result was disastrous for the northern army, as some units broke away from the Spanish charge as if under orders to retreat, while others turned to fight, only to become entangled in a field of maize that kept them from using their numbers to overwhelm their enemy. Still, scores of native soldiers threw themselves at their attackers, slowing down the cavalry's advance enough so that most of the Indians could retreat in good order. Skirmishes continued for the rest of that day and the next as squadrons of Spaniards harassed Inca columns marching toward Quizquiz's position 300 miles to the south, with Pizarro's men picking off stragglers, stealing whatever treasure they could find, and seizing sizable numbers of porters and servants. "The pursuit," writes Ruiz de Arce, who rode with Soto in one of these forward units, "continued for four leagues [sixteen miles] and many Indians were speared. We took all the serving people and the women . . . there was a good haul of both gold and silver."

The Quitoans must have been terribly discouraged by this first savage encounter. But the bloody skirmish had one positive outcome for the natives, since for the first time since the Europeans arrived, the captains and generals of Atahualpa's army were able to observe the Spaniards' use of weapons and strategies—including how they used their horses to such devastating advantage on flat ground—an insight seasoned commanders such as Yucra-Hualpa and Quizquiz would later incorporate into their strategies as they braced again to repel the enemy.

Pizarro rested his men in Jauja for two weeks, relishing the chance to stay in a city much larger and richer than Cajamarca. Once again, he ordered his men to restrain themselves from plundering, as Pizarro continued to play up his role as the supposed "liberator" to the powerful local *cacique,* a policy that later paid off when he provided several hundred soldiers to serve as auxiliaries against the Quitoans.

During the army's stay in Jauja, two important events occurred. First, the governor established the city as a Spanish town, laying out a plaza and church, and naming eighty men to serve as founding *vecinos,* under the command of the treasurer Riquelme. Second, the new Inca, Tupac Huallpa, suddenly died, possibly from poison.

The loss of this pliable young sovereign was a major inconvenience for Pizarro, who found himself once again having to cast about for candidates to fill the office of the Sun King.^ The leading choices included a brother of Tupac, named Manco, then living in Cuzco, and a teenage son of Atahualpa, who was the Quitoans' favorite. Pizarro, however, decided to wait, not wanting to slow his advance to Cuzco, where he would name a new Inca after the conquest was finished.

✝   ✝   ✝

While in Jauja, Pizarro dispatched Soto to scout out reports of troops massing to the south. What he found were soldiers of Yucra-Hualpa burning and destroying everything of use to the Spaniards along the road to Cuzco, including food stores and the all-important bridges.^

When Soto returned with the news of Yucra-Hualpa's scorched-earth policy, an alarmed Pizarro ordered him to organize a troop of seventy horsemen to dash south "with much speed" to secure supplies and capture key bridges. Soto was ready by October 24, 1533, when he and his outriders burst out of the Jauja Valley before dawn, riding fast, and planning to stay at least three days ahead of Pizarro and the main army.

According to eyewitnesses, Soto and his men covered an astonishing 250 miles in just five days,^ trying to reach the next major bridge at the Pampas River before Yucra-Hualpa could burn it. If this is true, it ranks among Soto's most impressive feats, particularly given the terrain in this central section of the Andes.^ John Hemming describes it as "wild, magnificent country, a vertical land of mountains deeply cut by fierce rivers plunging toward the Amazon. The topography changes with altitude, descending from snow-capped mountains to bare, misty puna high above the tree-line, down to pretty Andean valleys full of maize and flowers, and on down to suffocating heat and cactus in the depths of the canyons." Ruiz adds that the land to the south of Jauja "is rough with mountains and fields but there are no tall peaks . . . It is a land of many rivers . . . [and] sheep [llamas] . . . and there are many small deer."

Soto's route along the Royal Highway followed the Mantaro River for some fifty miles out of Jauja, where the river turns abruptly north to flow down into the Amazon. The road then continues to the southeast, passing over breathtakingly high ridges, and dropping into a series of river canyons. Some of the latter became so steep that the Inca highway became stairs cut into the rock. This worked well enough for a people with no horses or wheeled vehicles, but proved troublesome and exhausting for mounted riders, who faced the added peril of knowing that these precipitous stairways left them exposed to attack.

At first, the breakneck rush south seemed to pay off. Though Soto failed to reach the first bridge before Yucra-Hualpa torched it, local guards loyal to Huascar had hidden from the Quitoans "the materials which they had for mending it . . . and for this reason, they rebuilt it in a short space of time so the Spaniards might cross over it." This bridge spanned the Mantaro just below the town of Huancayo, crossing an "ugly gorge" of "crumbling yellow clay and outcrops of black rock." The new bridge, however, was poorly made. When Pizarro's army crossed it four days later, Pedro Sancho, traveling with the governor, said they found it full of holes from Soto's horses and "half destroyed. Still, the horses got over without endangering themselves, although nearly all stumbled because the bridge moved and trembled so."

Five days out of Jauja, Soto's exhausted force reached the outskirts of the last major Inca city before Cuzco, an administrative center called Vilcas. Cieza describes it as being "very important in this kingdom . . . having splendid edifices and a temple with great riches." Stopping five leagues north of Vilcas, Soto heard from Indian informants that Yucra-Hualpa's army was resting in the city on their way to meet Quizquiz. That night, Soto's men slept in their armor just beyond the outer perimeter of Inca sentries, waking up on October 29, 1533, five hours before dawn to launch what they hoped would be a surprise attack.

Soto split up his men into three squadrons, and then led the charge down into the valley, rushing along so quickly that the Quito sentries, who were on foot, had no time to raise an alarm.

As it turned out, this didn't matter, since the Quito army was off hunting in the surrounding hills when Soto arrived. "They had left their tents," reports Diego de Trujillo, one of Soto's outriders, "their women and a few Indian men in Vilcas, and we captured these, taking possession of everything that was there at the hour of dawn, which was when we entered Vilcas. We thought that there were no more troops than those who had been there then. But at the hour of vespers, when the Indians had been informed [of the Spaniards' attack], they came from the steepest direction and attacked us, and we them.

"Because of the roughness of the terrain," continues Trujillo, "they gained on us rather than we on them, although some Spaniards distinguished them-selves—for instance Captain Soto . . . and some others who won a height from the Indians and defended it strongly. The Indians on that day killed a white horse belonging to Alonso Tabuyo." Late that afternoon, Trujillo adds that the hard-pressed Spaniards, facing some twenty-five thousand Indian soldiers, "were forced to retreat to the square of Vilcas, and we all spent that night under arms."

The next day, the Quitoans attacked again "with great spirit," their morale boosted by the near victory the day before. "Carrying banners made from the mane and tail of the white horse they had killed," says Trujillo, the Indians swarmed into Vilcas and forced the Spaniards, in the haste of retreat, "to re-lease the booty of theirs that we were holding: the women and Indians who were in charge of all their flocks. They then withdrew."

But the battle was not yet over. As the Indians pulled back, Soto launched a ferocious counterattack, pursuing the Quitoans as they seemed to be retreating into the hills surrounding Vilcas.

This was, however, a trap set by a Quitoan high command—which was quickly adapting to *conquista* tactics. Yucra-Hualpa seems to have counted on Soto to give chase, hoping the Spaniards' predilection for bold forward thrusts would sweep them right into a series of steep ravines that would neutralize their horses—which, in fact, it did as Soto and thirty men rushed headlong "down a cleft in the mountain by a very difficult slope." Here Quito troops were waiting for him, abruptly shifting their mock retreat into an attack as thousands of footmen positioned above the horses rained down stones, javelins, and arrows. Those closest perched on boulders and in trees to batter the heads of horses and conquistadors with maces and battle-axes.

Stunned by the ferocity and ingenuity of this attack, Soto's troop was lucky not to be annihilated. Three Spaniards were badly wounded, one horse was killed, and two others were injured as the men fought their way out of the ravine, retreating to a more defensible position near the Royal Highway.

The Quitoans, however, were not finished. Chasing down the Spaniards once again, Sancho says they attacked "with more spirit and greater impetuos-ity than before, and in this way a sharper battle than the first was fought," though this time the Spaniards, in less-rugged terrain, were able to use their horses more effectively. Eventually, they forced the Indians to make a tactical retreat away from Vilcas, though not before another horse was killed and several more Spaniards wounded.

The battle resulted in six hundred Incas dead, two Spanish horses killed, and several of Soto's men gravely wounded—which seems a lopsided victory for the Spaniards. The reality, however, was that Soto was lucky he didn't suffer far worse casualties. He also had been tricked and manipulated by an enemy whose weapons were far inferior, though obviously their sense of strategy, and their ability to adapt rapidly in their tactics, were not. In his report to Pizarro, Soto called the skirmish at Vilcas a great victory.^ Yet the lesson of this battle was clear—that the Indians did not plan to let the Spaniards seize their empire without a vigorous and intelligent fight.

✢   ✢   ✢

No one understood the import of Yucra-Hualpa's tactical sense more than Francisco Pizarro. Receiving Soto's dispatches the day after the Battle of Vilcas, he sent an urgent message to his captain of the vanguard ordering him to halt immediately and wait, so they could face the newly invigorated Quitoans together.^ Indeed, his missive to Soto can be interpreted as something of a rebuke, its terse cordiality barely masking Pizarro's displeasure at what he considered Soto's recklessness in pursuing the enemy into the hills, where he not only came close to being defeated, but also revealed to the enemy the Spaniards' most glaring vulnerability—the ineffectiveness of the horse in rough terrain. In Pizarro's letter to Soto, Pedro Sancho says, the governor congratulated him and his men "on the victory they had won," but pointedly warned them next time to "be governed in these matters more by prudence than by confidence in their own strength."

Soto's actions make it clear what he thought of Pizarro's rebuke. Fired up by the blood-rush of fighting, and encouraged by the retreat of the Quitoans from Vilcas, he made a fateful decision—to ignore the governor's order, and keep rushing toward Cuzco. By now he was so obsessed with getting to the Inca capital first, he was willing to risk facing again an army that had nearly beat his tiny force, and next time would be even larger and better-prepared. Not even a report that Yucra-Hualpa was preparing an ambush up ahead,^ nor the fact his men and horses were exhausted, dissuaded the hotheaded Soto.

Soto's own explanation for breaching orders, sent by messenger in a letter to Pizarro,^ was that he wanted to save the bridges over the Abancay and Apurímac Rivers, and to prevent Yucra-Hualpa from linking up with Quizquiz. Trujillo and others with Soto, however, offer a more likely explanation—that Soto, Rodrigo de Orgóñez, and other firebrands got caught up in the excitement of the chase, and decided that since they had "endured all the hardships" in fighting the Indians, they should "enjoy the entry into Cuzco without the reinforcements that were coming behind." Another eyewitness riding with Soto, Pedro Pizarro, adds that "Soto was traveling with the evil intention of entering Cuzco before the [governor], on account of which we were all like to be lost."^

Furious when he learned of Soto's insubordination, Pizarro was forced again to split the army, ordering Almagro to march double-time with thirty horse to overtake and reinforce his renegade captain—and to stop him. This left Pizarro with a scant ten horsemen and twenty footmen to guard Chalcuchima, hundreds of slaves and porters, and what remained of the army's heavy baggage.^ It also meant the 350-man army was now strung out across two hundred miles in four small groups, with Soto in the lead, Almagro racing to catch him, Pizarro lumbering along behind, and the troops in Jauja taking up the rear. It was the Spaniards' most-precarious moment, and the Quitoans' greatest opportunity.

Once again, the Peruvians failed to take advantage. Either they were unaware of the Spanish situation, or knew about it but decided to stick with a strategy of massing all their troops near Cuzco for an ambush at a place called Vilcaconga. Named for a small feeder stream high above the Apurímac canyon, it was here that the Quitoans hoped the rough topography and difficult climb would exhaust and neutralize the Spanish horses, and allow the native forces to rain down stones and missiles from a secure height before attacking en masse in the style of fighting they knew best—hand-to-hand combat using their maces, clubs, and battle-axes.

The Quitoan strategy nearly worked as Soto rushed south, plunging directly into this fresh native entanglement. Leaving Vilcas after a brief rest, his troop dropped down into a deep canyon outside the city, leading their horses down steep stairs that cut the horses' hooves as they descended six thousand feet into "the hot, airless bed of the Pampas river." Here Soto found the bridge burned, though he was able with difficulty to ford the river, wading "with much fatigue because it was very full." Two horses died during this difficult crossing; when Pizarro came across their carcasses two days later, he "suspected some misfortune had befallen the captain," until letters arrived from Soto explaining that "the two horses had died of so many changes from heat to cold"—i.e., from exhaustion.

From the Pampas Soto charged east toward Cuzco, riding in and out of canyons, passing through (and plundering) several villages, and fording the great rivers of Andahuaylas and Abancay. In frequent dispatches to Pizarro he described his progress, reporting that the waters of the Andahuaylas had come up to the breasts of the horses, and that he had left behind ten men to guard treasure looted from villages along the way.^

By now, Soto knew Almagro was chasing him, but still he did not wait. Pedro Pizarro angrily writes that when "Soto received news of [Almagro's] coming . . . in order to carry out his intention, he went on with double marches, giving as a pretext to his soldiers his wish to hurry to capture that pass of Vilcaconga before the Indians should assemble, and this in the face of the fact that they had already been assembled there for some months. While Soto was proceeding in this manner, Almagro had news of it, and spurring on his horses, he went on at double marches without stopping day or night in order to catch up with Soto. It was the truth, then, that Soto urged on his horses so much that he wearied them."

Soto, now leading about fifty horsemen, arrived early on November 8 at the last major barrier on the Royal Highway to Cuzco—the great canyon of the Apurímac, which means "Great Speaker" in Quechua. According to John Hemming, "The Inca highway crossed this gorge on a high suspension bridge. The approaches to the ancient structure can still be seen half-way up the sides of the valley, with the narrow Inca road running through a tunnel before it turns, past massive stone buttressing, out into the present void. The bridge was burned by the time the Spaniards [under Soto] reached it, but they were able to ford the river despite its strong current and slippery stone bed," a feat the late-sixteenth-century historian Antonio de Herrera Tordesillas said "has never been seen since." Hemming adds that "the conquistadors' luck was partly due to the fact that they made their march at the driest time of year, just before the start of the rains. A few months later the rivers they swam and forded would become swirling grey torrents rising high up the walls of their canyons."

Soto crossed the frigid, quick waters while heavy morning fog blanketed the river. As the sun burned away the mists, he and his tired men began to climb the long, steep eastern slope of the canyon, a series of rocky, partially wooded rises that followed minor tributaries pouring into the river below. At midday, they stopped in the searing heat to rest at a small stream where they watered their horses and fed them maize provided by nearby villagers. Striking camp in midafternoon, they soon approached a high pass, where the highway rose above the head of the Vilcaconga River.

Now approaching twelve thousand feet, the Spaniards' path rose above the tree line, and into high, rocky meadows surrounded by ridges covered with shale, boulders, and scrub. "We were marching along with no thought of a line of battle," recalled Ruiz de Arce. "We had been inflicting very long days marches on the horses. Because of this we were leading them up the pass by their halters, marching this way in groups of four."

Hernando de Soto Commands the Spanish at the Battle of Vilcaconga Against the Incas, 1533

As they approached the summit, Soto was the first to see a line of dark shapes suddenly rise up above them, followed instantly by a shout that boomed and echoed across the canyon as the shapes abruptly poured over the top of the summit—three or four thousand of them, "coming down ... with great rapidity." Caught utterly by surprise, Soto shouted to his terrified men "to form a line of battle, but it was too late. The Indians were hurling a barrage of stones before them."

Most of the Spaniards scattered and ran for cover, while Soto and those immediately around him tried to rush upward to take the summit. But Sancho says the horses "were so tired that they could not get breath in order to attack with impetuosity such a multitude of enemies, nor did the latter cease to inconvenience and harass them," attacking them "continually with the lances, stones, and arrows which they hurled at them, so they were fatigued all to such an extent that the riders could hardly keep their horses at the trot, or even at [a walking] pace. As the Indians perceived the horses' exhaustion, they began to attack with greater fury."

Five Spaniards died in the initial crush and confusion—two on horseback, the others on foot before they could climb into their saddles. One man was killed when the Indians grabbed the tail of his horse and stopped him from reaching his companions. Unable to draw his sword in the hail of missiles and swarm of maces and clubs, he was overwhelmed, dragged off his saddle, and beaten to a pulp in a sea of painted wooden helmets, plumes, and brilliantly colored wool-and-cotton uniforms. Another man reportedly had his head cleaved in half by the force of a single blow from a stone mace. The Quitoans badly wounded six more men and eighteen horses; one of the horses later died.^

As this bloody afternoon wore on, Soto, showing his usual presence of mind in the midst of battle, managed to muster his surviving horsemen on a flat spot "near that mountain." Somehow, he held off the Incas long enough to water his horses in a small stream. This brief lull also gave him a chance to rally his troops and to propose a strategy. "Let us withdraw here step by step down this hillside," Sancho says he told the men, "in such a way that the enemy may think that we are fleeing from them, in order that they may come in search of us below, for, if we can attract them to this plain, we will attack them all of the sudden in such a manner that I hope not one of them will escape from our hands. Our horses are already somewhat tired, and if we put the enemy to flight, we shall end by gaining the summit of the mountain."

At first this strategy worked as Soto's men backtracked and lured down several hundred Incas onto a flat spot, where the horses could be used effectively. But the Incas quickly caught on to the ruse and retreated, after losing twenty men. The battle then continued as before until twilight, with the Spaniards being pummeled from above. If darkness had not intervened, the Indians might have killed them all.

When night fell, the two sides broke off fighting. The Quitoans positioned troops to seal off the trails and passes to the north, south, and east. On the west was the canyon and the Apurímac River. Under the cover of darkness, however, Soto was able to lead his weary men up to a nearby hillock, two crossbow shots away from the main Quito position. Here he "cared for his wounded and posted patrols and sentinels for the night, and ordered that all the horses remain saddled and bridled." He then attempted to rally his soldiers, telling them "he thought the day to come would not be as perilous as that just finished, and that God our Lord who had delivered them from danger in the past would grant them victory in the future, and he reminded them that even when their horses were weary on that day, they had attacked their enemies from a great disadvantage . . . even though their own number did not exceed fifty, and the enemy numbered at least eight thousand. Given this, should they not hope for victory?"

But Soto and every other Spaniard knew the situation was desperate. They were trapped on a frigid hillside at twelve thousand feet, battered and bleeding, and hemmed in by thousands of enemy troops. As if this weren't enough, Soto received intelligence that an enormous army under Quizquiz was advancing rapidly to reinforce Yucra-Hualpa. "Wait, Christians, until dawn," taunted the supremely confident natives that night, shouting from their nearby lines in words translated by Soto's interpreters, "when you are all to die!"

No one slept that night, as the stars twinkled in the cold, black Peruvian sky, and the Spaniards prayed and watched nervously for movements in the Inca camp. Then, suddenly, about one A.M., Soto's men heard a sound off in the distance, drifting up from the canyon below. At first, they must have thought they were dreaming. Then the noise became more distinct, and they knew exactly what it was—a Spanish trumpet.^

"By its notes the very much afflicted Spaniards were made to rejoice," says Pedro Pizarro, for they knew then that Diego de Almagro had arrived with reinforcements. The trumpet grew louder, sounding at regular intervals until Soto ordered his own trumpeter to respond. Soto's men then "came to where Almagro was, and this trumpet was sounded many times upon this night in order that some Spaniards who, wearied, had remained behind, might be able to guess where the camp of the Christians was."

When the next day dawned, the Quitoans were expecting a great victory, and quickly massed for an attack, only to find to their astonishment that Soto's troop had doubled overnight, and was dashing up the slope to attack them. Unprepared for such a vigorous assault, they took one look at the wall of steel and horseflesh charging toward them, and promptly retreated to a higher summit. Here they intended to make a stand, but never got the chance. For as Soto and Almagro topped the first hill and pressed their attack, the battlefield became immersed in a thick fog rising out of the Apurímac valley. This forced both armies to break off hostilities because "they could not see one another." The Quitoans then disappeared into the hills, continuing their march to rendezvous with Quizquiz. Almagro and Soto let them go, under orders to wait for Pizarro.

If Soto felt any remorse or embarrassment over the near debacle at Vilca-conga, no one mentions it. Nor is there a record of Pizarro's reaction when he caught up with his renegade captain two or three days later. One imagines that the governor at least censured Hernando de Soto, whose insubordination in this matter was serious enough that a less pragmatic general might have lopped off his head. But once again Soto's indispensability as a fighter and leader saved him. For Francisco Pizarro knew he could not advance against the combined armies of Yucra-Hualpa and Quizquiz without him. One senses that from this moment, however, Soto's days under Pizarro were definitely numbered, even as he and the others braced themselves for the final push to Cuzco.

✤ 15 ✤

The Navel of the World

ON NOVEMBER 14, THE combined armies of Quizquiz and Yucra-Hualpa made one last desperate effort to throw back the Spaniards in the umber-colored hills surrounding Cuzco. Once again, the native soldiers fought fiercely, at one point killing several horses and forcing a Spanish tactical retreat. But by the time darkness fell, the Spaniards and their Indian auxiliaries had pushed the armies of Quito into their final defensive positions outside the Inca capital.^

That evening, the exhausted Quitoans erected their tents and lit their fires feeling the intense despair of an army that on four occasions had come tantalizingly close to victory, but each time had failed. Battered, bloody, and eleven hundred miles away from their homes in Ecuador, the soldiers of Quizquiz, and the last hope of the many peoples of Peru, decided to give up the city they had fought so hard to capture throughout the long civil war, and had tried furiously to defend against this bizarre and unexpected assault by iron-clad warriors. Dressed in their warm multicolored wool cloaks against the cold, their faces downcast, the embittered soldiers slipped away that night quietly, under cover of darkness, retreating into a mountainous region southwest of Cuzco. In this wild, almost inaccessible country above the upper Apurímac River, the Quitoans hoped to rest and recuperate in a country too rugged and steep for Pizarro's horses to dislodge them.

At first light, the Spaniards rushed the abandoned Quito position, expecting a renewal of the previous day's fighting. Instead, they found an empty hillside of smoldering ashes, llama dung, and hastily discarded baggage. Suspecting a trick, Pizarro sent out scouts to comb the rocky hills above the Inca highway, on the lookout for an ambush as the main army crept along in a defensive formation all the way to the heights above the city. Here the Spaniards stopped to stare at the rooftops of Cuzco below, realizing that Quizquiz had indeed withdrawn and left them masters of a city more populous than any in Spain, with at least 100,000 people,^ spread out in a lovely, wedge-shaped valley.

As they marched down the broad royal highway toward the city, the people of Cuzco rushed out to meet them. Such a throng might have tried to block the Spaniards' entry. Instead, they welcomed it. Gathering by the thousands along the road, they cheered and waved at not only the Spaniards, but a young Inca not yet twenty years old, sitting on an elaborate litter at Pizarro's side—yet another claimant to the Inca throne, a younger brother of the slain Huascar, named Manco. A week earlier, Manco had appeared in Pizarro's camp at Vilcaconga, offering his support to the Spanish in exchange for being recognized by Pizarro as Inca—which the governor agreed to do. Later, Manco would become closely associated with Soto as the two of them chased Quizquiz across southern Peru, and Soto engaged the young prince as an ally in his political machinations against the Pizarros. Later still, Manco would launch a bloody revolt against the Spaniards. For now, however, he and his people remained tragically mired in the politics of the civil war, blinded to the true nature of the men they hailed that afternoon as saviors.

For the thirty-three-year-old Soto, the triumphant entry into Cuzco late on the afternoon of November 15, 1533, would be outshone only by his hero's welcome in Seville three years later. Riding at the head of his outriders, feeling supremely self-assured and more convinced than ever that his warrior God was guiding his destiny, he steered his mount down the wide, paved highway past fields of grazing llamas and intricately constructed terraces freshly turned and planted, headed toward the sprawling city the Incas called the Navel of the World—laid out in a huge, cross-shaped grid of small thatched houses on the outskirts and much larger and grandiose buildings in the center.^

Because the streets of Cuzco are as narrow as those of medieval Europe, the army was forced to break up into squads marching two abreast, passing through a sea of Incas gaping and cheering in the cool, thin mountain air. Still fearing a sudden attack from Quizquiz, or a change of heart among the city's people, they marched close together and in battle readiness past rows of rectangular one-story huts made of stone, with steep-sloped roofs of thatch. These outer suburbs of the great city can hardly have impressed the Castilians, though they knew what prize awaited them in the center—a fabulously wealthy district of royal palaces as large as any in Europe: block after block of mansions housing the Inca nobility, dazzling plazas, tribute houses, and gold-encrusted temples.

When they broke out of the dark, narrow streets and into the vast central plaza of Aucaypata, most of the Spaniards leaped off their horses and knelt to pray, resting their knees on a coating of finely crushed gravel glittering white in the late-afternoon sun. Others stayed mounted and watched the hills for signs of Quito infantry, while Pizarro dispatched men to seize major buildings. These included the great fortress of Colcampata, looming above the city on a steep crag, an enormous complex of thick walls and battlements erected over the centuries by Cuzco's rulers. Intended as an impregnable last stronghold against an overwhelming attack, it now fell without bloodshed as the unopposed Spanish cavalrymen rode through its trapezoidal portals and raised above its ramparts the flag of the Spanish king. This happened just as the last stray rays of sun slipped behind the hills on this final day of one great empire, and the first day of another.

Pizarro, still fearing a counterattack from Quizquiz, ordered his soldiers to bivouac in their tents on the plaza of Aucaypata—"the terrace of festivities and rejoicing"—and to keep guards posted and horses saddled around the clock. He then set up his headquarters in one of two three-story towers in the plaza, "built of the fine wood that was used in royal palaces." Rising from the southeast side of the plaza, it afforded a commanding view of the city and valley.

✣   ✣   ✣

As the days passed, and Quizquiz did not appear, the Spaniards gradually began to realize the enormity of what they had accomplished. Later, Pedro Sancho recalled that "The Spaniards who have taken part in this venture are amazed by what they have done. When they begin to reflect on it, they cannot imagine how they can still be alive or how they survived such hardships and long periods of hunger." Even the Incas were astonished by the Spaniards' stunning accomplishment. Soon after their arrival in Cuzco, they began calling them viracochas—children of the sun^—an appellation previously reserved only for the Inca emperor.

Within days, the Spanish leaders began behaving almost as if they *were* emperors, at least in terms of housing. Drawing lots, Pizarro and his senior staff wasted no time moving into the royal palaces facing the great square. The governor won the massive Casana palace on the northwest side of the main square, built by Atahualpa's great-grandfather, Pachacuti, the brilliant military strategist who led the first waves of Inca conquest outside the Cuzco valley in the mid-fifteenth century. Juan and Gonzalo Pizarro each won smaller palaces nearby, and Almagro the newly completed palace of Huascar.^

None of these equaled the splendor of the quarters won by Hernando de Soto^—the great palace of Amaru Cancha, built by Atahualpa's father, Huayna Capac. "It has a gateway of red, white and multicolored marble," wrote Pedro Sancho, who describes it as a complex of buildings, apartments, and a massive baronial hall that held up to four thousand people. Garcilaso claims it measured "two hundred paces in length and fifty to sixty in breadth," a pace being roughly three feet. Soto's friend, Miguel de Estete, also remembered it had "two towers of fine appearance" built of a dark, beautiful wood, and a gateway "faced with pieces of silver and other metals."

Sadly, nothing is known about Amaru Cancha's interior, because it was destroyed by fire three years later. One can imagine it filled with room after sumptuous room of beautifully carved furniture, luxurious clothing, frescoes of bright colors, statuary, tapestries, gold and silver effigies, plates, and cups. There were pipes carrying hot and cold running water, and hundreds of servants to maintain the palace and cater to the whims of its occupant—who, in this case, had been dead since 1527, though his mummified body had been preserved, permanently sitting in state, as had all the deceased emperors of the Incas in their individual palaces.

Soto had little time to enjoy his new lodgings, however, as fresh reports came in from Manco's scouts that Quizquiz's army had been sighted just twenty miles southwest of the city. This prompted Pizarro to dispatch Soto to investigate—and, if possible, to smash or at least drive away the enemy. Asking Manco to make this an allied effort, he ordered the prince "to assemble many warriors in order to go out and vanquish Quizquiz and drive from the land those of Quito." Manco, anxious to avenge the death of Huascar and most of his family, responded enthusiastically. In just four days, he raised an army of five thousand natives "in readiness with their arms."

Typically, Soto could hardly wait to give up his luxurious life to dash into the wilds. In fact, he moved so quickly out of Cuzco that he overran a small contingent of Quizquiz's retreating rear guard in a bad pass just before the Apurímac canyon. The Quitoans, however, were able to hold off his advance long enough for Quizquiz to finish moving his men across the river, and to burn the bridge behind them—a strategic victory that forced Soto into the highly vulnerable position of having to ford the Apurímac deep in a canyon where the Quito forces, perched up high on the bluffs, were able to hurl a steady barrage of rocks, spears, and arrows as the Spaniards attempted to cross the river. This gave Quizquiz enough time to pull back deep into a region of high, rugged valleys and ridges to the west. Once across the Apurímac, Soto pursued the Indian army for ten more days before calling off the chase, telling Pizarro when he returned to Cuzco that this region was "the wildest and most inaccessible they had ever seen." He also brought the good news that Quizquiz seemed to be moving away from the capital, and no longer was close enough to threaten it.

✛   ✛   ✛

With great relief, Pizarro ordered his men to stand down. He then began organizing a task the Spaniards had been anticipating for months, since first hearing about this wondrous city—the looting of the Navel of the World.

Great care had to be taken given that Pizarro's 200 Spaniards remained almost ridiculously vulnerable in a city of 100,000 people. This meant the governor had to keep a tight leash on his men, ordering them to pillage discreetly, and only in selected public buildings, palaces, storehouses, and monuments. In a city this sumptuous, this was hardly a burden—at least for the moment.

They started with the treasure closest at hand, rifling through the Incas' palaces, and the great Temple of the Sun, stuffing fantastic fortunes into bags and baskets as they collected the plates, armor, and personal effects of the Inca rulers, and the holy icons, statues, and relics of the temple, delivering everything to several storage rooms in Pizarro's palace for distribution at a later date. They also ransacked the fortress above the city, which still contained much of the late Huayna Capac's gold. "In short," reports the historian Francisco López de Gómara, "they took a greater quantity of gold and silver [in the temple] and in the surrounding district than they had in Cajamarca with the capture of Atahualpa,"^ though because there were more people to divide it among, the shares were smaller.

Amongst the vessels, idols, and statuary unceremoniously seized, ripped from walls, and hammered apart were expertly crafted treasures even finer than those melted down at Cajamarca. The artistry astounded even the conquistadors, whose chronicles are filled with awestruck descriptions of the Incas' work in gold and silver. "In one cave," wrote Pedro Pizarro, "they discovered twelve sentries of gold and silver, of the size and appearance of those of this country, extraordinarily realistic . . . They found shoes made of gold, of the type women wore, like half-boots. They found golden crayfish such as live in the sea, and many vases, on which were sculpted in relief all the birds and snakes that they knew, even down to the spiders, caterpillars and other insects." In the great Temple of the Sun, Soto's riding companion, Juan Ruiz de Arce, recalled seeing "many golden llamas, women, pitchers, jars and other objects in the chambers of the monastery." In one courtyard yet another eyewitness describes a spectacular garden made entirely of gold; and a golden font and altar standing before "an image of the sun of great size, made of gold, beautifully wrought and set with many precious stones."

Admiration for the artistic talents of Inca goldsmiths did not stop the plunderers from wrecking the greater portion of these treasures—a loss that at least one Spaniard in Cuzco that fall lamented, a young priest named Cristóbal de Molina. He wrote sadly that his compatriots' "only concern was to collect gold and silver to make themselves all rich . . . without thinking that they were doing wrong and were wrecking and destroying. For what was being destroyed was more perfect than anything they enjoyed and possessed."

In the hills above the city, the conquerors also found the tribute storehouses and supply depots of the empire, housed in seemingly endless rows of rectangular huts filled with "cloaks, wool, weapons, metal, cloth and all the other goods that are grown or manufactured in this country. There are shields, leather bucklers, beams for roofing the houses, knives and other tools, sandals and breastplates to equip the soldiers. All was in such vast quantities that it is hard to imagine how the natives can ever have paid such immense tribute of so many items."

Of course, this looting was not accomplished without offending certain Incas. For instance, Diego de Trujillo recounted the horror of the sun priests as the Spaniards in their great boots and armor violated the great temple of Coricancha, the most sacred shrine of the Inca religion. "As we entered," Trujillo relates, the high priest "cried out: 'How dare you enter here! Anyone who enters here has to fast for a year beforehand, and must enter barefoot and bearing a load!' But we paid no attention to what he said, and went in." By and large, the people of Cuzco, including Manco, chose for the moment to ignore these outrages in the euphoria of their supposed liberation—as long as they didn't get out of hand.

No one will ever know exactly how much plunder was collected in Cuzco during these early, hectic days, given the almost universal underreporting of the looters. The official tally, announced during the first division of the spoils the following March, totaled some 588,266 pesos of gold and 228,310 marks of silver,^ though this was just a fraction of a booty that would eventually total much more.^

✢ ✢ ✢

For most of December and January, Soto—ensconced in his palace, and living like a king—joined in the wild celebrations that consumed Spaniards and Incas alike as Pizarro's men piled up their spoils, and Manco and his followers relished their unexpected liberation. Even as the future of the empire and the freedom of the Incas hung in precarious balance, Spaniards and Incas alike plunged into a month-long bout of drinking, dancing, sex, games, and elaborate hunting expeditions as everyone seemed either too exhausted, or too overwhelmed by the enormous changes, to push onward to the inevitable next phase of the conquest—the confrontation with Quizquiz's still-formidable army.

From his rooms facing the Aucaypata plaza, Soto was ideally positioned to observe Manco's coronation ceremonies, the last ever for an emperor of Tahuantinsuyu. Indeed, Pizarro and his men watched with both fascination and repulsion at what they considered heathen rites,^ though the rituals must have seemed vaguely familiar to Spaniards used to their own religious festivals back home. Both began with the same ponderous parades of life-size icons dressed in flowing robes and carrying golden symbols. But instead of dead saints carved from wood, the Incas carried mummified bodies of their past emperors, whom they prayed and sang to, and showered with flowers before launching into the same frenzy of celebrating, drinking, dancing, debauchery, story-telling, and music one still sees in Spain during certain religious holidays.

Miguel de Estete, who was present at Manco's coronation, writes that "such a vast number of people assembled . . . could only crowd onto the square with great difficulty . . . [as] Manco had all of his dead ancestors brought to the fes-tivities . . . There was a litter for each one, with men in livery to carry it," with the train being followed by Incas marching behind and "singing many ballads and giving thanks to the sun." When they reached the square, the mummy of Huayna Capac, Manco's father, was set up "level with him, and the rest simi-larly in their litters, embalmed and with diadems on their heads. A pavilion had been erected for each of them, and the dead were placed in order, seated on their thrones and surrounded by pages and women with flywhisks in their hands, who ministered to them with as much respect as if they had been alive."

Estete also describes the drinking, a source of great interest among chroni-clers because of the massive amounts consumed by the Indians. "Both men and women were such heavy drinkers," Estete marvels, "and they poured so much into their bodies—for their entire activity was drinking, not eating—that it is a fact that two wide drains over [eighteen inches] in diameter emptied into the river beneath the flagstones . . . [and] ran with urine throughout the day from those who peed into them, as abundantly as a flowing spring." He adds that the festivities "lasted for over thirty days in succession."

✛   ✛   ✛

At the height of the celebrations in Cuzco, Pizarro received disturbing news—that the redoubtable Quizquiz was not pulling out of Peru, but was marching on the Spanish garrison at Jauja. Here Pizarro's royal treasurer, Alonso Riquelme, commanded about eighty men and a handful of horses guarding not only the city, but several tons of Cajamarca gold, a situation that looked like a disaster in the making. Indeed, Pizarro should have known that such a lightly manned Spanish outpost would present a tempting target for Quizquiz, who still had a capacity for causing great damage to the Spanish ef-fort—particularly if he should capture Jauja and strand the governor and his 150 men in Cuzco, far away from reinforcements.^

Again, Pizarro called on Soto to master a potentially calamitous situation, ordering him to take his fifty best men and to dash north, accompanied by Manco, Manco's brother Paullu, and a native army numbering this time some twenty thousand men.^

Originally, the army was to depart on December 31, 1533. But because the Spaniards were reluctant to miss out on the looting, and the Inca soldiers were loath to leave the coronation festivities, the army did not leave until February. It also was the height of the monsoon season, when southern Peru is drenched in torrential rains, and travel is difficult, even with a Royal Highway made of stone.^ This meant Soto and Manco arrived too late in Jauja, missing the Quitoan attack by almost three weeks.

The garrison held out anyway, reinforced at the last minute by the unexpected arrival of a small force from the coast led by Gabriel de Rojas, Soto's old friend from Panama and Nicaragua, and by a native army of several hundred men provided by the *cacique* of Jauja, a blood enemy of the Quitoans.^

Even so, the Spaniards in Jauja had come perilously close to defeat. Again, Quizquiz had demonstrated his strategic versatility by attempting to trap the city in a two-pronged pincer movement. First he sent one thousand men in a feint from the mountains in the west, with orders to draw off the Spaniards while the main army attacked from the plains below. It was a brilliant plan that might have worked, except for the swiftness of the Spanish horse, which allowed the Spaniards to discover the trick and rush back to inform Riquelme in time to redeploy his forces toward the main Quito attack. Nevertheless, the battle was fierce, with one Spaniard and three horses killed, and hundreds of Indians slain on both sides. In the end the combination of horses and steel, and the bitter hatred of the Jauja allies against the Quitoans, once again left Quizquiz's army bloodied and in retreat—this time to a fortress named Maracayllo, in a steep pass seventy-five miles north of the city.

Soto arrived in Jauja early in March, and wasted no time going after Quizquiz, taking a small squadron to reconnoiter the area around Maracayllo, and then returning to Jauja to organize a larger army from the forces of Manco, Jauja, Riquelme, and Rojas. Diego de Almagro also had just arrived from Cuzco with even more men, and with orders from Pizarro for Soto either to destroy Quizquiz's forces, or drive them out of Peru once and for all.^ Organizing an army composed of such disparate units, however, took several weeks, with Soto departing Jauja in early May 1534, leading perhaps one hundred Spaniards, augmented by some twenty thousand Inca soldiers.

Once again, Quizquiz proved elusive. For when Soto—now in command of a host as numerically impressive as any in Europe—arrived at the approaches to the Maracayllo fortress, the dispirited Quitoans were gone. Local Indians reported they were marching north, back to Quito—this time for good.

Soto, wanting to be sure, ordered his host to pursue the retreating Quitoans all the way to Huánuco,^ two hundred miles north of Jauja. Here he finally broke off the chase, and turned around his army for a triumphant march back through cities and towns that once again hailed the Spaniards and their allies as liberators, even as the long centuries of Spanish domination were about to begin.

✤ 16 ✤

Lord of Cuzco

RETURNING TO JAUJA IN late June, Hernando de Soto found Pizarro in town checking on his gold, and fuming over reports from Cuzco that the Spaniards there were disregarding his edicts to loot politely. They were harassing Indians, Pizarro's lieutenants wrote in urgent missives; they were fighting amongst themselves, and refusing to pay taxes. Pizarro, however, was on the way to the coast to found a new capital city,^ and did not want to be diverted back to Cuzco. He therefore did what was by now an almost reflexive action—he asked Soto to take charge and restore calm to the Inca capital. To give teeth to Soto's mission, Pizarro named him lieutenant governor of Cuzco, and appointed him to the office of royal corregidor.^ This made him, at last, the second-most-powerful man in Peru.

If Soto was surprised by this sudden turn of events, he does not let on. Nevertheless, this appointment represented a dramatic about-face for a governor who had long distrusted his blatantly ambitious *capitán*. Pizarro, however, had known Soto since he came to Panama as a boy, and was astute enough to know that for the moment, the two men shared a narrow, common goal—ultimate victory over the Incas. Pizarro and Soto would continue to be wary of each other, though for now the uneasy union of their talents remained intact, with the strengths and weaknesses of these two opposites balancing each other out—Soto being the quick, daring, and resourceful man of action, and Pizarro the steady, tenacious plodder with a will of iron. Yet Soto was under no illusions. He understood that this was a marriage of convenience only, and that Pizarro would push him aside the instant he no longer needed him.

Even in the instructions Pizarro handed to his dusty, perspiring captain that day in Jauja, he says he has faith in Soto to get the job done—to restore calm in the city, punish "acts of villainy," prosecute those who "have gone be-

188

yond what I commanded," and to protect the Indians. Yet he also warns Soto to remain impartial, telling him he "had learned to trust him in some things," but apparently not in others. He also orders Soto to serve "without getting involved" in his usual machinations and partisan schemes, instructing him to send frequent and detailed reports, and to follow his dictates exactly.

It's worth noting that Soto's appointment to Cuzco required not only a firm hand, but some capacity as an administrator and executive. Just three months earlier, Pizarro had established Cuzco as a Spanish municipality, when Soto was off chasing Quizquiz. This meant the task of making the city's new institutions work would fall to Soto, including the creation of a permanent city council, civil and military courts, a *nuncio,* a police force, and the agencies for distributing supplies and overseeing city services. Pizarro's trust in Soto to perform these functions, and his repeated assignment of Soto to senior administrative posts as early as Tumbez,^ suggest Soto's reputation as a poor administrator in Nicaragua was unfounded. He would soon amply demonstrate his capability as he gathered his belongings in Jauja, handpicked his own lieutenants to accompany him, and rode off to take command of one of the world's largest and wealthiest cities. There he would move back into his fairy-tale palace and assume the power of life and death over tens of thousands of people, and control of a plundering operation ultimately worth millions of pesos, including one thousand pounds of gold he would keep for himself—some of it, suggests Garcilaso de la Vega, taken on the sly.^

✝   ✝   ✝

When Soto arrived in Cuzco with Manco Inca late in July or early August, he moved quickly to restore order in the capital. Soto found the soldiers of Pizarro robbing, beating, and abusing the locals, torturing some to reveal the location of family heirlooms, and generally behaving as if they were far more than a few hundred men amidst 100,000 natives who conceivably could overwhelm them if they became enraged enough. Details are scant about Soto's exact methods in this "pacification," though he moved with typical dispatch and ruthlessness, quickly halting all unauthorized plundering. He also convinced his friend Manco, who was furious to find his so-called liberators looting and pillaging indiscriminately, that the abuses would stop. Not that the Spaniards ceased their plundering during the Soto regime. In fact, there appears to have been an understanding between Manco and Soto that the new overlords could continue to steal a certain amount of treasure discreetly. This was because Manco—who would launch a bloody revolt against the Spaniards eighteen months later—was not yet organized enough to fight

back, though by now he must have been catching on to the true intent of his
"allies."

As the situation calmed in Cuzco, Soto was sworn in as lieutenant governor
by the city council, which was using Soto's palace as the temporary city hall,
a situation that placed him in the center of power for most of the next year, until
his ouster the following spring.

Once again, we have few documents from Soto during this period, and
would have nothing at all if two Peruvian historians had not dug deep into the
dusty archives in Cuzco, and unearthed in 1926 a sheaf of yellowed manuscripts recording the minutes of the first council meetings held in the city—
documents that remain tantalizingly sparse in detail, though they provide us
some glimpses into life in the Inca capital during the brief regime of Lieutenant
Governor Hernando de Soto.^

During these mostly tedious meetings, which run from Soto's swearing in
on August 25, 1534, to February 5 the following spring, when the parchment
abruptly ends, Soto can be seen attending to the day-to-day details of governing—which is telling in itself, given that most of the records we have of Soto
show a man far more inclined toward action than administration. Yet even in
these dry, legalistic proceedings, Soto emerges as a strong personality, plunging into the realm of laws, decrees, and petty squabbling with all of the vigor
of a military campaign.

One of Soto's first actions as the all-powerful *señor* (lord) of Cuzco concerned not a major issue of state, nor the collection of treasure, but horse
dung—specifically, dung belonging to an animal owned by a certain Juan García Gaitero, whom the city council censured for defiling the small stream running across the main city square. Hardly an earth-shattering event, it was
typical of Soto's new job as he dutifully sat at the head of the council table on
September 4 and heard allegations of Gaitero's scandalous behavior in allowing his horse to deposit "dungheaps in the river where it should not have happened as there is a designated place." Soto punished the offender by ordering
him to pay a fine, and had his name and crime publicly read out by the crier "so
that all could hear." Other less-than-auspicious decisions included edicts de-
termining the distribution of firewood, the proper allotment of corn for the Indians, the assignment of a certain Anton Herradas as the new town crier, and
the censure of a council member for being frequently absent.^

More important were actions taken by the council to further placate the Indians—including, for example, an order by the council issued on October 29,
when Soto decreed that "no building or wall of a house belonging to . . . Indian
natives may be moved or torn down by anyone who finds them on his land
holding." Or an order issued in January 1535 to send out a punitive squadron to

certain mines outside the city, where Spaniards reportedly were stealing "all that they can" and abusing Indians. "The Lieutenant Governor," the minutes record, "answered that this was outrageous that everyone takes advantage, and that he had been meaning to send a person out before now" to correct the situation.^

The other big issue Soto tackled during his tenure was the distribution of property and *encomiendas* in the province of Cuzco. Up until now, the Spaniards in the city, including Soto, had lived in quarters assigned them just after the march on Cuzco, an ad hoc situation that had greatly contributed to the *vecinos'* indiscriminate seizure of Indian property, and to a number of scuffles and fights over which palace belonged to whom.

Obviously, this was a quagmire for Soto, particularly since he was working with a council composed almost entirely of Pizarro appointees. Interested mostly in showering favors on the governor's followers, they usually did so at the expense of everyone else—which makes it all the more remarkable that Soto remained aloof. Usually the first to try and take advantage when the politics became confused or chaotic, Soto's reticence suggests he either was preoccupied with his duties—and the ongoing looting, which was making him a rich man—or he was simply standing by to see who would prevail.

One outcome of Soto's neutrality was a reasonably fair distribution of property, despite the Pizarroists. It commenced after Pizarro agreed to a plan apparently proposed by Soto, which the city council passed on October 29, 1534. The record of that day's council meeting lists all ninety-three *vecinos* of Cuzco by name, and their allocations.^ According to the minutes, the standard share, or "plot," of land measured "two hundred feet"* along its front side, and included buildings, gardens, and patios, and any Indians living there, to be held in *encomienda*. Of course, Soto, Pizarro, and other senior officers got larger plots, with Soto receiving half of Amaru Cancha, the side "which looks out upon the entire plaza."^ Typical of a common soldier was the single two-hundred-foot plot near the Temple of the Sun that Soto awarded to one of his new cronies, a young footman named Juan Ruiz Lobillo, who would accompany Soto back to Spain, and later serve as a captain of the infantry in *La Florida*.

+ + +

With Soto now ensconced in his palace, eating from gold plates, attending to important state business, and counting his gold, it seemed only right for a man with such enormous appetites to seek out a mistress commensurate with his position.

Apparently, he had long ago discarded his lowborn Spanish mistress, Juana

---

*The "foot" referred to here measured close to a meter, meaning the standard plot equaled some six hundred modern feet.

Hernández,^ undoubtedly replacing her with various Inca women in what by now was probably a small harem. Yet none of these seems to have mattered to Soto as much as a woman named Tocto Chimpu, a daughter of the Inca Huascar, and supposedly the most beautiful woman in Peru.

She had a tragic love story attached to her name even before meeting Soto. This is told by Pedro de Cieza, and also by a Jesuit priest named Miguel Cabello de Balboa, who says he later learned the details from the product of Tocto Chimpu's affair with Soto, a daughter named Leonor de Soto.^* According to Cabello de Balboa, Tocto Chimpu was born to Huascar and one of his wives, named Chumbillaya, "of such a marvelous beauty that she excited the admiration of all those who saw her," including Huascar, who met her one day at a state function in her home province. Giving her the nickname Curicuillor, the "Golden Star," he took her into his harem. "There his constant attentions to her at the expense of his other wives led them to conceive such a great hatred that they resolved to destroy her using poison, and one day she was found dead in one of the compartments of the palace." Just before her murder, however, she conceived a child, Tocto Chimpu, whom an aunt spirited away with Huascar's blessing to a secret location, where as she grew "her beauty became so great, that she inherited the name Curicuillor that her mother had."

When Tocto Chimpu was fifteen, just before the civil war, she met and fell in love with a young general from Quito named Quilaco—an affair that quickly turned to tragedy for this Inca Romeo and Juliet as the war began, and the two were separated, and lost track of each other.

After Huascar's defeat and Atahualpa's death, Cieza tells us that Quilaco happened to be in Jauja, searching for his lost love, when Pizarro and his conquistadors arrived there during the march from Cajamarca to Cuzco. Somehow, Quilaco met up with Soto and told him his story—only to be informed that Tocto Chimpu was actually there in Jauja at that very moment, looking for him. "Quilaco-Yupangui was so surprised to find the one that he thought was lost forever," writes Cieza, "that he was unable to say a word. Hernando de Soto offered them his support and provided them with convenient protective clothing," whatever this means. "They were baptized," continues Cieza, "with the names Hernando Yupangui and Leonor Curicuillor and married according to the laws of the church." This outcome further indicates Soto's affection for certain high-ranking Indians. That Quilaco came to Soto in the first place suggests he was known among the Inca nobility as being sympathetic to certain native leaders, a reputation perhaps coming from Soto's support of Atahualpa. The relationship also takes on a paternalistic edge with Soto giving Quilaco the name Hernando, and Tocto Chimpu the name of his mother, Leonor.

---

*Soto confirms Leonor de Soto is his daughter in his will.

But the story of the Golden Star does not end here. For Cieza informs us that when Quilaco "died two years later . . . Hernando de Soto started sexual relations with the widow," whom Soto put up in an apartment near his palace, apparently under the protection of his new friend, Juan Ruiz Lobillo, who lived close by.^

When exactly Tocto Chimpu—now Leonor—became Soto's mistress is unclear. The proof came soon after, however, when their daughter was born, also called Leonor—a child who went on to live out her life in Cuzco, marrying a royal notary named García Carrillo, and having numerous children and descendants who carried on the Soto name in Cuzco for several generations.^

The final tragedy for Tocto Chimpu came when Soto abandoned her to return to Spain, and she died soon after. In a story with echoes of *Madame Butterfly,* Cabello de Balboa insists she died of heartbreak over her lover's departure, though it's more likely she succumbed as much to exhaustion and a life filled with calamity as from powerful feelings for a man who may or may not have actually cared about her. In any event, her death left her infant daughter destitute until an old friend of Soto's, a scribe named Juan de Herrera, adopted and raised her.^

✛   ✛   ✛

Besides his mistress, Soto surrounded himself in Cuzco with his usual clique of lieutenants, aides, hangers-on, and servants, though recently there had been some major changes among his closest cronies. Soon after the conquest of Cuzco, Pizarro had shrewdly authorized Soto's most loyal partisans, and many of his rank-and-file supporters, to depart Peru with their gold—including Pedro Cataño, Luis Maza, Ruy Hernández Briceño, and a childhood friend of Soto's from Badajoz, Alonso de Medina.^ This greatly weakened Soto's base of power in Peru, and left him more susceptible than ever to being pushed aside should Don Francisco decide he was no longer necessary—a highly likely outcome once Cuzco was settled.

Soto quickly formed a new inner circle of supporters, some culled from among Almagro's troops, and others from groups of Spaniards beginning to arrive from all over the empire to seek their fortunes. Among these were several men who would later return to Spain with Soto—and go on to serve as senior officers in *La Florida.* These included not only Juan Ruiz Lobillo, but also Luis de Moscoso, then a twenty-nine-year-old cavalryman from Badajoz who later became Soto's maestro de campo, and, after Soto's death, acting governor of *La Florida.* Soto also met at this time Nuño de Tobar. From Soto's hometown of Jerez de los Caballeros, he would serve as the first captain general of the Florida expedition. Other key Soto aides and confidants at Amaru Cancha included Alonso de Ayala, Soto's loyal *mayordomo* in Peru, Spain,

and Cuba; the Nicaraguan lawyer and cavalryman Pedro Bravo, who later testified that he was a "longtime friend and acquaintance"; Gonzalo Hernández,
a recently arrived priest and confederate of Almagro's; Pedro de Torres, the estate steward from Nicaragua earlier accused of murder; and Pedro Carrion, a
retainer in his forties who had known Soto in Nicaragua, and would later become the oldest conquistador serving in the Florida army.[^]

Soto's circle in Cuzco became complete with the arrival during the winter
of 1534–35 of Hernán Ponce de León, who sailed from León in one of the *compañia*'s ships, undoubtedly brimming with slaves and whatever portable
wealth Ponce was able to muster as he cashed in the partners' properties in
Nicaragua.[^]

Initially, the *compañeros'* reunion did not go well. Testifying years later in
the lawsuit he brought against Soto's widow, Ponce says that he and Soto
began arguing soon after he arrived, and that the relationship nearly went sour
then and there, though he does not specify the reason. Possibly, he was angry
at Soto's failure to send more than a token amount of gold to Nicaragua. They
also seem to have disagreed about the future direction of their partnership, trying to decide if they should embark on another *entrada,* settle in Peru, or cash
in their property and return to Spain.[^] The real reason for their animosity, however, probably had more to do with their respective roles. In Nicaragua, I suspect Ponce had been the senior member of the partnership, and was not pleased
to find their roles had been reversed in Peru.

Whatever their differences, they resolved them by July 27, 1535, when the
two men signed a contract reaffirming their partnership, and joining together
not only Soto's gold and properties, but new *encomiendas* Ponce received from
Pizarro, who had earlier promised him "the best to be found in the kingdom"
in exchange for the use of the *compañia*'s ships. This made these two men
among the richest in not only the Americas, but in the entire Spanish Empire.

Thanks to the massive lawsuit brought by Ponce after Soto's death against
his wife, Isabel de Bobadilla, we have a good idea of what this fortune was
worth. During the trial, which lasted from 1546–50, witnesses in Spain, Peru,
and elsewhere claimed the *compañia*'s total assets equaled some 200,000 to
250,000 ducats when Soto left Peru, including gold, property, Indians, and the
annual tribute paid by these Indians, "worth 30,000 gold pesos."[^] Ponce himself confirmed these figures, though he insisted Soto took almost everything
when he left Peru for Spain. He also alleged that Soto took this money without
his approval, an assertion denied even by his own witnesses.[^]

The partners found, however, that even as the ink dried on their new contract, their time to enjoy their wealth and property in Peru was fast coming to
an end as postconquest politics began to tear asunder Pizarro's realm, a situation that might have afforded a man such as Soto potential opportunities,

though as he would soon discover, not even an ante of 250,000 ducats was enough to keep him in the game.

✝   ✝   ✝

By late spring 1535, when Ponce arrived, Soto's prospects of conquering his own slice of the Inca Empire were already rapidly diminishing. In the north, two unauthorized campaigns set out in February to conquer Quito. The first was led by Soto's old rival, Sebastián de Benalcázar, who abandoned his post as garrison commander of San Miguel to march north, defeating the remnants of Quizquiz's army with two hundred recent arrivals from Panama. Then came Pedro de Alvarado, Cortés's former captain. Marching overland from the Ecuadorian coast to Quito with five hundred men, he lost one in five to starvation, cold, and high altitude crossing the Andes, arriving in Quito too weak to challenge Benalcázar, who soon had problems of his own as an enraged Pizarro dispatched Diego de Almagro with a huge force that demanded, and got, the renegade's surrender. Soto's prospects in the southern third of the Inca Empire likewise ended in the spring of 1535, when a ship arrived in Lima bearing orders from the king giving Almagro the concession to conquer Chile, and to be its first governor.

Up until this royal decree, Diego de Almagro must have been one of the most frustrated men in Peru. Since 1524, he had been Pizarro's partner, serving mostly as a subordinate organizing and outfitting the expeditions to Peru while Pizarro led operations in the field, and snatched away most of the titles, gold, and glory. Indeed, in 1529, when Pizarro returned from Spain with only a minor title of "marshall of Peru" for his partner, Almagro had become so incensed he quit the enterprise in disgust, though Pizarro was able to lure him back with promises of titles and heaps of treasure, not all of which he had honored.

By all accounts, Diego de Almagro was a highly capable commander and a natural leader who attracted fierce devotion among his supporters. Another old man of the *conquista*—he was now in his fifties, slightly younger than Pizarro—Almagro was also born a bastard and was probably illiterate. Said to be physically strong and intelligent, Pedro Cieza de León describes him as "a man of short stature, with ugly features, but of great courage and endurance. He was liberal, but given to boasting, letting his tongue run on, sometimes without bridling it." Others, primarily those who supported Pizarro in the coming conflict between the governor and Almagro, were less generous. They cast Almagro as a great villain, the man who "forced" Pizarro to execute Atahualpa, and who started the civil war between the Pizarroists and Almagroists.

In late March, however, when Almagro returned to Pizarro's headquarters at Lima after securing Quito, Pizarro at last awarded him a substantial title—

the lieutenant governorship of Cuzco—giving him orders to ride to the Inca
capital as Soto's replacement. This was an astute move by Francisco Pizarro.
For it may have occurred to him that Almagro and Soto, both independent political forces in Peru with strong personal followings, might someday see a
common interest in working against the Pizarros, a move he hoped to counter
by giving Almagro Soto's job. If this was Pizarro's strategy, however, it backfired when the news about Almagro's Chilean concession arrived in Lima
shortly after the newly appointed lieutenant governor departed for Cuzco. In
fact, the timing for Pizarro could not have been worse, to have one of his ex-
citable subordinates halfway between Lima and Cuzco when he received word
of his elevation to governor of Chile, even as his other less-than-trustworthy
senior captain was receiving word he was to be sacked. Adding to this potentially volatile situation was the fact that Almagro heard about his appointment
as a garbled rumor on the highway to Cuzco, which told him he had been given
authority not only over Chile, but Cuzco itself—hearsay that turned out to be
false, though only after Almagro had arrived in Cuzco, and insisted the city
was his.^

Almagro's claim, made as Soto, Juan Pizarro, Manco Inca, and a large
honor guard of Spanish *vecinos* and Incas gathered to welcome him, plunged
Cuzco into a crisis. Hotly disputing Almagro's claims, Juan Pizarro and other
Pizarro loyalists armed themselves in the governor's headquarters at Casana
Palace, on the central plaza. Likewise, Almagro and his men gathered weapons
and artillery and fortified Almagro's quarters nearby, in Huascar's palace.

This left Soto in an awkward and perilous situation. Since Almagro had not
been officially sworn in, he technically remained lieutenant governor, as well
as royal corregidor, which meant it fell to him to defuse the situation. Remaining cool, he quickly confronted both sides, ordering them to back down while
he sent one of his officials, Vasco de Guevara, to Lima to fetch back Almagro's
official royal orders, and to ask the governor to clarify Almagro's status.^

But the hotheaded Juan Pizarro could not sit tight and wait. Convinced Soto
was siding with Almagro, and that the mission to Lima was a delaying tactic,
he readied a small force to find and kill the messenger Guevara in the rocky
hills west of the city. Soto, however, found out in time to rush over to Casana
and prevent the attack, though only after "Juan Pizarro became haughty" and
threatened to lunge at Soto with a lance.

Soto didn't flinch, demanding "with all his restraint and charm" that Juan
put down his weapon and stop "looking for scandals." He then "admonished
them," says Cieza, "not to give rise to bad things and words," to which Juan responded with more "haughtiness and insults, saying that Hernando de Soto was
a friend of Almagro's and that he had shown a bias toward him."

Realizing that the situation was getting out of hand, and that the last thing the tiny band of Spaniards in this city of 100,000 Incas needed was a war amongst themselves, Soto showed considerable self-control by abruptly departing the scene, though he did so "in a huff," says Cieza, "as he was the chief justice in that city, and as such they had scorned and even threatened him."

This was not the end of the incident, however. For "when Almagro heard about this," continues Cieza, "he said that Juan and Gonzalo Pizarro were fickle and sniveling brats, and he sent many horsemen from among his allies" to protect Vasco de Guevara, the messenger. He also demanded that Soto, as the chief magistrate of the city, return to the Pizarros' palace and place Juan Pizarro under house arrest so that he would "not leave the city, because it was said that he wanted to go after Vasco de Guevara."

This demand forced Soto to decide between the two camps, since to arrest Juan Pizarro would make him an enemy of the Pizarros, and not to arrest him would alienate Diego de Almagro.

Actually, Soto's decision was an easy one, since Pizarro was obviously pushing him out, even as Almagro was becoming master of the next phase of conquest in the south, where everyone assumed there would be more Cajamarcas and Cuzcos filled with gold. Thus, as Pedro de Cieza notes, Soto at this point abandoned any semblance of impartiality and jumped "in bed with Almagro, and supported his interests."

Soto must have known that the bellicose Juan Pizarro would not give in meekly. Yet he walked across the hot, pebble-strewn plaza to Casana Palace anyway. Dressed in his magistrate's clothes, and accompanied by the city's constable and a small guard, he demanded the young Pizarro and his men turn over their arms and remain under house arrest. To which Juan responded "with bitterness and pride," screaming more obscenities and insults at Soto before once again grabbing a lance to wave in Soto's direction.

By now, Soto had had enough of this insolence. Always preferring action to talk, he grabbed a lance himself from one of his guards,* and challenged the young man to a fight in the plaza.

"Inflamed" and ready to brawl, the two men strolled haughtily out into the bright sunshine, under the peaks that surround Cuzco. Here Hernando de Soto and Juan Pizarro threw off their capes as a crowd of somber *vecinos* gathered to watch the spectacle of their two most senior leaders swinging heavy weapons at each other, glancing off blows and attempting to knock each other

---

*Long wooden pikes were often used in jousts and brawls between comrades who wanted to knock down their opponent rather than kill him, though fatalities still occurred.

down. Both men, however, were small and muscular, and expert lancers and fighters, which meant the duel continued for some time without either man gaining the advantage.

As the fight wore on, word spread quickly to followers of Pizarro, Almagro, and Soto, who armed themselves and rushed into the plaza, threatening to escalate the conflict.

What happened next is unclear. Cieza, who was not there, claims Juan Pizarro abruptly broke off the duel and retired to his palace when it became clear his followers were too few to defeat their enemies. Eyewitnesses claim that a recently arrived royal treasurer, Antonio Tellez de Guzmán, stopped the fight by dramatically grabbing a weapon of his own and leaping between Soto and Pizarro, holding up his lance and shouting to the combatants that "the Spaniards were too few in number to battle among themselves, and that if the two sides started fighting, the Indians would kill those who survived, and the city would be lost."

Hearing these words, Soto cooled down and realized his duty was to stop the fight, which he did, though he was "unwilling to excuse the scandal." Returning to his own palace in a rage, he issued orders forbidding the Pizarroists to leave the city, and then sent his constable (and presumably a large unit of armed deputies) to arrest Juan Pizarro, who apparently surrendered without a fight, and was taken to the city jail. Cieza adds that neither party acted with impartiality or wisdom in this incident, though he mostly blames the twenty-four-year-old Juan Pizarro, whom he says "was always turbulent and filled with envy for one or another." Even in jail, says Cieza, he threatened "to go out and kill everyone."^

Soon after, Francisco Pizarro himself arrived in Cuzco to defuse the situation, bringing with him the king's actual concession to Almagro. Typically, it was vague as to the geographical limits of Almagro's new domain. It seemed reasonably clear that Cuzco was to remain part of Pizarro's Peruvian colony, however—an interpretation Almagro agreed to after Pizarro gave permission to his former partner to recruit troops in Peru for his expedition. (No Spaniards could leave without the governor's consent.) Pizarro also offered to invest a large sum of money to help pay for the *entrada* to Chile.

✢   ✢   ✢

Once the situation calmed down in Cuzco, Pizarro wasted no time sacking Soto for openly siding with Diego de Almagro. He also made it clear that there would be no place for Soto in any future Pizarro venture, though this hardly concerned the ex lieutenant governor, who was now openly lobbying Almagro for a senior role in his upcoming conquest. Indeed, nearly everyone in Cuzco that spring assumed that Diego de Almagro would name Hernando de Soto to lead his campaign as captain general^—though as Soto would soon find out, the new governor had other ideas.

Little is known about the relationship between Soto and Almagro. They must have known each other in Central America. In Peru, they had frequently ridden together on campaigns, though often in an almost adversarial role as Almagro was either sent to restrain Soto's overly eager inclinations—which was the situation at Vilcaconga—or to reinforce Soto when the governor thought more men were needed—such as the recent campaign to drive Quizquiz back to Ecuador. At Cajamarca, we also see them representing opposing points of view on whether or not to execute Atahualpa. There is no reason to believe, however, that the two men thought badly of each other. Indeed, they now found themselves united by a shared animosity toward Pizarro, and the excitement of contemplating another conquest.

Yet Almagro seems to have been cool to Soto from the start. This is despite a Soto offer of 200,000 pesos if the new governor would name him to command the expedition to Chile^—a staggering sum that must have included not only some of Ponce's money, but also that of other investors willing to back Soto in Chile.

Diego de Almagro agonized over Soto's enticing offer, wanting the money, and knowing that militarily he was the best man for the job. In the end, he decided that behind Soto's outrageous offer lay an eagerness unseemly for a second-in-command. He therefore stunned everyone in Cuzco by announcing sometime in June that Soto would not participate in the *entrada* at all, and that he would lead the campaign himself, with a young, obscure officer—a former Soto outrider, Rodrigo de Orgóñez—serving as his captain general.^

Watching the Chilean expedition depart without him on July 5, Soto must have felt bitterly disappointed. For not only had he finally burned his bridges with the Pizarros with his support of Almagro, he now was faced for the first time in his life with no great task to accomplish—an intolerable condition for him. Even his whereabouts over the next few months are mostly unknown as he restlessly managed his properties and plotted his next move with Hernán Ponce and his cronies in Amaru Cancha.

A witness to these discussions, Soto's *majordomo* Alonso de Ayala, recalled years later that the two partners argued over what to do next.^ Apparently, their concept of the future had diverged a great deal since Soto departed Nicaragua, with Ponce, the more sedate of the two, wanting to take his money and settle down, either in Peru or back in Spain. Soto, however, was aching for a conquest of his own. The result was a compromise—with the two men agreeing that Ponce would remain in Peru and manage the *compañia*'s affairs, while

Soto returned to Spain to ask the king for fresh lands to conquer. Ayala and other witnesses said the partners further argued over where this concession should be,^ ultimately agreeing that Soto would ask for the still-unclaimed lands to the north of Quito in Colombia; or, if they were unavailable, for certain unexplored regions of Central America. They also decided that Soto would return to Spain with most of the company's gold, which would be needed to bribe court officials, and to pay for the expedition.

Soto departed Peru late in 1535, after transporting his gold by llama down the winding highway from Cuzco to the bustling new port at Lima. Here he boarded his own ship, the stalwart *San Geronimo,* filling its holds and cabins with his household, retainers, and a great pile of Inca treasures to give as gifts in Spain—clothing, tents, furniture, and slaves. He also carefully loaded his loot, "some in bars"^ of gold and silver, says a witness who sailed with him, "some packed in earthenware, and some in the form of women's figures." Traveling with him was the same core group he had gathered in Cuzco, and that would stay with him in Spain and *La Florida*—including Moscoso, Lobillo, and Nuño de Tobar.^

He probably sailed before the winter storms began in November, once again bidding farewell to a country he had helped alter beyond recognition, and carrying with him an enormous fortune. "Follow the adventures" of Hernando de Soto, says Oviedo, "taught in the school of Pedrarias de Avila in the scattering and wasting of the Indians of Castilla del Oro; a graduate in the killing of the natives of Nicaragua and canonized in Peru as a member of the order of the Pizarros; and then, after being delivered from all the paths to Hell and having come to Spain loaded with gold . . . knew not how nor was he able to rest without returning to the Indies to shed blood, not content with what he had already spilled . . ."

As he left Peru, Soto had acquired everything a conquistador dreamed of—riches, fame, and glory. He also had killed enough Indians, as Oviedo points out, to satisfy the bloodlust of the most rapacious conqueror.

But it was not enough. For Soto's obsession, as always, was with moving on to the next opportunity—with plunging ahead into the unknown, following El Cid's dictate always to seek greater glory, fortune, and success. And now, with his options exhausted in Peru, he was headed for the one place he knew of where he thought he might cash in his newfound fame and money for a fresh opportunity at conquest—at the court of His Cesarean Majesty, Emperor Charles V.

✣ 17 ✣

Back to Spain

SAILING UP THE WIDE, gray Guadalquivir on a spring day in 1536,* Hernando de Soto first glimpsed Seville as a cloud of smoke and dust rising into the blue sky of Andalusia. For him, it must have been a beautiful sight as the roofs and walls gradually came into view, topped off by the slender spire of the Giralda Tower. Just twenty-two years earlier, he had left this city as a no-name page. Now he was returning at age thirty-six a hero. For not only was he the most important captain from Peru to return home since Hernando Pizarro a year earlier—and one of the richest, carrying his one thousand pounds of gold^—he also happened to be arriving at a singular moment in Spanish history, when his countrymen felt more triumphant and less cynical than perhaps any time before or after.

As Soto's ship wound slowly through the freshly planted fields of spring wheat, grapes, and citrus groves south of the city, everything seemed to be going right for the Spanish. On their throne sat an energetic, if already weary, king-emperor who, at thirty-six, dominated Europe as no one had since Charlemagne, controlling scattered territories from Hungary and Germany to the Netherlands, and Italy to Spain. In the past five years his soldiers and conquistadors had humiliated his mortal enemy, the French, in Milan and Venice, turned back the Turks at Vienna, and conquered an immense new empire in the Indies. Within a decade, Charles's luster would dim as his Machiavellian maneuverings in Europe unraveled, and he plunged into a bloody, soul-wrenching campaign against Christian reformers led by Martin Luther. But for now, the Spaniards could gush over the exploits of a returning native son with absolute abandon.

---

*The exact date of Soto's arrival in Seville is not recorded.

✛   ✛   ✛

By the time the *Santa María del Campo* docked at the pier and stood down its sails, a great crowd had gathered, pushing and shoving to see who was on board, and to get a glimpse of the legendary *capitán*. At some point, the crowd parted as gendarmes cut a path for city officials and representatives from the Council of the Indies, who ordered port marshals to board the ships and insure that no gold or cargo was removed before being registered and taxed.

Once the official business was finished, Soto and his party stepped off the ships and onto shore. If they followed the usual custom, they climbed onto ox and donkey carts and were paraded through the city to the Casa de Contratación,^ where Soto and the others registered their arrival and then crossed a small plaza to the great cathedral, where custom further dictated they offer prayers, and gifts thanking God for their safe crossing.

In the crowd that day were several of Soto's friends from Peru, including his worshipful cavalry lieutenant, the thirty-two-year-old Pedro Cataño, who had returned to Spain a year earlier. According to Cataño, he invited Soto to stay at his house,^ where he apparently lived until finding a *casa* of his own later that spring or early summer.

According to witnesses, the palace Soto eventually acquired was enormous, containing a large courtyard and numerous apartments on two floors, with a grand staircase inside,^ and a staff befitting a high noble. "He employed servants," writes the anonymous Gentleman of Elvas, one of the Florida chroniclers who visited Soto in Seville, "including a majordomo, grand master of ceremonies, pages, equerry, chamberlain, footmen, and all the other servants requisite for an establishment of a gentleman."

Soto's friends later recalled that summer in Seville as a flurry of martial tournaments, gambling, parties, and cavorting. Alonso Pérez de Biberos, a crony who knew Soto in Nicaragua and in Seville, says Soto "spent much money on games, *cañas,* and other merriments." Luis de Moscoso also remembered that "when they went to Spain" they indulged in "things of passion and were quick-tempered," which probably means they spent a great deal of time strutting about and picking fights with anyone foolish enough to annoy or challenge them.

In between games and duels, Soto also attended to business. First and foremost, this involved his cache of gold, most of which was impounded by the Casa de Contratación upon his arrival. This was routine during the sixteenth century for returning conquerors, who often had to negotiate for months with officials over taxes and duties before their booty was returned. In Soto's case, the process seems to have gone smoothly, though the fact he stayed with his friend Cataño for several weeks suggests there may have been some delay.

What Soto ultimately paid for taxes is unknown, though we know the Casa de Contratación did force him into agreeing to an unspecified "loan" to the Crown—another common practice for the always-cash-strapped monarchy. This loan, however, was mostly repaid before Soto departed for Florida, partly in cash, and partly by providing Soto with an annual annuity based on the Crown's lucrative monopoly over the importation of silk, which by law entered Spain only through Granada. This amounted to an income of some eight hundred ducats a year, a very respectable income for a noble in Spain.^ Of course, Soto would have preferred to have his money returned as cash. But he understood that his "loan" was in essence a bribe to get the attention of the king—a necessity for anyone seeking favors from the Crown, particularly for something as audacious as permission to attempt a conquest.

Soto's obsession did not waver even amidst the pleasures of his new life in Seville, a state of mind no one describes better than Soto biographer Garcilaso de la Vega—also known as the Inca—whose insight into human behavior is often as penetrating as his facts are exaggerated and romanticized. Given Soto's success and money, the Inca suggests that most men would have settled down. Soto, however, "did not . . . Rather, his ideas and spirits being elevated by things that he experienced in El Peru, not content with what he had already done and acquired, [he desired] to undertake other similar and great exploits, if greater there could be." He adds that Soto was also motivated by "generous envy of . . . the Marquis del Valle Don Hernando Cortés . . . the Marquis Don Francisco Pizarro and the Adelantado Don Diego de Almagro." Nor could he tolerate being "inferior to those just named in valor and energy for war, or in prudence and discretion for peace."

✛   ✛   ✛

Almost immediately after arriving in Seville, Soto informed the Council of the Indies that he intended to ask Charles's permission to carry on a conquest. "Captain Soto of Peru arrived at this Court," reports an official document sent from the council to the king, "and he asked to finish the conquest [of the Indies] 200 leagues along the South Sea belonging to Don Pedro de Mendoza* [the viceroy of Mexico]. Note: he also offered to explore on the South Sea [the Pacific] passing to Peru. He is a man rich and they say of good reputation."

After this initial inquiry, Soto plunged into winning his concession. Indeed, during these months in Seville, Soto showed a great deal of skill in constructing a network of powerful allies among courtiers, the nobility, and other influ-

*This should be Don Antonio de Mendoza, viceroy of Mexico.

ential persons, shrewdly playing on his fame as a conquering hero, and on his skills as a "charmer" to make a remarkably smooth transition from the rough culture of the frontier to the burnished high society of Renaissance Spain.

Of course, he was aided immensely by his reputation as a dashing young man, renowned as a warrior in a warrior's culture. Mysterious, yet charming; tough, yet charismatic, he must have seemed irresistible as he dazzled the rich and powerful at dinners, tournaments, and parties, sweeping into a room dressed in great black capes and a flashy sword as everyone whispered stories about him that seemed lifted straight from *Amadis of Gaul.* Evidence of Soto's success in high society comes from a letter he wrote to an unnamed high-ranking official—probably written in the fall or winter of 1535—whom he apparently had impressed (or paid) enough to offer his support. I reproduce it below, because it is not only one of the few intact missives we have in Soto's own words, but also suggests Soto's frame of mind during this period.

Very Magnificent Lord:

That which Your Worship is to favor me in is as follows:

Inasmuch as His Majesty has not ceded to Francisco Pizarro more than two hundred and seventy-five leagues of the six hundred leagues granted [him] . . . there might be taken off from the beginning of his government to the town of San Miguel an extent of about one hundred leagues, starting from the town of Panama supposing now His Majesty should be pleased to grant it to me . . . even if it is the most sterile and unprofitable of that country, although I am of opinion that by way of Quito there is good opening into the interior, whereby to serve His Majesty in the Province from which I have just come.

Your worship not being able to get what I set forth, will try then for the government of Guatemala, with permission to make discovery in the South Sea, and for the title of Adelantado, with concession for His Majesty of the tenth part of whatever I may at my own cost discover in the sea and conquer, with patent and to my successors.

What Your Worship will send to the Señor Comendador, to be negotiated with His Majesty, is as follows:

The mantle of Santiago for Hernán Ponce de León.

All the Indians of apportionment which said Hernán Ponce de León and I hold by schedule from His Majesty, with other property in lands and houses, in fee simple, and if possible with a title.

Let whatever government may be given to me be given in perpetuity if possible, and if not, then for the longest term Your Worship may be enabled to secure. And when you shall have acted on these instructions and discovered where is the best chance of success, you will let me know I am to treat with these Lords of the Council in this business, and what I am to write to the Señor Comendador, and when.

Hernando de Soto^

It would be interesting to know who this letter is addressed to. The addressee's obvious familiarity with the court also suggests he is well-placed in Charles's administration.^ The letter itself is vintage Soto, written with a soldierly directness, and laying bare Soto's ambitions unvarnished by the usual niceties and flattery one almost always finds in such letters from this era. Soto's bluntness and self-confidence, however, seem to have been admired by his contemporaries, and remain a great constant throughout his life, whether he is plunging into battle, issuing edicts in Cuzco, exploring fresh territories, or asking favors as a supplicant.

Undoubtedly, Soto sent similar missives to other highly placed supporters, though none seems to have responded more vigorously than a woman he had met years earlier in Panama—Isabel de Bobadilla y Peñalosa, wife of his former mentor and nemesis, Pedrarias Dávila, and one of the most highly placed and formidable courtiers in Castile. Since the early 1520s, Isabel had been in Spain, first using her connections and talents to extricate her husband from his *residencia* in Castilla del Oro, and then serving as matriarch of the Bobadillas and Peñalosas, two of the most powerful and richest clans in Spain.^

Doña Isabel would have remembered Hernando de Soto as a rakish young captain in Panama—and, at the time, a close ally to her husband. Indeed, when she heard he was back in Spain and after a royal concession, she seems to have readily agreed to help with the king, adding an unexpected bonus for a formerly poor, unknown *hidalgo* from the back country—the hand of one of her daughters in marriage.

This was her third-born child, also named Isabel de Bobadilla, who in 1535–36 must have been at least in her late twenties.^ This suggests she may have been a widow, or somehow undesirable as a mate, since typically a woman in a highborn family was married by this age. Possibly, she had had trouble bearing children in a previous marraige, a theory borne out by the fact that she and Soto had no children during the three years they were together. She also may have been simply unattractive in some way, a notion suggested by the lack of effusive adjectives provided by any of the *La Florida* chroniclers. Even Garcilaso de la Vega says only that Isabel was "a woman of much goodness and discretion," a remarkably downbeat description for this romanticist.

The Inca's brief description was apt, however, for a woman who would serve as acting governor of Cuba in Soto's absence, and proved extremely capable as an administrator and woman of affairs. Garcilaso's assessment was also shared by Rodrigo Ranjel, Soto's private secretary in Cuba and *La Florida,* who tells us that the younger Isabel inherited her mother's fortitude, intelligence, and strength of character. "Like her mother," Ranjel writes, she was "a woman of great essence and goodness, and of very noble judgment and character." Soto himself confirms her abilities by the fact he named her acting governor, an unusual appointment for a woman in sixteenth-century Spain.^

My guess is that Isabel's physical demeanor mattered little in a marriage that was essentially a business arrangement, one that attached the lower-born Soto to a high noble family whose own stature was increased by allying itself with this very rich hero of the moment. The marraige took place in late November 1536, in the Bobadilla family chapel in Valladolid^—but only after Soto and his lawyers pounded out a marriage agreement with his betrothed's mother and her lawyers, giving Soto a large ranch in Panama as a dowry.^

The wedding was a high-society event in Valladolid, attended by courtiers in sumptuous capes, jerkins, satin leggings, and gold jewelry.^ The guest list also included Soto's friends Lobillo and Moscoso, and a new crony they met in Seville, a talented young pilot and *hidalgo* named Juan de Añasco—whose appearance here makes Soto's circle of high-ranking officers for *La Florida* nearly complete.

+   +   +

Before Soto left Seville for Valladolid, he purchased the clothing and furnishings required by his new status. Elvas claims he was not a flashy dresser, though the occasion of presenting oneself at the court of Charles V demanded a certain splendor. "They went well and costly appareled," writes Elvas, with Soto spending "very liberally" on clothes—which probably included decorative armor, brocades, velvets, gold embroidery, scented gloves, leggings edged in taffeta, and boots of colored leather as soft as silk. He also would have worn the heavy gold jewelry he was so fond of—chain necklaces, rings, and buckles—a glittering display of his success in Peru.

Elvas adds that Soto traveled with an enormous retinue in Spain that included not only Moscoso and his other sidekicks, but a train of servants: "his dependents, and many others who came about him." He also would have taken with him armed guards dressed in his livery to protect his train of coaches from bandits and wild animals during the dusty four-hundred-mile journey from Seville to Valladolid, and wherever else he traveled to meet nobles who might further his cause.

The sovereign that Soto came to meet did not arrive at court until February 1537. One of the most peripatetic kings in European history, Charles had been away from Spain for almost two years, first leading his victorious fleet in the capture of Tunis in Africa, and then conferring at the Vatican with Pope Clement VII, a Hapsburg ally. During the visit to Rome, Charles had issued a famous challenge that typifies a man greatly admired by conquistadors in the Indies for his haughtiness, ambition, and willingness to take chances. He had asked King Francis I of France, his greatest rival, to meet him one-on-one on a field to settle their differences once and for all—by jousting to the death. Francis, of course, turned him down, though the warrior culture of Spain loved their king for making such a gesture.

In 1536, Charles was almost exactly Soto's age, having been born in 1500 to the only daughter of Ferdinand and Isabel, named Juana, whose husband was the son of the Hapsburg emperor Maximillian I. This made Charles the heir to both dynasties, and to their extensive territories, beginning with Spain, which he inherited soon after Ferdinand's death in 1516. (His mother first inherited the throne, but was declared mentally unstable.) In 1519, when Maximillian died in Vienna, Charles also became ruler of Austria, the Netherlands, and Burgundy. That same year, he was elected Holy Roman Emperor, making him the dominant sovereign in Germany.

Charles was a brilliant, if overly serious, monarch who early on mastered what it took not only to administer his far-flung territories, but to parry and thrust against his enemies to gain even more. Machiavellian to a fault, his entire life was spent playing an enormous game of chess, with his opponents ranging from the French and the Lutherans to the Ottoman Empire, then at its height. Portraits show Charles as having a prominent nose, a heavy lower jaw, and a slight orthodontic deformity that prevented his teeth from meeting—which undoubtedly caused discomfort at mealtime. He dressed lavishly, though he said this was more out of duty than personal preference, a comment that dovetails nicely with Charles's most famous quip—that he ruled by using "an iron fist in a velvet glove."

✛ ✛ ✛

Apparently, the emperor was impressed by Hernando de Soto when they met in March or April 1537. We have no record of this meeting, or of Soto's days at court. Charles, however, always enjoyed spending time with notable conquerors from the Indies, whose stories and exploits offered a pleasant and, given the amount of gold flowing into his treasury from across the Ocean Sea, profitable diversion from his European entanglements.

Evidence of Soto's success with the king came on April 20, when the Crown issued the first of three documents providing Soto with his long-sought concession to conquer his own territory. This *capitulación,* however, contained a surprise for anyone following Soto's career up until this point. For instead of Colombia or Guatemala, the king granted him permission to invade a territory far away from either location—a place called *La Florida.*

How Soto's request for a position in Latin America became a mission to Florida is unknown, though apparently it came up when Soto discovered that Colombia and Guatemala had already been taken by others.^ Nor do we know who first suggested *La Florida,* though it almost certainly was the Crown, since for years they had been alarmed by the vulnerability of Spanish shipping as it passed close to the shoreline of North America, riding the Gulf Stream back to Spain. Lately, this coast had become a haven for French and British pirates. Soto may also have been enticed by tales of fantastic empires in this mysterious country.

To select just a few from a long list of fables then being circulated about *La Florida,* it's likely Soto was aware of claims it was home to the legendary Antillia Empire—founded, it was said, centuries earlier by seven Portuguese bishops who escaped the Moslem invasion of Iberia. He also would have heard legends about Amazons, people with eyes in their chests, and so forth, as well as stories linking *La Florida* with the kingdom of Prester John, a mythical Christian monarch who supposedly penned a letter circulated in the thirteenth century offering the services of his powerful army against Moslems and other Christian enemies.^ How much credence Soto gave these legends is unknown, though given a lifelong obsession with investigating every rumor he came across concerning gold and undiscovered empires, he undoubtedly listened raptly to every shred of information, true or false, he heard about his new concession.

Soto was not the first to try and conquer North America. The Crown already had launched three expeditions to seize the future United States. All had ended in disaster, with hundreds killed. Mostly, this was due to the incompetence of these *entradas'* leadership, though by now this vast territory of forests, mountains, swamps, and reportedly warlike natives had acquired a reputation as an evil and unlucky place.

First to try and conquer *La Florida* was Juan Ponce de León, of Fountain of Youth fame, though Ponce himself never mentions anything about a fountain. (The legend may have originated with Peter Martyr, a court historian who erroneously connects Ponce de León with a fountain of rejuvenating waters.) More likely, this former governor of Puerto Rico was after the usual gold and slaves. Ponce was so notorious for incompetence and cruelty toward the Indians in Puerto Rico that he had been dismissed by the *Audiencia* in Santo Domingo. Ending up back in Spain, he managed to secure the concession to Florida—he called it Bimini—from Ferdinand, setting sail in March 1513 in three small vessels. On Easter Sunday he made landfall, probably near Daytona Beach. Naming his new territory for the day he landed—which in Spain is called *Pascua Florida,* "the Feast of Flowers"—Ponce explored around the southern tip of the peninsula until being attacked by Calusa Indians outraged at Spanish attempts to seize them as slaves. This prompted a weary Juan Ponce and his bloodied party to give up and return to Spain, where he later organized a second effort to take Florida in 1519. This ended with Ponce being mortally wounded during an Indian battle near Charlotte Harbor. He died a few days later in Cuba.

The second attempt to conquer North America was more benign, being a genuine effort to establish a colony and settlement. It began in 1526, when a wealthy sugar plantation owner and high official on Hispaniola,^ Lucas Vázquez de Ayllón, convinced the king that a rich land called Chicora existed to the north of Ponce de León's *La Florida.* Insisting it had a moderate climate and large deposits of gold and silver, he talked up a rumor that a great kingdom existed in the interior ruled by a white king.^ Ayllón based his claims on information provided by an Indian captured in 1521 by slavers near Winyah Bay, north of present-day Charleston, South Carolina. Given the name Francisco de Chicora, this Indian quickly learned Spanish in Hispaniola. Apparently wanting more than anything to return home, he affirmed every wild rumor and speculation the Spaniards suggested,* attracting the attention not only of Ayllón, but also of the six hundred men and women who accompanied him to the future South Carolina in 1526. "Chicora," however, turned out to be decidedly un-European-like when the colonists arrived, the Carolina shore being a tangle of bogs and palmetto swamps. Despite this, Ayllón lingered there the entire summer, waiting until October to relocate to a better site in Georgia. By then, it was too late to grow food. This led to a horrific winter of starvation and disease. All but 150 people died. When Ayllón himself succumbed, the survivors gave up and fled back to Hispaniola.

The most recent attempt to conquer *La Florida* had come in 1527, when the one-eyed, red-haired Pánfilo de Narváez, a veteran of the Cuban conquest, cobbled together an ill-equipped force of four hundred men and eighty horses and headed north from his base in Santiago de Cuba to Tampa Bay. A bungler of the first order, whom Las Casa called "incompetent . . . cruel and stupid," Narváez a few years earlier had earned notoriety as the captain who took nine hundred men to arrest Hernán Cortés after his illegal conquest of the Aztecs, only to be soundly thrashed by the Mexican conqueror, and imprisoned for several months. This was followed by an inauspicious reign as governor of Cuba, where Narváez so incensed the local Indians that they launched a revolt still in progress when Soto arrived as governor of the island a decade later.

---

*Francisco de Chicora ran away soon after the Ayllón expedition arrived in "Chicora." Presumably he returned to his people.

True to form, Narváez had headed for Florida in the spring of 1528 without proper supplies or reconnaissance, and minus any native translators or guides. And if this were not bad enough, shortly after arriving, Narváez made the mistake of separating his land forces from his ships, whom he ordered to rendezvous with him at the end of the summer somewhere to the north. Tromping off into the interior one day in June 1538, chasing the usual rumors of gold, Narváez and his men disappeared without a trace, a loss so mysterious and chilling that in the dozen years since no one had dared try following in his footsteps.

Soto and the king signed the *capitulación* for *La Florida* on April 20, 1537, after weeks of haggling by each party's lawyers. The main issues were how much tax Soto would pay for any gold plundered or mined, whether or not he would be named governor for life, and how many years he would be given to complete his task.

The document itself, which presumes to give away an unexplored country whose inhabitants were unaware the Spaniards even existed, was similar to other concessions granted during the *conquista.* It starts by ceding to Hernando de Soto the right "to conquer and settle [from] the Province of Río de las Palmas [northern Mexico] to Florida, the government whereof was bestowed on Pánfilo de Narváez, and the Provinces of Tierra-Nueva, the discovery and government of which was bestowed on Lucas Vázquez de Ayllón." It then specifies that Soto take a minimum of five hundred men, including priests "for the instruction of the natives of that Province in our Holy Catholic Faith," certain officers, and "the necessary arms, horses, munitions, and military stores." The king orders Soto to build "three stone fortresses in the harbors and places most appropriate for them," to guard against pirates, and to supply provisions for his men to last at least eighteen months. As was customary, all of this was to be paid for by Soto, and not the Crown. Given four years to complete his conquest, from the time he departed Spain, he also was given the right to designate two hundred leagues (some six hundred miles) of coastline that he would govern "for all the days of your life, with an annual salary of . . . 2000 [ducats]," with twelve square leagues of his choosing to be owned by him and his family.

The rest of Soto's *cedula* mostly concerns two entirely contradictory commands. First, Soto is ordered to pay taxes and duties on whatever profits he realizes, or treasure he steals, including slaves, ransom collected from kidnapping *caciques,* and "all the gold and silver, stones, pearls, and other things that may be found or taken." Concurrently, he is instructed to see to "the good treatment of the Indians," and to avoid "the evils and disorders which occur in making discoveries and new settlements."

In the concession, and in subsequent documents signed over the next two weeks, the king also appointed Soto governor of Cuba, which he planned to use as a base for his expedition.

As a final honor, the king in late April laid across the shoulders of the new adelantado and governor-general a brilliant white tunic embroidered with the red crossed daggers of Santiago, Spain's most revered military order.^ One imagines a courtly ceremony with the king in his shimmering robes and crown, and Soto in a costly suit of armor, as the Knights of Santiago convene to hear the invocation of a new member. Charles then takes his sword in the familiar ceremony of touching each of Soto's shoulders with the blade,^ fulfilling a long-held obsession of a man who had spent his childhood in Jerez de los Caballeros watching the Santiaguines come and go from their castle in the middle of his city, and had probably dreamed about one day joining their ranks.

Book IV

Conquest

✧ 18 ✧

Armada

DURING THE SUMMER OF 1536, about the time Soto was moving into his new palace in Seville, far across the Ocean Sea in Mexico, Viceroy Antonio de Mendoza was receiving a gaunt, heavily tattooed medicine man who had appeared one day to the north of the city. His name was Álvar Núñez Cabeza de Vaca, formerly the royal treasurer of the Narváez expedition, which eight years earlier had disappeared without a trace in *La Florida*. Declaring Cabeza de Vaca's survival a miracle, Mendoza provided the former treasurer with clothes and housing and, the following year, a ship to convey him back across the sea, where he arrived in Lisbon on August 9. Journeying soon after to Valladolid Cabeza de Vaca met with King Charles and handed him a brief report on the fate of Narváez's expedition. He also conferred with the king in private, reportedly telling him about certain "secrets" he told no one else.

Of course, the very mention of secrets, combined with Cabeza de Vaca's claims to have seen emeralds and gold, plunged the court into a frenzy of speculation. Fresh rumors spread throughout the empire about the fantastic riches and great kingdoms hidden deep in the interior of *La Florida*. For Cabeza de Vaca, however, his own homecoming was not entirely satisfying. Having returned to Spain hoping to get Narváez's concession to *La Florida*, he was not pleased to find that another man had beaten him to it.

In the autumn of 1537, this lean *hidalgo,* his Indian tattoos now covered by the rich clothes of a minor Castilian noble, was nearing fifty years old. A small, intense man whose ordeal had left him moody and ill-tempered, Álvar Núñez Cabeza de Vaca remains one of the more paradoxical figures of the *conquista*—mystical yet pragmatic, moralistic yet highly ambitious, a proud *hidalgo* and longtime professional soldier who endured slavery and torture at the

hands of the Indians during his years lost in *La Florida,* only to become one of
their greatest defenders.

According to Cabeza de Vaca's brief *relación* of his Florida journey, he
joined Narváez as a senior officer for the usual reasons—quick profit, adventure, and glory. Yet even before the expedition began to fall apart, as Narváez
moved north from Tampa Bay to Tallahassee in the summer of 1528, Cabeza
de Vaca claims to have been openly criticizing his governor's frequent use of
torture, even against friendly Indians. Indeed, it was Narváez's wanton cruelty
that led to disaster near Tallahassee. There a Mississippian people called the
Apalachee became so infuriated with the Spaniards' bullying that they attacked
the poorly organized and equipped army, forcing them to retreat into the sterile, cane-choked salt marshes of Apalachee Bay. Trapped there without food,
a third of Narváez's soldiers became sick. Fifty died of starvation and disease
as their governor desperately searched for signs of his fleet, from which he had
foolishly separated at Tampa Bay with no clear instructions about where to
rendezvous.

When it became obvious the army would all die if they stayed much longer,
Narváez ordered his men to build rafts. They split logs of yellow pine to make
planks, used palmetto sap for tar, shirts for sails, horse manes and tails for rope,
and horsehides for water flasks. Meanwhile, Narváez's men melted down
spurs, stirrups, and other bits of metal, refashioning them into nails and axes.
Eleven years later, Soto's men would discover the remains of their bellows and
makeshift furnaces.

Narváez's idea was to sail across the Gulf of Mexico to Spanish Mexico.
But he had no idea of the distance involved. Nor had he brought along an experienced navigator, tools for shipbuilding, or a shipwright. (By contrast, Soto
brought along supplies and experts to build brigantines, and at least one accomplished navigator equipped with an astrolabe).^ The resulting "barges"
proved only marginally seaworthy, with "the sides . . . hardly a half a foot
above water when loaded," and nearly impossible to paddle and maneuver with
some 250 men crowded aboard.

With calm seas and fair weather, the vessels miraculously held together for
almost three hundred miles, until they reached the mouth of the Mississippi
River. There the powerful outflow of the great river scattered the shoddy fleet,
overturning some rafts and driving others out to sea. In a final act of abysmal
leadership, the red-bearded Narváez abandoned most of his men by taking the
strongest rowers and the best raft in a desperate attempt to overcome the currents and head toward the coast. This was the last Cabeza de Vaca saw of his
governor, who vanished without a trace. The royal treasurer's own raft floated
west for several more days, lost at sea as the forty or fifty men aboard were buffeted by storms. Nearly all died of hunger and thirst. Finally, they reached the

coast of Texas, on or near Galveston Island. Hitting a bank of waves crashing onto the shore, their barge capsized, scattering the dead and near dead along the beach.

Captured almost immediately by local Indians, most of the survivors were tortured to death or sacrificed in religious ceremonies. Cabeza de Vaca was enslaved, and almost certainly would have died except for a freak occurrence. Ordered one day to participate in a native healing ceremony for an important Indian leader, Cabeza de Vaca and three other Spanish survivors had the remarkable good fortune to mutter a few Ave Marias, only to have the dying man suddenly revive. The Indians were astonished by what seemed to them a miracle. They immediately freed Cabeza de Vaca and his friends, who soon gained a reputation as miracle healers among the tribes in the area. Taking their act on the road, they slowly trekked across Texas and northern Mexico, performing cures and becoming widely revered as great and powerful shamans.

For six years, Cabeza de Vaca and his colleagues wandered across the dry, often tortuous landscape along the present-day border between the United States and Mexico, moving from one Indian village to another, laying hands on the sick, selling charms, curatives, and wares, and searching for a sign they were nearing a Spanish colony. It was during this six-thousand-mile sojourn that Cabeza de Vaca acquired his deep respect for the Indians, identifying their struggle to survive in a harsh climate, and their intense pride in doing so, with his own ordeal.

Along the way, Cabeza de Vaca and his comrades became the first Europeans to see American buffaloes and opossums, and to taste pine-nut mash and bread made from mesquite-bean flour. They also were the first to hear legends about the supposedly rich and powerful city-states of the Zuñi and Anasazi to the north, in present-day Arizona and New Mexico. As their fame spread, Indians loaded them down with gifts, including turquoise—which Cabeza de Vaca apparently mistook for emeralds. Meanwhile, Cabeza de Vaca attracted quite a following of young men, who become disciples and servants to the strange white (and one African) medicine men, carrying their food, trade goods, and supplies, and protecting them with clubs, bows and arrows, and stone knives.

In March 1536, Cabeza de Vaca and his three companions finally happened upon a small gang of Spanish marauders hunting for slaves northwest of Mexico City. Believing the Spanish shamans to be Indians, the slavers started chasing them with their horses, only to have one of the "Indians" run toward them, waving and shouting in what sounded like Castilian. "Dumbfounded at the sight" of a naked man tattooed like an Indian speaking their tongue, the slavers

broke off their attack. Cabeza de Vaca explained he was a *hidalgo* from Andalusia, and demanded to be taken to their captain. This ended Cabeza de
Vaca's journey. But not before he had his first run-in with his countrymen over
his new attitudes toward the Indians. For no sooner had Cabeza de Vaca joined
the slavers in their camp, than he "had a hot argument with them, for they
meant to make slaves of the Indians in our train . . . and to think we had given
these Christians a supply of cowhides [i.e., buffalo skins] and other things that
our retainers had carried a great distance!"

For the rest of his life, Cabeza de Vaca would try to convince his fellow
Spaniards that the best way to conquer Native Americans was to be firm, but
also to show kindness and respect—a notion other Spaniards dismissed as the
Quixotic impulse of a man who had gone native far too long. Indeed, when
Cabeza de Vaca later tried to put his ideas into practice as governor of the Río
de la Plate colony in South America, the *vecinos* there bristled at his edicts banning the plundering of native towns, and making slavery illegal. In 1543, they
mutinied and sent him back in chains to Seville, where the Council of the
Indies chose to believe his enemies and exiled him to Africa. Eventually, he
was pardoned by Charles V, who allowed him to return to Spain. He died a
short time later, in 1556 or 1557, a broken and impoverished old man few remembered.^

✢   ✢   ✢

Sometime before Cabeza de Vaca's arrival in Spain, Soto and his new bride
climbed into a coach, undoubtedly emblazoned with the Soto coat of arms—a
golden eagle on a field of blood—and departed Valladolid for Seville. Most
likely surrounded by brilliantly attired aides, pages, ladies-in-waiting, and a
small troop of liveried servants and guards, the newly ordained knight and adelantado passed endless stands of wheat, beans, and olive trees withering in the
intense Mediterranean sun. Peasants sat laconically under shade trees and
thatched lean-tos, their faces red with the heat of high summer as they waited
for the comparative cool of the evening.

It was after he arrived in Seville, where he probably spent the worst of these
summer months in the cool chambers and gardens of his palace, that he heard
about Cabeza de Vaca and his "secrets." Accepting an invitation from Soto to
visit him in Seville, the old explorer showed up later that fall, spending several
days closeted with the new adelantado and his senior officers.

Patiently, Cabeza de Vaca answered Soto's eager questions about topography, climate, available food, and the disposition of the Indians. At some point,
he may have given Soto a copy of his *relación,* which he published in 1542.^

Yet Cabeza de Vaca remained tight-lipped and even contradictory about what most mattered to the would-be conquerors of Florida—the existence of wealth and great kingdoms. "In general" writes Elvas, Cabeza de Vaca "described . . . the wretchedness of the land and the hardships he had suffered." However, when several of his own kinsmen—including two important captains in the *La Florida entrada*, Baltasar de Gallegos and Cristóbal de Espindola—"urged him to tell them whether he had seen any rich land in Florida," he suggested they sell their property and join the expedition. "For in doing so," he said, "they would act wisely."

Soto and his men interpreted Cabeza de Vaca's reticence to mean he was hiding some great secret of untold wealth—which naturally redoubled every-one's belief that Florida "was the richest land in the world." It so stoked the imagination of young recruits that when Soto later departed Sanlúcar for *La Florida,* his problem was not the usual dilemma of having too few men, but too many. "Many men of good condition," says Elvas, "who had sold their es-tates, remained behind in Sanlúcar because there was no ship for them." For a time, it looked as if Cabeza de Vaca would join Soto in the expedition to *La Florida,* though Elvas says the agreement soon fell apart as Cabeza de Vaca balked at serving "under the banner of another." Soto, too, must have had second thoughts about a potential subordinate so independent-minded, partic-ularly one whose ideas about how to treat the Indians were so at odds with his own.

✛ ✛ ✛

By autumn in Andalusia, the Soto organization was gearing up for eight months of intense activity as the new adelantado of *La Florida* gathered up the necessary agents, accountants, recruiters, lawyers, pilots, and paymasters to prepare for one of the largest and most lavish enterprises the city had seen for some time.^ It also would be one of the more expensive in the *conquista* era, the total price topping 130,000 castellanos,^ six times what the king had spent on the Pedrarias expedition twenty-three years earlier. Soto himself directed his armada's preparations in Seville, aided by his majordomo, Alonso de Ayala; his wife, Isabel; and Juan de Añasco, whom Garcilaso describes as not only an exceptional leader and organizer, but a "mariner, cosmographer, and astrologer," among other things.^ He also dispatched Luis de Moscoso and Juan Ruiz Lobillo to tour the country and sign up recruits.

If the chroniclers can be believed, Soto paid most of the expenses himself—an unusual arrangement in an era when wealthy banking families in Seville fronted the funds for most expeditions, often at exorbitant interest rates.^ Soto also broke with tradition by paying expenses for many of his men, dis-pensing in some cases with the *cabalgada*-style contract in which a captain expected each man of the line to pay for weapons, food, and transportation. Wealthier recruits paid their own way, decking themselves out lavishly. One brother of the powerful marquis of Astorga spent thousands of ducats on slaves, horses, and finery. Another kinsman of the marquis—who may have been a Soto supporter at court—sold "a village of vassals he owned in the district of Campos." Likewise, Baltasar de Gallegos, the *hidalgo* captain from Seville related to Cabeza de Vaca, "sold houses, vineyards, a rent of wheat, and ninety *geiras* of olive orchard in the district of Seville," spending a staggering four thousand ducats to equip himself with armor, clothes, weapons, horses, slaves, and servants. He also transported to Cuba his wife and their entire household.^

+   +   +

As for the ships and masses of equipment bought by Soto for his venture, we have several dozen archival receipts and contracts made by Soto and his agents during the preparations in Seville. These chits detail transactions for everything from hardtack and wine barrels to the hiring of sailors, caulkers, and cabin boys for the fleet. The first of these records that on September 3, 1537, Hernando de Soto purchased the *La Magdalena,* a large ship of roughly eight hundred tons^ "with its *barcos,* rigging, and tackle" from a Triana merchant named Hernando Blas. The price was 1,212 ducats—paid for by Gregorio Castro, apparently one of Soto's agents. Two days later, Soto bought another ship, a large galleon named the *San Juan,* for 1,410 ducats. In a separate purchase, he paid three biscuit makers 653 ducats to prepare and deliver 800 *quintales* (about forty tons) of hardtack—enough to feed hundreds of men on the voyage across the Ocean Sea.^ And so it goes, with similar transactions continuing at a feverish pace throughout that winter and spring as Soto bought up everything from guns and crossbows to wine and olive oil.

By the time he was finished, Soto had purchased at least five large ships, and possibly seven—accompanied by three or more smaller and swifter caravels and brigantines tagging along as support vessels.^ He also hired experienced pilots to guide each vessel—and pursers, boatswains, and caulkers for the larger ships. We have records of him hiring thirty-eight sailors to man the fleet: twenty *marineros,* or general-duty sailors, seventeen *grumetes,* or shipboys, and one cabin boy.^ Rodrigo Ranjel says that the number of sailors was 130 by the time the fleet crossed from Cuba to *La Florida.*^

Soto also bought hundreds of tons of hardtack, salt-cured meat, olive oil, fresh water, and wine for the voyage. He amassed material available only in Europe—including, says Garcilaso, "much iron, steel, irons for saddlebows, spades, mattocks, panniers, ropes and baskets," arquebuses, gunpowder, crossbows, swords, chain mail, bucklers, boots, sacramental vessels for Mass, beads and other Indian trade goods, iron chain links and collars for freshly captured slaves and porters, and everything else required to equip the small, mobile village that the army would accompany across thousands of miles of unexplored country.^ Individual conquistadors took equipment of their own. So did those officials Soto would appoint as colonial officers in Cuba. Horses, seeds, and provisions for Florida itself Soto planned to purchase in Cuba.

✛   ✛   ✛

All that autumn, Soto's recruiters traveled far and wide in Castile. They even trekked into Portugal, where Luis de Moscoso "passed through Elvas," ten miles across the border from Badajoz, and recruited the anonymous Gentleman of Elvas and several other Portuguese. The recruitment drive in Elvas was typical of what happened in most towns, with Moscoso being approached by a wealthy *vecino* and former captain in the Portuguese army named André de Vasconcelos. He presented "patents" signed by a local nobleman, the marquis of Villa Real, vouching for him as a reliable captain, which Moscoso took to Soto in Seville. The new adelantado later wrote to Vasconcelos, telling him "he would favor him in every way and would give him men to command in Florida." In turn, Vasconcelos recruited seven others in his hometown, including our anonymous chronicler. Leaving Elvas shortly after Christmas, the group arrived in Seville on January 15. The Gentleman of Elvas says they went directly to Soto's house, entering "the patio upon which looked some balconies where he was. He looked down and went to meet them at the stairs . . . [and] ordered chairs to be given them so that they might be seated . . . [Soto] appeared well pleased with their coming and proffer. The table being already laid, he invited them to eat; and, while they were eating, he directed his majordomo to find lodgings for them near his house."

A few days later, André de Vasconcelos walked the short distance to the Casa de Contratación, near the cathedral, where he registered for the expedition, signing his name on a parchment and giving his parents' names as Gomez de Silva and Doña Guiomar Pacheca. He then entered his place of origin as Badajoz instead of Elvas—a common deceit in a period when foreigners were officially barred from participating in Spanish expeditions.^ At least four of his followers did the same,^ sealing their fate as participants in an expedition where only three of them would return home alive.

Sometime during the recruiting drive, Soto named the senior officials of his new government, and the captains and officers of his army. Mostly, he singled out men of high ability who were also loyal, and would not question his commands—as he had been wont to do when he was a subordinate. At least one of his officers would prove less than loyal, however—the royal treasurer, Juan Gaitan.* According to Garcilaso, Gaitan was plotting a mutiny after the Battle of Mabila, discovered by Soto and stopped before it happened.^ Other royal officers included Juan de Añasco, named royal contador, and Luis Hernández de Biedma, the royal factor (king's agent). Little is known about Biedma, other than he was the author of the official chronicle of the expedition written for the king—a terse account spare on details, but very useful as a guide to the main events of the *entrada.*^ Soto named his Peruvian crony Nuño de Tobar as captain general of the army, or second-in-command. Serving directly under him as adjuncts were Chief Constable Baltasar de Gallegos^ and Alférez General (Field Marshal) Diego Tinoco,^† a kinsman of Soto's on his mother's side, also serving as a Captain of the Horse.

Under these senior officers served Soto's permanent captains, each in charge of about one hundred men. To command the infantry units he named Francisco Maldonado of Salamanca and the Peruvian veteran Juan Ruiz Lobillo; for the cavalry he named Pedro Calderón, the Portuguese André de Vasconcelos, Diego Tinoco, and Alonso Romo. Soto assigned Luis de Moscoso to be *maestro de campo,* in charge of organizing and guarding the army and camps, and assigning daily rosters of duties for the troops.^ Soto's personal guard, composed of sixty halberdiers, was commanded by Cristóbal de Espindola, a native of Seville who would save Soto's life in the Battle of Mabila. Some years after Florida, he became a high official of the Inquisition in Mexico.^

Sometime during all of this activity, Soto undoubtedly trekked home to Extremadura, perhaps riding in a gilded coach beside his wife, and accompanied by his brilliantly attired retinue. Passing through the lichen-encrusted stone gates of Jerez de los Caballeros,^ and up the narrow, dirt-clogged streets of his boyhood, he rode slowly and solemnly into the glaring sun of the city's main square, basking in the adoration of a town that today is filled with statues and streets named after him, and even a trucker's restaurant called the Hernando de Soto Cafe.

In Jerez, Soto spent time with his family, whose formerly lackluster members could hardly believe their luck. His shadowy father, Francisco, about whom we know almost nothing, was probably dead in 1537–38;^ so was his mother, Leonor. His sisters, however, must have been on hand to greet him. Catalina was now married and living in the nearby village of Barcarrota. María

---

*Gaitan was appointed by the king, not by Soto.
†Also known as Diego Arias Tinoco.

lived with her husband in Badajoz. Soto also would have visited his older brother, Juan Méndez, who inherited his father's meager estate, about to be enriched. Indeed, in 1537, the new adelantado of *La Florida* arranged a sizable grant from the king for his big brother—a royal favor that apparently led to the older Soto brother being elected *regidor* on the city council in the late 1530s,^ probably the most prestigious position ever held by a Soto in Jerez de los Caballeros.

While in Extremadura, Soto recruited several members of his family^, including his thirty-three-year-old field marshal, Diego Tinoco, a kinsman on his mother's side from Badajoz. Another familial recruit was the field marshal's brother, Captain Alonso Romo. Recruiting in Barcarrota, fifteen miles north of Jerez, Soto signed up Diego de Soto, a nephew, who later became a field captain of some distinction, until he was killed during the Battle of Mabila. Garcilaso calls him "one of the best soldiers in the army and a very good horseman." He seems to have inherited his uncle's propensity for showing off, in one incident chasing down an Indian in a difficult spot "more to show his skill and courage than from any need he had for him."

Soto gained another recruit, and an in-law, when his niece, Isabel de Soto, married a prominent *vecino* of Jerez named Carlos Enríquez.^ Garcilaso describes him as a peacemaker within the Florida army, who "brought . . . concord" to the men in "their passions and private quarrels, setting himself to pacify and compose them . . . as their intercessor and patron with the General [Soto]." Soto's affection for this young man is proved by the fact that he himself gave away the bride to Don Carlos, and provided three thousand ducats for her dowry.^

✛   ✛   ✛

On April 1, Soto ordered his men to muster on the quay at Sanlúcar, a small village of whitewashed houses beside the mouth of El Río Guadalquivir. According to Elvas, the new adelantado became incensed when most of the men (excluding, of course, the Portuguese) appeared dressed not as soldiers, but "very elegantly, in silk over silk, and many plaits and slashes." Ordering them to muster again the next day in their armor, he was again displeased when most showed up wearing "poor and rusty coats of mail . . . [and] poor lances." The worst of these were immediately culled as Soto spent the morning walking up and down the ranks to make his final selections, choosing some six hundred men. These were ordered to stand "near the standard borne by his alférez," where they excitedly waited to be "counted and enrolled," and assigned to the ship that would take them to America.

Finally, on Sunday, April 7, Soto and his men heard Mass, had a last feast of fresh food, and then boarded their ships. They departed Sanlúcar "amid great festivity," with Soto "ordering the trumpets to be sounded and many rounds of artillery fired."

According to Garcilaso, Soto's armada was accompanied from Sanlúcar with another fleet of twenty "large ships . . . of Mexico." These were commanded by Gonzalo de Salazar, a newly appointed royal official to the court of Antonio de Mendoza. Soto, however, was in overall command of all the vessels.* Garcilaso further claims that during the first night out, Salazar's ship accidentally overtook the fleet's flagship, Soto's *San Cristóbal*—a severe breech of nautical etiquette that also put Salazar's ship in grave danger, since the fleet was on alert for a possible French attack, and was under orders to fire immediately on any unidentified vessel. When Soto's officer of the watch, Gonzalo Silvestre, spied Salazar's ship off his stern, he assumed it was the enemy, and ordered his gunner to open fire. "With the first shot all the sails were pierced through the center, from stem to stern," says Garcilaso, "and with the second shot the upper works of one side were carried away. They were preparing to fire again when they heard its people shouting loudly . . . that they were friends."

Soto, sleeping in his cabin, was awakened by the boom of the guns and ran up on deck just in time to see Salazar's crippled ship fall off and run up hard against the *San Cristóbal,* almost ramming her. The two ships' rigging became hopelessly entangled as the crews of both became terrified they would be pulled over and sunk. Soto, however, showing his usual composure, ordered his sailors to dash up the masts and cut loose Salazar's rigging, shouting at them to use the scythes attached to the yards for slicing ropes and sails. The plan worked. After the ships were separated Soto was so furious he ordered Salazar executed. Soon after, he calmed down and pardoned the young Mexican official, acknowledging that what had happened was an accident.

Nearly every major fleet from Spain during this period stopped at the Canaries to stock up on food and water before crossing the Ocean Sea. Dropping anchor off the mountainous island of Gomera on Easter Sunday, 1538, Soto and Isabel went ashore with the usual ceremony to meet the governor of the island,^ a cousin of Isabel's. In Gomera, Soto purchased "many provisions, bread, wine, and meat." He also made a request to Isabel's cousin for permission to take his teenage daughter, Doña Leonor de Bobadilla, with the armada as a lady-in-waiting to Isabel. This girl later became the source of a feud be-

*No eyewitness chronicler mentions the Mexican fleet.

tween Soto and one of his most-trusted officers, Nuño de Tobar, who soon after became Doña Leonor's lover and got her pregnant. Soto summarily demoted Nuño de Tobar for this indiscretion, possibly at the request of his wife.

In any case, the armada departed Gomera on April 28, as Soto turned his ships almost due west, toward the Spanish colony of Santiago de Cuba—and the massive, unknown continent to the north, which he, his king, and country had brazenly declared belonged to him. If he was able to seize and conquer it.

✣ 19 ✣

Cuba Bled Dry

EARLY IN JUNE 1538, anticipation grew in the fleet as the voyage took almost twice as long as usual to cross the Ocean Sea. It was on the thirty-eighth day that a lookout finally stared long and hard at a gray cloud looming ahead above the blue-emerald waters, and realized it was a shoreline. Not wanting to miss the reward given to the sailor who first sighted land, he undoubtedly shouted out the words every person in the cramped ships wanted to hear: *"Tierra! Tierra! Veo Tierra!"* Instantly, seamen in the other ships took up the call. Mariners, officers, prostitutes, servants, soldiers, pages, and doñas crowded the decks to see for themselves, and to breathe in the sweet scents of Cuba's sea grapes, cactus flowers, and other aromatic plants that still greet sailors as they approach the island's southern shore. Soto, hearing the news, would have ordered trumpets sounded and cannons fired.

Moments later, the fleet's master pilot, Alonso Martín de Lucas, would have begun shouting commands to the mariners to trim sails. Consulting his maps, and taking readings with his compass and astrolabe, he ordered the ship's signalman to raise flags telling the fleet to slow down and fall in line behind the *San Cristóbal.* As they drew closer, all could see the cliffs that rim the southern shore of Cuba, then called La Isle de Fernandina, as crew and passengers alike began singing the traditional "Te Deum," thanking God for their safe arrival.

If Alonso Martín's calculations in terms of latitude and longitude were correct, and the fleet had arrived where they were supposed to be, those on board would have seen a great gap in the cliffs ahead. This was the narrow channel leading into Santiago Bay, a protected natural harbor first discovered by Columbus in 1492. Nineteen years later it had been conquered by Diego de Velázquez, who began his rule over the peaceful shell-gatherers in the bay by enslaving and killing most of them within months of his arrival.

Entering this treacherous channel has always been nerve-racking, particularly for a pilot who had probably never been there before. At best, he carried a crude map haphazardly marking hidden shoals. Cautiously, Alonso Martín would have lined up his ships, coming up slowly to a steep and rocky headland to the right of the harbor's entrance, and a lower ridge to the left where rocky outcrops tumble into the sea. From a short distance out, he would have seen that the deepest part of the channel, where the water was darkest, turned in a wide sweep to the right, indicating shallows to the left, where the water was a lighter shade of blue. He could not see what these shallows held, however— a small, submerged inlet of rock, sand, and coral. Known today as Smith's Key, this hazard has wrecked many a vessel over the centuries—and nearly added Soto's ship to the list, thanks to a Spaniard on the shore who suddenly appeared to inexplicably wave them toward the rocks.

Riding a fast horse, the man deliberately signaled the fleet to bear left, a command that must have confused Alonso Martín, who clearly saw the deep water of the channel moving to the right.^ Nonetheless, he obeyed the signal from the shore, ordering the flagship to come hard to port. This brought the eight-hundred-ton vessel swinging slowly around—and headed directly for Smith's Key. At this point, the man onshore abruptly changed his mind. Even more frantically, he now signaled for the ships to turn hard to *starboard*. Garcilaso, who tells this story, adds: "To make himself better understood, he dismounted and ran to his right, making signs with his arms and his cape and saying: 'Turn, turn to the other side; you will all be lost!' Those on the flagship, when they understood him," continues Garcilaso, "turned as rapidly as possible to the left,* but as hard as they tried they could not prevent the ship from striking . . . against a rock."

The other ships of the fleet safely turned away, but the *San Cristóbal* scraped bottom, "striking so hard against a rock that all on board thought that it was stove in and lost." Fearing the hull was taking on water, many aboard the *San Cristóbal* panicked and hastily grabbed the ship's *batels* (skiffs) to escape. Because there was no protocol of women and children first in the sixteenth century, the strongest and quickest scrambled to make room for themselves, though Soto made sure his wife and her young lady-in-waiting, the lovely (and pregnant) Leonor de Bobadilla, got safely aboard. Soto was "importuned . . . to leave the ship," but refused to panic or abandon his vessel before investigating the damage. "By his own presence," says Garcilaso, for once not exag-

---

*Garcilaso is a bit mixed-up here. He actually says *a mano izquierda,* or "to the left," though he earlier tells us the command from shore was to turn *"a estribor,"* or starboard, which is to the right. The confusion, however, is settled by the topography of the Santiago channel, which clearly indicates a right turn to avoid the rocks of Smith's Key.

gerating, he was able "to prevent all the others leaving it." At this point, sailors searching belowdecks came running up to tell Soto there was no structural damage to the ship, and that the liquid sloshing in the holds was wine from broken casks, not seawater.

✛   ✛   ✛

The townspeople of Santiago, horrified at having nearly shipwrecked their new governor, sent over to the site of the accident "a very beautiful . . . roan horse for the Governor and a mule for Doña Isabel" to carry them to the settlement. Once there, the frightened *vecinos,* led by acting governor Gonzalo de Guzmán,^ "begged [Soto] to pardon them," explaining that they had mistaken his fleet for French *corsairs,* which had been attacking the island mercilessly off and on for several months. Just this past April, they said, a heavily armed French vessel had brazenly entered the harbor at full sail and would have burned Santiago to the ground if not for a lucky happenstance—the presence of an armed Spanish merchantman then at anchor in the harbor.^ Owned by one Diego Pérez, a trader from Seville, this Spanish ship had engaged the larger French vessel for several days in a running battle, finally forcing the *corsair* to withdraw—ominously headed in the direction of Havana.^

Satisfied with Guzmán's explanation, Soto presented his credentials to the city council, which accepted him as governor shortly after his arrival in early June.^ At the same time, Soto ordered the *vecinos* of Santiago to provide quarter to "all the men" in his party "free of expense. Those who wished to go into the country were quartered among the dwellings and farmhouses by fours and sixes, in accordance with the prosperity of the owners of the dwellings, and they were furnished by the latter with the provisions of which they had need." Of course, housing over six hundred newcomers in a town with a Spanish population of perhaps two hundred caused grumbling among the locals, though Soto did pay for food. He also tried to win over the *vecinos* by staging yet another round of lavish celebrations, games, and contests. These celebrations lasted "for many days," claims Garcilaso, "sometimes with dances, balls and masquerades, which were held at night; sometimes with games in which they ran and speared bulls with cane spears." There were "no jousts or tournaments," he adds, "on horseback or on foot, for lack of armor"^ in the city, and weapons among the townspeople.

Soto's propensity for grandiose celebrations deserves a brief comment. Everywhere he turns, he seems to be expending—and in the view of some of his followers, wasting—large sums of cash on games and fiestas.^ The simple explanation is that Soto was vain and loved the attention, which is true, though like most shrewd politicians and conquerors, Hernando de Soto also understood the practical side of staging such spectacles—that they provided drama, diversion, and excitement for his men, and greatly enhanced his reputation as a fabulously rich and successful conqueror. Everywhere Soto went after departing Peru with his fame and fortune—whether to court to meet the king, recruiting in the Spanish hinterlands, or touching down in a distant colony— Soto's aim was not just to impress, but to overwhelm. His flare for the dramatic is evident from the moment he first enters the history books, rushing into battle and performing showy feats of sword and saddle that by now, as he approached forty, had been deftly transposed into a highly successful political strategy to enhance his charisma.

These particular games, however, were inspired as much by horseflesh as vanity and politics. Because Soto needed mounts by the dozens, but knew local *vecinos* would keep their finest animals out of town to drive up the prices, the governor shrewdly arranged for a number of riding contests designed to lure in the owners of the best stallions and mares. This petty shopkeeper's ploy worked brilliantly as Soto, showing a flare for hard-nosed commerce, promptly purchased some 150 mounts, paying only about ten to twelve *castellanos* per horse, considerably less than the going rate.^

Guzmán and other leaders quickly picked up on this deceit. Complaining bitterly to the king, they claimed that the new governor was buying up every horse in sight, even their breeding stock. One official even called Soto a "shady dealer," insisting it would take years for the island to replenish a commodity that had been a highly profitable export to other colonies.

Their concern did not stop with horses, however. As the festivities continued, Guzmán and the older *vecinos* watched with mounting anxiety over the next several weeks as Soto bought up huge quantities of cattle, farms, food, and manufactured goods. He also began wooing the few young men remaining in Cuba, those who had not gone to Peru or Mexico.

Not all of Soto's would-be recruits on Cuba were young. One longtime *vecino* in Cuba, a rich landowner and slave trader named Vasco Porcallo de Figueroa, was impressed enough with Soto to offer not only his fastest horses, but himself.

Soto could not have been more pleased. One of the original conquerors of Cuba, Vasco Porcallo was locally famous for his brutality and grim effectiveness in conquering and controlling the natives residing in the center of the island, where he owned thousands of acres near Puerto Principe and Trinidad.

Almost immediately, this longtime Indian "pacifier," slaver, and *encomendero* became a friend and confidant of Soto, who must have greatly enjoyed the company of someone so like himself—a ruthless and successful product of the American frontier. Porcallo also became a font of information about *La Florida.* For a quarter of a century, he had lived close to this mysterious, dark continent. In 1528, he had helped outfit the expedition of his close associate, Pánfilo de Narváez. He also had known Juan Ponce de León, and had sponsored and outfitted numerous slaving and trade expeditions to the mainland.

In fact, Porcallo's knowledge of Florida should have made him the last man on Cuba to sign up for Soto's *entrada.* Knowing that no one had found so much as a single nugget of gold or silver in *La Florida,* Porcallo was also well aware of how fiercely the coastal tribes had fought against marauders looking for slaves. Presumably, he had been invited before to join expeditions and forays to the mainland, but had contented himself with getting rich selling supplies to everyone from Narváez to Hernán Cortés when he went to Mexico, and Juan de Grijalva when he left Cuba to explore the Yucatán.* Possibly, this former conquistador was simply bored. He also may have been more impressed with Soto than with Narváez or Juan Ponce, suspecting that if anyone was going to successfully explore and conquer *La Florida,* it was Don Hernando and his six-hundred-man army. Soto, for his part, shrewdly named Porcallo—whom he needed to supply provisions and horses—to replace the discredited Nuño de Tobar as captain general of the army.

✦   ✦   ✦

For three or four months, Soto stayed in Santiago, a crude but pleasant frontier town that must have reminded him of León, in Nicaragua, which was roughly the same size. Typical of early Spanish colonial enclaves, Santiago was arranged around a large, dusty plaza edged by a cathedral and public buildings made of stone, and backed by scattered houses, "large and well-apportioned." Behind the city and the bright turquoise bay, rolling hills spread some miles back, in those days covered with plantations of cattle and crops, which continued inland until they ran up against an abrupt ridge of mountains. Two decades before Soto's arrival, Santiago de Cuba had been one of the most important cities in the nascent empire of the Indies. But since the conquests of Mexico and Peru, it had devolved into a backwater. Soon enough, Cuba's fortunes would again improve as fleets began dropping by more frequently to resupply on their way back to Spain. This traffic, however, would end up benefiting not Santiago, but Havana, on the northern side and closer to the Gulf Stream shipping lanes.

---

*Grijalva later died during the Indian uprising in Honduras's Olancho Valley, put down by the young Captain Soto in 1527.

To Soto, anxious to get his grand expedition underway, the weeks in Santiago must have seemed unbearably tedious. Most of his time was spent organizing his *entrada,* though as governor of the Isle de Fernandina, he also had obligations to the Santiago *cabildo* (city council).

At first, the *cabildo* thought of Soto as a savior after years of official neglect from Spain. Six weeks after Soto arrived, Guzmán wrote to the king praising the new governor, saying he could see "a lot of ability and a man of good conduct . . . I think he will be of more consequence than those [officials] that came before him." But he added a note of caution. "God willing, the island will not be damaged by him taking *vecinos* away, because aside from having to maintain his own people, we know he will need to take away provisions from some of the *vecinos,* and without them we will live badly in this land, and we fear that he has his eyes and thoughts so set on Florida, that he cares little for us." Soto soon affirmed all of Guzmán's fears, quickly disabusing the *cabildo* of the idea he had been sent to attend to their problems. Indeed, the Crown all but affirms in its *capitulación* and other documents that Soto's appointment as governor was not intended to help Cuba, but to strip the island of its resources to support the goal of conquering *La Florida.*

Soto could not entirely neglect certain local crises, however, particularly those that might affect his preparations. Most pressing was the situation with the French. Their bellicose king, Francis I, remained Charles's mortal enemy as their struggle for domination in Europe spilled over into the Americas, where *corsairs* could stage random attacks almost with impunity. (England later dispatched Sir Francis Drake and other "Sea Lions" to similarly chip away at the imperial edges of the Spanish colossal.) Clearly, the days were over when every ship in the Caribbean was Spanish and friendly, and no seaward defenses were necessary. The Council of the Indies had discussed this very issue with Soto before he left, ordering him to build a stone fort in Havana, to protect the gold fleets carrying Crown taxes from Mexico to Spain.

Shortly after touching down in Santiago, Soto received word that the *corsair* chased away from Santiago in April had just attacked Havana, and burned it to the ground—a distressing development, if true, since Soto intended to use Havana as his base to explore *La Florida.* Dispatching Juan de Añasco on a fast caravel to investigate, he soon confirmed the attack. This prompted the governor to send another aide, Antonio Azeituno,* "with some men by sea to rebuild the city of La Havana."

In Santiago, Soto also launched an effort to build the stone fortress in Havana, as ordered by the Council of the Indies.^ His interest in this project was less civic-minded than either the council in Seville or the *cabildo* in Santiago

---

*Garcilaso gives his name as Mateo Azeituno.

would have preferred, however. Indeed, soon after the *cabildo* gave Soto three thousand pesos from its meager treasury to build the fort, the island's longtime royal treasurer, Lope Hurtado, wrote the king that he suspected Soto "has taken [this money] for his own necessities." But when the king responded, he censured Hurtado, not Soto, saying the royal treasurer should not have handed over the money to Soto. Suggesting that he had not read the *cédula* carefully, Charles noted that Soto had been ordered only to *build* the fort, while the *cabildo* was charged with *paying* for it. "Amazed" at this oversight, the king indicated that Soto had every right to keep the money.

Presumably, Soto *had* read the *cédula* carefully, and knowingly deceived the *cabildo* in a sleight of hand worthy of his days in Nicaragua. In the end, he did spend a small part of the three thousand pesos on the fortress of Havana, though it was so poorly constructed the city tore it down and replaced it a few years later. Soto pocketed what was not spent on the fort to help pay for his expedition, which finally was beginning to deplete even his enormous resources.

Meanwhile, Guzmán and the *vecinos* clamored for improvements to Santiago's defenses, noisily exclaiming to Soto (and to the king, God, and anyone else who might listen) that surely "no one wanted to see the church and other stone buildings, constructed at such great effort and expense, to be destroyed." Soto responded to these pleas by starting a small earthwork defense built above the town's landing, a project he left incomplete because of his own disinterest, and the squabbles in the *cabildo* over the bulwark's location, cost, and size. Eventually, the walls were built, but not until 1544, some months after the news of Soto's death had reached the island.^

The other pressing problem for the new governor of Cuba was the Indians, called Cubeños to distinguish them from the Spanish "Cubans." Grossly mistreated for a quarter century, and all but decimated by abuse, disease, and mass suicide, the Arawak on the mountainous far eastern edge of the island had recently taken advantage of the Spanish depopulation to revolt—spurred on, writes Soto's new alcade mayor in Santiago, Bartolomé Ortiz, by "the bad treatment of the Indians" by certain "bad elements" among the Spaniards.

In a series of brutal skirmishes, these so-called *cimarrónes,* or "wild Indians," had "committed many atrocities, killing Christians, Spaniards, Negroes, domestic Indians, and herds, and setting farms on fire." That spring, they had attacked and burned down the small Spanish settlement of Baracoa, and forced the Spanish to evacuate the entire region west of Santiago. Shortly before Soto's arrival, Guzmán had begun to fight back by dispatching squads of Spaniards and Africans to fight these *cimarrónes,* though he complained to the king that the lack of weapons on the island was greatly hampering these efforts.

Soto responded "directly upon his arrival at this city" by sending out more fighters to the western district, "a troop of Spaniards, with Negroes and tame Indians" from Santiago, and another from the nearby town of San Salvador. "We hope that these [*cimarrónes*] may be overtaken and chastised," reported the *cabildo,* "that the evil may cease." The letter then goes on to tell the king that "since there are no arms here nor on the island," they were making an urgent request for the Council of the Indies to dispatch on the next ship from Seville "crossbows, shafts, strings, and appurtenances," and "lances and bucklers."^ Soto supported this petition, though one wonders why he did not provide a few desperately needed weapons from his own vast stores aboard his ships.

The arms from Seville were a long time coming, with the revolt of the *cimarrónes* growing worse over the coming months. It spread across the island as Soto marched to Havana and lured away most of the young men of fighting age, whose presence had kept the desperate Indians in check. Shortly after Soto's departure that fall from Santiago, Bartolomé Ortiz dispatched a group of fighters to reconquer Baracoa. They proved so inept, however, that the Indians guiding them were able to turn on them in a surprise attack, killing them all.^

Guzmán and the *vecinos* were grateful for Soto, who was at least trying to cope with the problems of the *cimarrónes* and the French. Everything else he did made them furious, however. In August, for instance, Soto rammed through the *cabildo* an edict forbidding commerce between Cuba and the outside world, an economic disaster for islanders whose livelihoods depended on selling horses and food to passing ships and to settlements in Mexico and on other islands. Guzmán called this order "a very grave error" that "took away the major income of this island." Soto further crippled the long-term prospects for the local economy by ordering huge levies on imported slaves at a time when Guzmán and the others said they were desperate for laborers. "There is not one place in the Indies that charges duties on the Indian slaves brought to be sold, except on this island; for this reason, no one brings them here anymore." These edicts were blatantly illegal, as Soto must have known. He also knew that by the time the *vecinos* could appeal to the king, and the Crown could review the case and return a *cedula* overturning his edicts, Soto would have already stripped the country of everything he needed, and would be on his way to Florida.^

Sometime before departing Santiago for Havana, Soto dispatched his majordomo, Alonso de Ayala, on a long-neglected mission to Peru—informing his partner, Hernán Ponce de León, about everything that had transpired since they parted three years earlier in Peru. Soto had more than just a friendly report on his progress in mind, however. He also instructed Ayala to ask Ponce for an additional ten thousand ducats desperately needed to finance the expedition's final phase—a bold request considering Soto hadn't communicated for over a year with his partner. He shrewdly instructed Ayala to tell Ponce that as far as he was concerned, the *compañia* and their pact of brotherhood still existed, and that he would equally divide all plunder and wealth gained in Florida with his old comrade—provided, of course, Ponce sent him the money.

Ayala set sail that summer, but only got as far as Panama. Here he was told Ponce had already left Peru, and would be arriving any day in Panama on his way to Spain, having cashed out the *compañia*'s properties in Peru. While waiting for Ponce in Panama City, Ayala took care of another item of business for Soto: selling the ranch bequeathed him by Isabel de Bobadilla's mother as a dowry. Ayala later recalled he sold Pedrarias's ranch, which must have been enormous, for a staggering seven thousand pesos.^

Somehow, Ayala missed Ponce when he passed through the isthmus. The majordomo later insisted this happened while he was ill, though it is hard to believe that in this small colony Ponce slipped by Soto's servant undetected. Either Ayala really was very ill, or, more likely, Ponce purposely avoided him, having heard about his mission. For Soto's old partner seemed intent on returning to Spain as rapidly as possible, having decided he was through with frontier life—and, apparently, with his former partner.^ Later, he would explain his avoidance of Ayala by saying he was angry with Soto for accepting the concession to Florida without consulting him.^ This was, of course, a convenient point of view given the fact Ponce was taking back to Spain 60,000 to 100,000 pesos, and possibly much more, earned by selling off the partnership's estates in Peru, including property that belonged to Soto.^ Unfortunately for Ponce, however, his success at evading Alonso de Ayala in Panama would prove futile. For a few months later, when the ship taking him home to Spain ran into a storm, he was forced to make an emergency landing—in, of all places, Havana.

✛   ✛   ✛

Early that autumn, Soto mustered his army on the beach of Santiago. Much to the relief of the *vecinos,* he then departed for Havana 450 miles away, accompanied by Vasco Porcallo de Figueroa. Dividing his *entrada* into two groups, Soto assigned 150 cavalrymen to march overland with him,^ dispatching Isabel and the infantry by sea under the command of his new nephew by marriage, Don Carlos Enríquez. Soto had three reasons for leading his group overland across this sickle-shaped island the size of Pennsylvania. First, because he was governor, Soto wanted personally to check on the administration of each town and district; second, because he wanted to continue to buy up horses and supplies; and, finally, because he thought this trek through a known, but still difficult, frontier territory would be an ideal opportunity to train and harden his mostly green cavaliers, who would form the core of his army in *La Florida.*

In 1538, the island Soto and his men would march across consisted mostly of overgrown and unoccupied bush and savanna—vast grasslands punctuated by dense clumps of palms and flanked by forests, with districts of heavily wooded mountains in the south, and other scattered ranges in the middle and to the west. There were few mammal species here, the largest being the fleshy manatee. There also was an abundance of mice, shrews, squirrel-like jutías, long-snouted almiquies, and a variety of bats that came swooping through the Spaniards' camps at night, catching insects attracted by the horses and sweating men, and the light of the campfires. Reptiles were plentiful, with the usual tropical array of alligators, snakes, lizards, iguanas, and turtles. The army also was greeted everywhere by a cacophony of birds, particularly as millions upon millions of migrating geese, ducks, and songbirds from North America passed through the marshes and grasslands on their way to winter in South America. More permanent island species ranged from large populations of flamingos, wood ducks, and snowy egrets to dazzling macaws and the now-extinct royal woodpecker, an enormous *carpintero* the size of a heron, with a bright yellow fantail crest that looked so lovely in a woman's bonnet that hunters in the coming centuries killed every last one of them.

According to early chroniclers ranging from Columbus, who touched down on the island in 1492, to Bartolomé de las Casas, who once owned property there, Cuba was never heavily populated.^ This was probably because the clay savannas, deeply infused with dense mats of grass roots, were difficult to till with Indian digging sticks. Those natives who had lived on the island tended to inhabit the woodlands in the foothills of the mountains. Mostly Arawak, they had followed the customs of their cousins on Hispaniola and other Caribbean islands, living in small, orderly villages of large, round *bohios;* wearing little clothing; seldom fighting among themselves; and eating mostly homegrown cassava and fruit. When the Spaniards first arrived, the Indians greeted them with curiosity and gifts of food, only to be enslaved and overworked to the point that all but a few thousand had died by 1538. Most survivors worked the mines and on plantations, with several hundred *cimarrónes* hiding out in the mountains, desperately waging a guerrilla war, though already it was clear the original inhabitants of Cuba would become extinct within a few decades.

Elvas reports that Soto and his 150 men, accompanied by perhaps a hundred porters, first marched inland to the small Spanish settlement of Bayamo, eighty-five miles from Santiago.^ Normally, this journey took about five days in 1538, though the topography of rugged foothills on the backside of the towering Sierra Maestra may have slowed down the inexperienced cavalrymen. They probably made slow time marching up and down low hills and ridges, interspersed with grassy valleys. Still, it would have been a pleasant march, particularly for Soto. For not only was he back where he liked to be, marching on the edge of a frontier, but he also was, at last, leading his own forces as supreme commander.

Arriving in Bayamo, the troops found themselves in what would have been a small, sleepy cluster of *bohíos* and plantation buildings, with a mud-brick and thatch church set on a crude, half-overgrown plaza. Ordering the locals to house him and his men "by fours and sixes," Soto set about meeting with the town's officials and stripping the district of its food, horses, and young men. This pattern would be repeated at every town he stopped in on this journey, as Soto behaved almost like the general of a sixteenth-century army in Europe, living off the land by demanding that each village in their path quarter his soldiers, feed them at their own expense, and cater to their whims. As Elvas reports, in Bayamo Soto paid for "nothing . . . except maize for their horses," forcing the people in addition to pay him a special "tax" levied "on the tribute and service of the Indians." This was used as yet another source of income for outfitting the *entrada.* In Cuba, Soto treated the Spaniards almost as callously as he would the Indians in *La Florida,* where he also marched into villages demanding food, housing, and porters. But here Soto expected, and got, the acquiescence of the Spaniards in his *gobernación*—which meant he did not have to resort to the violence often inflicted on the Indians of Florida when they failed to obey.^

From Bayamo, Soto led his army fifty leagues across a belt of bushlike savanna to the next-nearest Spanish settlement, called Puerto Príncipe, near the northern coast. Here Elvas describes their highway, saying that "throughout the island, roads are made from town to town by means of the machete; and any year they neglect to do this, the thickets grow to such an extent that the road does not show. So many are the paths made by the cattle that no one can travel without an Indian of the country for a guide, for most of it is covered with a very lofty and dense forest."

In Puerto Príncipe, another drowsy enclave of *bohíos* and rough-hewn public buildings close to present-day Nuevitas, Vasco Porcallo invited Soto to visit his nearby estate, taking him there "by sea in a canoe."* Soto's trip with Porcallo was not entirely for pleasure, however. For as the troop approached the north coast, they were buffeted by a powerful hurricane that swept across the

---

*The location of Porcallo's estate is unknown; Elvas says only that it was "near the sea."

island from east to west—putting it directly in the path of Isabel, Don Carlos, and the fleet, then skirting the shore on the way to Havana.

At that moment, the armada was indeed "in great distress," having been blasted by strong winds and split into two groups by the storm. Elvas claims that two of the vessels got "within sight of the coast of Florida, and all suffered great need of water and food." All the ships eventually rode out the storm intact, though Elvas reports that after the hurricane they had no idea "wither they had been driven." Soon enough, they sighted Cape San Antonio, realizing they had been blown the full length of Cuba, beyond Havana to its westernmost tip, "an uninhabited district of the island . . . [where] they got water."^ Soto knew nothing about this as he visited Porcallo's estate, though he became so concerned about the fleet that he hastily returned to Puerto Príncipe and organized a small troop to escort him on a quick march to Havana.^ Ordering the rest of his men to keep traveling at the same slow pace, Soto arrived in Havana as early as October, and no later than Christmas. Relieved to find the fleet safe and at anchor in the harbor,^ he also found his wife, Don Carlos, and the infantry on hand to greet him—and to help begin the final preparations for the assault on *La Florida.*

✛   ✛   ✛

If Soto arrived at Christmastime, he sang his hymns and ate his holiday feast in a still-devastated city. Havana's leaders had begun repairs, but six months since the attack of the French *corsair,* the stone cathedral and public buildings remained mostly in ruins, caked in soot and ashes from the pirates' fire. According to Francisco de Ledesma, a priest in Havana, there were "no more than twenty-four *vecinos*"^ left in the city, down from three times as many before the attack. Most of the citizens fled to other cities, or to their estates in the country, and were only beginning to return to Havana.

Yet Juan de Añasco and Antonio Azeituno, dispatched by Soto from Santiago to rebuild the city, had not been idle. Local Indian and African slaves had been hard at work for weeks hammering together complexes of *bohíos* in anticipation of the army's arrival. Añasco also made sure the heavily damaged port was patched-up enough to handle the fleet and to store tons of expedition supplies. Havana's rudimentary shipyards had even managed to construct at least one new brigantine, fashioned out of Cuban hardwoods, and lathered in pitch made from Cuban pine.

In Havana, Soto plunged into the final phase of stripping the island of supplies, and making plans for his armada, with an eye toward sailing in late spring. Soon after arriving, he established his headquarters in a spacious house in town, almost certainly on the plaza. Here Isabel moved in their personal effects—a small mountain of clothes, furniture, and luxuries befitting an adelantado and governor-general, and the granddaughter of a marquis. In the first weeks of 1539, the first couple of Cuba also acquired at least four plantations near the city, the largest being at Cojímar, on the coast just east of the bay, a place famous for its white beaches, hungry sharks, and, before Fidel Castro's revolution, its casinos and resorts.

We know about Soto's holdings in Havana because in 1543, after his death, Isabel auctioned off thousands of items belonging to her husband before she departed Cuba for Spain. These included everything from a ranch at Maybeque, complete with native laborers, several hundred head of cattle, and five hundred yucca plants, to the Sotos' house in Havana, containing, among hundreds of personal effects, eighteen household slaves, a rosary made of thirty-two solid-gold beads, several pieces of bronze dress armor, twenty-four lances, eight books, and a collar and cape made of black velvet. The total money raised in this auction was more than four thousand pesos of gold—most of which Isabel pocketed and took home to Spain.^

Preparations proceeded smoothly until midspring, when several ships arrived in Havana's harbor on the way to Spain. Coming from Mexico, they brought Soto alarming news—that Viceroy Antonio de Mendoza was planning to lead his own expedition to lands north of Mexico, territories Soto considered part of his own concession. Ever since Álvar Núñez Cabeza de Vaca had emerged from the wilderness with his "secrets," Mendoza had been eager to send an *entrada* north. That spring, the viceroy and a young protégé, Francisco Vázquez de Coronado, had begun to raise an army, dispatching a priest named Marcos de Niza in March to reconnoiter what is now Arizona and New Mexico.^ This expedition would later create a sensation throughout the Spanish world when Fray Marcos returned and reported that he had seen with his own eyes a rich and highly advanced city named Cíbola, filled with gold—a report that would not be proven false until four years later.

Soto was furious. "Not knowing [where Mendoza] was sending [Coronado]," says Garcilaso, the governor began "fearing that the two might encounter and hinder one another, and that trouble might arise between them as had happened" in Peru between Pizarro and Almagro, and in Central America during the War of the Captains. Indeed, Cabeza de Vaca's reports were attracting two additional rivals more familiar to Soto—Hernán Cortés and Pedro de Alvarado—who over the next few months would themselves raise armies bent on conquering *La Florida*. In May 1540, Cortés dispatched one of his lieutenants north to explore the Pacific coast of California. A year later, Alvarado headed north overland from Mexico in the wake of Coronado. His expedition was cut short when this ruthless conqueror was killed not by the arrow of an Indian, or the sword of a rival Spaniard, but by being thrown from his horse.^

As quickly as a ship could be prepared, Soto dispatched one of his aides, Alvaro de San Jorge, to ask Mendoza his intentions. Meeting in the Viceregal Palace in Tenochtitlán, Mendoza explained to San Jorge that "he was sending the men whom he had recruited to another region far distant from where the Governor was going; [he also said] that the land of *La Florida* was so large and broad that there was room for all." Soto was not pleased by this answer, though he knew enough about North American geography to realize that Coronado's expedition would cover territory thousands of miles away, and that the two armies were unlikely to meet up.^ If Soto remained concerned about his competitors in Mexico, neither he nor anyone else in his party ever mentions the matter again.

It would be interesting to know if Soto later received word of Fray Marcos's claims of Cíbola and its supposed empire of gold, which the priest announced to the world in early September 1539—three and a half months after Soto arrived in *La Florida.* My guess is Soto did not know about the fray's claims, because something like this would have been mentioned in the chronicles. Soto, however, was still in close contact with his fleet and with Havana through that autumn. Possibly, he heard rumors of Cíbola and the Seven Cities of Gold, and kept them to himself. This may have been the "secret" he kept referring to throughout the *entrada,* and the source of his obsession to keep moving forward at all costs.

✛   ✛   ✛

Sometime late in 1538, Soto ordered Juan de Añasco to reconnoiter *La Florida* for a suitable place to land the army. Taking fifty men in two small ships for this important mission, Añasco later recalled sailing due north some seventy-five or eighty leagues, passing between Key West and the Dry Tortugas.^ Here he ran into early winter storms that made the sailing treacherous as he skirted the lower edge of the Florida Peninsula, and the vast, impenetrable swamps of the Everglades.

Because Añasco was an accomplished geographer and navigator, and undoubtedly carried with him whatever maps, logs, and descriptions of Florida were available from previous expeditions, he ignored as unsuitable the murky, cypress-choked marshes on the southern tip, heading for the more congenial coastal bays on the Gulf side. For years, mariners had known about two large natural harbors there, which we call Charlotte Harbor and Tampa Bay. Mapmakers in the 1530s labeled them the Bahía de Juan Ponce de León (presumably named after the site where Juan Ponce landed in 1521) and the Bahía Honda—the "Bay of Horses." Both harbors can be clearly seen on crudely drawn maps as early as 1519, when explorer Alonso Alvarez de Pineda became the first European to skirt the entire Gulf coast from Mexico to Florida.^

Exactly which one of Pineda's bays Añasco sailed to in 1538–39 remains a topic of spirited scholarly debate, since this is the same harbor Hernando de Soto would land in a few months later. Most historians believe it was Tampa Bay, supporting their claim with substantial archaeological and topographic evidence. A smaller but vocal group of scholars claim that Añasco—and Soto—landed in Charlotte Harbor, seventy-five miles south of Tampa Bay.* Archaeologists have not yet unearthed enough artifacts in either site to settle the matter. Nor are the chronicles much help, giving only vague distances and descriptions of a bay Soto would rename Bahía de Espíritu Santo—"Bay of the Holy Spirit."

Whichever bay it was, Juan de Añasco carefully explored it with a shallow-keeled caravel, scouting its tide and bottom depth to see if it could handle larger *naos,* and investigating its shoreline for a suitable place to land the armada. Somewhere in the harbor, he also dropped anchor and took a small squad of men to look for Indians. Under orders from Soto to return with natives to train as interpreters and guides, he managed to capture four Indians and to hustle them aboard his vessel. These were probably Timucuan speakers from tribes related to the great Mississippian culture to the north. Soon after, Añasco sailed back to Havana, the entire journey taking roughly two months.^

When Añasco's ships returned to Cuba, Soto greeted his friend with great enthusiasm. For not only did he report a rich and verdant land, he excitedly produced the four Timucuans he had captured, who by then had learned to repeat exactly what their captors wanted them to say. Speaking "by signs," because they had not yet had time to learn Castilian, they told a hushed and anxious governor "that much gold existed in Florida."^

When Elvas says speaking "by signs," he means that one of the Spaniards showed the Indians a ring or bracelet or some other item made of gold, pointed in the direction of Florida, and asked them to nod yes or shake their heads no. Of course they said yes, offering no other proof whatsoever. None, however, was required for these credulous men. "The governor and all the men were greatly pleased," reports Elvas, "and [impatiently] thought they would never see the hour of departure, for it seemed to them that was the richest land which had yet been discovered."

+   +   +

In April, with all of Havana rushing to finish preparations for the armada, a single ship appeared off the coast one day during heavy winds. According to Garcilaso, for four or five days the ship struggled to stay clear of the harbor,

---

*Another candidate for Soto's bay is San Carlos Bay, south of Charlotte Harbor.

coming "to the entrance of the port three times and as often [returning] to the open sea, as if avoiding that port, so as not to enter it." Finally, the ship's pilot gave up and steered his *nao* into the bay, where the *vecinos* onshore saw that the ship carried none other than Hernán Ponce de León, undoubtedly feeling angry at his pilot, and terrified of Soto. Years later, Ponce insisted he had tried to avoid landing in Havana because he was afraid his old partner would try to confiscate the gold that he was carrying back to Spain—which, in fact, Soto threatened to do.^

What happened between these two *compañeros* after Ponce arrived became the centerpiece of the massive Ponce-Bobadilla lawsuit. Commencing shortly after Soto's death, the suit had Juan Ponce and Isabel de Bobadilla both claiming the other had failed to properly divide his or her share of the *compañia*'s fortune, according to partnership contracts dating back to Panama. During the trial, over one hundred witnesses—expedition survivors, servants, priests, aides, and longtime acquaintances of Ponce and Soto's from Central America and Peru—testified about Ponce and Soto's close and profitable relationship from 1514 to Soto's departure from Peru, and how it broke apart in Havana.

When Ponce arrived, witnesses say Soto greeted him warmly, and then promptly asked him for ten thousand pesos of gold. Ponce answered by lying, claiming he had left his treasure in Nombre de Dios. Soto didn't believe him, but went along with the deception, inviting him to come ashore and offering him a suite of rooms in his own house.

Ponce demurred, saying he was ill, though in fact he was anxious to off-load at least one, and possibly two, heavy chests of treasure, so he could hide them before Soto searched his ship. Depending on whose story you believe, that night Ponce either ordered his men to bury the chests onshore,^ or to spirit them secretly to a Havana *vecino* and friend of Ponce's named Luis de Luna.^ But Soto, having secretly placed guards near the ship, caught his partner in the act, seizing the treasure and Hernán Ponce, and taking both to his hacienda on the central plaza.^

Hernán Ponce remained in Soto's power for several more weeks—treated, according to most witnesses, cordially by the governor, even as he tried to squeeze out of his longtime partner whatever money he felt was owed him, and probably more. Witnesses said he threatened Ponce repeatedly, eventually dropping his pleasantries to warn his former *compañero* not only to turn over his treasure, but to sign a document reaffirming their partnership. One witness says Soto threatened to tear apart Ponce's ship into small pieces, and to take him to Florida against his will if he failed to comply. Another man, a field captain named Alvaro Nieto, testified in the Ponce-Bobadilla trial that Soto was

fully capable of this sort of coercion, since he already had "brought to the
fortress" of Havana "a barber, a lawyer, and a ship's pilot,"^ apparently incarcerated to ensure that they would not desert the army.

Ponce refused to be bullied. Arguing that Soto had already spent over
100,000 pesos of partnership money, he insisted that whatever was left belonged to him. But as Ponce himself noted dryly in the trial, in the end he was
powerless to resist a governor-general commanding an army of six hundred
men.^ He therefore handed over eight thousand *castellanos,* and, on May 13,
signed the contract reaffirming his *compañia* with Hernando de Soto. Witnesses add that Soto also took from his partner a set of silver stirrups worth one
thousand *castellanos,* and a brilliantly colored Peruvian tent—the sort Soto
had probably used himself during his campaigns with Manco Inca in 1534.^
These items were taken from among a rich assortment of personal effects witnesses recalled seeing in Ponce's rooms in the Soto *casa*—including a large
gold tray worth two thousand ducats, a gold saltshaker worth one thousand
ducats, two gold pitchers, a gold set of pots, cups, and plates, and two Incan
figurines of a husband and wife from the waist up, fashioned out of gold. Other
servants said Ponce had gold and silver everywhere, wrapped up in sacks, and
packed in earthern containers.^

After Soto's departure for *La Florida,* Ponce tried to renege on his contract
with Soto, claiming he had signed under duress. While this was perhaps true,
he got nowhere with the new acting governor, Isabel de Bobadilla, and the authorities in Havana. When Soto heard about this in Florida, he flew into a rage,
shouting that he should have brought Hernán Ponce with him to Florida in
chains, and left him in the wilderness to die.^

Ponce finally departed Havana late that summer, sailing to Seville, where he
tried to conceal his remaining treasure to avoid paying taxes. Once more he
was caught, this time by agents from the Council of the Indies, who levied a
large fine before releasing most of his money. Only then was Soto's old partner able to do something he obviously had craved for some time—he bought a
large house, married into a prominent family, and settled down to enjoy his
money. Eventually, he was appointed a *venticuarto* (alderman) of Seville, living out his life in a manner that would have bored Soto to death—as a rich and
powerful man of affairs in Spain.

As Soto and Ponce sparred in Havana, the armada's senior officers were
making the final counts of ships, supplies, horses, and men. Since arriving in
Cuba, the number of recruits had changed slightly, with some from Spain dropping out, and several Cubans joining up. We have no exact count, though the
number was probably about six hundred officers, soldiers, tradesmen, servants,

and non-Indian slaves. In addition, there were some 130 sailors in the fleet,^ most of whom returned to Havana. The final count of horses was about 240 mounts, plus an undetermined number of mules and packhorses.^* As for provisions, Soto's royal officers in a letter to the king said the governor provided food "at the cost of much money, to be employed solely in affording us sustenance." This included "more abundant provisions than could be gotten out of Spain for an armada. There are 3,000 loads of cassava, 2,500 shoulders of bacon, and 2,500 *hanegas*† of maize." In Cuba, Soto left behind large herds of cattle, pigs, goats, and sheep on his farms to transport later, when he established a settlement on the continent.

The fleet ferrying everything across the Straits of Florida was roughly the same that had sailed a year earlier from Sanlúcar—five large ships, two caravels, and two brigantines^—though at least one of the original ships was gone, replaced by another vessel Soto "borrowed" from Ponce to transport horses to the Bahía de Espíritu Santo. This ship ended up being scuttled in Florida when it began to leak because of worm damage. But Soto, perhaps at last feeling as if he had abused his old comrade enough, replaced the beached ship with one of his own vessels, the much sounder *La Magdalena,* which Ponce used to sail to Spain. Another change in the fleet's composition was the addition of a brigantine, probably the one built in the Havana shipyards and used by Juan de Añasco during his explorations.

In mid-May 1539, Hernando de Soto signed his final will and testament, and a power of attorney for Isabel. On May 18, the adelantado set sail from Havana, leaving behind forever the settled world of the Spanish Empire, and headed once again for an unexplored territory, where he was convinced he would find a golden empire greater than any yet discovered.

---

*Soto took along a personal contingent of nearly one hundred guards, pages, secretaries, lawyers, servants, stablehands, and a chamberlain named Luis de Fuentes. He also brought several dozen horses of his own, and a small herd of pigs that he planned to breed and save for food in emergencies.
†About 3,800 bushels.

✣ 20 ✣

Landfall

SOTO'S "SPLENDID COMPANY" FIRST saw the shoreline of *La Florida* as a thin, gauzy line on May 25.^ As the fleet drew near, it slowly grew into a thicket of green palms and shrubbery, the edge of a vast continent from which most of Soto's men would not return. This included the dark, imposing figure probably pacing the high poop of the *San Cristóbal,* his eyes blazing with anticipation and a lust to plunge in and see what was beyond the coastal thickets.

By now, this ritual of arrival at the precipice of the unknown was second nature to Hernando de Soto. But for most of the uneducated medieval peasants he was leading, just dimly aware of what they were facing, the sight of that narrow band of green abruptly shifted this place of giddy rumors and bold predictions into something real, tangible—and, for some, terrifying.

The majority of these young, raw recruits remain anonymous, other than their names, parents' names, and places of origin, recorded on yellowed archival manifests. For a few we have more—those who are mentioned in the chronicles or went on after the expedition to leave a paper trail of contracts, letters, and testimonies. The latter include one Gonzalo Martín, then a twenty-two-year-old shoemaker from Seville. Eight years later, in 1547, he would testify on behalf of Hernán Ponce in the *Ponce v. Bobadilla* lawsuit. Claiming that Soto had cheated Hernán Ponce in Havana, he told the court that Soto had commandeered Ponce's ship to use as a transport for horses to Florida.^ There was also an eighteen-year-old named Juan Sayago, a tailor from Zafra, near Seville. In 1547, he testified in Mexico City that the land in Florida was "very good, and if Soto had not died, he would have settled the land to the profit of His Majesty." Sayago did not sign his name because "he said he did not know how to write." Yet another was a *hidalgo* named Luis Daza, who had been named by the king to serve as a *regidor* on Soto's governing council, once the governor built a settlement in *La Florida.*^

Regrettably, the records tell us nothing about what these men were thinking that day as the fleet cut through the Gulf waters toward *La Florida,* though we can be sure that nearly all shared one powerful emotion—a blind faith in the governor-general pacing the deck of the *San Cristóbal,* whom they all had come to fear and admire so much that virtually every one of them was willing to follow him anywhere, even to almost-certain death.^

With the fleet still miles away from the coast, lookouts were already searching for a broad natural harbor Añasco had scouted as the debarkation point for the armada. This was the inlet Soto would later call Bahía de Espíritu Santo, Bay of the Holy Spirit, to commemorate the fleet's arrival on Whitsuntide. As suggested earlier, this was almost certainly Tampa Bay—and not Charlotte Harbor, seventy-five miles south of Tampa, or San Carlos Bay, fifteen miles south of Charlotte. Again, the chronicles are frustratingly vague about where Soto made his landfall, though the few clues they do provide clearly favor Tampa. Most telling is Soto's own observation that Espíritu Santo ran thirty miles inland—which conforms only to Tampa Bay, the other two being much smaller. Tampa and its surrounding region also best fit the configuration of Indian villages, rivers, mounds, and other topographic features mentioned in the accounts. Yet there are inconsistencies. According to eyewitnesses, Soto's bay was so shallow his larger ships touched bottom and had to be lightened by off-loading men and supplies. Tampa Bay, however, should have been plenty deep for sixteenth-century *naos,* even before it was dredged in modern times. (Early U.S. survey records suggest Charlotte Harbor and San Carlos Bay were even more shallow.) One final clue came in 1612, when a young explorer named Juan Rodríguez de Cortaya arrived at a large inlet he says was located at 27.3° latitude—the true location of Tampa Bay. There he met Indians who told them this was the place where Soto landed.^

As disappointing as this mystery remains, it's hardly the last time we will be confronted with an enigma concerning Soto's route. Where exactly the governor-general placed his polished boot in North America at any given time remains elusive, even with numerous tantalizing hints that suggest at least a general routing. Over the next few chapters, I base my reconstruction on a close reading of eyewitness accounts, archival materials, archaeological finds, and relevant theories; and on a careful retracing of Soto's journey by car, mountain bike, and foot. Still, nearly all of what I propose remains at best an informed conjecture.

Mostly, I concur with the so-called Hudson Route, named for Georgia anthropologist Charles Hudson. A feisty, broad-shouldered academic with a thick white mustache—he looks like a brawny William Faulkner with white hair—Hudson's passion for proving his Soto theories occasionally leads him to overstate his case, espousing his points in an impatient and sometimes combative style. Yet this frequently puts him right where he seems to enjoy being most—in a heated, even sharp defense of his hypotheses at Soto symposiums, lectures, historic-association meetings, and in private debates and conversations. Yet no other Sotoist in the past half century has attempted such an in-depth, comprehensive, and passionate effort to track the governor-general across *La Florida*. To find someone else as singularly devoted one must go back to the 1930s and another towering anthropologist and Sotoist, John Swanton, who at the height of the Great Depression convinced a cash-strapped Congress to spend tens of thousands of dollars on an exhaustive four-hundred-page study of Soto's route, which he mostly wrote and edited. Titled *Final Report of the United States De Soto Expedition Commission*—though Swanton himself admits it is hardly final—its purpose was to map out as definitive a course as possible for Soto's expedition, so that the U.S. Park Service could erect markers for a historic trail. Fifty years later, this Park Service project remains mostly on the drawing board, stalled by continuing controversy over Soto's route. But this has not prevented towns and counties along Swanton's proposed route from raising memorials and statues, and holding parades and fetes to celebrate Soto's supposed passing.

Charles Hudson first became interested in the Soto chronicles as raw source material for his anthropological work on southeastern Indians. Quickly realizing that recent archaeological and archival finds had rendered Swanton's route obsolete, Hudson set off on what has become a tireless and somewhat Quixotic quest to visit every possible Soto locale in North America, and to consult with hundreds of local experts and laymen, crisscrossing the Old South in a red 1965 Karmann Ghia with his wife, the writer Joyce Rockwood Hudson.^

Hudson's hard work has mostly paid off. He has even managed to convince most Soto scholars to agree to his substantial alterations of Swanton's route—including his belief that the Spaniards marched farther north than Swanton proposed, particularly as they moved from the Carolinas toward Arkansas. Hudson also suggests new sites where several key Soto events took place, including the point where he "discovered" the Mississippi River, and where Soto's army was nearly obliterated in the Battle of Mabila. In his office at the University of Georgia, Hudson keeps track of his latest ideas about Soto sites on a wall-size map of the Southeast, peppered with inch-high flags mounted on toothpicks. Arrayed like a field marshal's campaign map, the red flags identify probable places Soto visited. The yellow ones mark sites Hudson is less sure about.

Predictably, Charles Hudson's realignment of Soto locations long held sacred has not always been warmly received by town boosters, tourist agencies, and local Soto enthusiasts—particularly as this peripatetic anthropologist treks about in the South coolly informing townspeople proud of their association with Soto that he may not have passed their way. Hudson's compulsion to find the truth about Soto's route has shades of Soto's own quest—a notion Hudson, in one of his reflective moods, might agree with, admitting with an ironic laugh that despite his efforts, his quest seems at times as much an Eldorado as was Soto's obsession with finding his golden empire.

✛   ✛   ✛

As Soto's armada drew alongside the coast that late spring day in 1539, dolphins probably chased the wakes of the vessels. Gulls circled overhead, unaccustomed to the feast of scraps and refuse their noisy descendants take for granted along the heavily populated coast of present-day Florida. By now, most of the voyagers crowding the decks were undoubtedly straining to see the lush shoreline dense with coconut palms, live oaks, palmettos, mangroves, white-blossomed magnolias, and a tangle of grapevines so thick that Spaniards would later joke there was a single stem running the length of *La Florida*. They also saw birds—tens of millions of them, four times the number one sees today—pelicans, ducks, seagulls, terns, egrets, and herons so numerous that early explorers say they sometimes blocked out the sun when they flew overhead. Soto was less interested in this natural bounty, however, than in several thin, wispy puffs of smoke he would see over the next few days rising along the coast. This meant Indians were nearby—and that they knew the Spaniards were here.

But where, exactly, was here? The master pilot, Alonso Martín, had set a course to sail from Havana^ to the bay Soto would call Espíritu Santo—which Juan de Añasco had discovered during his scouting expedition a few months earlier. But now that they had arrived, Añasco did not recognize this stretch of coastline. Nor did he see any sign of the great bay as the navigators scoured their charts and took readings with their instruments. When they still came up blank, a frustrated Soto decided to send a party in a brigantine to reconnoiter closer to shore, since the *navíos* were in as close as they dared in these shallow coastal waters. Soto himself, unable to resist the chance to plunge into his new territory after so many months of waiting, announced that he would personally lead the expedition, though it was highly unusual for a governor-general to do a scout's work. He took with him Añasco and Martín, and several lightly armed soldiers.

If Soto's Bahía de Espíritu Santo really is Tampa Bay, the fleet at this moment probably stood at anchor two miles off the southern end of Longboat Key. This thin coastal island is just south of the entrance to Tampa Bay, not far from a modern resort Floridians have misnamed Cortez Beach.^ Departing the fleet, Soto and his companions would have steered their open, one-masted vessel to run just off Longboat's beach, heading north until they reached the end of the island. Slipping between Longboat and Anna Maria Island to the north, they would have disappeared from the armada's view through a narrow sea pass now connected by a low steel bridge rumbling with beach traffic. Abruptly finding themselves out of the wind, they manned the oars in the quiet, weed-choked waters, paddling until a few minutes later they entered Sarasota Bay—which at first they mistook for Añasco's harbor, until realizing it was much too small.^

By now, the sun was dropping fast. Not wanting to get caught away from the fleet after dark, Soto ordered the rowers "to return to the ships." But when they emerged from the narrow passage between the two islands, they found that the wind had shifted direction, and stiffened to a light gale that nearly prevented them from paddling out into the open sea. Once free of the inlet, the tiny craft could make no headway toward the fleet as the wind pushed them repeatedly back against the beach on Longboat Key. Finally, as the sun dropped into the sea and the sky darkened into twilight, the governor gave up and ordered his men to run the brigantine up onto the beach for the night, in a protected spot out of the driving wind. This could have been either on Longboat Key itself, or possibly back inside Sarasota Bay. Wherever it was, Rodrigo Ranjel says they found a small Indian village hastily abandoned, containing "a hut like the large ones that have been seen in the Indies, and other small ones."^

Apparently, the natives had fled the town as the Spaniards approached, alerted to their presence by the smoke signals passed from village to village along the coast, "which the Indians made in order to give information to one another." Later, Soto learned the Indians in the area had run away "because of some fears of us." Garcilaso adds that this fear may have come from the natives' experience eleven years earlier with Pánfilo de Narváez, who had treated these Indians as cruelly as he had those in Cuba—chopping off their hands and noses, burning them, and throwing them to the dogs to be torn to shreds.^

With Soto now stranded onshore, miles away from the fleet, Oviedo notes that the lightly armed party was lucky not to have been attacked and obliterated by Indians. "The Governor and those who were with him," Oviedo writes in his *Historia,* interjecting his own opinion into the section where he paraphrases Ranjel's account, "were in no little danger, because they were few and without weapons . . . In short, to personally take so much care was carelessness and too much diligence or lack of prudence on the part of the Governor, because those things are the responsibility of other persons and not the person who has to govern and rule the army . . ."

To the immense relief of Soto's men, lookouts the next morning sighted their governor and his brigantine "well leeward of the ships," where strong winds continued to impede their progress as they labored to rejoin the armada.

Realizing the governor would never reach them in this wind, Field Marshal Baltasar de Gallegos, a steady man whom Soto would rely heavily on throughout the expedition, shouted from his ship to Captain General Vasco Porcallo de Figueroa aboard the *San Cristóbal.* He said something should be done to rescue the governor.

Vasco Porcallo either ignored Gallegos, or didn't hear him. So the field marshal himself—a veteran of the conquest of Tabasco in southeastern Mexico, and one of the wealthiest and most experienced men in the army—ordered one of the fleet's caravels "to weigh anchor" and take him personally "toward where the brigantine appeared." The caravel, being larger and more maneuverable than a brigantine, was soon able to come alongside Soto's smaller vessel and tow it back toward the armada. "By this time," continues Ranjel, "the port was already reconnoitered" by a scouting party in the fleet's other bergantine—which was now anchored as a marker on one side of the bay's main channel—probably Tampa Bay's southwest channel. Word of their discovery reached the fleet about the time Gallegos returned with Soto.

Excited by this news, Soto ordered Gallegos's caravel to turn around and go quickly to the other side of the main channel, "so that the ships [of the fleet] might pass through the middle" of the two vessels. Soto himself led the armada from his flagship into the Bahía de Espíritu Santo, first under sail, and then, because the heavier ships scraped bottom, by the more painstaking method of "kedging"—that is, running out the anchor line with a skiff, planting it on the bottom, and heaving the ship forward on the line. Damage from this operation was minimal because the bottom was sand and mud, though it was tedious work. The shallowness also meant this bay might not work as the harbor for a new colony. Indeed, Soto was not pleased with Juan de Añasco, who had promised this inlet would easily accommodate any ship. "This day the Governor and Juan de Añasco . . . had hard words," relates Ranjel, though Soto as usual cooled down and "concealed and endured" his feelings.

For four more days the fleet slowly proceeded into the bay, the sailors continuing their tiresome kedging, aided by riding tidal currents, as Soto searched out a suitable landing place.^ On May 30, Soto ordered his men to unload the horses, both to lighten the ships for the kedging, and because it was becoming unhealthy to keep the horses confined in their straps on board. Already, nineteen or twenty mounts had died after two weeks below decks. That same day and the next, all the men but the sailors disembarked, probably near Piney Point, between Cockroach Bay and Bishop Harbor.^

Once ashore, if Soto followed normal *conquista* procedure, he ordered his men to clear out a broad space for a makeshift camp, dispatching work crews to cut down trees and hack away underbrush. As they worked, Maestro de Campo Luis de Moscoso assigned guards to patrol the perimeter, and others to

Soto Lands at Tampa Bay, 1539

organize food, supplies, and mess groups. Meanwhile, page boys and servants gathered grass in great bunches for the hungry horses, which were off-loaded and led directly on wobbly legs to drink from freshwater creeks running down the beach.

In the midst of off-loading, Soto dispatched a small squadron to sweep the area for Indians. Almost immediately, they ran into a small band of six to ten natives Ranjel says had approached the camp out of curiosity, "to reconnoiter these Christian guests and learn what people they were." This first encounter between Soto's Spaniards and the Indians of *La Florida* did not go well, quickly devolving into a harbinger of things to come as the two groups fought a sudden, bloody skirmish. Casualties were two Indians killed and two horses wounded. The other natives, says Elvas, "escaped, for the land being obstructed by woods and swamps, the horses, because of weakness from voyaging on the sea, became mired there and fell with their masters."^

The following morning, Soto took a hundred more men in the brigantines to look for a site where he could properly bivouac the army.^ He found it some eight miles to the north, in another Indian village hastily abandoned, located near the modern village of Ruskin. The Indians called this town Ocita, which also was the name of the *cacique* ruling the area. According to Elvas, Ocita was composed of seven or eight round huts made out of timber, straw, and mud daub, the biggest and grandest belonging to the *cacique* and standing "near the beach on a very high hill which had been artificially built as a fortress." There also was an ornate temple topped by "a wooden bird with its eyes gilded"; a common motif among southeastern Indians, who considered birds to be symbols of heaven. Deciding to make this village his temporary headquarters, Soto ordered the rest of the army to march to Ocita. This took two days because of the dense thickets and swamps. Meanwhile, the ships, still painstakingly kedging and riding tidal currents "arrived near the town . . . and thus they unloaded all the clothing and supplies that they carried."

Everyone, including stragglers, arrived in Ocita by June 3, most of them muddy, hot, and none to happy to find themselves in a primitive village lacking in gold and Indians, and hardly suggestive of a sophisticated culture. The locals did not even seem to grow maize; a depressing fact for those in the army who understood the correlation between corn and advanced civilizations.

But Soto remained undaunted, deciding it was time to stage another of his elaborate entertainments. That same day, he dressed in his richest clothes, walked to the nearby beach, and raised the banner of His Cesarean Majesty high above the sands and swamps, claiming the entirety of North America for the Spanish Crown, and for himself. The fact that two others had already made the same claim—Juan Ponce de León and Pánfilo de Narváez—made no difference to the adelantado of *La Florida.* Nor did the minor disappointments of the past few days. For Soto, having already committed his fortune and prestige, had long ago convinced himself that this mysterious continent he faced with upheld arms on that early summer evening, as mosquitoes and flies swarmed above the blazing torches of his men, contained riches and fame beyond his wildest dreams.

✛ 21 ✛

Ocita

WHEN HERNANDO DE SOTO planted the purple-and-gold standard of Castile and Aragon on the Florida coast, what exactly was he claiming?

According to the king, his *gobernación* combined the concessions given to Pánfilo de Narváez and Lucas Vázquez de Ayllón. Theoretically, this encompassed the entirety of North America above Mexico, all 7.3 million square miles of it—quite a piece of real estate to be claimed by one person standing on a beach, who had no real idea of this continent's size. Even if he had, it would hardly have stopped him from making his audacious claim.

Nor was Soto alone. As he off-loaded his men and material late that May near the Indian village of Ocita, other explorers were making their own bids to penetrate deep into the interior. In Mexico, Francisco Vázquez de Coronado was about to launch his invasion of what is now the southwestern United States. And far away to the northeast, in the St. Lawrence River Valley, the French explorer Jacques Cartier two years later would begin his third and final expedition trekking deep into Canada, where he had already claimed the homelands of the Huron, the Algonquian, and the Iroquois for France. Meanwhile, off to the west, Francisco de Ulloa and, later, Juan Rodríguez Cabrillo^ were beginning explorations up the Pacific coast from Mexico, which would eventually take Cabrillo as far north as present-day Oregon.

In 1539, North America remained a mostly Dark Continent to Europeans, though Soto had at least a vague awareness of what he might find. By contrast, the Indians of the Southeast, numbering perhaps one million as Soto raised his banners on that long-ago day,^ knew nothing about the maelstrom about to sweep over them. A few coastal tribes had encountered Spaniards. But the majority of natives Soto would come upon were still living as they always had—

253

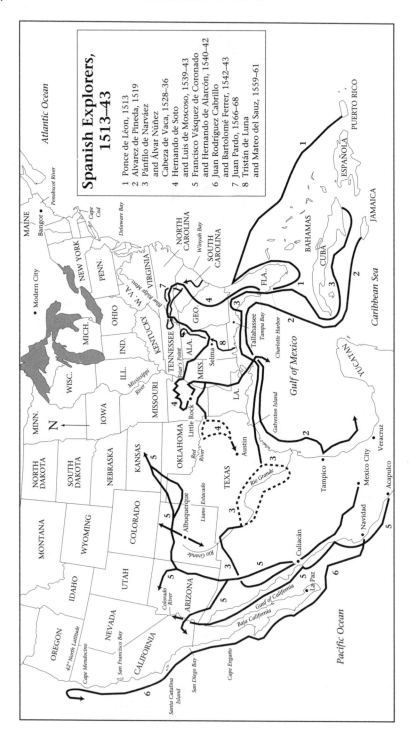

Spanish Explorers, 1513–43

1 Ponce de Léon, 1513
2 Alvarez de Pineda, 1519
3 Pánfilo de Narváez
   and Álvar Núñez
   Cabeza de Vaca, 1528–36
4 Hernando de Soto
   and Luis de Moscoso, 1539–43
5 Francisco Vásquez de Coronado
   and Hernando de Alarcón, 1540–42
6 Juan Rodríguez Cabrillo
   and Bartolomé Ferrer, 1542–43
7 Juan Pardo, 1566–68
8 Tristán de Luna
   and Mateo del Sauz, 1559–61

working their fields, worshiping their gods, making love, and fighting battles, for the moment ensconced in a world where plague, steel, and bearded warriors were beyond comprehension.

Already, Soto and his men had met—and killed—Timucuan Indians, a people then inhabiting the upper half of the Florida Peninsula, from perhaps Tampa Bay to the Aucilla River. Little is known about this long-extinct people. Shortly after Soto's visit, they began dying by the thousands from disease and the aftermath of Soto's *entrada,* dwindling to only a few hundred by the time a combined British and Creek army invaded north Florida in the eighteenth century, and finished them off. Thanks to Soto's chronicles and archaeologists' digs, we know the Timucuans worshiped the sun, built earthen mounds to elevate their palaces and temples, etched tattoos of birds, snakes, and geometric designs on their bodies, and were dominated by *caciques* who ruled clusters of towns and villages that provided him tribute. In many ways, they resembled the High Mississippian cultures Soto would encounter later on, though their art was cruder, their political structures less absolute, and their cities smaller, the Timucuans being the equivalent of country cousins to the highly sophisticated kingdoms and empires to the north.

We do not know exactly what the Timucuans looked like. Presumably, they looked like Mississippians, whom the Italian explorer Giovanni de Verrazano described in 1524 as having skin the "color russet," and "hair black, thick, and not very long, which they tie together in a knot behind and wear like a tail. They are well featured in their limbs, of mean stature, and commonly somewhat bigger than we are. They are broad breasted, with strong arms . . . great and black eyes, with a cheerful and steady look. They are not strong of body, yet sharp witted, nimble, and great runners."

What the Timucuan looked like mattered far less to Soto than snatching a few to interrogate; not only about the lay of the land, but also about a growing concern of the Spaniards at Ocita—where were the great cities and piles of loot? Where was the evidence of a second Inca Empire hidden somewhere in the interior?

So far, Soto's men had been unable to capture a single Indian who could tell them anything about empires or gold—or even about the world beyond his own village. To make matters worse, three of the Timucuan interpreters captured earlier by Juan de Añasco escaped within the first few days—two of them slipping away the first night in Ocita, and the other bolting into the forest during a mission to find more Indians. This left Soto with only one interpreter; and, as the days went by, a handful of other Timucuans the Spaniards had managed to seize, hoping to use them as guides. All, however, had proved either unable or unwilling to help. Some purposely led small scouting parties astray, guiding them deep into swamps and thickets, where the Indians escaped as their captors became bogged down in canebrakes and quickmud.^

On June 2, the Spaniards moved into the abandoned town of Ocita, chief city of a province that seems to have stretched across southern Tampa Bay, from the Alafia River in the north to Sarasota Bay in the south. Soto, however, had yet to capture the local *cacique*, even as he moved into Ocita's *bohío* palace, built atop the town's largest earthen mound. For the next six weeks, Soto would live there, surrounded by lavish household items undoubtedly brought over from Spain and Cuba—chairs, trunks of clothes, weapons, bedding, china, and majolica jars filled with wine and olive oil, all of it set up in the cool half-light beneath eaves of thick pine logs overlaid with palms, the massive chamber illuminated by a hole in the center of the roof where smoke from cooking fires billowed out into the sky.

According to the chroniclers, the mound where Soto made his headquarters was large enough to hold not only the *cacique*'s palace, but numerous outbuildings, and a palisade encircling the top. Elvas speculates that the "high hill ... artificially built" was erected primarily for defense. It also served to enhance the prestige of the *cacique* by physically placing him above everyone, and closer to the sun. Other mounds in Ocita and elsewhere were used to bury *caciques* and other important people.^ Some farther north towered thirty or forty feet high, built by hand over the decades and centuries, the dirt carried in baskets and laid down inch by inch.^

✛   ✛   ✛

Scholars have offered several possible sites for Soto's Ocita in Tampa Bay—and in Charlotte Harbor and San Carlos Bay. Again, our eyewitness accounts offer no definitive details, though they provide the usual clues to help narrow down the possibilities. For instance, the chroniclers tell us Ocita is located at the mouth of the small river the army crossed after disembarking, and that it was located within sight of the ships. This means that any prospective site must be located on the north bank of a shallow stream near the bay.^ The site also should conform to Elvas's description of the town, with its seven or eight houses and a "very high" mound on a "beach," topped by a flat top large enough to accommodate Soto's *bohío* and a ring of defensive palisades.

Another requirement is that artifacts from the site date to the mid-1500s, and contain not only the proper styles of Indian pottery and statuary used by Timucuans in 1539, but also European artifacts Soto and his men would have left behind during an extended stay—broken pots, loose coins, bits of metal, and trade goods such as beads, mirrors, knives, and other trinkets. In the Tampa Bay area, the archaeological site corresponding most closely to these requirements is near Ruskin, at the mouth of the Little Manatee River, eighteen miles inside the bay. Called Thomas Mound, it was excavated in the late 1890s by a Philadelphia archaeologist named Clarence B. Moore, and then in the 1950s by Florida archaeologist Ripley Bullen.^ Soon after Bullen's dig, the site was destroyed by bulldozers building a highway, though they collected enough data to convince two leading Soto scholars, Charles Hudson and Jerald Milanich, to conclude Thomas Mound is Ocita.

I happen to agree with them, though this is as good a place as any to point up the problems with making definitive statements about where Soto laid his head to rest in *La Florida*. Indeed, these two dedicated scholars, who have spent more than a decade at the center of the stormy controversy over Soto's route, want so badly to solve the mystery of where their protagonist made his first camp—and, in the larger scheme of things, to solve the puzzle of Soto's entire route—that they do not stop with declaring Thomas a "possible" site for Ocita. They want us to believe it *is* Ocita, a certainty that is not entirely supported by the evidence.^

Hudson and Milanich base their claim on a number of clues. These include Thomas's location deep in Tampa Bay, its proximity to a small river, the existence of an earthworks they speculate may have been built by Soto's men, and so forth. But their smoking gun supposedly rests on two bits of archaeological evidence—Ripley Bullen's sketch of the Thomas Mound site, which they insist offers a strong correlation to Elvas's description of the village, and several European artifacts dug up over the years, including a single glass bead dug up by Ripley Bullen. They suggest this glass bead was manufactured during the first half of the sixteenth century, and that it may have been deposited at Thomas by Soto's expedition.

Analyzing their claims takes us into a world of scholarly minutia, where archaeological mysteries are scrutinized and, sometimes, solved, by a single tiny artifact—assuming an archaeologist is correct about the importance of such minutia. Take the sketch.^ Penned in 1952, it clearly shows a typical Tampa Bay Indian village of the proper period. But instead of the one "very large" mound mentioned by Elvas, Bullen has drawn in five mounds, the most sizable being only six feet high—a modest height in relation to what Elvas saw farther north, and would have recalled as points of comparison when he wrote his *relación*. As for the single glass bead,^ Hudson and Milanich take a large stash of artifacts unearthed at Thomas and surrounding sites over the years—beads, pendants, bits of copper, and so forth—and rightly conclude that most of them are not traceable directly to Soto. Indeed, the sixteenth-century European items are mostly standard trade paraphernalia that could have been given to the people of Thomas Mound either by Soto—or by other expeditions, including those led by Narváez, various slaving captains, and officers from St. Augustine, after it was established in 1565. Some of this material might also have been washed up from a shipwreck, or given to someone else by Soto, and then traded to the people of Thomas Mound. Despite these doubts, Hudson and Milanich cite this single artifact from these digs to buttress their claim, suggesting this "may be a Nueva Cadiz Plain bead, a type known to date from the Soto era." Manufactured in the city of Nueva Cadiz, in Venezuela, these distinctive beads are used by archaeologists as distinctive Soto-era "markers" because they were widely used by Spanish explorers during the 1530s, but not after 1541, when the factory in Venezuela was destroyed by an earthquake.

Ripley Bullen, however, believed that this particular bead and the other material he dug up with it postdates Soto, perhaps by several centuries.^ But even if it is from the sixteenth century, there is no proof Soto himself, or one of his men, handed it over to an Ocita Indian at Thomas Mound. In fact, the paucity of definitive Soto-era Spanish artifacts from Thomas casts some doubt on this site, particularly since an extensive search by archaeological teams in 1987–88 failed to turn up a single additional Spanish item in a place where Soto spent over a month off-loading and organizing supplies—not so much as a single nail, or a chip from a shattered olive jar.^

+   +   +

Soto's early frustration at being unable to capture knowledgeable Indians—or any Indians, for that matter, other than a few stragglers—became a major problem as the summer proceeded, and the natives continued to elude his men. In part this was because the inexperienced Spaniards had not yet properly learned to sneak about in the swamps and forests. But even when Soto's men managed to find Indians, they proved to be among the most formidable fighters Soto had ever seen, including the Incas. Their secret was a weapon unheard-of anywhere else in the Indies—the longbow. Indeed, the governor-general had not faced such deadly bows and arrows since his late teens in Colombia, during the disastrous Juan de Tavira *entrada* up the Atrato River, where the seventeen-year-old Soto and his fellow conquistadors were turned back by fighters shooting tiny dartlike arrows tipped in poison. Timucuans and other Mississippians used no poison. What made their bows so formidable was their size—"as thick as an arm, six or seven feet long"—and their deadly accuracy when fired from as far away as "200 paces."

Soto's men had great difficulty even bending these bows as tall as a man, used by the Indians to shoot arrows capable of piercing iron mail "as deeply as a crossbow." "Made of certain reeds like canes," Elvas says the arrows were "very heavy and so tough that a sharpened cane passes through a shield. Some are pointed with the fishbone, as sharp as an awl, and others with a certain stone like a diamond point. Generally when these strike against armor, they break off at the place where they are fastened on. Those of cane split and enter through the links of mail and are more hurtful."

The Timucuans' skill as fighters became evident that first week, when several Spanish parties sent out to capture Indians were soundly thrashed and routed. For instance, on June 2, Soto sent out Juan Ruiz Lobillo with fifty footmen—"most of them armed with swords and shields"—with orders to find and kidnap Indians. Passing through "a swampy land, where the horsemen could not go," Elvas tells us "they came upon some Indian huts near the river," only to have most of them escape by plunging into the river. Riding after them in hot pursuit, Ruiz Lobillo managed to grab several Indian women.^ This provoked a ferocious charge by twenty warriors, and a hasty retreat back to Soto's camp, where sentries heard their shouts, and sent out reinforcements. This saved Ruiz Lobillo's troop from possible annihilation, but left several of the men badly wounded. One of them soon died—an unnamed Spaniard who became the first, but certainly not the last, of Soto's *hombres* to be killed by the Indians of *La Florida.*^

Not all of the scouting parties failed. One day early in June, Baltasar de Gallegos led forty horse and eighty infantry several miles north of the camp, where they happened upon a group of twenty Indians in a clearing. They "saw [them] from afar," says Ranjel, "painted red (which is a certain red ointment that the Indians put on when they go to war or wish to make a fine appearance),* and they wore many plumes and carried their bows and arrows."

Not wanting to waste an opportunity where he could use his horses in a broad, open space, Gallegos ordered his cavalry to charge. Easily outrunning the startled Indians in this terrain, the horses caught up with a group of four Indians, whom the lead riders began to knock down one by one with their lances. Reaching the fourth man, however, they were stunned to see him suddenly throw up his arms and shout to them in Castilian, saying, " 'Sirs, for the love of God and of St. Mary do not kill me: I am a Christian, like you, and I am a native of Seville, and my name is Juan Ortiz.' " He also implored them not to kill his Indian companions, who he said " 'have given me my life.' "

As usual, the hyperbolic Garcilaso adds dramatic details to his version.^ He tells us that the lancer who nearly ran down Juan Ortiz was named Alvaro Nieto, a cavalryman from Albuquerque, supposedly "one of the stoutest and strongest Spaniards in the whole army." According to the Inca, this Nieto charged the young Spaniard and began "vigorously [thrusting] a lance at him. [But] Juan Ortiz had good luck and dexterity, so that, warding off the lance

*Red and black were widely used Indian symbols for discord, often used during war.

with his bow and jumping sideways, he avoided at the same time the blow of the lance and an encounter with the horse." Garcilaso says Juan Ortiz then tried to shout something to Nieto, but had gone so long without speaking Castilian, he could not remember how to say anything but "Xivilla, Xivilla," by which he meant to say, "Seville, Seville."

This was enough to stop Nieto, who somehow had heard there might be a marooned Spaniard in the area. He asked Ortiz if he were this man. Ortiz nodded vigorously, prompting the burly Nieto to seize him "by one arm," throwing him "behind his horse as if he were a child." He then carried Ortiz back to Gallegos and the others, who at that moment were "scouring the woods" and hunting down Juan Ortiz's companions "as if they were deer." Gallegos called them off "before they should do any injury" to Ortiz's friends, much to the young castaway's relief, since he seemed to have grown fond of them during his years of captivity.

According to Elvas, Juan Ortiz was a young *hidalgo* from a noble family in Seville. He had come to Florida with Narváez, but had returned to Cuba with the sailors when the army marched inland. In Havana, he had been recruited by Narváez's wife to join a mission to search for her missing husband in *La Florida*. Sailing in a brigantine to Soto's Bahía de Espíritu Santo, he and the others one day came within sight of a Timucuan village where they "saw . . . a cane sticking in the ground with its top split and holding a letter." Thinking this was a message left by Narváez, Ortiz and another man went ashore to fetch it, only to be attacked by Indians. They killed the other man during the fighting, and captured Ortiz.

Carrying him back to their village, they tortured the boy by flaying him over a fire on a "grill laid on top of four stakes," a cruelty Garcilaso blames on the same Ocita who was now eluding Soto. Garcilaso insists that this was no wanton torture, however, but revenge for cruelties inflicted on this *cacique* by Narváez—who, among other atrocities, cut off Ocita's nose and murdered his mother.

Ocita's vengeance nearly killed Juan Ortiz. "Half roasted" over the fire, the heat against his skin seared "blisters on that side as large as half-oranges." He would have died, except for the intervention of a most unlikely intermediary—the *cacique*'s daughter. In a story that predates the tale of Pocahontas and John Smith by several decades, this young woman apparently took a liking to Juan Ortiz in the short time he had been a captive, to the point that this native princess begged her father to spare the boy's life—which he did, though reluctantly.

Ortiz's life continued to be miserable, however, as Ocita enslaved him and forced him to endure hard labor—and intermittent torture and abuse. "Every time he remembered that they [the Spaniards under Narváez] had thrown his mother to the dogs and left her to be eaten by them," says Garcilaso, "and when he went to blow his nose and could not find his nostrils, the devil possessed him to avenge himself on Juan Ortiz, as if he had cut them off."

One day, three years after Ortiz's capture, Ocita's rage reached the point where he decided to sacrifice the young Spaniard to the Timucuan gods—who apparently required human blood on very rare occasions.^ Elvas, in his recounting of the story, says this sacrifice was called for because a rival *cacique* named Mocoso had attacked and burned down one of Ocita's villages, prompting Ocita's priests to declare their gods were "thirsty" for the "blood of their Indians or of any other people they can get."

Juan Ortiz learned of Ocita's plans from the same Timucuan princess who had saved him before. Warning him the dread event would happen the following day, the princess implored the young Spaniard to flee to Mocoso's territory, where she told him he would be safe. This remarkable young woman then helped the young Spaniard sneak away late one night, guiding him beyond the edge of the village through the dense foliage, and showing him the road to Mocoso's country, "since he did not know the way."

By morning, Ortiz was in Mocoso's capital, where he was welcomed by the *cacique* and treated with great respect—because, insists the romantic Garcilaso, this young chieftain was in love with the princess who had helped Juan Ortiz.^ It's more likely that Mocoso welcomed Ortiz because he knew it would irk his enemy, the *cacique* Ocita. For the next nine years, Ortiz lived with Mocoso, who treated him with "kindness" and "honor . . . and kept him constantly with him day and night, doing him much honor." Meanwhile, Juan Ortiz became, for all intents and purposes, an Indian, dressing in a breechcloth and short grass skirt, tattooing his arms, and carrying "a bow and some arrows in his hands" as he gave up all hope of ever again seeing Spain or Spaniards.

That night, Gallegos took the befuddled but overjoyed Juan Ortiz back to camp to meet Soto, who greeted him "with . . . rejoicing." For Juan Ortiz offered not only a stirring tale of courage and survival of the sort these Spaniards relished, but also a fantastic stroke of luck for an expedition floundering because they lacked interpreters and guides familiar with the area. Soto wasted no time sitting Ortiz down to ask the always-burning question, repeated again and again in the narratives—had he "heard of any land where there was gold or silver[?]"

One can imagine Soto and his senior officers in their smoky *bohío,* sitting on campaign chairs drinking wine from the ships' stores late that night of June 4, leaning close to hear the answer as Juan Ortiz tried to form the words in

Spanish. To their great disappointment, however, "he said no." Nor had he seen any other treasure, though he admitted that "he had never gone more than ten leagues round about from where he was." But Ortiz had heard from other Indians in Mocoso's village about a *cacique* named Urriparacoxi, who lived some thirty leagues (ninety miles) to the northeast, and was said to be so powerful and wealthy that both Mocoso and Ocita paid tribute to him.

Willing to grasp at even the slimmest hope, Soto welcomed this news as if he had just been told Urriparacoxi were Cuzco itself. He also was pleased to hear that Urriparacoxi abounded in maize and other foodstuffs, since he knew his ships' stores would not last forever, and he soon would be faced with the formidable task of keeping several hundred people fed by stealing provisions from the Indians. For this, he would need a country more fertile and populous than this coastal region of swamps, where they had seen no maize grown.

Soto was sorely disappointed about the lack of gold. But now that he had information on a supposedly more sophisticated kingdom in the interior he could at least contemplate a move inland, telling his men "there could not but be a rich land" somewhere "at one end or the other" of this enormous continent. Moreover, the army now had an interpreter and an expert on Indian affairs in the *hidalgo* from Seville, a young man who would prove indispensable until his death from fever two years later in Arkansas—still far away from a home he briefly thought he would see again.

✛   ✛   ✛

During these first busy weeks in *La Florida,* as the army's scouts fanned out to investigate the Espíritu Santo region, Soto organized the army into permanent squadrons—four of cavalry, commanded by Pedro Calderón, André de Vasconcelos, Arias Tinoco, and Alonso Romo, and two of foot, commanded by Francisco Maldonado and Juan Ruiz Lobillo. Soto also assigned sub-units of crossbowmen, riflemen, lancers, and loosely organized engineering squads for building bridges, boats, and fortifications.^

By now, Soto had also arranged his camp in a standard *conquista* deployment, assigning "footsoldiers as sentinels, in couples at each position along the roads and at proper places, who stood watch for four hours," and horsemen to ride back and forth among the sentinels; still others in the camp were assigned to be awake and on alert. For a month and a half, the camp remained a hubbub of activity as slaves and conquistadors labored to unload the ships, and to erect and maintain palisades of earth and timber. Soto also sent out work crews to clear out a defensive perimeter the distance of a crossbow-shot around the camp, hacking away at the "vast and lofty forest" so that "the horses might run and the Christians have the advantage of the Indians if the latter should by chance try to attack them by night." Somewhere in the camp, Soto's priests also would have assigned a team of laborers to build a makeshift place of worship with an altar to hold Masses—complete with glittering sacramental vessels of gold and silver, candlesticks, velvet altar clothes, and ornate robes and miters for the twelve priests sent along to see to the spiritual needs of the Spaniards,^ and to Christianize any Indians who survived the ordeal of capture, enslavement, and hard labor.

✢　　✢　　✢

Still unable to locate the *cacique* Ocita and his people, Soto led a small squadron on Saturday, June 7, to visit Juan Ortiz's patron, the *cacique* Mocoso, "to make peace and bring him to the friendship of the Christians," and to thank him for his good treatment of Juan Ortiz. In turn, Mocoso greeted Soto with great ceremony—and asked him a favor. Explaining that he was surrounded by enemies, including Ocita and Urriparacoxi, Mocoso asked for an alliance with the Spaniards. According to Elvas, he made his case in a long, decorous speech, one of several monologues inserted into Elvas's account that read more like bad dialogue from a third-rate chivalric novel than words spoken by a real Indian chieftain.^ Yet the intent was clear—to flatter Soto into crushing Mocoso's adversaries.

Anxious to gain this *cacique*'s cooperation, Soto immediately agreed to "help him against his enemies." But he also had a price—as many porters, guides, and women as the *cacique* could spare.

Note that Soto here does not *demand* these things—possibly because he did not want to risk having another group of Timucuans disappear into the jungle, but also because Soto appears to have been genuinely grateful to Mocoso for his favor to Juan Ortiz. Indeed, this *cacique* seems to have been one of those rare Indian leaders Soto held in high esteem, either because they behaved with great courage and haughtiness—such as Atahualpa or Manco—or performed some notable act Soto considered chivalrous by his own exacting *hidalgo* code.

Soto's regard for Mocoso was demonstrated the next day when he invited the *cacique* to dine with him at the Spanish camp—and, more importantly, let him return home a few days later, loading him down with Castilian clothing and other gifts. This was one of the very few times during the entire *entrada* Soto willingly released a *cacique* while still in his own country. On virtually every other occasion, Soto ended these dinner parties by seizing his guest, and ordering him (or her) to obey his demands, or face torture and the destruction of his people.

The same weekend Soto visited Mocoso, he dispatched yet another squad, this one under the command of Vasco Porcallo, to investigate a rumor that the *cacique* Ocita was hiding out and massing his warriors in a nearby village.

Porcallo, however, found the village empty, as Ocita once again was a step ahead of his would-be conquerors. Angry and frustrated, Soto's captain general—already known for his cruelty as a plantation owner in Cuba—ordered the village burned, and the Indian guide who had brought them there torn to shreds by an Irish greyhound.^

Garcilaso adds that Vasco Porcallo during this raid embarrassed himself by charging into a swamp after Ocita, only to run into a quagmire of "slime and mud" that nearly drowned him and his horse. He escaped, says the Inca, "more through Divine mercy than human assistance, for those on foot could not swim out to reach him quickly and aid him because . . . they would have sunk in the mire . . . and those on horseback could not come to his assistance for the same reason.^

"Covered with mud and with his hopes of taking the *cacique* gone," Garcilaso concludes, "(and being beaten and ashamed of himself and full of grief and melancholy), he ordered his men to return."

Soon after Vasco Porcallo returned from this raid, he and Soto had a fierce argument over something all of the chroniclers refuse to talk about.^ Presumably, it concerned either Porcallo's ineptitude at capturing Ocita, or his disillusionment with the expedition, and the apparent lack of riches in this part of Florida, which he may have blamed on Soto. Whatever the reason, Soto was angry enough that he refused to talk to Porcallo—except to request that the captain general resign his position and return to Cuba. Porcallo agreed, deciding he was too old to be a conquistador, and wanting to return to his "large possessions and the ease and pleasure he had left behind." He departed on July 9, sailing back to Havana in *La Magdalena,* the ship Soto provided to Hernán Ponce to replace his partner's worm-eaten ship, which he had scuttled in the bay.

✛   ✛   ✛

As Soto organized the army, his men debated whether or not their governor should build a permanent settlement in the Bahía de Espíritu Santo. Soto, who usually let his men openly talk over such matters before making his final decision, cut off the discussion in mid-July. He told them there would be no colony here, because the soil was too swampy and sterile. He did not dismiss the idea of an inland settlement, however—provided what the Indians told him about the province of Urriparacoxi, with its rich fields of maize, was true. To find this out, he dispatched Baltasar de Gallegos on June 20 with eighty horsemen and one hundred footmen to investigate—and, of course, to look for signs of precious metals.

According to Elvas, the *cacique* of Urriparacoxi found out the Spaniards were coming, and sent out a party of thirty men to greet them in a small village some sixty to eighty miles from Ocita, west of present-day Orlando. Carrying gifts of maize and furs, they brought a titillating message from their ruler—that up north, in a place called Ocale, the Spaniards would find all the treasure they could carry. "That land," the Urriparacoxi told Gallegos, "had gold in abundance," so much so that when they "came to make war on the people of Ocale, they wore hats of gold resembling helmets." Gallegos, being a shrewd pragmatist, understood that "these messages were pretense" to delay or get rid of the Spaniards—and to give the *cacique* time to hide out should the Spaniards decide to march on his own territory. Yet Gallegos felt duty-bound to send back messengers to Ocita, informing the governor about what the Indians had said about Ocale. Typically, Soto received the news not with Gallegos's skepticism, but with elation. Elvas tells us "all those in the port . . . believed that what the Indians said might be true."

Ranjel tells a different story about Gallegos's message, and the governor-general's response. In his chronicle—which, remember, is paraphrased and edited by Soto's old enemy, Gonzalo Fernández de Oviedo—Ranjel claims Gallegos wanted to report back to Soto and the army that Urriparacoxi was actually a poor land, and that there seemed to be little of value in this region of *La Florida*. But Soto, knowing his men would never march inland after such bad news, ordered Gallegos to lie. "Even though he [Gallegos] might not find good land," writes Ranjel-Oviedo, Soto told him to "write good news, in order to inspire the people," a command Gallegos, "a man of truth," had great difficulty fulfilling, it "not of his disposition to lie." Yet he also was not in a position to disobey a direct order from the governor.

Gallegos dealt with the situation by writing two letters—"one of truth and the other of lies, but those lies, stated with such cunning, and with equivocal words, could be understood one way and the other . . . And thus the Governor did not reveal the truthful items, saying rather that [these letters] . . . were news of great secrets, which later on would demonstrate much utility for all." Meanwhile, when Soto read out loud the "false" letter about the riches of Ocale, it had the intended effect, stirring the men's "desires to go forward" as "all fell into conformity and unanimously asked for entrance into the interior, which was what the Governor was scheming."

It is difficult to know what to make of this story told by Soto's secretary, and interpreted by Gonzalo Fernández de Oviedo. Is it true? Did Soto lie to his men at Ocita? And how much of this account is from Ranjel, and how much from Oviedo?

In general, historians consider Oviedo's voluminous *historia* reasonably accurate—inasmuch as a conquistador of the sixteenth century writing about people and events of his own time can be fair and truthful. This means that the core of this story—that Soto ordered Baltasar de Gallegos to lie—might very well be true. Certainly, Soto was capable of such a deception, as proved by his corrupt dealings in Nicaragua and Peru.

Before departing the Bahía de Espíritu Santo, Soto ordered Pedro Calderon to stay with forty men to guard the harbor and the remaining ships of the fleet—and to keep open communication lines between Florida and Havana. This was on July 9, the same day that Hernando de Soto wrote a long letter addressed to the *cabildo* city council of Santiago. In this missive, the last we have written in his own hand, Soto gives not only a highly optimistic account of the expedition's first weeks, but also a vivid demonstration of his ability to believe in what he wanted. After telling the council about his landfall, skirmishes with local Indians, and the discovery of Juan Ortiz, he describes Gallegos's mission to Urriparacoxi in glowing terms. Gallegos, he says, "has found fields of maize, beans, and pumpkins, with other fruits, and provision in such quantity as would suffice to subsist a very large army without its knowing a want."

He adds that Gallegos seized twenty-seven Urriparacoxi Indians, among them "some old men of authority, as great as can be among such people, who have information of the country farther on. They say that three days' journey from where they are, going by some towns and huts, all well inhabited, and having many maize-fields, is a large town called Acuera, where with much convenience we might winter; and that afterwards, farther on, at a distance of two days' journey, there is another town called Ocale. It is so large, and they so extol it, that I dare not repeat all that is said," though he happily suggests this Ocale is not only rich in maize, but also has a culture that is highly advanced, with "many trades," "much intercourse," and, of course, "an abundance of gold and silver, and many pearls."

"May it please God," Soto concludes, "that this may be so; for of what these Indians say I believe nothing but what I see, and must well see; although they know, and have it for a saying, that if they lie to me it will cost them their lives."

✤ 22 ✤

The Swamp of Cale

FROM HIS VANTAGE POINT high on Ocita's mound, Hernando de Soto had an excellent view of his army preparing to leave shortly before dawn on July 15, 1539. By the light of enormous bonfires, and a faint bluish-white glow in the eastern sky, he would have seen the men breaking down their tents, sliding into coats of mail, strapping on swords, and attaching heavy neck-rings and chains to Indian slaves and porters. Some of the slower *hombres* were still eating, chewing another day's ration of the ship's vile-tasting hardtack. This was the final allocation of free food from Cuba—a week's worth of cured meat and moldy, rock-hard bread that would have to last until the army reached the supposedly corn-rich province of Urriparacoxi.

Later that morning, Soto may have taken a final look from his height on the mound, watching with great satisfaction as the men formed into lines, and the lead units set off briskly to scout and secure the road into the interior. Beyond the camp, he would have seen the sun slowly rising in early morning, its light still mostly obscured by vapors rising off the river, bay, and swamps, a thick fog that always made morning marches in Florida eerie as the marsh became a frightening place of dark, looming shapes—was it a tree? The horse of a *compañero*? A Timucuan sharpshooter?

The army departed Ocita arrayed in standard *conquista* marching order, beginning, as always, with the vanguard. Behind them came the main army, called the battle line. Divided up into squadrons, some of these men would have been on alert in case of attack; others protected the senior officers; still others guarded the porters, slaves, prisoners, and noncombatants snaking along the trail in a procession that sometimes stretched for several miles. Typically, Soto rode at the head of this large, ungainly center—when he wasn't galloping

267

off to join the vanguard—surrounded by aides, standard-bearers, and his personal guard. Flanking this central column, outriders on horse and foot traveled in pairs and small units, on constant lookout for Indian attacks—and for native snipers, whose deadly accurate arrows would keep the army constantly on edge throughout the four years of the *entrada*. This became the army's greatest terror, that native bowmen would sneak up with no warning to shoot silent missiles into their necks or chests as they slept, ate, or ducked into bushes to relieve themselves. Lastly came the rear guard, a unit of horsemen on watch for an unexpected assault from behind. It was also their job in these early days to keep open communications with the garrison at Ocita, dispatching fast riders back and forth carrying messages.

From the Bahía de Espíritu Santo, the army planned to march north to the "River of Mocoso," the boundary between Ocita and the territory controlled by the *cacique* Mocoso. Then they would swing inland to the northeast toward Urriparacoxi,^ where Soto would again head almost due north, marching quickly up the spine of west-central Florida toward the kingdom of Ocale, probably situated some forty miles south of Gainesville.^

That first morning, the cumbersome, inexperienced army traveled only about five miles, held up by the Río de Mocoso—probably today's Alafia River in northeastern Tampa Bay.^ Arriving here late in the morning, Soto halted his force and ordered his chief engineer, a Genoan known only as Maestro Francisco,^ to build a bridge. He did—by felling two large loblolly pines and laying them side by side across the water for the infantry and others on foot. The horsemen crossed by plunging with their mounts into the river and holding onto the logs as their horses struggled through medium-quick waters.

It should be noted that Soto, unlike many *conquista* leaders—including Balboa, Tavira, and others he had served under—planned ahead for such aquatic obstacles, bringing along Maestro Francisco and other experts, and also the tools and critical materials (iron nails, pitch, canvas for sails) for constructing elaborate bridges and, for larger rivers and lakes, brigantines. By now Hernando de Soto was an old hand at dealing with recalcitrant bodies of water, having several times nearly drowned in them—on the Atrato, with Balboa on the South Sea, with Benalcázar on the San Juan River in Nicaragua, and under his own command when he forded the Pampas, Apurímac, and other rivers in Peru.

After crossing the Mocoso, the army halted on the sandy north bank of the river, probably near *cacique* Mocoso's village. As slaves cleared out space under palms and tall cypresses, the Spaniards set up their first overnight bivouac of the march. Arranging the men in mess groups of four or six,

Soto's Route Through Florida, 1539
(After Hudson and Milanich)

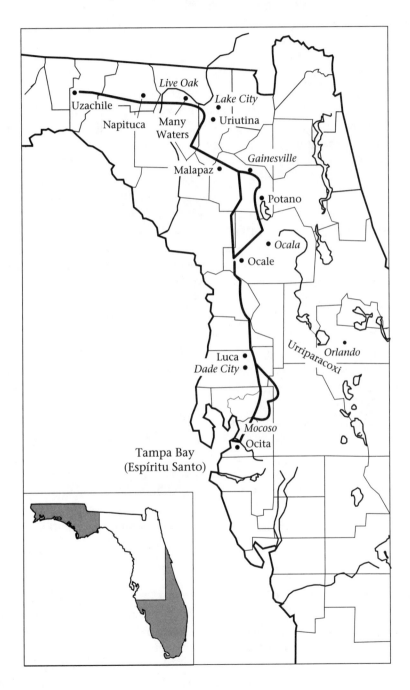

Live Oak

Uzachile

Lake City

Napituca

Many Waters

Uriutina

Gainesville

Malapaz

Potano

Ocala

Ocale

Luca

Dade City

Urriparacoxi

Orlando

Mocoso

Ocita

Tampa Bay
(Espíritu Santo)

Maestro de Campo Luis de Moscoso announced rosters for everything from latrine-digging duty to posts for that night's patrol. It was on this stopover that Soto probably first erected his magnificent Peruvian tent, appropriated in Cuba from Hernán Ponce de León. It must have looked dazzling and exotic against the Florida jungle and the Renaissance finery of the camp—an enormous, colorful structure woven from cotton, *vicuña,* and llama wool, and dyed in brilliant reds, oranges, greens, and yellows. Divided into compartments, it must have required several men to carry and raise it each day—an extravagance Soto felt he not only deserved, but one that also emphasized his great wealth and past success—won, he repeatedly told his men, only after great toil and hardship. Years later, several expedition survivors remembered with awe this sumptuous tent, which gives us some idea about how Soto paraded about the Florida countryside in these early days, acting not only like a European king, but also a high Inca noble of the sort he had cavorted with as the powerful lord of Cuzco.

Soto's grandiose style of travel in Florida was reminiscent of another upstart *conquista* Señor—Hernán Cortés—when he led his 1524 *entrada* into Honduras, after his success in Mexico. Historian Salvador Madariaga has described him as marching "with the luxury and even the extravagance of a Renaissance prince; his household comprised a steward, two toastmasters, a butler, a pastry cook, a larder-master, a man in charge of his gold and silver services, a chamberlain, a doctor, a surgeon, many pages, including two spear-pages, eight grooms, two falconers, five musicians, two jugglers, and three muleteers."

Soto, too, carried with him all the servants and luxuries a fortune in plundered gold could buy. This included at least one steward, three pages, a meat carver, a personal secretary, a chamberlain, seventy bodyguards, cooks, two African slaves, stablehands, and, undoubtedly, many more servants and household specialists not listed anywhere.

Like Cortés, Soto would end up watching his princely procession gradually unravel, eventually being reduced to tatters by hardships, floods, fire, and Indian attacks. Indeed, within a few weeks of Soto's departure from Espíritu Santo, eyewitness Francisco de Castejon says Soto's Peruvian tent—built for the high, cool, and dry atmosphere of the Andes—was wearing out,^ the cloth breaking apart and ripping as it became an early casualty in Soto's glittering procession.

✛   ✛   ✛

Soto's exact route through the southeastern U.S. remains a mystery, though it's less of one in Florida than elsewhere. This is in part because this modern state has been unusually generous in spending money on archaeology over the years. It's also because Rodrigo Ranjel, Soto's secretary, provides an almost daily record of the army's progress through the Sunshine State—which Gonzalo Fernández de Oviedo paraphrases in great detail. Indeed, though Ranjel's original diary is lost, one can read Oviedo's version and still imagine the young secretary, then in his late twenties or early thirties, sitting down each evening after supper to scrawl down a few impressions by firelight before dropping off to sleep.

We don't know what Rodrigo Ranjel looked like.^ It's clear from the chronicles that he was an excellent soldier as well as a man of letters. He once saved Soto's life, during the disastrous Battle of Mabila in Alabama the following autumn, when Ranjel mounted a horse and single-handedly held off a charge of Indian infantry, giving the foot-bound Soto time to escape. We also see the governor-general frequently entrusting Ranjel with dangerous missions to convey messages—most recently the notes passed between Soto at Espíritu Santo and Gallegos at Urriparacoxi.^ Soto's fondness for his secretary was evident even in Havana, when he bequeathed Ranjel three hundred ducats in his will, a sizable fortune for a retainer in the sixteenth century.^

In his account, Rodrigo Ranjel seems to repay Soto's generosity with a scathing critique of his former employer—though to be fair to Ranjel, it's virtually impossible in his narrative to know where the secretary ends and the historian Oviedo begins. Indeed, the Hernando de Soto springing from the Ranjel-Oviedo narrative is singularly arrogant, devious, and cruel. He is a liar to enemies and friends alike, a man addicted to abusing and killing Indians, and despoiling frontiers simply because he enjoyed it—and to get rich. Intense, temperamental, and impulsive, Ranjel-Oviedo's Soto is an exceptionally gifted but flawed soldier and conquistador; a man who is insanely reckless, plunging into one rash escapade after another, and senselessly exposing himself and his men to dangerous situations.

We have heard these criticisms before—from Pedrarias Dávila and Sebastián de Benalcázar in Nicaragua, and from the Pizarros and others in Peru, all of whom had political and personal reasons to denigrate Hernando de Soto. Oviedo is no different. During the 1540s, when he was writing the Ranjel section of his *historia,* Oviedo was having great difficulty acquiring the necessary royal sanction to publish part two of his massive narrative. This was because part one, published in 1535, had been loudly condemned by moralists at King Charles's court—including the fiery Bartolomé de las Casas, who bitterly denounced the *historia* as failing to condemn properly *conquista* savageries against the Indians. By now, Oviedo was out of favor at the court, and more than willing to sermonize and even embellish the sins and excesses of a dead adelantado leading a failed expedition, if that's what it took to see his book in print.* Oviedo also has a literary agenda as he uses the Ranjel narrative to spin a droll morality tale about excessive greed and hubris inevitably leading to disaster—themes that Oviedo, late in life, embraced with great fer-

*Oviedo was unsuccessful in his bid to see part two of his *historia* published in his lifetime. For three centuries, the manuscript languished in the Spanish archives, being finally published in 1851.

vor as he assessed his own less-than-upright role as a conquistador in his youth.

We will never know what Rodrigo Ranjel really thought of his governor, separate from Oviedo's opinion. Yet we can assume that the antipathy at the core of this *relación* comes at least in part from Ranjel, since the details of certain Soto transgressions—including the story of the recent letters sent by Gallegos to Soto—could only have come from a close associate of Soto's who somewhere along the way got terribly disillusioned about the man he served so diligently for half a decade.

During the first few days of the *entrada* through Florida, Oviedo's paraphrasing of Ranjel reads like a series of diary entries, almost as if he is quoting verbatim, with slight alterations, from Ranjel's original. If we tinker just a bit with Oviedo's words—for instance, exchanging the paraphraser's *they* with the chronicler's *we*—it is possible to create a daily diary-like account of the expedition's first week, which probably read something like this:

Tuesday, July 15. *With the Governor we set out from the village and the port at Espíritu Santo, and that night bivouacked at the Río de Mocoso, where we made two bridges for the army to cross over the river.*

Wednesday, July 16. *We marched to the Lake of the Rabbit, so named because a rabbit suddenly started up in the camp and frightened all the horses, which ran free, spreading out behind for over a league, not one remaining, and all the Christians scattered to recover the lost horses; and if there had been any Indians around, even a few, they would have had us at their mercy and, as a result of our lack of caution, the war would have ended here shamefully.*

Thursday, July 17. *The horses having been recovered, today we reached St. John's Lake.*

Friday, July 18. *Under a very strong sun we came to a savannah, and the soldiers arrived much exhausted and a steward of the Governor's, who was named Prado, died of thirst; and many of the foot soldiers were hard-pressed.*

Saturday, July 19. *We came to the Plain of Guazoco, and the men went into the cornfields and gathered the green maize, which greatly cheered us, for this was the first time we had seen maize in this country.*

Sunday, July 20. *We came to Luca, a pretty town, early in the day, and there Baltasar de Gallegos came to meet the Governor.*

Monday, July 21. *We are joined by the people that Baltasar de Gallegos had. The Governor sent a messenger to Urriparacoxi, and a reply did not come.*

Unfortunately, Ranjel's scant account is nearly useless in terms of where the army marched that week in Florida. We can assume that Soto headed north from Mocoso's village, possibly following an old Indian trail roughly corresponding to today's U.S. Highway 301.^ This would have taken them through thick bands of wetlands and shallow palmetto marshes surrounding Tampa Bay, though by midsummer, these swamps were probably becoming so baked and desiccated by the sun that the surface water was receding into hundreds of shallow ponds and lakes. Among these may have been the two large bodies of water Ranjel calls the Lake of the Rabbit and St. John's Lake. Likewise, the hot, arid plain the army suffered through on their fourth day out may have been a long stretch of shallow, grassy wetlands where a punishing sun had evaporated away the water, and baked its sandy-clay soil hard as stone.^

By now, the army was leaving behind the marsh country and marching gradually uphill probably toward the modern-day towns of Zephyrhills and Dade City.^ There they would have passed into a broad corridor of loamy, fertile soil that runs up central Florida from Lake Okeechobee to the Panhandle, and was home in the sixteenth century to scattered concentrations of Indians, villages, and fields of maize.^ Doubtless, the "Sabana de Guazoco" was an artificial clearing made by the Indians to grow the green maize that so excited the army on the fifth day out from Ocita. For the appearance of maize was the first clue that they might be approaching a more advanced civilization.

✛　✛　✛

On July 20, the army reached Luca, meeting up with Gallegos and his troops. Again setting up his magnificent Peruvian tent, Soto waited two more days for the main body of Gallegos's troop to ride in from Urriparacoxi. While in Luca, Soto sent out messengers to the *cacique* of the Urriparacoxi, asking him to come in from his hideout in the forest. The governor promised the usual favors and good treatment should he voluntarily give himself up. Nothing worked, however, as this aboriginal king continued to send the Spaniards messages about the golden land of Ocale—but refused to surrender.

Normally, Soto, the master "pacifier" in Panama and Nicaragua, would have listened to this *cacique's* stories, and then gone after him, if for no other reason than to provide an example to other Indians in the area that the Spanish were not to be trifled with. Fortunately for the Urriparacoxi, Soto was in a hurry to see the treasure of Ocale for himself, and had no time to waste chasing down a recalcitrant *cacique* whose kingdom was well-off in terms of maize, but poor in everything else. Soto may also have been trying to emulate Pizarro's highly effective strategy in the early days of the Peruvian campaign, when the grim old conquistador ordered his men to act as amicably as possible toward the Incas, to trick them into believing the Spaniards had come with friendly intentions.^

Departing Luca, the army at first made good progress toward Ocale. Three days out, however, they ran into a formidable natural barrier—a congested system of marshes, reed-infested ponds, quickmud, and rivers that Ranjel calls "the swamp of Cale." "Large and very difficult to cross," says Garcilaso, this swamp was "a league in breadth," and "contained a great deal of very deep mud . . . up to the very edge." This means the entire wetlands stretched some eight to twelve miles—if Garcilaso was correct—a swath of topography not only difficult to cross, but also devoid of food for an army running out of the week's rations of hardtack given to each soldier at Tampa Bay. This marsh is probably today's Withlacoochee Swamp,^ which indeed stretches some ten to twelve miles across a depression of stagnant cypress bogs, freshwater lakes, and hammocks. Camping first near a small village named Visela, and then, on July 24, at Tocaste, a slightly larger hamlet, the army plunged into the swamp in typical Hernando de Soto style—with him so obsessed to see his golden city that he abandoned the main army late that morning, ordering eleven of his best riders to arm themselves and join him in a mad dash to Ocale.

Rodrigo Ranjel, one of the eleven, says they spent most of that afternoon skirting the southern edge of the swamp, following a narrow trail congested by thick mud and fallen trees, where several small bands of Indian fighters popped up to fire arrows and then scamper away. None of these quick attacks slowed down Soto, who kept skirting the swamp until the trail suddenly widened into a broad and well-maintained highway.^ Probably a choke point in the swamp—a spot where numerous small trails converged into one well-traveled path on a high, narrow strip between two marshes—Soto convinced himself that this was the start of a great roadway, and a sure sign they were drawing near a large and prosperous country. Rushing ahead at full gallop, says Ranjel-Oviedo, Soto behaved as if "his hands were already on the prey."

Deciding he had too few men to storm into Ocale, Soto twice dispatched Ranjel to dash back and order Moscoso to send up more men. Eventually this would swell his vanguard to some fifty-six men as the governor plunged forward, behaving as recklessly as ever, even as the trail again became narrow and difficult, and Indians harassed them at every turn.

In 1539, the area in and around the Swamp of Cale was populated with hundreds of Indians living on small hammocks and islands amidst the marshes, where the soil was thick and black, and the bogs offered a natural defense against attack—and ample opportunities for ambush. Indeed, most of these Indians staged their hit-and-run attacks and easily got away in the dense cane-brakes and marshes. Soto's men managed to chase down a few, killing some and capturing others to use as guides. These proved as guileful as the Indian guides Soto had seized at Ocita. "As they were enemies," says Garcilaso, they led their captors astray, taking them "into difficult passes and places where there were Indians in ambush, who came out to discharge arrows at the Christians."

Infuriated by these deceptions, Soto finally ordered four of the captured guides thrown to his bloodhounds after they led the army straight into an impenetrable bog. The war dogs greedily ripped the men to pieces while a fifth guide was forced to watch. "Fearing death," he was terrorized into directing "them faithfully, and taking them out of the bad passes through which they were traveling, he put them on a clear, plain and wide road" leading to the true passage through the swamp. This trail proved only slightly less treacherous as the men waded through a wide, shallow, grass-choked stretch of water. "It was of great current and broad, and they crossed it with great difficulty," says Ranjel, "and where there was no need of a bridge, they crossed with the water at their chests and at the chin, with their clothes and saddles on their heads." When "the current carried off a horse, and it drowned . . . the rest crossed with ropes, as those who crossed first with the Governor had."

Finally emerging safely from the swamp on the other side of the river, Soto reached a small village named Uqueten, on the southern edge of a vast crop of ripe maize. Because the mud-drenched men by now had gone two or three days without food, they ran hungrily into the fields and gathered as much maize as they could carry, ordering their servants to build fires, cook the grain, and grind it into maize patties, which they ate with great relish.

Once everyone had eaten and rested, Soto ordered them back out into the fields to gather maize to send back to the main army on the other side of the swamp, which he knew was also low on provisions, their Urriparacoxi corn having run out.

The main army, as it lumbered toward Soto's position, was indeed close to starving. Some of the recently captured native porters had already died from lack of food, weakened by carrying heavy loads—an exhausting form of labor they were unaccustomed to. Even Soto's officers were down to eating roots and green stalks of half-grown corn, as the army grew more desperate by the hour, waiting for word from the governor about Ocale and its supposed bounty of food.^

Up until this point, the slow journey in Soto's wake through the Swamp of Cale had been a nightmare for the Spaniards in the main army. "Many men developed raw wounds from the weight of their armor and other loads they had to carry" wrote Cabeza de Vaca, who marched through here in 1528, slogging through mud so thick it was a monumental struggle to take each step. At times, Soto's men sank in the muck up to their knees. Even worse, they were in a place where one could see nothing behind the thick, dark veil of foliage flush against the trail. But they could hear the eerie calls of cats, wolves, alligators, and birds as every man remained tensely on guard for the slightest rustle of cane or the crack of a twig—anything that might reveal the presence of Indian *guerrillas,* waiting to launch volleys of silent missiles. Several Spaniards were wounded by native sharpshooters on the way to Ocale, with one man, a crossbowman named Diego de Mendoza, dying of his injuries.

None of this would have mattered if Ocale had really been the rich city Urriparacoxi had promised—a place where warriors wore helmets made of gold, and "its people, by shouting, made flying birds fall." But it was not.

Ocale turned out to be little more than another village of several dozen palm-thatch lodge houses. There was no gold, no great city, and certainly no Inca-like empire. For Ocale, like Urriparacoxi, was wealthy only in one thing—its great expanses of ripe maize, enough to feed the army for three months, according to Elvas. Otherwise, this Timucuan town must have been a bitter disappointment. Yet if anyone in the army felt betrayed by Soto and his talk about "secrets" and rich countries, none of our eyewitnesses mentions it. Nor does Soto seem overly put off as he orders his men to rest for a few days, before setting off again ever deeper into the interior.

✛ ✛ ✛

As Soto approached Ocale, the *cacique* had already fled his village in what was now becoming a maddening pattern for Hernando de Soto. Once more, he sent out messengers trying to lure this local native king into the Spaniards' camp. This time, however, the *cacique* responded not with silence, or with stories about gold in some distant country, but with a scathing and passionate speech condemning the Spaniards and their savagery in a startlingly insightful assessment of Soto's true intentions—probably too insightful, given that this was recounted (if not concocted) by Garcilaso de la Vega.

This speech is different from most of Garcilaso's monologues, however, because it denigrates rather than glorifies Soto and his Spaniards. Every so often the half-Indian in Garcilaso peeks through in his narrative to give a Native American's point of view. Usually, this comes across as a romanticizing of the Indians Soto met, who appear in Garcilaso to be as lovely, handsome, strong, brave, and as militarily brilliant as Soto and his men. On this occasion, however, Garcilaso provides us with a darker, more brutally honest portrayal of the Indians' point of view vis-à-vis the Spaniards, and their role as invaders.

Garcilaso claims this *cacique* said he "already had much information from other Castilians who had come to that country years before as to who they were, and he knew very well about their lives and customs, which consist in occupying themselves like vagabonds in going from one land to another, living from robbing, pillaging, and murdering those who had not offended them in any way. He by no means desired friendship or peace with such people, but rather mortal and perpetual warfare, and even though they might be as brave as they boasted of being, he had no fear of them because he and his vassals considered themselves no less valiant, as proof of which he promised to wage war against them during all the time that they might see fit to remain in his province, not in the open nor in a pitched battle, although he could do so, but by waylaying and ambushes, taking them off guard."

The Ocale *cacique* also replied to Soto's version of the old *Requerimiento*, declaring that he already was king of his land, and would serve no other, adding that "he and all his people protested that they would die a thousand deaths to maintain their liberty and that of their country."

The chroniclers say nothing about how Soto reacted to this speech—if, in fact, it happened. Yet recent archaeological finds near the Withlacoochee Swamp suggest the Ocale did not come away from their encounter with Soto unscathed. At an excavation called Tatham Mound, archaeologists in 1984 discovered a mass grave—including ten bones with deep divet marks apparently cut by a sharp blade. One victim had his arm completely severed; another had his shoulder blade cleaved off.^ Dozens of other Tatham corpses also found in this grave seem to have died en masse within a few weeks or months of each other, possibly from disease introduced by the Soto *entrada*.^

✣ 23 ✣

Onward to Apalachee

AS THE LAST STRAGGLERS arrived in Ocale, the Spaniards wearily gathered maize, squash, pumpkins, and beans, plundering the Indians' fields. Because they had even fewer servants left alive after the march through the swamp, most were forced to prepare their own food. Elvas describes the "plight" of these rugged soldiers trying to pulverize corn "in a mortar cannon ... with a pestle like a window bar," and then attempting to sift "the meal through their coats of mail." Apparently, this produced a passable flour that the men "baked in some flat pieces of earthen vessels which they set on the fire." Some found this process so difficult they gave up, eating "the maize parched and sodden."

While his men ate and regained their strength, Soto pondered his situation, dismayed to find himself already two months into his expedition, with several men and horses killed, and nothing to show for it. But this hardly dampened the enthusiasm of a man who had survived grueling *entradas* from Darién to the Andes, who remained convinced that these past eight weeks were merely a prelude to a successful quest.

Soto's next would-be Eldorado, after the disappointments at Ocale, was a kingdom to the north the Spaniards had already heard about even in Spain, from Cabeza de Vaca. This was Apalachee, which Biedma says "was widely known in all the land." Garcilaso describes it as a place "concerning which they had heard so many amazing and great things, both as to the abundance and fertility of the land and the deeds of arms and bravery of the people."

In his *relación,* Cabeza de Vaca indicates Narváez found no gold when they attempted to invade Apalachee. Nor do Soto's chroniclers make any mention of gold or the expectation of gold in Apalachee. This suggests Soto's aim was primarily to find food for the coming winter. Crushing the Apalachee was also a point of pride, given the bold talk among the Indians about the ferocity of the Apalachee, and the fact they had chased away Narváez.

On August 11, Soto departed Ocale with a vanguard of fifty horse and one hundred footmen, again leaving Moscoso in command of the main army still resting at Withlacoochee. Soto's party departed without guides. Biedma writes that "some excursions were made to capture some Indians who might guide us to the Province of Apalachee." But he notes that even "the one who knew the most" of the three or four men captured "did not know two leagues farther from that town." But Soto knew Apalachee lay to the north, which is where most of the major trails leading out of Ocale were headed.

For once, the main path was wide and easy to follow. In fact, Soto was almost certainly marching along one of the oldest tracks in this region of North America.^ Used for centuries, and probably much longer, by Florida's Indians—who first arrived in the Southeast thousands of years ago, probably during the last Ice Age^—these ancient highways always took a traveler along the highest and driest topography, the least strenuous inclines and declines, and the most convenient river crossings. (Even today, Florida's major north-south highways follow the basic routing of these ancient trails.) Cleared so that three or four persons could walk abreast, these paths and others throughout his trek would not only allow Soto to move with incredible speed, but also with the assurance that these roads must lead someplace.

According to the chroniclers, the army marched for three days out of Ocale without incident, except for a few minor skirmishes with Indians in a country the Spaniards called Potano.^ Here Soto saved the life of one of his senior captains, Francisco Maldonado, when "an Indian attacked" Maldonado "and badly wounded his horse." The Indian, says, Ranjel, "would have pulled the lance from [Maldonado's] hands if the Governor had not arrived by chance of fortune," presumably spearing the Indian with his own lance, or hacking off critical body parts with his sword. Soto's passage through Potano country was hardly an easy one, however. According to Elvas, who came through here with the main army several days behind the vanguard, the men suffered great hardship because "the land over which the Governor had passed was destroyed and bare of maize."

Little is known about the Potano Soto met.^ Nor is there a strong archaeological presence of beads, ceramics, and other Soto-era markers to provide us with clues about his trek through their territory—possibly because the army was moving so quickly. Yet the Spanish presence in the land of the Potano made a strong impression on at least one *cacique* in the region. Sixty years later he adamantly rejected a request by a Franciscan priest, Father Martín Prieto, to establish a mission in his village. When the priest asked why, the elderly *cacique* explained bitterly that he had suffered greatly at the hands of Hernando de Soto and his men, and wanted nothing more to do with the Spaniards.^

+   +   +

A few miles west of modern Gainesville, on Soto's fourth day out from Ocale, Juan de Añasco and a small troop were riding patrol when they suddenly came upon a party of about thirty Indians working a small field of maize, plucking the tiny ears of corn and dropping them into large, round, flat-bottomed baskets. With the army desperate for Indians to use as guides and servants, Añasco could hardly believe his luck as he shouted to his men to overtake the Indians before they could run away.

Imagine the terror of these thirty natives, their work abruptly interrupted by strange men on huge, never-before-seen beasts who swept across the field to sling ropes around some, and bodily lift others onto their animals, while rapping still others on the head and shoulders with the backsides of their swords and lances. Within minutes, the battered men, women, and children would have been tied together with hemp rope or chains as the white-faced men forced them to start marching.

Soto was ecstatic when Añasco arrived back at camp. He was even more pleased when the *cacique* who ruled this area suddenly showed up, offering to exchange himself for the captives, and promising that if Soto released them, "he would order provisions taken to him and would give him a guide for the onward journey." Soto happily agreed, releasing the prisoners and ordering "a guard put over" the first *cacique* he had managed to acquire in the entire three months of his *entrada*.

Soto's revelry, however, was premature, however. For the truth was their *"cacique"* was an impostor. The trick was discovered the next morning, when the alarm was sounded by the perimeter guards that a large force of Indians was gathering "about the town, near the forest." According to Elvas, this prompted Soto to summon the bogus *cacique*, who "asked to be taken near them as he wished to speak to them and assure them, and [he said] that they would do whatever he ordered them." But as soon as the *cacique* drew near the Indians, he abruptly turned on his guards and "attacked the Christians stoutly and escaped and no one was able to overtake him; and all the Indians went fleeing through the woods."

These Indians, however, had not counted on a Spanish weapon they probably had not seen in action—the war dog. As the false king dashed away from the Spaniards, Soto himself "ordered loosed a hound," which went charging into the midst of the native warriors—and, "passing by many other Indians, went to seize the pretended *cacique* who had fled from the Christians," recog-

Indians Thrown to the Dogs
Theodore de Bry, c. 1600

nizing his scent. The dog "held him by the fleshy part of the arm in such a manner that the Indian was thrown," but not harmed. What happened afterward to this counterfeit *cacique* is unrecorded, though Soto had tortured and killed Indians for much less. Because of this incident, Soto named this village Mala Paz, or "Bad Peace."^

By now, the country the Spaniards were passing through had shifted almost completely to dry savannas and forest as they left the swamps behind and headed north, probably along the corridor of today's I-75, which traces an ancient Indian route. Here Soto and his vanguard pressed on into pleasant country where Soto's army began to eat very well, the reputation of the South for good food being a gratifying fact of life even then. James Adair, who lived among the Indians of the Southeast in the eighteenth century, writes about the foods the Spaniards must have eaten. For instance, Adair describes a tasty bread made by mixing white cornmeal flour, beans, and sweet potatoes, and refining the mixture by sifting it through finely sliced cane. "Baked either in thin cakes moistened with bear's oil, or as large loaves," he wrote, "the results were excellent." He describes with great relish how the Indians roasted various roots and potatoes, and barbecued pumpkins. They made cakes out of dried persimmons, figs, and black mulberries mashed with nuts, raisins, acorns, and corn, and soaked in bear and venison fat.^ Game and fish were also plentiful, he says, though the Spaniards missed beef, having to satisfy their carnivorous yearnings with deer and other wild game.^

As for beverages, when Soto and his people were thirsty for something other than water, which was pure and sweet throughout most of the Southeast,^ they drank teas made from sassafras and other herbs. When they wanted something stronger, they concocted a frothy, wretchedly bitter "day" beer made from fermented corn, and sweetened with honey. If this was not enough, more adventurous Spaniards may have tried the Indians' "black drink," a potent and intoxicating beverage made from boiling a holly rich in caffeine, and typically consumed by adult male Indians before council meetings and major events.^ Drunk rich and thick, and for hours on end by the natives, this precursor of strong coffee produced a caffeine high that the Indians claimed heightened their awareness, and improved their physical acumen in dances, ceremonies, ball games, and warfare. It also was used as a purgative, with Indians wanting to "purify" their bodies purposely ingesting copious quantities until they vomited, spurting forth with great show and ceremony.^*

On August 16, the vanguard's journey through the Middle Florida Ham-

---

*This explains why this holly is called *Ilex vomitoria*.

mock Belt was abruptly interrupted by the troop's arrival at a river Ranjel calls El Río de las Discordias, "The River of Discords." Here Ranjel indicates a crisis occurred among the members of the vanguard, which he refused to elucidate in his narrative, even when Gonzalo Fernández de Oviedo asked him for details. However, the fact that he uses the word *"discordia"* suggests the incident involved a dispute; perhaps a flare-up between the volatile Soto and a faction of his men over a matter of routing, or how to cross the river, or even whether or not the expedition should continue. One source of this *discordia* may have been news delivered by local Indians about the travails suffered by the Narváez expedition, which had passed this way on its way to disaster in Apalachee. "All were saddened" when they heard about the suffering of Narváez, says Elvas soon after the incident at the river occurred, "and advised the governor to return to the port and leave the land of Florida; so that he might not get lost as had Narváez; that, if he went on, when he might wish to return he could not; that the Indians would end by seizing the little maize that was to be found."

Dismissing their pleas—probably by reminding them of the suffering he had endured in Central America and Peru, and by intimating that Narváez was a fool—"the governor answered that he would not turn back until seeing with his own eyes what they said, which he could not believe." Elvas adds that the governor abruptly ended the discussion by ordering the men to "be ready saddled," so they could keep on marching.

El Río de las Discordias was almost certainly the Santa Fe River, which Soto would have crossed where it runs through the present-day O'Leno State Park.^ This is one of dozens of flourishing state parks in the South on or near the Soto route, most of them Depression-era projects that over the past six decades have grown into excellent sample plots of what the country looked like when Soto came through. Typical of these parks, O'Leno is essentially a six-thousand-acre glimpse into the aboriginal condition of north Florida centuries ago; a world dense with longleaf pines and sweet gums towering one hundred feet high, mangroves with man-size buttresses, and hordes of dogwoods, Carolina willows, sparkleberries, honeysuckles, and holly.

Had Soto arrived earlier in the summer, he would not have had to worry about crossing the Santa Fe. For right in the middle of O'Leno Park is a "natural bridge," where the thirty-foot-wide Santa Fe suddenly drops out of sight into a limestone sinkhole, running underground for three miles before reemerging to continue flowing aboveground to the west. This crossing is obscured only in August and September, when heavy rains often bury the natural bridge under high water. This is apparently what Soto and his men found in August 1539, when the road they were following led them straight into the river. "That day they made a bridge of pines," says Ranjel. Garcilaso adds that Maestro Francisco "laid out the bridge by using geometry." He then directed his engineering team—four or five Basque carpenters and another Genoan who had supposedly learned to use a saw while a captive of the Moslems at Fez^— to throw great beams of wood across the river, binding them together with heavy ropes, and then attaching "thick planks thrown out over the water and fastened together with heavy ropes." The crossing itself then proceeded without incident.

✛   ✛   ✛

The day after the vanguard crossed the River of Discords, the dispirited Spaniards finally had a bit of luck. It happened when Baltasar de Gallegos was scouting the area and stumbled onto an unfortunate group of seventeen Indians, whom he captured—including the daughter of a local chieftain.^ Gallegos rushed back to Soto with this girl, knowing that the governor would appreciate this sudden and unexpected prize. For it meant he finally had a chance to snatch himself a genuine *cacique*.

That very afternoon, the girl's father, named Aguacaleyquen, greeted Soto as the army moved into his capital, also called Aguacaleyquen, turning himself over to the Spaniards in exchange for his daughter's freedom. Archaeologists believe this capital was situated near the small Ichetucknee River, twenty-five miles west-northwest of Gainesville, at an expedition dig where they have unearthed Soto-era trade beads, and the remains of mid-sixteenth-century Indian settlements.^

Aguacaleyquen seems to have been one of several allied chieftains in a district bordered by the Suwannee River to the north and the Santa Fe to the south, in modern-day Suwannee and Columbia Counties. This unnamed province's other major towns were Uriutina, Napituca, and a village Ranjel calls *Muchas-Aguas*—"Many Waters"—because it rained so hard there for two days that Soto was forced to halt his march. Apparently, the *caciques* of these towns were related by blood, or kinsmenlike alliances, with all of them paying tribute to the most powerful chieftain in the region, Uzachile. His main city was located near the Aucilla River, sixty miles west of Aguacaleyquen's domicile.^

For years, historians have linked this nation with the Utina people in the St. Johns River valley, seventy-five miles to the east, an Indian nation that became well-known in early Florida history when they allied themselves in the 1560s with a small French army trying to claim *La Florida* for the Fleur-de-lis. In 1564 and 1565, the French and Utina fought two bloody battles against the Potano, conflagrations later immortalized in a famous engraving by Dutch artist Theodore de Bry, who depicts Frenchmen in armor shooting guns amidst multitudes of perfectly proportioned, tattooed Indians dressed in flowing capes, robes, and helmets, most of the details plucked out of de Bry's imagination.^ Anthropologists now believe the Utina etched by de Bry were probably a different people from the group Soto was now about to visit with such devastating results. Indeed, by the time Europeans returned a generation later, they were not only unavailable to ally themselves with the French, but were either extinct, or no longer a distinctive polity.^

On August 22, the beginning of the end for Aguacaleyquen's people started when "a great multitude of Indians appeared" near the Spanish camp. Hoping to intimidate the Spaniards into releasing their *cacique*, they instead prompted Soto to put the camp on full alert, and to dispatch eight fast horsemen back to Ocale, with orders for Luis de Moscoso and the main army to march double-time to reinforce the vanguard. "The Maestro de Campo," says Ranjel, "had no small diligence in carrying out that command, and on the fourth day of September he arrived where the Governor was, and all were delighted to meet together; because as they had imprisoned the *cacique*, it was feared that the Indians would ally themselves" and attack the Spaniards. It was during this journey that the main army nearly starved, because "the land over which the governor had passed was destroyed and bare of maize." They also heard at this time the same reports as the vanguard concerning Narváez's miseries, and his failure to find riches in Apalachee.^

Despite the general grumbling and unhappiness, Soto kept moving, leaving Aguacaleyquen on September 9. He took with him "the *cacique* and his daughter," the latter of whom he had not yet released, despite his promises. Crossing the rain-swollen River of Aguacaleyquen—probably the Ichetucknee River, near Lake City, Florida—they slept that night in a small village near the river, arriving the next day in Uriutina, a village "of pleasant view and with much food" dominated by "a very large hut, in the middle of which there was a large courtyard." This was a Timucuan council house, where local Indians gathered for important meetings and ceremonies, and to gorge themselves with black drink. These buildings could be enormous, with archaeologists unearthing evidence of round structures over one hundred feet in diameter, capable of holding hundreds of people.^

Moving on the next day, Soto and the army were delayed in the soggy village of Muchas-Aguas,^ a stopover as miserable for the men as crossing the swamps to the south, since most were either camping in the open as the rain poured down in great sheets, or under canvas tents that quickly became saturated and useless. When the rain finally stopped on September 15, Soto led the army to the next major city, called Napituca^—a place that few Americans

have heard of, though this is where one of the greatest massacres in early-
American history was about to occur.

During these six days of travel, large groups of Indians sent by Aguaca-
leyguen allies and kinsmen continued to mass around the edges of the army.
Playing flutes and drums, dancing, cajoling, and imploring the Spaniards to release their captive, the atmosphere shifted back and forth from festive to threatening and back again. "Every day," says Elvas "they came to the road playing
on flutes, which is their sign . . . that they come in peace." Aguacaleyquen's
aides also supplied the army with porters, guides, food, and servants—which
was not only a relief to the army, but proof that Aguacaleyquen and his kinsmen ruled a state in which a *cacique* had the authority to order large numbers
of subjects to perform even onerous tasks, and be obeyed.

By now, the most important chieftain in this unnamed province, Uzachile,
had heard about the kidnapping of his kinsman. He dispatched his own high-
ranking ambassadors to parley with Soto, dressed in colorful feather capes, the
skins of pumas and martens, and shell and mica jewelry, their bodies richly
decorated with tattoos. Soto, however, "dismissed them with good words,"
saying he would release his prisoner when the army arrived at Uzachile's main
village, on the other side of the province.

This prompted the anxious Indians to consider another course of action—a
surprise attack.

The Indians' scheme was simple. At Napituca, probably located southwest
of present-day Live Oak, Florida, they would offer a face-to-face parley between Soto and one of Uzachile's kinsmen, Uriutina, the *cacique* of the village
the Spaniards currently occupied. Sweetening the lure of their trap, the Indians
would also tell the Spaniards they wished to discuss the possibility of becoming allies and auxiliaries against the Apalachee—a shrewd proposal they suspected would be very attractive to the Spaniards as they contemplated their
conquest of this powerful kingdom to the north. However, because "they were
afraid to enter in the camp and be detained," says Ranjel, they asked Soto to
bring Aguacaleyquen "to a large savanna" near the village for their conference.

Fortunately for the Spaniards, just before the conference one of their native
interpreters divulged Uriutina's true intentions to Juan Ortiz, who rushed over
to the governor as he was departing for the parley. Warning Soto it was a trap,
Ortiz declared that "[the Indians] had decided to assemble and to come against
him in order to give him battle and to take from him the *cacique* whom he was
holding." Garcilaso, who says there were four native interpreters involved, insists that Uriutina, whom he calls Vitachuco, had ten thousand warriors waiting to ambush Soto—a number considerably higher than the few hundred
Indian troops indicated by eyewitness accounts.

Garcilaso devotes several pages to profiling this "Vitachuco,"^ creating a remarkably unflattering portrait of an Indian in a book that generally treats Native Americans as near equals to the Europeans in terms of intelligence, valor, and worth. In this story, Vitachuco becomes a stereotypical villain of high romance—a man not only evil, but vain and stupid, who spends the days leading up to the meeting with Soto bragging to his Indian friends about how he planned to torture the Spaniards once they had been defeated. "He [Vitachuco] said that he intended to roast some of them alive," Garcilaso has Vitachuco declare, "boil others alive, and bury others alive with their heads outside; and that still others would be poisoned with poison from the yew tree so they could see themselves become corrupt and rot away. Some would be suspended by the feet from the highest trees available, to become food for the birds."

Armed with Ortiz's intelligence, Ranjel says Soto scrambled late in the afternoon of September 15 to prepare his own counterstrategy, ordering his men "to arm and mount" and to be on the alert in case the Indians tried to attack. The signal for a Spanish charge, he said, would be a blast on a trumpet, delivered by the army's young trumpeter, Rodrigo Corona.^ Soto then went to meet Uriutina, accompanied only by a small guard, "taking the *cacique* [Aguacaleyquen] by the hand and talking with him."

At this point, Garcilaso launches into a lengthy description of what will be, in his florid account, a magnificent pitched battle fought beside two lakes between two brilliantly attired and courageous adversaries. He describes the Indians as being "brave and of fine appearance . . . They had their bows and arrows on the ground covered with grass, in order to make it appear that as friends they were unarmed. The squadron was drawn up with all military precision, not square but elongated, the files straight and somewhat open with two projecting wings at the sides, arranged in such good order that certainly it was a fine thing to see." Against this native host Soto's forces "advanced handsomely equipped, armed, in battle array, formed in squadrons, the cavalry and the infantry separate."

Ranjel and Elvas describe a smaller and less grandiose affair, where three or four hundred Indians and six or seven hundred Spaniards armed themselves and then hid in their respective camps while their leaders tried to outwit each other. The advantage, however, was with Soto, since Uriutina was unaware he had discovered the Indians' secret plan to attack.

The Indians made the first move. Ranjel tells us that no sooner had Soto arrived "and the conversation was beginning, when he saw himself immediately surrounded with Indians with their bow and arrows, and from many directions came innumerable others, in such a manner that the danger that the governor

Indian Caciques Lead Their Armies into Battle

Theodor de Bry, c. 1600

was in was manifest." Having anticipated this attack, Soto ordered the trumpet sounded. This triggered a full-scale Spanish charge, as Soto's cavalry came rushing across the field to smash into the massing Timucuans, hacking with swords and "lancing many Indians."

They took the Indians completely by surprise, though Ranjel says Uriutina's men fought well, battling the Spaniards for "a good period of time." They killed one of Soto's own horses, and wounded several other horses and men. But the outcome of a battle fought in a cleared, flat space was inevitable as the Spanish horse carried the day, forcing Uriutina and his warriors, as night approached, to flee toward the two ponds on the edge of the plain.

The Spanish were not about to let them escape, however. Fired up by finally fighting the sort of battle they preferred, units of cavalry hotly pursued the Indians, who out of desperation dove into the water to save themselves. Still, Soto's men did not relent, rushing to surround the smaller of the two ponds, and to post sentries as best they could around the other much larger body of water.

All night, the Timucuans stayed in the frigid water, with Spanish riflemen and crossbowmen taking potshots at them, and Juan Ortiz shouting at them in Timucuan to surrender. "Forced by necessity and the coldness of the water," says Elvas, "they did," feeling the bitter humiliation of defeat as "one by one . . . the suffering from the cold conquered them, [and] they would cry out to Juan Ortiz" that they were coming in, and not to kill them.

The last to surrender was Uriutina, compelled to come in only after some of his own men were sent out by Soto to convince him further resistance was futile. Upon coming ashore, this abased, waterlogged cacique composed a message to be sent to his kinsman, the paramount cacique Uzachile, telling him the Indians had failed, and warning all other Indians in the area to avoid these strangers at all costs, "these Christians, who are devils and who are more than a match for them."

✝   ✝   ✝

As individual Indian soldiers emerged from the cool, black water that night of September 15–16, with their war paint smeared and their skin wrinkled from being soaked, the Spaniards bound them up with rope and marched them back to Soto's camp at Napituca. Once in town, Soto ordered them put in chains and imprisoned in a huge lodge house in the village. As the sun rose, Elvas says the Indians "were allotted among the Christians for their service," with individual prisoners being led off in ropes and chains to the personal areas of soldiers, where they were put to work grinding corn, carrying equipment, fetching grass for the horses, and obeying whatever commands given them.

Nothing could have been more debasing to these proud warriors. Indeed, as the morning wore on, the Indians' stunned compliance must have changed to outrage as the Spaniards forced them to perform tasks they considered beneath them. Their anger reached the breaking point when Soto entered the council-house prison early that morning to separate out the *caciques* and leaders. "Encouraging them in order to bring them to peace and harmony," Soto ordered them untied so that they might be better treated than the common Indians.

Apparently, Soto was used to Indians crushed this decisively in battle being docile and dejected, at least for a while. But not these Timucuans. For no sooner had the first *cacique* been released from his chains than he turned on Soto and punched him in the mouth, delivering "such a great blow that it bathed [Soto's] teeth in blood and made him spit out" more blood^—a singularly suicidal, if enormously satisfying, action for this Native American. Indeed, this sudden, defiant act almost instantly ignited a revolt by the other captive warriors, which spread out to engulf dozens of prisoners throughout the camp. According to Elvas, the Indians grabbed whatever they could find to use as weapons, with one man snatching "the pestle for crushing maize," which he used "with all his might to kill his master." Others grabbed swords and lances carelessly left about, and "so handled [themselves] as if [they] had used [them] all [their lives]. An Indian with a sword surrounded by fifteen or twenty men on foot in the public place, uttered [a] challenge like a bull, until some halberdiers of the governor came up, who killed him. Another one with a lance climbed up on a cane floor which they make to hold their maize (which they call *barbacoa*) and there he made a noise as if ten men were inside; and while defending the door, he was struck down by a javelin."

Again, the outcome was never in doubt as Soto's Spaniards rallied against prisoners mostly unarmed and chained, or otherwise encumbered. Within minutes, the conquistadors had grabbed weapons and were battling back, cutting down the most recalcitrant Indians, and recapturing the others. This time, the prisoners were not spared, however, as a bloodied and furious Soto ordered most of the survivors executed, culling out only the youngest Indian boys to be trained as servants. "All the rest," says Elvas, "he ordered to be punished by being fastened to a stake in the middle of the plaza," and shot through with arrows delivered by a firing squad of Indian collaborators captured near Tampa Bay.

Apparently, these former subjects of the *cacique* Urriparacoxi had proven themselves loyal enough to the Spaniards to be released from their own chains, and given weapons, which they now turned on their Timucuan cousins. Whether or not this was done willingly, or under duress, is not known.^ In any case, the sight of two hundred men tied up and shot must have been terrifyingly effective as a deterrent against further uprisings.

Yet one wonders why Soto chose to kill so many men when, if any had to die, a small demonstration might have sufficed. This wholesale execution is the first time we see Soto abandoning his usual pragmatism in such matters. For Soto at this moment was desperate for native servants to keep his army going, and could ill afford to slaughter potential slaves and porters.

Some of Soto's own men considered the punishment excessive and wasteful. Elvas calls it a "massacre." Ranjel also disapproved, telling us that as Soto watched the warriors of Uzachile killed, he turned to his aides and wistfully spoke of the "hardships" he and other Spanish leaders had to endure to conquer new countries—including the intransigence of certain Indians, who, he said, forced captains and generals to torture and kill them because of their unwillingness to acquiesce. Recalling long discussions on Indian policies with the Council of the Indies in Seville, Ranjel says the governor then exclaimed to his friends, "[I]f only those lords of the Council were here so that they might see how His Majesty is served in these parts!" To which Ranjel replies, in a comment made later to Oviedo, that it was precisely because of men such as Soto that the council had repeatedly ordered "the tyrannies and cruelties to cease, and to have better order in the pacification of the Indians . . . so that . . . the consciences of the conquistadors are at peace, and the natives of the land are not maltreated."^

✛ ✛ ✛

On September 23, seven days after the executions at Napituca, Soto and the army broke camp and marched some ten miles to a sizable river, probably the Suwannee.^ Cool, swift, and deep, Garcilaso claims it had "precipices on either side as high as the length of two pikes and as perpendicular as walls." If this is a reasonably accurate description, then it's likely the army crossed in the vicinity of Dowling Park, Florida,^ where State Highway 250 spans the river at one of its narrowest points, and the banks are high and steep—in some places as high as "two pikes," or about twenty-eight feet.

Soto's men called this stream El Río de los Venados, "The River of the Deer," because Uzachile, who now had no army to defend himself as the invaders approached his capital, sent several slaughtered deer as a peace offering. He hoped this might in some small way mitigate the maelstrom now headed directly at his own city thirty miles to the west.

While feasting on this meat, the Spaniards took two days to build another large bridge to cross the Suwannee. Ranjel says it was constructed out of "three large pines in length and four in breadth," the trees being "perfect and like the very large ones from Spain."

In Garcilaso's version, the Indians on the other side of the river did not come bearing gifts of venison, but bows and arrows, which they used to attack Maestro Francisco and his crew as they tried to complete their bridge. Eventually, the attackers succeeded in driving away the Spaniards, forcing Soto—his face still "bandaged" from the Indian's blow at Napituca—to build "six large rafts on which a hundred men crossed, including crossbowmen, harquebusiers, and fifty armed cavalrymen." He also describes a fierce skirmish as the Spaniards landed on the opposite shore.

As usual, no other chronicler mentions this story—or anything about belligerent Indians, rafts, or sallying forth. Garcilaso also fails to explain why Soto would have been so foolish as to send men into the highly vulnerable position of being shot at while in their rafts—unless he ordered his men to cross at another location up or down the river, without the Indians on the other side realizing it. Nor does the Inca tell us where these Indians came from, given that most of the warriors, *caciques,* and *principales* in the area had just been killed at Napituca.

From The River of the Deer, Soto pushed his army hard to reach Uzachile's capital in a single day. Marching some twenty miles, they trekked along another broad trail, passing by frequent farmsteads and villages surrounded by "large fields of maize, beans, and calabashes of the kind called in Spain romana." By dusk, they reached Uzachile, possibly located at or near a seventeenth-century Spanish mission site archaeologists have located beside Lake Sampala,^ some forty miles east of Tallahassee.

In a final desperate gambit to avoid destruction, King Uzachile evacuated his capital as Soto approached. "For because of the news which the Indians had of the massacre of Napituca," says Elvas, "they dared not remain." Uzachile, however, left behind "an abundance of maize, beans, and pumpkins," still apparently hoping to turn aside Soto's wrath with gifts.

Garcilaso claims Uzachile's capital (he calls it Osachile) contained two hundred large houses made of wood planks and thatch—almost certainly an exaggeration. More credibly he writes that Uzachile, like most Timucuan cities, was surrounded by a palisade of thick wooden posts planted close together, and dominated inside by large, grassy plazas edged by earthen pyramids rising "two or three pike lengths in height."* These were flat on top, he says, with enough room on the major mounds to hold "ten, twelve, fifteen or twenty dwellings" belonging to "the lord and his family and the people in his service." Their size, he adds, varied "according to the power and grandeur of [the Lord's] estate." Below the great mounds the Indians built temples and charnel houses, usually raised on lesser pyramids. High nobles also lived on or near this plaza, their dwellings raised slightly above the commoners who lived in clusters of huts inside and outside the palisade. Scattered about the center city

---

*Twenty-eight to forty-two feet.

were storage huts filled with food, hothouse-saunas, markets, and a system of small lakes and irrigation canals for supplying water.

In Uzachile, Soto dispatched two captains to scour the country around the town for Indians. "They captured a hundred head," says Elvas, "among Indian men and women." From the latter, Soto chose "one or two," either to cook his food, or to serve as mistresses, or both. The others were divided amongst the rest of the men, secured "in chains with collars about their necks" to avoid a repeat of the Napituca rebellion. These wretched Indians were then "used for carrying the baggage and grinding the maize and for other services which so fastened in this manner that they could perform."

Elvas implies that the "spirit" of these Indians was not broken by these harsh measures, however. "Sometimes," he reports, "it happened that when they went with them for firewood or maize they would kill the Christian who was leading them and would escape with the chain. Others at night would file the chain off with a bit of stone which they have in place of iron tools, and with which they cut it." Those caught in these desperate acts suffered the same fate as the "rebels" of Napituca—instant execution.

On September 29, with the ranks of the army now swelled by two or three hundred Indian porters and servants captured before and after Napituca, Soto departed his temporary headquarters atop the principal mound in Uzachile. With winter not far off, he was anxious to march on Apalachee, the object of his latest fantasy concerning great empires, even if it didn't have any gold. Indeed, he still felt compelled to conquer this country, if for no other reason than it was in his way, and he needed its reportedly ample food and supplies.

Not far from Uzachile, the army plunged into a dense wilderness of pines and shrubbery—obviously a natural buffer maintained by Uzachile's people to keep the militaristic Apalachee as far away as possible, a purpose that cannot have been lost on Soto. For it confirmed what he had been hearing about all these months—that he was about to confront his first serious military challenge of this *entrada,* a prospect he undoubtedly relished as he rode on his high saddle under a pine canopy at least eighty feet above him, with his flanking sentinels riding through the woods on either side, on maximum alert for Indians guarding the Apalachee border.

❖ 24 ❖

Anhaica

THE PINE FORESTS OF NORTH Florida are pleasant in late September, as the humidity eases off and the temperature becomes tolerable, even for men wrapped in thick quilted armor, chain mail, and metal jackets. Yet Hernando de Soto was clearly on edge as his guides from Uzachile and elsewhere became gradually more terrified approaching the Apalachee border. Go back, these Timucuans pleaded, regaling the interpreter, Juan Ortiz, with gruesome stories about legendary Apalachee atrocities, and the fierce, maniacal bravery of warriors feared for hundreds of miles beyond their domain.^

For some Spaniards, the terror among their guides undoubtedly whetted their appetite for a good fight. The Timucuans' unease cannot have been entirely shrugged off by the army's rank and file, however. After four months of unremitting and sometimes vicious attacks by Indians, compounded by heat, swamps, misery—and, of course, a troublesome lack of profit—the average soldier may have been less than enthusiastic about facing an even more formidable foe. There also was continued muttering among the men about the fate of Pánfilo de Narváez's army at the hands of the Apalachee a dozen years earlier.

Soto's preoccupation with the coming campaign—and the high stake he had in winning it—seem to have made him more irritable than usual, as a young infantryman named Alvaro de la Cadena found out the day the army departed Uzachile. Sneaking away from his unit "without permission" to fetch a sword he had left behind, his absence was noticed, and reported to the governor. But instead of exacting the usual fine, demotion, or flogging for the breach of military discipline, a tense Soto ordered Cadena hung. The sentence stunned the army, and is reminiscent of Pedrarias's summary hanging of his servant, San Martín, on the Isle de Dominica in 1514. Lacking Pedrarias's cold-bloodedness against his own people, Soto soon cooled down. "Through the entreaties of good persons,"^ he cancelled the execution. One suspects, however, that young Cadena did not get off completely, but was severely punished, though none of the chroniclers provides any details. There are no further reports of swords being left behind.

On September 30, the day after Cadena's transgression, Soto and the army arrived at a small village called Agile, probably nestled in the woods on or near the Aucilla River.^ Ranjel says this *pueblo* was subject to the Apalachee, though if it was, there was no sign they intended to defend it. Elvas says that the Indians in the village "had not heard of the Christians." This allowed Soto's vanguard to approach undetected, giving the villagers barely enough time to throw down what they were doing and flee into the woods, where "most of them escaped." The Spaniards managed to capture a few Agile women, however. These were assigned, as usual, to cook food and perform other servants' duties, with the youngest and most supple undoubtedly reserved as concubines.

Throughout this narrative, I have noted the dismal treatment of women—by Spaniards and, at times, by Indians. A chronic shortage of details has forced me to skim the surface of what must have been, at times, a nightmare of rape and abuse. In Agile, however, I am able to provide at least a brief glimpse into one Indian woman's ordeal—and how she fought back.

It happened on September 30, when a young lawyer named Pedro Diaz de Herrera^ tried to rape one of the Agile women in the bushes, only to discover that she was as ferocious and unwilling to be subjugated as the warriors who rebelled at Napituca. This woman, says Ranjel, "was such" that when Herrera stayed "alone with her and behind his other companions" she "seized him by the genitals" until she had "him very fatigued and submissive." Possibly, she grabbed a knife or blade to cut him, since Ranjel adds she "would have killed him" had he not screamed bloody murder, attracting the attention of his comrades.*

Ranjel insists that Pedro Diaz de Herrera had not "wished to have intercourse with her as a lustful man," though this is hard to believe. For he took the substantial risk of taking her by himself into woods probably filled with hostile Indians, an act of insubordination coming just a day after Soto had nearly hung a man for leaving his unit. Moreover, it hardly seems likely that a man would casually expose his genitalia in front of a woman for reasons other than sex. It's worth noting that Ranjel makes no mention of the *bachiller* Herrera being punished for his foray into the bushes. Perhaps Soto, when he heard about the incident, considered Herrera's humiliation at literally being caught with his pants down penalty enough. Herrera's compromising position may have given every-

*None of the chronicles tells us the fate of this woman.

one a good laugh, though deep down this incident, like Napituca, cast yet another pall over an army with dozens of Indians in their midst who might turn on them anytime—even, as Señor Herrera discovered, during sex.

✛   ✛   ✛

By now, the Apalachee leadership knew the Spaniards were coming. For weeks, their scouts had undoubtedly been relaying information to their capital at Anhaica, in present-day Tallahassee, where the *cacique* of this powerful Indian nation was devising his own strategies in tense consultations with his advisors. Already, the Apalachee had dispatched a large force of warriors to stop the Spaniards. Numbering at least in the hundreds, and possibly in the thousands, they were marching in highly disciplined battalions down wide trails across their country, with orders to defend their eastern border at the Aucilla River.

According to Garcilaso—who is, unfortunately, our chief source for the coming campaign—the Apalachee's preparations were aimed primarily at countering the Spaniards' most effective weapon: the horse. Unlike most Indian nations Soto would confront in *La Florida,* the Apalachee already had direct experience fighting Spanish cavalry, thanks to Narváez. They also had firsthand knowledge about Spanish armor, weaponry, and battle tactics—none of which seemed to impress them, armed as they were with longbows as deadly and accurate as those of the Timucuan.

Garcilaso indicates the Apalachee strategy rested on a series of carefully planned hit-and-run attacks to be mounted along a succession of fronts, starting at the Aucilla. Here the Apalachee either would rout their enemy, as they had Narváez, or they would fall back on another defensive position a few miles to the west, where they would keep trying to defeat the enemy as they fell back from one position to the next. Each of these sites was meticulously selected, says the Inca, most being choke points along the narrow trail through the marshlands west of the Aucilla, or defensible positions within the cleared agricultural land beyond the swamps. If all else failed, they would adopt a slash-and-burn policy, torching their own towns and food supplies as they fell back toward Anhaica, and then to wilderness strongholds and hideouts to the west, near their western border at the Apalachicola River.

Garcilaso suggests that the Apalachee chose their positions mindful of the Spanish horse. Like the Quitoans in Peru, who quickly learned to engage the Spaniards in country too rough for mounts to charge effectively, the Apalachee planned to fight only in heavily wooded and swampy areas, avoiding confrontations in the open. They also hoped to stop the horses, and perhaps to capture some alive, by constructing rope-and-cane fences across narrow paths and arroyos.

Another critical component of the Apalachee war effort was their famed belligerence. For what they lacked in sophisticated weaponry, they more than made up for with a suicidal courage that even the haughty Spaniards feared and respected. Ranjel, for one, describes them as "most valiant men," whose ambushes and traps would kill "many Christians" over the days and weeks to come, and whose pride kept them from surrendering, "although the Spaniards pursued them and burned them," and hacked off their noses and hands.

Other eyewitnesses say the Apalachee were convinced they would triumph—which in fact they did, in the sense that they ultimately survived Soto's bloody and destructive incursion. For another century and a half, they would remain a powerful political entity in Florida, until an allied army of British-and-Creek fighters swept down from the English base at Charleston in the early eighteenth century and decimated them so utterly that within a generation, the Apalachee ceased to exist.

The proud Indians Soto was about to confront were the first true Mississippians along the Spaniards' route—that is, the first highly organized kingdom with a strong central authority; standing army; elite classes of politicians, priests, and warriors; and a complex network of trade with other Mississippian kingdoms as far north as the Great Lakes—and, perhaps, as far south as Tenochtitlán in Mexico.

Details about the Apalachee are sketchy in the chronicles, though modern archaeology has recently augmented the written word with numerous illuminating, if frustratingly incomplete, discoveries. We also have archival reports and narratives written in the seventeenth century by Spanish priests and administrators who set up missions among the Apalachee. These accounts tell about a people far removed from those Soto met, however—a nation Christianized and living in mission towns, and more connected with the Spanish colonial capital at St. Augustine than with the then rapidly disintegrating Mississippian kingdoms and religious centers to the north.

What we know for sure is that when Soto came through, the Apalachee king ruled a prosperous kingdom that worshiped the sun, grew an abundance of food, and built large cities filled with pyramids, temples, and large, round lodge houses. We also know that this kingdom was only some forty miles square, centered in modern Leon County—one of the most fertile counties in Florida, where underground cisterns of fresh water still rise up regularly from limestone sinkholes to replenish a thick crust of alluvial soil.

In 1539, this country was fertile enough to feed some 25,000 Apalachee, and possibly as many as 100,000.^ It also was rich in game, fish, and shellfish, which the Apalachee ate with great relish, given the great heaps of animal remains they discarded in garbage pits dug up over the years by archaeologists. They also used furs and bones of fish and animals to fashion elaborate clothing and jewelry—everything from feather capes and marten-skin shawls to painted-bone earrings and decorated breastplates made from seashells. Garcilaso tells us the Apalachee were as well-known among other Mississippian kingdoms for the jewelry they fashioned from shells, which they collected on the coast, as they were for their fighting ability. Apparently, the Apalachee operated a booming business in trading conches, fantail shells, coral, whelks, and jewelry to inland kingdoms, bartering for everything from crockery to copper.^

The only written description we have about Apalachee culture was penned by a priest in residence at Anhaica in the 1670s, one Juan de Paiva, who decided to record in detail the Apalachees' most popular game.^ He did not do this out of historic curiosity, however, but to convince the colonial authorities in St. Augustine that this game was a pagan rite that should be banned. Called simply *el juego de pelota*—"the ball game"—it was played by two teams, usually rival clans or villages, who tried to score goals by kicking and slapping a small, hard buckskin ball toward a goalpost topped by a stuffed eagle in the middle of a playing field. Hitting the post scored one point; hitting the eagle scored two. Played exclusively in the summer, the game involved elaborate ceremonies to set up the goalpost, paint the contestants in their clan colors, and to perform rituals such as fasts, chanting, dream interpretation, charms, and countercharms.

According to Father Paiva, the game could be extremely violent. It started with what sounds like a scrum in a rugby game going after a ball, but quickly devolved into a free-for-all. The players fell "upon one another at full tilt," writes Paiva, "aiming kicks without concern whether it is to the face or to the body, while at other places still others pull at arms and legs with no concern as to whether they may be dislocated or not, while still others have their mouths filled with dirt." After this melee was finished, as the "pileup begins to become unentangled," it was common to "find four or five [players] stretched out [unconscious] like tuna; over them, others are gasping for breath . . . and over there lie others with an arm or leg broken." Paiva says the violence spilled over into the audience, with virtually every game he witnessed erupting in "a live war." In some cases, Indians died of their injuries. "How can these wretches stay alive thus?" Paiva asks, claiming that this game was the root cause of every social ill afflicting the Apalachee of the seventeenth century—including a series of catastrophic epidemics that had steadily reduced a people who had once numbered in the tens of thousands to only a few thousand.

By 1682, the government in St. Augustine had officially proscribed the game—something the Apalachee must have greeted with the same horror and sadness as modern Americans being told that baseball or football had been banned. (Many Indians in Florida continued to play it clandestinely.) Of course, Father Paiva never mentions that his own countrymen played equally lethal games with their tourneys, *cañas,* and wrestling matches. He also fails to note the devastating psychological impact of banishing the national pastime of a people already grappling with their own obvious decline, who had seen their great armies, their religion, and now even their favorite form of play snatched away.

Anthropologists believe the people who eventually became the Apalachee first appeared in north Florida sometime around A.D. 800, seven hundred years before Soto's arrival.^ But it was not until about A.D. 1240 that they built their most impressive city. This was not Anhaica, but an unnamed enclave near Lake Jackson, Florida, which the Apalachee abandoned in the mid- to late fifteenth century, two or three generations before Soto's *entrada.*^

According to archaeologists, the city at Lake Jackson at its height was dominated by a central earthen pyramid three stories high and over 250 feet on each side at the base, with an enormous rampway running down one side and into the central plaza.^ On top, the king lived and held court in a complex of buildings that included his palace, servants' quarters, religious buildings, and, possibly, the large council chamber where the king met with generals, nobles, and aides. Facing the pyramid, on the south side of the plaza, was a smaller mound some nine feet tall and ninety feet on each side. Other less dramatic mounds—seven in all—were scattered throughout the city, which covered one square mile, with a population of up to several thousand.

It's a mystery why the Apalachee abandoned Lake Jackson. Possibly, the move to Anhaica represents the succession of a new dynasty wanting to make a break with past regimes. Another explanation is that food distribution somehow became disrupted; or, perhaps, some religious imperative forced the move. It is also possible that the Apalachee in 1539 were still using their complex at Lake Jackson for religious rites, even as the population shifted west to Anhaica, and that they kept its location secret from Soto and his army. This would explain why the chroniclers fail to mention the Lake Jackson site, and also why Anhaica lacked the usual pyramids and ceremonial centers one would expect in a major Mississippian city.

Inside the largest mound at Lake Jackson, archaeologists have unearthed a remarkable cache of pots, beads, clothing, and, most spectacular of all, four beaten copper breastplates buried in the mid-thirteenth century with certain highborn individuals, probably kings. The copper most likely arrived as chunks of rock from north Georgia, the closest source for this metal. It then would have been beaten flat and painstakingly etched by local artisans, who carved sophisticated religious images into the soft metal. These breastplates are as graceful and skillfully wrought as the finest reliefs and paintings Soto saw in the Inca Empire, though the Mississippians lacked even the most rudimentary knowledge of smelting precious metals.

Three of the breastplates show Indians dressed up as hawks, which represent war. Heavily tattooed and draped with feather capes like wings, two of these depictions show warriors wearing hawk-head masks and carrying sleek war clubs; the third shows a skeletal hawk-man lying down as if he has been dead for some time. The fourth plate, the most beautiful unearthed at Lake Jackson, shows a finely rendered peregrine falcon, revered by all southeastern Indian peoples because of its swiftness, and its technique of killing prey by swooping downward so quickly (up to 180 miles per hour) that it strikes its victim dead not by grabbing it with talons, but by smacking a sudden blow to its head, much as a warrior bashes his opponent with a mace or war club. Undoubtedly, the king and his court in Anhaica dressed in similar garb as they performed rituals, ceremonial dances, blood sacrifices, and prayers as they prepared their troops to meet the rapidly approaching Spanish army.^

✣   ✣   ✣

Late on October 1, Soto reached the forest bordering the east side of the Aucilla River, entering a low-lying valley of marshes and backwaters. Garcilaso says there were "woods that were on either side"—and, nearer the river, "a forest with a great deal of thick and tall timber and much undergrowth consisting of blackberry vines and other small growth, which, being interwoven with large trees, so thickened and closed up the forest that it had the appearance of a stout wall." Normally, the Aucilla is about thirty feet wide, though in the fall of 1539 it was apparently flooded well beyond its banks. Elvas tells us the army had to march across flooded marshland a "crossbow-shot's distance where the water came up to the waist."^ Garcilaso insists the river was flooded an incredible three to four miles wide—clearly an exaggeration, given the topography.^

According to Garcilaso, the Indians began their attack as soon as Soto's vanguard ventured "a few steps" into the swamps and thickets. "There was a lively combat," he says, as the Spaniards in front struggled down the only passable trail in the woods, "a path the Indians had made, so narrow that two men abreast could scarcely go along it." Under orders to reach the river itself and to determine how best to cross it, the vanguard soon became so hard-pressed by the Apalachee in the bottleneck of the trail, where it was impossible to maneuver in the surrounding marshes, that they were forced to send back for reinforcements from the main army, camped on the plain just outside the forest.

As usual, Soto responded by gathering up a force under his personal command. Quickly marching into the woods, he joined the battle, which became ever more "cruel and bloody" as the Spaniards pushed hard into the waist-high water, slashing and lancing and firing their guns, headed inexorably toward their target—the main channel of the river. They managed to reach it by the end of the day, but only after both sides suffered "deaths and wounds." With night falling, Soto ordered his men to stand fast and pitch a makeshift camp. He then ordered Maestro Francisco and his team to lay a bridge across the deep channel, "made of two fallen trees and other timbers fastened together."

In describing this battle, Garcilaso tells yet another colorful story, ripe with romance and drama, but contrasting with eyewitness accounts that describe it as far less grandiose. According to Ranjel, this "battle" was actually a minor skirmish occurring not at the entrance to the forest, but at the main river channel, where three of Maestro Francisco's bridge builders were ambushed and killed by a small band of Apalachee hiding "in the canebrake on the other side." Elvas also describes this incident as being somewhat less then a full-fledged engagement, adding that after the initial ambush other small groups of Apalachee attacked those building the bridge from "a very high, thick wood" across the main channel. These warriors were chased away, says Elvas, when Soto deployed a crack unit of crossbowmen to come "to their aid." They "made the Indians take to flight." Both Ranjel and Elvas claim Soto then crossed the river without further difficulty once the bridge was completed. Ranjel says the army took two miserable days to cross the channel, march through the swamp, and reach the next large town, called Ivitachuco.

The Inca's account describes in much more vivid detail a hellish march through a seemingly endless swamp where a large force of Indians was deployed to attack in lightning-quick assaults against both sides of the Spanish column. At one point, he says, Soto was forced to order his hundred best cavalrymen to dismount and fight on foot in a tight wedge to protect his crossbowmen and gunners, because the horsemen, with their superior armor, "received less injury from the arrows." This desperate strategy, intones the Inca, was necessitated by the Indians' highly organized style of fighting. They "observed some order and plan," he says, lining up on either side of the trail, "so that when those on one side were attacking, the others did not do so until the first had withdrawn, so as not to wound one another with stray arrows." The Apalachee clearly had the advantage in this sort of close fighting, the Spaniards being saved only by their armor and their numbers, and because they kept relentlessly moving forward in order to free themselves from the tangle of foliage. If Garcilaso's story is true, one wonders why the Spanish weren't badly mauled by the the Apalachee who went "in and out among the Christians so boldly that they paid no attention to them."

Eventually, Garcilaso allows his hard-pressed Spaniards to fight their way to the edge of the woods, where they finally break out into open fields, their preferred terrain for fighting. Here, says the Inca, the inevitable occurred as Soto and his men "gave rein to their horses and showed well the anger they felt against the Indians, because in the more than two leagues of open country that intervened before they came to the maize fields, they did not meet a single Indian whom they failed to capture or kill."

This slaughter—if Garcilaso is not making all of this up—must have been horrific, with Soto determined to teach the Apalachee a lesson as he and the army "undeceived them regarding their opinion of themselves and their boast that they would kill and destroy these Castilians as they had" the army of Pánfilo de Narváez.

Late on this same day, the Spaniards arrived at the town of Ivitachuco, situated a few miles west of the river, probably in a cluster of archaeological sites just south of present-day Lake Iamonia.^ Ivitachuco was in flames when Soto approached. "For the Indians," says Elvas, "had set fire to it."

The exhausted Spanish vanguard must have rushed down the broad Apalachee roadway when they first sighted the smoke. Galloping hard, they tried to reach the town as the thatch roofs roared high with flames, and soot rained down on fields of ripe, yellow corn. Unable to stop the flames in the village, the Spaniards at least stopped the fire from burning the crops as Soto ordered his men and servants to pick as much corn and other vegetables as they could carry. Later, as the fire burned itself out and the sun went down, Soto ordered Luis de Moscoso to organize guards and messes, finally allowing his weary men to rest. The Apalachee, says Garcilaso, continued to harass the army that night, shouting and hooting "at all hours" to keep the men from sleeping, and launching "sudden attacks . . . shooting many arrows into the camp."

Soto rested his men in Ivitachuco for an entire day before departing on October 5, marching the army into the rich agricultural heartland of the Apalachee kingdom—a land of "good quality," says Garcilaso, where there were "large fields of maize, beans, calabashes, and other vegetables, the fields on both sides of the road extending across the plain out of sight, and it was two leagues through them. Among these fields," adds the Inca, "were scattered a large number of separate houses at a distance from one another and not in the form of a pueblo." Using these farmsteads as temporary bases, the Indians persisted in assaulting the Spaniards, says the Inca, to the point that "the latter, offended by such pertinacity and angered by the obstinacy and rancor they perceived in them, lost patience and speared them without mercy all through the maize fields, to see whether they could overcome or punish them by force of arms."

Still the tenacious Apalachee attacked, even as the Spaniards pressed forward and plunged deeper into their kingdom, stopping the next night in a village called Calahuchi, near the St. Marks River.^ Here they had one guide run away, and a second one, an old woman, lead them momentarily astray. By now, however, the outcome of their march was now certain. For slowly, and relentlessly, the grinding efficiency of the Soto war machine moved onward, headed toward the Apalachee capital.

On Monday, October 6, Soto and his army arrived at Anhaica. Predictably, the capital was emptied of its king and his people, though the Indians departed without setting it afire—either because they had no time, or because they were reluctant to destroy their chief city.

According to Garcilaso, Anhaica consisted of "two hundred and fifty large and substantial houses," which Soto distributed to his men, while "he settled himself in those belonging to the *cacique,* which were on one side of the pueblo." The Inca adds that these "ruler's dwellings were superior to all the others," which means that the king's palace may have been not only sumptuous by the standards of aboriginal Florida, but also was built up on a pyramid— perhaps a small, newly built mound constructed in the half century since the Apalachee had moved from their old capital at Lake Jackson.

✢   ✢   ✢

We have now reached the only place in the *entrada*'s entire four-thousand-mile route where there is incontestable proof Hernando de Soto was there. This is Anhaica, and its location is in downtown Tallahassee, about a half mile from the Florida state capitol building—specifically, in the front yard of a mansion that once belonged to Florida State Governor John Martin.

My certainty comes from a remarkable discovery made in 1987 by archaeologist Calvin Jones,^ a colorful former Texan who spends much of his time roaming around north Florida looking for early Spanish sites, which he has an uncanny ability to find. Jones discovered Anhaica one afternoon during his lunch break—he is a staff archaeologist at the Florida Bureau of Archaeology—when he took his usual brown-bag sandwich and drove by the Governor Martin estate. For a long time he had considered this place to be a prime candidate for a Spanish-Apalachee site, given its location on a high plateau over a stream, its fertile soil, and the fact that several ancient Indian and Spanish-era highways once intersected here. To his surprise, Jones that day found earth-

movers and bulldozers parked on the mansion's lawn, about to dig a foundation for a new office complex. Fearing he might miss his chance to check his
hunch about this site, Jones stopped and asked the developers if he could grab
a shovel and make some test digs. They agreed.

That very afternoon, he unearthed a thumb-size fragment of a baked-clay
wall, and then a broken shard of a Spanish olive jar. Jones was elated, though
his first thought was not of Soto's camp. He thought this was probably a long-
lost Spanish mission—possibly the seventeenth-century mission of La Purifi-
cación de la Tama.

In the days to come, Jones's exhilaration turned to bafflement as he began
digging up pieces of green and yellow pottery of a type he had never before
seen in a Spanish mission site. Then a friend brought over a metal detector,
and located what turned out to be rusted bunches of small, hand-wrought nails,
and other bunches of tiny, interconnected rings of iron. "I had no idea what
these rings were at first," says Jones. "Then it dawned on me that they might
be chain mail."

X rays of the iron rings, which Jones found all over the site in rusted clumps,
confirmed that they were, in fact, the remains of iron-mail shirts. This led Jones
to the conclusion that the Governor Martin Site might be Anhaica, since Soto
was the only Spanish military force to pass through this area before chain mail
became obsolete in the Indies after the mid-sixteenth century.^ In fact, the
presence of so much iron mail corroborates at least one of Garcilaso's stories,
which may explain why the army left behind such a seemingly valuable stash
of Renaissance technology for archaeologists to dig up four and half centuries
later. According to the Inca, while the army bivouacked in Anhaica over the
winter of 1539–40, Campmaster Luis de Moscoso was wounded by an arrow
in the right side during one of the incessant skirmishes with the Apalachee. The
wound, though minor, astonished the Spaniards because Moscoso, being a notorious spendthrift, was wearing one of the finest coats of mail money could
then buy, a hauberk "so highly burnished [that it] had cost 150 ducats in Spain.
The rich men had brought many of these, because they were so highly regarded."

The arrow, says Garcilaso, passed through not only the mail, but a thick
leather jacket and a quilted doublet, and would have killed him had it not been
fired at a slant. "Amazed at such an unusual shot, the Spaniards wished to see
just what these highly burnished coats of mail, upon which they depended so
much, could withstand." So they summoned one of the strongest Apalachee
archers from among their prisoners, and strapped "the best coat of mail that
they had" to one of the large, thick baskets the Indians used to collect maize in
the fields. Firing a longbow at fifty paces, this Indian "shot the arrow, which
passed through the coat of mail and the basket so clean and with such force that

if a man had been on the other side it would have passed through him also."

Repeating this test with two, and then three hauberks, the Spaniards were, from then on, "undeceived with regard to the little defense that their much-esteemed coats of mail afforded against arrows. Thus the owners themselves made fun of them, calling them linen from Flanders, and in place of them they made loose quilted jackets, three or four finger-breadths in thickness, with long skirts that would cover the breasts and haunches of the horses. These jackets made from blankets would resist the arrows better than any other defensive armament; and the thick and unpolished coats of mail, which were not highly valued ... were a better defense against arrows than the very elegant and highly burnished ones. Thus the cheaper ones came to be more valued and the expensive ones laid aside"—literally, as the dig at Governor Martin has proved.

Later in 1987 and in 1988, a full-blown excavation^ at the Anhaica site, led by Jones and archaeologist Charles Ewen, yielded a large quantity of material left behind by Soto's army—more olive-jar fragments and iron mail, blown-glass beads, wrought-iron nails, an iron crossbow quarrel (pointed metal tip), and five coins of small denominations someone in Soto's army obviously kept as pocket change, and dropped accidentally on the ground. Nearly all of these artifacts can be traced to the early and mid-sixteenth century—including a tell-tale Nueva Cadiz bead^ and the olive jars, which were fashioned and glazed in a style popular during Soto's era. The crossbow quarrel is also a date marker, since by the late sixteenth century, soldiers stopped using the crossbow when improvements in rifles made them obsolete. The most convincing artifact of all was the mandible of a pig. Soto brought with him a large herd of swine from Cuba, introducing the first pigs onto a continent where they were not native, and none had lived before. This means that a hog's jaw dating from around 1540 most likely came from one of Soto's animals.

✢   ✢   ✢

Soto quickly set about transforming Anhaica into a military fortress designed to protect the army from continued Apalachee attacks. He ordered the existing Apalachee fortifications strengthened, and established patterns of sending out heavily armed units to gather food, reconnoiter, and patrol the region around the city. At the same time, Soto sent out messengers to try and coax the Apalachee king to surrender.

Garcilaso describes this *cacique,* whom he calls Capafi, in almost comical terms, claiming he was so grossly obese he could not walk. "Capafi was a man with an extremely large body," writes Garcilaso, "so much so that because of being excessively fat and because of the indispositions and impediments that this always caused him, he was so helpless that he could not take a single step or stand on his feet. His Indians carried him on a litter, and wherever he wished to go in his house he went on all fours."^

One develops a certain fondness for Garcilaso de la Vega. His descriptions continue to entertain, even as we scratch our heads and wonder about just how much to believe. For here we have Garcilaso relating another story uncorroborated by eyewitness chroniclers, who never mention Capafi by name, and barely talk about him at all, much less his obesity and his propensity to crawl. In fact, the chroniclers devote almost no space to the army's sojourn in Apalachee, a strange omission considering Soto bivouacked here for almost five months, as he waited for spring to arrive.

Thus we are left with Señor Vega and a long-winded story about how Soto personally led a platoon to capture Capafi in his secret jungle hideout, only to have him later escape when his Spanish guards became careless one night and fell asleep, assuming the lame and corpulent *cacique* would not get far even if he managed to slip past them. They were, of course, wrong. For no sooner had they begun to sleep than the king, with astonishing dexterity, "dared to escape from them, and did so by passing on all fours through the sentries." He struggled on until he reached the woods, where his warriors found him and carried him off to safety, "where he was never seen again, then or later." The delinquent soldiers, says Garcilaso, claimed they had been vigilant and lied about falling asleep, telling Soto "that the thing was impossible unless he had been carried through the air by demons," an excuse Garcilaso says Soto, in a fit of dubious chivalry, "pretended to believe . . . in order not to affront these captains and soldiers."

✛   ✛   ✛

As the weeks passed, the Apalachee continued to launch raids against the Spaniards, with snipers slinging arrows at parties gathering food and grass for the horses, and small bands staging raids and attacks at all hours of the day and night. Still Soto managed to launch a series of large, armed squadrons sent out to explore the region. Soto's kinsman, Captain Arias Tinoco, led one of these missions; André de Vasconcelos, the Portuguese captain, led another. Both traveled north, returning after eight or nine days to report they had found no evidence of gold or great empires. They also reported that Cabeza de Vaca was wrong about the interior. For the farther Soto's captains marched inland, the more they saw prosperous settlements, towns, people, and land planted with crops—observations that the beleaguered Soto, still hoping to find great kingdoms to the north, welcomed with considerable relief.

To explore the south, Soto dispatched Juan de Añasco and a squad with orders to locate the sea, and to scout out a site where the ships might be brought up from Tampa Bay. Añasco found a spot about twenty miles south of An-

haica, in a well-stocked but abandoned Apalachee village called Aute, probably near present-day St. Marks, Florida^—at the junction of the Wakulla and
St. Marks Rivers, just above Apalachee Bay. Marching farther south into the
dense coastal marshes, Añasco's road changed from wide and well-maintained
to a narrow, swampy trail winding precariously through a maze of quickmud
and cane thickets, palmettos, and palms.^ This was slow going, though by the
sixth day out from Anhaica, he arrived as close to the sea as the swamps allowed. There he was able to discern through the foliage "a very wide and spacious bay," which he began skirting, looking for a place to camp.

They didn't go far, however, before stumbling on a horrific sight—an overgrown clearing where they found scattered about "skulls of horses . . .," "mortars . . . to grind the corn," and "a large tree which had been cut down and made
into troughs [*couches*] fixed with some posts which were used as mangers."
This was, of course, the camp of Pánfilo de Narváez, where dozens of
Spaniards in 1528 had perished from disease, starvation, and the shellacking
they received from the Apalachee, and where the survivors had built their
shoddy rafts and tried to escape *La Florida*.

The camp deeply affected Añasco, his men—and, when they saw and heard
about it, everyone in Soto's army. For they could see with their own eyes how
quickly an *entrada* could go from muddling along to disaster. Standing quietly
on the edge of the old camp where so many Spaniards had died, Añasco and
his men must have shared some of Cabeza de Vaca's despair twelve years earlier when he wrote: "[Y]ou can imagine what it would be like in a strange, re-
mote land, destitute of means either to remain or to get out. Our most reliable
help was God our Lord; we had not wavered in this conviction."

While at Narváez's camp, Juan de Añasco also sent out strong swimmers to
take soundings of the bay, and carved crosses and other "signals" on "trees
standing near the water," in case Soto decided to bring ships here to reopen his
communication line to Havana. Armed with all of this information, Añasco returned to the relative safety of the fortress at Anhaica to meet with Soto.

✦   ✦   ✦

It's difficult to know what sort of relationships Soto had with his chief advisors and captains. The chroniclers provide little insight in such matters. But
in many cases they do tell us which captains Soto chose to take on difficult missions, a strong indicator of whom he most depended on and trusted. During this
period, two gifted captains stand out—Baltasar de Gallegos, who seems to
have been Soto's expert on missions to parley with Indians, or to fight battles;
and Juan de Añasco, whose assignments typically involved either the sea,
ships, or exploration. This is why we see Añasco in charge of sizing up
Apalachee Bay; and why Soto assigned him to carry out perhaps the most per-

ilous mission to date after he returned from Narváez's camp—to trek back to
Ocita in the Bay of the Holy Spirit, some three hundred twenty miles away
through enemy territory.^ There he was to tell Pedro Calderón and the garrison
to leave Ocita and come to Anhaica. Soto also ordered Añasco to sail the remaining ships of the fleet into Apalachee Bay.

Accompanied by thirty of the army's best horsemen, Añasco departed Anhaica on October 17, plunging back into territories where the Indians could
hardly have been more hostile. Indeed, Añasco knew his only hope of surviving was to run his horses so swiftly through populated areas that the Indians
would have no time to organize an attack, or to warn the next village. This is
exactly what Añasco did, completing in just ten days^ a journey that had taken
Soto and the army eleven weeks. This was a feat matched only once in *conquista* history that I am aware of—when Captain Hernando de Soto in Peru
rode 250 miles in five days, averaging some fifty miles a day. Elvas describes
Añasco's tactics, telling us "he passed through the towns at night," resting out
in the open three or four hours at a time "at a distance from habitation."
    Garcilaso de la Vega devotes twenty-two action-packed pages to Añasco's
journey. This is in part because the Inca's chief informant, a cavalryman
named Gonzalo Silvestre,^ was one of the thirty who participated in this mission. Specifics of the squadron's mad dash, however, are less interesting in
Garcilaso than material he provides about how a lightly armed Spanish unit in
the Indies organized itself on such a march. For instance, he tells us the men
traveled "with only helmets and coats of mail over their clothing, their lances
in their hands, and a pair of knapsacks on their saddles containing some horse-
shoes and nails and the food that they could put into them for horses and riders." He also explains how the men set watches as they raced south, with
two-thirds of the troops sleeping while the remaining third stood guard, pa-
trolling the area in pairs. Garcilaso even offers up a theory for why Spanish
horses in the Indies were able to "withstand the excessive labor they have un-
dergone and now undergo in the conquests of the New World." It was maize,
says the Inca, which "all Spaniards of the Indies" agreed offers "a great deal of
substance and is much liked by them and by all animals."

    During the first two days out from Anhaica, Añasco's troop retraced in re-
verse the route taken earlier by the main army, galloping unimpeded across
Apalachee and the wilderness barrier dividing it from the kingdom of
Uzachile. On the third day, they reached Uzachile itself. Here, says Garcilaso,
they "passed through the pueblo, going at a canter," which was apparently fast

enough to keep the Indians from attacking. Only when they had ridden "a league beyond the pueblo," he adds, did they rest for "the remainder of the night" at a place off from the road. Continuing their race south, they sped through villages and past startled Indians, reaching the Suwannee River on the fourth day. That afternoon, they ran into a grisly sight—the battlefield and execution site at Napituca. Garcilaso says the troop approached with some apprehension, fearing that the Indians there would be particularly vexed and in a mood for revenge. But when they arrived, they found the place eerily empty of people, "entirely burned and destroyed."

"The walls," writes the Inca, basing his narrative on Silvestre's recollections, had been "leveled to the ground; and the bodies of the Indians who had died on the day of the battle and those whom they killed on the day that the *cacique* Vitachuco [Uriutina] struck the Governor were all heaped together in the field, no one having desired to bury them. The Indians said later that they had abandoned and destroyed the pueblo because it was founded on an unlucky and unfortunate site; and the dead Indians, as ill-fated men who had not carried out their pretensions, they left unburied as food for birds and wild beasts." Garcilaso adds that it was a custom here to inflict this "very infamous punishment" for those unlucky in war.

For six more days, the troop rode south, fending off several inconclusive Indian attacks, forging swamps and rivers, and enduring "many . . . hardships and dangers." By the time they crossed the Swamp of Cale, Garcilaso-Silvestre describes the men as "fatigued and exhausted by the long labor they performed," and "so broken and weary that they could scarcely stand." The men became so miserable and irritable that they began verbally lashing out at one another. One young cavalryman, Gomez Arias, screamed at Juan de Añasco that he "rewarded so poorly the unendurable hardships that he and his companions were suffering," vocalizing with extraordinary insolence the age-old complaint of the grunt to his officer. " 'Confound you and the evil bitch that gave birth to you!' " Garcilaso says this young man screamed at the top of his lungs. " 'You are on your horse, fully dressed and wrapped in your coat, and you don't consider that we have been in the water for more than four hours, stiff with cold and doing all we can. Get down and come in, and we shall see if you can do better.' " Overlooking Arias's outburst, Añasco convinced the men to press on. They finally arrived at Ocita ten days after departing Anhaica, minus two cavalrymen who died suddenly and mysteriously of an unknown illness, one of them expiring while still "on his horse."

Pedro Calderón, who must have been feeling very lonely during the three months since Soto departed, greeted these exhausted emissaries in his fortress-camp with "many embraces and common rejoicing by all." Their first questions, however, were not about the disposition of the governor or their friends and comrades, but about gold. In one of the more truthful statements in his narrative, the Inca informs us that "the hunger and craving for this metal often alienates and denies relatives and friends."

Garcilaso fails to mention how Calderón's men reacted to the news that not a single nugget of precious metal had been found—information that must have been terribly disappointing to men who had just spent weeks on end sitting idly and dreaming of the great wealth they would take home as their share in another great Soto victory.

After a brief rest at Ocita, Juan de Añasco, following Soto's orders, dispatched two caravels still in the harbor back to Havana with letters from Soto—and with twenty female Indian slaves Añasco captured in Potano, earmarked as gifts to Isabel de Bobadilla.^ The remainder of the fleet he boarded himself, with Calderón's infantry, setting sail for Apalachee Bay to rendezvous with Soto and the main army.

Calderón was not so lucky. Soto had ordered him to march the cavalry—those of the garrison and those who had accompanied Añasco—back along the very same trail that Añasco and his thirty men had just taken. According to Garcilaso, Calderón's trek was every bit as miserable as Añasco's, with at least two men and seven horses killed by Indians, the worst coming at the end when the Apalachee came out in force to challenge their passage through the Swamp of Ivitachuco. Battered and bleeding, Calderón's men finally arrived in Anhaica at the end of November, shortly after Añasco arrived in Apalachee Bay near Aute, where Soto had established a small garrison to guard the highway between his winter headquarters and the sea.

Before winter set in, Soto dispatched one more reconnaissance mission. He ordered Captain Francisco Maldonado to skirt and investigate the Gulf coast to the west in Añasco's caravels. This mission was part of a grand strategy Soto planned to commence the following spring. His idea was to march inland to the north and then to the west in a great, sweeping arc that would end, he hoped, in Maldonado's newfound harbor, where ships would be waiting with fresh supplies from Cuba.

For two months, Maldonado and fifty men coasted "along toward the west." "Entering all the coves and inlets and rivers that he saw . . . he arrived at a river where he found good entrance, a good port and a town of Indians on the sea coast." This harbor, and an Indian town Maldonado calls Achuse, was either at Pensacola Bay or Mobile Bay, with the latter the more probable.^ According to Biedma, local Indians came to investigate the strange men and vessels, and to offer the Spaniards presents and goods to buy. These included "a good blanket of sables" of finer quality than those found in Apalachee. But in typical *conquista* style, Maldonado was friendly with the natives only for as long as it took to lure them onto their ship. Then "he captured one of those Indians" and spirited him back to Anhaica, where this hapless trader from Achuse was never heard from again.

+ + +

As Juan de Añasco and Francisco Maldonado were away, Soto continued his attempts to "pacify" the Apalachee, using every trick and terror tactic he knew to bludgeon, cajole, and frighten them into obedience. Nothing, however, seemed to work against an enemy as uncooperative as any he had met during his twenty-five years in the Americas. Ranjel says that a highly frustrated Soto pursued the Apalachee with great intensity and ruthlessness, torturing them mercilessly, cutting off their hands and noses, burning them at the stake, and throwing them to the dogs. Still, says Soto's secretary, expressing both the stress felt by the beleaguered Spaniards, and perhaps a personal disdain for Soto's tactics, "never did they wish to come in peace."

Twice, says Ranjel, the Apalachee succeeded in launching serious attacks against the palisaded Spanish camp, flinging torches and shooting flaming arrows that ignited major fires within the city. Elvas adds that the Apalachee managed to sneak into the camp one night "through the sentinels without being seen." They set a fire that caused "two thirds" of the town to burn before the Spaniards could put it out. Other bands of Apalachee warriors routinely attacked Spaniards when they went out of the village to fetch food, hunt, or to relieve the garrison at Aute. Garcilaso tells harrowing stories about men being overwhelmed and scalped while picking fruit off trees, and others being shot dead by arrows. According to one of Garcilaso's informants, Alonso de Carmona, twenty Spaniards lost their lives during the five months at Anhaica. No chronicler, however, ventures a guess about how many Apalachee may have perished.

Despite Soto's inability to "pacify" the Apalachee, at Anhaica we see him finally shaking off the frustrations and disappointments of the long, wet, unproductive Florida march as he once again convinces himself—and his men— that great riches lie inland. His optimism came from several indicators about the country to the north.

First, there was the fertility and natural opulence of the Apalachee region— which, his scouts continued to tell him, got better the farther they rode into the interior. By now, he also had Indian informants telling him about the great

Mississippian cities and the network of highways and trade to the north, where he was told powerful *caciques* ruled sizable populations and large swaths of territory. Soto also heard about the mountains we now call the Appalachians, after the Apalachee, which was good news to conquerors whose experience with the Aztecs and the Incas had convinced them that there was a link between gold and mountains.

But none of this information aroused Soto and his men more than the words of a teenage Indian boy Elvas says was captured at Napituca. First interrogated by Soto's royal treasurer, Juan Gaitan, the boy, called Perico, was brought to Soto after claiming he came from a distant inland country rich in gold. Garcilaso says that Perico was "sixteen or seventeen," and was one of two boys captured not at Napituca, but in Apalachee. Both boys, says Garcilaso, had been accompanying traders "who were accustomed to enter with their merchandise, selling and buying, many leagues into the interior country."

Whatever his origins, Perico astonished first Gaitan, and then Soto, by describing in great detail his own country, called Yupaha. Claiming it was ruled by a queen living in a city of "wonderful size," a twelve- or thirteen-day march to the north, he said that this "chieftainess collected tribute from many of her neighboring chiefs, some of whom gave her clothing, and others gold in abundance." At first incredulous, Garcilaso says the Spaniards showed him "gold jewelry and pieces of silver and fine stones set in rings that were found among some of the captains and principal soldiers, so that he might better understand the things that they were asking him about."

"He replied," continues Garcilaso, "that in a province called Cofachiqui,* which was the most distant one that he had visited, there was a great deal of metal like the yellow and the white, and that the chief traffic of the merchants, his masters, was to buy those metals and sell them in other provinces." Elvas adds that Soto did not completely believe the boy until Perico described to the Spaniards what seemed to be the process of how the gold was "taken from the mines, melted, and refined, just as if he had seen it done, or else the devil taught him; so that all who knew anything of this said it was impossible to give so good an account of it unless one had seen it; and all when they saw the signs he made believed whatever he said to be true."

Garcilaso says that the Spaniards were so "pleased . . . at this news," that all "[desired] to see themselves at once in Cofachiqui in order to be masters of so much gold and silver and so many precious pearls." Biedma insists that the only reason the army waited was because Francisco Maldonado was still away exploring the Gulf coast. "He spent two months on this journey," says Biedma,

*This should be Cofitachequi.

"yet to all of us it became a thousand years through detaining us there so long, since we had news of the interior."

+   +   +

In mid-February, Maldonado finally returned. Adding to Perico's extravagant claims his own good news of a harbor and populous lands to the west, he showed off his kidnapped Achuse Indian and stolen sables to a Spanish camp suddenly exuberant over the prospects for success.

As it turned out, the reliable Maldonado, whom Soto had first met at court in Valladolid, would not be present in *La Florida* for the march north to Cofitachequi. Within days of his return, Soto ordered him back to Cuba with final letters explaining his plans, and orders for Maldonado and Isabel to organize a fleet the following fall to meet up with the army at the harbor of Achuse. If Isabel and Maldonado heard nothing from the *entrada* that fall, Soto ordered them to keep returning to Achuse, and "to cruise the coast as far as the River of Espíritu Santo"^—the Mississippi—until he reconnected with the army.

Soto himself may have accompanied Maldonado to Apalachee Bay, to see off the fleet. Under towering cypresses, and against a bright green backdrop of canes, marsh grasses, and shrubs, Soto probably watched as these small vessels, looking so alien against the aboriginal coast of Florida, hoisted their sails and moved slowly away, maneuvering out of sight toward the Gulf. They took with them the last news the world would hear of Hernando de Soto for another three years.

Later in life, Francisco Maldonado probably considered himself lucky to have missed the horrors Soto and his men would face in the interior. But on that long-ago spring in 1540, as he arrived at the frontier pier of Havana, he must have felt terribly disappointed at being left out of what looked to be a most profitable enterprise. This regret, however, soon changed to relief when Maldonado sailed that autumn to rendezvous with Soto at the Bay of Achuse, and found no trace of the expedition. Years later, Maldonado recalled that "he removed with certain ships to wait in the sea so as to provide from this country [Cuba] certain men and provisions to resupply the army in Florida . . . [but] could not find him."

For three years, Isabel and Maldonado would organize small fleets of men and provisions as Maldonado returned each season to search for the lost *entrada*. Indeed, the army disappeared without a trace after that spring of 1540, when Soto and his men turned north in a buoyant, hopeful mood, marching toward Cofitachequi—and the golden empire they were once again convinced they would find.

Book V

Obsession

✤ 25 ✤

Idylls of Georgia

TURNING HIS BACK FOREVER on the outside world, Hernando de Soto departed Anhaica on March 3, 1540. According to the Gentleman of Elvas, he "ordered all his men to provide themselves with maize" stolen from the Apalachee, "for a journey of sixty leagues through uninhabited land." The men had to carry these provisions themselves, since "most of the Indians" they had captured to use as slaves and carriers, "being naked and in chains, had died because of the hard life they suffered during that winter."

In other words, several hundred Indians from as far away as Urriparacoxi had expired that winter at Anhaica from the lethal neglect of a governor long accustomed to treating slaves as perishable commodities. One pictures these wretched Indians, distributed to Spaniards as servants and laborers, weighed down by heavy iron chains chafing their necks, wrists, and ankles. Forced to sleep on the bare ground during a wet, frigid season, with little shelter or warm clothing, and minimal food, they one by one had grown weak, dying from overwork, malnutrition, and fatigue—and from the intense, suicidal despair that killed so many Native Americans in the Indies. During the five-month bivouac at Anhaica, the Spaniards must have found fresh bodies nearly every morning among the Indians, a grisly sight that after a while became chillingly commonplace for Soto's men. This carnage was not only a human tragedy. It also was misguided from a practical point of view—as each soldier early that morning was finding out, hoisting knapsacks filled with heavy loads of grain on top of their already-heavy loads of armor, weapons, tents, clothing, and personal effects. But not even these burdens could lessen the enthusiasm of the army as they deployed that day in their usual formation, marching north toward the legendary kingdom of Cofitachequi.

As for the weary and hungry Apalachee, most of whom had spent the winter hiding in the woods, they apparently allowed the Spaniards to leave their

country peacefully. Satisfied that at last their belligerence had chased off the
invaders, they continued to persist as a people for another century and a half,
making them the exception among most polities unfortunate enough to be in
Soto's path.

Guided now by the Indian boy Perico, the overloaded army marched about
ten miles that first day through an unpopulated pine forest. He halted late in the
afternoon near the Florida-Georgia border, probably on the shore of the
present-day Ochlockonee River. From there, the army plunged into a thick but
pleasant piedmont forest of pines and sweet gums, where they spent the next
few days marching toward the broad valley of the lower Flint River, in southern Georgia.* In 1799, a traveler exploring the Flint's floodplain described this
area as swampy and flat, and filled with "bay galls and dwarf evergreens, cypress ponds, with some live oak." The soil, he noted, is a thin layer that barely
covers a bedrock of limestone, pocked here and there with sinkhole ponds, and
frequently covered with swamps and marshes.

The chronicles disagree about the number of days it took to march through
this mix of swamp and forest, where the first buds of spring were appearing,
and the nights in mid-March remained cool, if not cold. Ranjel says the army
marched from the Ochlockonee to the Flint River covering the thirty or forty
miles in just one day,^ an unlikely feat even if the army was not weighed down
by knapsacks full of grain.^ Ranjel may have been riding ahead with a faster-
moving vanguard, however, possibly led by Soto. This may also explain why
Elvas says this trek took four days, since he was probably traveling with the
slower-moving main army, dragging their loads through water, canes, silt, and
sludge.

The army had great difficulty crossing the Flint,^ arriving when the runoff
from snow in the Appalachian Mountains was at full flow. According to Ranjel, "the river was so broad that Cristóbal Mosquera, who was the best thrower,
tried but did not manage to throw a stone across it." He says Soto ordered a *piragua*† built to help guide the men and horses through the water. Using it to
cross to the other side, the Spaniards linked up the shores using a long chain
made by joining "the chains in which they brought the Indians" into one long
strand. Thanks to the mass deaths at Anhaica, these restraints were available.
The men then ferried themselves across in the *piragua,* holding on to the chain.
The water, however, was so swift "the current . . . broke the chain two times;
and seeing this, they attached many ropes and from these made two, and they

---

*The chroniclers call this waterway the Río de Capachequi.
†A large canoe usually made from a single enormous log, with plank gunwales tacked on.

Eastern Portion of Soto's Route, 1539–40
(Hudson Route)

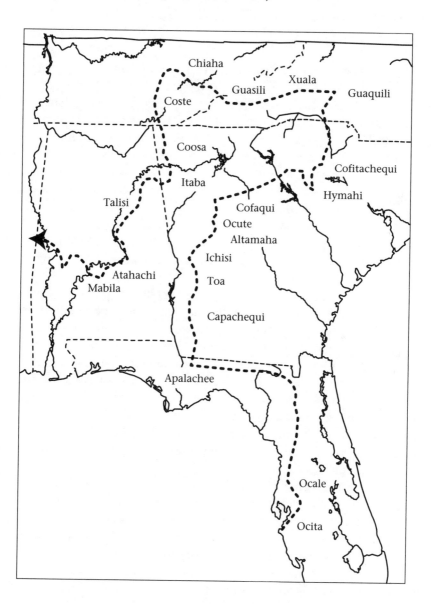

attached one to the stern and the other to the prow." It took four days to painstakingly pull over men and supplies on this single vessel, as the men heaved the craft back and forth, the cold spray soaking hair, clothes, armor, food, and weapons. For the horses, "they made long ropes and attached them to the neck; and although the current pushed them down, pulling the ropes drew them out, but with difficulty, and some half drowned."

Once across the Flint, the army on March 11 found themselves on a narrow but well-established trail through a country undulating between dry hills and wetlands. That night, they found their first major village since Anhaica. Called Capachequi, this was a small enclave of huts situated on a large hammock, possibly on the Chickasawhatchee Creek a few miles west of the Flint. Finding it "well supplied" with provisions, but abandoned by its inhabitants, Soto stopped only long enough to plunder the *barbacoas* of food before plunging into another swamp where the water "came to the cinches and saddle pads of the horses." With night coming on, some of the foot soldiers spent a very wet and cold night bogged down in this marsh—a miserable experience not only because of the dampness, but also because even today this swampy area is infested with alligators, rattlers, copperheads, coral snakes, leaches, ticks, and, of course, dense clouds of mosquitoes.

That night, the men would also have been kept up by the noise of opossums, squirrels, raccoons, bears, and perhaps an ocelot or bobcat rummaging for food—and, occasionally, getting into shrieking battles as they either hunted or were themselves hunted. Then, as morning dawned, came the calls and songs of birds by the millions, some returning north in great flocks after the winter. There would have been Carolina chickadees and wood thrushes chattering, yellowthroats and song sparrows bellowing out their repetitive calls, cardinals and yellow warblers singing from the trees, and red-tailed hawks, falcons, and eagles cawing, flying in great circles high up in the sky.

As if this weren't enough, it was on that same night that the army encountered its first Indians since leaving Anhaica—a band of warriors who attacked five infantrymen slogging through the marshes. Elvas says the Spaniards were rifling through an abandoned Indian camp in the swamp, looking for mortars to grind their corn, when five Indians suddenly pounced. Caught in a soggy thicket without horses or crossbowmen, the soldiers abruptly found themselves struggling hand to hand with natives charging from every direction as they tried to draw swords and fend off blows from battleaxes, maces, and arrows. One Spaniard had his head instantly crushed by a powerful blow. Three others were badly mauled; the fifth man escaped to sound the alarm. This brought relief in time to save the three wounded men, though the Indians managed to retreat with no casualties, fleeing "through a swamp with a very dense wood where the horses could not enter."

According to Garcilaso, there were seven, not five, Spaniards who departed from Soto's camp "without orders from the officials of our army, simply for recreation and to see what was in the other little pueblos" in the swamp. Five of these, he says, were members of Soto's personal guard. Lightly armed and "not recalling the great vigilance and care that the Indians . . . always exercised in killing those who strayed away," they came to a large hammock planted with maize. There Garcilaso says a band of Indians killed all five of the men from Soto's guard, "each with his body pierced with ten or twelve arrows." A sixth was fatally wounded, one Andrés Moreno, nicknamed Angel because on the road he was known for often repeating admonitions to angels. The seventh and final victim, one Francisco de Aguilar, was also badly hurt. But he was able to keep fighting and somehow fend off the attackers, despite having "two arrow wounds which passed through both thighs, and many blows over the head and the whole body." When his comrades found him, says the Inca, he was single-handedly repelling a crowd of Indians, who had "knocked his shield to pieces, only the handles being left."^

Little is known about the shadowy Capachequi Indians who lived and thrived in this swamp. Archaeologists have found enough material to confirm they lived in several small villages erected atop easily defensible hammocks, where they grew corn and, in at least two instances, built modest pyramids. Garcilaso claims the Capachequi were politically connected to the Apalachee, though our eyewitnesses hint they were a different people, with different customs and, perhaps, a different language^—a contradiction that may have recently been settled by archaeologists digging along the lower Flint. Unearthing an abundance of native pottery and artifacts from the mid-sixteenth century, they have determined that the styles more closely resemble pieces dug up at Apalachee than those excavated to the north^—meaning Garcilaso, this time, may have been right. Having tromped through these swamps myself, wading in gaiters through stagnant, mosquito-infested wetlands to reach isolated hammocks, it seems likely these mysterious swamp Indians kept mostly to themselves; a somewhat backward but proud and belligerent people who had little contact with the more-advanced kingdoms to the south or north.

✢   ✢   ✢

After the attack, the *entrada* moved more cautiously through the marshes, once more alert to every movement in the dark, brooding jungle. Thankfully, this ordeal ended a few days later as the army passed through a series of small, peaceful Mississippian kingdoms not only surprisingly congenial and cooperative, but apparently more advanced than even the Apalachee.

Ancestors of the Lower Creeks, these people lived in large, comfortable, and secure cities surrounded by palisades, and built alongside the great rivers of south, central, and northeast Georgia. They had a highly developed agriculture, were governed by powerful *cacique*-kings, and crafted lovely and sophisticated pottery, statuary, baskets, and jewelry. At night they slept in neat, round cabins plastered inside and out with a stiff mortar-and-cane mixture that looked like tile to the Spaniards, and differed markedly from the less sturdy and sophisticated grass-and-thatch *bohíos* to the south. Built out of planks split from trunks of cypress and pine with wood wedges, the finest of these houses were gabled, and the walls whitewashed with ground oyster shells, or white clay and chalk, and topped off with elegantly carved statues of hawks, falcons, and cats. *Caciques* lived in large complexes of rooms and buildings, built atop earthen pyramids larger than any the Spaniards had seen among the Timucuan in Florida. In front, says Elvas, these palaces had "large balconies" with "seats resembling chairs made of canes" used as thrones, or seats of honor. Surrounding these palaces were "many large *barbacoas* in which they gather together the tribute paid them by their Indians, which consists of maize and deerskins and native blankets."

For clothing, women in aboriginal Georgia dressed in blankets woven from fine thread "as good as the most precious thread from Portugal." Made from the middle layer of mulberry bark, and "from a plant like daffodils which when pounded becomes like flax," Elvas says they wore these blankets by "draping one from the waist down and another over the shoulder with the right arm uncovered in the manner and custom of Gypsies." Georgian men wore one long robe thrown over the shoulder, and underneath a small "truss of deerskin resembling the breech clouts" to cover their genitals. Everyone wore jewelry—carved and painted earrings, pendants, necklaces, beads, and amulets made from wood, bone, and shells.

On March 23, after marching through another uninhabited forest and recrossing the Flint, probably near Montezuma, Georgia,^ Soto arrived at Toa, capital of the first of the four advanced kingdoms he would pass through during this phase of his exploration in Georgia. The most sizable city the Spaniards had yet seen in *La Florida,* Toa was so impressive it once more convinced Soto that he was nearing some great and wealthy kingdom.

Garcilaso says the people of Toa abandoned their city as the Spanish army approached, "taking their women, children, and possessions" into the woods. Our eyewitnesses suggest this withdrawal was halfhearted, however, and that the Toa people showed little of the fear the army had come to expect in *La Florida*. In fact, when Soto's men detained several Indians in a village near Toa—captured, says Biedma "unawares," because they "had not heard about us"—the incident was quickly resolved to everyone's satisfaction when the Indians offered to provide "some interpreter guides" in exchange for their release.

According to Garcilaso, when Soto arrived in Toa's major city, his men scoured the empty town for Indians, and found several nobles and captains whom the Inca portrays as gallantly staying behind to insure that all the "common people" safely escaped. Soto ordered these *principales* arrested. This prompted a group of Indians to stride up to Soto "without any sign they felt uneasy at finding themselves captives" and demanded to know Soto's intention. "Do you wish peace or war?" they asked. Through Juan Ortiz, Soto claimed he desired peace—which for once was true, since he was simply passing through to Cofitachequi, and required only guides and fresh provisions. The Indians responded by mildly chastising this strange foreigner, telling him, "[I]t was not necessary to capture us for this purpose; we will give you here all the supplies that you need for your journey, and we will treat you better than they treated you in Apalachee, for we know very well how you fared there." The Indians quickly made good on their promise by dispatching messengers to fetch the Toa king, who ordered his captains to supply the Spaniards with food and housing in a nearby town.

✢   ✢   ✢

Soto stayed in Toa only a few hours. He suddenly became obsessed once again with wanting to keep moving, inspired by the sophistication of the Toa people. His exhausted men refused to budge at such a late hour, however, having by now grown weary of their governor's chronic overenthusiasm. As Garcilaso notes: "[I]t was a constantly observed custom of his that he must go himself to any new discovery of provinces because he was not satisfied with the reports of others, but wished to see it with his own eyes." This prompted Soto to set off secretly "at midnight," according to Rodrigo Ranjel, "with up to forty noblemen and gentlemen on horseback, and those whom for diverse reasons he had not wished to put under another Captain."

Usually, Hernando de Soto was able to count on the loyalty of his army. Throughout the *entrada,* however, there are these moments when he seems to lose a measure of control. None of the chroniclers provides details about who within the army led the grumbling—or, in this case, delivered the resounding "no" when Soto wanted to keep marching past Toa. Ranjel, however, makes the point that Soto's forty loyalists were "nobles and gentlemen." This suggests that if there was a mild dissension within the ranks, it probably involved

commoners and foot soldiers who simply balked at moving one step farther—
even as the army's *hidalgos,* mounted on horses and better-rested, felt compelled to follow their fellow aristocrat when he gave the order. Whatever
happened, at moments like this, Soto undoubtedly wished he were not encumbered with such a large army. Clearly, he preferred leading the small, quick,
highly mobile squadrons he had commanded so effectively in Central America
and Peru, consisting of partisans as hot-blooded as he, who could get fired up
on the slightest pretext of gold or adventure.

Among our eyewitnesses, only Ranjel accompanied Soto's mad dash to
Ichisi,^* the next Georgian kingdom to the north. He tells us the governor led
his weary followers on a hard march all that night and the next day, pushing
them to travel some thirty miles in eighteen hours. Stopping at last on the second night to bivouac in the swamps of the Ocmulgee River, south of Macon,^
they all fell exhausted amidst the noise of insects and croaking frogs, and the
strong odor of mud, water, and rotting vegetation.

That next morning, Soto and his *hidalgos* finally arrived at the border of
Ichisi. Half swimming across a wide branch of the Ocmulgee, they stormed the
first village they found, situated on an island in the river. Once there, "they captured some people and found food," but saw no gold or evidence of Inca-style
grandeur. This prompted Soto to halt later that day and send word to the main
army to join him. While waiting on the west shore, near modern-day Macon, a
delegation from the Ichisi king arrived to ask three provocative questions similar to those asked in Toa. "Who are you? What do you want? Where are you
going?"

According to Ranjel, Soto answered by reciting a summary of the old *Requerimiento,* the first known instance where the adelantado of *La Florida*
obeyed this long-standing royal edict, dating back to King Ferdinand's day.
Saying he was a "Captain of the great King of Spain," Soto told the emissaries—presumably dressed in white robes, dyed leather breeches, and feather
bonnets—that he had come in the name of the emperor Charles V "to give them
to understand the sacred faith of Christ . . . that they should know him and be
saved." He also intimated that they should give obedience to "the Emperor and
King of Castile . . . [and to] Rome and to the Supreme Pontiff and Vicar of God
who resides there," insisting that the emperor "would treat them all well, and
with peace and justice, like his other Christian vassals." Elvas adds that Soto
at Ichisi used, for the first time in Florida that we know about, the old *conquista*

---

*Biedma calls this kingdom Chisi; Elvas calls it Achese. Garcilaso calls Ichisi by the name Altapaha, which
he may be confusing with Altamaha, a village the Spaniards visited a few days later. In most instances, I use
Ranjel's spelling for places and names.

tactic of claiming godhead. He said he was "a son of the sun and came from where it dwelt." This affirms for anthropologists that the Mississippians of Georgia held the sun in high regard, though there is no evidence the Ichisi treated Hernando de Soto any differently, despite his claim.

By March 29, the army was reunited and being guided by a delegation of brightly garbed Ichisi ambassadors toward the kingdom's capital, probably located at the well-known Lamar Site, on the outskirts of Macon. The going was slow, since the next day the army woke up to a heavy rainstorm. It fell in great sheets all day long, at one point swelling a stream into a torrent that the army had to cross quickly before it became flooded and impassable.^ Despite the inclement weather, the inquisitive Ichisi people came out to crowd around the Spaniards, turning the march through the Ocmulgee bottomlands into a festival of the sort Soto had not seen since the early days of the Inca campaign, when Pizarro's policy of nonbelligerency had attracted crowds of Peruvians coming out to marvel and gawk at the strangers. "This day," says Ranjel, "Indian men and women came forth to receive them. The women came clothed in white, and they made a fine appearance, and they gave to the Christians tortillas of corn and some bundles of spring onions exactly like those of Castile, as fat as the tip of a thumb and more . . . and they ate them" from then on "with tortillas, roasted and stewed and raw."

Resting that night at "a pretty town" subject to Ichisi,^ with "plenty of food," Ranjel says they crossed the main Ocmulgee channel on March 31 in war canoes provided by the king of Ichisi, "who was one-eyed." Meeting the Spaniards on the east bank of the river, King Ichisi then led them into his capital. There he "gave them very good food and fifteen Indians to carry burdens," and "a guide and interpreter" for their journey to the north. Ranjel notes that this King Ichisi was "the first [Indian king in *La Florida*] who came in peace . . . [and who] did not wish to be tiresome."* This one-eyed prince of the Ichisi also informed them there was a "great lord" who lived to the north, in the next kingdom along the Spaniard's intended route, "called Ocute."

Biedma has a different recollection of Ichisi, saying it was a poor kingdom. They were "well served by the Indians," he says, but the people had little to give in terms of food and porters. The royal factor's account is contradicted by the archaeological record at Lamar, however. For on a short rise above the Ocmulgee just south of Macon one can still see a sizable complex of mounds and ruins, behind a screen of cypress and canebrakes just a few meters off Interstate 16. Excavated in the 1930s, the Mississippian town at Lamar was encir-

*The word Oviedo uses is *fatigar,* which means "to tire" or "to be weary," as well as "to annoy."

cled in the mid-sixteenth century by an oblong-shaped palisade made from thick logs planted vertically in the ground, side by side. The entire wall measured some twelve hundred by eleven hundred feet—a space nearly as large as Soto's hometown, Jerez de los Caballeros, inside its city walls. The most impressive sight at Lamar is a mound unique among Mississippians—a circular edifice eighteen feet high and fifty feet in diameter on top, with a circular ramp cut into its sides in a spiral from top to bottom. Another larger mound sits about five hundred feet to the west, across a broad plaza.

At its peak in the late fifteenth and early sixteenth centuries, several hundred Mississippians lived here, though it's possible the city was in decline when Soto visited. This may explain Biedma's insistence on this kingdom's poverty, and why the one-eyed Ichisi king could supply only fifteen porters when most High Mississippian kings gave or were forced to hand over hundreds. Within a few years of the Spaniards' visit, archaeologists say the Ichisi abandoned this city, and began a rapid devolution from a High Mississippian kingdom to the collection of comparatively primitive Creek villages later found in central Georgia by British settlers.

Soto stayed in Ichisi only one day, though for some reason he took the time to erect a large wooden cross atop a mound "very high in the middle of the public place"—perhaps the strange beveled mound still at Lamar today. Presumably, this project was suggested by Soto's priests, who urged the governor to do his duty by the *Requerimiento,* which theoretically compelled him to introduce Christianity to peaceful Indians. But Soto was in such a hurry he explained to the baffled Ichisi only "that the cross was a memorial of that on which Christ suffered, who was God and man and created the heavens and the earth and suffered to save us, and that they should reverence it." The Ichisi king, perhaps wondering where Soto's earlier claim to be the son of the sun fit in with this god-man Christ, nonetheless played along, promising to revere the cross after the strangers left—which the Spaniards soon did, much to the relief of the one-eyed king and the Ichisi people.

✢   ✢   ✢

From Ichisi, Soto led the army along a broad trail connecting the Ocmulgee to the Oconee River, where they arrived on April 3 at a village of abandoned cabins. Here Luis Hernández de Biedma notes that the river "did not flow to the south like the others that we had crossed. It flowed east, to the sea, where the licenciado Lucas de Ayllón had come." This indicated not only that they were nearing the Atlantic Ocean, but also that they at least had a rough idea of where they were vis-à-vis Ayllón's failed colony. Biedma also tells us this easterly flowing stream seemed to corroborate the claims made by the boy-guide Perico, who insisted that Cofitachequi was near the coast of the Ocean Sea.

The terrain changed as the army moved into higher ground, shifting from the scattered pine forests and dense, difficult-to-surmount wetlands of central and southern Georgia to pure piedmont, where longleaf, loblolly, and other pines began to blend in with red maples, chestnut oaks, black walnuts, cedars, and sycamores. Hardwoods were particularly dense in places left alone by the Indians, whose practice of burning expansive areas to clear them off for hunting and growing crops gave faster-growing pines an eco-advantage over oaks and walnuts. Today, pine continues to dominate in this country, as intensive farming in years past has given way to cattle pastures and "crops" of fast-growing softwoods favored by paper companies, who own much of this land. Conditions for marching also greatly improved as the ground became less spongy and soft, and the banks of rivers and creeks more solid. The topography was more hilly, though on balance this region—which stretches from northeast of Macon well into the Carolinas—would prove to be one of the more pleasant the Spaniards encountered during the entire *entrada,* even considering that the intense heat and humidity of a typical Southern summer were fast approaching.

The same day Soto arrived at the Oconee River, he was met by ambassadors from the next kingdom in his path, called Altamaha. The Indians welcomed the Spaniards and told them their king, Camumo, had ordered a town up ahead prepared for them, and outfitted with "an abundance of food." The following day, this Camumo further ingratiated himself to the Spaniards by sending out war canoes to ferry the army across the Oconee—undoubtedly hoping to follow the same strategy as the people of Toa and Ichisi, who had successfully gotten rid of the Spaniards by giving them everything they wanted in terms of fuel, servants, and housing. On the east bank of the Oconee, Camumo himself met the Spaniards in his capital city, probably situated near the sleepy town of present-day Milledgeville, Georgia.^

Ranjel indicates this king was unusually astute, responding to Soto's gift of "a large feather colored with silver" with comments that sound almost sarcastic in their excessive adulation. "You are from heaven," he remarked, holding the feather aloft for all to admire, "and this your feather that you give me, I will eat with it; I will go forth to war with it; I will sleep with my wife with it." Probably amused by the king's prodigious blandishments, Soto affirmed he could do all of these things with his new feather, if he wished. Later, Camumo further impressed the Spaniards with his shrewdness by asking to whom he should "give the tribute in the future"—Soto, or a powerful kingdom to the north he was subject to, called Ocute. Suspecting "this question might have been asked with cunning," Soto responded by claiming "he held Ocute as a brother," and that Camumo "should give Ocute his tribute until the Governor should command something else."

During this same meeting, Soto sent word to Ocute, ordering him to appear at Altamaha. He did on April 7, acquiescing without a fight, just as the others had throughout Georgia. To reward him for his obedience, Soto gave Ocute "a hat of yellow satin, and a shirt, and a feather." He then raised yet another cross in Altamaha, apparently on a mound in the central plaza.

Two days later, Soto was in Ocute,^ having marched up the east bank of the Oconee River south of the present-day Oconee National Forest. Here one can still find a small sample of the great piedmont forests that once covered the clay hills of northeastern Georgia, and later became the rich heartland of Georgia's cotton-growing region before the Civil War. Biedma says this area was "well populated with Indians." So much so that Elvas claims the Ocute king sent "two thousand Indians bearing gifts, namely many rabbits, partridges, maize bread, two hens, and many dogs." Elvas adds that these "dogs," which were probably opossums, "are esteemed among the Christians as if they were fat sheep, because there was a great lack of meat and salt. Of this there was so much need and lack in many places and on many occasions that if a man fell sick, there was nothing with which [to give him] to make him well; and he would waste away of an illness . . . and he would die from pure weakness, some saying: 'If I had a bit of meat or some lumps of salt, I should not die.' " In other words, the army in *La Florida* suffered terribly from a diet lacking in salt, critical vitamins, protein—and, if they were exclusively eating corn for too long, essential amino acids. Indeed, the "weakness" described by Elvas sounds as though the men suffered from malnutrition of the sort that greatly weakens victims of famine today, making them prone to viruses and other maladies that a healthy body would easily throw off.

Yet one might ask, why didn't the Spaniards take advantage of the rich game of the southeastern United States? Elvas in this section supplies an answer, first off admitting that the Spaniards were terrible hunters. "The Indians," he says, "do not lack for meat; for they kill many deer, hens, rabbits, and other game with their arrows. In this they have very great skill, which the Christians do not have." Elvas adds that the men were moving too quickly, at Soto's insistence, to stop and hunt. They also "did not dare to turn aside from the paths" for fear of ambush.

At Ocute, Soto and the king apparently had a disagreement concerning how many porters the Indians would provide. The matter was resolved when Soto "got angry with him, and he [Ocute] trembled with fear." In the end, the king provided some four hundred porters loaded up with food. Soon after this, Soto again raised a large, crude cross in the middle of this town. Ranjel says the Indians "appeared" to receive it "with much devotion," falling "on their knees, as they saw the Christians do." Of course, Soto's fulminations against Ocute, and the fact that Soto now controlled four hundred of the kingdom's young men and women, undoubtedly contributed to the devoutness of those Indians.^

On April 12, the army marched north toward another kingdom subject to Ocute, called Cofaqui.^ There they met an aged *cacique* with a full beard and his nephew, "who governed for him." They provided the army with more porters and food. Another local king, Patofa,^ who was independent of Ocute, but at peace with him, later arrived in Cofaqui and provided even more porters, whom the Spaniards called *tamemes*.* These men also were to double as warriors if Soto needed auxiliaries. This brought the total number of carriers and warriors accompanying the army to at least eight hundred Indians, and as many as twelve hundred^—including Patofa himself, who agreed to accompany Soto on the march.

The reason the Indians cooperated so readily was simple—the Spaniards were marching on Cofitachequi, long a hated and feared enemy of the people of northeastern Georgia. Indeed, as the Spaniards made their final preparations in Cofaqui, the Indians regaled them with stories both ancient and fresh about the dreaded warriors of Cofitachequi, whose military might was as famous here as the Apalachee's prowess in Florida. Moreover, the Cofitachequi were rumored (of course) to live in great cities filled with gold—and ruled, it was said, by a young woman, who was their queen.

*This term originated in Mexico.

✤ 26 ✤

The Pearls of Cofitachequi

AS THE ARMY REACHED the northern edge of the Georgian kingdoms, Hernando de Soto summoned the boy-guide Perico to ask how far it was to Cofitachequi. Arriving dressed in Spanish clothes and affecting the regal manner of the *hidalgos* he now spent time with,^ the Indian youth solemnly turned and gazed off to the east and announced that the great empire the Spaniards sought was "four days' journey thence toward the rising sun."^

Perico owed his exalted position—which was probably on the order of a mascot—to the fact he was the army's sole guide to Cofitachequi. He also had become important to the Spaniards as a translator, being the only person in the *entrada* capable of understanding not only Timucuan, the language of north Florida, but the various Muskogean tongues the army had been encountering in Georgia, and would find in the Carolinas. This facility with languages meant Perico had joined Juan Ortiz as a critical link in the army's translation "chain"—a progression that started with Ortiz speaking Spanish and Timucuan, and continued with Perico speaking Timucuan and Muskogean. This chain would grow longer as the *entrada* penetrated deeper into *La Florida,* with Soto's questions and comments being passed from Ortiz to Perico and on down a line of translators in a dizzying relay of Mississippian tongues.

Perico's position in the army remained highly precarious, however. It was wholly dependent on his information being correct—which, the army was about to discover, it was not. For even as this precocious boy stood back after majestically pointing to the northeast, he was immediately challenged by the assembled emissaries from Cofaqui and Patofa. Stepping up to Soto in their white togas and brilliant feathers, they informed the governor that Cofitachequi was much farther than four days away, and could be reached only by passing through an uninhabited wilderness where there were no trails, and no villages with food supplies. Nor could they confirm the existence of gold or silver to the north.

Confronted with this contradictory information, Perico—rather than admit his information was faulty, and risk losing his newfound status—responded by staging one of the great early theatrical performances in American history. For what was the one thing he could do to fend off the suspicions of his newfound patrons?

By claiming the devil made him do it, of course; and by putting on a great spectacle for the superstitious Spaniards. Elvas says that Perico "began to foam at the mouth and to throw himself on the ground as if possessed." His performance was real enough to attract Soto's priests, who came running over to perform a quick field exorcism, offering up their prayers and holy mutterings, which soon drove out the evil spirits.

Of course, Garcilaso de la Vega was unable to resist embellishing such a bizarre story. In his version, Perico is not playacting, but is actually possessed by the devil—who appears one night "with a horrible visage, and accompanied by many servants" to demand Perico stop guiding the Spaniards toward Cofitachequi, or be killed. "As he said these words," Garcilaso says, the devil "hissed at [Perico] and dragged him through the room, giving him many blows all over the body." The devil "would have ended by killing him if two Spaniards had not been able to come so quickly to his assistance. As the big devil saw them . . . he had left him immediately and fled," for "the demons fear the Christians." Naturally, says Garcilaso, Soto was initially incredulous when his men told him this story. But when the young Indian showed him the "marks of the lashes" inflicted by the demons, and bruises and "swelling they found all over his face and body," Garcilaso says everyone believed him. That same day, the Inca adds that Perico was baptized, so that if the devil returned, he would fear him as much as he did the two Christians who saved him.^

Devil or not, Soto had invested too much in getting to Cofitachequi to turn back or deviate. Therefore, sometime during the week of April 12—the exact date is unclear—the army gathered up food to last for several days, formed up in their standard marching order, and headed off toward the wilderness. Guided by Perico and *cacique* Patofa, they set out on a trail well-known to the local Indians. It led to one of their distant hunting grounds some sixty miles to the east, where the Savannah River comes rushing down from the Blue Ridge Mountains along the modern border between Georgia and South Carolina. Just beyond this watery barrier, the Spaniards hoped to locate their elusive golden city, while the Indians hoped to benefit from the military might of their newfound allies to crush their ancient enemy.

+ + +

The forest the Spaniards were about to enter was a natural buffer zone of uninhabited wilderness perhaps 130 miles wide. Apparently, the Ocute and other local tribes maintained it to keep the dreaded Cofitachequi as far away as possible. Indeed, archaeologists have uncovered evidence—villages, farmsteads, and mounds—that up until a century before Soto arrived, the Savannah River valley had been inhabited by a Mississippian-style people, who had abruptly departed.^ It's not clear why they left or where they went. Given the deeply ingrained fear among the Ocute for the people to the northeast, it's possible that at least some of the Savannah River people relocated in northeastern Georgia, possibly after flee-ing from attacks by the Cofitachequi army. This would explain why the Ocute talked about having had "no dealings with" this distant people—whose location they did not even know for sure—yet insisted they "were at war" with them.^

At first, Perico and Patofa led them along a well-defined trail, which Patofa said the locals had used for decades on long-range hunting and fishing expedi-tions into the Savannah River valley. After a few days this trail began to peter out, even as the men became anxious about their dwindling supply of food—and the obvious fact that there was no great empire in the area, or even a single tiny vil-lage or family hut. "We were already beginning to see the lie of the Indian," says Biedma. Nonetheless, Soto was now committed, and did not turn back. But he did order everyone to "save as much food as they could," since it was becoming evi-dent that they must locate a well-stocked Indian town or face starvation.

On April 17, the army reached a great river that was almost certainly the Sa-vannah. Ranjel describes it as "an extremely large river, divided into two branches, broader than the shot of an arquebus, and it had many bad fords of many flat stones [*lajas*], and it came up to the stirrups, and in places up to the saddle pads. The current was very strong, and there was not a man on horse-back who dared to take a footsoldier on the rear [of his horse]." This meant the infantry had to cross in a different part of the river, where the water was deeper, but the current a little less stiff. "They made a string of thirty or forty men tied one with another," continues Soto's secretary, "and thus they crossed." For four more days, the allied army of Spaniards and Ocute struggled to cut a trail through swamps and thickets. Heading roughly northeast "without a road," and now completely out of food, they crossed a second "very large" river and then arrived on April 21 at a third—probably the Broad.^

After yet another strenuous and miserable crossing, Soto's frustration fi-nally erupted into anger. Ordering the army to bivouac in a pine grove near the river, Soto called for Perico and "threatened the youth and made as if he would throw him to the dogs because he had deceived him, saying that it was a march of four days, and for nine days he had marched making seven or eight leagues on each day; and now the men and horses were becoming weak because of the great economy which had been practiced with regard to the maize." For Perico, this was the moment of truth he must have dreaded since concocting his fan-tasy about this distant city of gold, which he had cleverly parlayed into his spe-cial status. Now the illusion was shattered, and Perico was forced to admit that "he did not know where he was"—and to plead for his life, undoubtedly begging on his knees before the enraged governor. In fact, Soto did spare the boy. But only because he was a critical link in the Spaniards' interpreter chain. "That there was no other whom Juan Ortiz understood," writes Elvas, "availed in preventing him from being thrown to the dogs." Soto did order him put in chains, abruptly ending Perico's brief moment of grandeur.

Ordering the army to stop where they were, Soto decided to personally lead a scouting party of horse and infantry in search of a road or signs of inhabitants. But he found nothing, covering some twenty miles before returning to camp that night "greatly disheartened."

"Next day," says Elvas, Soto called a conference of his hungry and increasingly desperate advisors and captains to consider options—undoubtedly with the rank and file milling about close at hand under a warm, blue Carolina sky. "Different opinions were expressed as to whether he should turn back or what he should do," says Elvas. Ranjel adds that "some said that they should turn back." This was quickly vetoed, "inasmuch as the land behind through which they had come was left very desolate and lacking in maize." Soto himself "proposed, as he had always done, that it was better to go forward." Of course, none of this talk satisfied men whose stomachs were empty, who "were in great doubt as to whether they could reach a place where they might be aided. Moreover, they considered that if they went on like defeated men, if any Indians dared to attack them, they could not escape."

As always, Soto was at his best in an emergency—whether it was at the height of battle, putting down a rebellion, or facing seemingly insurmountable hardship. Even now, with his *entrada* on the verge of ruin, he kept his cool, issuing two rapid-fire orders. First, he told Patofa to return home with his Indians, because there was no longer food to feed the Indian porters and warriors.^ Next, he gathered his four best captains and supplied each with eight horsemen, "men who could swim, in order to cross mud and streams which they might come to, and he chose horses, the best in the camp." The four captains included Soto's most reliable officers, whom he repeatedly turned to in crises. There was Juan de Añasco, who went downstream along the Broad; Baltasar de Gallegos, who went upstream; Soto's old Peruvian friend, Juan Lobillo, who led his squad inland; and, finally, Soto's kinsman from Badajoz, Alonso Romo, who also headed into the interior, away from the river.^

Before these men left, Soto gave everyone in the army a nutritional boost by slaughtering some of his three hundred pigs, brought along for such a contingency. "He ordered half a pound of flesh to be given to each man daily,"^ says Elvas. This was added to a diet consisting of a few grains of maize a day, "the tendrils of wild vines that grew in the woods and along the streams," and whatever herbs and roots the men could scrounge, which they "boiled with considerable trouble." Garcilaso adds that Patofa's Indians, before they left, helped some by hunting game and fish.^ Still, Ranjel reports that the men suffered "great conflict and hardship, and the horses without any food, and they and their owners dying of hunger, without a road, with continual rain, the rivers continually swelling and narrowing the land, and without hope of towns or knowledge of where they had to look, calling and asking God for mercy."

For two days, the despairing men waited, hearing nothing from the four captains. Then, on Sunday, April 25, Añasco's platoon burst into camp on their exhausted, rickety horses to announce they had found a small town twelve or thirteen leagues away. Strapped onto the rear of two of the strongest horses were Indians the squad had snatched away from the vicinity of the village—"an Indian woman and a boy."^ Garcilaso says that Añasco's men also brought back all the grain they could carry—and, curiously, "some horns of cattle" they had found in the village, perhaps a reference to buffaloes, which may have existed in the sixteenth-century Southeast, in small numbers.^ "With his coming and with the news," says Elvas, "the Governor and all were so glad that it seemed to them that they had then come back from a most greedy death."

The next morning, Soto wrote letters explaining where they were going for the other three units still out searching for food. Placing them in a pumpkin under a well-marked pine tree, he led the army toward Añasco's village, called Himahi,* probably located near the confluence of the Congaree and Wateree Rivers near present-day Wateree, South Carolina. As the day wore on and the hungry, despondent men struggled to reach the village, Soto rode ahead with a small company to organize the food. Unable to make the village by dark, the exhausted men dropped in their tracks to sleep "sprawled out" on the ground several miles away from Himahi, "some at a distance of two, and others at three or four, leagues from town, each one according as he could march and his strength aided him." In Himahi, Elvas says they found a *barbacoa* filled with corn. Biedma says it held some fifty *fanegas* (about five thousand pounds). They also found "some flour of toasted corn, and many mulberry trees loaded with mulberries, and some other small fruit." Ranjel says they also found "*morotes* . . . which are like delicious and very fragrant strawberries" and "infinite roses, and native ones like those in Spain . . . but rather more delicate and mellow."

The following day, as the Spaniards ate their newly plundered food, and savored the beauty of rose-filled meadows in this place that had saved them from almost-certain death, Captain Alonso Romo arrived with four or five more In-

---

*This is Ranjel's name for this village. Elvas calls it Aymay.

dians. These were taken to Soto, who tried to coerce them to guide the army to Cofitachequi. When they refused, Soto ordered one of them burned alive. Not even this gruesome torture persuaded the others to talk, though they were tied to a stake one by one and burned. Ranjel says none revealed the location of his sovereign's capital.^ The very next day, Gallegos arrived with a woman who willingly told them how to reach Cofitachequi. Lobillo, too, came in that day with news of roads to the north, and word that "the chieftainess of that land had already heard of the Christians and was awaiting them in one of her towns." This information prompted a relieved Soto to dispatch the usual message to this queen, telling her he had come in peace, and would be arriving shortly in a domain he hoped would be laden with the sort of riches that would make him and the army forget the misery of the past few days.

✣   ✣   ✣

Fired up once more by plundered food and dreams of conquest, Soto gathered his strongest horsemen and headed north to the banks of another large river, guided by the woman brought in by Baltasar de Gallegos. This was probably the Wateree River, which Soto most likely reached in the vicinity of Lugoff, South Carolina, twenty miles east of Columbia.^

It was there, on May 1, 1540, that Soto first encountered the queen of Cofitachequi, though our eyewitnesses differ on exactly what happened. Elvas says a sister of the queen and several *principales* crossed this river in four canoes to confer with Soto before the queen herself arrived sometime later, borne regally in a litter and conveyed across the stream in "a canoe with an awning at the stern and on the bottom of which was already spread a mat for her and above it two cushions one on top of the other, on which she seated herself." Once across, this *"cacica"* welcomed Soto "with very sincere and open good will . . . present[ing] him with a quantity of clothing . . . namely blankets and skins. And from her neck she drew a long string of pearl beads and placed it about the neck of the governor, exchanging with him many gracious words of affection and courtesy." Ranjel essentially agrees with Elvas's account, though Biedma says the queen sent a niece to welcome Soto, and that "some Indians brought her on a litter with much prestige," after which she offered Soto five or six strands of pearls. He adds that three or four days later, the queen's niece "went away to the woods," and that neither she nor the queen appeared again during the army's eleven-day stopover in the Cofitachequi area.

Garcilaso positively gushes about the queen of Cofitachequi, claiming that she was a woman of "great beauty" and "extreme perfection." He compares her to Cleopatra crossing "the River Cydnus in Cilicia" to meet her lover, Mark Antony. In his version, the pearls she gives Soto are "as large as hazelnuts" and strung up as "a great rope . . . that was wound three times around her neck and hung down to her thighs." Soto was so charmed by this gift, adds the Inca, he took "from his finger a gold ring that he wore, set with a very handsome ruby," and gave it to her—a gift reminiscent, as the Inca well knew, of a similar gift given by Soto to Garcilaso's late kinsman in Peru, the emperor Atahualpa, during Soto's famous meeting in Cajamarca.

That same day, Hernando de Soto and his party crossed the river in canoes provided by the queen, who most eyewitnesses say escorted him to her capital at Cofitachequi. This was probably located near present-day Camden, South Carolina, possibly at an archaeological dig known as the Mulberry Site.^ On May 3 the main army arrived at the Wateree, which they crossed over the next two days. Ranjel says seven horses drowned while trying to swim across.

The grandeur of the queen, and her pearls, made the Spaniards instantly put behind them the miseries of the past few days as the men buzzed about the possibility their governor had been right all along about *La Florida.* They were also relieved to find a *cacica* willing to welcome them peacefully and to offer food and housing—a reception they had not anticipated after Patofa's talk about Cofitachequi's warlike reputation, and the torture of the Indians a few days earlier. But there was a reason for the Cofitachequis' friendly response. As Soto quickly discovered, this great kingdom, the first truly extensive Mississippian "empire" he would encounter in *La Florida,* had recently suffered a catastrophic plague that had so decimated its population, and its ability to raise an army, that its demise as a great power in the ancient Southeast was already a foregone conclusion.

When Soto arrived, the plague was so recent that the political situation had not yet adjusted itself to Cofitachequi's weakened status. This means the queen still ruled at least the northern half of South Carolina, and probably maintained her empire's preplague dominance over an area that may have stretched from the Atlantic coast to the foothills of the Blue Ridge Mountains in North Carolina,^ a region roughly the size of the modern Netherlands. How much authority Cofitachequi actually exerted over this territory before the plague is a matter of debate among anthropologists. In fact, Cofitachequi may have been more of a dominant kingdom among rival polities than a rigid central authority. This means the royal house of Cofitachequi would have directly controlled only its home region in the Wateree-Catawba River valley. More distant vassal states probably remained locally autonomous, paying tribute to the lords of Cofitachequi. Meanwhile, various kingdoms probably jockeyed for political advantage over their neighbors in a situation reminiscent of medieval Europe, where kings tended to dominate only a small area, with their influence over powerful nobles in outlying duchies, baronies, and earldoms waxing and waning depending on the circumstances of the moment.

Ranjel describes the people of Cofitachequi as "covered down to the feet in very excellent hides, very well tanned . . . and blankets of sable and blankets of mountain lions." They also wore "breeches and buskins, and black gaiters with laces of white hide, and with fringes or edgings of colored hide, as if they had been made in Spain." Elvas adds they were "well set up and proportioned, and more well-mannered and civilized* than any who had been seen in all the land of Florida; and all were shod and clothed" in a similar manner to the toga-clad Mississippians of Georgia. The warriors wore "breastplates, as well as corselets and helmets, made from raw and hairless hides of cows, and from the same [hides] very good shields." These "cows" are buffalo, which Fray Sebastián de Cañete, another eyewitness who accompanied Soto, calls *vacas pequeñas,* or "small cows," adding that they roamed "plains" in a "certain part"—presumably the Great Plains to the west—"that extend more than 300 leagues." Cañete further tells us in the all-too-brief fragment of his lost chronicle that these *vacas pequeñas* produce "very good meat, and there is a trade in the hides inland," which may explain how their horns and skins ended up in South Carolina.

The towns and houses of the Cofitachequi people, like their clothing, were similar to what the army had seen in Georgia, though reportedly more elaborate. In the nearby city of Talimeco, "a town of great importance" that may have been the capital of the empire before the plague, Ranjel recalls seeing a "very authoritative temple on a high mound," and a palace for the *cacique* that was "very large and very tall and broad, all covered, high and low, with very excellent and beautiful mats," presumably woven with brilliant colors, and hung like finely woven wallpaper to decorate the outer walls. Garcilaso de la Vega takes a particular delight in describing this city he calls Talomeco, saying it was composed of five hundred houses,^ "all large and of better materials and workmanship than ordinary ones . . . In the middle of the pueblo, facing the lord's houses was the temple," which the Inca spends nine pages describing. "Earnestly" admonishing us to believe his account, he insists the temple was "more than a hundred paces long and forty wide," with outsized walls and a steep-pitched roof covered in several layers of canes split and tightly woven. The roof was covered almost completely with intricately arranged skeins of pearls and seashells, and by

---

*The word Elvas uses is *polida,* which can mean "civilized," but also "polite" and "well-mannered."

"many periwinkles, extraordinarily large . . . With the sun reflected on them, they made a beautiful sight."

Just inside two enormous doors, the Inca tells us, "twelve giant figures carved from wood" stood guard, six on a side, with each face carved in "a fierce and bold posture." These giant sentries held war clubs, wooden broadswords, battleaxes, longbows, and arrows, all elaborately carved and embellished with mica, copper, pearls, deer antlers, and shells. Near the floor were rows of benches holding the remains of Cofitachequi's royal families, contained in large chests painted with portraits of the deceased, the coffins themselves holding not only bundled bones, but a wealth of pearls, deerskin, dyed cloth, and pelts of native cats, deer, and martens. Surrounding the temple, Garcilaso describes eight marvelous rooms stacked high with weapons—one with pikes, some of which had heads of brass, and others filled with clubs, axes, broadswords, staffs, bows, arrows, and more shields made from buffalo hides "brought from distant countries."

Whatever the grandeur that was Cofitachequi, it was all crashing down in 1540. Indeed, the Spaniards found themselves marching through a settled country "very pleasant and fertile," with "excellent fields along the rivers," but almost entirely emptied of people. "About the town [of Cofitachequi]," says Elvas, "within the radius of a league and a half were large uninhabited towns, choked with vegetation, which looked as if no people had inhabited them for some time." He also notes that these eerily empty towns were full of *barbacoas* loaded with a "considerable amount of clothing—blankets made of thread from the bark of trees and feather mantles (white, green, vermilion, and yellow)," all of them elegant, and suitable for winter. "There were also many deerskins, well tanned and colored with designs drawn on them and made into pantaloons, hose, and shoes." Alonso de Carmona, one of Garcilaso's informants, says that in Talimeco, "where the burial place and rich temple was, they found four long houses full of bodies who died from the plague that had raged there."

Garcilaso informs us that the queen herself first told Soto of the plague when they met at the river. Apologizing for the lack of food on hand, the queen told him "the pestilence of the year before had deprived her of the provisions" she might have given Soto in previous years. She was able to give him enough maize for his immediate needs, though food supplies in the capital region were minimal enough that soon after the men had regained their strength, Soto ordered Baltasar de Gallegos to take most of the army northeast to a vassal city of Cofitachequi, called Ilapi. This was probably located near present-day Cheraw, South Carolina, fifty-five miles away. There, the queen said, she had seven large cribs of grain stored that she would give the Spaniards.

✢   ✢   ✢

Soto stayed on at Cofitachequi with a small guard to search for treasure. He became ecstatic one day when the queen told him she could bring him precious metals colored yellow and white, though it would take her a few days to have them brought in. When the "metals" arrived, however, they turned out to be "a large quantity of copper" instead of gold, and "large slabs as thick as boards" of mica instead of silver. "At first sight," says Garcilaso, the mica "shone like silver, though . . . they weighed almost nothing, and when handled they fell apart like a clod of dry earth." The adelantado of *La Florida* was further let down when he and Rodrigo Ranjel entered a temple near Cofitachequi,^ and found among the bodies "a thing like a green and very good emerald." Soto, writes the secretary, "was very delighted," though when they called in Juan de Añasco, the royal treasurer, to record their find, he had to inform them this was no emerald, but a piece of green glass.

Poking around more in the dark temple, among corpses and piles of bones, Soto and Ranjel soon found additional bits of glass in the form of beads and rosaries with crosses. "They also found Biscayan axes of iron," and "two Castilian axes for cutting wood," says Biedma, "and . . . some *margaritas* [beads] of the kind they carry from here [Spain] to barter with the Indians." Apparently, these artifacts originated in Lucas Vázquez de Ayllón's aborted colony.^ According to the Indians, his ill-fated settlement had been located nearby, on the coast, "up to thirty leagues from here"—that is, roughly ninety miles.^

In the end, Soto had to satisfy himself with just the pearls of Cofitachequi, though they were flawed from having holes cut into them, and from the Indians' practice of removing them from freshwater oysters by using fire, which turned them black.^ This didn't stop Soto from plundering large numbers of them from Indian temples,^ however, though he claimed to have left behind the bulk of this treasure, pledging to his men that they would fetch it later, on a return visit.

Of course, Soto failed to make good on this promise to return, though another Spanish explorer did come here some twenty-six years later, a young captain named Juan Pardo. Ordered by Pedro Menéndez de Avilés, then the new governor in St. Augustine, to build a settlement on the Carolina coast and to explore inland, Pardo spent three years marching up and down the Carolinas and across the Blue Ridge Mountains into Tennessee, establishing small garrisons here and there. Ultimately, he hoped to establish a route to Mexico—an effort that soon failed because of attacks by Indians, too few men, and Pardo's belated realization that New Spain was farther away than he thought. It was during these forays that Pardo visited some of the towns Soto had seen a quarter century earlier, including Cofitachequi.^ Pardo's Cofitachequi, however, was greatly diminished from the grand city visited by Hernando de Soto. In the space of just a quarter of a century, this powerful Mississippian Empire had almost completely disintegrated, the fields having gone fallow, and the towns greatly reduced in population. As for the handsome and gracious queen described so admiringly by the chroniclers, she and her imperial clan seem to have disappeared, melting away with their empire.

+   +   +

Everyone in the army felt let down by the meager treasure in Cofitachequi. As Soto's men rested and regained their strength, however, eating fine Southern cooking, and living in sturdy *bohíos,* they began talking amongst themselves about how appropriate this place was for establishing a colony. "All the men," says Elvas, "were of the opinion that they should settle that land as it was an excellent region," being not only rich agriculturally, but strategically located near the sea at a point where the Gulf Stream carried fleets returning home to Europe. "All the ships from New Spain, and those from Peru, Santa Marta, and Tierra Firma," says Elvas, "would come to take advantage of the stop there." He adds that this was not only "a good land and suitable for making profits," but it was also rich in pearls, some of which "were worth their weight in gold and, if the land were to be allotted in *repartimiento,* those pearls which the Indians would get afterward would be worth more" than those damaged by fire.

Elvas's comments are echoed by expedition survivors, who later extolled the natural abundance of *La Florida,* particularly the region of Cofitachequi. Some survivors testifying in the Ponce-Bobadilla trial suggest that had Soto lived, he might have returned there to establish a colony—a fascinating "if," considering the impact on the subsequent history of the Old South had an *entrada* as rich and powerful as Soto's built a permanent colony in what became South Carolina. Later groups tried, but none had anything approaching Soto's resources. During Menéndez's *gobernación* in St. Augustine, Pardo and others managed to erect small missions and settlements as far north as the Chesapeake Bay,^ though none lasted more than a few years.

Hernando de Soto, however, had little interest in the tedious process of building colonies; not when he still believed he could score the sort of huge overnight success he had grown accustomed to in Central America and Peru. As Elvas dryly notes, "the governor's purpose was to seek another treasure like that of Atahualpa, the Lord of Peru, he had no wish to content himself with

good land or with pearls." Indeed, Soto was willing to listen to his men's entreaties to settle here. But in the end, he insisted that they keep going, both because Cofitachequi was low on food, and because "it was necessary to hasten
to the port of [Achuse]" to rendezvous with Maldonado and the fleet.

But as Elvas points out, there was plenty of food in the general region to
keep them fed for several weeks. They also could have grown more, since it
was still early in the growing season. Others note that had Soto built a colony
in the Carolinas, with a port on the sea, he could have used it as a base for
launching campaigns of conquest wherever he wanted. He also could have
dispatched a troop to meet up with Maldonado at Achuse, with orders for the
Havana fleet to make haste and sail up the coast to the Carolinas.

Soto simply did not want to stop in a place with no gold and a small population of potential laborers and slaves. Indeed, when he heard that twelve days
inland there lived a great king ruling a country called Chiaha, he refused to listen to any more talk about staying in Cofitachequi, "determined to go in search
of that land." Because "he was a man hard and dry of word," and because they
all knew that once "he had voiced his own opinion he did not like to be contradicted . . . all conformed to his will. And although it seemed a mistake to
leave that land," Elvas notes with an uncharacteristic wistfulness, "no one had
anything to say to him after his determination was learned."

So it was with great regret that the *entrada* packed up before dawn on Thursday, May 13, almost a year to the day since they had departed Havana, and
again plunged into the vastness of *La Florida*. Nearly everyone lamented their
departure—with some already beginning to wonder if Don Hernando de Soto,
adelantado of *La Florida,* member of the Order of Santiago and hero of Peru,
was losing his mind.

✣ 27 ✣

Lost Opportunities

JUST BEFORE DAWN ON May 12 or 13, as the mists stood thick against Cofitachequi's damp savannahs and overgrown maize fields, Hernando de Soto mounted one of his horses and turned his back forever on his best chance for success in *La Florida*. His departure did not go smoothly, however, being marred by an incident with Indians that Elvas describes as a "revolt." He provides few details, except to say that certain men "of little quality" had committed "offenses . . . against the Indians." Whatever this was, it not only provoked a violent response from the people of Cofitachequi, but it also infuriated the queen, who already had been having second thoughts about cooperating with these brutish strangers. She did not act on her anger quickly enough, however. For just as Soto was about to leave, informers told him "the *cacica* was minded to go away if she could without giving guides or *tamemes* for carrying"—an action that to the Spaniard's way of thinking bordered on treason.

Soto ordered her arrested, despite everything she had done to help the army, particularly when they were starving and vulnerable. Both Elvas and Ranjel disapproved, with Ranjel (or is it Oviedo?) noting sarcastically that "they took with them" the queen of Cofitachequi "in payment of the good treatment that they had received from her." She was placed under heavy guard, but like Atahualpa in Peru was allowed to keep her aides and servants, and to administer to her religious and political duties. She also was allowed to indulge in the aboriginal luxuries of a High Mississippian sovereign throughout her captivity, attended to by her servants and retainers.

Little is known about the famous queen of Cofitachequi other than she was young, and seems to have recently inherited an extensive empire about to crash down around her. According to our eyewitnesses, she was beautiful, though this is an adjective so freely dispensed in the sixteenth century to describe queens, princesses, and noblewomen that it only proves this sovereign was not exceptionally ugly, tall, short, fat, or otherwise abnormal. She was remarkably generous to Soto and his men, providing them food from the meager stores available in her plague-ridden country, and even acquiescing when they asked to ransack her nation's temples and charnel houses in search of pearls. Obviously, this was part of a strategy of giving the Spaniards whatever they wanted, though hints in the narratives suggest she had more on her mind than hurrying these strangers on their way. Indeed, she behaves with a fatalism that suggests she knew her empire was doomed. This may explain why she seemed so nonchalant about allowing Soto to plunder her people's holy places—which, after all, were shrines to gods and ancestors that had proved useless against Soto's army, and against the recent onslaught of disease.

There also is the matter of whether or not the queen of Cofitachequi and Soto became lovers, as a few romantics have suggested. No evidence exists to support this, though we do get a whisper of a clue about the queen's love life when Elvas informs us she fell in love with "a slave of André de Vasconcelos,"^ who escaped from the Spaniards to join her after she herself absconded from Soto's company some weeks later. "And it was very certain that they held communication as husband and wife," says Elvas.

Of course, Garcilaso has something to add to the legend of the woman known among Soto enthusiasts as the Lady of Cofitachequi. Informing us she was a "young marriageable woman who had recently inherited" her position, the Inca describes her as a highly capable leader, though already weary with the burdens of an office beleaguered by overwhelming problems. This attitude becomes clear early on in Garcilaso's story, when he describes her offering food to Soto and his starving men, but with the caveat that he not take everything. When Soto brusquely asks why not, the Lady explains she has but two storehouses filled with grain, "which she had collected to succor the vassals who had escaped the plague." One, she says, contains 950 bushels of maize, which she will offer to Soto. She "begged that he be pleased to leave her the other for their own need, which was great." If he needed more grain, she said, she could supply it in other villages. As always in the Inca's account, the chivalric Soto behaves magnanimously, telling the queen that because she had offered so much "during a time when her country was suffering ... he and his people would endeavor to get along with as little food as they could, in order not to give her so much inconvenience."^ He seems to have kept this pledge, sending his men to surrounding towns and villages as far away as Ilapi, seventeen leagues to the northeast.

Soto's chivalry abruptly ended when he ordered his hostess placed under guard on that long-ago May day,^ and told her she would be accompanying him on his journey as he trekked across her empire, toward present-day Tennessee. According to the chroniclers, Soto regretted having to kidnap the queen. This may be true, given that his last kidnapping had led to the battle and massacre at Napituca. Soto also seems to have genuinely felt affection and even a sense of fairness with certain Indians who had helped him in some way, or acted favorably toward him. Yet this hardly stopped him from using the queen's imprisonment to his advantage, forcing her over the next several weeks to order local leaders to provide the Spaniards with food, guides, and porters. "In all the towns through which the governor passed," reports Elvas, this queen was "well obeyed" as she "ordered the Indians to come and carry the loads from one town to the other."

✛   ✛   ✛

With his captive traveling under heavy guard, "on foot with her slave women," Soto roared out of Cofitachequi the morning of May 13, determined to march as quickly as possible to the next major kingdom beyond the borders of Cofitachequi, called Chiaha. If we can believe Charles Hudson, the army averaged a remarkable twenty miles a day between Cofitachequi and their arrival on May 18 at Guaquili, the next major city to the north.^* This seems an almost impossibly quick pace for a troop encumbered by porters carrying heavy loads, and men and horses still weak from the ordeal in Ocute. Soto may have been able to march faster than usual because he was traveling with only a small part of his army—those who remained in Cofitachequi and did not march north with Baltasar de Gallegos, who was then preparing to depart Ilapi to rendezvous with the governor several days later.^ Ranjel might also be referring to the movements of a vanguard sent out by Soto, which the impatient governor may have led in a quick march ahead of the main group departing Cofitachequi.

From Guaquili, as the army journeyed almost due west into Tennessee, Ranjel-Oviedo's account once more reads like a diary, and is clearly based on

---

*Subject to the queen of Cofitachequi, Guaquili may have been located near present-day Hickory, North Carolina.^

brief entries scrawled by the young secretary at the end of each grueling day's march. Again, I offer a few entries below, slightly modified from Oviedo's paraphrased version^ to give a feel for what this eyewitness saw and felt during this portion of Soto's journey.

Tuesday, May 18. *In Guaquili. Here the Indians came forth in peace and gave us corn, although little, and many hens roasted on* barbacoa, *and a few little dogs,* which are good food. They also gave us* tamemes.

Wednesday, May 19. *We went to a canebrake.*

Thursday, May 20. *We went to a small savannah where a horse died. Some foot soldiers of Baltasar de Gallegos arrived, making it known to the Governor that he was approaching.*

Friday, May 21. *Today we reached Xuala, which is a town on a plain between some rivers; its* cacique *is so well-provisioned that he gave us much of what we asked for:* tamemes, *corn, little dogs,* petacas, *and however much he had.* Petacas *are baskets covered with leather for carrying clothes and whatever they might wish.*

Saturday, May 22. *Baltasar de Gallegos arrived with many sick and lame, and since we are about to cross mountains, we need them healthy, so we rested here three days.*

Tuesday, May 25. *We left Xuala and crossed a very high mountain range, and spent the night in a small forest.*

Wednesday, May 26. *We were in a savannah where we endured great cold, though it was already late May; and we crossed, in water up to our shins, a river that our navigation charts indicates is [a tributary of] the River of Spíritu Sancto.*

If Charles Hudson is right, the army during these eight days marched from Hickory, North Carolina, following the modern Interstate 40 corridor as it heads toward the Blue Ridge Mountains at Marion. There they crossed the Swannanoa Gap and dropped down into the upper valley of the French Broad River at present-day Asheville^—which is, as Ranjel indicates, a distant tributary of the Mississippi, which the Spaniards called Spíritu Sancto—or Espíritu Santo.[†]

Ranjel's reference to this geographic point should be of great interest to anyone who believes this expedition was poorly run from a navigational standpoint—or for those who believe Soto had no idea where he was, or where he was going. Given that no European had yet explored much beyond the mouth

---

*These may indeed be dogs, or possibly opossums.
[†]Biedma calls the Mississippi Espíritu Santo; Ranjel calls it Spíritu Sancto.

of the Mississippi, it's remarkable that Ranjel and the expedition's geographers were able to conjecture (possibly in retrospect, after the entire journey was over) that the French Broad eventually connects with the Mississippi, via hundreds of miles of twists and turns along the Tennessee and Ohio Rivers.

Soto was now marching across stunningly beautiful country, bathed in hues of green as fresh leaves grew to their full size in late May. This was a land of low, rippling, ancient mountains that rise from one thousand feet on valley floors to peaks nine thousand feet high, interspersed with limestone crags and waterfalls, and supporting such a profusion of plant life that nearly every species of tree, shrub, vine, and lichen found in the eastern half of the United States grows here. Looking up from the valleys, Soto would have seen largely what we see today—ridges covered on their lower and middle slopes with dense bands of hardwoods giving way to shortleaf pines and, in higher elevations, thick bands of red spruce, Fraser fir, and yellow birch. On the humid valley floors, Soto was passing through dark, damp forests of black oaks, chestnuts, sugar maples, magnolias (in bloom in May, perfuming the air), and scattered hickories. In the mid-sixteenth century, these valleys were mostly cleared by the Indians. This means they would have looked similar to what we see now in many Blue Ridge valleys, where loggers and farmers until recently kept the lower elevations largely shorn of trees. Soto would have seen more climax forest growth up on the mountainsides. Otherwise, as timber and agriculture decline and forests begin to grow back in modern-day eastern Tennessee, one sees the same sort of meadows Soto did, filled with fast-growing grasses and shrubs broken up by scattered clumps of pines and hardwoods. The Indians liked this sort of vegetation because it supported large populations of deer and other game they hunted better than climax forests, with their high canopies and shadowy floors almost devoid of leafy foods.

To Soto, the Appalachian Mountains meant more than beauty. They also meant gold might be nearby. As suggested earlier, Spaniards in this era believed that precious metals occurred most often in mountainous regions, given what they had found in the Andes and in the sierras of Mexico and Central America. By now, Soto himself must have known something about the geology of precious metals, having spent over a decade in Central America seeking out and running mines. (In at least two instances in Nicaragua, Soto was dispatched on missions specifically to seek out mines.^) He also must have brought along an expert or two specifically assigned to look for evidence of naturally occurring metals. In Cofitachequi, Ranjel reports that a man named

Alaminos seemed to know something about gold and silver. "A native of Cuba, although Spanish," says Ranjel, this Alaminos claimed to have "found a bit of gold" in the river that ran through Talimeco, "and such a rumor became public in the army among the Spaniards, and for this it was believed that this was a land of gold, and that good mines would be found there." There is no evidence that Soto followed up on this specific lead, though Ranjel tells us he and his men believed this area to be in "better disposition . . . for gold mines than all that they had passed through and seen."

Twenty-six years later, Juan Pardo's men concluded the same thing when Juan de la Bandera, Pardo's chronicler, reported they "found a trace of metals" when some soldiers climbed a steep ridge in these mountains. "The alchemists swore," writes Bandera, "that it was silver." Later, Pardo himself picked up a small reddish stone, which one of his metal experts declared "might be silver ore" of the sort the Spaniards had recently discovered in Mexico, known as ruby silver because it was bright red. Charles Hudson has suggested the stone was really a chunk of red jasper or hematite (iron oxide).^ In 1567, Pardo's men also claimed to have found traces of diamonds,^ which fed stories for centuries afterward about rich lodes of *los diamantes* hidden somewhere in the southern Appalachians. Even today, these legends have not been entirely put to rest, though no one has ever found anything more than quartz crystals, which the Indians in Soto's day sometimes used to temper their pottery.

When Soto came through here, he was also looking for copper, having found in Cofitachequi "some copper hatchets . . . they said had a mixture of gold." The Indians said this metal had been mined in a place called Chisca, deep in the mountains to the north. The Spaniards also heard from the Indians that at Chisca "there was a foundry for copper and other metal of that color, except that it was finer and of much more perfect color." When Soto dispatched two men to find this place, however, they came back empty-handed, saying that the country to the north was so rugged it could be crossed only with great difficulty.^

Of course, there is great irony in all this talk and rumors of precious metals. For the truth is, there was—and still is—a small amount of naturally occurring gold in this region, recovered mostly by panning in creeks and streams. First discovered in 1820 by a Carolina farmer named John Reed, mines in north Georgia, the Carolinas, and eastern Tennessee produced as much as a million dollars a year worth of gold until 1848, when the miners literally pulled up stakes and rushed off to the California gold rush. Soto also failed to locate copper deposits that still exist in the area—some of which were worked by prehistoric Mississippians—when he inexplicably turned away from Chisca. Indeed, one would have expected a man obsessed with finding precious metals to have pursued this lead more vigorously, though I suspect that Soto, like

most plunderers, had far less interest in finding gold he had to work for—if he
thought he could steal it from others, or force them to collect it for him.

When Soto reached the French Broad River valley late in May, he was nearing the western border of Cofitachequi's influence, where the captive queen
hoped to be set free. Not willing to trust these men who had turned against her,
she decided to flee while still in her own territory. She planned her escape carefully, aided by four accomplices, including the slave who, during the long
march from her capital, had become her lover. This man is not identified by
race, though he was probably a nominally Christianized Indian, perhaps from
one of the provinces in Georgia.

They made their move on May 26, near modern Knoxville. Announcing she
needed to go with "her slave women who were carrying her . . . into a wood . . .
to attend to her necessities," the queen stepped into a thicket where she was
then met by her friends. Quickly striking off her chains, they plunged deep into
the woods—possibly with the help of local natives awed by the presence of the
great lady who ruled them from far away.

After eluding Soto's platoons, the fugitives headed back to Xuala, the city
Soto had passed through a few days earlier. There the queen and her party ran
into none other than that same Alaminos who had discovered the gold tracings
in Cofitachequi—who apparently had deserted from the army. According to
Elvas, he explained his presence to the queen by claiming he had come down
with a fever that caused him to be left behind when he became disoriented and
wandered off the road. Ranjel mentions nothing about a fever, insisting that
Alaminos de Cuba "stayed behind" in Xuala with another Spaniard, Mendoza
de Montanjes, "with deception"—a comment the secretary does not explain.^
But the reason seems obvious. The two young men were after gold, and either
did not want to share whatever they found with the rest of the army, or had been
rebuffed by Soto in their request to look further, perhaps because the senior officers had concluded that whatever tiny amounts of gold existed in the area
were not worth pursuing at that time.

On May 26, when Hernando de Soto was told these men had deserted, he ordered the renegades' captain, Alonso Romo, to take a squad and bring them
back. Late on May 27, he did, arriving in camp with the two terrified fugitives,
undoubtedly wishing they had never seen the tiny little nuggets of metal
Alaminos de Cuba had panned in Cofitachequi.

Ranjel glosses over what happened next. He says only that Soto "wanted
to hang" the two men, without telling us whether the sentence was carried
out. But because desertion was almost always a capital crime in this era, I suspect that Soto either did hang the men, or ordered them severely punished—

if for no other reason than that he was leading an army already disgruntled about the decision to leave Cofitachequi. In just two weeks four others had deserted, among them a young foot soldier named Alonso Rodríguez, who had slipped away back in Chalaque, a day or two out of Cofitachequi. The three others were a slave from Cuba, a Moor from North Africa, and "a very shrewd black man"^ belonging to Vasco González. Needing badly to restore discipline, I suspect Soto ordered Alaminos and Montanjes brought before him, heard Alaminos's lame excuse about his supposed fever and disorientation, and pronounced his sentence—death by hanging. The execution of these two men would have sent a chill through the army, and restored some discipline. Certainly, there are no more reports of desertions for some time to come.

✟   ✟   ✟

In Xuala, Baltasar de Gallegos and his soldiers finally arrived, reuniting the entire army so they could proceed on down the valley of the quick-flowing French Broad River. Again, the army was moving as rapidly as possible through country sparsely populated and provisioned. With many of the men still recovering from the ordeals of the past few weeks, and again facing the prospect of running out of food, Soto's haste was less an effort to fulfill his quest than to put food in the bellies of his men. Again, Ranjel gives us a day-to-day account of the weary march down the valley, from the vicinity of Asheville, where the deserters were punished on May 27, heading northeast over the Tennessee border toward Chiaha, located some twenty-five miles east of Knoxville.^

Friday, May 28. *We spent the night in an oak grove.*

Saturday, May 29. *We marched alongside a large creek, which we crossed many times.*

Sunday, May 30. *In the morning messengers came in peace, and we arrived early in Guasili, and the Indians gave us many* tamemes, *many little dogs, and corn; and because this was a good resting place, the soldiers afterward called out the term House of Guasili when they threw the dice, for good luck.*

Monday, May 31. *The Governor left from Guasili and took the army to an oak grove alongside a river.*

Tuesday, June 1. *We passed through Canasoga and spent the night in the open.*

Wednesday, June 2. *We spent the night alongside a swamp, and ate a very great number of mulberries.*

Thursday, June 3. *We followed a large creek next to the river [the*

French Broad] we had crossed in the savannah where the cacica *[from Cofitachequi] went away, and now it was large.*

    Friday, June 4. *We went to a pine forest and a creek, where Indians from Chiaha came in peace and brought corn.*

    Saturday, June 5. *In the morning, we crossed the very broad river, across a branch of it, and entered Chiaha, which is on an island of the same river.*

This island capital, which Hudson places near Dandridge, Tennessee,^ was exactly what the ailing army was looking for. It had no gold, but it had bountiful supplies of food, starting with twenty *barbacoas* of maize, which Soto accepted with relief from the *cacique*. But corn was just the beginning. All of the chroniclers, even the economical Biedma, praise the cuisine of ancient Chiaha. "In that town, there was an abundance of butter in gourds, in melted form like olive oil," says Elvas, made from "bear's grease." They also enjoyed the first and only pot of bee's honey mentioned on the entire journey, and "considerable oil of walnuts and acorns." All agree these were delicious, though Ranjel complains that they caused "flatulence."

Elvas says Soto lodged himself as usual in the *cacique*'s *bohío,* while his men camped in the fields surrounding the town. The horses, which were "so weak that they were unable to carry their owners," were put out to pasture, where they soon "grew fat because of the luxuriance of the land." For twenty-two days, the Spaniards rested in the closest thing to paradise they had seen for a long time. Ranjel says the Indians were not only peaceful, but they also "played" with the Spaniards—whatever this means—and they "swam in the company of the Christians," splashing and enjoying themselves in the cool, clear waters of the French Broad. "They served them very well," he adds.

But inevitably trouble flared as the Spaniards, with their strength returning, blundered about asking for more and more, until their hosts finally had enough. As often was the case, it was the Spaniards' libido, restored by tortillas drenched in walnut oil and bear's fat, and flavored with mulberries, that was the immediate cause of rancor when Soto himself demanded thirty women from the *cacique* and his *principales*.

Remarkably resolute in following their strategy of giving the strangers what they wanted so they would go away, the Indians did not respond with violence. By now, the word was out among the Mississippians, passed up and down the highways of ancient America, that these strangers seemed intent not on invasion and wanton destruction, but on finding yellow and white metals, and on exploration. Resist them with force, the multilingual network of Mississippian messengers, spies, and runners warned, and face a brutal war, torture, and the loss of homes and crops—which is what happened to the Apalachee.

Greet them peacefully, obey their demands, and the strangers would remain mostly nonaggressive—if one could tolerate their indignities and outrageous demands.

In the case of Chiaha, they followed the plan right up until the moment Soto asked them to give up large numbers of their women, something they decided they would not allow. Understanding that it would be foolish to challenge their visitors militarily, however, early on the morning of June 20 the people of Chiaha "left the town with their wives and children," hoping the Spaniards would go away and leave them alone.

This was not Soto's style. He responded by leading thirty horse and thirty infantry himself to ferret out the Chiaha people, destroying a few maize fields on the way to give them a sample of the punishment in store for them should they remain in hiding. Late that same day, he found them holed up on another islet, probably in the French Broad, chosen by the Indians because it was inaccessible to the horses. Soto might have tried to attack the island anyway. But he knew the Indians would defend themselves, which would not only mean loss of life for Spaniards and Indians, but also might ignite a situation like Apalachee the previous winter. There, constant warfare had worn down both sides, and ended up with Soto having no porters to carry his food and supplies. Therefore the governor, whose primary goal was to keep moving, offered the Indians a compromise. He agreed not to attack or punish them if they would honor their previous agreement to supply porters. In exchange, he would drop his request for women, "since it cost them so dearly to give them to him." The Indians quickly agreed.

That night, the people of Chiaha returned to their island enclave under the watchful eyes of Soto's Spaniards, bivouacked in tents around campfires. Happy to have been spared a war, but embittered over their treatment at the hands of their visitors, one imagines these Native Americans walked past Soto's men stone-faced and barely able to conceal their rage. Certainly, they were no longer in the mood to "play."

✤ 28 ✤

The Empire of Coosa

REFRESHED AFTER THEIR RESPITE in Chiaha, Soto's men on June 28, 1540, plunged back into their journey, the full army traveling together for the first time since they crossed the wilderness of Ocute, in the Savannah River valley. For eighteen days, the Spaniards trekked roughly 150 miles across low mountain passes and down river valleys, their path alternating from wide highways to narrow trails. Now numbering some 550 men,^ plus hundreds of *tameme* porters, slaves, and servants, the *entrada* moved either single file or two to three men abreast, depending on the terrain, with *caballeros* on horseback carrying their lances, swords, maces, flags, and heralds, and the infantry shouldering not only weapons, but whatever personal effects the *tamemes* could not carry, loaded into packs of canvas and leather.

Marching in the long, serpentine column were units of arquebusmen with their wax wicks smoldering, ready to ignite fuses in case of attack; crossbowmen with shafts placed and levers ready to crank; and men of the line with their light, quilted armor, sweating and red-faced under the hot summer sun. There were slaves in chains, some tattooed on the forehead with the royal mark; Indian men with bare backs struggling under loads of dried meat, maize, and equipment; dozens of young, supple women taken along as concubines, and less attractive ones delegated to prepare and cook the Spaniards' meals; and hundreds of pigs squealing and scurrying about, chased by pages and Indians pressed into service as swineherds. By now, the Spaniards' brilliant attire—their silks, great capes, satin-trimmed shirts, and everyday shirts, breeches, hose, and boots—must have been starting to fade and fray. Their corselets, gorgets, and pointed *cabasset* helmets also must have been losing their burnish, with some rusting around the edges. Yet the Spaniards still presented a remarkable spectacle for the Indians as they wound their way alongside the French Broad River to the Little Tennessee, and then due south over a

352

series of low mountain ranges into the northwest corner of Georgia^, headed for the heartland of the next major Mississippian empire—the Coosa.

During this steamy summer march, which would eventually take the army beyond Coosa toward the planned rendezvous with Soto's fleet on the coast of Alabama, Soto finally established the marching rhythm he had been after since making landfall in *La Florida*. This involved the usual *conquista* method of quickly bringing the local *cacique* under his power, so the Spaniards could use his authority to demand food, lodging, porters, and women until Soto had passed through his kingdom and on to the next, where the process would begin again.

Soto's smooth and largely uneventful progression across the southern Appalachians was hardly a coincidence. He chose this route specifically because he had been told the army would find the stores of food they needed, and large numbers of Indians to impress as *tamemes* and servants. The Indians, too, were continuing to operate under their tactic of giving the invaders what they asked for to get rid of them. None of the native leaders, however, fully appreciated how much luck contributed to their design. For had Soto found any sign of treasure existing among the natives of Tennessee and Georgia, this march would have instantly ceased to be relatively benign, with Soto grabbing what he wanted, whether or not the Indians cooperated.

During this trek, Hernando de Soto, perhaps for the first time in years, seems to have relaxed. In the absence of gold or obvious Cuzco-like cities to seize, and confident he would easily reach his fleet on schedule, the adelantado of *La Florida* after Chiaha became, if briefly, less obsessed and more at ease with himself than perhaps at any other time in his career. One sign of this is the fact he allowed the army's daily mileage to drop from an average of some sixteen miles a day between Ocita and Chiaha to a more manageable twelve miles a day.^ This included frequent stops to rest, negotiate with *caciques*, and enjoy the food, cool rivers, and other pleasures of the march through this country.

Clearly, Soto during this trek had a plan in mind for when he met up with Francisco Maldonado, though what this was remains a mystery. Eyewitnesses testifying a few years later in the *Ponce v. Bobadilla* trial insist their governor-general had planned first to explore the land, then to establish a base in the Gulf, which he would use as a stepping-off point to return to the most promising sites in the interior to build settlements.^ If this is true, then his meeting with Maldonado was not only intended as an opportunity to off-load fresh supplies, but also as a first step in establishing a colony, possibly with its port city situated in Mobile Harbor.

For centuries, historians have assumed that when Soto later turned inland after the Battle of Mabila, without building a Gulf colony or even meeting up with his fleet, he proved without a doubt his lack of interest in colonizing. Gonzalo Fernández de Oviedo, for one, roundly condemns Soto, even as he trekked south that summer toward the Gulf, for failing to halt and build a settlement. In his massive *historia,* Oviedo insists that Soto's sole purpose during this march, and throughout the Florida *entrada,* was "neither to populate nor to conquer, but rather to disturb and devastate the land and to take away the liberty of all the natives, and not to convert or make one Indian a Christian or friend." If this were not bad enough, Oviedo contends that Soto did not even know or care where he was going, "except that his intent was to find some land so rich that it might sate his greed, and to find out about the great secrets that the governor said he had heard about those places . . . And as regards the disturbing of the land and not settling it, nothing else could be done until they came upon a site that satisfied him."

It's true Hernando de Soto spent most of his time scouring the countryside for treasure, and was willing to destroy anyone who tried to stop him. But this was never his entire purpose. Indeed, Oviedo fails to note the subtlety of Soto's style—that he was a consummate pragmatist who frequently attempted to avoid violence for the practical reason that it slowed down his progress, and put at risk his greatest resource if he was to succeed: his own army. The censorious historian also misses the fact that Soto, despite his obsession with conquest and treasure, was during this phase of his *entrada* chiefly an explorer—and quite a good one—in addition to being a *cabalgador* and conquistador.

Soto's steady, confident procession that summer of 1540 also suggests he was feeling reasonably pleased with the expedition thus far. Otherwise, why would he so deliberately head to the sea and the rendezvous point? Of course, the outcome in *La Florida* had been modest in terms of treasure. But being a consummate schemer and propagandist, he undoubtedly believed he could convince the outside world that his year of exploration had been highly promising. He could show off his pearls, talk up the rumors of gold and copper, and parade around captured Mississippians in their sophisticated regalia. He could leave it to his men to extol *La Florida*'s potential in terms of crops and land, and of peaceful Indians whose settled societies offered a large and pliant source for slaves and laborers.

With three years left on his royal contract, and vast stretches of *La Florida* remaining to be explored, Soto had every reason to be content, if not satisfied. Particularly since he had proven his mettle as an *entrada* general by leading his men across an astonishing thirteen hundred miles of unknown territory in just over a year, with minimal casualties. For sheer organizational acumen and the number of people and distances involved, this was more than Pizarro had accomplished during his march from Puná to Cuzco in Peru. It was, in fact, rivaled during the *conquista* only by other large inland expeditions then under way—including Coronado's exploration of the southwestern United States, which had begun that spring, and Francisco de Orellana's monumental trek down the length of the Amazon, which had been in progress for over a year in the fall of 1540.

Soto's march to Coosa was not entirely blissful. In Coste, the next major kingdom south of Chiaha, Soto saw his peaceful sojourn nearly turn violent when he and eight Spaniards entered Coste's capital, probably situated twenty-eight miles southwest of modern Knoxville, on an island in the Little Tennessee River.^ Looking for corn, some of his party began plundering *barbacoas* near the *cacique*'s palace. This was despite a friendly welcome from the Indians,^ and with no regard for the fact that the group was vastly outnumbered and lightly armed, and the main army was in a camp about a half mile away.

The callous behavior outraged the *cacique* of Coste and his people, who seized the looters and "began to beat" them, while others grabbed "their bows and arrows" to "come forth to the plaza." Normally, Soto would have met such an assault against his men with deadly force—if only to drive home the point that Indians who dared lay hands on a European faced automatic punishment, even if the European was at fault. But because Soto had "entered in the town carelessly and unarmed," he abruptly found himself in a position where he was likely to be the one penalized—or even killed.

He first heard the fracas between his men and the Indians when several natives breathlessly rushed up to the *cacique* to report that the Spaniards were trying to plunder the royal stores. They were quickly followed by the bloodied looters themselves, who ran up to join Soto's party. Angrily turning to his guest, the king demanded an explanation as native soldiers began to assemble on the square with their weapons.

A conquistador with less experience might have panicked, or attacked in a suicidal charge. Soto did neither. Instead, he proved once more the nimbleness of his mind during a life-threatening crisis. As the Indians closed in, he suddenly turned on his own men and "began to quarrel" with them, pretending to chastise them for stealing the natives' corn. He whispered to them to play along and "suffer it and be tolerant, because of the evident danger in which they were, and that no one should put a hand on his weapons." He "thrashed some of them" as "he flattered the *cacique* and told him that he did not wish that the Christians should anger them." This ruse convinced the Indians to disperse quietly and put away their weapons. Relieved to have avoided warfare with the Spaniards, the *cacique* even consented to accompany Soto back toward the savannah where the army was setting up camp.

This time, the *cacique* was being overly complacent. For no sooner were they out of range of Coste's longbows than Soto turned on their leader, ordering his men "to lay hands on the *cacique* and ten or twelve of his principals, and they put them in chains with their collars, and he threatened them and said he would burn all of them, because they had laid hands on the Christians." Apparently, Soto did not carry out his threat to burn them, though it's likely he exacted some sort of punishment unrecorded in the chronicles.

✛   ✛   ✛

As Soto moved from Chiaha to Coste and onward toward the Gulf of Mexico, he passed through the northernmost provinces of what may then have been then the largest aboriginal empire in the Old South, the empire of Coosa. How large remains a matter of dispute. According to the Gentleman of Elvas, Coosa ruled in the north as far as Tali, just south of Chiaha on the Tennessee River. Historians have interpreted this to mean Coosa held sway in the north over not only Tali, but possibly Chiaha, Coste, and the other small kingdoms in the Tennessee River valley visited by Soto as he approached the Coosa capital itself, most likely located in northwestern Georgia.

There is ample evidence linking these northern cities along the Tennessee basin with one another. To begin with, Coste's king was visiting Chiaha when Soto came through, apparently as a familiar friend.^ Archaeologically, there is also proof of close ties, not only between Chiaha and Coste, but also their neighbors in the Tennessee Valley to the southwest, Tali and Tasqui—in terms of the pottery the Indians of this era left behind, their style of dwellings, burial patterns, and so forth.^

The evidence is less clear for linking these northern kingdoms along the Tennessee with Coosa itself, located farther south, probably on the Coosa River near Carters, Georgia. Again, it's Elvas who suggests the connection. He tells us that once Soto left Tali, situated a few miles south of Coste, the army "marched for six days, passing through many towns subject to the *cacique* of Coosa, and as he entered his lands, many Indians came to him on the way on the part of the *cacique* with messages, some going, others coming." There also is a single but compelling archaeological link connecting this region with not only the Coosa heartland in northwestern Georgia, but also with other polities along the Coosa River as it flows into Alabama. This is the presence in burial mounds from Tennessee to Alabama of large, flat shell gorgets incised with a uniform depiction of a rattlesnake—drawn as a series of circles (coils) with a giant head and teeth in the middle, and a large rattle. Buried exclusively with elite women and their children, and dating to the early and mid-sixteenth century, these gorgets have been unearthed in a pattern that geographically coincides almost exactly with the extent of the Coosa Empire as reported in the chronicles. It's possible these gorgets were used as identity markers for the Coosa emperor, whose personal symbol may have been the rattlesnake, king of the snakes and master of the underworld, and a source of great power to the Indians of the Southeast. But it's equally plausible these gorgets were simply popular ornaments traded along an established route that just happens to coincide with the reported extent of greater Coosa.

Beyond the two remarks in Elvas, and the intriguing mystery of the rattlesnake gorgets, no other conclusive evidence exists of a political or even a strong cultural link between Coosa and the Tennessee Valley. None of the other chroniclers mentions any association, other than vague comments made by Ranjel that Coosa ruled over "much land," and Garcilaso's offhand statement that Coosa's domains extended "more than a hundred leagues" in length—equal to some three hundred miles—a stretch of land that, if true, included not only Chiaha in the north, but also kingdoms along the Coosa River well into Alabama.

Even if the Coosa emperor ruled such a vast domain, it hardly means his sway in the north or south was as a highly centralized power ruling every aspect of life. Like the queen of Cofitachequi, Coosa's authority beyond his heartland was more likely minimal, with the emperor demanding occasional tribute in corn, furs, and laborers, coerced by dispatching the Coosa army every so often for a show of force. In fact, this exact situation happened when the Spanish explorer Tristán de Luna, coming out of Mexico, dispatched a small party to visit Coosa in 1560, and ended up accompanying a Coosa army on a punitive raid against a subject province called Napochie, fifty miles north of the Coosa capital. Apparently, this polity had refused to pay tribute, and was attempting to break away.^ Another indicator that Coosa and the northern kingdoms were connected is suggested by their joint efforts to fend off common enemies—in particular, the Cherokee, whose Iroquois-speaking ancestors may have been pushing south at this time, bumping up against the northern boundary of the Muskogean speakers near Chiaha.^ The close proximity of the Muskogeans and the Cherokee may also explain why Biedma says that "in this province we began to find the towns palisaded"—that is, defended by walls, moats, towers, and barricades. It may be that the threat of invasion from the north was what catalyzed a loose federation among Coosa and the kingdoms of the Tennessee Valley in the first place—with the ancient and highly respected House of Coosa the dominate partner. But it's also possible the palisades were originally built in an attempt to fend off not the Cherokee, but a conquering Coosa army.

South of Coosa—if, in fact, the Carters site *is* Coosa—Soto would find his road taking him past another series of small Mississippian kingdoms along the Coosa River. Closely linked archaeologically to one another, they also are more obviously tied culturally to Coosa than the cities to the north, in terms of pottery and other artifacts. We also have direct evidence from the chroniclers of the Coosa emperor's power and sway over the southern flank of his empire. They describe in some detail how, after being kidnapped by Soto, this sovereign was able to command large numbers of porters for Soto's use all the way to a city called Talisi, probably near present-day Childersburg, Alabama, which the chroniclers tell us was on the southern frontier of Coosa. The Coosa emperor attracted a near-fanatical devotion among Indians along this southern route. Everywhere he went, crowds came out to greet him, with one group attempting to launch a spontaneous raid to rescue him.

The chroniclers suggest that south Coosa was no more secure from outside threats than was the north. Ranjel describes one southern city near the empire's frontier as being encircled in a double wall of palisades, adding that the Indians there and in other walled cities built their enclosures by sinking "many thick poles, tall and straight, next to one another; they weave them with some long sticks, and daub them within and without, and they make loopholes at intervals, and they make their towers and turrets [*cubos*] spread out along the curtain and parts of the ramparts as suits them; and at a distance, they appear to be one very excellent wall [*muralla*], and such walls are very strong." The enemy to the south is easier to identify than the one in the north. Called the Atahachi, they were a Mississippian people who had apparently been making aggressive moves toward Coosa, most recently led by their king, Tascalusa, a name Soto would soon regret ever hearing. For Tascalusa, like Coosa, built strong-walled cities to defend his frontier, including a small fortress-town called Mabila, where the Spaniards would soon fight their disastrous battle—and, in the process, change not only the course of Soto's *entrada,* but quite possibly the history of North America.

✣   ✣   ✣

As problematic as Coosa's size is the location of its capital, which Soto reached on July 16, after marching seven days from Coste. The debate over where, exactly, Hernando de Soto laid his head to rest in this ancient Indian metropolis is almost as fierce as the controversy over Soto's landfall in Florida, and where he first glimpsed the Mississippi River. Over the years, several candidates have been suggested, though only two are now taken seriously.

The first was proposed by John Swanton and the 1939 De Soto Commission. He placed ancient Coosa near Childersburg, Alabama, at the site of an old Creek town called Coosa. At the time, Swanton reasoned that the Creeks, as descendants of the ancient Mississippians, had continued to occupy the same locales as their ancestors—a not entirely logical claim given the dislocations and migrations that occurred after the collapse of the Mississippians, and the turmoil that surrounded the encroachment of British, French, and American settlers into the Old South. Since Swanton, the notion that Coosa was situated in Alabama, and not in Georgia, has been championed by a prolific Alabama archaeologist, Caleb Curren. His intimate knowledge of this state's archaeology has lent considerable weight to Swanton's general placement of Coosa in this state, though Curren and his colleague Keith Little now place Coosa not at Childersburg, but at the Terrapin Creek Site near Gadsden, Alabama.^ Curren and his associates have also constructed a hypothetical route from Coste to Mabila—one that is completely different from Charles Hudson's itinerary in this area. Curren's route, however, is as carefully researched as Hudson's, making it not only plausible, but maddeningly so, given that he and Hudson have both come up with Mississippian sites dated to the sixteenth century spaced just about the right distances apart, with rivers, mountains, and plains appearing where the chroniclers say they should be. In fact, nowhere else in the entire muddle of where Soto may or may not have been in *La Florida* do we find two such probable candidates, lined up almost as if one were seeing double. The Curren and the Hudson tracks start off about sixty miles apart in the north, with Curren's line running south and west of Hudson's as the two routes move in a parallel sweep along the general direction of the Coosa River. Hudson's course turns due west at Montgomery, Alabama, while Curren's continues south to within fifty miles of the Gulf before it veers off to the west and north.

There is a serious complication with Curren and Little's route, however. For if they are right, and Coosa is located as far south and west as Terrapin Creek, then we would have to throw out the rest of the Hudson route I have been describing since the army left Tallahassee—which most scholars now agree on. This is because Hudson and his colleagues, in taking Soto through Georgia and the Carolinas, and across the French Broad River valley into Tennessee, have placed Coste—the spot where Soto turned south toward Coosa— too far north to link up in any meaningful way with Curren's proposed route in Alabama. Hudson's placement of Coste in Loudon, Tennessee, some 30 miles southwest of Knoxville, means that Soto would have had to march nearly 220 miles in just eight days to reach Childersburg, equal to an impossible 28 miles a day.

I should point out that Little and Curren do not locate Coste near Knoxville, but farther south, near Chattanooga. They suggest that a well-known cluster of archaeological sites in and around this modern city comprised the Mississippian kingdom Soto visited early in July 1540.^ Unfortunately, their route considers only Soto's progress in Alabama, and a small portion of Tennessee, and does not address the larger question of Soto's itinerary before Coste—which

effectively neutralizes their argument, since they do not explain how Soto got
to "their" Coste at Chattanooga.^

The second and more likely site for Coosa is Charles Hudson's candidate, located
near Carters, Georgia, at a dig known as Little Egypt—which today is inundated
under the waters of the dammed-up Carters Lake. Built at the juncture of Talking
Rock Creek and the Coosawattee River, Little Egypt seems to offer a reasonable fit
given the few clues available concerning the location of the Coosa capital.

Soto's chroniclers offer few hints about Coosa's location. Elvas says only that
it was "very populous and had many large towns," and was a "charming and fertile land, with good cultivated fields stretching along the rivers." He adds that "in
the open fields were many plums," which were delicious, and wild grapes "along
the rivers and on vines climbing up into the trees." Biedma contributes nothing
more, and Ranjel notes that besides plums and grapes, there were "some small,
sour apples, like those that they call *canavales* in Extremadura." These were
probably crab apples. Even Garcilaso is brief, telling us there were three large
mounds in Coosa, and that the town consisted of "five hundred large and good
houses, which showed clearly that it was the head of a province so large and important." As always, however, we cannot be sure about the Inca's numbers.

Fortunately, these sparse descriptions are augmented by a letter penned later
by Fray Domingo de la Anunciación, a priest who accompanied one of Tristán
de Luna's captains—Mateo del Sauz—to Coosa in the summer of 1560. Written on August 1 of that year, as Sauz's troop of forty cavalry, one hundred infantry, and two priests settled in for a stay of several months in Coosa,
Anunciación describes this aboriginal capital twenty years after Soto's visit as
being still "densely populated," and located in a valley cleared of trees and
planted extensively with crops. "There is a mountain range to the north of the
town," writes the priest, "which runs east and west. It is fairly high and well-
wooded, but up to this time we do not know where it begins or ends. This town
is situated on the banks of two small rivers which unite within it." Other descriptions of Coosa by Sauz's men also verify Elvas's brief comment that Coosa
was not one large city, but a cluster of towns—eight towns, according to Luna's
men, five small and three large. It is possible that Luna was describing a different Coosa than Soto, one the Indians founded after abandoning the original, possibly due to disease. But even if this happened, the new Coosa would not have
been removed far enough from the old to alter the scenery around it greatly.

The descriptions of Soto's and Luna's men do not provide definitive indicators for where to find Coosa; they just narrow down the possibilities. They
also happen to match up well with the conditions at Little Egypt, which is lo-

cated in a valley of the right size where two small rivers intersect, and is within sight of the Cohutta range, a prominent east-west ridge of mountains with peaks over one thousand feet high. Archaeologically, the site sits in the middle of a drainage basin rich in alluvial soil that supported a sizable population in the sixteenth century, and consisted of at least seven Mississippian towns, including three with earthen pyramids.^ In Little Egypt itself, there are (under the water) two mounds extant, with a third destroyed sometime after 1932, when the site was investigated by archaeologist Warren Moorehead.^ This third mound count offers us a rare chance to vindicate Garcilaso de la Vega, who writes that the Coosa emperor "lodged the governor in one of three houses that the *curaca* had in different parts of the pueblo . . . situated on a height." Another important archaeological feature at Little Egypt is the mix of pottery styles dating to Soto's era. These include both clay-fired pots distinctive to Chiaha and other northern kingdoms, and shell-tempered pottery favored by polities south of the Carters Site.^ This supports the idea that Coosa was at the very least a major center of trade in the Tennessee and Coosa River valleys, if not the overlord of these domains.

The final piece of evidence supporting Little Egypt—and Hudson's route through Georgia and Alabama—comes from numerous sixteenth-century European artifacts unearthed exactly where they should be if Soto (and Tristán de Luna's group) followed the Hudson route. Those items have been uncovered in sites ranging from Hudson's Chiaha to his proposed site for Mabila (near Selma, Alabama). These include iron celts, wedges, and chisels, as well as a telltale Nueva Cadiz bead dug up inside one of the mounds at Little Egypt. At one site on Hudson's route through Georgia, the King Site, a local collector has even unearthed a double-edged sword, identified by an expert at New York's Metropolitan Museum of Art as a rapier manufactured in Europe during the mid-sixteenth century.^ The mere presence of several 450-year-old Spanish artifacts does not conclusively verify Soto was here, given that these items were highly portable. But their presence in a general pattern corresponding to Soto's probable route, and that of Luna's troop, lends considerable weight to the idea that these conquistadors passed this way. In contrast, European artifacts are notably sparse in most of Curren's sites.^

+   +   +

Given the importance of Coosa, and its status as a major High Mississippian polity, it's strange the chroniclers devote such a paucity of space to the *entrada*'s stay there, particularly since they spent most of the summer marching through Coosa, and over a month resting in Coosa itself—from mid-July to August 20. From what little our eyewitnesses tell us, the Spaniards' introduction to these people and their emperor on July 16 was every bit as spectacular as the arrival of the queen of Cofitachequi two and a half months earlier. Ac-

cording to Elvas, the Coosa sovereign "came out to welcome" Soto a half mile
or so from his capital. He was carried, as was the great lady to the northeast,
"in a carrying chair borne on the shoulders of his principal men, seated on a
cushion, and covered with a robe of marten skins of the form and size of a
woman's shawl. He wore a crown of feathers on his head; and around him were
many Indians playing and singing." Ranjel adds that the emperor's litter was
"covered with white blankets of the land," and was borne by "sixty or seventy
of his principal Indians . . . and none was an Indian of the plebeians or commoners, and those that carried him took turns from time to time, with great ceremony." Garcilaso, in another unusually brief account, tells us the Coosa
emperor's entourage included "more than a thousand nobles"—almost certainly an exaggeration—"adorned with mantles made of various kinds of skins.
Many of them wore fine marten-skins that gave off a strong odor of musk.
They wore long plumes on their heads" that "stood up half a fathom high and
were of many and varied colors; and they were stationed in the field in order
in the form of a squadron, with twenty men to a file."

The description of this powerful Mississippian sovereign, however, ends
here with this tantalizingly fleet glimpse, making it impossible to construct any
sort of meaningful profile. Only Garcilaso adds a detail or two more, telling us
"this lord was twenty-six or twenty-seven years of age, of very elegant bearing, as are most of those in that country, and of good understanding. He spoke
with discretion and gave good replies to all the questions that were asked him;
he appeared to have been brought up in a most enlightened and polished court."
But all this tells us is the emperor was young, and behaved like every other native *señor* in Garcilaso's chivalric version of *La Florida,* where nearly every
important Indian was noble, handsome, fair, brave in battle, and an accomplished conversationalist. In his enthusiasm to encourage Spaniards of his day
to colonize North America, the Inca even has Coosa begging Soto to stay on
and establish a Spanish settlement there—an invitation he says Soto graciously
declined.

The truth of what happened in Coosa is considerably less cordial. Both
Elvas and Ranjel tell us that Soto, after being welcomed with great pomp, and
having the emperor clear out a town for the use of his army, thanked his host
not with grand speeches, but by taking him prisoner, and by making his inter-
minable demands for food, *tamemes,* servants, and women. This in turn
prompted most of the people of Coosa to run away and "hide themselves in the
woods," until a contingent of soldiers commanded by four captains flushed
them out and, in what was by now a cruel and routine exercise, imprisoned
them "in collars of iron and in chains." Dragged back to camp, these Indians

The *cacique* of Coosa greets Soto.

were distributed among Soto's men "as slaves," and not only were taken with the army when they left, but never allowed to return home, "except some whose good fortune and assiduous industry . . . managed to file off their chains at night; or some, who were able, while on the march, to wander away from the road upon observing any lack of care in their guard, who went off with their chains and with their loads and the clothes they were carrying."

None of our eyewitnesses describes the Coosa emperor's reaction to his sudden incarceration, and the enslavement of up to hundreds of his subjects. Yet one can guess the humiliation felt by a monarch who ruled or dominated at least five other kingdoms, and possibly as many as seven spread out over 250 to 300 miles, with a combined population perhaps in the tens of thousands,^ an army numbering in the the upper hundreds or thousands, and an extensive and profitable network of agriculture, trade, and tribute. Indeed, the emperor's distress and anger may have motivated him to begin spreading the word to *caciques* far and wide, warning about the danger presented by these outsiders, with their false promises, metal weapons, horses, and strange appearance. His admonitions may even have reached the ears of Tascalusa, Coosa's most potent enemy to the south—a highly aggressive Mississippian king ruling a relatively new and expanding empire in southern and western Alabama, who at that very moment was probably trying to determine how to react to the Soto juggernaut when it reached his domain.

+ + +

On August 20, Soto and his prisoner—accompanied by a retinue of his *principales* and at least one of his sisters—departed Coosa with the Spanish army rested, well-fed, and carrying with them more slaves, servants, and *tamemes* than ever before or after in *La Florida*. Inadvertently leaving behind another deserter, a Levantine named Feryada^ (who was not missed for several days), the army marched for two days in a heavy rainstorm over highlands between the Coosa River valley and the next major kingdom to the south, called Itaba. According to Charles Hudson, this was the famous assemblage of Mississippian pyramids we now call the Etowah Mounds, located near Cartersville, Georgia. This High Mississippian city reached its apogee centuries before Soto's arrival, and was now reduced to perhaps a thousand people where many thousands once lived. Yet Ranjel still describes the city they visited as "a large town alongside a good river." At Itaba, Ranjel adds that the Spaniards "bartered for some Indian women," trading mirrors and knives for them.

Soto was delayed in Itaba for seven or eight days while the army waited for the rain-swelled river to subside. Once they dried out, the Spaniards proceeded down the heavily populated Etowah River valley, one of the densest areas of Mississippian archaeological sites in Georgia. On August 31 they arrived in

Ulibahali, a walled city probably located near present-day Rome, Georgia. They were met by several local *principales* loyal to Coosa, Ranjel says, who approached the army with an "evil intent," threatening to attack the Spaniards and free their prisoner. They were few in number, however, and agreed to disperse when Coosa, under orders from Soto, asked them "to lay down their weapons, and so they did." The *cacique* of Ulibahali then provided the army with *tamemes* and twenty or thirty women "as slaves," again at the direction of Soto's hostage. In this city, yet another soldier deserted, a Salamanca *hidalgo* named Francisco Rodríguez el Manzano. According to Ranjel, "it was not known if it was from his own will or from losing his bearings going alone to pillage, inasmuch as he went on foot." Ranjel adds that "he was unhappy," and a melancholy sort who liked to be by himself. This is why it was several hours before they missed him. Elvas says Manzano "was lost in that place" when he "wandered away to look for grapes, which are abundant and excellent there." Apparently, an African slave, Joan Vizcaíno, also escaped during this period, a man who belonged to Captain Juan Ruiz Lobillo.

From Ulibahali, Soto moved quickly along broad highways with the Coosa River to his right. He crossed the Alabama border west of Rome, Georgia, and then turned southwest at a small town subject to Ulibahali called Piachi, probably located at an archaeological dig known as the King Site. He lost a day waiting there for Juan Lobillo, who went back to look for his slave without permission, a transgression for which Soto "reprimanded him severely."

For the next thirteen days, the Spaniards continued marching across the ridges and valleys of piedmont country toward the Gulf. They averaged five to six leagues—thirteen to twenty miles—through populated areas, and moved faster through unpopulated areas, "in order to avoid the necessity of a lack of maize." This pace seems to have been quicker than it had been since leaving Chiaha, because it was now autumn, and time for Soto to rendezvous with his fleet.^

On September 16, the army reached the first villages of the next large province, called Talisi, probably located near Childersburg, Alabama.^ Two days later, they reached Talisi itself, which was "large and fertile with much corn, and next to a big river," most likely the Coosa River. The Spaniards found this city abandoned, the Indians having run away, presumably into the rugged piedmont hills to the south.

Talisi was either the last town under Coosa's nominal sway, or was independent, depending on which chronicler one believes. Whatever the case, it was here that ambassadors sent by Tascalusa, "a powerful lord and very feared in that land," arrived to meet with Soto. One of these emissaries was Tascalusa's son, whom Garcilaso says was eighteen years old—and, of course, carried himself with "elegance and fine bearing." The Inca also says "he was head and shoulders taller than any of the Spaniards or Indian in the army," which sounds believable given that numerous eyewitnesses describe Tascalusa himself as being of gigantic stature. Because Soto had apparently been hearing about the Atahachi's fierceness for some time, he greeted the prince and ambassadors by staging for them a show of Spanish martial acumen. According to Ranjel, "the Governor commanded the Spaniards to mount, and that those on horseback should gallop, and sound the trumpets." This display was "more to impose fear," adds Ranjel, "than to make ceremony." Soto also departed from his usual tactics at Talisi by dispatching with the prince and his emissaries "two Christians instructed to observe and spy, in order that they [the Spaniards] might take counsel and be prepared."^ Apparently, this was done out of deference for the Atahachi's reputation as warriors. It is also possible Soto sent these two men because he had heard hints from his many native informers that the Indians of the region might be planning some sort of surprise attack.

✛   ✛   ✛

In Talisi, Soto finally released the emperor of Coosa, "so that he might return to his land." For some reason, Soto refused to free his sister, which so saddened Coosa that he was "tearful," suspecting that he would never see her again, and because "they had brought him so far from his land." He also was undoubtedly lamenting the disgrace of his captivity, and the denigration of his stature as a semideity and ruler to his people. For it must have been damaging, if not disastrous, for a man considered to be a son of the sun to be treated like a slave and carried about, possibly in chains, by foreign invaders whose power and invincibility far outshone his own.

How much Coosa's humiliation affected his prestige is unknown. So is the extent of violence and physical destruction inflicted on Coosa and its provinces during Soto's four months marching from Chiaha to Talisi. In fact, the chroniclers do not record a single violent death among the Spaniards or Indians during this march. There are hints of violence, however—in the incident at Coste where Soto pretended to beat up his own men, and then clapped the *cacique* and his *principales* in chains. There also is the free-for-all capture and enslavement of the Coosa people after they ran away from their capital, and the close brush with battle when warriors threatened to attack at Ulibahali. Recently, archaeologists have unearthed dramatic physical evidence of European violence against Indians. Digging in the 1970s at the King Site^—which may have been Piachi—archaeologists Patrick Garrow and David Hally found numerous bones pocked with slash marks, obviously inflicted by sharp-edged metal blades. These included cuts made deep into skulls, and divots cut into the bones of victims' arms. Who inflicted these wounds is a mystery. It could have been Indians using European weapons, though the blows tend to be made against the upper bodies of the victims, as if the attackers were slashing down-ward—say from a horse. And if the attackers were European, there are only two candidates—Soto's army, or Sauz's squad, which came through here in 1560, though the latter group was small, starving, and hardly in a position to be engaging in battle.

There also is the puzzle of the victims' identity. Nearly all are either women or old men. Possibly, the men were wounded in their warrior youths during battles with the Spanish, or they and the women were servants or slaves wounded or killed as punishment for some infraction. Charles Hudson also has suggested they might have been involved in a battle against Soto's army some-place other than Piachi—since there is no evidence of a battle being fought there—and either returned home wounded, or had their remains carried back for burial. If this is true, then these people may have fought at Mabila, which the Spaniards, as they continued their quick pace, were fast approaching.

The impact of Soto's 105-day march through Coosa territory was far greater than the specific number of Indians violently killed, abused, and degraded. When Luna's party came this way just twenty years later, accompanied by sev-eral men who had been there with Soto, they found a country greatly dimin-ished from its previous glory. Soto's former soldiers—including an ex–field captain, Alvaro Nieto, and at least two others^—told Luna's men they must have been bewitched to have thought Coosa was such a rich and powerful land. In what had been the southern flank of the Coosa Empire, Luna's men found the great roadways Soto had marched along so effortlessly now overgrown, and the once heavily populated river valleys devoid of people. Lacking guides and food, Luna's men nearly starved during a journey that took them two months, whereas Soto had taken only three weeks, and had no trouble keeping his army well-fed, and served by hundreds of servants and porters.

Eyewitnesses in Sauz's party likewise insist the Coosa they saw as being far less impressive than what Soto's men claim. This may be because the Coosa the Spaniards visited in 1560 was not the same city that Soto saw two decades earlier. Sauz's men mention nothing about the magnificent towns and cere-mo-nial centers depicted by Soto's chroniclers. The 1560 party describes the towns of Coosa as being composed of crude clusters of huts, with those for the win-ter being little more than sod huts "covered with earth," and topped by grass, weeds, and crops. Temples are likewise "rudely constructed" and "uncouth," with Anunciación telling us that the religious shrines were "little frequented"—which may indicate that the people had either lost faith in their religion, or felt these new, less-grandiose temples lacked the spiritual weight of old ones left behind. (Anunciación, as a priest and missionary, may also have been simply denigrating the pagan religious rites.) Nor is there any mention of the earthen pyramids described by the Soto chroniclers—except when the Coosa *cacique* stops at an abandoned, overgrown mound on the way to fight a battle, and climbs it to enact a war ceremony on what is obviously a sacred, if no longer occupied, spot.

There also is the matter of palisades. Anunciación says his party found walls built around most villages, whereas Soto's men mention none in the central Coosa area. Moreover, the walls in 1560 were apparently as crudely and hastily constructed as the houses and temples, as if there had been a rapid breakdown in the security of the region as traditional power bases collapsed, and individual villages fought among themselves, or were forced for the first time in centuries of High Mississippian dominance to fend for themselves. Anunciación says these walls were only about the height of a man, and marginally effective as true defensive barricades, particularly when compared with the high, intricate palisades Soto's men describe at Chiaha, Ulibahali, and Mabila.

Clearly, some sort of disaster had occurred between the two expeditions that radically altered the population, agricultural base, cities, villages, and ceremonial centers. One obvious explanation is disease—planted either by Soto's men, or spreading westward from Cofitachequi.^ Greater Coosa may have been devastated by Soto's theft of food so near the winter, which could have led to mass starvation. Soto also kidnapped large numbers of the most able Indians to use as *tamemes* and servants, many of whom probably died. Moreover, there must have been a massive disruption in trade occurring after the annihilation of the Atahachi and other Mississippian kingdoms at Mabila, which plunged the entire region between central Alabama and the Gulf into an abrupt dark-age that utterly cut off Coosa from the sea—and from the tribute and trade it was used to receiving from its southern vassals.

Perhaps worst of all was the loss of Coosa's political and military supremacy in the region, caused by the emperor's degradation as a hostage, and also because Coosa may have lost a large number of warriors dispatched to aid Tascalusa at Mabila—if, in fact, he contributed soldiers to the battle,^ as Garcilaso insists. Coosa's military might also may have been strained by a sudden flurry of uprisings and wars waged by its tributary kingdoms, and by outside powers trying to take advantage of Coosa's disabilities and loss of prestige. This would have not only taxed Coosa's military capabilities, but also would have severely disrupted the flow of food and other tribute the central government depended on to maintain its population, fields of maize, and its army. As I mentioned earlier, Luna's Spaniards happened to arrive in Coosa as the *cacique* was preparing a punitive campaign against one of its subject states, the Napochies, a breakaway kingdom to the northwest, which had announced it would no longer pay tribute. With the help of the Spaniards, the Coosa *señor* was able to reassert his authority after a show of force—including a blast from a Spanish arquebus in front of the main Napochie city. Yet Coosa's domination over even this close-by kingdom seemed, by 1560, tentative at best.

Our final glimpse of Coosa comes seven years after Sauz's foray, when Juan Pardo in 1567 came marching across South Carolina and over the Blue Ridge Mountains to arrive at the Indian town of Satapo, on the banks of the Little Tennessee River, north of the modern Georgia state line in Tennessee.^ There Pardo's men found houses painted with images of pale men on horses carrying lances and swords. One of Pardo's party, Juan de Ribos, later testified that he saw in this same village samples of Spanish arms, mail, and clothing, possibly collected when Soto marched through these mountains. Or they were carried there from somewhere else, perhaps even as booty from Mabila, where Soto lost a great deal of equipment amidst ashes and fire.^ It was during his stay in Satapo that Pardo was dissuaded from continuing onward in his efforts to reach Mexico, being warned that "a grand *cacique* who was called Cosa [Coosa]" was organizing an ambush to the south, composed of several kingdoms—including Satapo, Coste, and Chiaha. This suggests that as late as 1567, Coosa's ability to influence polities on its northern flank remained intact enough for them to spearhead a military coalition against a common enemy. It also tells us that by now, with a third Spanish army on its way, the Coosa leadership was scrapping the policy of cooperation it had used to deal with Soto and Sauz, and was now opting for war. In a final reference to Soto, one of Pardo's soldiers claimed to have later spoken with a Portuguese pilot named Almeydo, who told him he had traveled inland hundreds of miles, supposedly to the place where Soto had died.

After Pardo's unsuccessful probe into Coosa's northern flank, there were no more European expeditions to the Coosa region until almost a century later, when the British at Charleston began exploring the interior in the 1670s. By that time, the Coosa glimpsed by Soto and Luna had disappeared completely, their cities abandoned, and the civilization of the Mississippians a distant and fading memory of the Upper Creeks, their descendants.

✤ 29 ✤

Tascalusa's Fire

AS SOTO HEADED SOUTH, King Tascalusa of the Atahachi weighed his options about what to do with these powerful, deadly strangers moving toward him, with the inevitability of a tornado gathering to vent its fury on a hot Alabama afternoon. Yet Tascalusa probably knew more in advance about the strangers than most Mississippian rulers because he may have already met a European—a Greek named Doroteo Teodoro (also called Don Teodoro). Thirteen years earlier, Teodoro had become a castaway on the coast to the south, during the desperate voyage of Pánfilo de Narváez from Florida across the Gulf of Mexico. Cabeza de Vaca explains how he had disappeared when Narváez's tawdry fleet sent him to fetch water in the vicinity of Mobile Bay. Nothing was known about his fate until the Indians showed Soto a *puñal*—a small dagger—that belonged to the Greek, who had apparently lived for a period of time in the Atahachi town of Piachi. Whether or not Tascalusa met Don Teodoro is unknown. But it seems likely the king would have at least received a detailed report about him—and about the Spaniards he came with. But this information would have been very misleading, since Narváez's shabby fleet and emaciated army hardly provided an accurate example of Spanish might. Tascalusa also may have received sketchy reports about Narváez's routing by the Apalachee in Florida; and, over the past few weeks, about Soto's largely peaceful march from Chiaha—all of which may have contributed to the course of action this king was about to take in regard to his approaching visitors.

By all accounts, Tascalusa was an enormous man. Elvas says he was "very tall of body, large limbed, lean, and well built." Ranjel-Oviedo compares him to a man in King Charles's personal guard called Antonico, apparently famous in Spain for his size and height.^ Even the terse Biedma says it was the opinion of most that "he was a giant." Garcilaso, who tells us Tascalusa was about forty years old—roughly Soto's age—adds that this king was so huge that when Soto ordered a saddle horse brought for him to ride, none could be found big enough to carry him. He had to settle for one of Soto's larger packhorses.^

There is evidence that the Atahachi dynasty of Tascalusa had been ruling southern Alabama for only a short time, perhaps two or three generations. This comes partly from archaeological clues, which suggest that most of central Alabama was dominated until about 1450 by another powerful empire, this one centered on the Black Warrior River near modern Tuscaloosa. The capital of this aboriginal empire was one of the largest cities built during the six centuries the Mississippians flourished in North America. Known today as Moundville, because of its twenty large, flat-topped mounds, this great city held at least three thousand people at its height in the thirteenth and fourteenth centuries, and perhaps ten thousand more in villages and towns in its immediate vicinity.^ Beyond this, Moundville's influence probably extended the length of the Black Warrior, and to parts of the Tombigbee and Alabama Rivers, where "colonies" containing Moundville-style pottery and artifacts have been unearthed in several sites.^ Inexplicably, a century before Soto's arrival, Moundville had suddenly collapsed—possibly because of a military defeat by the Atahachi. Their decline was so rapid that this magnificent city is not even mentioned in the chronicles.

The Atahachi had been at their chief city long enough, however, that when Soto came through, Tascalusa greeted him sitting on a balcony perched on the side of a pyramid, the sort that would have taken at least two or three generations to build. Yet Ranjel calls this a "new town," perhaps meaning that this capital was considered "new" by the Indians because it had usurped and replaced the more ancient capital of Moundville.

According to Garcilaso, the Atahachi displayed the military vigor of a young kingdom in a phase of conquest and expansion. Indeed, the Inca insists that the *cacique* of Talisi—where Soto met Tascalusa's ambassadors—was then in the process of switching allegiance from Coosa to the Atahachi.^ None of the other chronicles mentions much about the politics of the Coosa-Atahachi frontier, though eyewitnesses make it clear that Talisi marked the end of Coosa's influence in the south, since it was here they released the Coosa emperor. Tascalusa's authority in the area is also conspicuous in these accounts since his son, and not an anonymous messenger, came to meet with Soto.

Our eyewitnesses make it clear the Atahachi king enjoyed considerable power and authority in the area, even if we compensate for the fact that the chroniclers may have exaggerated his might to explain away the approaching debacle at Mabila. All of the chroniclers devote considerable space to playing up the wealth and regality of Tascalusa, describing the hundreds of servants and retainers who "gathered around him" when he held court, "so that they formed a courtyard and open space where he was." Among his retainers was a nobleman, "a very graceful Indian on foot," who always stood in front of the king "with a sunshade, on a pole." Elvas says this sunshade, "which was the device he bore in his wars," was made from deerskin that "from a distance it looked like taffeta, for the colors were very perfect."^ Tascalusa held audiences seated either on or below a balcony "made on a mound," and situated on one side of Atahachi's main plaza, where the king sat on high cushions.^ He was crowned with what Ranjel calls "a certain headdress like an *almaizar,* worn like a Moor," and "a *pelote* or blanket of feathers down to his feet." In sum, says Soto's secretary, this gigantic Mississippian king in all of his trappings conveyed "an appearance of great authority." Elvas adds: "He was greatly feared by his neighbors and vassals," and was "lord of many lands and many people."

Little is said about the city of Atahachi itself, other than it had at least one mound and a plaza. According to Garcilaso, it was too small to quarter the entire army.^ But all the chroniclers agree that the area around the city and along the Coosa River was well-populated and extensively planted with maize and other crops. There also is little said about the role the military played among the Atahachi, though events would soon reveal that Tascalusa had at his disposal a large and highly disciplined group of warriors. It's likely the Atahachi had developed a well-organized warrior class, given the speed and sophistication with which their army was about to be mobilized, and the attention to detail evident as the Indians stored weapons for the upcoming battle, made repairs to fortifications, and issued orders to troops perhaps numbering in the thousands.

✛   ✛   ✛

Soon after Soto entertained Tascalusa's son at Talisi, the king launched preparations for what he hoped would be a daring surprise attack—one as brilliant, and audacious, as Pizarro's unexpected assault against Atahualpa at Cajamarca. The Indians felt a great deal more confident than the tiny band of *cabalgadas* had in Peru, however. For Tascalusa apparently had at his disposal thousands of warriors to launch his assault. He was also defending his own country, not invading it.

How, exactly, the Atahachi readied themselves for their assault is only vaguely apparent from the sketchy descriptions in the chronicles. Garcilaso claims that Tascalusa had been planning to kill the Spaniards at Mabila for a long time, and that "for this purpose he had assembled the warriors that he had there, not only from among his own vassals and subjects but also from the neighboring and outlying [provinces], so that all might enjoy the triumph and glory of having killed the Castilians and might have their part of the spoils that they carried. Those who were not his vassals had come on this condition." If this is true, then Tascalusa's effort went far beyond his own realm. It also means the Indians in this part of the South were sophisticated enough to organize what amounts to a grand Mississippian alliance, setting aside their own rivalries and wars to join like the ancient Greeks at Thermopylae to fight their common enemy. It also makes the outcome of their effort much more devastating, since the massive losses suffered by the Indians at Mabila would have impacted not just the Atahachi, but kingdoms and polities across the entire region—perhaps as far away as Coosa and Chiaha.

None of the eyewitness chroniclers gives the slightest hint of a grand Mississippian coalition. Elvas suggests that the preparations for the attack were made hastily, triggered not by a long period of strategizing, but because Soto angered Tascalusa by detaining him in Atahachi. According to Elvas's account, a Spanish scout sent ahead to investigate the situation at Mabila informed the governor that Tascalusa's soldiers had begun arriving only a day or two before the Spaniards were to arrive at the city, and that "they had made great haste to strengthen the stockade" around Mabila.

Other evidence exists that soldiers from distant Indian polities may have participated, though it's circumstantial. For instance, there is the Spanish weaponry Juan Pardo found in the Tennessee town of Satapo in 1567, which could only have been captured in a battle where the Spaniards were at a disadvantage, since Soto was not in the habit of voluntarily giving weapons to natives. Possibly, warriors from Tennessee fought at Mabila—the only large-scale battle waged that summer between the Spaniards and the Indians—and returned home with swords and lances as war trophies. We also know from Juan Pardo's accounts that High Mississippian kingdoms had the capacity to form large regional confederations, given Coosa's alliance of vassals and neighboring states assembled to drive out Pardo and his small band of explorers.

Whatever happened, it's clear the Atahachi had developed a high level of organization in warfare, capable of readying a large army on a moment's notice. As we'll see, the strategies used by the Atahachi, and the skill and innovation they would show during the battle, suggest this sort of attack was not entirely impromptu for Tascalusa's people. Moreover, the king's tactics suggest that he knew something of his adversary, and how the Spaniards would behave. For instance, Tascalusa seemed to know that it was Soto's style to enter a new city first with just a few men, as if to prove his boldness. He also seemed to realize that the Spaniards had grown careless in the months since they fought their last battle against the Apalachee—and that they could probably be lulled into a false security with food, drink, women, and a promise of obedience.

✢   ✢   ✢

Watching his men entertain the Atahachi ambassadors at Talisi, Soto probably was thinking ahead to an easy march through what appeared to be another cooperative Mississippian kingdom. With little prospect of finding gold or other treasure, the governor's first impression of Atahachi was relief that it was reportedly rich in food and well-populated, in case he decided to form a coastal colony, or to bivouac his men there during the coming winter. My guess is he was thinking more about his impending contact with Francisco Maldonado and the fleet than with his reception by yet another Indian nation. Carefully considering what to announce to the outside world about his seventeen-month sojourn in *La Florida,* he may even have taken a moment to smile, realizing that he might not have found any gold and silver, but he did have chests of pearls, an intact army, knowledge of a sophisticated culture and heavily peopled regions, and vast territories he had yet to explore—which might yet yield great quantities of precious metals.

Tascalusa's son personally guided the Spaniards from Talisi to Atahachi, traversing a roadway that Charles Hudson says left the Childersburg area and headed almost due south, following the east side of the Coosa River.^ This took the army through a lightly populated area of small villages—and, according to Luna's party in 1560, a region heavily forested. Though no chronicler mentions a crossing, Hudson says the army must have forded the Tallapoosa River at some point, since Tascalusa's chief city was probably on the southern bank of the Alabama.^ Hudson places the Atahachi capital at the Charlotte Thompson Site, near Montgomery, or on one of several other mid-sixteenth-century sites arrayed in a tight cluster near where the Coosa and the Tallapoosa join to form the Alabama. Archaeologically, these sites contain mounds, city layouts, and artifact styles similar to patterns found at Moundville,^ indicating a past connection with that society, though by 1540 Moundville itself had ceased to be a factor in the region. There also is a second style of pottery prevalent among the mid-sixteenth-century artifacts, which archaeologists call the Shine II culture, found throughout the lower Tallapoosa valley, and up the Coosa into Georgia. These artifacts suggest at the very least that this area was a buffer region between large Mississippian entities, one to the north, probably Coosa, and Moundville to the west before its collapse. It also suggests that these Indians were once vassals or trading partners with Moundville, or possibly descendants of Moundville colonists who settled in the area and retained older traditions of pottery and cultural styles, while developing styles of their own Shine II culture. But this is just more speculation. Trying to construct a history of a long-departed people based on how they manufactured a few pots, figurines, knife blades, and ceremonial pyramids would be like digging up a half dozen ruined towns and homesteads in Greece and, knowing nothing more about ancient Greek art, language, or politics, trying to reconstruct, say, the political and social history of the Greeks leading up to Peloponnesian War.

+   +   +

Soto arrived in the Atahachi capital—which was also called Atahachi—on October 10, when the leaves begin to turn in central Alabama, and the air is comfortably cool. His meeting with Tascalusa is described in detail by all the chroniclers, though what they write must be viewed with some skepticism, since these men are describing the prelude to a major military embarrassment. This gave them every incentive to puff up the power and majesty of an enemy that nearly crushed them. Even the usually reticent and succinct Luis de Biedma inserts at least a trace of hyperbole in his description of Tascalusa as a "giant"—and later in his claim that the Atahachi army numbered five thousand warriors. This may be true, though Ranjel tells us the number was a more believable three thousand plus, and Elvas some twenty-five hundred.^

According to Elvas, Soto first dispatched his old friend, Luis de Moscoso, with fifteen men to meet the Atahachi sovereign in a scene that seems lifted directly from accounts of Soto's meeting with Atahualpa eight years earlier. Moscoso found the king dressed in his turban-crown and his brilliant feather cape, and sitting in state before his pyramid, ensconced on his throne of two cushions, surrounded by retainers and soldiers. Galloping up on his Spanish mount, Moscoso "talked with him," but seemed to get little response from the haughty king. This prompted Moscoso to put on a show of horsemanship, ordering his men to charge their horses in front of Tascalusa, "turning them from one side to the other, and at times toward the *cacique*."

Still paying him no mind, Tascalusa "with great gravity and unconcern from time to time raised his eyes and looked as if in disdain," which is exactly how Atahualpa had reacted to the young Soto's charges and flourishes at Cajamarca. Even when Soto arrived, Ranjel and Elvas tell us the Atahachi king remained in his regal pose, refusing to rise even after the governor dismounted "and went up to him." The entire time, says Ranjel, Tascalusa remained "quiet and composed, as if he were a king, and with much gravity."

Soto then either embraced Tascalusa, took him by the hand, or simply stepped up to him, depending on whose account one believes. He then spoke with him before settling down to a feast provided by the Indians, and an evening of entertainment. Ranjel recalls that the Atahachi danced "well in the way of the peasants of Spain," with Biedma saying that the Spaniards, too, "made much festivity," organizing jousts and horse races—though Tascalusa "seemed to think little of all this."

When the festivities were over, Hernando de Soto confronted the Atahachi king with his usual demands "to give us Indians to carry the burdens"—and, of course, women. True to form, Tascalusa "responded that he was not accustomed to serving anyone, rather that all served him before." To which Soto responded that night by ordering the king detained and put under guard in the palace the Atahachi had provided for the governor. Tascalusa, says Ranjel, "scoffed at such a decision, being lord, to give him so suddenly a restraint or impediment to his liberty." Like Elvas, Biedma suggests that it was this arrest that triggered Tascalusa's resolve to launch the attack at Mabila, and "the ruin that afterward he inflicted on us." Indeed, it was on the very next day that Tascalusa began the first part of his strategy by handing over four hundred men to serve as *tamemes,* while putting off Soto about supplying females and food—which he insisted he would provide at one of his other cities, called Mabila. There, said the king, brilliantly playing his deception, he would provide the Spaniards with one hundred women, "and those which they most desired."

✢ ✢ ✢

The next day, Soto and the army departed Atahachi, with the gigantic Tascalusa mounted on Soto's largest packhorse, still a prisoner, and dressed up gaudily in a crimson Spanish cape. For six days they marched along the Alabama River through the heartland of Atahachi, passing through fields and villages, including Piachi, a "high town, upon the bluff of a rocky river," where the Spaniards were given Don Teodoro's dagger. In Piachi, there also was an incident that must have hardened Tascalusa's resolve—if any hardening was needed. As the army moved to cross the river, a band of local Indians killed two Spaniards, one of them a member of Soto's guard^—the first casualty we know of since southern Georgia. Predictably, Soto was furious, and immediately demanded that Tascalusa bring in the culprits responsible, or face punishment by torture. "In a fit of anger," says Biedma, Soto "treated the *cacique* badly and told him he was going to burn him unless he gave him the Indians who killed the Christian." Tascalusa haughtily replied that he would turn over these Indians at Mabila—even as he was dispatching a messenger to Mabila "to assemble there all the warriors whom he had in his land."

According to Garcilaso, the death of the two Spaniards at Piachi, and Tascalusa's angry response, also convinced some of Soto's men that the Atahachi king "was not as true and loyal as he pretended to be." This was why Soto dispatched the two scouts with some of Tascalusa's men to reconnoiter the highway between Piachi and Mabila, and to report back on the Indians' disposition at Mabila in supplying the porters, women, and provisions. Apparently, Soto made this move to assuage his own men's misgivings, assuming that the scouts would return and report all was well up ahead. If this was his intent, it misfired. For on October 16, one of the scouts rode back and breathlessly informed the governor that the Indians up ahead "were evilly disposed, because when he was there many men and many arms had entered the town." They also were working frantically at Mabila to reinforce the palisades around the city, and demolishing houses and clearing out the foliage around the walls, as if preparing for battle.

This news led to a heated meeting with Soto's alarmed senior officers. They advised him not to enter Mabila. Luis de Moscoso, for one, told the governor "it would be well to camp in the open field since the Indians were so disposed," particularly since the army at this point was not marching in disciplined ranks, but was spread out among the several villages and farmsteads in the area, "pillaging and scattering themselves." Soto listened to their warnings but as usual decided he knew best—behaving with the same reckless certitude that had gotten him in trouble before. He brushed off Moscoso and the others, telling them he was tired of camping in the open, and preferred to sleep in the house Tascalusa had promised him inside the city. He also told his men that he did not want to appear weak in front of the king and his warriors.

Thus he spurred his mount forward and shouted orders for a small unit of men and advisors to follow. These included a contingent of his guard, led by its captain, Cristóbal de Espindola; his senior advisors Luis de Moscoso and Baltasar de Gallegos; the interpreter Juan Ortiz; and Rodrigo Ranjel, the secretary whose skill with a sword was about to be proven.^ Several servants and retainers also accompanied them—two priests, a page, a cook, several of Soto's female slaves, and other soldiers and their retainers.^

Riding with the usual Renaissance pomp and majesty, Soto and his company—Ranjel says there were forty, Elvas says ten to twelve—soon came within sight of Mabila's high beam-and-mud-daub walls, arriving in front of its main gate about nine A.M. the morning of October 18, 1540. If the forty-year-old governor of *La Florida* paused momentarily outside the gates to reconsider his decision, or to study the defenses, or to take stock of what might lay before him, there is no record. But if he did, one wonders what he was thinking in these final hours before the battle that would transform the quest of this brash, heretofore highly successful conquistador from conquest into folly.

Approaching the entrance to Mabila, Soto was greeted by the local *cacique* of this town. He "came out to welcome him with many Indians playing music and singing." He also gave the governor gifts of blankets of marten skins. Soto, with his guard, then dismounted and followed his hosts, including Tascalusa, through the gates and into the city. Three or four hundred Atahachi were on hand to greet the Spaniards. Dressed in ceremonial feathers and body paint, they cheered and welcomed their guests as Soto and his company walked past long, whitewashed cabins topped in steep cane roofs, moving toward a spacious plaza that opened up just inside the gate. There Soto ordered some of his guards to stand watch over the horses, while he, Moscoso, Gallegos, Ranjel, Ortiz, Espindola, and a few bodyguards followed Tascalusa and local town officials to the place of honor at the head of the plaza.

✛ ✛ ✛

Biedma gives us a thumbnail sketch of Mabila as "a small and very strongly palisaded town" situated on a plain. "The pueblo," adds Garcilaso—whose description here is reasonably accurate, based on what archaeologists have unearthed in similar Mississippian towns in this area—consisted of approximately eighty large houses, and "was situated on a very beautiful plain and had an enclosure three estados high, which was made of logs as thick as oxen.* They were driven into the ground so close together that they touched one another. Other beams, longer and not so thick, were placed crosswise on the outside and inside and attached with split canes and strong cords. On top they were daubed with a great deal of mud and packed down with long straw, a mixture that filled all the cracks and open spaces between the logs and their fastening in such a manner that it really looked like a wall finished with a mason's trowel." The Inca says the stockades were reinforced with towers holding seven or eight men on top, and that loopholes and slits were cut into the walls for shooting arrows at attackers. There were also two portals leading in and out of the city—one to the east, and one to the west. "In the middle was a spacious plaza," he wrote, "around which were the largest and most important houses."

Mabila's location is yet another great mystery of Soto's route, even though it should be more conspicuous than most. After all, this is where the expedition lost a great deal of equipment to fire, and where there should be a prolific heap of trash, burned walls, and charred European artifacts—including obvious Soto markers such as half-melted crossbow tips, lance blades, bits of armor, and arquebus balls.

For years, scholars and local Soto enthusiasts assumed Mabila was located where John Swanton and the 1939 De Soto Commission said it was—just north of Mobile Bay, somewhere near the confluence of the Alabama and Tombigbee Rivers. Alabama archaeologist Caleb Curren still places Mabila in this general vicinity, among the cluster of sites near in southern Clark County, Alabama.^ Archaeologists have unearthed an abundance of sixteenth-century European artifacts in this area, particularly at a dig known as the Pine Log Creek site. The items include a brass candlestick, a brass holy-water container, an iron gun-barrel, fragments of a sword, a pike head, an iron bridle and cheek plate, and beads from Soto's era. The religious items, Curren notes, are particularly significant, since Elvas and Ranjel both mention that items used for Mass were lost to the fires at Mabila.

There are problems with Curren's hypothesis, however. First is the already-mentioned difficulty with Soto marching in the time allotted from Hickory, North Carolina, all the way to southern Clark County. There also is the question of portability of artifacts. Curren concedes that the Pine Log Creek Site is probably not Mabila itself, since there is no evidence of a battle. He suggests

---

*The archaeological evidence suggests that these "logs" in Mississippian cities were of a diameter considerably less than that of an ox. Garcilaso also claims the houses of Mabila held fifteen hundred people, which is too many. An estado is equal to five feet two inches.

that the artifacts might have been taken to the Pine Log Creek area as war trophies after the conflagration, where they were then buried with notables. This doesn't prove Mabila was nearby, however, since the "trophies" could just as easily have been carried a great distance. It's also possible that these artifacts originated not with Soto's *entrada,* but in shipwrecks along the Gulf coast. This may explain the presence of sacramental objects in an Indian burial site.

Charles Hudson and his associates also have had trouble locating a candidate for Mabila. They can only say where it *should* be in relation to their overall route^—in the vicinity of Selma, Alabama, some ninety miles north of Curren's Clark County locale. Hudson admits this is a weak link in his Soto itinerary, since there is no site in the area yet discovered that looks remotely like a place where a major Spanish-Indian battle was fought. So far, archaeologists working along the Alabama River near Selma have found several palisaded villages from Soto's day, though none has more than a scattering of European artifacts.^

✝   ✝   ✝

Wherever Soto was, he and his party soon found themselves having a good time, entertained by Indian dancers as Tascalusa and his *principales* chatted amiably, and everyone feasted and drank fermented beverages. According to the soldier-chronicler Alonso de Carmona, the dances were "performed by marvelously beautiful women, because as I have said those Indians are very well favored, and the women so much so that afterward, when we left that country and went to México, Governor Moscoso* took an Indian from this province of Mauvila,† who was a very handsome and graceful woman. She could compete in beauty with the most elegant from Spain who were in all México." Biedma says that there were fifteen or twenty women dancers, whose beauty was used "in order to dissemble" the Spaniards: to divert their attention from the secret preparations then underway beyond the plaza, and from Tascalusa, who quietly slipped away to join his generals as the mesmerizing dancers swirled and dipped.

Garcilaso describes what happened next, saying Tascalusa went to a hut where his aides were holding a council of war. "When Tascalusa was among his captains," writes Garcilaso, "and the chief men of his army, he told them that they must determine quickly . . . whether they would immediately cut the throats of the Spaniards who were then in the pueblo and of the others after them as they arrived, or whether they would wait until all of them had come." For some time, the council argued over which option was best, until Tascalusa,

---

*Soto, shortly before his death, named Luis Moscoso his replacement as acting governor.
†This town is known by numerous spellings, including Mabila, Mauvila, Mauilla, and Mavila.

rising to his full height, threw his considerable weight in favor of killing at once any Spaniards that came within their power. He then issued the order to his troops hiding in the houses around the plaza to attack Soto and his party immediately.

Eyewitness chroniclers report only that Tascalusa slipped away into a nearby house, and then refused to come out when Soto asked him to, telling the governor that "he would not come out of there and that he would not leave that town." Elvas says he then issued a warning: "[I]f [the governor] wished to go in peace he should go immediately and should not insist on trying to take him out of his lands and dominion by force." At this point, say the chroniclers, the Spaniards began to look around, realizing the houses were not empty, as they had assumed, but filled with Indian soldiers armed for battle. Ranjel says some members of the governor's guard first noticed things were amiss when they saw natives hiding bundles of bows and arrows "secretively in some palm leaves." This sent them rushing back to warn Soto, who must have frowned as he grabbed his helmet and strapped it on, while ordering his guard to fetch the horses so they could leave. Biedma says it was Cristóbal de Espindola who first noticed the houses around the plaza were filled with warriors, and were "ready for war."

About this same time, says Elvas, Baltasar de Gallegos was trying to grab one of Tascalusa's principal men to ask him to fetch his sovereign. As the man haughtily refused, Gallegos noticed there were Indian soldiers hiding nearby. This prompted him to draw his sword and cleave off the man's arm, spilling the first blood that day in Mabila.

The battle began moments later when the Indians answered Soto's repeated demands for Tascalusa's return by suddenly bursting out of the houses and swarming into the streets and the plaza of Mabila, shouting war cries and brandishing clubs, maces, and loaded bows. "Immediately," says Elvas, "the Indians came out," charging toward Soto's position, and leaping up to man the walls and the towers guarding the city. Depending on which account you believe, Tascalusa had hidden three thousand, five thousand, or eleven thousand warriors in the huts, which he now threw against Hernando de Soto and his small band of aides and bodyguards. They found themselves suddenly cut off from the city's gates, and from the rest of the Spanish army—which remained sprawled out across several miles along the Alabama River.

Soto and his party were fully armed, but found themselves ensnared in a situation very unfavorable to their style of fighting—trapped in a cramped fortress-town with their horses across the plaza, and masses of Mississippians surging toward them, eager to engage them using the close-in style of fighting they excelled in.

During the first confusing minutes of the assault, five Spaniards of Soto's guard were struck down by arrows and a crush of well-aimed blows from maces. The others survived this initial wave of attackers, though some were wounded, including Baltasar de Gallegos, who was struck repeatedly on the head by a young Indian warrior until the "blood flow[ed] from under his helmet." Soto, too, was hit with some twenty arrows, though none penetrated his heavy quilted armor as he hacked away with his sword.

As the Spaniards fought to free themselves and escape out the gate, two of them—Rodrigo Ranjel and Juan Méndez de Solís, a member of Soto's guard—managed to fight their way to two of the horses, tethered across the plaza. Solís was shot dead as he climbed into one of the saddles. But Ranjel, as he himself relates, managed to mount his horse and rear it up against the Atahachi. This caused the charging Indians to pause long enough for Soto to dash over to another mount and jump into the saddle.

Soto could have escaped the city through a nearby gate. But this was not his way. Instead, he turned abruptly back into the fray, blasting into the midst of the Indians to clear a path for the bloodied Gallegos and his bodyguards, using the old *conquista* tactic he was famous for—the sudden thrust forward into the midst of unarmored Indians. Miraculously, Soto, Gallegos, and most of the remaining guards escaped Mabila alive, battling their way to the gate, where they ran out into the surrounding field and raised the alarm among the soldiers then arriving on the outskirts of town. However, they were forced to leave behind a priest and some of Soto's servants, who holed up in a house, where they tried to defend themselves with a single sword.

As the governor and his party retreated in chaos, the Indians made a move that would later prove disastrous for the Spaniards—they invited the army's *tamemes* (porters) to join them. Having stopped not far from Mabila's walls, these Indians, some of them Atahachi warriors pressed into service just two days earlier, and some from as far away as Florida, responded eagerly to the defenders' request as they carried their loads inside the gates, helped each other strike off their chains, and grabbed weapons from the stockpiles in the city. They also rifled through the *entrada*'s baggage, grabbing weapons, clothes, and everything from iron pots to leather shoes. As soon as the *tamemes* were all inside, Biedma says the Indians "closed the gates of the town and began to beat their drums and to raise banners with a great yell, and to open our trunks and bundles and display from the top of the wall all that we had brought."

Out in the field, the Spaniards were in disarray as Soto, probably looking like a porcupine with arrows sticking out of his armor, galloped hard to the nearest soldiers, shouting furiously to them to arm themselves. Biedma says

the governor then organized a troop to encircle the town to prevent any Indians from escaping, taking an additional "sixty or eighty" men to form into four
squadrons so they could "assault the town on four sides," break through the
walls, and set the town on fire.

Elvas says the signal for this Spanish counterassault was the blast of an arquebus, which boomed over the Alabama plains as the four squadrons threw
themselves against the palisaded town. The Indians repelled this first onslaught, with the Spaniards pulling back in exhaustion, most of them so tired
from this unexpected combat after weeks of comparative inactivity that they
paused for a moment to assuage their "great thirst" by finding a nearby pond.
But when they bent down to drink, they saw "it was tinged with the blood of
the dead" from their initial attack, flowing from a creek that first passed
through Mabila.

After this brief pause, the Spaniards attacked again—and again, as this give-
and-take of Spanish attacks and Indian parries continued for some time. Elvas
says the Indians "fought with so great a spirit that they drove us outside again
and again." Ranjel adds that at one point the Indians even tried an offensive
thrust outside their walls, rushing out as the Spaniards appeared to be falling
back. But this was only a ruse by Soto to try to draw them out, which failed
when the defenders quickly retreated back behind their walls. It was during this
action that Ranjel reports one of the army's favorite captains was killed, Soto's
in-law, Don Carlos Enríquez. He stopped to pull an arrow out of his horse in
front of the city walls, only to be struck by another in the neck between his
armor's collar and the bottom of his helmet. "Asking for confession," Ranjel
says, "he fell dead."

The battle continued well into that cool autumn afternoon, though as more
and more Spanish troops heard the alarm and rushed forward as reinforcements, it became clear the Castilians would prevail. Repeatedly, they threw
themselves against the walls, hacking with swords and axes against the plaster,
cane, and branches. Each time they were beaten back, only to return to hack
away more of the palisades. Finally, as the afternoon waned, they breached the
wall enough for a few men to rush inside, and to set the nearest houses on fire.

Instantly, the flames caught on the cane-and-thatch roofs as a deadly wall of
fire exploded across the city—and in a flash of heat and smoke shattered the
Indians' defense. Hundreds of Atahachi were trapped and obliterated by the
flames within minutes. The rest ran for their lives, either into the central plaza
or over the walls and into the fields outside. Either option brought the warriors
face-to-face with Spanish lances as Soto's cavalry stood ready to cut them
down in what devolved into a massacre like the slaughter at Cajamarca, when

Soto and his outriders spent the night of Atahualpa's capture killing Incas. But unlike the Peruvians, the Atahachi fought on until the cause became so hopeless a great number of them committed suicide by fleeing "into the burning houses, where, piled up one on top of the other, they were suffocated and burned to death."

Garcilaso describes a much more dramatic Battle of Mabila in what amounts to a fourteen-page mini-epic. Offering a profusion of details left out by the other chroniclers, he writes, for instance, that when Baltasar de Gallegos cut off the Indian's arm to start the fighting, he did not merely sever the poor man's limb. He slashed him "from the left shoulder downward," and "laid open his whole side, and with his entrails protruding he immediately fell dead." Likewise, Garcilaso describes Soto's escape as high melodrama, writing about the disarray of the Spaniards as the Indian army burst out of the houses and followed the governor and his party in hot pursuit. Attacking "our men rashly, even grasping the cavalrymen's lances," they inflicted serious damage on the Spanish army as the two sides engaged in what the Inca describes as a fantastic and courageous duel between two armies lined up in squadrons and crashing against each other again and again, until the Indians were forced to retreat back inside their fortress.

At this point, says the Inca, Soto ordered a "squadron of two hundred cavalry" to breach Mabila's gate, which they did after much effort, hacking it to pieces with axes as the Indians rained down stones and arrows from above. Breaking through, the Spaniards then rushed in, only to be confronted with a vicious house-by-house battle, which lasted four hours. During this phase of the battle, Garcilaso says Soto himself was shot in the buttocks as he lifted up "in his stirrups to throw a lance at an Indian." This exposed "the small unprotected space between the saddlebow and the breastplate, and though he wore a coat of mail, the arrow broke through it and penetrated some six inches into the left hip." Soto, notes the Inca, continued fighting "through all the rest of the battle, which was almost five hours, without being able to sit in the saddle, which was no small proof of the valor of this captain and of his skill in horsemanship."

As the fighting spread, Garcilaso claims that the wives and daughters of the Atahachi warriors joined in the battle, some of them grabbing weapons dropped by both Indians and Spaniards. These they turned on their enemy "with no less skill and ferocity than their husbands."

Meanwhile, says the Inca, the Spaniards lit a fire to clear a path to attack, which quickly surged out of control and spread across the city as the battle raged on "most fiercely and cruelly," with "no lack of blood, fire, and death, for the whole pueblo was filled with savage combat." Eventually, says Garcilaso, the Indians knew they had lost, but they kept fighting, wanting to take "vengeance for the death of their people; and, if they could not avenge them, they could at least see to it that all of them should die before becoming slaves of the Spaniards."

This battle, one of the bloodiest fought in five centuries of warfare between Europeans and Indians on what would become United States soil, ended at sunset with Mabila in flames, and heaps of Indians lying dead or dying as men moaned and coughed, and blood soaked the ground. One of the last of the Indians died as twilight came, and the first cool breeze of night blew over the battlefield. It happened as a group of Spaniards, themselves wounded, exhausted, and drenched in blood and sweat, chanced to look up on what remained of Mabila's smoldering ramparts. There they saw an Indian warrior wake up after lying unconscious for most of the battle. Reviving just as a line of fire was closing in on him, threatening to burn him alive, the man desperately tried to escape the flames by running up a bastion, only to look out onto the plain, where he saw heaps of dead Indians, and units of Spanish cavalry chasing down those still alive, and running them through with lances. Overwhelmed by despair, and what he probably knew was the end of his people and his civilization, this unnamed Mississippian quickly unstrung his bowstring and, before the Spaniards watching him could scramble up the wall to stop him, threw it over the branch of a nearby tree, wrapped it around his neck, and hung himself.

Book VI

Madness

✢ 30 ✢

Aftermath

ONLY GARCILASO, THE GREAT romantic, writes about the aftermath of Mabila with the proper blend of repulsion, pathos, and respect for the thousands killed—not because he was there, but because he understood the horror of war's aftermath both as a writer and a soldier, having served as a high-ranking officer in King Philip II's army. Claiming that one could not walk down the streets of Mabila "for the dead bodies," Garcilaso writes that "the fire consumed more than 3,500 souls in the houses . . . the fire cutting them off from the door and suffocating and burning them inside without their being able to get out . . . it was pitiful to see." Most of the dead, he says, "were women" who had come as wives "in obedience to their husbands, who had commanded them to do so. Others, who were single, said they had come at the importunity of their relatives and brothers who had promised to bring them so they might see some . . . great celebrations . . . after the death and destruction of the Castilians." Still other women had arrived as lovers, fiancées, and girlfriends to watch "their gallants and sweethearts . . . who begged and persuaded them to come and see the valiant deeds and exploits they expected to perform against the Spaniards."

Outside the smoldering walls the horrors continued, says the Inca, with the fields and streams around the city filled with the dead and dying. "For four leagues round about in the woods, ravines and streams," he writes about the day after the battle, "the Spaniards on going through the country found nothing but dead and wounded Indians, to the number of two thousand persons who had been unable to reach their houses. It was pitiful to hear them groaning in the woods, entirely helpless."

We will never know how many Indians died at the Battle of Mabila. Presumably, all the chroniclers exaggerate their tolls—which range from twenty-five hundred to eleven thousand—in order to make their own losses and stupidity look less awkward. Given what is known archaeologically about southern Alabama, the Indian army probably numbered no more than one to three thousand, even if allies from far away participated. This means that Elvas's body count of twenty-five hundred is not inconceivable, though my guess is the number of Indians killed was more likely in the upper hundreds, with a thousand being the upper limit.

Whatever the number, this was a devastating loss for the Mississippians of Alabama, and beyond. In a single bloody conflagration, the Spaniards had killed or wounded virtually every fighting man in the region, including Tascalusa's son and heir, "found lanced," and the king's aides, generals, and priests. As for Tascalusa himself, "nothing was ever learned of the *cacique*, either dead or alive," though he almost certainly perished, his body burned beyond recognition. Even more disastrous was what died with these Mississippian leaders—the centuries of collective knowledge about how to grow crops, build cities, worship gods, and administer the Atahachi government.

By the time the next Europeans visited southern Alabama nineteen years later, during the 1559–61 Tristán de Luna expedition, the only trace of Tascalusa's kingdom was a few survivors living among the ruins of an Atahachi city. Reduced to a society of primitive agriculturists quickly devolving into hunter-gatherers, they told the Spaniards that their country had once been great and powerful, until strangers looking like them had come and destroyed their crops and cities, and killed their people. The former kingdom of Atahachi proved so barren of food and essentials that Luna's small group of soldiers and colonists nearly died of starvation after their provisions were destroyed in a hurricane. Forced to search inland to find food, these Spaniards journeyed to a place called Nanipacana, where Luna found barely enough corn to survive the winter. Indeed, this region Soto had found populous and rich in food was now rapidly becoming a wilderness, with one of Luna's men reporting the forest was still "open" enough that "the cavalry might skirmish." It would not be long, however, before the clearings formerly tended by Atahachi farmers and hunters would become choked with small trees and underbrush—and, eventually, disappear as the great forests of the South reestablished themselves.

For Soto, the blood-soaked bodies and moans of the dying were all too familiar. Countless times before that dark evening of October 18, 1540, he had seen Indian bodies piled up in heaps—in Darién and Natá in Panama, under the volcanoes in Nicaragua's Great Valley, and in Peru at Puná, Cajamarca, Vilcas, and Vilcaconga. In fact, the morning after the battle, Soto was far more concerned about his own dead and dying. All that night, as Soto grimaced in pain over his own wound in the buttocks^—if, in fact, Garcilaso was right about the governor being shot—his men brought in Spanish bodies. By the light of several massive bonfires, built to keep the wounded warm, he could probably see them laid out side by side on the grass, the dead men's faces turning pale and gray-white—a gruesome testament not only to the ferocity of the battle, but also to the blunder made by Soto in going into Mabila in the first place.

According to the chroniclers, the total number of Spaniards killed at Mabila was between eighteen and twenty-five.^ Among the corpses was Don Carlos Enríquez, the husband of Soto's niece, known as a conciliator and calming force in the army who would be sorely missed over the coming months. Also laid out was Captain Diego de Soto, the governor's nephew, killed when he tried to avenge Don Carlos's* death by rashly plunging into the thick of battle as the Indians overran a Spanish forward position, overwhelming Diego de Soto and several men with their arrows, clubs, and maces. Other prominent soldiers killed that day included at least four *hidalgo* cavalrymen from Castile—Juan de Velez of Tordesillas,^ Juan de Espinosa of Ubeda, and Pedro Blasco and Juan Vázquez, both from Barcarrota, the small town near Jerez de los Caballeros where Soto gave away his niece, Isabel de Soto, in marriage to Don Carlos. The rest of the dead, says Elvas, were footmen, including a man from Badajoz that Garcilaso claims died of cowardice, "a common man, very uncouth and rustic, whose name has been forgotten." The Inca says this man turned his back and fled when the Indians launched one of their attacks, only to fall dead soon after he reached a place of safety, "without a wound or any sign of a blow . . . All the Spaniards said that he had died of fright."

✛   ✛   ✛

Near the bodies of the Spanish dead, the army's only surviving surgeon-barber^ struggled frantically to treat the wounded in a makeshift hospital set up among a scattering of huts the Atahachi had apparently built for the Spaniards to sleep in. Handicapped because the army's medicines and bandages had been destroyed in the fire, the surgeon and other helpers tore up the shirts of the dead "to make bandages," and used "the adipose tissue of the dead Indians" to treat and seal the wounds, "since we had no other medicine, because all had burned that day." Garcilaso adds that certain soldiers took on the grisly task of "cutting open the dead Indians and taking the fat to use as ointment." Apparently, this was a contingency occasionally resorted to on European battlefields before the modern era. According to legend, it also had been used at least one other time in the Indies, when Cortés supposedly melted Indian flesh at Tenochtitlán to seal up his brigantines during *La Noche Triste,* "the Night of Sorrow," when he was forced to retreat from the Aztec capital across the shallow lake encircling the city.

In all, Biedma says, "two hundred and fifty of us escaped with wounds, for we had seven hundred and sixty arrow wounds." This means almost half the

---

*Carlos Enríquez and Diego de Soto were brothers-in-law.

army was pierced by arrows, with the injured averaging three serious arrow wounds apiece.^ Within the next few days, at least thirteen, and as many as thirty-five more, injured Spaniards would die, raising the losses in the Battle of Mabila to roughly one in fourteen of Soto's army on the eve of the battle. The Indians also killed twelve horses, and wounded seventy more.^

Most devastating to the expedition, however, was the almost total loss of the army's baggage—including most of Soto's grand possessions, and the precious pearls of Cofitachequi,^ the only tangible sign of Soto's portable wealth in *La Florida.* "All the clothing carried by the Christians" was lost in the fires, reports Elvas. So were "all the clothes and ornaments and chalices and moulds for wafers, and the wine for saying mass," and a small store of wheat flour they had been "carefully and reverently" hoarding for Communion during Mass. Garcilaso says this raised a fine point of theology among the priests "as to whether or not they could consecrate bread made of maize." The assembled holy officers finally decided that what "the holy Roman church, our Mother and Lady, in her holy councils and sacred canons orders and teaches us, is that the bread shall be of wheat and the wine from the grape." This forced the priests to organize what the Spaniards came to call a "dry mass," which was conducted like a regular service, except that there was no Eucharist—a frightening omission for men who believed a Christian must have a formal Communion with God every so often to be assured a place in heaven, particularly when they had the blood of battle on their hands, and at any moment they might die.

Nothing in Soto's career so far equaled the blunder of losing his equipment and treasure at Mabila. In terms of lives lost, he had suffered losses of this magnitude before. He also had survived other embarrassments at being taken by surprise when he should have known better. But by allowing his *tamemes* to bring up the army's equipment so close to Mabila without an adequate guard violated one of the fundamental rules of warfare—that a commander never leaves his supplies exposed. This is particularly true for a battle Soto easily could have won without losing his equipment, or so many Spanish lives. He might even have been able to rout the army of Tascalusa without a serious loss of life among the Indians—whom he had hoped to preserve in adequate numbers to serve as slaves and laborers for a colony that just a few hours earlier had seemed a sure thing.

✝   ✝   ✝

For three or four weeks,^ the Spaniards convalesced in the fields around the smoldering city of Mabila, tending to their wounded, searching for food in nearby villages, and living in constant fear that the Atahachi or some other kingdom would launch a crushing attack against the greatly weakened army. Soto himself impatiently waited for his hip and perhaps other injuries to heal as he gathered intelligence about the country surrounding his makeshift camp, and whether Maldonado's ships had arrived off the coast.

The chroniclers offer differing accounts about whether or not the army found the ships. Elvas claims Soto did hear about them from Indians on the coast, who sent word to Juan Ortiz that Spanish vessels were at anchor six days' march to the south.^ This chronicler insists, however, that Soto did not contact Maldonado's fleet, worried that his men might desert him and return to Cuba. Accordingly, the governor arranged "with Juan Ortiz that he should keep still about it, so that the men might not oppose his determination [to stay in *La Florida*], and because the pearls which he desired to send to Cuba as samples had been burned; for if the news [of the ships] was noised about the men might desire to go to that land [Cuba]. And fearing that if news were heard of him, unless they saw gold and silver, or anything of value, it [Florida] would acquire such a reputation that no man would desire to go thither when people might be needed; consequently he determined not to give news of himself so long as he did not find a rich land."

According to Biedma, Soto *did* mention the ships to his men, but refused to let anyone make contact. But the reason Biedma gives has nothing to do with a fear of desertion. He says Soto vetoed the request because the army was low on provisions. "Many wished that the Governor would go to the sea," he writes, "because they [the Indians] gave us news of birgantines, but he did not dare" go to the ships, because "the month of November was already half over and it was very cold, and he felt it advisable to look for a land where he might find provisions in order to be able to winter." But this seems an odd reason. For even if there was a paucity of food in southern Alabama, it seems incredible that Soto would move off without contacting Captain Maldonado, or offloading desperately needed supplies that might have helped alleviate the lack of provisions. Nor does it seem likely that if the army knew about the ships, someone didn't slip away to find them, and beg passage to Cuba—something Maldonado says did not happen. Curiously, Ranjel does not mention the ships at all— a perplexing omission, given that Soto's secretary would have been far more likely to have known about them than Elvas, who was not in Soto's inner circle.

In the end, I suspect the real reason Hernando de Soto turned away from his ships was that he continued to believe in his ultimate success. Of all people, he knew that every major conquest had suffered setbacks, with most losing far more men and horses by now. Soto also was well aware that only the most iron-willed and tenacious conquerors were successful. His choice at Mabila, then, was probably not based on the availability of maize, or even on his own reputation, but solely on a simple question. How could he best insure the continuation and ultimate success of a quest he was obsessed with finishing at all costs? In the mind of this consummate gambler, the answer was obvious. As Elvas suggests, he had to ignore Maldonado and the fleet if he was to maintain the integrity of an army that was still overwhelmingly powerful by Mississippian standards—but could not afford to lose more men if it was to retain its edge.

Still, we are left scratching our heads at why Soto's men continued to follow him beyond Mabila. Only Garcilaso suggests there was any true dissension in the army, when he recounts the story about a half-baked mutiny led by
Juan Gaitan, the royal treasurer. In a story that rings as true as any in the Inca's
narrative, he describes Hernando de Soto after Mabila as facing an army
"frightened and disturbed" by "the incredible ferocity of the battle," with a sizable number of men now wishing "to leave the land and go away from it as
soon as they could." "A few" of these grumblers conspired to desert to the sea,
says Garcilaso, to look for whatever ships they could find. (The Inca makes no
mention of Maldonado.) Before they could leave, however, their plan was
leaked to Soto—who, Garcilaso says, disguised himself to investigate the allegations personally, making "the rounds at night as thoroughly as he could," and
at one point overhearing "the treasurer, Juan Gaitan, and others who were in
the hut with him saying that when they reached the port of Achusi"* they
would find ships and "go to Mexico or El Perú, or . . . return to Spain, because
they could not endure such a hard life to win and conquer such a poor and miserable country."

"This hurt the governor exceedingly," says the Inca, "for he understood
from those words that his army was disintegrating and that his men, in finding
a place to go, would all desert him . . . These things, considered by a man so
zealous of his honor as was the governor, produced in him hasty and desperate
resolutions." Thus, concludes Garcilaso, Soto "gave orders that they would
again go inland, and withdraw from the coast, so as to deprive the ill-disposed
of the occasion for . . . stirring up all his men to rebellion."

So according to Garcilaso, it was Soto's men, not Soto himself (who seldom
does anything wrong in the Inca's narrative) who forced their governor-
general to embark on a disastrous course. For had Gaitan and the others not
"betrayed his hopes and cut off the road to his ambition," says Garcilaso, then
Soto would have followed what the Inca insists was his plan all along—to establish a base and settlement on the coast before moving inland. As it was, the
adelantado was forced against his better judgment to plunge back into the unexplored frontier. The Inca adds pensively in one of his few overt criticisms of
his hero that Soto should have stuck to his plan anyway, and "put down that
mutiny by punishing its leaders." He says this would have frightened the others
into obeying him. Instead, relates Garcilaso, Soto allowed himself to be "governed only by his own passionate feelings . . . which he could not control and
govern . . . with the clear reasoning and unbiased judgment that serious matters
demand," a deficiency that would eventually cause "his own destruction."

*Ranjel calls this port Achuse.

✣ 31 ✣

The Wilderness

IN MID-NOVEMBER, WITH WINTER fast approaching, the army was finally able to limp its way inland in search of food to pillage. Moving slowly in the cold and damp, with heavy flakes of wet snow falling on black, sodden leaves, the once-grand army of Hernando de Soto now looked more battered, ragtag, and weary than ever. A few men still wore European clothes, rapidly wearing out since virtually every spare shirt, boot, and legging had been lost in the fire at Mabila. Most of the men now dressed themselves in native blankets and scraps of clothing. These included, says Ranjel, "a nobleman named Don Antonio Osorio, brother of the Lord Marquis of Astorga." Having an annual income of two thousand ducats back in Spain, he was now reduced to wearing "a doublet of blankets of that land, torn on the sides, his flesh exposed, without a hat, bare-headed, bare-footed, without hose or shoes, a shield at his back, a sword without a scabbard." "I could not help laughing," adds a sardonic Oviedo, "when I heard him say that a nobleman had left . . . the aforementioned income in order to go to look for this life at the sound of the words of Soto" and his "sweet talk."

When Soto left Mabila, he crossed a river, probably the Alabama, near Selma. He then led his army to the northwest, presumably marching through the rolling, pine-covered hills between this river and the Black Warrior, reaching its deep, blue-gray waters on November 17.^ The chronicles give no clue as to why Soto took this particular route. Most likely, the Indians in the area told him, through Juan Ortiz, that if the Spaniards wanted food, they should travel in this direction, toward present-day Tuscaloosa, Alabama. For as every Indian in the area knew, this had been the home region of the great Mississippian empire we now call Moundville. Soto was about a century and a half too late, however. For sometime late in the fifteenth century the Moundville culture had inexplicably collapsed, devolving into a much smaller post-

Mississippian polity that may have been the people Soto's chroniclers call the Apafalaya. Soto may even have passed through Moundville itself, though by that time this complex of twenty mounds, great plazas, moats, and irrigation channels was overgrown enough with trees and scrub that no expedition members mention seeing anything out of the ordinary—if, in fact, they came this way.^

By the time the Spaniards reached the first town in the province of Apafalaya, called Talicpacana, four or five days out from Mabila, they urgently needed food, having now marched four days on just two days' provisions. They found some corn at Talicpacana, but not nearly enough. Nor did the Apafalaya people in the next town, Mozulixa, make it easy for Soto to steal what he needed. As the *entrada* approached, the locals evacuated Mozulixa, situated on the east bank of a river—probably the Black Warrior—and crossed over to the opposite side in canoes. Taking with them their maize and beans, they promptly put it on display under mats across the river. It was almost as if they were daring the Spaniards to cross and take it as they massed warriors up and down the steep, muddy banks.

Reading the chronicles at this point, one senses an overwhelming weariness permeating every word, as if they cannot quite believe they are once again facing starvation, and confronting a band of enraged Indians brandishing longbows and spears, determined to make a difficult river-crossing potentially deadly. Worn down by eighteen months of marches, fording streams, snipers, and warfare, the men of the line must have stood on the east bank of the Río de Apafalaya wondering if they would ever escape this torment of cold, wet, hunger, and hostile natives. As usual, Soto came up with an energetic plan to save his frazzled men. Scouting up and down the riverbank on one of his horses, growing thin from lack of feed, he decided to build a *piragua* raft capable of transporting thirty *hombres* and several mounted riders, which he planned to launch secretly farther up the stream, beyond where the native sentries patrolled. Eating whatever food they could find, the Spaniards built the *piragua* in just four days, using nails forged from metal retrieved after the Mabila fire. When it was finished, Soto "ordered it to be transported one night a half league up stream" on "a large cart," where sixty men^ early that morning—including several on horseback—heaved this flat vessel made of planks and heavy logs into the cold, black water. Climbing aboard, they held their lances and swords ready so they could burst off the barge the moment it touched the other shore.

According to Garcilaso, the first two men off the raft were Diego García, son of the alcalde of Barcarrota back in Spain, and Gonzalo Silvestre, the Inca's erstwhile hero and probable informant. Supposedly, these two went rushing off the raft so quickly they soon found themselves alone "more than two hundred paces back from the landing place," surrounded by no fewer than eight thousand warriors! But of course they managed to hold off the horde anyway until help arrived, escaping without so much as a scratch—or so says Garcilaso.^

"The Indians," says Elvas in his more modest recollection of the landing, "perceived what was being planned, and those who were nearest ran up to forbid the crossing," shooting "innumerable" arrows. But as "this great canoe landed, they fled" through a stand of canebrakes. Soto himself then crossed over with a large contingent of cavalry, and secured the heaps of grain and dried vegetables on the shore, which the hungry men eagerly cooked and feasted on.

+   +   +

The next day, as snow and cold rain soaked the miserable army, Soto pushed on, seizing food in two more Apafalaya villages,^ including its capital, where the Spaniards captured the *cacique* as their "guide and interpreter." This Indian led the army onward through a sparsely populated region, probably in Pickens County, Alabama, and then across the modern Mississippi border. Again headed west, they were looking for an Indian people called Chicasa, well-known in the area for their prosperous fields of maize.

First the army had to cross yet another swift, frigid river on December 17, 1540—probably the Tombigbee. Once again, Indians opposed their passage, and had to be chased away after Soto's engineers built another *piragua*. That same afternoon, Soto's harried troops arrived in the Chicasa capital, "a small town of twenty houses." But the region itself was rich enough to feed the army for the remainder of the winter, the Indians having abandoned most of their maize, some of it still in the fields when they fled the Spaniards' approach.

Little is known about the Chicasa of the sixteenth century. The trader and explorer James Adair described them in the 1770s as being unusually large in size, fond of playing a spirited, Mississippian-style ball game, and so warlike that several forays against them by the French, supported by Choctaw allies, ended in crushing defeats. "The name of a Chikkasah became as dreadful, as it was hateful to [the French settlers'] ears," reports Adair, an assessment Soto, after spending a winter in Chicasa country, would have wholeheartedly agreed with. Recently, anthropologists have speculated that the Chicasa in the 1530s and 1540s were in the midst of a gradual devolution from a High Mississippian culture. According to the archaeological record, they had recently abandoned several medium-size cities with ceremonial mounds, and were slowly migrating from eastern Mississippi across the Tombigbee basin north toward Tupelo, where James Adair says they were living by the early eighteenth century. This makes it difficult to know where, exactly, Soto made his 1540–41 winter camp, since these Indians were living in more or less temporary villages lacking in mounds or other structures that might help us establish a location.^ This doesn't mean Soto scholars haven't tried to find Soto's camp—with one particularly innovative anthropologist named Jay Johnson talking NASA into loaning him a sophisticated imaging device he hoped would help him find buried archaeological material from the air. Unfortunately, these thermal sensors found nothing obvious. But Johnson intends to keep trying.

✛   ✛   ✛

Two centuries after Soto, James Adair said "the Chikkasah live in as happy a region as any under the sun. It is temperate; as cool in the summer, as can be wished, and but moderately cold in the winter. There is frost enough to purify the air, but not to chill the blood; and the snow does not lie four-and-twenty hours together." This description is reasonably accurate for the Mississippi of today, though anyone who has spent even a day there in July or August would be hard-pressed to call the climate cool. Nor would Soto's chroniclers have agreed with Adair's assessment of a Chicasa winter. Perhaps it was a last gasp of the so-called Little Ice Age—which climatologists believe descended on the Northern Hemisphere in the sixteenth and seventeenth centuries—but the winter of 1540–41 could hardly be considered moderate. Biedma says "more snows fell there than in Castile," and Ranjel remembered that "it snowed with as much wind as if they were in Burgos, and with as much or more cold." Elvas adds that the men "suffered great hardships and cold, for it was already winter, and most of the men were lodged in the open field in the snow before having any place where they could build houses."

At first, the Chicasa stayed away from the Spaniards, who were too exhausted and uncomfortable to make much of an effort to go after them. Then, in early January, the Chicasa *cacique* and several of his chief men arrived at Soto's camp on their own, bringing "one hundred and fifty rabbits and some clothing of their land, namely blankets and skins." This began several weeks of interaction between Soto and this unnamed Chicasa chieftain, who "came to visit him frequently," sometimes being conveyed from the Indians' camp a mile and a half away on a small horse Soto loaned him. At one point, after the Spaniards had settled in and built houses and more or less secured their camp, Soto "invited the *cacique* and certain of the principal Indians [to visit him] and gave them some pork to eat," the first known pork barbecue in Mississippi.

These friendly relations were a ruse by the Chicasa. For they were as incensed as any other Indian people over the outrages committed by the invaders, who had stolen their homes and appropriated their food supply, leaving them and their families to fend for themselves in the snow and cold during this unusually harsh winter. Elvas and Biedma both contend the Chicasa were just pretending to be peaceful so they could observe and analyze the Spaniards' defenses, and the disposition of the army.

The Chicasa's first attempt to strike back at the Spaniards came when the *cacique* asked Soto to help him rein in a vassal village, hoping to trick the invaders into dividing their army. Soto suspected a ploy, however, and remained "very watchful and prudent," so that the Indians "did not dare attack." Tensions continued to mount as the Spaniards, now well-fed and rested, if chronically cold, began to get restless, and the Indians became ever more desperate to avenge what must have been a season of dreadful suffering, as warriors watched their small children grow sick and emaciated, and revered elders could not stay warm, even under thick blankets of bearskins. At one point, a band of Indians sneaked in at night and tried to steal some of Soto's precious hogs, housed in "certain houses a crossbow shot away from the camp." Elvas insists their motive was an overfondness for pork, though more likely they were desperate for food. "Three Indians were seized in the act," says Elvas, "two of whom the governor ordered to be shot with arrows and the hands of the other cut off. In that condition he sent them to the *cacique*" as a warning. Apparently it worked, since no more is said about hog thievery.

In another incident, it was a party of Spaniards who rode secretly to the Indian camp to seize "some skins and blankets," probably because they were cold. This infraction so infuriated Soto he ordered the ringleaders executed—not because they had robbed from the Chicasa, but because they had violated his orders to leave the Indians in peace. Two of the plunderers were Soto's own servants—his page, Ribera, and his chamberlain, Fuentes—both of whom had probably lost their cold-weather clothes and blankets when Soto's household gear was burned at Mabila.

Before Chicasa, Soto had several times ordered severe punishments in the heat of anger, only to cool down and retract his orders. But this time, perhaps still smarting over the near insurrection of the army after Mabila, he did not relent, even when the expedition's priests and several senior officers pleaded for the men's lives. Undoubtedly, they would have been hung or beheaded if Baltasar de Gallegos hadn't quietly asked Juan Ortiz to mistranslate a statement by the Chicasa *cacique,* altering it to say that the men "were not guilty nor had they done any wrong to him; that if he [Soto] would do him a favor, he should let them go free." "The governor," adds Elvas, then "ordered the prisoners released."

All this was a prelude to what happened in early March, when the snows cleared and Soto decided to depart the Chicasa capital. As usual, he demanded the *cacique* supply him with porters for the march, to which the Indians re-

sponded with "such an uproar" late in February that Soto backed off the request for the moment, demanding instead that the *cacique* bring him *tamemes*
by March 4. The *cacique,* threatened with death should he fail to comply,
agreed, though Soto strongly suspected he would rather fight than give in. The
governor was so sure the Indians were "engaged in evil intrigue," that he assembled his men that evening and "said publicly . . . 'I will sleep armed and
[with] my horse saddled [this night].' And all said that they would do the same;
and he called to the maestro de campo," Soto's old friend from Peru, Luis de
Moscoso, "and told him that he should take extra precautions with the sentinels
that night."

Soto's instincts were correct. According to Ranjel, however, neither he nor
his men actually remained vigilant that night. "The Governor," he says, "lay
down undressed in his bed, and neither his horse nor any other was saddled,
and all in the camp lay down to sleep without care and unarmed." As for the
men assigned the watch, the dour Ranjel calls them "the worst of the worst"
riding the "worst horses in the whole army."

For weeks, the Indians had been planning an attack. "Each day," says
Biedma, "Indians came and went . . . who, under the pretense of being at peace,
came to see the manner in which we slept and how we guarded ourselves." This
made it easy for more than three hundred Chicasa to steal undetected into the
Spanish camp by twos and fours late that night, during the second watch just
after two A.M., carrying with them "some little jars in which they brought fire,
in order not to be noticed or seen." Garcilaso adds that "they brought faggots
made of a certain herb that grows in that country, which, when made into a rope
or thin cord and lighted, smolders like the match-cord of a harquebus, and
when waved through the air it bursts into flame that burned steadily like a wax
taper . . . They [the Indians] had twists made of the same herb on the points of
their arrows so as to shoot them while burning and set fire to the houses from
a distance."

The Indians, dressed in their feathers and masks and painted for war,
sneaked through the savanna-like meadows surrounding the camp, hugging the
shadows, and slipping in behind the sentries as they made their familiar rounds.
Barely breathing, and clutching earthen containers burning with the sweet
scent of the smoldering "herb," they approached the first huts of the sprawling
camp. There they listened for a moment to the silence of men sleeping, horses
grunting, and the first insects and birds of spring chattering and whistling.
Then a signal was given and the assault began, with the lead Indians touching
the straw roofs of the nearest huts with the smoldering ropes, and the Chicasa
shouting battle cries and "beating their drums."

Caught utterly by surprise, most Spaniards were driven "out of the houses without having time to arm themselves; and as they rose, maddened by the noise and blinded by the smoke and flame of the fire, they did not know where they were going nor did they succeed in getting their arms or in putting saddle on the horse; neither did they see the Indians who were shooting at them. Many of the horses were burned in their stables, and those which could break their halters freed themselves. The confusion and rout were of such a nature that each one fled wherever it seemed safest, without anyone resisting the Indians."

Only Soto succeeded in grabbing a lance and throwing a saddle on his horse, though he did not cinch it tight enough, and fell off his mount as he rushed over to lance the nearest Indian. The force of the blow knocked him backward with a thud onto the ground. Yet he did manage to kill his target—the only Chicasa who died that night.

Fortunately for the Spaniards, the Indians were so successful in their efforts to create chaos that they themselves were put off by the confusion, mistaking the horses escaping from the flames for an attack by lancers. Thus they abruptly broke off their assault, an action Biedma called "a great mystery of God," since "not a man of all of us would have escaped" if the Indians had continued to fight. As it was, the Spaniards' literally had been burned a second time as "the town was consumed with fire," taking with it fifty-seven horses, eleven Spaniards, and over four hundred of Soto's five hundred pigs. "If, perchance, any one still had any clothing left from the fire at Mabila," says Elvas, "it was now all burned up in that place; and many were naked as they had no time to snatch their jerkins." Even worse, the Spaniards had let the Chicasa get away, a disaster that now left the burned, bleeding, and mostly defenseless survivors terrified the Indians would return to finish them off. For some reason the Indians stayed away, however, giving the men a chance to recoup.

Typically, Soto's reaction to this catastrophe was to take immediate action. Ordering his men to move two to three miles away, to the Chicasa's now-abandoned winter hideout, he organized a hospital for the many wounded, and dispatched units of uninjured soldiers to chop down ash and other suitable trees to replace lances, javelins, and saddles burned in the fire. Keeping his stunned troops busy preparing for the assault everyone expected, Soto also "made haste to set up the forge, and they made a bellows from the hides of bears" to re-fashion metal blades, lance and crossbow tips, horse tackle, and shields.

Despite Soto's encouragements, however—which must have been wearing very thin by now—the Spaniards found themselves thrust into fresh miseries far worse than before the Chicasa fire. For it was still so cold on the broad plains of Mississippi in March that they had to build huge bonfires just to keep warm, as they spent the first few nights after the Chicasa disaster "turning from one side to the other without sleeping, for if they were warmed on one side they froze on the other. They managed to make some mats out of dry grass woven together," adds Elvas, "and placed one mat below and the other above. Many laughed at this contrivance, but afterward necessity forced them to do likewise."

Inexplicably, the Chicasa waited almost a week to renew their attack, coming "at the hour of dawn," as the sky turned light blue in the east, and birds migrating north filled the air with a wild cacophony of noise. They rushed Soto's camp from three directions, though this time, the Spaniards were ready. "The governor," says Elvas, "with great quickness, drew up his men in order in three companies, with some men staying back to guard the camp, and hastened to the attack." Chasing the Indians onto a flat plain, which favored their horses, the army soon routed the Chicasa, slaughtering many of them in a fit of pent-up rage, as the Mississippi dawn came up "bright and clear."

✛   ✛   ✛

It took two months for the 450 or so survivors of this fresh debacle to recuperate and rebuild as an effective fighting force. But they would remain forever weakened, and would no longer be able to operate with the overwhelming impunity of the days before Mabila and Chicasa—a reality Elvas says caused the Spaniards to be greatly "demoralized" as they tried to pick themselves up on that field in Mississippi. Yet still Soto convinced them to keep marching— though by now they had little choice, since Maldonado's boats were long gone from the bay far to the south, and to their back was a countryside either destroyed by the Spaniards, or lacking enough food for an *entrada* that still numbered, with all of its servants and porters, as many as seven or eight hundred people. They also knew that somewhere up ahead lay the Río de Espíritu Santo, which flowed into the Gulf of Mexico. At this point, it offered their best chance for reconnecting with the outside world.

Little the Spaniards did went smoothly in Mississippi, however. Just a few days later, as they headed northwest across the gently rolling hills of the north-central portion of this future U.S. state, following a trail that local Indians said would take them to an important empire on the Mississippi River, the Spaniards came upon yet another fierce band of Indians determined to block their progress. "Here," says Biedma, "something happened to us that they say has never happened in the Indies, which was that in the middle of the road where we were to pass, without having food to defend nor women to guard there, but rather only to prove themselves against us, they made a very strong barricade* of poles ... and about three hundred Indians placed themselves there, with determination to die before they relinquished it." Deploying his weary men in battle order, Soto charged this barricade, thinking there must be food or something there of value. However, after he routed the Indians, and lost as many as fifteen men now lacking decent armor, and suffered twenty-five or twenty-six wounded, he discovered the barricade was nothing more than a provocation.

Soto's travails were still not over. For as he and his bloodied men buried their dead and built slings to carry the freshly injured, he found himself plunging into yet another vast wilderness of the sort he had crossed in Florida, and in the Savannah River valley. In a forest composed of dense pines, some towering 150 feet, the Spaniards suddenly found themselves marching under a canopy that must have left the trail dark, gloomy, and cavelike—exceedingly humid by day and cold by night. Later, as their trail petered out into an uninhabited thicket, this aboriginal forest gradually shifted to a mix of hardwoods and pine, and later still, of thick swamps filled with towering cypresses, ferns, magnolias, laurels, rotting trees, and a rich variety of birds, lizards, snakes, and small mammals. The Spaniards were forced to swim across some of these swamps, though Elvas says the woods were mostly "passable on horseback," a small consolation to men once more facing starvation as their already scant food supplies ran out. Once again, they were forced to dig for roots, and to attempt to shoot whatever game was not frightened away by the movement of several hundred people. Only the knowledge that the army was fast approaching the great river, and another Mississippian kingdom where they hoped to find food, kept the men from giving up out of despair, or from launching another attempted mutiny against Hernando de Soto.

✢   ✢   ✢

On the morning of May 8, coming off a low bluff above the broad Mississippi River valley, the Spaniards finally broke out of the wilderness—and beheld below them exactly what they had been praying for: a medium-size town obviously Mississippian. Probably located near modern-day Walls, Mississippi,^† about thirty miles south of Memphis, this town contained at least one small mound, and was surrounded by fields of maize.^ Off in the distance, they

---

*Biedma's translator offers a footnote about the word *barricade,* saying "The term *albarrado* may refer to an earthen wall or trench, implying more than a simple wall of timber."

†The exact location where Soto sighted the Mississippi River is disputed. Other candidates include Sunflower Landing near Rena Lara, Mississippi, and Friar's Point, both a few miles south of Walls.

could also see a great gray ribbon of muddy water stretching nearly a mile wide. Eager to seize what food they could, Soto led a contingent of horsemen so quickly into the town, called Quizquiz, that he took it by surprise, and rapidly seized everyone they could find. Because the men were off working in the fields, these were mostly women, including the mother of the local *cacique*. Previously, Soto would have clapped these prisoners in chains and demanded the *cacique* and his remaining people bring the Spaniards food at once. But this time, "inasmuch as his men were ill and weary for lack of maize and the horses were also weak, [Soto] determined to pleasure [the *cacique*]" by freeing the women, "in order to see if he could have peace with him."

Releasing the women did not mollify the Indians. The next day they returned "with their bow and arrows with the intention of attacking the Christians," who lined up to fight, only to have the leaders of Quizquiz suddenly approach for a parley, "a crossbow flight from where the Governor was, near a stream." To Soto's surprise, six *principales* announced they were surrendering, explaining that they "had learned from their ancestors that a white race would inevitably subdue them; and that they were about to return to the *cacique* to tell him to come immediately to render obedience and service to the governor." The *cacique* then dutifully appeared, bringing pelts and a small cache of maize. He suggested that Soto march on to the river, where there was another town filled with maize, apparently affiliated with his own village. This all happened on May 8 or 9 as a prelude to the event Soto is best known for—the "discovery" of the Mississippi River. As I have mentioned before, Soto was actually discovering the inland portion of the river, the mouth having been sighted, mapped, and explored years earlier by numerous mariners and slavers.

If this had been the eighteenth or nineteenth century, and Soto had been a David Livingstone or a Meriwether Lewis, steeped in a culture obsessed with the romance of discovering new rivers, mountains, and lakes, we might have seen some indication that the adelantado cared even a little bit about what he was "discovering." But the truth is, the chroniclers report only that Soto and the army arrived at a "large river." What we hear about most on this supposedly auspicious day in American history is the relief of our eyewitnesses at finding large stores of maize in the second village of Quizquiz. For men more practical than romantic about matters of geography, all that really awed them about the river was its size, which seemed truly daunting to an army who somehow had to cross it. Ranjel says it was "a larger river than the Danube." Elvas describes it as being "a half league wide, and if a man stood still on the other side, one could not tell whether he were a man or something else. It was of great depth and of very strong current. Its water was always turgid and continually

Soto at the Mississippi, 1541

many trees and wood came down it borne along by the force of the water and current."

The other thing that impressed the Spaniards about the Mississippi was the appearance on its waters a day or two after Soto set up camp of an armada of Mississippian warships unlike anything any of them had ever seen. Sent out, they were told, by a large polity across the river called Aquixo,^ the chroniclers claim this fleet comprised some two hundred vessels arrayed in battle formation. Elvas describes them as "very large and well built," looking like "a beautiful fleet of galleys," with thousands of warriors "painted with red ochre and having great plumes of white and many colored feathers on either side [of the canoes] and holding shields in their hand with which they covered the paddlers." He adds that "the canoe in which the *cacique* came had an awning spread in the stern, and he was seated under the canopy." Other Aquixo notables also sat under colorful awnings, surrounded by men bearing longbows, arrows, and war clubs.

At first, the Aquixo *cacique* sounded as if he wanted peace with the Spaniards, though as usual this was a pretense for sending envoys to size up Soto and his army. Soon after, as the Spaniards built their camp, feasted on Quizquiz's maize, and began to build several *piraguas* to make their crossing, Aquixo's highly disciplined ranks tried to land and stage an attack—which they attempted more than once. Soto's crossbowmen were ready each time, however, with volleys of arrows that sent the beautiful ships back out into the river at a safe distance.

For the entire month Soto spent constructing rafts and resting his men, the fleet appeared nearly every day to challenge the Spaniards should they try to cross. But as the army regained its strength, these daily visits by the Indian armada grew less fearsome as the invaders began to realize that a culture capable of building such impressive vessels, and maintaining them in the river with such discipline, was as advanced as any they had seen in *La Florida*. Though hardly a replay of the resplendent Inca ship Bartolomé Ruiz had sighted years earlier off the Peruvian coast, which signaled to the world the existence of the Inca Empire, these Mississippian canoes inspired Soto's men with fresh hope that perhaps, after all they had suffered, the golden empire Soto had been promising might finally exist across this great river.

✢ 32 ✢

Last Chance

FOR NEARLY A MONTH, Soto's half-starved army rested under shade trees along the Mississippi. They feasted on local corn, and game fried in bear fat and corn flour—including a huge aquatic beast Elvas calls a " *'bagre,'* a third of which was head; and it had large spines like a sharp shoemaker's awl at either side of its throat and along the sides." This was, of course, a catfish, which the Spaniards caught on a hook. They undoubtedly ate it with squash, beans, and bread made of persimmons, relaxing in their makeshift camp of open-walled summer huts. Nearby, Soto's engineers had erected a primitive dry-dock, where they were constructing four flat *piragua* rafts to transport the army across the great river. Built with gunwales high enough to avoid being swamped in the current, and caulked with hemp and flax^ cut with tree sap, the vessels held up to sixty or seventy men, and their horses and baggage. The idea was to cross as quickly as possible, to avoid an extended battle with the Indians of Aquixo.

The *piraguas* were finished on June 17. Wasting no time, Soto dispatched a unit of scouts on mounts and on foot that very night to secure a beachhead on the opposite shore. Knowing that the Indians nearly always came out in their war canoes in midafternoon, the Spaniards sailed at three A.M. "Because the current was strong," says Elvas, "they went upstream along the shore for a quarter of a league and in crossing were carried down with the current of the river and went to land opposite the place where the camp was." Debarking without incident on a bank of hard sand, the *piraguas'* pilots and oarsmen quickly recrossed the river, transporting over the rest of the army, pigs and all, by seven or seven-thirty in the morning. This was a remarkable operation. For not only is the Mississippi swift and difficult to cross, but Soto also had to have built exceptionally large and maneuverable vessels to transport so many people and animals in just a few hours. It was worth it, however, to avoid a battle on the water with a native armada that probably could have decimated the army. Incredibly, not a single person was lost, nor a horse nor piglet, though Ranjel says the men all agreed "nothing so difficult could ever be offered them again."

The next day, a Sunday, Soto marched to Aquixo, unchallenged by the splendidly attired warriors in the war canoes, whose disappearance goes unexplained by the chroniclers. Moving on to another small town that had a canal connecting it to the Mississippi, Soto dismantled the rafts to preserve the precious nails before plunging on that next Wednesday into what Ranjel calls "the worst road of swamps and water they had seen in all of Florida." This was probably one of the naturally occurring backwater marshes choked with canebrakes that still exist outside West Memphis, Arkansas.^

A day later, Soto began searching for a kingdom called Pacaha, where Indians told him "there was gold." That same afternoon, the Spaniards finally reached dry ground, arriving in a heavily populated area dense with maize and "many walnut trees with soft nuts shaped like acorns." These were probably pecans. They also found "mulberry trees and plum trees . . . like those of Spain, and others gray, differing, but much better, and all the trees as verdant all year as if set out in gardens and in a clear grove." Now marching along a natural alluvial levee, the army was probably headed for the St. Francis River—and one of the largest Mississippian cities they had seen since Tascalusa's capital of Atahachi, called Casqui, most likely situated at a well-known site outside of Parkin, Arkansas.^

Archaeologists at Parkin have unearthed a Mississippian town built in the shape of a rectangle, enclosed by remnants of an earthen wall and a deep moat, and dominated inside by a twenty-one-foot pyramidal mound with a ramp large enough to drive a car up—a layout that corresponds closely to the Casqui described by Biedma. He says the town was "well palisaded and with a moat of water around it," and contained a sizable mound shaped like a pyramid, and several smaller mounds.^ On top of this mound, Ranjel tells us the *cacique* had hung "many heads of very fierce bulls" over the door of his *bohío,* arranged the way Spaniards "put heads of wild boars or bears at the doors of the houses of the hunters." These were, of course, buffaloes—which, some weeks later, scouts sent out by Soto would observe grazing in herds on fingers of the Great Plains stretching into western Arkansas.

In Casqui, the *cacique* seemed so anxious to please the Spaniards that he showered them with gifts of pelts and food, and ordered huts made available to the men. He even agreed to let Soto's priests erect a large cross on the central pyramid for the first time we know of since Ocute. Following the Spaniards'

Soto's Route Through Arkansas, 1541–42
(Hudson Route)

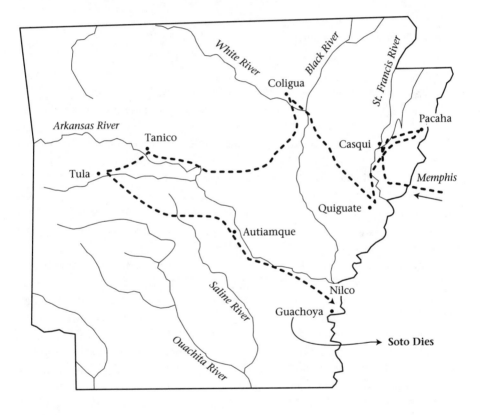

example, the Indians knelt to pray^—even as the *cacique* insisted Soto "was a man from heaven." In fact, the governor's alleged divinity gained considerable credence among the Indians when shortly thereafter, rain fell in great sheets to break a local drought so severe that the Casqui said their "children were dying of hunger."^ But Soto the god was unable to help when the *cacique* brought two blind men who begged to be cured. The *cacique* had a reason for ingratiating himself to Soto, however—he was at war. His enemy was the very Pacaha that Soto was searching for, whom he hoped the Spaniards would help him conquer.

Perhaps deluding himself that Pacaha was the sort of rich prize he had long been looking for, Soto agreed. He even ordered his men to restrain themselves in their treatment of Casqui's people, a standard *conquista* protocol when the Spaniards enlisted native armies to serve as their auxiliaries.

✛   ✛   ✛

Following his usual method, Soto began the conquest of Pacaha by dispatching messengers demanding the king there give himself up. But the sovereign of Pacaha had already fled when the messengers arrived. This prompted Soto to order his men to form up in a battle line and march on the city, probably located in a broad pasture near the Arkansas city of Turrel, not far from present-day Interstate 55.^ Blasting into Pacaha three days later, on June 29, Soto quickly seized the heavily stockaded but abandoned town, himself leading a troop of outriders to catch up with Indians reportedly fleeing from the city.^ Capturing several of these Mississippians, the governor sent them back as prisoners to Casqui, his ally. Elvas says this *cacique* was greatly disappointed when Soto refused them permission to kill the prisoners. This chronicler adds that another Spanish troop, paddling in canoes and led by Don Antonio Osorio, captured more Pacaha Indians trying to escape up the river. Several of these—"principally women and children"—drowned as they tried to swim and paddle away, and were swept under by the Mississippi's currents.

Little is said about the Indians of Pacaha, other than that they obviously were High Mississippian, and sustained a population probably numbering in the thousands. The next time Europeans came through here, during the 1673 expedition of Jacques Marquette, the region had reverted to wilderness, with almost no people.^ Soto's role in this depopulation is unknown, though archaeologists know the area had been heavily peopled for at least one thousand years before he came.^ Possibly, the drought mentioned by the chroniclers had something to do with the rapid demise of these people—or, perhaps, disruptions in the growing season caused by the Little Ice Age.

In Pacaha, Soto's chroniclers do mention an irrigation system built into the city's moats, which they say flowed from the Mississippi into a series of ditches and artificial ponds containing "many very good fish of different kinds." These included catfish, spadefish, and a fish "the size of a hog, called *'pexe pereo.'* " In Pacaha, Soto's men also found "many blankets, deer, lion, and bear skins, and many cat skins." Elvas says Soto's men snatched these up, because many of them "were still poorly clad" after the fires of Mabila and Chicasa. "From the blankets," says Elvas, "were made loose coats and cassocks . . . From the deerskins were also made some jerkins, shirts, leggings, and shoes and from the bear skins very good cloaks, for water would not go through them. They found there shields made of raw cowhide with which the horses were provided with armor." One can imagine what all this looked like, with Soto's men now more closely resembling Davy Crockett in his buckskins and moccasins than Renaissance knights and infantrymen.

Otherwise, the "plunder" at Pacaha was minimal. Of course, there was no gold, the only items of value being some of the richer furs, a few beads made out of seashells, "and some corn that there was in the town." Soto gave most of this plunder to the *cacique* of Casqui, with Biedma saying these things were "of much wealth for them." The Spaniards also must have found some of the lovely, haunting pottery archaeologists and pot hunters still dig up in Pacaha and Casqui—water casks fashioned into the heads of men and women; statues of warriors; gorgets etched with scenes of warriors carrying the heads of enemies, and ballplayers running; and pots colored in bright red swirls and topped with handles shaped like rabbits, turtles, and birds.

Only Ranjel insists this was a rich country, telling us that Pacaha, Casqui, and Aquixo were "the best towns that they had seen up to then, and better palisaded and fortified, and the people of more beauty, except for those of Cofitachequi." Possibly, Ranjel's praise comes from the fact that the expedition had not seen anything this good for several months—at least since Atahachi—which must have given the dispirited men at least a tinge of hope things might improve.

Settling into the heavily fortified city, and in two other fortress-cities nearby, Soto bivouacked the army at Pacaha for nearly a month. He used it as a base for a somewhat desperate series of forays north, south, and west to reconnoiter the country in search of gold and powerful empires. Biedma also suggests Soto sent a troop out looking for the "South Sea"—the Pacific Ocean—having no idea how much farther *La Florida* stretched to the west. (If this sounds far-fetched, keep in mind that if Soto still had on hand any sort of astrolabe or geographic measuring device, and was able to calculate his longitude at Pacaha, he would have come up with a line that in Nicaragua places one just off the coast, a few miles into the Pacific Ocean.) Biedma accompanied one of the forays to the northwest, where the Indians of Casqui told them there "were large villages through which we could go. But we traveled eight days through an uninhabited land of very great swampy lakes," reports this chronicler, "where we did not even find trees, but rather some great plains, where was grass so tall and so strong that even with the horses we could not force our way through it."^ Biedma adds that they found a tribe called the Calusi living on this prairie, a hunter-gatherer people living in portable *"ranchos"* made of sewn grass and poles. Garcilaso describes yet another foray into some mountains to the west,^ where Indian merchants near the Mississippi claimed the Spaniards would find salt, which the Spaniards were in need of—and "much of the yellow metal they asked for." Indeed, they found both, returning to Pacaha after eleven days carrying "six loads of rock-salt crystals." The yellow metal turned out to be copper, however, which Soto might have gone on to investigate, except that the scouts reported the land was "sterile and thinly populated."

While these scouting parties were out, the cacique of Casqui abruptly left one day from Soto's camp without permission—something the Spaniards frowned upon. This happened, moreover, when the cacique of Pacaha was making overtures of peace to the Spaniards from his hiding place deep in swampland near the Mississippi. Furious with Casqui's departure, Soto decided to ally himself with Pacaha, and agreed to organize an attack on Casqui's capital. But no sooner had he ordered his men to prepare for battle, than Casqui showed up again, bringing with him not only gifts, but an entertainer Ranjel describes as a jester. "Saying and doing witty things," says Ranjel, this jester "gave occasion for much laughter to those who saw him." Soto's secretary also tells us Casqui delivered a spirited speech telling Soto that he had meant no offense, and asking him why the Spaniards "wish to destroy me, your friend and brother?"

"My Lord," Ranjel reports him saying, "now that God heard us, by means of the cross; that the women and boys and all those of my land knelt down to it to ask for rain from the God who you said suffered on it, and he heard us and gave it to us in great abundance and saved our cornfields and seed beds; and now . . . you wish to destroy those children and women who love you and your God so much? Why do you wish to use such cruelty without our meriting it?" Soto, says Ranjel, was uncharacteristically moved by such an outpouring, and supposedly wept in front of his men. The governor explained that he had meant to destroy Casqui only because he ran away, and had showed what seemed to be excessive "pride"—which, Soto insisted, "our God most abhors, and for which he punishes us most." Now that Casqui had returned, Soto (whose own expansive pride sounds as undiminished as always) said he would forgive the wayward *cacique*, explaining that "if you believe what you say, God Our Lord commands that we love you like a brother." Soto emphasized that what he said was not a lie, telling Casqui—presumably with a straight face—that to "lie is a very great sin among us."

That night, Hernando de Soto invited both Mississippian kings to supper, and demanded they make peace—a move that might have been motivated by respect for the two *caciques* as Christian "brothers," though more likely, Soto was growing weary of their inter-Mississippian conflict, and wanted to end the fighting so he could concentrate on reconnoitering the area, and figuring out what to do next. Proving that American Indians could be as petty as Europeans, however, the two native leaders used even this occasion to bicker. Pacaha insisted he should sit beside Soto in the place of honor, because his family's lineage was more ancient and revered. Casqui did not deny this claim. Yet he insisted on sitting beside Soto because he was older^ and his kingdom more powerful. The governor, being a good *hidalgo,* chose blood over muscle, and ordered Pacaha to sit at his right side, "because he was a greater lord and more ancient in Estate."

At dinner, the two kings continued their attempts at one-upmanship by giving Soto gifts. First, Casqui gave him "a daughter, a pretty girl" from Casqui. Not to be outdone, Pacaha offered one of his own wives, "fresh and very virginal," and also "a sister and another principal Indian woman." An outraged Oviedo reports that Soto accepted these gifts, commenting that Soto, in his speech about "the greatness of the cross and of the faith," apparently had failed to mention "he was married," and that Christians were "not to have more than one wife or access to another." Oviedo also condemns Soto and his men for once again failing to stop and build a settlement in a country rich in maize and Indians.

✛ ✛ ✛

After sending out several more scouting forays, Soto departed Pacaha in late July. He headed south, probably marching across the high, flat alluvial delta region between the Mississippi and the St. Francis River. Returning to Casqui, he trekked from town to town in this heavily populated area, arriving at Quiguate on August 5, "the largest town that we found in Florida." Most likely, this was situated on the south bank of the St. Francis near its confluence with the Mississippi, at a site just north of the present-day St. Francis National Forest. Soto rested there for twenty-one days, claiming it was because the army needed to capture more porters, servants, interpreters, and guides. But the real reason he stopped had more to do with his gathering quandary about where to go next. To the north, his scouts reported a vast prairie. To the east, there were the kingdoms and empires he had already visited. To the south, he heard about more cities like Casqui, Pacaha, and Quiguate, though he did not yet want to march in that direction, since it led back to the sea and the outside world. This left only one option—to head west, where native informants claimed the Spaniards would pass through an uninhabited wilderness before coming to "a province where they killed some cows [buffaloes]." Here, said the Indians, Soto would find interpreters and guides to take them "to the other sea"—that is, the Pacific Ocean, supposedly close by.

Setting off from Quiguate on August 26, the army soon plunged into a series of small, swampy river valleys* where the men frequently slept in the mud and water. Later, a writer traveling in this same area described one of these "bayous" as running "a hundred feet wide at the most. Its muddy banks are hidden by high tufts of reed and rush, behind which rises a beautiful forest of sumacs, cotton woods, and walnut trees of various species, covered with black creepers and long twigs, which hang from the higher branches. White creepers with fragrant flowers, ivy, and convolvulus surrounded the trunks of old trees and rejuvenated them with their green shoots; and on younger trees *herbe-à-la-puce* [trumpet vine?] opened its red bell-flowers. The bayou water, thick and reddish, was very quiet and reflected the rays of a beautiful sun. Many alligators were asleep on the surface like stumps of trees rather than living creatures."

To Soto's men, this trek was as miserable as any they had endured, with the chroniclers so tired by now of reporting every swamp and mud-drenched crossing that they provide few details. Elvas notes only that the army did not go hungry, since there were so many fish in these Arkansas marshes that they could kill all they needed "by striking them with clubs." Even the Indian *tamemes* ate well, he says, since all they needed to do was to roil their chains in the mud. This caused the fish to become "stupefied," and to rise to the surface, where "they caught as many as they wished."

As August turned to September, the *entrada* continued to march slowly through this swampy backcountry of rural Arkansas, presumably headed toward present-day Newport, near the confluence of the White and Black Rivers.^ On September 4, they arrived at a place called Coligua—"a pleasant town amidst some mountains, on a gorge of a large river." Taking it by surprise, the Spaniards snatched the *cacique*, numerous people, clothes, food, and something they were greatly in need of: large quantities of salt. They also hunted buffalo for the first time, going out "at midday to kill cows, since there are many wild ones." A few days later, crossing some "rugged mountains" on the eastern edge of the Ozarks,^ they arrived at Calpista, where "there was a spring of water from which very good salt is made," which the Indians cooked "until it cakes."

---

*These were probably the L'Anguille River, Big Creek, Bayou de Vue, and Cache River.

Turning again toward the south, Soto finally left behind the marshy country and headed into the thick, luxuriant pine and hardwood forests of the Ozarks, his men stumbling over loose shale and rocks scattered across the eastern approaches to this ancient range. For a while, Soto seems to have followed the southerly flowing White River. Then he began to zig and zag, turning west and then north again, possibly following the Little Red River before cutting due west once more, marching across the present-day counties of White and Faulkner. Throughout this journey, Soto continued to march deliberately from town to town, stealing food and capturing Indian servants. Yet tracing his probable route on a map suggests an *entrada* marching tentatively this way and that, almost as if one can see in the meandering line a growing sense of desperation. By early September, Soto was headed for central Arkansas, leading his buckskin-clad army toward the Arkansas River valley, where he had heard there was yet another Mississippian kingdom, called Cayas. Again, the chroniclers provide only the barest of details. Ranjel does little more than list towns, noting that on September 14, a Wednesday, they came to "a large river"—the Arkansas—which Biedma says "flowed into the great river [the Mississippi]."

By now, the weight of Soto's gathering failure must have been truly bearing down on him. Indeed, the bitter realization that he was not going to be successful must have confronted him every time he looked in the haggard faces of his men, or watched the unsteady gait of his lean horses, scarred by battle wounds and bites from swarms of insects, and ridiculously armored in dried hides of buffalo. But the forty-one-year-old adelantado kept going. In mid-September, he reached the tilled fields and small villages of Cayas, most likely arriving at the Arkansas River some thirty miles north of Little Rock. He entered this verdant valley where the river narrows slightly, flanked on the north and south by tree-clad mountains and hills that fade into the distance in hazy shades of purple and green.

On September 15, Soto broke off from the main army with a small vanguard and rode ahead to Tanico, one of Cayas's major towns.^ Probably located in the Russellville/Dardanelle area of Arkansas, about seventy miles northwest of Little Rock, the Spaniards once again found a natural source of salt being worked there by the natives, "of high quality and delicious."^ According to Elvas, the Indians made the salt to trade for "skins and blankets" in other regions. "They gather it along the river," he says, "which leaves it on top of the sand when the water falls. And since they cannot gather it without more sand being mixed with it, they put it into certain baskets which they have for this purpose, wide at the top and narrow at the bottom. They hang the baskets on a pole in the air and put water in them . . . After being strained and set on the fire to boil, as the water becomes less [evaporates], the salt is left on the bottom of the pot."

Soto rested his men there, and let loose the horses to eat their fill of the autumn maize then ripening in the fields, until they "grew fat and throve." Over the next month, he also sent out forays to capture what appeared to be exceedingly passive Indians. This included the Cayas *cacique*, whom Soto had dragged to him in chains so he could inquire, with gloomy longing, "whether he had knowledge of any great *cacique* and where the most populated land was." This sheepish *cacique* replied that there was a "well-provisioned province" to the southwest, called Tula. Again ordering his men to prepare to march, Soto told them he wanted to set up a winter camp at Tula, since it was now October, and the temperature was quickly dropping as the leaves turned color, and fell in great heaps across the fields and highways.

✛   ✛   ✛

On October 1, Soto led a troop of outriders and as many as fifty infantry^ to investigate Tula. They discovered a people as militant as any the Spaniards had yet seen in *La Florida*. "We crossed some rugged mountains and arrived at the town without their having heard anything of us," says Biedma, who was with Soto on this foray. As they started to "apprehend" some Indians, however, the Tula "began to call to arms and make war on us," surprising the small group of Spaniards by pouncing on them "like wounded dogs." "Such was their ferocity," says Biedma, that they wounded nine or ten horses and seven or eight Spaniards. Soto's men killed thirty or forty Indians before retreating to sleep that night in "a clearing in a lowland that the river made."

The next day, Soto gathered reinforcements from the main army and marched back to Tula, only to be confronted by "three very large squadrons of Indians that came upon us at dawn, on three sides." According to Ranjel, this was a surprise attack in more ways than one, since these Indians "brought long poles like lances, the points fire-hardened." Developed by the foot-bound Tula to kill buffalo, these Indians quickly realized their use against the strange animals the Spaniards rode. Setting themselves up with the butts of their long staffs planted firmly in the ground, they waited for Soto's cavalry to charge— a tactic that made the Tula one of the few native peoples in the Americas to devise an effective defense against the horse. Because of this, Ranjel says "these were the best warriors that the Christians came upon." That day, he adds, "they wounded Hernandarias [de Saavedra], grandson of the marshal of Seville,^ and thanks to God that the Christians behaved so gallantly, so that they did not receive much damage."^

According to all the chroniclers, the Tula represented a dramatic change from the Mississippians of the Arkansas River valley. Living near modern

Ozark, or perhaps farther south, near Bluffton,^ in the Ouachita National Forest, they were hunter-gatherers first and agriculturists second, supplementing the game they hunted with small plots of maize and vegetables. Probably ancestors of the Caddo Indians,^ they not only fought differently from the Mississippians, they also lived in smaller and cruder villages, and spoke a language so different from Muskogean that the people of Cayas had trouble finding interpreters who understood the Tula.^ In part, said the *cacique* of Cayas, this was "because he and his forebears had always been at war with the lords of that province," and "they had no converse." The people of Tula also had a strange custom of greeting the Spaniards by crying profusely, something later explorers remark on when they visit the Caddo.^

But this was not all. As Soto pressed on down the valley, and sent parties scouting as far west as Oklahoma, a few miles from Fort Smith, Arkansas, the Spaniards found themselves entering an entirely different topography from anything they had seen before—a sea of grass where the soil was chalkier and less rich, the land was flat, and there seemed to be so little water that no trees could grow. Obviously, it was a place unsuited for any sort of large-scale Indian kingdoms or empires. Nor was there any evidence the Pacific Ocean was anywhere nearby.

Faced with the reality of dead ends to the west and north, even Soto had to admit the *entrada* had reached the end of the line. Yet he was still not ready to give up, having one final card to play—the Ouachita Mountains, a rocky, steep range that reminded Soto of highlands in Darién, Nicaragua, and Honduras, where the Spaniards had found traces of gold in the streams and in shallow, narrow veins. Praying that these mountains, too, contained gold nuggets, he ordered his men on October 19 to plunge into the Ouachita hills, where he wandered about for the next five days, sifting through the silt of the many creeks and rivers. But he came up empty every time.

✛   ✛   ✛

On October 23, Soto reluctantly left the mountains, unable to spend more time searching for gold because "winter had already come . . . the cold, rains, and snows." Having most likely followed the upper Ouachita River for a time, before crossing over to the headwaters of the Saline River basin, the army marched as quickly as possible back toward the Arkansas River, suddenly less concerned about gold than in finding a large, well-provisioned city they could seize and live in during what was to be their third winter in *La Florida*.

According to Elvas and Biedma, Soto had by now made a pivotal decision to return to the Mississippi, where he at last wanted to establish a base, build ships, and send men back to Cuba "to give information of himself . . . for it was three years and over since Doña Isabel, who was in Havana, or any other person in a Christian land, had heard of him." Tallying the dead so far at 250 men and 150 horses, Elvas explains that Hernando de Soto still had no intention of giving up his quest. "In the following summer," Elvas writes, Soto planned "to reach the sea and build two brigantines and send one of them to Cuba and the other to New Spain [Mexico], so that the one which should go safely might give news of him." He then told his men that "from his property in Cuba" he hoped "to refit, take up his expedition again, and explore and conquer [the land] farther west than he had yet reached." Undoubtedly recalling the "emeralds" and "gold" mentioned by Álvar Núñez Cabeza de Vaca—and perhaps the stories of Fray Marcos de Niza about the Seven Cities of Gold—Elvas says Soto wanted to go "whither Cabeza de Vaca had gone."

Soto, however, was unaware that the region to the west was being explored at that very moment by Francisco Vázquez de Coronado. A month earlier, this young conqueror and protégé of the Mexican viceroy Antonio de Mendoza had arrived at his easternmost point, in central Kansas, at a village called Tabás. Feeling a desperation and sense of failure Soto would have fully understood, Coronado had at Tabás decided to call it quits, too, having determined that Fray Marcos's legendary Cities of Gold were a fantasy. It was while Coronado rested his exhausted army in Tabás that Soto, who was then at Coligua, came as close as he ever got to his countryman. Marching within three hundred miles of each other, the two explorers afterward drew farther apart, as Coronado turned toward the panhandles of Oklahoma and Texas as he headed back to Mexico, and Soto, after marching west another 175 miles, turned around and headed back toward the Mississippi.

There is no evidence the two men knew of each other's presence deep in the interior of North America. Yet there is a strange story told by Coronado's chief chronicler, Pedro de Castañeda, about a slave girl who escaped from one of Coronado's captains in the Panhandle of Texas, only to be captured weeks later by Luis de Moscoso, then trying to escape to Mexico after Soto's death. No mention of the girl is made by Soto's chroniclers, though Castañeda reports she told Moscoso "she had fled from other Spaniards nine days distant and she named the captains." The mystery of how Castañeda could have known this has caused some scholars to wonder if this ever happened.^ Yet it remains intriguing to think that this unnamed girl may have been a link between the two *entradas,* and that through her the expeditions of Soto and Coronado spanned virtually the entire continent, even as they both degenerated into dispirited bands of survivors praying to make it home alive.

✢ 33 ✢

March of Death

NEAR REDFIELD, ARKANSAS, AT an Indian town called Autiamque,^ Soto and his men suffered terribly through another bitterly cold winter. They had plenty of food—maize, "as well as beans, nuts, and dried plums." But this was little solace against the cold and incessant snowfall that virtually trapped them for several weeks inside the stockade. Digging their way out of the thick drifts, the men had to content themselves with patrols able to travel no more than "two crossbow flights from the town" because of the snow. It was so thick that Elvas says they allowed their servants to move about "unshackled," knowing they could not escape under such inclement conditions.

During this fierce winter, yet another tragedy struck the ailing Spanish army when Soto's brilliant young translator, Juan Ortiz, fell ill and died. The governor, says Elvas, felt his loss "deeply," not only because of Ortiz's sorrowful experience as a castaway in Florida, but because Ortiz was the linchpin for what was now an extraordinarily complex system of communication critical to the *entrada*'s survival. Garcilaso tells us that by Mississippi, Ortiz was leading a chain of translators numbering between ten and fourteen persons, captured in the "many provinces that [Soto] passed through, almost every one of which had a language different from the others."* Consequently, every time Soto wanted to communicate with a new *cacique,* he would speak to Ortiz, who translated the words to one of the interpreters he understood. This person in turn would pass the message down the line "like a chorus to receive and pass on the words." Elvas says Ortiz was replaced by "a youth who had been seized in Cofitachequi, and who now knew something of the language of the Christians," though

*This was not entirely true, as most of the people Soto met spoke one dialect or another of Muskogean.

he cannot have made up for Juan Ortiz's skills and knowledge of both the Indian and Spanish cultures.

It is impossible to know what Hernando de Soto was thinking during that long winter in Arkansas. Reading Elvas at this point, the adelantado seems like an animal pacing in a cage as he lunges this way and that, trying desperately to make sense of what was happening to him. Biedma, however, offers no indications at all about Soto's state of mind, devoting only a paragraph more in his terse narrative to the army's comings and goings before he abruptly announces Soto's death. Nor does Rodrigo Ranjel offer us any clues, since Oviedo's manuscript suddenly ends just after Tula, with the great historian leaving only a bare outline of two more chapters he intended to write, but never did. As for Garcilaso, he continues to depict his hero as a man full of hope and determination to the end.

Garcilaso is not being entirely hyperbolic. For Elvas and Biedma—and numerous witnesses in the *Ponce v. Bobadilla* trial^—insist that Soto was still operating under a clear plan as the snows receded and the army began to head toward the Mississippi on March 6, 1542. All of our eyewitnesses reiterate that Soto was determined to establish a colony on the Mississippi, where he would build his brigantines, send them to Cuba and Mexico, and await reinforcements. Nor had he completely given up on the notion that a golden land still existed in *La Florida*. In fact, there were still *entrada* members who preferred to risk "death in the land of Florida than to leave it poor," who still hoped "to find a rich land . . . , because of what Cabeza de Vaca told the emperor." These men, like Soto, wanted to keep exploring to the west, where Cabeza de Vaca had claimed to see people dressed in cotton tunics, and "gold and silver and precious gems of much value."

Yet Soto knew his once-invincible army had become too weak to pursue his quest properly, a harsh reality that even the most optimistic talk about gold and silver in the direction of the Great Plains, and reinforcements from Cuba, could not change. For the truth was, Soto had squandered a fantastic opportunity—not only because he hadn't found precious metals, but also because he had wasted half his army and a fortune in equipment and supplies, and hadn't established a single mission village, garrison, town, or trade route. As he must have known, even if he had lived to contact Cuba, the reinforcements, weapons, and provisions available there were not of sufficient quantity to re-create anything approaching his glorious army of three years back. And this assumes he could coerce and sweet-talk more than a handful of diehards to continue the quest to find Cabeza de Vaca's gold.*

✛   ✛   ✛

From Autiamque, Soto led the army down the Arkansas River toward the Mississippi. They passed through yet another densely populated valley, punctuated here and there by swamps, and by Mississippian towns and villages whose people mostly ran away as the strangers approached, sometimes taking their maize with them. Several times, Soto sent out parties to try and capture these runaways, and to steal their food. But the Spanish army in its weakened state had little luck as they continued to march toward the great river, anxious to find a place to make a settlement, and to build their brigantines—preferably in a populated area where there was ample food, and affable Indians.

By mid-April, the Spaniards found what they were looking for in a small kingdom called Guachoya, located near present-day Arkansas City, a few miles south of where the Arkansas pours into the Mississippi River. There Soto found a pliable *cacique* and plenty of maize, beans, and dried plums. The situation, however, was not entirely bucolic. For looming just across the river was another large, powerful Mississippian empire called Quigualtum. Just a few days later their war canoes began massing near the Spanish camp, demanding to know what they were doing in this country. Earlier, Soto would have reacted to such provocation by instantly launching a devastating attack, thundering into the cities of Quigualtum with his horses and steel to plunder, rape, and destroy as he saw fit. But the army was long past inflicting such damage, diminished to the point that they might not survive a determined assault by a full-scale Mississippian army, particularly if the Indians attacked them on the river as they tried to float downstream in their brigantines.

For a man whose entire being was centered on his sense of invincibility, who had always operated from a position of overwhelming strength, this must have been devastating. Indeed, the nightmare Soto was now living seemed to manifest itself in a sudden and desperate conviction that the Gulf of Mexico must be just to the south, and that he need only sail downriver a short distance to find the sea and return to Cuba, where he could fetch reinforcements and return like a phoenix to smash Quigualtum and any other native lord. Appearing to be slightly unbalanced, Soto was sure the *cacique* of Guachoya was lying when he claimed to know nothing about the sea, insisting there was only swampland and wilderness to the south.

Fervently wanting to prove the *cacique* wrong, Soto sent "Juan de Añasco

---

*Had Soto lived and reconnected with the outside world, any efforts to explore west would have been dashed once and for all by the news of Francisco Vásquez de Coronado's failure to find gold.

downstream with eight horse to see what population there was and to ascertain whether there was any knowledge of the sea." For a week, Soto waited, undoubtedly pacing the high earthen pyramid where he was living in the Guachoya capital. Scanning from his height the riverbank to the south, he kept waiting for his old friend to appear with the good news he craved. Añasco's reconnaissance was not encouraging, however. He reported finding no trace of the sea. Nor had he found any settlements where the army could steal food as they searched for the Gulf of Mexico. In fact, said the frustrated captain, he had been unable to "proceed more than fourteen or fifteen leagues because of the great arms leading out of the river, and the canebrakes and thick woods lying along it."

With Ranjel's account now finished, we have no one in Soto's immediate entourage to tell us the adelantado's reaction. Elvas reports that "The governor's grief was intense on seeing the small prospect he had for reaching the sea," a response that suggests Soto was at last losing his self-confidence, this man who was famous for his icy resolve, and his unalterable belief he would win in the end. Even worse, says Elvas, was Soto's despondency over "the way in which his men and horses were diminishing," and his bitter understanding that "they could not be maintained in the land without succor."

"With that thought," says Elvas, "he fell sick," even as he tried a gambit he had often used as a standard ploy in his conqueror's repertoire—the claim that he was a god. This time, the pronouncement was made not to awe a recalcitrant *cacique* into surrendering, but out of necessity, due to his vincible position. "Before he took to his bed," says Elvas, "he sent an Indian to tell the *cacique* of Quigualtum that he was the son of the sun and that wherever he went all obeyed him and did him service. He requested him to choose his friendship and come there where he was, for he would be very glad to see him."

Quigualtum further humiliated Soto by answering this pronouncement of godhead with the haughtiness of a *hidalgo*. He said that if the governor was able to "dry up the great river he would believe him" about being a god. "With respect to the rest, he was not accustomed to visit any one. On the contrary, all of whom he had knowledge visited and served him and obeyed him and paid him tribute, either by force or on their own volition. Consequently, if he [the governor] wished to see him, let him cross there. If he came in peace, he would welcome him with special good will; if he came in war, he would await him in the town where he was, for not for him or any other would he move one foot backward."

When this reply was delivered, Soto was "already in bed, badly racked by fever. He was very angry that he was not in condition to cross the river forthwith and go in quest of him [Quigualtum] to see whether he could not lessen that arrogant demeanor. However, the river was now very powerful there . . .

Burial of Hernando de Soto Mural, De Soto County
Courthouse, Hernando, Mississippi, c. 1900

and very furious because of its strong current. On both sides of it were many Indians; and his strength was now no longer so great that he did not need to take advantage of cunning rather than force."

Soto's position worsened as his fever increased, even as the *cacique* of Guachoya seemed to be conspiring with Quigualtum against the Spaniards. "Noting how many Indians came to the town daily," says Elvas, "and how many people were in that land, and fearing lest some of them conspire with others and plan some treason against him . . . [Soto] ordered that men of horse be stationed at . . . the gates. All night long the horses were left bridled and from each company mounted men rode by [in] couples and went to visit the sentinels who were stationed on the roads at their posts outside the town, and the crossbowmen who were guarding the canoes by the river." This call to action was like the old Soto, though what he did next was more the act of a cornered beast than a seasoned conquistador. As the tension mounted, and his fever grew ever worse, Soto in a fit of frustration dispatched Nuño de Tobar with a mounted band of outriders, and Juan de Guzmán leading a unit of infantry to give a demonstration of *conquista* brutality. With the horses traveling overland, and the foot soldiers by canoe, Soto ordered this troop to sneak up at night on the nearby town of Nilco and to attack them without warning or provocation, "in order that the Indians might fear him . . . by treating them cruelly."

Tobar reached Nilco first as the sun began to rise over the mudflats beside the Arkansas River, only to be seen by an Indian who ran wildly back toward town to raise the alarm. But it was too late. "Before the Indians of the town had all come out," says Elvas, "they were on them." Because Nilco was situated on a level plain, there was no place for the "five or six thousand souls in that settlement" to flee against the onslaught of horses at full charge.

Elvas recounts the assault with a disgust uncharacteristic of him. He had taken this posture once before, when he described the massacre three years earlier at Napituca, in Florida. "The people," he says, "came out of the houses and went fleeing from one house to the other," running for their lives as Tobar ordered "that no male Indian's life should be spared." What followed was a sickening slaughter. "The cries of the women and little children were so loud that they deafened the ears of those who pursued them," writes Elvas, who apparently was at Nilco. "A hundred or so Indians were killed there and many were badly wounded with the lances, who were let go in order that they might strike terror into those who did not happen to be there." Elvas calls some of the Spaniards "butchers" and "inhuman" because they killed old men, women, and children. He also says there was a great deal of "cowardice" that day. The bloody demonstration did succeed in terrifying the Indians of Guachoya, however, who had sent representatives to watch the massacre. They reported back to their *cacique* "with great fear everything as it happened." Whether or not

Quigualtum reacted with equal trepidation is not known, though I suspect he was not overly impressed by a surprise attack against a sleeping village unaware they were being targeted.

✛   ✛   ✛

By now, in mid-May 1542, Soto's fever was racking his forty-two-year-old frame, turning him gaunt and pale. What he felt as he slipped farther into the delusions of fever is unknown. Gathering his close friends together, he told them "he was about to give an accounting before the throne of God of all his past life," though as Elvas tells it, he didn't seem particularly concerned about this. Indeed, he was dying the way he had lived, worshiping his warrior God, and undoubtedly feeling as though he had served such a deity well. He thanked his soldiers for remaining loyal, despite "the hardships they had suffered." He asked them to forgive any "offense they might have received from him." His men, in turn, asked him to chose a successor. Soto named his comrade from Peru, Luis de Moscoso, probably because he knew his old friend was both a savvy leader, and was anxious to flee this country. Garcilaso and several witnesses at the *Ponce v. Bobadilla* trial insist that Soto, even on his deathbed, remained optimistic about *La Florida*.^ Yet his choice of Moscoso, a sometime dandy with no interest in starting or running a new colony, suggests the opposite, that Soto in the end had soured on this land that had failed him, and led to his ruin.

There is some speculation about exactly what killed Soto. Elvas and Biedma suggest despondency was as much to blame as illness, with Biedma saying simply that "The Governor, from seeing himself cut off and seeing that not one thing could be done according to his purpose, was afflicted with sickness and died." Garcilaso, true to his style, describes an elaborate deathbed vigil where virtually every man in the army filed past to say good-bye as "this magnanimous and unconquered gentleman" died "like a Catholic Christian," muttering prayers.

Some have suggested Soto was killed by his men, perhaps being poisoned with some concoction that caused his body to seem feverish. Soto must have had enemies in the army capable of murdering him, though the conspiracy theorists fail to take into account that if Soto's men ever needed their leader, it was at Guachoya, where they were surrounded by hostiles, and in a truly desperate situation. Moreover, Soto was planning to depart *La Florida* when he died, which removes the major motivation among the disgruntled in the army, who wanted only to escape back into the Spanish world.

In the end, Soto is the sort who should have died fighting, overwhelmed by Native Americans on a hill such as Vilcaconga, or on any number of other battlefields where he could have gone down in a blaze of blood and savagery. Instead, he quietly receded deeper into fever, which lasted for several days before Hernando de Soto slipped into unconsciousness and death.

The date was May 21, 1542.

✛   ✛   ✛

Hernando de Soto's death does not end his story. For gods do not die, which put his men in an awkward and perilous position with the Indians massing outside their camp, and Quigualtum hovering in the background, perhaps preparing to strike at any moment. "Luis de Moscoso," says Elvas, "determined to conceal his death from the Indians, for Hernando de Soto had given them to understand that the Christians were immortal." Soto also had convinced the Indians of Guachoya that he knew what they were thinking at any given time, having shown them a mirror, which he said revealed "whatever they were planning and thinking about," a ruse that had helped keep a peace the new acting governor was determined to maintain. Thus Moscoso "ordered [Soto's corpse] to be placed secretly in a house where he was kept for three days; and from thence he ordered him to be buried at night inside at a gate of the town." The Indians, however, noticed "the earth had been disturbed," and suspected Soto had been buried there, knowing he had been sick.

This prompted Luis de Moscoso and a small band of Soto's friends to disinter him and carry his body to one of the army's dugouts at the river's edge. They loaded the already rotting corpse of the adelantado of *La Florida* into a large hollow log (Elvas says they used blankets and heavy sand),^ and carried it out into the middle of the great river. There, in an almost impossibly poetic finale to this savage conqueror's life, his friends heaved the log containing his body into the swirling, writhing waters, where it quickly sank beneath the surface, plunging to the depths of the river Hernando de Soto supposedly discovered a year earlier, when he still believed his march of death was a great quest, and that it would be many years before he died as a hero, having achieved a fantastic success.

EPILOGUE

IT TOOK MORE than a year for Luis de Moscoso to lead the remnant of Soto's army out of *La Florida,* and to return 311 of them safely to Mexico.^ Fearing Quigualtum, Moscoso first tried to reach Mexico overland that summer of 1542. He marched over one thousand miles across Arkansas and Texas, turning back near modern-day Dallas when the country became too dry and sparsely populated to feed and maintain the army. In September 1542, they arrived back at the Mississippi near Guachoya, where Soto had died. Here they spent the winter in a nearby city before building rafts to float down the Mississippi. Harassed by floods and fierce attacks on the river by Quigualtum and by another powerful Mississippian kingdom in southern Mississippi—possibly the Natchez—Moscoso and his exhausted troop finally made it to the Gulf. They then sailed to Mexico, astonishing the *vecinos* of Panuco by arriving on September 10, 1543, after having been long ago given up for dead.

ACKNOWLEDGMENTS

SO MANY PEOPLE have helped me with this book over the past five years that I hope I remember them all. First is my wife, whose patience and encouragement has shown no boundaries. I also am grateful for the support of my children, my mother and father, Sandy and Jeanne Robertson, Court and Margi Catron, Bill Brown, and my late grandmother, Evelyn Duncan Brown.

Thanks to Ignacio Avelleneda, a quiet, astonishingly perceptive archivist and scholar; David Dye, who generously gave me his time and good conversation in Memphis; Charles Hudson, who knows more about Soto's march in the Deep South than anyone alive; and numerous archaeologists and historians, professional and amateur, some of whom entertained me in their homes and spent time showing me Soto sites—Jerald Milanich, Mike Gannon, Paul Hoffman, John Hann, Jeffrey Mitchem, Doug Jones, Jay Johnson, Vernon Knight, Gene Black, Lawrence Clayton, Chester DePratter, Charles Ewen, Eugene Lyon, Fred Limp, Michael Mossley, Ed Moore, Dan Morse, John Scarry, Tom Sever at NASA, Rufus Ward, Jr., and Gail Wagner. Thanks to Pat Galloway for keeping me honest, and making me look critically at every aspect of Soto's experience; and Richard Kagan for keeping me straight about Spain in the sixteenth century. I also thank Elizabeth Alexander and Bruce Chappell of the P. K. Yonge Library of Florida History for their invaluable assistance; the librarians and researchers of the Library of Congress; and the researchers at the Archivo de las Indias in Seville. In Spain, thanks also to Rocío Sánchez Rubio and José Luis Pereira Iglesias. In Panama, thanks to Eduardo Navarro and Juan Carlos Navarro; in Nicaragua, thanks to Jorge Eduardo Arellano; in Mexico (and elsewhere), thanks to Stuart Cornew.

In Baltimore, thanks to Steve Vicchio, friend and fellow voyager in matters of good, evil, and other assorted presumptions; and to my assistants—Jana Miser, Ami Cantrell, and ace translator Samara Jaffe; and Denise Hawkins and Amy Dean, who elevated fact-checking, copyediting, and researching into an art form. Of course, none of these friends, experts, advisors, and assistants are responsible for errors, omissions, or absurdities in this text.

At William Morris, I am indebted to Pam Berstein, who first encouraged me to pursue this long quest; and Mel Berger, who can say more in one or two words than anyone else I know.

At Crown, I deeply appreciate the patience, wit, and breadth of knowledge of my editor, Jim Wade; the good humor and deligence of his assistant, Paul Boccardi; and the contributions and enthusiasm of Peter Ginna, who helped shepherd a complex project at the eleventh hour. Also thanks to Señor Pat Sheehan, and to Brian Belfiglio; and to Jim Walsh and the production department at Crown, who showed me undeserved patience on a complicated text.

NOTES ON ILLUSTRATIONS

Cover: Hernando de Soto, from *Retratos de los Españoles ilustres con un epítome de sus vidas* (Madrid, 1791); Soto Coat of Arms, from *Narratives of De Soto in the Conquest of Florida . . .*, trans. by Buckingham Smith, 1866; Signature of Hernando de Soto, from a document stored in Madrid's Biblioteca Nacional, reprinted in *El Adelantado Hernando de Soto . . .*, by Antonio del Solar y Taboada and José de Rújula y de Ochotorena, 1929; xxvii: "The Soto Map," attrib. to Alonso de Santa Cruz, ca. 1544; 1: Knights Jousting, from an early sixteenth century woodcut; 3: El Cid, woodcut; detail from Christopher Columbus Meets the Arawak on Hispaniola, British Library; 17: View of Seville, attrib. to Antonio Sánchez Coello, courtesy of the Museo de América, Madrid; 28: detail from The Quevi Lacenta, from *A New Voyage and Description of the Isthmus of America,* by Lionel Wafer, 1934; 45: Horses Transported by Boat, detail from illustration in *Historia General y Natural de las Indias . . .,* by Gonzalo Fernández de Oviedo, 1526; 54: Crested Dragon, motif from ancient Panamanian gold plaque, from the Sitio Conte; 65: Soto, from *De Gedenkwaarie Voyagie van don Hernando de Soto,* 1706; 67: Ancient Nicaraguan Idol, from *Nicaragua: Its People, Scenery, Monuments, Resources, Condition, and Proposed Canal,* by Ephraim George Squier; 80: Cortés, from the Lienzo de Tlaxcala, 1550–64; 97: Spaniards Receiving Tribute from Indians, from the Codex of Duran, 1560–80; 109: Spanish Conquistador, from the Lienzo de Tlaxcala; 116: Spanish Ship, from the Codex of Duran; 122: Ancient Peruvian Warriors, painted on a Moche pot; 137: Soto and Hernando Pizarro meet Atahualpa, from *Nueva crónica y buen gobierno,* by Felipe Guaman Poma de Ayala, ca. 1580–1620; 139: Atahualpa, from *Nueva crónica y buen gobierno,* by Felipe Guaman Poma de Ayala, ca. 1580–1620; 150: Atahualpa Captive, from *Nueva crónica y buen gobierno,* by Felipe Guaman Poma de Ayala, ca. 1580–1620; 164: Death of Quizo Yupanqui, *Nueva crónica . . .,* by Felipe Guaman Poma de Ayala; 176: Soto at the Battle of Vilcaconga, John Judkyn Memorial, Bath, England; 180: Chavin Warrior, after a drawing in *Chavin Art,* by H. H. Rowe, 1962; 188: Cuzco Plaza, from *Libro Primero de Cabildos de la Ciudad del Cuzco,* 1534–35, ed. by Raúl Rivera Serna (Lima, 1965); 201: Symbol of Knights of Santiago, from *Narratives of De Soto in the Conquest of Florida . . .*, trans. by Buckingham Smith, 1866; 213: Soto, from

Historia General . . . , by Antonio de Herrera, 1615; 215: Caravel from *Arte de Navegar,* by Pedro Medina, 1545; 226: Indian Hatchet, from *Historia General y Natural de las Indias* . . . , by Gonzalo Fernández de Oviedo, 1526; 250: Soto Lands at Tampa Bay, from *Ballou's Pictorial Drawing Room Companion,* 1855; 253: detail from The Natchez Temple, from *Histoire de la Louisiane,* by Antoine S. Le Page du Pratz, 1758; 267: detail of Timucuan Indians Cooking, engraving by Theodore de Bry, in *Narrative of Le Moyne* . . . , by Jacques le Moyne, 1564, reprint and trans. in 1875; 278: detail of Timucuan Warriors, engraving by Theodore de Bry, in *Narrative of Le Moyne* . . . , by Jacques le Moyne, 1564, reprint and trans. in 1875; 281: Indians Thrown to the Dogs, engraving by Theodore de Bry, in *Americae pars quarta . . . historia . . . Occidental India* (Part IV of *Historia Americae sive Novi Orbis*), by Girolumo Benzoni, 1594; 288: Indian *Caciques* Lead Their Armies into Battle, engraving by Theodore de Bry, *Brevis narratio eorum quae in Florida Americae* (Part II of *Historia Americae sive Novi Orbis*), by Jacques le Moyne, 1591; 294: Hawk Man Excavated at Lake Jackson, Florida, by permission of The Kent State University Press, first appeared in *Midcontinental Journal of Archaeology,* 1982; 317: Serpent Men, from a conch shell drinking cup at Spiro, Museum of the American Indian; 330: Native Woman, possibly enslaved, from *Le Fleur de la Science de Pourtraicture,* by Francisco Pellegrino, 1530; 342: detail from Conveyance of the Great Sun of the Natchez, from *Histoire de la Louisiane,* by Antoine S. Le Page du Pratz, 1758; 352: Coosawatte Plate, recovered in northwest Georgia, an artifact possibly left by the Luna Expedition when they visited Coosa; the Coosawatte Foundation, drawing by Julie Barnes Smith and Jodie Lewis; 363: The *Cacique* of Coosa, from *De Gedenkwaarie Voyagie van don Hernando de Soto,* 1706; 370: Soto at Mabila, from *Historia General* . . . , by Antonio de Herrera, 1615; 385: Soto, from *Historia General* . . . , by Antonio de Herrera, 1615; 387: Museum of the American Indian Bird-Man, Plate 203 Drawing, Philip Phillips and James A. Brown, *Pre-Columbian Shell Engravings*, Paperback Ed., Part 2, from the Craig Mound at Spiro, Okla., Peabody Museum Press, © 1984 by the President and Fellows of Harvard College; 393: Soto Battles the Alibamu, from *Historia General* . . . , by Antonio de Herrera, 1615; 403: Discovery of the Mississippi River by Hernando de Soto, published by Johnson Fry and Co., 1888, from a 1853 painting by William Henry Powell now filling a panel in the rotunda of the U.S. Capitol; 405: Bird Image on Ceramic Vessel at Moundville, from *Indians and Artifacts in the Southeast,* by Bert Bierer, 1978, courtesy of Mrs. Betty M. Bierer; 417: Spear Point, from *Archaeology of the Central Mississippi Valley,* by Dan and Phyllis Morse, 1983, courtesy of Dan and Phyllis Morse; 421: Burial of Hernando de Soto, Mural in De Soto County Courthouse, Hernando, Mississippi, ca. 1900.

REFERENCE NOTES

Sources listed in the bibliography are cited below in an abbreviated form. When multiple versions appear in the bibliography, the version listed first is the one cited in these notes, unless otherwise indicated. Occasionally in the text, I have slightly altered translations, spellings, accents, and so forth to either clarify meanings, or to avoid the confusion of multiple spellings of names and places.—D.E.D.

Foreword: Heroes, Demons, and Conundrums

xvii *of six hundred men:* The exact number of men who landed in *La Florida* with Soto in 1539 may never be known. Ignacio Avellaneda has prepared the most recent and up-to-date analysis of this question. In his *Los Sobrevivientes de la Florida,* Avellaneda cites all known sources, including the chronicles and testimonies by expedition survivors, and comes up with a range of 600 to 950 men who departed Seville for Cuba, and a range of 513 to 1,000 who departed Cuba for Florida. (The highest count comes from the biographer and romanticist Garcilaso de la Vega, who almost certainly exaggerated his numbers.) Preserved in the Archives of the Indies in Seville are two official registers of passengers, the first listing 651 persons, including a double entry. The second lists 657 persons. See AGI, 45-1-1/17. Contratación 5,536. Libro 5o, Folio 271 a 296 v y 301 a 522 v; from Solar y Rújula, 275–334. Both include slaves and women, but exclude Soto, his wife, and his entourage. Swanton studied the three chronicles and Garcilaso's biography and counted 793 persons who left from Spain and Cuba and debarked in Florida, including several repetitions. Avellaneda compiled the following tables comparing the various numbers offered by chroniclers and expedition survivors. (The chart is divided into two groups, those who left Spain, and those who left Havana, because some recruits from Spain left the expedition and others joined in Cuba.) I have slightly modified the table heading from Avellaneda.

Number of persons who departed for Florida, 1539

From Spain to Cuba:

Gentleman of Elvas	600
Official passenger register, Seville	657
Garcilaso de la Vega	950 plus
Juan López (survivor)	700
Sebastián de Villegas (survivor)	700

From Cuba to Florida:

Royal officials in Havana	513
Luis Hernández de Biedma	620

Rodrigo Ranjel 570
Garcilaso de la Vega 1,000
Pedro de Arevalo (survivor) 650
Francisco de Guzmán (survivor) 650
From Spain and Cuba to Florida:
J. R. Swanton 793
—from Avellaneda, *Los Sobrevivientes,* Table 1, 8–9.

In this narrative, I use a range of 600 to 700 as a very rough approximation of how many persons Soto started with in *La Florida.* This includes soldiers, artisans, servants, women, and all non-native members of the *entrada.*

xvii *and heavy metal:* De Soto was a division of Chrysler Motor Company discontinued in 1960.

xix *"to the savages":* Bell, J. B., *The Hernando de Soto Narrative,* 4. This children's book, written by the former mayor of Hernando, Miss., was published by the Committee to Honor Hernando de Soto in Hernando, county seat of De Soto County.

xix *on the Indians:* I consider "Indian" to be an odd appellation for the natives of the Western Hemisphere, a name that has persisted despite the fact we now know Columbus did not arrive in India in 1492, as he claimed. Unfortunately, more accurate names—such as Native American or perhaps Amerindian—have yet to catch on, and sound forced at this stage in history. I make every effort to refer to individual tribes and peoples by their proper names— Cueva, Apalachee, Coosa, etc.

xix *half his men:* No one knows for sure how many men perished in *La Florida.* Elvas says 311 survivors reached the port of Pánuco in Mexico on September 10, 1543. Biedma lists 221 survivors, though his list is incomplete. Garcilaso puts the number at under 300. Members of the expedition who later testified in legal depositions indicate the number was between 300 and 350. Avellaneda says he can verify only 257 survivors, though he indicates this is not a final tally.

Number of survivors

Gentleman of Elvas 311
Garcilaso de la Vega . . . . .under 300
Hernández de Luis Biedma 221
Pedro de Arevalo (survivor) 350
Francisco de Gutierrez (survivor) 300
Luis de Moscoso (survivor) 350
Sebástian de Villegas (survivor) 350
John Swanton 194
Ignacio Avellaneda 257
—from Avellaneda, *Los Sobrevivientes,* Table 2, 10.

xix *had no immunity:* The total Indian death count resulting from Soto's incursion is unknown. Chroniclers usually describe Indian casualties in vague terms, saying "some," "a few," or "many" natives were killed. At times, they mention specific numbers killed in military operations. For instance, at Mabila, Ranjel-Oviedo says 3,000+ died; Elvas says 2,500; Biedma says 5,000; and Garcilaso says "nearly 11,000." See Swanton, 88. Even though we can assume these figures are exaggerated, Indians killed in combat certainly numbered in the thousands over the course of the four year expedition.

xx *them to pieces:* The evidence for Soto's cruelty is extensive. A good place to start is an essay written by the great Peruvian historian, Raúl Porras Barrenechea, sarcastically titled "Soto the Good." See Trujillo, *Relación,* ed. by Raúl Porras Barrenechea, n120, 119–20.

xx *accuracy and scholarship:* The most noteworthy of these include John Abbott's *Ferdinand de Soto, the Discoverer of the Mississippi,* F. Blanco Castilla's *Hernando de Soto, El Centauro de las Indias,* Theodore Irving's *The Conquest of Florida,* and Theodore Maynard's *De Soto and the Conquistadors,* all of which glorify Soto as unrivaled among conquistadors. See bibliography for a complete listing of Soto biographers.

xxii *"a small man":* Pedro Pizarro, *Relación,* 341.

xxiii *"so is mine":* Tuchman, xviii.

xxiii *he was literate:* Illiteracy was not necessarily a hindrance to high office in the Spanish Indies, where self-made men lacking a formal education employed secretaries to handle their paperwork. The most famous example is Francisco Pizarro, who could neither read nor write, and dictated his missives and edicts to aides.

xxiv *document, now lost:* Evidence suggests that three other chronicles once existed, but are now missing. The first is a memoir written by a cleric with the Soto expedition, Alvaro de la Torre, mentioned in a letter dated October 25, 1559, from the viceroy Luis de Velasco of Mexico to Tristán de Luna, who was about to begin a failed attempt to conquer part of *La Florida.* Two other Soto expedition survivors, Juan Coles and Alonso de Carmona, wrote short memoirs used by Garcilaso de la Vega in his biography of Soto. Every so often, Garcilaso quotes directly from both men's records, offering fragments of the complete versions, now lost.

xxiv *Portuguese in 1557:* See Swanton, 4–11, for extensive notes on the publication histories, authenticity, and reliability of Elvas, Ranjel-Oviedo, Biedma, and Garcilaso. For some time now, reconstructionists have attacked the validity of using memoirs, period histories, and particularly chronicles as anything but highly suspect works of subjective reality. I tend to agree with this, though I find certain chronicles to offer valuable information, particularly when two or more agree on a particular observation or fact. Chronicles also provide a glimpse into what the people of an era were thinking and feeling. Historian Patricia Galloway and her colleagues have commented extensively on the drawbacks of the Soto chronicles, insisting that they are little more than "campfire tales" hopelessly compromised by the writers' prejudices, blustering, and faulty memories. Galloway has also argued, with some success, that Elvas's account may not have been written entirely by a participant in the expedition, but was perhaps rewritten by its first publisher, who may have lifted certain key stories from Oviedo's chapters based on Ranjel's account. Though I am not convinced this is true, I have attempted whenever possible to identify the prejudices of my sources, and to acknowledge the skepticism introduced by Galloway and others about accepting information in the chronicles at face value. See Galloway et al., *Studies in the Historiography of the Hernando de Soto Expedition* (in manuscript).

xxv *Soto's private secretary:* Ranjel is sometimes spelled Rangel.

xxvi *the "Hudson route":* Besides Hudson's, the other important hypothesis concerning Soto's route is rendered in John Swanton's 1939 *Final Report,* which Charles Hudson and others

say is flawed because Swanton and his commission did not have available the wealth of archaeological and archival data uncovered since 1939. (In the absence of definitive proof for
any route, Swanton retains his devotees.) In 1985, Jeffrey Brain of Harvard came up with a
compromise "corridor" theory, which draws a map with large shaded areas that encompass
all possibilities for where Soto might have gone. See Swanton, *Final Report,* introduction
by Jeffrey Brain, xlvii.

Prologue: Soto "Discovers" the Mississippi

xxi *Near Walls, Mississippi:* See note on Walls below.

xxiii *early as 1510:* At least three decades before Soto's "discovery" mariners and slavers coasting the Gulf shore probably knew about the Mississippi. The first officially reported sighting of the river's mouth was on June 2, 1519 by Alonso Alvarez de Pineda, who clearly
delineates the great river on a map he (or his pilot) sketched of the Gulf coast that year. Soto
can be credited with the first European sighting and exploration of the river upstream, and
of the Mississippi Valley. See Weddle, 99–101, for information on Alonso Alvarez de
Pineda's expedition.

xxxiv *by the Spanish emperor:* According to Elvas, King Charles I also named Soto a marquis,
though he is the sole source for this claim. See Elvas, 47.

xxxv *of "great secrets":* Ranjel-Oviedo, 289.

xxxv *(book was published):* For the story of Juan Gaitan's abortive mutiny, see Garcilaso,
357–58.

xxxv *"of the land":* Elvas, 89.

xxxv *"abounding in maize":* Elvas, 168.

xxxv *"Vast Dark thunderstorm":* Bartram, *Travels;* in Bakeless, 32.

xxxvi *"cone-like buttresses":* Bakeless, 335.

xxxvi *"devastate the land:"* Ranjel-Oviedo, 289.

xxxvi *town of Walls:* This scenario of Soto's entry into the Mississippi River valley was suggested to me by archaeologist David Dye, during two afternoon tours of the Walls, Miss.,
area, twenty miles south of Memphis. Though controversy continues to rage over where, exactly, Soto "discovered" the Mississippi, Dye offers what I consider a convincing argument
in favor of Walls. As Dye has pointed out in a still unpublished paper, the archaeological
sites and topography in the area seem to best fit what is described in the chronicles. Other
possible sites in northwestern Mississippi include Sunflower Landing, near Rena Lara;
Friar's Point, a few miles north of Sunflower Landing; and Memphis, Tenn.

xxxvii *in the 1950s:* According to David Dye, a local farmer told him this mound was destroyed
in the 1950s. See Dye, Interview, 1990. Also see Morse, *Archaeology of the Central Mississippi Valley,* for a description of the Walls site, its artifacts, and the probable layout of its
aboriginal structures.

xxxvii *king called Aquixo:* Anthropologists remain uneasy about what political descriptive to
use when referring to Mississippian polities. Most prefer to call them "chieftainships"—a
pre-state political unit where kinship and hereditary rulers loosely dominate an area, with
authority only to demand tribute and to be supplied with fighters should they go to war. The
largest chieftainships are ruled by a "paramount chiefs," a kind of aboriginal emperor who
demands tribute and fighters from several subservient chieftainships. A "chieftainship" is

more than a "tribe" ruled by a "chief," but less organized than a "kingdom," which one anthropologist (David Dye) defines as a system of hereditary rulers organized into an identifiable state, with a bureaucracy separate from the kinship and clan alliances that distinguish a chieftainship. Anthropologists define an empire as one state or individual ruling over other states or tribes. Neither Dye nor anyone else, however, considers these definitions to be hard and fast for the Mississippians or for other peoples. (For instance, many of the "kingdoms" of the early Middle Ages in Europe were technically chieftainships, though we popularly call them kingdoms.) Because I find the use of "chieftain" and "chieftainship" a bit cumbersome and ill-defined, I have chosen in this text to use "king" and "kingdom" and "emperor" and "empire" to describe certain High Mississippian polities. This is in part because the simple definition of these terms, as defined in *Webster's*, almost certainly apply. For instance, *Webster's* describes a king as being merely a hereditary ruler of a people, and an emperor as ruling a collection of states, tribes, or peoples. Certainly, these definitions apply to certain Mississippian entities. Finally, "chieftainship" is too often used to describe non-Euroasians, while we more freely apply the term "king" in referring to, say, the "kingdom" of Scotland in the Middle Ages, which was almost certainly a "chieftainship." For more information on chieftainships, see Helms, *Ancient Panama,* and Johnson and Earle, *The Evolution of Human Societies.*

xxxvii *in the region:* Important Mississippian rulers dominated polities outside their home province by forcing subject peoples to pay tribute in food and goods, and by demanding they provide warriors in time of war. Coercion was exacted by threat of force, actual raids, and by the reputation of a powerful polity developed over a period of time.

Book I: Youth

Chapter 1: Soto Is Born

3 *"Close in, Spain!":* I have no proof Soto actually shouted these words, though this was one of several popular battle paeans shouted by conquistadors and soldiers in Soto's day. It was first used in the early years of the *Reconquista* against the Moors. See Crow, *The Root and the Flower,* 84, for the story of how St. James, Spain's patron saint, appeared in a dream and saved a Christian force against a superior Moslem army in A.D. 813. Later in his life, Soto is described as invoking Santiago's name during two battles—the Battle of Vilcaconga in Peru, and the Battle of Mabila in Alabama.

3 *"more or less":* Testimony of Hernando de Soto, during a hearing about the services of Alonso Martín de Don Benito, October 26, 1535, Lima; AGI, Patronato, 1-6-1/24; DOP II, 355–67.

3 as *"about forty":* AGI, Justicia 719, 9, 1536.

4 *about his future:* Boys in the late Middle Ages were expected to come of age very early by our standards, particularly in a poor region such as Extremadura, where the second-born in a *hidalgo* family seldom lingered at home longer than was necessary. Fourteen was the age at which Hernán Cortés, the future conqueror of Mexico and a second-born son, was sent off by his *hidalgo* family from their home in Medellín, in northern Extremadura, to study law at the University of Salamanca. Fourteen tended to be the age at which a European prince was crowned as the designated heir to his father's throne.

4   *sometime around 1500:* See Garcilaso, 499.

4   *more easily resolved:* The evidence for each town claiming to be Soto's birthplace is as
    follows:

> *1. Jerez de los Caballeros, home of Soto's father's family.* Soto considered himself
> a *natural*, or native, of Jerez de los Caballeros, his father's family's town, affirming this
> fact in several documents. Numerous friends, associates and contemporaries also con-
> firmed he was a *natural* of Jerez. Some examples:

Soto was a "native of Jerez near Badajoz."
                    —Probanza of Lope Vélez, 1536, Seville; AGI; Trujillo, 92.

"Soto was a native of Jerez situated 4 leagues from this village of Barcarrota."
                    —Testimony of Gonzalo Vázquez, July, 1550, Barcarrota; PB I, 52.

"Captain Soto was the son of an esquire of Jerez de los Caballeros."
                    —Elvas (Smith), 97.

During an investigation into Soto's lineage conducted by the Order of Santiago,
eight prominent citizens of Badajoz, all of whom knew Soto, testified that Jerez de los
Caballeros was Soto's place of origin. See *Expediente de Hernando de Soto;* Solar y
Rújula, 123.

The Soto family probably belonged to the parish of San Miguel in Jerez de los Caballeros. In his *Testamento,* he orders his corpse after death to be taken to: ". . . the city
of Jerez, near Badajoz, where it shall be consigned to the sepulcher where lies my
mother, in the Church of San Miguel; and in that church I order . . . a chapel to be built
. . . where my body shall be . . ."
                    —*Testamento de Hernando de Soto;* AGI, Justicia 750A; *The De Soto Chronicles,*
                                                                        Vol. I, 366–67.

> *2. Badajoz, home of Soto's mother's family, capital of southern Extremadura.* The
> only document I am aware of identifying Soto as a native of Badajoz, the capital of
> southern Extremadura, fifty miles north of Jerez, is the dowry agreement made be-
> tween Soto and Isabel de Bobadilla in 1536, which says: "Señor Hernando de Soto . . .
> native and resident of Badajoz. . . . " (AGI, Justicia 750A, P. 1, F. 64–69; Solar y
> Rújula, 157–66.) But this must be placed against dozens of documents that claim Jerez
> as Soto's native city. Certainly, Soto as a boy frequented Badajoz, his mother's home-
> town. Numerous prominent citizens in Badajoz recalled knowing Soto and his family,
> though all of these witnesses affirm he was a native of Jerez. (*Expediente de Hernando
> de Soto;* in Solar y Rújula, 123.) Long after Soto's death, Pedro Pizarro wrote in his
> *Relación:* "They say Soto was a native of Badajoz" (Pedro Pizarro, 229), though he was
> probably referring to the region of Badajoz, a common shorthand of the period for any-
> one who came from villages near Badajoz, the region's capital.

> *3. Barcarrota.* Virtually no evidence exists linking Soto's birth or upbringing to

Barcarrota, known in the sixteenth century as Villanueva de Barcarrota. The sole evidence comes from an almost certainly erroneous statement by Garcilaso de la Vega, writing almost a half century after Soto's death. See Garcilaso, 447. Unfortunately, numerous historians and biographers over the centuries have accepted Garcilaso's error as fact, including Herrera, Irving, Abbott, and others.

4 *no proof whatsoever:* Garcilaso's confusion may come from the fact that Barcarrota is in the same province as Soto's real place of origin, Jerez de los Caballeros. The two towns are only about eleven miles apart. Soto also had family in Barcarrota.

4 *other definitive documentation:* Standardized birth records did not exist in Spain until late in the sixteenth century, when cities and towns began recording births.

4 *early sixteenth century:* According to a 1492 census, Jerez had 2,150 *vecinos,* or property owners, and a total of some 8,000 inhabitants, making it a large city by late-fifteenth-century standards. See Ordax, 347–48.

4 *place of origin:* Soto hints he is from Jerez in his will. See Soto, *Testamento,* 366–67.

4 *of his family:* The weight of the evidence in favor of Jerez has not deterred the city fathers of Barcarrota and Badajoz from erecting monuments to the region's thrice-claimed native son—including statues, schools, streets, cafes, and even a house in Barcarrota identified as the "Birthplace of Hernando de Soto."

4 *"village of Barcarrota":* Testimony of Gonzalo Vázquez, July, 1550, Barcarrota; PB I, 52.

4 *House of Soto:* All genealogical information about Soto comes from Solar y Rújula, 41–46. Some have questioned whether or not there is a direct link between Hernando de Soto and the lineage cited by Solar y Rújula, who base their findings on possibly dubious eighteenth-century genealogies.

4 *early tenth century:* Alfonso IV ruled c. A.D. 925 to A.D. 931.

6 *"Moors, no peasants":* Expediente de Hernando de Soto; Solar y Rújula, 123–56.

6 *"sword and shield":* Elvas, 47. This quote comes from the so-called Gentleman of Elvas, the anonymous author of one of the chronicles from Soto's Florida expedition. His comment about Soto's poverty is not as an eyewitness, since Elvas was not present in Panama when Soto arrived.

6 *early sixteenth century:* Several historians in Extremadura have informed me about the omission of the Soto family in the Jerez archives. A brief inspection of my own also turned up nothing. This does not preclude a future researcher turning up documents that mention Soto's family at this time. Another *hidalgo* family in Jerez, that of the conquistador Vasco Núñez de Balboa, is mentioned frequently in the Jerez archives c. 1490–1515, particularly as financial patrons of the San Miguel church, which also was the parish church of the Sotos. See Ordax, 349.

6 *in the 1490s:* See Testimony of Hernando Romo, April 12, 1538, Badajoz, *Expediente de Hernando de Soto;* Solar y Rújula, 141.

6 *"city of Badajoz":* Testimony of Juan Mexía, April 12, 1538, *Expediente de Hernando de Soto,* Solar y Rújula, 148. According to Spanish genealogical records, the Tinoco family originated in Portugal, where Leonor's ancestors were prominent knights before crossing the border into Extremadura. After Soto's death, several Tinocos married into the titled nobility of Badajoz. This elevated the family into the ranks of viscounts and marquises in two or three generations.

7   *pounds of gold:* See Solar y Rújula, 59.

7   *of his estate:* See Soto, *Testamento,* 366–72.

7   *council in Jerez:* See Ludeña, appendix 5.

7   *Don Alonso Enríquez:* Soto had another nephew, Captain Diego de Soto, whose parents are
    unknown, and who accompanied his uncle to *La Florida,* dying at the Battle of Mabila in
    Alabama on October 18, 1540. There is some confusion over Diego's name. Ranjel identi-
    fies him as Francisco de Soto; Solar y Rújula and Garcilaso call him Diego. (See Ranjel-
    Oviedo, 294; Solar y Rújula, 44; Garcilaso, 343.) Diego's sister, Isabel de Soto, married
    another of Soto's captains recruited in Badajoz, Don Carlos Enríquez, who also died at Ma-
    bila (See Ranjel-Oviedo, 294; Elvas, 104.) Soto himself gave the bride away at their wed-
    ding held at Barracota. This occurred sometime during the two years (1536–38) when Soto
    was in Spain before sailing to Florida.

7   *"appear most becoming":* See Soto, *Testamento,* 367.

8   *of the Conquistadors:* Seventeen percent of Spain's emigrants to the Indies came from Ex-
    tremadura during the sixteenth century, though it accounted for only seven percent of the
    total Spanish population. See Kamen, *Spain 1469–1714,* 92.

8   *in* La Florida: Swanton lists 341 men. See Swanton, 372–77.

8   *"three months' hell":* Davies, 23.

8   *eaving the womb:* Hale claims 50 percent of all children born in Renaissance Europe died
    during their first year. See Hale, 17.

8   *one square mile:* Jerez inside its old city walls is 750 meters long by 225 meters wide, or
    about 20 hectares. See Ordax, 350.

9   *daylight travel hazardous:* Throughout rural Castile, town documents repeatedly record the
    dangers beyond a town's fortifications. For instance, on July 2, 1510, when Soto was ten years
    old, a Jerez sheep owner petitioned town officials to send armed men (and boys) to kill a wild-
    cat "who has numerous times attacked and devoured the sheep, and has a reputation . . . for
    great ferocity." (Archivo Municipal de Jerez, 1512.) Also see Altman, 56. Florentine diplomat
    Francesco Guicciardini (1483–1540) toured Spain in 1512–13 and wrote about his astonish-
    ment at the emptiness of the country between cities. See Gibson, *Black Legend,* 32.

9   *"on their backs":* Hale, 19. For more about the plagues and famines, see Pike, 10, and
    Matute y Gavira, *Noticias,* 54.

9   *week in May:* See Pike, 10.

9   *thirty-five thousand people:* In 1534, a census taken in Seville, Spain's largest city (Toledo
    and Barcelona were close seconds) indicates a population of 30,000 to 50,000. See Pike,
    5–11. Spain's entire population in 1500 was some 7.5 million, compared to 40 million
    today. Other major European cities in 1500 included Paris and London, with about 80,000
    people each, and Naples, with 100,000. See Hale, 320–22.

10 *"won the day":* *Poema de Mio Cid,* 112–13, trans. Rita Hamilton and Janet Perry.

11 *"are as beautiful":* Anonymous, *Auto da Sibila Cassandra;* in Brenan, 143.

12 *the daily Mass:* The infamous Spanish Inquisition executed far fewer people than is gener-
    ally suspected, a total of perhaps two thousand between 1480 and 1504. See Durant, VI,
    215. In Soto's day, the number of religious executions in Spain was typical of those per-
    formed in other European countries, where inquisitions could be equally exacting and
    cruel.

12 *a "good hidalgo": Expediente de Hernando de Soto;* Solar y Rújula, 123–55.

12 *"man of truth":* Ranjel-Oviedo, 258.

12 *"man of worth":* Ibid., 296.

13 *the town council:* See Altman, 79–80 for information on education of *hidalgos* and nobles.

14 *"hoofs and . . . blemishes":* Cervantes, *Don Quixote,* 27–28.

Chapter 2: Across the Ocean Sea

15 *wo thousand colonists:* Most of Pedrarias's fleet arrived off Santa María la Antigua de Darién on June 26, 1514.

16 *between 1513 and 1519:* For instance, see Testimony of Alvaro Alonso Prieto, December 1546, Madrid. PB I, 11.

16 *"more or less":* Soto gave this information as a witness in the Probanza of his longtime friend Alonso Martín de Don Benito. See Testimony of Hernando de Soto, Probanza of Alonso Martín de Don Benito, October 26, 1535, Lima. AGI, Patronato 1-6-1/24; DOP II, 160.

16 *Pedrarias arrival date:* The theory that Soto sailed with Pedrarias in 1514 was given a strong boost in 1939 when anthropologist John Swanton unearthed statements by two of Soto's associates offering what seemed irrefutable evidence. In his landmark *Final Report of the United States De Soto Expedition Commission,* Swanton first quotes Arias de Villalobos, who knew Soto in Panama and Nicaragua, as saying Soto and his friends Hernán Ponce de León and Francisco Compañón "went to those parts with Pedrarias." Swanton then paraphrases Juan de Rojas, Soto's longtime associate and his lieutenant governor in Havana, saying that Rojas "affirmed" that Ponce, Soto, and Compañón "crossed . . . in the same ship," and that this ship also carried Pedrarias. See Swanton, 67–68. However, careful scrutiny of the original documents by archivist Ignacio Avellaneda reveals that the usually careful Swanton misinterpreted, or possibly mistranslated, the statements of Villalobos and Rojas. Villalobos, it turns out, was reporting hearsay about Soto's arrival. In his 1550 statement, he clearly says he did not witness the crossing himself, because he arrived in Panama long after Hernando de Soto. His comments are further muddled when read in the Spanish version, which indicated Soto, Ponce and Compañón crossed in the *era* of Pedrarias's regime, but not necessarily *with* the new governor. As for Rojas, he never mentions Soto at all in his statement about crossing to Panama, saying only that he himself traveled on Pedrarias's ship.

16 *above the city:* In the early sixteenth century, the familiar crown of the Giralda we see today had not yet been built. Soto would have seen a comparatively plain-looking bell tower sitting atop the original Moslem minaret. The exact height of the tower at this time is unknown. See Casariego, *The Giralda of Seville,* for more information.

16 *official court* artistas: Historian Richard Kagan, for one, disputes this attribution.

16 *ray of sunlight:* In Coello's painting, the Giralda is depicted as it looks today, with its splendid Renaissance top.

18 *north of Cuba:* Juan Ponce de León did not "discover" Florida, though his expedition was the first official *entrada* sanctioned by the Crown. The distinctive peninsula of Florida began appearing on maps in Europe as early as 1507. By then, it had probably been visited several times by anonymous mariners, slavers, and merchant men, some of whom believed Florida was an island.

18 *men young again:* Peter Martyr first reported Juan Ponce's claims of a fountain of youth in 1514. "At three-hundred and twenty-five leagues from Española," he writes, "those who have explored closely tell of an island, named Boiuca or Agnaneo, having a celebrated spring, by drinking the waters thereof old men are rejuvenated." Martyr, *Second Decade;* quoted in Sauer, 190. Oviedo, however, dismissed this rumor as an Indian fable.

19 *as a "pacifier":* Nicaraguan Historian Jaime Incer has this to say about the Spaniards' use of the word "pacification" in Nicaragua: "The wars of conquest being finished and there being no more pretext for obtaining slaves, the name 'pacification' was invented. The Spaniards thus marched to pacify Indians in villages they claim were rebellious." Incer, 114.

19 *in numerous expeditions:* For the lists of men crossing with Pedrarias in 1514, see AGI, 9-3-1/25; DOP II, 422–28. A perusal of the personnel in the Pedrarias Armada reveals at least two men who Soto may have commanded in the 1524 invasion of Nicaragua—Alonso Sánchez, listed as a bricklayer in 1514, and Pedro de Torres, possibly a future overseer on one of Soto's ranches in Nicaragua.

19 *politician and strategist:* In *The Prince,* Machiavelli offers Ferdinand as a model of how a militarily "weak king" from a country poor in resources can advance to fame and glory. See Machiavelli, 81–82.

20 *and suicidal despair:* Hispaniola's pre-Columbian native population is unknown. Columbus reported 1 million inhabitants on Hispaniola in 1494. Other period estimates ranged from several hundred thousand to 3 million. Certainly, the island was heavily populated, a contention backed up by archaeological findings. By 1518, Alonso Zuazo, a royal agent sent by the Court to investigate conditions on Hispaniola, reported 1.13 million natives had died since 1508, and that only 11,000 remained alive. He correctly predicted they would be extinct within a few years. See CDI I, 310. Also see Peter Martyr, Decade III; quoted in Sauer, *The Early Spanish Main,* 202.

20 *a rival power:* In four edicts issued in 1493, the Pope—claiming to be God's agent in certain matters of geography—granted Spain dominion over virtually the entire Western Hemisphere. This was thanks to quick action taken by Ferdinand just after Columbus's return from discovering the Indies, and to a large bribe paid to Alexander VI, the Spanish-born pontiff who owed his position to the Catholic king.

20 *disgrace to Spain:* Once in Spain, Hojedo is said to have joined a monastery, where he became a recluse the rest of his life.

20 *failing to return:* Nicuesa and 580 men left Urabá in 1510 and headed west along the coast of Panama, where they disappeared.

21 *"[cribs] like maize":* Balboa, Letter to the King, Jan. 20, 1513, CDHE, III, No. V, 375, trans.: Clements R. Markham (Hakluyt Society, Andagoya, *Narrative,* v. 34), xii–xiii.

21 *"being always pacific":* Balboa, Letter to the King, Jan. 20, 1513; in Sauer, *The Early Spanish Main,* 229.

21 *"of the world":* Balboa, Letter to the King, Jan. 20, 1513; in Markham, *Narrative of Pascual Andagoya,* xiii.

21 *"to the country":* Ibid.

21 *"a great loss":* Balboa, Letter to the King; in Romoli, 178. Pedrarias, when he sailed to Castilla del Oro, had orders to engage the Portuguese if he found them, which he did not.

22 *next five centuries:* Most of Ferdinand's ideas are embodied in his *Royal Instructions to Pe-*

Reference Notes

441

drarias Dávila; in Angel de Altolaguirre, 37–45; Serrano y Sanz, cclxxix–cclxxxviii; NIW 3, 50–53.

22 *"of these kingdoms":* Ibid.

22 *"in my life!":* quoted in Romoli, 198. The Dominican priest, Father Montesino, delivered a famous sermon in Santo Domingo on the last Sunday of Advent in 1511 before a congregation of the governor, officials, and *vecinos,* telling them they were living in mortal sin because of how they were treating the Indians. The sermon was not well received. See Sauer, *The Early Spanish Main,* 197.

22 *Laws of Burgos:* Ferdinand cleverly defused, for the moment, the mounting criticism of the pro-Indian Dominican priests led by Montesino by calling together a council at Burgos in 1512–13 to debate not only Indian treatment in the colonies, but whether or not the Crown even had a right to conquer Indian lands. This was an extraordinary proposition, to have an absolute monarch embarking on a new wave of imperial expansion and opening a debate on the fundamental morality of his policy. Not surprisingly, the council, after rancorous debate, sided with the king, though they wrote a detailed set of rules for fair Indian treatment in the colonies. This document was widely scorned and ignored in the Indies. Contrary to the myths of the Spanish Black Legend, however, Indian rights remained an important topic of discussion at the Spanish court throughout the century, debated with a frequency and vigor unheard of in other European capitals during this era.

22 *infamous El Requerimiento:* See *El Requerimiento,* 1513; for the full text of the version of this document used by Pedrarias, see Serrano y Sanz, ccxcii–ccxciv. Quoted in Romoli, 200–201. Other versions of the *El Requerimiento* exist, with slight differences, in DOP II, 287–89; Oviedo, bk. XXIX, chap. 7; Las Casas, bk. III, chap. 57; and Herrera, Decade I, bk. VII, chap. 14.

23 *"and without servitude":* El Requerimiento, 1513, in Romoli, 210.

23 *"who accompany me":* El Requerimiento, 1513; full text in Serrano y Sanz, ccxcii–ccxciv. Quoted in Romoli, 201.

24 *"Castilla del Oro":* Ferdinand, *Cédula Appointing Pedrarias Dávila as Governor of Castilla del Oro;* in Alverez Rubiano, 522.

24 *blank before 1509:* See Alverez Rubiano for a detailed history of Pedrarias's life, and key documents.

25 *in* La Florida: When Soto returned to Spain from Peru in 1536, he moved in with Pedro Cataño, formerly one of his outriders in Peru, and a member of one of Seville's most prominent Genoan banking families. According to Mary Pike, Soto took advantage of this relationship to borrow money for his expedition. See Pike, *Enterprise and Adventure,* 102; note on 194.

25 *endorsing the Requerimiento:* See Serrano y Sanz, cclix–cccxxxviii and appendices for detailed information on the armada's preparations and a study of how the new government was planned; also see Romoli, chaps. 17 and 18. Other sources: Oviedo, bk. XXIX, chaps. 1, 6; Las Casas, bk. III, chap. 53, 59; Martyr, Decade II, bk. 7; Angel y Altolaguirre, app. 9–17; DOP II, 39–76; Alvarez, chap. ii and app. 5. For information on ships and personnel of the fleet: FAAP, vols. IV, V; CDHH-A, vols. X, XIV; CPI (1930 and 1940).

25 *"one of brocade":* Zuazo, *Letter from Alonso Zuazo to Monsieur de Xévres;* CDI I, 247–411; quoted in Sauer, *The Early Spanish Main,* 248.

25 *"ever left Spain"*: Quoted in Romoli, 209.
26 *three thousand*: See Romoli for Oviedo's number, and for her own estimate, 210.
26 *their third try*: See Romoli for a description of send-off and voyage, 210–13; also Oviedo, bk. XXVI, chap. 10 and bk. XXIX, chap. 1, 6, 7; Las Casas, bk. III, chap. 3–18; and Martyr, Decade II, bk. 7; Decade III, bk. 5.

Chapter 3: The Scourge of God

28 *"impression of dignity"*: Oviedo, bk. XXVI, chap. 10; paraphrased by Romoli, 215.
28 *says of "heartbreak"*: Ibid.
29 *orders to disembark*: Malaria, which was apparently carried by Europeans to the Western Hemisphere, was not yet a factor in Panama. Biohistorians theorize that Spanish soldiers who had served in Italy and North Africa, where malaria was rampant, brought the infectious disease with them in their blood and passed it on to American mosquitoes, eventually causing regions such as eastern Panama to be virtually abandoned until modern antimalarial drugs and pesticides were invented.
29 *it an "evil"*: Andagoya, 6.
29 *where "sickly vapors"*: Zuazo, Letter to Xévres, January 22, 1518, CDI I, 247–411; quoted in Sauer, 249.
29 *"quantity of gold"*: Columbus, Letter to Ferdinand and Isabel, July 7, 1503, Jamaica; quoted in J. M. Cohen, *The Four Voyages of Christopher Columbus*, 287.
29 *and small idols*: Oviedo says Cosa plundered 182 marks (9,100 pesos) of booty in Urabá. See Oviedo, *Historia*, bk. XXVII, chap. 1–4; quoted in Sauer, 162–64.
30 *of boundless riches*: See Sauer, 116–19.
30 *highly toxic herbs*: See Oviedo, *Natural History*, 27. Oviedo says the Indians also used acids derived from ants and certain plants to concoct some poisons.
31 *de las Casas*: Las Casas began his career as a conquistador/settler on Hispaniola. In 1515 he abandoned his *encomienda* near Santo Domingo and became a priest, launching a fifty-year career as a fiery and influential advocate for the Indians, serving as a bishop, writer, historian, and advisor to two kings.
31 *"a majestic throne"*: Las Casas, *Historia*, III, 35.
31 *"clean-limbed and strong"*: Las Casas, *Historia*, bk. II, chap. 5, 62; quoted in Romoli, 14.
31 *of San Miguel*: See Ordax, 349.
32 *Spaniards and Indians*: Herrera says he was "fair with his men, generous, severe," a man who had "incredible foresight in all things relating to war, or civil government, and he was the first himself to set a good example." Herrera, Decade 2, bk. I, chap. 3. Peter Martyr called him a "Hercules, the conqueror of monsters," Martyr, *De Orbo Novo*, from F. A. McNutt, I, 281–315; quoted in NIW, 48. Even the critical Las Casas called him "a man of clear understanding." Las Casas, *Historia*, bk. II, chap. 2, 5; quoted in Romoli, 14.
32 *than one mistreated*: Nothing better exemplifies Balboa's attitude than a casual reference made in a 1513 letter to the king, in which he tells Ferdinand he knows certain information is correct because he had received identical answers from Indians by "putting some to the torture, treating others with love, and giving to others presents of things from Castile." Balboa, Letter to the King, CDHE III, 358–76; quoted in Sauer, 228.
32 *cruelty and contempt*: One of many examples of Balboa's capacity for cruelty toward the

Indians occurred during the march to the South Sea in 1513. Peter Martyr describes him hacking off limbs of intractable natives and ordering his dogs to tear apart others. (See Martyr, *De Orbo Novo,* from F. A. McNutt. I, 281–315; from NIW III, 37. 2). In another example, he worked at least five hundred porters to death during his South Sea boat-building project in 1518. See Las Casas, II, 87–88.

32 *heard from again:* This was a very serious offense, one that discredited Balboa with the king before the discovery of the South Sea, after which the king forgave him. The death of Nicuesa was later used by Pedrarias as evidence against Balboa in the mostly sham trial conducted before his execution for treason in 1519.

32 *"as he wished":* Zuazo, Letter to Xévres, January 22, 1518; quoted in Sauer, 219–20.

33 *"very good order":* Quoted in Romoli, 220.

34 *"paragraph of bombast":* Romoli, 220.

34 *"or long grass":* Oviedo, *Natural History,* 39.

34 *paucity of food:* See Balboa, Letter to the King, January 20, 1513; quoted in Romoli, 146.

35 *suggested, bubonic plague:* See Romoli, 225–26.

35 *"exhaustion and illness":* Oviedo, *Historia General,* III, 232–39, 252–56; quoted in NIW, 65.

35 *fully "two thirds":* Zuazo, Letter to Xévres; quoted in Sauer, 249. Andagoya says seven hundred died in a single month from starvation and *modorra.* Andagoya, 6.

35 *"of corn bread":* Las Casas, bk. III, chap. 61, 199.

36 *their bloody business:* By late autumn, Spanish casualties had dropped to what the Spanish considered an acceptable minimum, with Andagoya reporting the *entradas* were not only bringing back ample food plundered from the Indians, but "all the gold they could lay their hands on" and "great troops of captive natives in chains." He adds that these slaves were immediately put to work digging for gold. Others were forced to build houses and plant crops. "They all died," says Andagoya. Andagoya, 7.

36 *"up among themselves":* Oviedo, *Historia General,* III, 232–39, 252–56; NIW, 65.

36 *of the sun:* See Helms, chap. 1, 3 for information on Panamanian tribal systems and customs.

36 *"loins by cords":* Andagoya, 9.

36 *and gold ornaments:* See Romoli, 97–98.

37 *by cotton cords:* See Oviedo, *Natural History,* 37; Andagoya, 15; Romoli, 98, 111–12; Sauer, 240 for information on Cuevan structures and funerary customs.

37 *to satisfy Ayora:* See Zuazo, Letter to Xévres, January 22, 1518. Ayora netted only 1,393 pesos' worth of gold items from Comogre, and from the nearby *queví* of Tubanamá, another ally of Balboa who was rewarded for his loyalty on the South Sea expedition by a brutal execution at the hands of Ayora and his butchers. See DOP II, 397.

37 *a "hellish hunting":* Oviedo, *Historia,* bk. XXIX, chap. 10; from Sauer, 253.

37 *"lost and desolate":* Zuazo, Letter to Xévres, January 22, 1518.

37 *"in this question":* Probanza of Alonso Martín de Don Benito, AGI, Patronato 1-6-1/29; DOP, II, 160.

37 *this disastrous expedition:* Las Casas tells the story of the Tavira expedition. See Las Casas, III, 203–6. Also see Oviedo (Pérez de Tudela), III, 240, 243. Romoli says two hundred soldiers accompanied Tavira. See Romoli, 314.

38   *gold, called Dabaibe:* Rumored to be "a strong and glittering place of palaces and treasures
     . . . , where a tutelary mother-goddess was worshiped in a temple of fabulous splendor."
     (Romoli, 123.) Balboa originated the legend of Dabaibe in a letter to the king. Balboa first
     heard about the place from Indians near the mouth of the Atrato when he explored there in
     1512. (Oviedo records the date of Balboa's sighting of the Atrato as June 24, 1510; this has
     caused some discrepancy as to the date of the expedition. However, since Balboa had not
     yet departed Hispaniola at this time, it has been commonly accepted that Oviedo intended
     to write "1512." See Romoli, 122–3.) The first "El Dorado" story coming out of South
     America, *Dabaibe* was well-known in Europe as a legendary city of gold for several
     decades in the sixteenth century. See Balboa, Letter to the King, January 20, 1513, in
     CDHE, III, 358–76; Altolaguirre, app. 8; further information in Martyr, Decade II, bk. 4, 6;
     Oviedo, *Historia,* bk. XXIX and in his *Natural History,* chap. 10. The Indians told Balboa
     that a certain "Lord of Dabaibe" lived far up the river, and that he controlled "all the gold"
     in the entire Atrato Basin, including "certain chests of gold each of which requires several
     men to lift." (Balboa, Letter to the King, CDHE III, 358–76; quoted in Sauer, 227.) The leg-
     endary Dabaibe was never found, and the truth about its gold and people remains a mystery.
     By the time the area was thoroughly explored later in the sixteenth century, the people of
     Dabaibe had disappeared, and their cities were lost to dense jungle. Dabaibe was probably
     a major stop on the pre-Colombia trade route that carried gold from the mines in Colombia
     and Peru north into Panama and Costa Rica, and as such was mistaken as a source of the
     gold itself by the Indians living in Urabá. There is no evidence of magnificent palaces and
     golden temples having existed. Much of this lore was embellished by Peter Martyr. Bal-
     boa's informants told him Dabaibe was a center of goldsmiths who fashioned raw metal into
     small and exquisitely worked pendants and charms of the sort archaeologists still unearth
     now and then in tombs in Colombia, Panama, and on up the isthmus.

38   *to the Atrato:* Tavira reportedly spent 8,000 gold pesos of his own money on outfitting his
     expedition, a sizable fortune in Darién at the time.

38   *"in Indian canoes":* Balboa, Letter to the King, CDHE III, 358–76; quoted in Sauer, 225.

39   *death within hours:* Herrera describes how poison was extracted from frogs and snakes, pre-
     pared for use on arrows, and its effects on victims. See Herrera, Decade I, chap. 14–16.

39   *the Spanish feared:* See Hemming, *The Conquest of the Incas,* 112–16, for detailed de-
     scriptions of Indian and Spanish weaponry and armor.

40   *"covered in leather":* Hemming, 114.

40   *"three large canoes":* Las Casas, 204.

40   *lances, and crossbows:* See Las Casas, 204.

40   *against future attacks:* In 1512, Balboa described the lower Sucio as being so swampy that
     he and his men had to march several leagues at a time "in bogs and water, naked, with our
     clothes bundled together on bucklers on top of our heads." Balboa, Letter to the King, 1513;
     DOP III, 358–76.

40   *"heavy forest rains":* Las Casas, 204.

41   *they could overboard:* Oviedo, who knew Tavira and had a low opinion of his corrupt deal-
     ings, claims he drowned while transferring from one ship to another, a less dramatic and, if
     true, a far more embarrassing demise. See Romoli, 314.

41   *"[of] Pedrarias Dávila":* Probanza of Alonso Martín de Don Benito; AGI, Patronato, 1-6-
     1/24; DOP II, 360.

41 *pesos of gold:* See Romoli, 313.

43 *"[with more gold]":* From Porras Barrenechea, in his notes in Trujillo, *Relación,* n 120, p. 119. I have been unable to find the source of the testimony cited by Porras Barrenechea; he says it was given in Panama in 1526.

43 *"Castilla del Oro":* Ranjel-Oviedo, 289.

43 *"to kill Indians":* Oviedo, *Historia,* bk. III, chap. 33; from *Nicaragua en los Cronistas de Indias,* 222–23.

43 Oviedo, *"perfect justice":* Oviedo, *Historia General,* 205. The captains quoted come from Oviedo, *Historia General,* 205–23.

44 *interior of Darién:* See Helms, citation, for a good overview of archaeological data on Panama.

44 *1511 to 1526:* See Góngora, *Los Grupos,* 21.

44 *of fifteen years:* See Góngora, ibid. This figure is the officially reported tally; undoubtedly there was more treasure taken that was not reported.

Chapter 4: Balboa Is Dead

45 *Sea, not Balboa:* See Pedrarias, Report to the King, undated (c. autumn, 1515); Altolaguirre, app. 52; DOP II, 256; Romoli, 278.

46 *"in the world":* Balboa, Letter to the King, October 16, 1515, Santa María; Medina, II, 139, 235–36, 237; Altolaguirre, app. 39; quoted in Romoli, 276.

46 *"the South Sea":* Royal *Cedula* naming Vasco Núñez Adelantado of the South Sea and Governor of Panama and Coiba, September 23, 1514, Valladolid; Altolaguirre, app. 29, p. 63. In 1515, "Coiba" referred to the domains of the Coiban people, who lived west of the Cuevans in west-central Panama. "Panama" referred to the area of present-day Panama City.

46 *"also served us":* Supplementary Instructions from the King to Pedrarias, 1515; quoted in Romoli, 263.

47 *gesture of reconciliation:* Bishop Quevedo joined Pedrarias's wife to convince the governor it would be in everyone's best interest to make peace with Balboa. See Oviedo, III, 232–39, 252–56; NIW, 68–69; Romoli, 288–90.

47 *back in Spain:* See Alverez Rubiano, 377, for information on Isabel and Pedrarias's children.

47 *de los Caballeros:* Soto in his will asked to be buried in the Cathedral of San Miguel in Jerez de los Caballeros, a cathedral built, in part, with money provided by the family of Vasco Núñez de Balboa. See Ordax, 349.

48 *the Pacific side:* "Acla" meant "place of bones" in the Cueva language. This name took on new meaning in 1515 when at least a dozen Spaniards under Lope de Olano were killed to a man by the Cueva Indians of Careta, who became incensed at attacks by Pedrarias's captains in their region. See Romoli, 289. Today, the site of Acla, once the gateway to the mountain passes in the interior of eastern Panama, is uninhabited, the Spanish town Balboa founded having been long ago abandoned.

48 *"that of Darién":* Espinosa, *Relación,* 1515–17; Altolaguirre, app. doc. 59; CDI XXXVII, 73–74; quoted in Sauer, 260.

48 *"is with you":* Herrera, Decade I, bk. 10, chap. 2; quoted in Markham, 830.

49 *(Havana in 1539):* The original 1535 document is lost, though it is referred to in the 1539 version signed by Ponce and Soto in Havana. See Solar y Rújula, 79–89.

49   *"brotherhood was founded":* Conciertos de Hernando de Soto con Hernán de Ponce de
     León, PB, P. la, F. 56 a 62; Solar y Rújula, 79–90.

49   *years 1513–19:* The Havana document is vague as to whether the eighteen or nineteen years
     should be figured from 1535, when the original document was signed in Cuzco, or from
     1539. Counting backward from 1535 places us in the period of Balboa's expedition. Count-
     ing back from 1539 takes us to c. 1520, when Soto, Compañón, and Ponce lived in Natá, in
     western Panama.

49   *second-in-command:* Little is known about Francisco Compañón's early life. He was a *hi-
     dalgo* and nephew of Diego de Albítez, who came to Darién with Diego de Nicuesa, and
     served as a captain and regidor in Santa María before the arrival of Pedrarias. In 1513, Al-
     bítez accompanied Balboa on the expedition that "discovered" the South Sea. He later be-
     came one of Pedrarias's most successful captains during the bloody *montería infernal,* the
     "hellish hunting" that decimated the Cueva of Panama. It is not known when Compañón ar-
     rived in Panama. His name does not appear on any documents prior to 1517, though it is rea-
     sonable to assume that he either arrived with his uncle in 1509, perhaps as a young page or
     aide in his retinue, or joined his uncle sometime prior to 1517. The fact that he was a cap-
     tain in 1517 indicates he had been in the Indies long enough to establish himself. Las Casas
     calls Compañón one of Pedrarias's "chief executioners" of the Indians. (Las Casas, *Histo-
     ria,* 249.) Oviedo adds he was as wicked as any of Pedrarias's men, though he was a "bet-
     ter talker" than Soto or Ponce. (Oviedo, III, 169–70.)

49   *of western Panama:* Ponce served as a pilot and captain on the first Espinosa expedition to
     western Panama, which passed through Acla on its return to Santa María. Hernán Ponce
     may have been among the several men from the Espinosa group who stayed on in Acla to
     join in Balboa's project, though he is not specifically mentioned.

49   *"silk and finery":* Conciertos de Hernando de Soto con Hernán de Ponce de León, PB, P.
     la, F. 56 a 62; Solar y Rújula, 79–90.

49   *"conveying the timber":* Herrera, Decade II, bk. I, chap. III.

50   *just as well:* See Romoli, 337–39, for a detailed description of Balboa's boat-building ex-
     pedition.

50   *"excess of 2,000":* Las Casas, *Historia,* III, 80. Las Casas writes that the official death toll re-
     ported to the Crown by the Bishop of Darién was five hundred Indians; however, he says that
     the notary that reported this figure to him confided that officials "did not want to put in a higher
     number because apparently it was something incredible, but the truth is that they amounted to
     in excess of 2,000." Andagoya, an eyewitness, adds that "In this river we made two ships; and
     we brought many Indians to Acla, to carry the materials for the ships, and the food for the car-
     penters and other workmen. We conveyed these ships down to the sea with great labor, for we
     met with many torrents forming hollows, which we had to cross." (Andagoya, 19.)

50   *a "chief executioner":* Las Casas, *Historia,* III, 49. Las Casas says Compañón "robbed
     everything of the land and food of the Indians that they (the Spaniards) captured, treating
     them like beasts of burden, forcing them to carry every cargo."

50   *perhaps helped with:* In 1535, Soto testified that he was with Alonso Martín on the boat-
     building expedition, and that he witnessed Martín's actions there. See Testimony of Alonso
     Martín de Don Benito, 1535, Lima; AGI, Patronato 1-6-1/24; DOP II, 360.

51   *"were hardly safe":* Herrera, Decade II, bk. I, chap. III.

51   *Balboa to "despair":* Ibid.; also see Andagoya, 19–20.

51 *"mention the Indians":* Las Casas, *Historia,* III, 82.

51 *"on many Indians":* Herrera, Decade, II, bk. I, chap. III.

51 *"cordage or pitch":* Andagoya, 19–20.

51 *"wealth of Peru":* Herrera, Decade II, bk. I, chap. III.

52 *the next year:* This was Pedro de los Ríos, the aged Governor of the Canary Islands, who would end up mysteriously dying within hours of arriving at Santa María, leaving Pedrarias to rule as governor of Castilla del Oro for another seven years.

52 *"come to Acla":* Oviedo, *Historia;* NIW, III, 70.

52 *"had him arrested":* Ibid.

52 *"against the Indians":* Statement of the Proceedings Against Vasco Núñez de Balboa, January 12, 1519, Santa María; Altolaguirre, app. 66; see Romoli, 330.

52 *"for many days":* Oviedo, *Historia;* NIW III, 71.

Chapter 5: The Southern Sea

54 *"in his house":* Romoli, 308. The Spanish population for the entire colony was 600 at the end of 1515, with 435 men away at that time on *entradas* or at Acla. See DOP II, 246.

54 *"up quite comfortably":* Oviedo, *Natural History,* 40.

54 *find fresh supplies:* According to tax receipts collected from 1514 to 1519, out of a total take in plunder, slaves, and mining of 190,436 gold pesos, mining accounted for 32,245 pesos, *cabalgadas* for 128,758 pesos, and slaves for 29,433 pesos, the low amount for slaves reflecting the fact that most were divided as booty and were never actually bought or sold for cash. See Góngora, *Los Grupos,* 21.

55 *"the South Sea":* Andagoya, 22.

55 *"abounding in fish":* This is according to a note in Andagoya, 22. Sauer translates this word as "fishermen." See Sauer, 255.

55 *"and a woman":* Espinosa, *Relación,* 1517. For the origin of Panama's name, see Las Casas, *Historia,* III, 59.

55 *of the city:* Andagoya, 22. My description of the assembled company is based on a passage in Romoli, 220.

56 *"fifty, or forty":* Andagoya, 23. Below is an example of a typical *encomienda* granted in 1522—in this case to Soto's future Peruvian commander, Captain Francisco Pizarro, and Pizarro's retainer, Cristóbal Deleva:

The Cacique *of Taboga*

This *cacique* was found to have 206 adult persons, 84 men and 122 women, who were granted in *encomienda* to the following persons:

To Captain Francisco Pizarro, a native of Trujillo, who came with the Governor Alonso de Hojeda and served as his deputy and captain and has been a councilor and magistrate in this city and also a *visitador* in it, and who has served Their Highnesses very well during all this time in these kingdoms: 150 Indian men and women with the person of the said *cacique.*

To the said Cristóbal Deleva, because he is an old settler and a person who has served and because he has a tame Indian woman *(india mansa)* born in this chiefdom: 12 persons [Indians].

—DOP II, 446–57; NIW I, 84. The original list of those *vecinos* receiving *repartimientos* in 1519 is in Góngora, *Los Grupos,* 70–75.

56 *taxed, and regulated:* Today, the ruins of Panama *Viejo,* Old Panama, rise above the beach ten miles east of the modern city of a half-million people, which was moved to a more defensible position in 1671, after being sacked by Henry Morgan, the English buccaneer. Little remains of Pedrarias's city, other than the massive stone tower of a cathedral built after Soto's time, and the ruins of several walled buildings. Most of these are now inhabited by squatters, who lean their makeshift huts against the broken stones.

56 *in the Americas:* This highway was paved so that it could be used year-round, even during the prodigious rainy season, when earthen trails can become impassable.

56 *of his captains:* We know Ponce was there because his name appears on the official report of the expedition. See DOP II, 154–83; NIW I, 71–79 for information on the first Espinosa campaign to western Panama.

56 *of the expedition:* This *relación* was dictated by Gaspar de Espinosa to a scribe. The report is comprised of several sections, one of which Soto signed, describing operations against the *caciques* Susa and Queco. He also signed at the end of the entire document. Espinosa, *Relación,* October 14, 1519, Panama City; CDI I, 20, 44–56.

57 *the* San Cristóbal: See Medina, II, 276; Romoli, 401.

57 *of Spanish steel:* For information on Coiban customs and warfare, see Sauer, 269–77. For information on Badajoz's failed expedition, see Romoli, 265, 285–87, 310–11.

57 *Gonzalo de Badajoz:* For information on this expedition, see Espinosa's *Relación,* 1517; DOP II, 154–83; NIW, 71–79.

57 *"garment of cotton":* Ibid.; quoted in Sauer, 271.

57 *"among the dead":* Ibid.

58 *"punished and destroyed":* Ibid.

58 *"of the Christians":* Ibid.

59 *"trembling all over":* Ibid; DOP II, 294–96; NIW, 79.

59 *"for the Christians":* Ibid.

59 *"about the legs":* Sauer, 276.

59 *in Espinosa's group:* In 1524, an almost identical amount of plunder was distributed in Nicaragua—35,000 pesos—with minor captains receiving between 100 and 300 pesos. See CDI II 42, 72.

59 *"noses hacked off":* Las Casas, *Historia,* III, 76. In all, Las Casas accuses Espinosa of killing forty thousand natives in Coiba. He concludes that "the spirit of Espinosa" was no better than Pedrarias, and that "el furor Domini (the wrath of God) possessed them both." As always, this figure of natives killed by the sword during Espinosa's campaigns is probably inflated, though it is likely the chief justice, who conducted three large-scale, systematic campaigns in western Panama, probably killed thousands of Indians, with more dying from the usual indirect causes of disease, starvation, displacement, hard labor, and despair.

60 *in western Panama:* The story of this *entrada* is in Las Casas, *Historia,* III, 392–95.

60 *"noise of battle":* Ibid.

60 *"courage nor strength":* Herrera, Decade II, bk. VII, chap. III.

62 *"to the ships":* Ibid.

62 *to the capital:* In Natá's quiet city square, a bronze bust of Gaspar Espinosa declares him the "founder" of Natá. The bald, mustached man depicted looks more like a lawyer than a conqueror, with his high lace collar and cool, calculating expression.

62 *the tiny settlement:* This story is told in Las Casas, *Historia,* III, 395.

63 *"free many men":* Ibid.

63 *"arrived in time":* Ibid.

63 *man, in 1531:* Several years ago, the Republic of Panama memorialized Urraca by etching his profile into their one-cent coin, and by naming a small park in central Panama City the Urraca Freedom Park.

63 *new Spanish municipality:* See PB I, 47, for information regarding Soto's sojourn in Natá, and the partnership there of Soto, Ponce, and Compañón.

Book II: Consolidation

Chapter 6: The Invasion of Nicaragua

67 *"call it* Mexica": this is an imagined scene, though something like it almost certainly happened.

67 *worm-eaten brigantines:* González Dávila sailed with four brigantines, but was later forced to scuttle one when it became unseaworthy. See NIW I, 95.

67 *pesos of gold:* For more information on the *entrada* of Gil González Dávila, see his *Relación;* DHN I, 89–107; NIW I, 90–94.

68 *"damaged by shipworm":* González Dávila, *Relación;* NIW I, 90.

68 *"force of arms"* Ibid., 92.

69 *the Spaniards' guns:* Three of González Dávila's riflemen were severely wounded at Nicoya when a lit arquebus fuse accidentally ignited a keg of powder and blew up the Indian hut where they were staying. See NIW I, 92.

69 *boarded their ships:* It was here that González Dávila scuttled one of his ships, which had become too rotten and worm-eaten to sail.

69 *captain and conquistador:* The evidence for Soto living in Natá from 1520 to 1523 is mostly circumstantial. We know from Las Casas (*Historia,* III, 397) he was there during the siege of Urraca in 1520, though there is no record of him returning after escaping the siege and riding back to Panama City to raise the alarm. Most likely he came back to Natá to be with his partners, and was not only present when Pedrarias founded the city, but also was one of the sixty *vecinos* to receive *repartimientos* in the town as a reward for his role in the Urraca campaign. In 1550, a witness who knew Soto in Panama, Arias de Villalobos, testified he remembered seeing Soto and his two partners staying in a house in 1525 they had apparently lived in before going to Nicaragua in 1523. (Testimony of Arias de Villalobos; PB I, 47.)

69 *and high collar:* No known likeness of Espinosa was rendered during his lifetime, though the artist who rendered this bust seems to have captured Espinosa's exacting, cool, lawyer-like personality.

70 *"served, but adored":* Las Casas, *Historia,* III, 395.

70 *Diego Albítez:* After Pedrarias declared Natá a Spanish city, he named Compañón's uncle, Diego Albítez, lieutenant governor of the city. Soon after, Albítez gave up the post to his nephew, Compañón, who remained lieutenant governor of the city until he moved to Nicaragua in 1524.

70 *"and tyrannical ways":* Las Casas III, *Historia,* 397–98.

71 *killing "many Spaniards":* Ibid.
71 *a generation earlier:* See López de Velasco, *Geografía,* 1571 and 1574; and Sauer, 284.
72 *the invasion force:* Initially, the investors spent two thousand pesos to pay for "the ships, tackle, Negroes, horses, and other things" left behind in Panama by Gil González Dávila when he fled the country. The abandoned assets were sold at auction, the proceeds going to González Dávila's partner, Andrés Niño, who also sold his services as pilot. See *Contrato de Compañia;* in Melendez, 199.
72 *Córdoba's initial invasion:* This is according to a list of participants and their share of booty. See CDI II, 42: 72; and Melendez, app. 3, 217–20. Both Ponce and Compañón appear in the early archival records of the new colony shortly after the invasion.
73 *five for Puente:* See CDI II, 42: 72. There may have been more horses.
73 *ransom at Cajamarca:* For Pedro Díaz's role as silversmith and evaluator of the gold and silver collected at Cajamarca, see CDI I 10, 239–40; and Lockhart, 468–69.
73 *"Paradise of God":* Las Casas, in *Nicaragua en los Cronistas de Indias: Bartolomé de las Casas,* No. 1, 71; quoted in Incer, 62.
73 *"in the Indies":* Oviedo, *Historia; Nicaragua en los Cronistas de Indias:* Oviedo, 203–204, 302; quoted in Incer, 62.
74 *"they are saved":* Andagoya, 34–35.
74 *away as Tenochtitlán:* For information on the origins of the Nicaraguan natives, see Newson, 26–33.
74 *and dozens more:* For information on Nicaraguan customs and cosmology, see Incer, chap. 4.
75 *"this so willingly":* González Dávila, *Relación;* NIW I, 92–93.
75 *courtier's conversational skills:* Diriangen launched a surprise attack against González Dávila and his men after the Nicaraguans as they rested from a feast provided by the Indians. See ibid., 93.
75 *sent by Córdoba:* Pedrarias, Letter to the King, April, 1525, Panama; DHN 1, 130.
75 *he left Urutina:* Ibid.
76 *success in battle:* When González Dávila was attempting to convert Nic-atl-nahuac to the Christian God, one of the king's chief worries was that he and his warriors would have to give up two of their favorite pastimes if they embraced Christianity and became Spanish vassals—"dancing when they were drunk" and wearing the "colors, weapons, and plumes of feathers" of their military squadron, ranks, and orders. There is no record of how González Dávila responded, though one wonders if he and his men felt any empathy, bedecked in their own Castilian plumes, heralds, and garish clothing.
77 *"of the dead":* Oviedo, *Historia;* from *Nicaragua en los Cronistas de las Indias: Oviedo,* 444–45.
77 *"severe northeast winds.":* Squier, *Travels in Central America:* quoted in Anderson, n230.
78 *many populated islands":* Pedrarias, Letter to the King, April, 1525, Panama; DHN 1, 130.
78 *was not navigable:* Pedrarias reports that "the brigantine" sailed by Soto and Benalcázar took a *barco* canoe and tried to run the rapids anyway, traveling downstream several miles before the white water forced them to give up and turn back.
78 *"Gil González Dávila":* Oviedo III, 368; NIW, 97.
78 *"through that land":* Ibid.

Chapter 7: War of the Captains

81   *"men of Cortés":* Pedrarias, Letter to the King, April 1525, Panama City; DHN 1, 130.

81   *never took place:* Years later, Alvarado and Soto would find themselves again competing for the same territory when they both made claims on *La Florida.* This time, however, the region was so enormous that the two never came close to meeting, with Soto confining his explorations to the southeastern U.S., and Alvarado to California. Alvarado's movements into Soto's territories precipitated a long lawsuit brought by another old rival from Central America, Hernán Cortés, who also claimed *La Florida* as his own. See CDI I 15, 300–51.

81   *back to Guatemala:* According to Pedrarias, Soto received the news of Alvarado's pullback shortly after arriving at this Spanish captain's recently abandoned camp outside Nequepio. Here "they found some things" left behind by an obviously well-off Mexican army, including "red cabbage," i.e., cabbage seeds, and "boots" that some of Soto's men were later seen wearing when they returned to León. Pedrarias, Letter to the King, April 1525, Panama City; DHN 1, 130. Incer says Alvarado and Soto did not personally meet each other at this time, because Alvarado was already headed north. See Incer, 71.

81   *of central Honduras:* Nicaraguan historian Jaime Incer has reconstructed Soto's route through El Salvador and Honduras in his excellent *Viajes, Rutas y Encuentros, 1502–1838,* 71–72.

81   *beautifully carved animals:* For information on the Lenca and other tribes of the mountainous interior of Honduras and Nicaragua, see Incer, chap. 10.

81   *"will to live":* Gil González Dávila, Dispatch to Bishop Fonseca, 1518, Santo Domingo; CDI I 34, 237; quoted in Sauer, 206.

83   *through Lenca territory:* This method of travel foreshadows Soto's later debacle at Mabila, where the Indians got plenty of advance warning about Soto as the Spaniards marched noisily through Alabama.

83   *Soto knew his:* According to Oviedo, González Dávila had "heard from Indians in the area how Hernando de Soto and many Spaniards were coming." (Oviedo III, 191–92.)

83   *"in four regiments":* Pedrarias, Letter to the King, April 1525, Panama City; DHN 1, 130.

83   *than they were:* The Mississippians in *La Florida* were particularly adept at using the tactic of attacking by rushing in from the four cardinal points, most notably against Soto at the Battle of Chicasa, where the Chicasa launched a devastating surprise attack the night of March 4, 1541, by rushing Soto's camp from three or four sides.

83   *"of the Emperor!":* Oviedo III, 191–92.

83   *"to the other":* Andagoya, 37.

83   *González Dávila's "cunning":* Herrera III, 171; quoted in Swanton, 69–70.

83   *"certain [other] spoils":* Pedrarias, Letter to the King, April 1525, Panama City; DHN 1, 130.

83   *"with two arquebuses":* Andagoya, 37.

83   *"Puerto de Caballos":* Herrera III, 171; quoted in Swanton, 69–70.

83   *it for himself:* See Pedrarias, Letter to the King, April 1525, Panama City; DHN 1, 130; Andagoya, 37; Herrera III, 171; Swanton, 69–70.

84   *"and a negro":* CDI II 42, 72.

84   *pesos of gold:* Soto apparently shared his prize with the two men who helped sponsor him, Hernán Ponce and the royal treasurer Alonso de la Puente. The other division captain, Francisco de la Puente, also received 1,000 pesos of gold. Only three men received higher

shares—Córdoba (12,000 pesos), Juan Téllez (2,000 pesos), and Alonso de la Puente (1,200 pesos). Sub-captains, including Soto's second-in-command, Sebastián de Benalcázar, were awarded between 300 and 500 pesos; horsemen received between 100 and 300 pesos; and footmen as little as 12 pesos, with a man's share depending on his initial investment and his performance during the invasion. Father Diego de Aguero, as the representative of the church, received 510 pesos. This is the only existing record of gold distributed during the conquest phase in Nicaragua. Apparently, other gold was distributed, given that on September 26, Córdoba sent 185,000 pesos to the king "in payment for past fifths [taxes already owed] and an advance payment on the future" (CDI II 42, 72)—an amount that suggests the total take was closer to one million pesos, if the king was sent one-fifth of all present and anticipated plunder. Part of this royal payment, however, may have been a "gift" that far exceeded the required "fifth." As the archivist Mario Góngora points out, conquistadors in the Indies frequently overpaid the fifth "to please the King and to solicit his favor"—particularly when they had just seized a territory without permission.

84 *alcalde of León:* The evidence for this appointment is in DHN 2, 467–556.

84 *of the region:* For information on the chaotic politics in Trujillo and northern Honduras during this period, see Chamberlain, chap. 1.

84 *"Audiencia on Hispaniola":* Herrera IV, 324; quoted in Meléndez, 101.

84 *and public buildings:* According to Pedrarias and other sources, Córdoba plunged into the building of Granada and León with great enthusiasm.

85 *independent of Panama:* It is possible that if Córdoba gave a favorable response to Moreno's letter, it was motivated as much by a desire to gain the crown lawyer's support for the highway project as it was to launch a rebellion against Pedrarias.

85 *de Olid's insurrection:* This was a disastrous and unnecessary march for Cortés, who spent months slogging through desolate mountain ranges and unhealthy and uninhabited swamps when he could easily have sailed to Honduras to discipline Olid. During the march, he lost dozens of men to disease and starvation. Cortés himself nearly died, and permanently damaged his health.

85 *night at supper:* Oviedo says González Dávila beheaded him; Las Casas says he was wounded with a table knife. Soon after, González Dávila returned to Spain, where Oviedo says he died of "hardships he had suffered." See NIW, 99.

85 *sticking with Pedrarias:* See Incer, 82.

86 *about his plans:* Andagoya, 36–37.

86 *"anger against him":* Oviedo III, 247–48; NIW, 99–100.

86 *"elimination of Hernández":* Meléndez, 109.

86 *"out of prison":* Andagoya, 36–37.

86 *"took the field":* Ibid.

87 *"to kill him":* Ibid.

87 *"abandoned their horses":* Ibid.

87 *or December 1525:* See Meléndez, 110, who notes that routine dispatches from Córdoba on October 26 and November 3 indicate the situation was normal in León, suggesting the incident with Soto occurred after these dates.

87 *late January 1526:* Soto's arrival is noted in AGI, Justicia 1043, no. 1; see Meléndez, 110.

89 *"far as Natá":* Andagoya, 36–37.

89   *Natá's city square:* Years later, a *vecino* in Natá named Arias de Villalobos recalled that he saw Soto and Compañón in Panama "when they arrived there after fleeing the captain Francisco Hernández . . . and he saw them living in a house they owned in Natá." PB I, 47.

89   *was predictably enraged:* The governor already knew about the revolt from the trader Juan Téllez, who had just returned from Nicoya by sea with the news. See Meléndez, 110–11; DHN 1, 307.

89   *as captain general:* See ibid.

89   *their small army:* The army Soto commanded cannot have been large, given that Panama had already been drained of men for the invasion of Nicaragua, and for Francisco Pizarro's first voyage to Peru, which had departed Panama City late in 1524.

89   *Gonzalo de Badajoz:* See Peralta, 707–14; Meléndez, 111.

89   *of his own:* In Tenochtitlán, after a long period with no news from Cortés, his rivals among the royal officials dispatched from Spain declared him dead, and began to dismiss and abuse Cortés's followers in the Mexican capital.

89   *El Furor Domini:* The execution was officially reported to the royal court on a document dated June 20, 1526. See DHN 1 12, 85; Meléndez, 118.

89   *Hernando de Soto:* Because González Dávila was well known at Court, and was a sometime confidant of King Charles, word of his clash with Soto undoubtedly reached the ears of the King, who also had been hearing disturbing reports of violent episodes and revolts among the captains of Cortés in Honduras, and Cortés's rivals in Mexico.

90   *gold and slaves:* Pedrarias sent Soto off on at least one minor *entrada* to "pacify" the Cosiguina Peninsula to the north. See DHN 5, 570; Incer, 568.

90   *his port city:* See Chamberlain, 20.

91   *of the Yucatán:* See DHN 1, 318–77.

91   *least two dozen:* See ibid.

91   *"to captain Compañón":* Letter of Francisco de Castañeda to the King, October 5, 1529, León; AGI Patronato, L. 26, R. 5; DHN 2, 196–214.

92   *at 104 pesos:* See Residencia de Pedro de los Ríos; AGI Justicia, 360, F. 1844; also see García, 230.

92   *testify against him:* The exact date of the former governor's departure is unknown. He was probably in Panama by late autumn, 1526, arriving in the capital of Castilla del Oro with a ship full of illegal Nicaraguan slaves to sell in the market of Panama. See Oviedo 3, 302, 304, 307, 365–68; NIW, 98; Anderson, 231.

92   *recruited in Hispaniola:* See Chamberlain, 20–24.

93   *the Great Valley:* These events are described in DHN 1, 318–71; also see Chamberlain, 20–24; and Newson, 103. In Olancho alone, Salcedo punished by death and mutilation two hundred Indians for allegedly participating in the uprising against Hurtado. He also grossly mistreated his own porters and slaves. Having departed Trujillo with three hundred Indian porters, and capturing two thousand more while on the march, Salcedo arrived in León with only one hundred Indians still alive.

94   *"collected much property":* Oviedo III, 222.

94   *the Governor's Guard:* See ibid.

94   *"of His Majesty":* Testimony of Bartolomé de Celada, Hearing Concerning the Indian Uprising in Olancho, May 6, 1528, Trujillo. DHN 1, 318–71.

94 *of Indian "pacification":* Ibid.
94 *of ten thousand pesos:* Hearing Held by Pedrarias About the Disorders Caused by Salcedo, July 13, 1528, León; Alvarez, app. 135.
94 *(scenes in Valladolid):* Real Cedula, June 1, 1527, Valladolid; Alvarez, app. 125.
95 *royal alcalde mayor:* Real Cedula, November 29, 1527, Burgos; Alvarez, app. 128.
95 *of his tenure:* See Alvarez, 374.
95 *governor of Nicaragua:* Real Cedula, June 1, 1527, Valladolid; Alvarez, app. 125.
95 *Indians in* encomienda: See Alvarez, app. 128.
95 *Gulf of Nicoya:* See DHN 1, 379.
96 *"the best buildings":* Oviedo III, 222.
96 *one thousand pesos:* See Alvarez, app. 135.

Chapter 8: Lord of Tosta

97 *"with many Indians":* DHN 2, 467–555.
97 *sizable "mining estates":* DHN 2, 520.
97 *in the Pacific:* Before 1529, most slaves were shipped to Panama via the island of Chira in the Gulf of Nicoya; afterward, shipping was routed through the port at La Posesión on the coast of León. In 1529, Las Casas and others say there were five or six ships involved in the slave trade; it appears that one and possibly two were owned all or in part by Soto and Ponce. They also may have owned shares in other ships.
97 *"collected much property":* Oviedo III, 222.
97 *thousand Indian vassals:* This number of Indians is an educated guess based on estimated populations for Tosta and other areas where Soto and Ponce owned large estates, and on known *encomiendas.* For instance, Diego López de Salcedo owned some thirty-five thousand Indians in 1527, the largest known estate in Nicaragua. In 1531, Pedrarias owned about nine thousand Indians. Numerous sources attest to the large size of the partnership's holdings in land and Indians. Three specific *encomiendas* are cited in available documents. These are (1) the Indians and estates in and around the native town of Tosta, near the Tezoatega volcano, some forty miles north of León (see Trial of Pedro de Torres, DHN 4, 531–56); (2) the *repartimiento* at Maliguaque, composed of "a huge quantity of Indians," which Ponce acquired from Hernando Caera in 1531 as payment for Caera's berth on Soto's Peruvian armada (see *Residencia,* Francisco de Castañeda, DHN 4, 71); (3) an unidentified *encomienda* which, formerly belonging to Rodrigo Moriel, was given to Soto and Ponce during Salcedo's administration. Later, Francisco Castañeda ordered Moriel compensated by commanding Ponce to give him "other Indians and one horse and some other things" (see DHN II, 116–77). The partnership seemed to have owned numerous other *encomiendas* for which no records exist.
98 *distrusted* los capitáns: According to Las Casas, there were five total slave fleets sent from Nicaragua in 1529, meaning that Soto and his company were involved in at least three, and possibly more. Las Casas, *Breve Relación,* 45.
98 *taken advantage of:* See DHN 2, 82–85; 219–77.
98 *realized "great profits":* DHN 1, 492.
98 *Ponce gladly supplied:* This cargo was not authorized by Pedrarias. In fact, the *Santiago* left the port at La Posesión with guns blazing as the governor attempted to seize the illegal cargo of 240 slaves and 30 or 40 Spanish debtors fleeing the colony, most of them smuggled

aboard by Soto and Ponce. For the story of Bartolomé Ruiz's visit to Nicaragua in 1529, see DHN 2, 28–71.

98 *in meticulous detail:* Information on this shipment of slaves is in DHN 2, 82–85 and DHN 2, 219–77.

98 *"of the king":* Under the rules of the *Requerimiento,* Indians could be legally enslaved if they violently resisted Spanish authority, and refused to acquiesce to Spanish rule. These "rebels," if captured, were branded—usually on the forehead—with the seal of the king to show they had been "legally" enslaved.

99 *occasionally much more:* See Newson, 104.

99 *four thousand pesos:* See ibid., 104. Historian Linda Newson says that conditions aboard slave ships were so abysmal during this period and later that as few as fifty Indians out of four hundred would survive the journey, which could take as long as a month round-trip. If this was true, then the profits for Ponce's shipment might have been considerably less than one thousand to four thousand pesos. Note that Soto and Ponce undoubtedly were involved in additional slaving shipments. The slave trade from Nicaragua to Panama reached a peak of fifteen to twenty ships by the mid 1530s. In 1536, the Crown banned all exports of slaves in the colonies, which slowed, but did not stop the trade.

99 *or seventeen pesos:* Ibid.

99 *as three times:* These expeditions occurred in 1527 (DHN 5, 187); in 1529 (ibid.); and in 1531 (DHN 4, 268).

99 *supplies became exhausted:* See Newson, 103.

99 *for tiny nuggets:* According to Las Casas, the technique in Nicaragua in his day was to scratch stream beds and runoffs with wooden hoes, and to dig out terraces in the hills. Dirt was collected in wooden bowls with holes in the bottom, called *bateas,* which Indians used as sifters.

99 *from their villages:* So many Indians from the valley were sent to the mines that reports in the late 1520s complain that *vecinos* in the Great Valley began running out of laborers and servants to grow food and perform chores.

100 *"and without ceasing":* Las Casas, *Breve Relación,* 43–45.

100 *a majority interest:* The partners' role in the mines began in earnest in 1526, when Gabriel de Rojas was replaced as commandant by Francisco Compañón. He took over both as governor of the Spanish settlement, and warden and chief tormentor of the Indians working the mines. A few months later, Compañón was joined by Hernán Ponce de León, who abandoned his duties as that year's elected alcalde of León to help organize the *compañía*'s mining operations. Later, legal records in León indicate that colonial officials considered Ponce to hold a virtual monopoly on running the mines. (See DHN 2, 467–556).

100 *pesos of gold:* AGI Patronato 26–5; see Newson, 107, n114, p. 381.

100 *"Grace of God":* The gold of Gracias a Dios did not even equal the paltry total mined in Panama during the decade from 1514 to 1524, where some 150,000 pesos was dug up by Cueva and Coiba Indians. The total take at Gracias a Dios, in the bloody accounting of gold versus lives, totaled perhaps five to ten gold pesos per Indian killed.

100 *"fever and sickness":* AGI Patronato 26-5; quoted in Newson, 119.

100 *for their lives:* Castañeda says this plague, which may have been a form of virulent pneumonia, killed "many Indians and some Spaniards."

100 *as "many perished"*: Letter of Pedrarias to the King, January 15, 1529, León; AGI, Patronato, L. 26, R. 5; DHN 2, 449–557. The mines remained abandoned until late 1529, when Ponce took over as the new commandant in Gracias a Dios, with a man named Pedro de Robles as overseer of the *compañia*'s holdings. How well Ponce performed his job, however, was a matter of opinion in the heated politics of León. His enemies insisted that once he and Soto become interested in leaving Nicaragua for Peru, Ponce had "not maintained the mines under his rule as commanded . . . nor has he extracted gold that is in there." Others claimed he embezzled gold from the Crown's taxes, "not reporting all he should have." Supporters, of course, maintained the opposite, saying that Soto and Ponce had done so well in the mines that they were "financing their expedition" to Peru "with gold from the Gracias a Dios mines." (DHN 2, 467–555.)

100 *in high flood*: Compañón, however, apparently made it back to León, where witnesses say he brought the fever with him, and died "in just a few days of a violent fever" "in the hacienda of the partnership," undoubtedly with his friend Hernando de Soto at his side. (Oviedo III, 222; Testimony of Juan Reales, 1550, PB I, 47.)

100 *"the Captain Compañón"*: Soto, *Testamento,* 368.

100 *no one else*: Upon Compañón's death, Soto and Ponce, according to their *compañia* contract, divided up the partnership's total holdings into three parts. Ponce and Soto kept their parts together and re-formed themselves into a dual partnership, while Compañón's third went to his mother, Mari Alvarea, who apparently lived in León. See Testimony of Juan Reales, 1550, PB I, 47.

100 *a spectacular decline*: See Las Casas, *Breve Relación,* 43–45; and Newson, 85–88 for a detailed analysis of the aboriginal population of Nicaragua. Newson cites numerous sources who speculated on the pre-conquest population of Nicaragua, with estimates ranging from under 100,000 to millions. She also makes a convincing case that the Great Valley was fertile enough to support a sizable population.

100 *"kill the delinquents"*: Las Casas, *Breve Relación,* 43–45.

101 *his "own vassals"*: Oviedo, Cronistas, 442–43.

101 *"or eighteen caciques"*: Ibid.

101 *shores of Nicaragua*: See Las Casas, *Breve Relación,* 43–45. See Newson, *Nicaragua,* 84–87.

101 *100,000, or more*: Specific instances of Spanish cruelty by Soto and other slavers is abundant, and makes horrific reading. For example, in 1531 Soto was ordered by the royal alcalde Francisco Castañeda to put down an alleged "rebellion" on several islands in the Gulf of Fonseca. Making short work of the uprising, Soto and his men reportedly amused themselves on their way home by branding Indians destined for the slave markets "with red hot irons . . . in the face." (This story is told by Incer, 114; see DHN 5, 186–87.) On other occasions, Soto undoubtedly participated in such common practices as "dogging" recalcitrant Indians, slicing off noses, hands, and feet, and lopping off heads of Indians chained neck-to-neck when they flagged during the brutal marches to the slave markets in León and elsewhere.

101 *in some areas*: See Newson, 84–85.

101 *during this period*: See Herrera, *Historia General,* 10 dec. 5 lib. 1 cap. 10:72; quoted in Newson, *Nicaragua,* 120. There is evidence that an epidemic, possibly involving smallpox, ran through parts of Central America in 1520–21, just before Córdoba's invasion.

This may partly explain why the Spanish so easily conquered the previously warlike Nicaraguans.

101 *"thirty thousand people":* Las Casas, *Breve Relación,* 43–45

102 *"of the Maribios":* DHN 1, 475.

103 *"Ponce de León":* DHN 2, 308. Though this description could apply to any of three stone houses situated near the corners of the cathedral, two can be eliminated because records clearly identify them as belonging to other *vecinos.* (One of these, located behind the cathedral, was owned by Martín Estete.) This leaves, by process of elimination, the *casa* facing the northeast corner of the cathedral.

103 *(María de Soto):* "I order that to . . . Doña Maria de Soto," Soto wrote in his will, "married to Hernán Nieto, be given one thousand ducats from my goods." He also provided for a son in his will, who may have been born in Nicaragua—Andrés de Soto, "a boy, who they say is my son." Soto, *Testamento,* 369.

103 *a high gate:* See DHN 2, 116–77.

104 *"Lord Pedrarias Dávila":* DHN 4, 63–135.

104 *"the alcalde mayor":* DHN 2, 467–555.

104 *"the Royal Treasurer":* DHN 5, 63–91.

104 *"other small things":* Testimony of Juan de Quiñones, *Residencia* of Licenciado Francisco Castañeda, January 3, 1546, León; DHN 5, 63–91. Quiñones also testified that Castañeda once overturned a death sentence handed down by Pedrarias for Juan Hernández, master pilot of the *San Geronimo,* a ship owned by Soto and Ponce. Hernández's crime is not mentioned. Hernández's death sentence may have had something to do with the fact that Ponce's ships conveyed Pizarro's army to Ecuador from Panama late in 1530, in violation of Pedrarias's orders. Though the pilot who captained the vessels is not mentioned in any documents, it is likely this person was Juan Hernández. His freedom cost two thousand pesos, a sizable sum paid by friends of Soto and Ponce as a bribe to the royal alcalde and other magistrates. See Pedro Pizarro, *Relación,* 11–12 for information on Ponce providing Pizarro with ships.

105 *expand their fleet:* See DHN 2, 196–214.

105 *"his passing fancy":* DHN 2, 116–77.

105 *"to His Majesty":* Ibid.

105 *in a chair:* See Letter of Castañeda to the King, October 5, 1529, León; DHN 2, 196–214. There is no evidence King Charles reacted to these missives any more than his grandfather Ferdinand had responded to those sent earlier by Pedrarias and Balboa.

106 *former mentor, Pedrarias:* See DHN 2, 116–77.

106 *historians allow him:* For instance, at a city council meeting held in 1530, Soto praises Castañeda's efforts to build adobe walls in León, saying these sorts of public-works projects are "a good precedence to start in a new land." In the same meeting, he criticizes Pedrarias's attempts to publicly discredit Castañeda, saying he feared this move "would result in the people of this land becoming insolent and looking unfavorably upon the execution of justice . . . and they will no longer take the law seriously." DHN 2, 116–77.

106 *at La Posesión:* We know the partners had an *encomienda* at Tosta because of a murder that occurred there on February 24, 1529. The fact that Soto and Ponce employed as many as a half-dozen overseers and tribute collectors at Tosta—a number suggested in the records of the murder investigation—indicates their holdings at Tosta were extensive. See DHN 4, 531–49.

106 *allied with Tezoatega:* The Maribios spoke an entirely different language from the Nicarao, and may have been related to the Sioux of North America, though some scholars dispute this. See Newson, 29.

107 *"Pedro de Torres":* DHN 4, 531–49.

107 *"his own hand":* Ibid.

107 *"man," "well respected":* Ibid.

108 *"Pedrarias de Avila":* Ibid.

Chapter 9: Conspirator

109 *"fish, and trees":* Porras Barrenechea, *Cronistas del Peru,* 54; quoted in Hemming, 25.

109 *of their country:* The taking of natives as translators was standard procedure during the *conquista.* In 1539, while Soto was in Cuba preparing for *La Florida,* he sent his master pilot, Juan Añasco, on a reconnoitering expedition to the Florida coast intended, in part, to fetch Indians to train as translators.

110 *to a marquis:* This happened in 1537, after Pizarro successfully put down the rebellion of Manco Inca.

111 *all other "cargo":* See DHN 2, 28–71.

111 *"make an agreement":* Cieza (Cantu), 75.

111 *three hundred slaves:* An eyewitness, Pedro Bravo, described in a later deposition how the operation was carried out, saying the Spaniards and slaves were collected at night on barco skiffs dispatched from *Santiago* and from *San Geronimo,* Soto and Ponce's galleon. According to Bravo, Soto's men rowed these barcos "to shore with shots of artillery" fired as a signal to co-conspirators on land, who then unloaded as many recruits and slaves as possible to be conveyed to the *Santiago.* Bravo adds that most of the Spaniards were debtors banned by law from leaving the colony until their bills were paid. These included Francisco García, "that owed this witness [Bravo] ninety-three pesos for a debt . . ." Another man smuggled out was the overseer of Soto's and Ponce's mines at Gracias a Dios, Pedro Zapatero, who presumably left with Soto's permission. See the hearing record concerning the Ruiz incident, held on July 3, 1529, in León. See DHN 2, 28–71.

112 *"crossbows, and arquebuses":* Ibid.

113 *"in the kingdom":* Pedro Pizarro, 11–12. Pedro Pizarro's recollection of this agreement follows the Pizarro party line in what became a bitter dispute over what, exactly, the Pizarros originally promised Soto. The Pizarros later claimed they promised him the lieutenancy of the major city in Peru, while Soto and Ponce understood he would be named lieutenant-general, or second-in-command, of the invasionary army. Soto obviously expected the latter when he arrived in Peru, only to discover that Pizarro's half-brother, Hernando, already had been named lieutenant general. This issue of command remained a serious point of contention between Soto and his Nicaraguans and the Pizarro brothers and their followers during the early conquest of Peru.

113 *"them to Peru":* DHN 2, 467–555.

114 *"the year passed":* Ibid.

114 *"trouble paying attention":* Testimony of Sebastián Benalcázar, City Council Meeting, December 31, 1530, León; DHN 2, 467–555. How much of this criticism is partisan rhetoric, and how much is fact, is difficult to know. Certainly, Benalcázar and other Pedrarias stal-

warts were not alone in accusing Soto of being overly passionate and easily distracted from administrative matters. Yet their accusations that Soto ignored his post as alcalde in 1525 are not entirely fair. He was away much of the time that year conducting military operations, including the confrontation with González Dávila in Honduras and on long campaigns to Cosiguina and Lake Nicaragua. Toward the end of his term, Soto was not even in the country, as he marched through Costa Rica to warn Pedrarias of Córdoba's insurrection.

114 *"and responsible men":* Ibid.

114 *tried something foolish:* Soto apparently took out his frustrations on the Indians during this brief campaign, abusing captives with a wantonness unusual for a man who tended to be cool and systematic in his "pacifications." According to Jaime Incer, this is the *entrada* where Soto amused himself by torturing Indians with hot irons. This was not the only time Soto took out his rage against the Indians. Twice in La Florida, Soto ordered massacres of unarmed natives in fits of rage—at Napituca, near modern-day Gainesville, Florida, and at Nilco, in today's eastern Arkansas.

115 *live another year:* This tale is told in Albornoz, 96.

Chapter 10: Isla de la Puná

116 *fleet turned armada:* The exact identity of Soto's ships is not certain. Witnesses testifying in the Ponce-Bobadilla lawsuit in 1550 recalled that Soto ordered home the *San Geronimo* from Peru in 1532, though it is unclear whether he personally conveyed his army in this ship, or if the ship was already in Peru, having earlier transported Pizarro's men from Panama. A treasury record in Seville (AGI Contaduría, 1825) records the arrival in Peru at the Isla de Puná on December 1, 1531 of two ships from Nicaragua, with a stopover in Panama. Though this document does not mention Soto by name, no other vessels traveled to Puná at this time. The document, however, does not mention the *San Geronimo.* Instead it lists two ships named *La Concepción.* The masters of the two *La Concepcións* were Juan de Avendaño and Cristóbal Quintero. See Lockhart, n407.

116 *or fifty horses:* Lockhart says twenty-five horses. However, if one considers the number of horses reportedly on Puná before Soto's arrival, and the number after a more likely figure is forty to fifty horses.

116 *illegitimate daughter, María:* See Trujillo, *Relación,* in notes by Raúl Porras Barrenechea, 93; also see Soto, *Testamento,* 369.

116 *wealthy* vecino *investors:* Investors still in Nicaragua received at least one payment in return for their investment in 1532, when Soto dispatched the *San Geronimo* back to Nicaragua with five thousand castellanos taken from his share of the Inca's ransom. See Testimony of Juan Reales, PB I, 9. Reales says most of this money went to cover the expenses of the Soto-Ponce company, though it might also have been intended to reimburse other investors. Reales testified that "Soto was in Peru and he sent Ponce the ship *San Geronimo* that was there and five thousand castellanos necessary for the expenses of the company." (PB I, 9).

116 *in Puerto Realejo:* See Letter of Francisco de Castañeda to the King, October 5, 1529, León; DHN 2, 196–214.

116 *"of the ships":* Pedro Pizarro (Means), 150. Among the owners were Soto, Ponce, and Castañeda.

117 *tents, and horses:* For instance, a rich *vecino* named Hernando Caera sold his *encomienda*

at Maliguique to Hernán Ponce, who served as a broker in many of these deals, "and he left with a huge quantity of Indian slaves and free Indians, and many left in a like manner" (Residencia of Francisco de Castañeda, January 3, 1536, León; DHN 4, 71).

117 *"to these parts":* Pedro Pizarro (Means), 150. This gold was conveyed on one of the ships Ponce provided the Pizarros to take their men to Peru. "Having got this treasure, Don Francisco Pizarro sent one of the ships of Hernán Ponce de León to Nicaragua under García de Aguilar," writes Pedro Pizarro. (Pedro Pizarro, ibid.) Part of this gold may have gone toward the two-thousand-peso bribe arranged by Castañeda to overturn a death sentence imposed by Pedrarias against Soto and Ponce's master pilot, Juan Hernández. Apparently, his crime was to help convey Pizarro's men to Peru in violation of Pedrarias's orders.

117 *"hundred [Spanish] men":* Ibid.

117 *years or less:* See Lockhart's *The Men of Cajamarca* for his brilliant study about Pizarro's men—who they were, where they came from, and where they went.

117 *could do anything:* Because virtually all of Soto's followers on board those small, overcrowded ships were about to become rich and famous beyond their wildest dreams, we know more about them than just their names. For instance, there was Miguel de Estete, a 24-year-old notary and a relative of Martín Estete, Soto's longtime colleague and sometime rival in León. Miguel served as both a cavalryman and an accountant. Originating in Santo Domingo de la Calzada in Old Castile, he arrived in Nicaragua in 1526. In Peru, he accompanied Soto on most of his dangerous assignments, wrote a pithy chronicle of the Peruvian conquest, which includes eyewitness accounts of Soto's exploits, and served at times as Soto's advisor, secretary, and accountant. He returned to Spain in 1534 with many of Soto's men, and settled in Valladolid a wealthy man. (See Lockhart, 265–67.) Others may have included Sebástian de Torres, an important *vecino* in Nicaragua who rode with Soto against the Incas and later became one of the wealthiest men in Peru; Luis Maza, a 28-year-old constable and former Pedrarias crony turned Soto loyalist; Pedro Ortiz, a *hidalgo* with one of the fastest horses in Peru; Lope Vélez and his friend Pedro Cataño, plebeian merchants and business associates of Ponce and Soto in Nicaragua, and Iñigo Tabuyo, a 25-year-old Basque footman who bought a white horse after Cajamarca, and rode at Soto's side in the vanguard of the invasion. Other less prominent Soto supporters from Nicaragua included Francisco de Quiñones, Juan de Porras, Francisco de Fuentes, Alonso Beltrán, and others. See Cieza (Sáenz), 122.

117 *"destroy this country":* DHN 2, 467–555.

117 *early autumn 1531:* Soto's departure date is unknown, though he openly began preparations after Pedrarias's death in March and arrived in Puná on December 1. See AGI, Contaduría, 1825.

118 *north of Tumbez:* This bad weather may have been an early European experience with an el Niño, an enormous and often devastating weather pattern that occurs every few years off the Pacific coast of South America. It may even have been Pizarro's second run-in with El Niño weather. Early in his second voyage to search for Peru, his ships were also buffeted by powerful northerlies and storms that kept them from sailing farther south than Colombia. This storm pattern, which often has proved disastrous to the coastal cities of Peru, may have been partly responsible for the destruction of Tumbez between the second and third voyages, a destruction generally attributed to the Inca civil war and plague. Interview with historian Michael Mossley, 1990.

118 *"the neighboring forests"*: Prescott, 892.
118 *Soto in Nicaragua:* Pedro Pizarro (Means), 150.
118 *"body swelled up"*: Ibid., 151.
118 *"escaped having them"*: Ibid.
118 *"doublets of cotton"*: Prescott, 894.
119 *swarms of mosquitoes:* Cieza says there were "more mosquitoes than soldiers in the army of the Grand Turk."
120 *"and wealth unbounded"*: Anderson, 162.
120 *brothers was Hernando:* For a biographic sketch of Hernando Pizarro, see Lockhart, 157–68.
120 *among the troops:* For a biographic sketch of Juan Pizarro, see Lockhart, 168–75.
120 *against the crown:* For a biographic sketch of Gonzalo Pizarro, see Lockhart, 175–89.
121 *"to do so"*: Pedro Pizarro (Means), 156.
121 *"was not pleased"*: Cieza, 103.
121 *of the army:* The Pizarros consistently downplay Soto's role in their letters and accounts. See Pedro Pizarro (Means) and Hernando Pizarro's *Letter to the Royal Audiencia in Santo Domingo,* his account of the conquest. Soto's role was also not given its proper due because of his early departure from Peru, where chroniclers and historians quickly forgot him amidst the wars, rivalries, and revolutions occurring in the generation after the invasion.

Chapter 11: Empire of the Four Quarters

122 *gold at Cajamarca:* See Lockhart, *The Men of Cajamarca,* for biographies of individual conquistadors in Pizarro's army, and their occupations.
123 *early in 1532:* Exact dates of events during the Peruvian conquest are difficult because of discrepancies among the chroniclers. Pizarro's secretary, Francisco de Jerez, says the army departed Puná in January, others say February or March. The Spaniards retained a presence on the island at least until February 3, according to a shipping record signed on Puná. See AGI, Justicia 724, no. 6.
123 *the Puná Islanders:* See Cieza, 104. It is unclear whether Pizarro's "alliance" with Tumbez was mutually agreed to, or was coerced by the Spaniards. Given the events about to take place, one suspects the latter.
123 *"in great torment"*: Ibid., 104–5.
124 *being warned away:* See Zárate, 63.
124 *and the coast:* See Pedro Pizarro, 157–59. Pedro Pizarro says the Indians guiding a party of Spaniards on rafts stopped on some small islands between Puná and the mainland "to sleep, and when they [the Indians] believed them to be asleep, they went away . . . and later they returned with more [Indian] troops and killed those [Spaniards] whom they had left there." Pizarro says the same thing would have happened to his party, except that one of his companions in his *balsa* was ill, and remained on the raft all night, under the guard of Pedro and another man.
124 *"so few Spaniards"*: Cieza, 105.
124 *very first assignment:* Another explanation for Cieza's comment is that it never happened, and that Cieza invented this moment of introspection to gain a dramatic effect.
124 *"they could find"*: Cieza, 106–8.
124 *"the Emperor's service"*: Zárate, 63–64.

125 *"peace without conditions"*: Cieza, 106–8.

125 *"chiefs and Indians"*: Pedro Pizarro (Means), 162–63.

125 *"so traitorously massacred"*: Zárate, 63–64.

125 *"about . . . the Inca"*: Buenaventura de Salina y Córdoba, 64.

125 *"to come here"*: Sancho, 29.

125 *"Nicaragua or Panama"*: Cieza, 107.

125 *governor of Tumbez:* Soto's duties in this position are not clear, given that Tumbez was never named a municipality, and that Soto spent most of his time riding around in the mountains. From a hearing in 1536, we do know that one of his tasks in Tumbez was to oversee the accounting of whatever gold was plundered in this recently impoverished city. (See Inquiry made into the conduct of Francisco Pizarro and other royal officials, August 20, 1535, Lima; CDI 10, 257.) According to witness Geronimo de Aliaga, an accountant who worked with Soto, Soto saw Pizarro order officials in Tumbez to burn royal tax receipts so they would not have to pay the royal fifth for some of the gold.

127 *"direction of Quito"*: Pedro Pizarro, 162.

127 *Pizarro's original army:* It appears that the army—composed mostly of Extremeños— divided during these early days of the conquest along lines of regional loyalties, with Spaniards from northern Extremadura siding with Pizarro (who originated in Trujillo), and those from southern Extremadura siding with Soto. See Lockhart's analysis on this topic of *Men Of Cajamarca,* 82–85.

127 *"and Gonzalo Pizarro"*: Pedro Pizarro, 162.

127 *"men on foot"*: Buenaventura de Salinsa y Córdoba, 68.

127 *and commissar, respectively:* See ibid. for information on Pizarro's assignments for his senior officers.

127 *"with 64 men"*: Ibid.

128 *a hasty retreat:* In *La Florida,* Soto would establish a similar base camp where he made his landfall in Tampa Bay, though he later abandoned it when he plunged into the interior.

129 *"and no fruit"*: Cieza, *Travels,* 215.

129 *"and noisy deer"*: Titu Cusi Yupanqui, 8.

129 *in full regalia:* This standard still exists in the Museo del Ejército, Madrid.

130 *"of the land"*: Cobo, *Historia del Nuevo Mundo;* quoted in McIntyre, 114.

130 *"until nearly night"*: Ibid.

131 *Prince Ninan Cuyuchi:* See Hemming, 28 and n547 for information and sources on the plague that almost certainly killed Huayna Capac and many other Peruvians.

131 *"them all up"*: Hernando Pizarro, Letter to Oidores, 87; quoted in Hemming, 45.

131 *crowds that autumn:* Though seasons in the southern hemisphere are reversed from those in the northern hemisphere—with our summer being their winter, and so forth—I am using seasons as they would be called in the northern hemisphere, to avoid confusion. Thus when I say "autumn" in this passage, this refers to the time of year northerners call autumn, which would actually be the spring in southern latitudes.

131 *"of the earth"*: The Spaniards called the Tahuantinsuyu people "Incas" because the Spaniards had long been in the habit of confusing the names and titles of *caciques* with the names of countries. In fact, "Inca" was a title like "Emperor," and comes from the Quechua word *Iunca,* originally used by Tahuantinsuyus to differentiate sophisticated valley

dwellers from the more primitive *Serranos,* who lived high in the mountains. See McIntyre, 12.

132 *of the Americas:* For detailed information about the Inca culture in modern texts, see Hemming, McIntyre, and Prescott.

134 *"horse and foot":* Jerez, 26.

135 *"more than 3,000":* Mena, 27.

135 *"for the troops":* Cieza, *Travels,* 217.

135 *"fear of Atahualpa":* Mena, 27.

135 *"of unrefined gold":* Ibid.

136 *"ahead like these":* Ibid.

136 *"to the Spaniards":* Trujillo, 54; quoted in Hemming, 32–33.

136 *"into many pieces":* Cieza, 109–11.

136 *"will remain alive!":* Trujillo, 54; quoted in Hemming, 33.

Book III: Fame

Chapter 12: Cajamarca

139 *"to see him":* Mena, 28.

139 *and 62 cavalry:* See Hemming, 27; and Lockhart, chap. 2. Both authors come up with their counts based on lists of those who received shares of the Inca's ransom, as compiled by Pizarro's two secretaries, Francisco de Jerez and Pedro Sancho, and by period historian Pedro de Cieza de León.

140 *"very difficult passes":* Hernando Pizarro, 114.

140 *"give him battle":* Ibid.

140 *"some 13,500 feet":* Hemming, 31.

140 *"by the roads":* Hernando Pizarro, 114. Hemming notes that four years later, during Manco Inca's uprising, a Spanish troop was in fact obliterated in these same mountains by a far "less professional Inca army." See Hemming, 31.

140 *"high, infertile savannahs":* Hemming, 31.

140 *"a lovely cathedral":* Ibid., 32.

141 *many as eighty thousand:* Mena says that Soto and Hernando Pizarro, after visiting the Inca, estimated the troops to be 40,000, so as not to frighten the men, though in reality the number was closer to 80,000. See Mena, 30.

141 *other key locations:* At roughly this same time, one of Atahualpa's generals, Quizquiz, was capturing Cuzco and destroying what remained of Huascar Inca's army. Atahualpa's other chief general, Chalcuchima, was occupying the major southern city of Jauja with his army.

141 *"have killed us":* Ruiz de Arce, 359; quoted in Hemming, 32.

141 *Hernando de Soto:* Soto was still the captain of the vanguard, and is always mentioned as a division commander during this phase of the conquest.

141 *"the open space":* Hemming, 33.

141 *"pitchers of* chicha": Mena (Sinclair), 29.

142 *"and jingling bells":* Poma de Ayala, 390.

142 *"lodging of Atahualpa":* Jerez, 48.

142 *"a great lord":* Ibid., 66.

142 *"at his feet":* Ibid., 48.

142 *with glittering weapons:* The number of troops in the Inca's courtyard comes from Jerez.

142 *"to the ground":* Estete, 26.

143 *"his entire forehead":* Pedro Pizarro, 249; quoted in Hemming, 34.

143 *"of the Christians":* Mena, 236; quoted in Hemming, 34.

143 *"at the Captain":* Jerez, 48.

143 *"men and horses":* Hernando Pizarro, 116.

144 *"submit to him":* Ibid.

144 *"who concealed themselves":* Ibid.

144 *"cups of gold":* Mena (Sinclair), 30.

144 *"good to him":* Estete, 28; quoted in Hemming, 35.

144 *"which it wheeled":* Ibid.

144 *"had shown fear":* Ibid.

144 *"star-studded sky":* Ibid., 28–29; quoted in Hemming, 35–36.

145 *"all were knights":* Mena, 238; quoted in Hemming, 36.

145 *"spirit they had":* Pedro Pizarro, 236; quoted in Hemming, 36.

145 *"and twenty doors":* Mena (Sinclair), 31.

145 *divisions of cavalry:* See Cataño, 282, who writes that Pizarro's squadron of footmen were "hidden under the livery."

145 *capture the Inca:* Pizarro also assigned smaller units to station themselves around the town to block escape routes. Up in the small fortress, Captain of the Artillery Pedro de Candía stood ready with the army's eight or nine riflemen and four small cannon.

145 *frighten their guests:* Originally, Atahualpa planned to come with his guards armed; he then changed his mind.

146 *"on their heads":* Mena, 238; quoted in Hemming, 38.

146 *"sweeping the road":* Jerez, 53.

146 *"of many colors":* Ibid.

146 *"of pure terror":* Pedro Pizarro, 227.

146 *fled in fear:* Atahualpa later made this comment to Pizarro.

146 *"all were concealed":* Mena (Sinclair), 32.

146 *"in the other":* Jerez, 54.

146 *"advance no further":* Mena (Sinclair), 32.

147 *his new masters:* See Jerez, 54.

147 *"our sacred law":* Mena (Sinclair), 32.

147 *"go two salvos":* Ibid.

147 *"began to kill":* Pedro Pizarro, 227, 229; quoted in Hemming, 42.

147 *"suffocated one another":* Ruiz de Arce, 363.

147 *"he had committed":* Jerez, 55. Note that Jerez is casting Atahualpa as a tyrant deserving of his fate, a common assertion made later by Pizarro partisans such as Francisco Jerez in trying to defend their subsequent murder of the Inca.

148 *"seized the* cacique . . .*":* Cataño, 282.

148 *and* " 'Spear them!' "*:* Ibid.

148 *"in the fields":* Ruiz de Arce, 363.

148 *seven thousand died:* See ibid.

148 *"he was sad":* Mena (Sinclair), 33.

149 *prisoner by us:* Ibid.

149 *"guarding his women":* Estete, 33; quoted in Hemming, 45.

149 *of the Spaniards":* Jerez, 57.

149 *"wrought this day":* Jerez, 58.

Chapter 13: 13,000 Pounds of Gold

150 *"from the square":* Jerez, 59.

151 *order of Atahualpa:* See Mena, 246–48.

151 *"to get killed":* Gaspar de Gárate, Letter to his Father, July 30, 1533; Lockhart, 460.

151 *"to their homes":* Hernando Pizarro, op. cit., 119.

151 *crowned in rosewood:* See Jerez, 61–62, for a complete description of Atahualpa's palace.

151 *"large drinking vessels":* Jerez, 59.

152 *"of the moon":* McIntyre, 8.

152 *"within two months":* Jerez, 65.

152 *"left to him":* Mena, 250; quoted in Hemming, 49.

153 *"in a litter":* Gárate, Letter to his Father, July 30, 1533; Lockhart, 460.

153 *"sign of pleasure":* Jerez, 66.

153 *"spat into it":* Ruiz de Arce, 361; quoted in Hemming, 50–51.

154 *become adept at:* See Espinosa, Letter to the King, August 1, 1533, Panama; CDI I 42, 70.

154 *"he had promised":* Jerez, 69.

154 *"satiated with it!"":* Espinosa, Letter to the King, July 21, 1533; CP, 60.

154 *"without his permission":* Mena, 252.

154 *of the world:* Some later historians, including Augustín de Zárate, claimed Soto was one of the men who traveled to Cuzco at this time. But eyewitnesses list three other men as having made the journey—Martín Bueno, Pedro de Moguer, and a man named Zárate.

155 *of an attack:* The fact that Pizarro sent his brother, Hernando, on a far-flung mission to Pachacámac during this period, but kept Soto in Cajamarca, suggests two possibilities: that Pizarro did not trust Soto enough to give him a unit of men to make an exploration; or, more likely, that the governor preferred to have his most able combat commander close by, in case of an attack.

155 *"it pleased him":* Mena, 264; quoted in Hemming, 69–70.

155 *"had no gold":* Ibid.

155 *"was therefore removed":* Ibid.

156 *"would kill him . . .":* Ibid.

156 *"were his servants":* Ibid.

156 *"in my lodging":* Hernando Pizarro, *Confesión*, 408. Hernando Pizarro claims Almagro and the treasurer Riquelme tortured Chalcuchima; he doesn't mention himself or Soto as being participants.

156 *"blessedness and meekness":* Porras Barrenechea, from Trujillo, notes, 119.

158 *and tiny litters:* For examples of eyewitness descriptions, see Jerez, 69, 98–99; and Mena (Sinclair), 36–41.

158 *twelve thousand pesos:* See Mena (Sinclair), 37; Hemming, 65.

158 *pesos a day:* See Hemming, 73.

158 *"of good silver":* Ibid.

158 *marks of silver:* These numbers come from a document signed by Francisco Pizarro that was found by Rafael Loredo. See Loredo, *Los Repartos,* 72–74. Francisco Jerez and Pedro Cieza León also give these exact figures. See Hemming, n556.

158 *committee of* repartidores: See Porras Barrenechea, *Las Relaciones Primitivas de la Conquista del Perú,* n97–98, for the list of committee members.

158 *appointed royal officers:* These were Treasurer Alonso Riquelme, Veedor García de Salcedo, and Paymaster Antonio Navarro.

159 *marks of silver:* See Sancho, *Report on the Division of the Inca's Ransom;* in Markham, 131–43; for a list of who got what amount of the Inca's ransom. Most of the 168 men received roughly a standard share for horsemen and infantry, though outlays varied widely according to a man's contribution, rank, and class. Generally this meant junior captains, notaries, merchants, and *hidalgos* got more than footmen, commoners, pages, and artisans, though in the tradition of the Spanish *reconquista,* even the lowest men in some cases received sizable shares for an exceptional performance. Almagro's men, who came after the Inca's capture, received nothing of the ransom. Nor did the *vecinos* who stayed behind to settle in San Miguel.

159 *pesos of gold:* It is telling that certain senior captains did not receive a senior captain's share, apparently because they either failed to live up to expectations, or because Pizarro wanted to push them aside. Topping this list was Cristóbal Mena, who received less than a standard horseman's share, though in the early days of the *entrada* he was one of Pizarro's chief lieutenants. Luis Hernández Bueno and Juan de Salazar were also snubbed, receiving more than Mena, but less than Candia and the rest of the senior staff. Mena apparently understood he was no longer wanted; at the first opportunity he departed for Spain.

160 *"hundred thousand natives":* Jerez, 99–100.

160 *"horses remained saddled":* Jerez, 101. The watches included Almagro's men.

160 *"neck of Atahualpa":* Jerez, 100.

161 *the Rumiñavi rumor:* "Wishing to know the truth," writes Oviedo, "five notables volunteered to go in person to investigate and see whether those warriors were in fact coming to attack the Christians . . . The Governor agreed, and Captain Hernando de Soto, Captain Rodrigo Orgóñez, Pedro Ortiz, Miguel Estete, and [Lope] Velez went to find those enemies."

161 *"us to die?":* Cataño, 284; quoted in Hemming, 77.

162 *"before Soto's return":* Andagoya, 52.

162 *"on the conquistadors":* Ruiz de Arce, 364.

162 *ceremony and baptismal:* Atahualpa took "Francisco" as his Christian name. It is not known whether this was intended as an irony or an honor directed at his kidnapper and executioner, Francisco Pizarro.

162 *"wet with tears":* Oviedo, pt. 3, bk. 5, chap. 22; quoted in Hemming, 80.

162 *"upon the sea":* Pedro Pizarro, 220. Nearly all of the eyewitnesses, even those who wrote their accounts long after the events occurred, seem unsure about how to explain themselves as participants in the Inca's death. Most gloss over the execution, failing to mention the results of Soto's investigation, and insisting that the threat of Rumiñavi's attack was real.

163 *after Soto's death:* Luis de Moscoso was a relative of the conquistador Pedro de Alvarado, Cortés's former captain and the Governor of Guatemala. On the way to Peru, Moscoso met Hernán Ponce de León in Nicaragua. After the conquest of Peru, Moscoso is listed as re-

ceiving a modest *encomienda*. Later, in Lima, he became a prominent land owner and aide to Pizarro, until departing for Spain sometime after Soto left in 1535.

163 *"or other person"*: Espinosa, Letter to the King, October 10, 1533, Panama; CP, 66; quoted in Hemming, 80.

163 *"death of Atahualpa"*: *Royal Decree*, July 29, 1533, Toledo; CP, 64. King Charles specifically condemned the execution on two counts—first, because "it was done in the name of justice," and second because Atahualpa "was a monarch," and thus should have been tried by the king.

163 *"it great opportunities"*: Lockhart, 196.

163 *"and spoken to"*: Garcilaso, 61.

Chapter 14: The Dash South

164 *Ponce and Soto:* This is speculation, based on the fact that Soto and Ponce owned a ship called *La Concepción*, which was probably one of the vessels Soto took to Puná.

164 *the Peruvian invasion:* Mena's account was apparently published anonymously in Seville in 1534, the first account of the conquest to reach the public. In 1935, Peruvian historian Raúl Porras Barrenechea proved this "anonymous" *relación* was almost certainly the work of Captain Cristóbal de Mena. See Hemming, n548.

165 *"of [His Majesty]"*: Sancho, 21.

165 *from Atahualpa's assassins:* On orders from Atahualpa, his generals had murdered hundreds of members of the Cuzco royal family after capturing Cuzco. Only a few escaped—including the future Inca and rebel leader Manco Inca, and the mother of Garcilaso de la Vega, author of *The Florida of the Inca*, about Soto's journey through Florida.

166 *"a great feast"*: Sancho (García Icazbalceta), 121; trans. Hemming, 87.

166 *"the Governor's house"*: Sancho (García Icazbalceta); trans. Hemming, 88. Also see Cabildo de Jauja, Letter of July 20, 1534; CL III, 2.

166 *"a rear guard"*: Sancho, 33.

166 *"that they needed"*: Cabildo of Jauja, Letter of July 20, 1534; CL III, 2.

167 *"above the water"*: Estete, 37; quoted in Hemming, 91. Estete wrote about this bridge when he accompanied Hernando Pizarro seven months earlier on an expedition to explore Peru to the south. Sancho, Hernando Pizarro, and others note that Inca bridges were constructed in two spans, one for commoners and one for important persons and royal messengers.

167 *must take action:* As in Cajamarca, the nervous Spaniards again began hearing rumors of native troops massing to attack. According to the rumors, General Chalcuchima was the mastermind organizing these attacks—despite being a prisoner of the Spaniards, and under heavy guard. These suspicions led to another round of abuse and torture inflicted by Pizarro's men against the old general. See Sancho, 34.

167 *and Juan Pizarro:* Juan was considered the best fighter among the four Pizarro brothers. It was during this march, riding in the vanguard with Soto, that he began to distinguish himself as a talented outrider.

168 *"and difficult forest"*: Sancho, 38.

168 *"clothes were drenched"*: Ibid.

168 *"league from Jauja"*: Ibid.

168 *to twenty thousand:* Ruiz de Arce says the Spaniards confronted 25,000 Inca warriors in a

subsequent engagement with this same army. Soto later put their number at 8,000 in a dispatch to Pizarro (Sancho, 80). Both may be exaggerations. Ruiz de Arce's estimate seems too high, written years later, when he could afford to be boastful. Soto's was recorded in the thick of battle, as he tried to calm his men and assure them that the forces massed against them were not so numerous as they feared.

169 *"gold and silver":* Ruiz de Arce, 365.

170 *the Sun King:* After the humiliation and execution of Atahualpa, the position of the Inca had rapidly declined from an almost all-powerful demi-god to a political post to be haggled over, a process that greatly weakened the ruling class of the Inca, and contributed to what would become a growing anarchy as ancient enemies of the Inca reasserted themselves across Peru and Ecuador. All of this would prove very useful to the Spaniards, who took advantage of the disunity and internal conflict to strengthen their rule.

170 *all-important bridges:* For the Quito army, this scorched-earth strategy was risky. For not only were they stripping the land bare of resources for the Spaniards, but for themselves, should they decide to retreat back to Quito, 1,500 miles to the north. Cieza de León says that during this sortie, Soto and Almagro were spotted by Indian scouts, who caught the Spaniards hiding in the hills surveying the destruction. "When some [Incas] came back to inspect the road," says Cieza de León, "they heard the snorting of the horses, and became terrified. They tried to escape for their lives, but the Spaniards cruelly killed them." (Cieza de León, 194.)

170 *"with much speed":* Cieza de León, 195.

170 *just five days:* See Sancho, 59–73.

171 *of the Andes:* If this pace sounds improbable, note that Soto was traveling extremely light along a broad, paved highway stocked with provisions. Moreover, this dispatch is not unheard of in modern endurance horse races, where riders sometimes cover a hundred miles in a single day.

171 *"of the canyons":* Hemming, 100–101.

171 *"many small deer":* Ruiz de Arce, 366.

171 *"cross over it":* Sancho, 59.

171 *"of black rock":* Hemming, 103.

171 *"and trembled so":* Sancho, 62.

171 *"with great riches":* Cieza de León, 213.

172 *"and we them":* Trujillo, 60–61; quoted in Hemming, 103.

172 *"night under arms":* Ibid.

172 *"They then withdrew":* Ibid.

172 *"very difficult slope":* Ibid.

172 *"first was fought":* Sancho, 60.

173 *a great victory:* The letters exchanged between Soto and Pizarro during the conquest of Peru are lost, though much of the critical information contained in them was written down by Pedro Sancho, Pizarro's secretary, in his official chronicle of the expedition.

173 *invigorated Quitoans together:* See Sancho, 73–74.

173 *"their own strength":* Ibid.

173 *ambush up ahead:* Pedro Pizarro, 235.

173 *in a letter:* See Sancho, 75.

174 *"were coming behind":* Trujillo, 61.

174 *"to be lost"*: Pedro Pizarro, 235. Apparently, Pedro Pizarro and others strongly advised Soto to wait for the Governor. But Soto, a man who seldom heeded advice good or bad from subordinates, ignored them, just as he had rejected his lieutenants' warnings a decade earlier in Honduras during the disastrous incident with Gil González Dávila, and would later dismiss his captains' advice in Florida.

174 *army's heavy baggage:* The gold of Cajamarca had been left in Jauja with Riquelme's garrison.

174 *"the Pampas river"*: Hemming, 105.

174 *"heat to cold"*: Sancho, 79–80.

175 *along the way:* This information must have greatly distressed Pizarro, since it suggested Soto was more interested in small, local caches of gold than in the decisive battle ahead. Some of the villages Soto plundered were allies of the Spaniards, being loyal to the Huascar faction during the civil war.

175 *"he wearied them"*: Pedro Pizarro, 237–38.

175 *"slippery stone bed"*: Hemming, 106.

175 *"been seen since"*: Herrera, Decade V, bk. 5, 349–50.

175 *"of their canyons"*: Hemming, 106.

175 *"groups of four"*: Ruiz de Arce, 366.

177 *"with great rapidity"*: Sancho, 82.

177 *"stones before them"*: Hemming, 106.

177 *"with greater fury"*: Sancho, 83.

177 *horses later died:* One of the dead men was the young correspondent I have quoted now and then, Gaspar de Gárate, whose letter to his father at Cajamarca is the only piece of personal correspondence surviving from the early Peruvian conquest. Another young man killed was Hernando de Toro, originally brought over from the Pizarro's home town of Trujillo to serve as a squire and bodyguard for the governor, though lately he had become more his own man, riding with Soto as one of the hotheads who decided to ride ahead against the Governor's orders. The others killed included a notary named Juan Alonso, his mulatto friend Miguel Ruiz, and an illiterate footman who bought a horse at Cajamarca, named Francisco Martín. All these men died rich. The cocky Toro was worth 12,000 pesos at Cajamarca; the others had received at least 4,000 pesos apiece from the Inca's booty. Some sources suggest a sixth man died, identified only as "Hernández."

177 *"of the mountain"*: Sancho, 84–85.

178 *"hope for victory?"*: Ruiz de Arce, 365.

178 *"all to die!"*: Ibid.

178 *a Spanish trumpet:* James Lockhart notes that this incident was reported by all the chroniclers in heroic-sounding prose, though "it was less cinematic and more typically Spanish than might appear. Soto's men had gotten into trouble by rushing too far ahead, trying to reach the riches of Cuzco before the rest. The rescuers were hurrying, not so much to save their comrades as to keep them from getting to Cuzco first. And [the trumpeter Pedro de] Alconchel was not trying to signal that help was coming, but to inform some stragglers where camp had been made for the night." Lockhart, 370.

178 *"the Christians was"*: Pedro Pizarro, 239.

179 *"see one another"*: Sancho, 92.

Chapter 15: The Navel of the World

180 *the Inca capital:* For information on the Spanish entry into Cuzco, see Sancho, chap. 10; Estete, 44–46; Trujillo, 63–64; also Hemming, 109–21.

181 *least 100,000 people:* The exact size of pre-conquest Cuzco is not known. Scholars have proposed estimates ranging as high as 200,000. (See Stannard, 43.) Estete and others claimed that in the largest Inca cities, over 100,000 people gathered at one time for festivals. See Estete, 41; also Cook, 39, 200.

181 *in the center:* See Hemming, 119–20.

182 *"in royal palaces":* Garcilaso, pt. I, bk. 7, chap. 10; pt. 2, chap. 32; quoted in Hemming, 122.

182 *"periods of hunger":* Sancho, 201; quoted in Hemming, 120.

182 *of the sun:* This appellation did not necessarily mean the Inca believed the Spaniards were gods. The name comes from a legendary Inca king named Viracocha, a son of the sun who reportedly wore a beard (native Peruvians normally cannot grow facial hair) and performed various miraculous feats, including driving away certain enemies of the Incas, just as the Spanish had driven away the forces of Atahualpa and Quito.

182 *palace of Huascar:* See Acta de fundación del Cuzco, para. 4; also Pedro Pizarro (BAE), 192.

182 *Hernando de Soto:* When lots were drawn by the senior officers for palaces, Amaru Cancha was won by both Soto and Hernando Pizarro, who divided the palace between them. Soto occupied the rooms facing the square. See Acta de fundación del Cuzco, para. 9. Hernando Pizarro gained control of the entire palace after Soto departed Peru in 1535. Amaru Cancha burned down in 1536, during the Inca revolt. Later, Hernando Pizarro sold the property to the Jesuits for 14,000 pesos. In 1572, Soto's Peruvian daughter, Leonor de Soto, and her notary husband, García Carrillo, sued the Jesuits to recover Soto's portion of the palace. The outcome of the suit is unknown. In Quechua, Amaru Cancha means "place of snakes" and refers to the district of the snakes in Cuzco. Other districts were named after lions and other animals.

182 *"and multicolored marble":* Sancho, 192; quoted in Hemming, 122.

182 *"sixty in breadth":* Garcilaso, *Royal Commentaries,* 320. Garcilaso defines a pace as "two feet," 540.

183 *"and other metals":* Estete, 45; quoted in Hemming, 122.

183 *"with their arms":* Sancho, 107–8.

183 *"had ever seen":* Ibid.

184 *"capture of Atahualpa":* Gómara, chap. 37, 123; quoted in Hemming, 122. The nineteenth-century Peruvian historian Rafael Loredo discovered documents detailing this first haul of Cuzco treasure, which totaled 700,113,880 *maravedíes,* compared to 697,994,930 *maravedíes* distributed at Cajamarca. (See Hemming, n565, for detailed analysis.)

184 *"and other insects":* Pedro Pizarro (BAE), 195–96; quoted in Hemming, 122.

184 *"of the monastery":* Ruiz de Arce, 372.

184 *"many precious stones":* Trujillo, 64.

184 *"enjoyed and possessed":* Molina of Santiago, 118; quoted in Hemming, 134–35.

185 *"so many items":* Sancho, 195.

185 *"and went in":* Trujillo, 64.

185 *marks of silver:* This is according to Rafael Loredo, who analyzes the distribution of treasure at this division of Cuzco spoils in his *Los reportos,* 95–107. Also see Hemming, n565.

185 *total much more:* The exact total of gold and silver collected in Cuzco and in the surrounding valley will never be known. For years after the initial conquest, Spaniards kept searching, and finding, caches of treasure.

185 *considered heathen rites:* With his tiny army, Pizarro did not yet feel secure enough to try and stop the "pagan" ceremonies.

186 *"had been alive":* Estete, 54–56. (Hemming, 127.)

186 *"days in succession":* Ibid.

186 *away from reinforcements:* Gómara says that strategic considerations and the fate of the eighty-man garrison vexed Pizarro considerably less than what mattered most to him in Jauja. "For it stung him greatly," says Gómara, "that he had left a great treasure in Jauja with a tiny garrison." López de Gómara, *Historia,* 2:42–43.

186 *twenty thousand men:* See Cabildo of Jauja, Letter of July 20, 1534; CL 3:5.

187 *made of stone:* Soto's force was further delayed by Quizquiz's destruction of whatever bridges remained across canyons and rivers then at full flood along the royal highway. It took twenty days for Manco's engineers just to repair the bridge spanning the raging Pampas river below Vilcashuaman.

187 *of the Quitoans:* See Hemming, 139 for a description of this battle.

187 *and for all:* See Sancho, 133–35 for a description of this campaign.

187 *way to Huánuco:* The Cabildo of Jauja (Letter of July 20, 1534; CL 3:5) says Soto marched 70 leagues before turning back. Sancho says Soto was ordered to pursue Quizquiz as far as Huánuco (Sancho, 142–43). Pedro Pizarro says Soto went only as far as the Atavillos region, south of Huánuco (Pedro Pizarro, 285–86).

Chapter 16: Lord of Cuzco

188 *new capital city:* Pizarro's name for his capital was La Ciudad de los Reyes, the City of the Kings. "Lima" comes from a corruption of the area's original Indian name.

188 *of royal corregidor:* A corregidor represented the king's authority in a colony, and oversaw all royal business, including the management of crown properties, and taxation. Pizarro, as a royal governor, had the authority to name Soto corregidor, pending approval by the king. Pedro Pizarro is the source for Soto's appointment as corregidor, though it is not clear when the governor named him to this post. See Pedro Pizarro, 293.

189 *"without getting involved":* Instruction of Francisco Pizarro to Hernando de Soto, July 27, 1934, Jauja; AGI, Patronato 1, 4, 1; CDII 42, 132–34.

189 *early as Tumbez:* See CDI 10, 246.

189 *on the sly:* See Garcilaso, 61. The Spaniards first major division of Cuzco loot was on March 19, 1534, while Soto was away chasing Quizquiz. Soto's exact share in this melting is not recorded, though it was probably substantial. That October, there was a second division, presided over by Soto, who presumably gave himself a hefty share, though a specific amount was never recorded. Because there is a large discrepancy between Soto's total reported take in treasure and his fortune at the time of his departure for Spain in 1535, it seems that Soto acquired gold and silver above and beyond what is recorded—and what he would have earned from his *encomiendas.*

190 *Hernando de Soto:* The scholars who found this document were Horacio H. Urteaga and Carlos A. Romero. They discovered it by accident, slipped into another unrelated document dated 1572. See Libro primero de cabildos de la ciudad del Cuzco, introduction by Raúl Rivera Serna, 1.

190 *"all could hear":* Libro primero de cabildos de la ciudad del Cuzco, 31.

190 *being frequently absent:* See Ibid., 42.

191 *"out before now":* Ibid., 32–33; 42.

191 *correct the situation:* Soto ordered his friend Gabriel de Rojas, who had come with him from Jauja, to take on this delicate task, as someone "that in other regions has been used for honored responsibilities, and he will know what to do." Ibid., 42.

191 *and their allocations:* See ibid., 32–37.

191 *"the entire plaza":* Cabildo de Cuzco, 33. Soto also received as part of his share of property in Cuzco half of the Convent of the Virgins of the Sum, which he sold to an apothecary named Segovia, who later discovered 72,000 pesos worth of treasure buried underneath it. See Jerez (Markham), n73.

192 *mistress, Juana Hernández:* See Trujillo, 52. Trujillo says that when Soto arrived at Puná, he brought a certain Juana Hernández with him from Nicaragua. Nothing more is heard of her. I am assuming she was a low-born mistress, or perhaps a mistress-servant.

192 *Leonor de Soto:* See Cabello Balboa, 131–43 for the story of Soto's affair, and Cabello Balboa's sources.

192 *"her mother had":* Ibid.

192 *"of the church":* Cieza de León, 181–83.

193 *"with the widow":* Ibid.

193 *lived close by:* Hemming writes: "The Acta de Fundación said that a plot was awarded to one Pedro de Ulloa in 'the enclosure in which lives the *palla* [lady] of the Lieutenant Hernando de Soto, behind Lobillo's lot.' (Porras Barrenechea, 'Dos documentos esenciales')." Hemming, n571.

193 *for several generations:* See AGI, Patronato 109 1-5-20/4; Solar y Rújula, 185–90. In 1572, Soto's daughter and her notary husband made a claim on property once owned by Soto—the site of the Amuru Cancha palace, which the Jesuits now occupied. The record of their suit is in the Biblioteca Nacional in Lima, dated September 26, 1572.

193 *and raised her:* See ibid.

193 *Alonso de Medina:* Alonso de Medina was a *hidalgo* roughly Soto's age. Medina probably knew Soto as a boy in Extremadura, where the Medinas were close friends of Soto's mother's family in Badajoz. (See Testimony of Alonso de Medina, 1538, Badajoz, *Expediente of Hernando de Soto;* Solar y Rújula, 152–54.) Having arrived in Nicaragua in 1524, Medina quickly acquired a modest *encomienda,* giving it up in 1529—probably because he was in debt—to escape with twenty other Spaniards to Panama. (He departed on a ship belonging to Bartolomé Ruiz, who smuggled out the men with the help of Soto and Hernán Ponce.) From Panama, Medina joined up with the Pizarro expedition, eventually being reunited with Soto on Puná. During the conquest, Medina served as one of Soto's outriders, proving to be one of his most loyal followers. See Lockhart, 226–27, for biography of Alonso de Medina.

194 *"friend and acquaintance":* PB I, 13.

194 *the Florida army:* PB I, 9–10.

194 *properties in Nicaragua:* Ponce had arrived in Peru by May 20, when he collected 18,033 pesos of gold for Soto in the final distribution of plunder in Cuzco. (Report to the King, May 20, 1535; CDI 9, 504.) Pedro Bravo testified in the Ponce-Bobadilla suit that Ponce came to Peru with "many horses," and presumably gold from cashing out the partner's estates in Nicaragua. "It was said they both resided together [in Peru] and had a partnership . . ." PB I, 13. Luis de Moscoso mentions at least one *encomienda* owned by Ponce, at the Indian town of Gualuchiari. See Moscoso's testimony in PB I, 7. Ponce apparently was given numerous additional properties as part of his original agreement with the Pizarros. See Pedro Pizarro, 11–12.

194 *return to Spain:* See PB II, 7, 10. Ponce testified in the Ponce-Bobadilla trial that he was upset with Soto's decision to conquer *La Florida,* saying this was a bad idea. At the same trial, Soto's majordomo, Alonso de Ayala, testified that Soto and Ponce had agreed while still in Peru that Soto would go back to Spain and attempt to acquire a royal concession for a governorship in "the South Sea"—i.e., on the Pacific coast of South or Central America— "and not in anywhere else." See PB II, 7. This suggests Ponce and Soto may have been at odds in Peru over the future direction the partnership should take. Ponce's subsequent return to Spain, where he settled down to live a comfortable life in Seville with his Peruvian fortune, further suggests he did not share Soto's enthusiasm for launching more conquests and adventures.

194 *"in the kingdom":* Pedro Pizarro, 11–12.

194 *"30,000 gold pesos":* Testimony of Isabel de Bobadilla, PB I, 44. Estimates of the Soto-Ponce fortune mentioned in the *Ponce v. Bobadilla* suit ranged from 130,000 ducats to 250,000 ducats. Isabel de Bobadilla testified that the "gold, silver, coinage, and other things that were valued" totaled "200,000 ducats." (PB I, 36.) Moscoso confirms this amount, saying that this was the total amount of gold held by the partners. (PB I, 7.) Several witnesses placed the total value of the partner's gold, silver, and properties in Peru at 250,000 ducats. See PB I, 36.

194 *his own witnesses:* See PB II, 8.

195 *"without bridling it":* Cieza de León, *War of Las Salinas,* chap. 70, 223; quoted in Hemming, 234.

196 *city was his:* Numerous sources describe these events. See Cieza de León, *Cronistas,* 255–70; Pedro Pizarro, 285–95.

196 *clarify Almagro's status:* Cieza de León, 265.

196 *"Pizarro became haughty":* Ibid.

196 *"bias toward him":* Ibid., 266.

197 *"even threatened him":* Ibid., 267.

197 *"Vasco de Guevara":* Ibid.

197 *"supported his interests":* Ibid.

197 *"bitterness and pride":* Ibid.

197 *"Inflamed" and ready:* Ibid.

198 *"would be lost":* Tellez de Guzmán Report to the King, May 5, 1536, Seville; CDH Chile 4, 60.

198 *"excuse the scandal":* Cieza de León, 269.

198 *"one or another"*: Ibid.

198 *"and kill everyone"*: Pedro Pizarro, 293–94. Naturally favoring his family in this incident, Pedro Pizarro makes Soto the villain. "One day," writes Pizarro, after Almagro arrived, and the Pizarroists and Almagroists began to arm, Soto "came to where Juan Pizarro was with his friends in order to incarcerate him in his dwelling, though he failed to do the same to Don Diego de Almagro. On account of this, Juan Pizarro and Soto had words, for Juan Pizarro told him that he was unfairly partial, and Soto replied this was not so, whereupon Juan Pizarro seized a lance and stuck Soto with it, and, had not [Soto] quickly fled upon the horse he was riding, he would have been overthrown by the blows of the lance. Juan Pizarro then followed him until he chased him into the place where Almagro was, and, had not the friends and soldiers of Almagro saved him, [Juan Pizarro] would have slain him, for Juan Pizarro was a very valiant and ireful man." He adds that Juan and Soto did eventually fight, and that this was broken up by a certain Gómez de Alvarado.

199 *as captain general*: See Cieza de León, *La Tercera Parte*, 387.

199 *expedition to Chile*: Letter of Rodrigo Orgóñez to his father, July 2, 1535, Cuzco. Porras Barrenechea, *Cartas del Peru*, 167.

199 *his captain general*: This young horseman wrote two letters to relatives in Spain that reveal Almagro's state of mind as he made his decision. "I came to this city," Orgóñez writes, meaning Cuzco, "and afterward the Lord General [Almagro] came and said that he wanted to grant me what I wanted, and he said to tell others that he could not be had for money, and that he has said that I am his son and that whatever it will cost him he will name me [Lieutenant] Governor." Letter of Rodrigo Orgóñez to Antonio de Vergara, July 1, 1535, Cuzco; Porras Barrenechea, *Cartas del Peru*, 165.

199 *to do next*: See Testimony of Alonso de Ayala; PB I, 11.

200 *concession should be*: See ibid.

200 *"some in bars"*: PB II, 8. The witness was Gonzalo Hernández, a cleric who sailed with Soto from Panama to Spain.

200 *Nuño de Tobar*: See PB II, 8.

200 *"had already spilled . . . "*: Oviedo, in Ranjel-Oviedo, 289–90.

Chapter 17: Back to Spain

201 *pounds of gold*: Several Peruvian conquerors had already returned home, the most prominent being Hernando Pizarro, who had come to deliver gifts and information to the king shortly before Atahualpa's execution in June, 1534. Other major returnees included Cristóbal de Mena and Francisco de Jerez. Both had published *relaciónes* about the march to Cajamarca, in which Soto figured prominently. Hernando Pizarro, as the Governor's brother, had been greeted with particularly enthusiastic fanfare, though his dour demeanor, and the shock felt in the Iberian world when Francisco, his brother, ordered the Inca's execution, greatly diminished his status as hero.

202 *Casa de Contratación*: One thousand pounds of gold, or one hundred thousand pesos, was almost twice what even the richest man in Seville, the Marquis de Valle, reportedly earned in a year from his properties—that is, some 60,000 ducats a year. The richest seven men in Seville earned an average of about 35,000 ducats a year from rent and properties. See Pike, 27.

202 *at his house*: According to Cataño, Soto stayed with him during the spring and part of the

summer of 1536. If this is true, then we know approximately where Soto lived during these first weeks in Spain. Archival records indicate Cataño's house was located near the Guadalquivir in Seville, in the parish of San Miguel, a small area occupied today by the University of Seville and the city's theater district. In the sixteenth century, this was a small but wealthy parish of merchants and petty nobles who had become rich from trading with the Indies. This group included Cataño, who had returned home from Peru with most of his loot intact. (He received a double horseman's share of Atahualpa's ransom—362 pesos of gold and 880 marks of silver, plus whatever gold he collected after Cajamarca.) Cataño came from a Genoan family of merchants and ship owners who were already well off, having benefited from the Indies trade since they loaned a small amount of money to Columbus for one of his expeditions. Pedro was also the first of the Cataños to win from the king a coat-of-arms—a yellow field with a black eagle bordered by eight gold stars, which he had painted proudly above the entryway to his house for Soto and everyone else to see.

202 *grand staircase inside:* Elvas says: "They . . . went to the Governor's [Soto] lodgings. They entered the patio upon which looked some balconies where he was. He looked down and went to meet them at the stairs . . ." Elvas, 50.

202 *"of a gentleman":* Elvas, 47.

202 *"and other merriments":* PB I, 13.

202 *"were quick-tempered":* PB I, 8.

203 *noble in Spain:* Elvas says that "the Emperor took [by loan] a part" of Soto's fortune, "which was repaid to him by six hundred thousand reales with interest in [duties on] the silks of Granada, and the rest was delivered to him [in cash] at the Casa de Contratación in Seville." Elvas, 47.

203 *"discretion for peace":* Garcilaso, 62.

203 *"of good reputation":* Notice of Officials of Seville to the Emperor, undated (probably summer, 1536); Porras Barrenechea, *Cartas del Peru,* 185–86.

205 *"Hernando de Soto":* Soto to unknown Señor, date unknown (probably late 1536 or early 1537); Porras Barrenechea, *Cartas del Peru,* 273. The original letter is in the Biblioteca Nacional in Madrid. Only the signature is obviously in Soto's handwriting. See *The De Soto Chronicles* I, 358–59.

205 *in Charles's administration:* This Señor may also have been hired by Soto as a well-placed advocate at the Court.

205 *clans in Spain:* the elder Isabel's grandparents included the Marquis of Moya and Francisco de Bobadilla, the latter a favorite of the Catholic kings. Isabel also had a famous aunt and namesake, who was a close and trusted confident of Queen Isabel the Catholic. There is a story that this aunt was so beautiful that Ferdinand, who frequently strayed from the Queen's embrace, took a fancy to her, forcing Isabel to hastily arrange a marriage with the governor of a colony far removed from the Court—in the Canary Islands.

205 *her late twenties:* Isabel the younger is listed in her father's will of 1514 as the third of his eight children, all of whom had been born by that date. This suggests that she was born c. 1508, and possibly earlier. But whatever her exact age, she appears to have been considerably older than most señoritas in high society, who were often married while still children. Possibly, she was a widow, though if this were the case, it is likely one of the chroniclers or historians would have mentioned it.

205 *"goodness and discretion":* Garcilaso, 91.

206 *"judgment and character":* Ranjel-Oviedo, 251.

206 *sixteenth-century Spain:* Only one other woman served in high office in the Spanish colonies during this period—Aldonza Manrique of Venezuela, who inherited the governorship when her father, Marcelo Villalobas, died in 1526. This Doña Aldonzo ruled Venezuela for at least thirteen years—compared to Isabel's five-year reign in Cuba.

206 *chapel in Valladolid:* During the *Ponce v. Bobadilla* trial, several witnesses testified they had seen or heard about Soto's wedding in Valladolid. The priest who married them, Alberto Gallego, describes himself as the Bobadilla priest at the family chapel at the time. See his testimony in PB I, 16. Also see PB II, 9.

206 *as a dowry:* See Letter of dowry and pledge of Doña Isabel de Bobadilla in the marriage of her daughter to Hernando de Soto, November 14, 1536, Valladolid. AGI, Justicia 750 A; Solar y Rújula, 157–66. Also see PB I, 15.

206 *and gold jewelry:* See PB I, 16. No detailed description of Soto's wedding exists; however, one can assume the guest list included prominent members of the Valladolid society, given the importance of the Bobadilla family, and Soto's fame and notoriety. Elvas reports that several of Soto's well-dressed friends traveled with him to Valladolid (See Elvas, 47).

206 *spending "very liberally":* Elvas, 47.

206 *"came about him":* Ibid.

207 *"a velvet glove":* Attributed to Charles V by Thomas Carlyle, *Latter-Day Pamphlets,* 11.

208 *taken by others:* Guatemala was apparently denied to Soto because Bartolomé de las Casas was lobbying the king to send a more humane governor, one that the aging bishop hoped would be able to convert the natives by peaceful means. See Henke, 77–81. The crown also had others in mind to govern Ecuador and Colombia, including Soto's old rival, Sebastián de Benalcázar.

208 *other Christian enemies:* The legend of Prester John may have had some basis in fact, perhaps referring to the Christian kingdom of Ethiopia in Africa, where Coptic Christians managed to fight off the Moslem faith that seized the remainder of northeastern Africa during the European Middle Ages. The letter supposedly written by John was almost certainly a hoax.

209 *official on Hispaniola:* Garcilaso says Ayllón was a judge on the Audiencia of Santo Domingo, and was a Knight of Santiago. See Garcilaso, 64.

209 *a white king:* This may be a reference to Prester John.

209 *"cruel and stupid":* Las Casas; quoted in Weddle, 26.

210 *"of . . . 2000 [ducats]":* Concession made by the king to Hernando de Soto of the government of Cuba and conquest of Florida, April 20, 1537, Valladolid. AGI, Patronato 50-2-55/10; Solar y Rújula, 119–22; *The De Soto Chronicles* I, 364.

210 *"and new settlements":* Ibid.

211 *revered military order:* It is not known if the king literally participated in Soto's induction ceremony, though Charles was in Valladolid at the time, and, as both king and the leader of the Knights of Santiago, it would have been customary for him to personally induct a new member into the order.

211 *with the blade:* This is one of several ceremonies the king might have used to induct a new knight.

Book IV: Conquest

Chapter 18: Armada

216 *with an astrolabe:* Garcilaso says Soto brought along a Genoan shipbuilder named Maestro Francisco, 152, 392. He also brought nails and tackle to be able to quickly construct brigantines and other vessels. See Alonso de Carmona's comments about Añasco's abilities as a navigator in Garcilaso, 526–27. Also see Dan Morse, "Scientific Instruments and Early Exploration in the United States," *The Florida Anthropologist,* 43:1:45–47 (March, 1990).

216 *"water when loaded":* Cabeza de Vaca, 47.

218 *"a great distance!":* Ibid., 125, 127.

218 *man few remembered:* See Cyclone Covey's preface to *Cabeza de Vaca's Adventures in the Unknown Interior* for a good, and brief, biography of this explorer's life, his attitudes toward the Indians, and the disastrous failure of his Indian policies in the Río de la Plate colony.

218 *published in 1542:* Later, when the expedition was traveling through Texas after Soto's death, the chroniclers several times mention having read a "report" given to Soto by Cabeza de Vaca.

219 *"would act wisely":* Elvas, 48.

219 *"banner of another":* Ibid.

219 *for some time:* The 1530s was a busy period for large expeditions, after a hiatus that extended back to Pedrarias's venture in 1514. Just two years earlier, Pedro Fernández de Lugo commanded perhaps fifteen vessels and 1,200 people to assume the governorship of Santa Marta; a year earlier, in 1535, Pedro de Mendoza sailed in twelve ships carrying over 1,000 people to explore and settle the Río de la Plate on the border of modern Argentina and Uruguay.

219 *topping 130,000 castellanos:* According to witnesses in the *Ponce v. Bobadilla* trial, Soto told Ponce in Havana he had spent 130,000 castellanos on the expedition, and needed an additional 8,000. See PB I, 2.

219 *"cosmographer, and astrologer":* Garcilaso, 89.

219 *among other things:* Añasco also had influence at the court, obtaining a special permit dated May 4, 1537, to traffic slaves in *La Florida.*

219 *exorbitant interest rates:* See Pike, *Enterprise and Adventure,* 102; n1; and 194.

220 *"district of Seville":* Elvas, 49.

220 *their entire household:* See AGI: Mexico 204, Probanza de Baltasar de Gallegos, 1545.

220 *eight hundred tons:* See AGPS, L. 1, 1537, F.6; Ludeña, app. 5.

220 *"rigging, and tackle":* Ibid.

220 *the Ocean Sea:* See ibid.

220 *as support vessels:* Soto's fleet consisted of six or seven ships with at least forty-two sailors and eight pilots; his chief pilot was Alonso de Lucas. (AGPS, L. 1, 1537, F.6; Ludeña, app. 5). Different sources give different numbers of ships in Soto's fleet:

Garcilaso . . . . .7 large, 3 small
Elvas 7
City officials, Santiago de Cuba 5
Letter of Gonzalo de Guzmán, Lieut.
Governor, Santiago 6

Other witnesses testifying in probanzas and in the *Ponce v. Bobadilla* trial claimed the number of ships ranged from 3 to 6 ships. According to archival records in Seville, the ships were as follows, with the names of their pilots and any officers or sailors specifically assigned. (These records are incomplete; see AGPS, L. 1, 1537, F.6; Ludeña, app. 5.)

1. *San Cristóbal,* "nao"
   Master: Luis Pérez
   Boatswain: Juan Suárez
   Purser: Juan de la Fuente
   6 sailors assigned.
   Garcilaso says the *San Cristóbal* was the fleet flagship, with Soto in command.

2. *San Juan,* Galleon
   Master: Juan de Cheaga
   2 sailors assigned.
   Garcilaso said this ship was commanded by Diego García.

3. *Pequeño San Juan,* Galleon
   Master: Juan Rodríguez
   Purser: Rodrigo Alonso
   6 sailors assigned.

4. *La Magdalena,* "nao"
   Master: Pedro de Solís
   Purser: Juan Sánchez
   Caulker: Marco Alemán
   9 sailors assigned.
   Garcilaso says Nuño de Tobar commanded this ship.

5. *San Martin,* "nao"
   Master: Cristóbal García

6. *San Cristóbal,* "nave"
   Master: Miguel de Aragocés

7. *La Veronica,* barco
   Master: Pedro Guillén

According to the archival record, 23 sailors listed in the archives are not assigned to specific ships; also, out of 37 common sailors listed, 20 are *marineros* (sailors), 16 *grumetes* (ship boys), and 1 a *paje* (cabin boy). There are 3 men listed as pilots, but not assigned to ships. They are Rodrigo de Hermosi, Juan López, and Gonzalo Porto. They either worked on ships already named, or piloted smaller ships or caravels not named.

Garcilaso says the fleet consisted of seven large ships, and gives names for each of them, though only three names match up with those in the archival records. These are the *San Cristóbal, La Magdalena,* and *San Juan.* He names four ships not cited in the archival records. These are *La Concepción,* commanded by Luis de Moscoso; *Buena Fortuna,* commanded by André de Vasconcelos; *Santa Bárbara,* commanded by Arias Tinoco; *San Antón,* commanded by Alonso Romo de Cardeñosa; and two more unnamed ships. It is possible that Soto renamed some of the ships after he purchased them, which would account for the discrepancies. (Garcilaso, 73–74.) Garcilaso offers the following description of the ships listed in his narrative:

1.	*San Cristóbal*	800 tons
2.	*La Magdalena*	"no smaller"
3.	*La Concepción*	500+ tons
4.	*Buena Fortuna*	"equally as large"
5.	*San Juan*	another large ship
6.	*Santa Bárbara*	"another large ship"
7.	*San Antón*	"a small galleon"
8.	1 unnamed caravel	
9. & 10.	2 unnamed brigantines	

I wish I could describe in detail what Soto's ships looked like. But because ship designs were a closely held secret in sixteenth-century Europe, specifics about vessels of this period remain sketchy. Models of ships and paintings offer a few clues, as do manifests of tackle, crews, and cargo. These tell us that a *nao* or *navío,* which I have translated as a "large ship," was a vessel of 100 to 1200 tons burden with at least one closed deck and often more—and high bulwarks, three masts, square sails, a high poop and, sometimes, a high prow.

220 *one cabin boy:* See AGPS, L. 1, 1537, F.6; Ludeña, app. 5.

220 *to* La Florida: Ranjel-Oviedo says there were 700 men aboard the fleet that left Havana in 1539, with 570 fighting men, and the rest sailors. See Ranjel-Oviedo, 253.

220 *"ropes and baskets":* Garcilaso, 72.

221 *of unexplored country:* For information on supplies conveyed from Spain, see AGPS, L. 1, 1537, F.6; Ludeña, app. 5; also see Garcilaso, 73–74; Elvas, 50–51. Additional evidence of goods brought from Spain occurs throughout the narratives, as Soto uses nails, tools, weapons, and other Spanish-made equipment.

221 *"near his house":* Elvas, 49–50.

221 *in Spanish expeditions:* See Solar y Rújula, 288. In the Archivo de las Indias in Seville, the list of recruits for the Soto expedition is arranged by date, with the first recruits signed in on January 26, and the last on March 15. See AGI: 45-1-1/17. Contratación 5,536. Libro 5, folios 271–96 and 301–522; and Solar y Rújula, 275–334 for the complete list.

221 *did the same:* See Garcilaso, 409. Gaitan was not the original treasurer named for the expedition. On May 4, 1537, a royal decree details the duties of the treasurer, on Diego de Corral. Another decree in the same *legajo* is addressed to Jorge Gaitan. Only four of Vasconcelos's followers are listed in Solar y Rújula's register of expedition participants. See AGI: 32-4-29/35.

222 *before it happened:* See Garcilaso, 408–9.

222 *of the* entrada: Elvas says Biedma's first name is Antonio, which is incorrect. Appointed Factor by royal decree on December 10, 1537, in Madrid, Luis Hernández de Biedma's duties were later described in a *cedula* dated January 14, 1538, in Valladolid (AGI: 32-4-29/35). His manuscript remained unpublished until 1841, when it was published in French in Paris. In 1851, Buckingham Smith published it in Spanish, and in 1866 for the first time in English.

222 *Baltasar de Gallegos:* Gallegos was one of the most experienced officers in Soto's army. Originating in Seville, he arrived in Mexico in 1526, participating sometime later in the conquest of Tabasco by Baltasar de Osorio. He was wounded during this campaign; afterward, he was given an *encomienda* in this district, where he lived for three or four years before returning to Spain to marry. While in Seville, he learned his property in Mexico had been taken from him. Soon after, he signed up with Soto, spending over 4,000 ducats on servants, horses, and equipment. In *La Florida,* he became one of Soto's most important captains. Besides the Soto chronicles, sources for Gallegos's life include: Probanza of Baltasar de Gallegos, 1545, AGI, Mexico 204; he also testified in the *Ponce v. Bobadilla* trial.

222 *Diego Arias Tinoco:* Garcilaso provides this man's name and title, Garcilaso, 450. This is apparently the man referred to as Diego Tinoco in the other chronicles. None of the these other sources confirm that Diego was Alferez General. Nor is it clear when Soto appointed him to this position. Diego had two brothers, named Arias Tinoco and Alonso Romo. All three were captains. See Avellaneda, *The Survivors of the De Soto Expedition,* 56.

222 *for the troops:* Below is a list of Soto's senior officials and officers for his administrations in Cuba and *La Florida,* and for his army, upon his departure from Spain.

Royal Officers (appointed by the King):
Treasurer: Juan Gaitan
Contador: Juan de Añasco
Factor: Luis Hernández de Biedma

Soto's Administration in Cuba:
Alcalde Mayor: Juan de Ortiz
Lieutenant in Havana: Juan de Rojas
Lieutenant in Santiago: Francisco de Guzmán (already in Cuba)

Soto's Officers:
Captain General: Nuño de Tobar
Maestro de Campo: Luis de Moscoso
Chief Constable: Baltasar de Gallegos
Alférez General: Diego Arias Tinoco

Captains: Francisco Maldonado/Infantry
Juan Ruiz Lobillo/Infantry
André de Vasconcelos/Cavalry
Pedro Calderón/Cavalry

Arias Tinoco/Cavalry
Alonso Romo de Cardeñosa/Cavalry
García Osorio, Captain of Harquebusiers

Captain of the Guard: Cristóbal de Espindola
Private Secretary to Soto: Rodrigo Ranjel

Clerics (12 total*):

Priests (7 total) including:
Rodrigo de Gallegos
Diego de Bañuelos
Francisco del Pozo
Dionisio de París
3 unnamed

Friars (5 total):
Luis de Soto
Juan de Gallegos
Francisco de Torres (Soto's personal confessor)
Francisco de la Rocha
Sebastián de Cañete

222 *Inquisition in Mexico:* See Avellaneda, op. cit., 27.

222 *de los Caballeros:* There is no direct evidence Soto returned to his boyhood town, though it is certain he was present at Barcarrota, located about 15 miles north of Jerez; and in Badajoz, some 50 miles to the north.

222 *dead in 1537–38:* This seems evident because in 1537, when Soto arranged a special grant of money from the king for his family, it was his brother, Juan, and not his father, cited in the royal favor. Witnesses testifying in the *expediente* to determine Soto's eligibility to join the Knights of Santiago also refer to Francisco Méndez de Soto as if he had long been dead. See *Expediente of Hernando de Soto,* in Solar y Rújula, 123–56.

223 *the late 1530s:* Solar y Rújula say that in 1537, Juan Méndez was awarded a *merced de maravedís,* or "favor of money," from the Crown. The amount is not known, nor is the reason, though one can surmise the grant was given as a result of Soto's negotiations with the king, and was perhaps connected with the Crown's repayment of the gold the king borrowed from Soto. For information on Juan Méndez de Soto's stint as *regidor,* see Ludeña, app. 5.

223 *of his family:* Out of some 600 men in Soto's army, 321 were from southern Extremadura, then referred to by the name of its capital, Badajoz. See Swanton, 82.

223 *"had for him":* Garcilaso, 250.

223 *named Carlos Enríquez:* There is some confusion about Isabel de Soto's relationship with Soto. Elvas calls her Soto's niece, but later refers to her husband, Don Carlos, as Soto's

---

*This is according to Garcilaso; see also testimony of Fray Francisco de Torres, PB I, 19.

brother-in-law. Garcilaso agrees with Elvas's comment that Don Carlos was married to Soto's niece. Soto himself, in his will, describes Isabel de Soto as a "cousin" (Soto, *Testamento,* 369). Because the will is more authoritative than either Elvas or Garcilaso in this matter, I have called Isabel a "cousin." It should be noted, however, that terms such as "nephew," "niece," and "cousin" were often used interchangeably.

223 *"the General [Soto]":* Garcilaso, 350.

223 *for her dowry:* See Soto, *Testamento,* 396.

223 *"counted, and enrolled":* Elvas, 50.

224 *"of artillery fired":* Ibid., 51.

224 *"ships . . . of Mexico":* Ibid.

224 *"they were friends":* Ibid., 75.

224 *of the island:* The Count was the grandson of Isabel's great aunt, also named Isabel, who was the queen's favorite lady-in-waiting. When King Ferdinand began to show amorous interest in this great aunt, who was very beautiful as a young woman, the queen reluctantly married her off to the Governor of Gomera, the current governor's grandfather, to remove her from the Court.

224 *"wine, and meat":* Elvas, 51.

Chapter 19: Cuba Bled Dry

227 *to the right:* This story is told by Garcilaso. None of the eyewitnesses mention it.

227 *"against a rock":* Garcilaso, 79.

227 *"in and lost":* Ibid.

228 *"others leaving it":* Ibid.

228 *"for Doña Isabel":* Elvas, 51.

228 *Gonzalo de Guzmán:* Guzmán had officially resigned as alcalde mayor of Santiago, de Cuba a year earlier, on May 20, 1537, following a general order issued by the king that an alcalde had to wait two years before being eligible for reelection. However, because Cuba had so few men qualified for high office, Guzmán had continued on unofficially. At this time in Cuba, there had been no governor since Velázquez's death in 1524. Apparently, the Crown had considered the island of too little importance to take the time to appoint a replacement. In letters and documents, Guzmán is sometimes called Lieutenant Governor of Santiago, this position having been conferred on him in 1526 by the city council.

228 *"to pardon them":* Garcilaso, 84.

228 *in the harbor:* There are two sources for this story. The first is in Garcilaso (80–84), who insists in his romanticized account that the French captain and Diego Perez fought a chivalrous battle that included greetings, presents of wines and dried fruit, and salutations in between "valiant" and hard fought battles. Guzmán's less romantic version is contained in a letter to the king dated August 28, 1539 (CDI II, 59–60).

228 *direction of Havana:* See Guzmán, Letter to the King, August 28, 1539; CDI II, 59–60.

228 *in early June:* There are two dates given for Soto's arrival at Santiago. According to the *cabildo* of Santiago, and in a letter written to the king by Gonzalo de Guzmán, the date was June 7. Elvas, however, says the fleet arrived on Pentecost, which was June 9, a date also given by Bernardo de Quesada, Royal Attorney for Santiago, in a letter to the king. The confusion over this date illustrates once again that precise dates—and distances,

heights, and so forth—simply were not as important to people of the sixteenth century as they are to us today.

228 *"they had need":* Elvas, 51.

228 *"lack of armor":* Garcilaso, 85–86. Apparently, the armada's armor and weapons had not yet been unloaded from the ships, and was off-limits to the townspeople.

228 *games and fiestas:* Alonso Pérez de Biberos, a longtime colleague of Soto who served in his battalion during the invasion of Nicaragua, and accompanied Soto on the famous visit to Atahualpa at Cajamarca, recalled in 1547 that he had spent time with Soto in Seville during the preparations in 1537–38 for the Florida Armada. Testifying in the *Ponce v. Bobadilla* trial, he said that Soto had "spent much money on games, *cañas,* and other merriments . . ." Testimony of Alonso Pérez de Biberos, January, 1547, Seville; PB I, 13.

229 *the going rate:* This is according to Gonzalo de Guzmán in a letter to the king. See CDI II 6, 2. Also see the *residencia* of Hernando de Soto; AGI, Justicia 62, 2, R. 2.

229 *a "shady dealer":* Letter from Lope Hurtado to the King, January 20, 1539, Gibraltar; CDI II, 6, 337.

230 *"large and well-apportioned":* Elvas, 52.

231 *"little for us":* Letter of Gonzalo de Guzmán to the King, July 20, 1538, Santiago; CDI II 6, 2.

231 *"of La Havana":* Garcilaso, 87.

231 *of the Indies:* This is according to an order issued to Soto from the Casa de Contratación on March 20, 1537, shortly before he sailed from Seville. See Wright, 220.

232 *"his own necessities":* Letter from Lope Hurtado to the King, January 20, 1539, Gibraltar; CDI, II, 6, 337.

232 *for it. "Amazed":* Quoted in Wright, 221.

232 *reached the island:* See Wright, 175–77.

232 *certain "bad elements":* Letter from Bartolomé Ortiz to the Council of the Indies, March 30, 1539, Santiago. CDI, II, 6, 49.

232 *"farms on fire":* Letter from the Cabildo of Santiago de Cuba to the King, July 26, 1539, Santiago; *The De Soto Chronicles,* 379.

233 *"lances and bucklers":* Ibid. On March 7, 1539, the Crown in Toledo issued an order to the Council of Indies to send 50,000 *maravedíes* worth of weapons. (CDI II, 6, 338.) Later, as the rebellion spread, the king ordered the cabildo of Santiago to raise whatever funds it needed to "pacify" the *cimarrónes,* expressing displeasure that the authorities had allowed the uprising to occur, which interrupted the flow of gold from the Cuban mines.

233 *killing them all:* See Wright, 174.

233 *"them here anymore":* Letter of Gonzalo de Guzmán to the King, August 28, 1539, Santiago; CDI II 6, 59–60.

233 *way to Florida:* This cedula was issued on October 3, 1539. See Wright, 207.

234 *seven thousand pesos:* Ayala's mission to Panama is detailed in his testimony during the *Ponce v. Bobadilla* trial. Ayala describes his attempt to meet with Ponce, and the sale of the ranch in Panama. See PB I, 11–12. García Osorio adds that Ayala was away from Cuba for eight or nine months. See PB I, 19–20.

234 *his former partner:* Ponce's decision to abandon life in the colonies was probably influenced by the 1536 rebellion in Cuzco of Soto's old ally, Manco Inca, whose forces trapped Ponce and 189 other Spaniards in the city for over three months. During this siege Ponce

served as one of three cavalry captains; Soto's other old friend, Gabriel de Rojas, and Juan Pizarro served as the other two, with Hernando Pizarro in overall command. The siege was a nightmare for the Spaniards. The Inca torched most of the city and came close to forcing a Spanish retreat from the city. Eventually, Pizarro's men put down the rebellion and restored order. Soon after, Ponce sold off his holdings in Peru, having decided to retire from the frontier and return with his gold to Spain.

234 *without consulting him:* Ponce made this comment during testimony in the *Ponce v. Bobadilla* suit. See PB II, 10.

234 *belonged to Soto:* See ibid; also see PB I, 21, 27–28. When Ponce arrived in Seville, he attempted to smuggle in some of his gold without registering it for taxes. The authorities caught him, and charged him a hefty fine.

234 *overland with him:* Elvas, 55. Garcilaso puts the number at 350.

235 *never heavily populated:* See Sauer, 183 for information on Cuba's original native population.

235 *miles from Santiago:* Elvas says the distance between the two settlements is twenty-five leagues. The distance in miles is based on the present distance between Santiago and Manzanillo, the original site of Bayamo. See Elvas, 54; Wright, 45.

236 *"fours and sixes":* Elvas, 54.

236 *"of the Indians":* Ibid.

236 *failed to obey:* It is worth noting that towns in Europe sometimes resisted the demands of armies for food and housing as they marched to and from battle, with violent results not unlike what Soto and other conquistadors inflicted upon recalcitrant Indian villages.

236 *"and dense forest":* Elvas, 54.

236 *"in a canoe":* Ibid.

237 *"they got water":* Ibid., 55. Some historians have suggested Soto's fleet sailed south around the island, and that the storm blew them not within sight of Florida, but Yucatan. If the fleet had sailed south, however, then why would Soto have gone to the north coast to inquire about its progress? As for being blown to Yucatan, and not Florida, this is possible even if the ships took a northerly route, though Florida is much more likely given the direction hurricanes tend to blow in that region. Nor is it strange that they ended up that far west of the island, beyond Havana, given that hurricanes blow clockwise, with a large storm system pushing them in a westerly arc.

237 *march to Havana:* See Elvas, 54–55.

237 *in the harbor:* Elvas says the fleet took forty days to reach Havana. This means that if they departed Santiago in mid-September, they were in Havana by late November, though a report by Alcalde Bartolomé Ortiz says the fleet arrived at Christmas time, 1538 (CDI, II, 6, 50). It is possible that the fleet did not leave Santiago until several weeks after Soto and the cavalry departed traveling by land. In this case, if Elvas's forty days is correct, the fleet must have left Santiago in mid-November. However, even with a storm, this is a very long time to make this trip by sea.

237 *"twenty-four* vecinos*":* Testimony of Francisco de Ledesma, February, 1550, Havana. PB I, 53–54. Ledesma said he knew this number of vecinos was correct because he was "in charge of their souls."

238 *home to Spain:* The inventory of items auctioned in the Soto estate is contained in the *Ponce*

v. Bobadilla suit, AGI: Justicia 750 A; Solar y Rújula, 223–73; *The De Soto Chronicles* I: 489–98.

238 *and New Mexico:* In 1540, Cortés filed a massive, and pointless, lawsuit against Soto, Pedro de Alvarado, and Mexican Viceroy Antonio de Mendoza, claiming he had the right to conquer *La Florida.* See Suit of the Hernán Cortés against the Adelantados Hernando de Soto and Pedro de Alvarado, and the Viceroy Antonio de Mendoza, 1541; CDI, I, 15, 300–51. This was one of many suits filed by Cortés in the final years of his life, as he struggled in obscurity to regain his power and fame, and to get even with his many enemies.

238 *"as had happened":* Garcilaso, 90.

239 *from his horse:* As Alvarado prepared his expedition to explore north of Mexico, he was asked by Mendoza to divert his army to assist the viceroy in putting down a rebellion in Jalisco, known as the Mixtón War. It was during the fighting in June 1541 that Alvarado died after a bad fall from his horse. See Sauer, *Sixteenth Century North America,* 153.

239 *"room for all":* Garcilaso, 90.

239 *to meet up:* In July 1541, the expeditions of Hernando de Soto and Francisco Vásquez de Coronado later came within three or four hundred miles of one another, when Coronado reached the area he called Tabás, on the Arkansas River in central Kansas, and Soto was exploring northeastern Arkansas from his base at the Indian city of Pacaha. Apparently, Coronado heard rumors of another group of Spanish explorers to the east. Early in July, he asked Indian messengers to take a letter to these unknown Spaniards explaining who he was, and asking them to identify themselves. As far as we know, this letter never reached Soto. Nor is any mention made by Soto's men of another group of Spaniards to the west. Soon after reaching Tabás, Coronado gave up on finding a golden empire in Kansas, and began marching home to Mexico. See Bolton, *Coronado, Knight of Pueblos and Plains,* 303–4.

239 *the Dry Tortugas:* See Probanza of Juan de Añasco, May 30, 1544, Pueblo de Los Angeles; AGI: Patronato 57-1-3.

239 *Mexico to Florida:* For information on the Pineda expedition and other early explorations of the Gulf Coast, see Weddle, 38–54.

240 *roughly two months:* The best source for Añasco's voyage is his probanza, taken in Pueblo de los Angeles, Mexico on May 30, 1544 (AGI: Patronato 57-1-3). Numerous other expedition survivors, and official reports of the period, agree with Añasco's basic recollections, with slight variations on the number of months Añasco was away, how many ships he took, and how many natives he captured. Only Garcilaso de la Vega's account is greatly at odds with these other records. He claims that one of the expedition's survivors, Alonso de Carmona, told him that Añasco took two trips to Florida—the first a brief sail-by in late winter, 1538, and the second a more serious journey in the early spring, during which he determined the landing site and kidnapped several Indians. This second trip, according to Garcilaso and Carmona, nearly ended in disaster "because of their having been lost for two months on a desert island without anything to eat save sea snails and booby birds, which they killed with cudgels." Eventually, say these two sources, Añasco and his men were rescued (Garcilaso, 89–90). It sounds as if Carmona himself may have been among the shipwrecked, which makes it even odder that no one else mentions this near calamity, including Añasco, who surely would have recounted it in his probanza in 1544, if for no other reason

than to add yet another example of his courage and fortitude. Yet Añasco clearly says there
was only one trip, and that it lasted two months.

240 *"existed in Florida"*: Elvas, 56. Ranjel, in testimony given at the *Ponce v. Bobadilla* trial,
adds that these Indians said Florida was rich in maize. Testimony of Rodrigo Ranjel; PB:
Avellaneda, Notes, 35. Pedro Calderon, another witness in the trial, adds that pilot Juan
Pérez accompanied Añasco; this is probably the same man listed in Seville as Luis Pérez,
pilot of Soto's flagship, the *San Cristóbal.*

240 *"yet been discovered"*: Elvas, 56.

241 *"to enter it"*: Garcilaso, 91.

241 *threatened to do"*: Several witnesses in the *Ponce v. Bobadilla* trial give this number. See
PB II, 10, 12–13.

241 *the chests onshore*: See Garcilaso, 91–93.

241 *Luis de Luna*: Testimony of Francisco de Ledesma, February, 1550, Havana; PB I, 53–54.

241 *the central plaza*: See ibid.; also PB II, 10–13.

242 *"a ship's pilot"*: Testimony of Alvaro Nieto, January, 1547, Mexico City; PB I, 10.

242 *six hundred men*: See Testimony of Hernán Ponce; PB II, 12.

242 *Inca in 1534*: Numerous witnesses in the *PB* trial testified that they saw this tent. It probably was made in the usual Inca style, with a mix of cotton and llama wool brightly died into
patterns. Ponce in his testimony mentioned the stirrups.

242 *in earthen containers*: See PB II, 12.

242 *wilderness to die*: See Testimony of Bartolomé, Ruiz, January, 1547, Seville; PB I, 11.

243 *in the fleet*: Ranjel-Oviedo says there were 700 men total who sailed to Florida: 570 of them
disembarked, the rest were sailors. See Ranjel-Oviedo, 253.

243 *mules and packhorses*: Ranjel-Oviedo says 223 or 224 horses arrived in Florida; the Letter
of Soto's Royal Officers says 237; Elvas says 213; Biedma says 223; Garcilaso says 250
to 350. In addition, at least one caravel load of horses was brought from Havana in
August, 1539.

243 *"hanegas of maize."*: Letter to the King from Soto's Royal Officers, May 18, 1539, Havana;
Smith, 281–282.

243 *and two brigantines*: The sources are in an unusual agreement about the composition of the
fleet departing Havana, though there is some confusion over the identity of the larger ships.
At least one of Soto's original ships brought from Spain had returned to Seville, replaced by
Ponce's ship. Garcilaso also says Soto bought a ship that arrived in the harbor one day. Called
the *Santa Ana,* it had once belonged to Pedro de Mendoza, Governor of the Río de la Plate
colony, who had recently died of syphilis. In the *PB* trial, witnesses also say Soto bought a
ship from Pero Augustín in Havana. This means Soto may have sent back an additional one
or two ships to Spain, replacing these with the *Santa Ana* and the ship purchased from Augustín. This may also explain why the names of the vessels given by Garcilaso do not always
match up with the names listed in the receipts of Soto's ship purchases in Seville. Another
explanation is that Soto changed the names of the ships after purchasing them.

Chapter 20: Landfall

244 *on May 25*: All of the eyewitness chroniclers agree that Soto first sighted land on May 25,
1539. Garcilaso cites the date as May 31. Throughout the Florida expedition, dates given by
various chroniclers are remarkably consistent, with numerous exceptions. Where chroniclers differ in matters of dates, I usually defer to Ranjel-Oviedo, since his account is appar-

ently based on a day-by-day journal. Second-best is Biedma, who wrote his brief narrative as an official report to the king shortly after the expedition ended. Elvas's dates are least reliable because he wrote his *relación* several years after the *entrada.*

244 *horses to Florida:* Martín described himself as a shoemaker from the parish of Santa María in Seville. See PB I, 14.

244 *"how to write":* Testimony of Juan de Sayago, January, 1547, Mexico City; PB I, 10. Also see Avellaneda, *Los Sobrevivientes,* 52.

244 *in* La Florida: See PB I, 9. Also see the Probanza of Rodrigo Vazquez, 1554, AGI: Patronato 60, N. 5, R. 7; Probanza of García Osorio, 1560, AGI: Patronato 63, R. 9; and Avellaneda, *Los Sobrevivientes,* 26–27.

245 *to almost-certain death:* A witness in the *Ponce v. Bobadilla* trial, Alvaro Nieto, claimed that at three men went unwillingly to *La Florida*—a barber, a lawyer, and a ship builder he says were imprisoned in Havana, probably after they tried to desert. See PB I, 10.

245 *where Soto landed:* See Swanton, 122. For a thorough analysis of where Soto may have landed—and an argument in favor of Tampa Bay—see Milanich and Hudson, *Hernando de Soto and the Indians of Florida.* For alternative views proposing Charlotte Harbor and San Carlos Bay, see Rolfe Schell's *De Soto Didn't Land at Tampa Bay;* Lindsay Williams's "A Charlotte Harbor Perspective," in *The Florida Anthropologist,* 42:4 (December 1989); Warren H. Wilkinson's "Opening the Case Against the U.S. De Soto Commission Report and other De Soto Papers," from *Papers of the Alliance for the Preservation of Florida Antiquities,* 1:1 (Jacksonville Beach, Florida, October, 1960); and "The Case for Concluding that de Soto Landed Near Present-Day Fort Myers, Florida," reviewed by Louis D. Tesar, in *The Florida Anthropologist,* 42:4 (December 1989).

Though no one is able to say with absolute certainty which inlet is Soto's Bahía de Espíritu Santo, I lean toward Tampa Bay for the following reasons:

1) According to Soto, in a report sent back to the *cabildo* in Santiago, the channel of his bay "runs up twelve leagues or more from the sea"—i.e., at least thirty miles (Soto, Letter to the Cabildo of Santiago, in Smith, 285). San Carlos Bay's channel is at best twelve miles long. Charlotte Harbor is also less than thirty miles long. Only Tampa Bay is this large.

2) Archaeologically and topographically, the arrangement of villages, rivers, islands, and swamps in the Tampa Bay area corresponds better to what is described in the chronicles than either San Carlos or Charlotte. Likewise, the layout of towns and villages cited in the chronicles as the *entrada* moved north from Bahía de Espíritu Santo toward modern Tallahassee match up with astonishing exactitude with those archaeologists have dug up in recent years. See Milanich and Hudson, *Hernando de Soto and the Indians of Florida,* for a thorough analysis of this question.

3) By 1539, mapmakers and mariners had identified two major bays in Florida. They called these Bahía de Juan Ponce de León—named for the bay where Ponce was probably fatally wounded—and Bahía Honda. Though maps in this era were crude and highly inaccurate, most modern scholars believe Bahía Honda is the present-day Tampa Bay, and Bahía de Juan Ponce is Charlotte Harbor. If this is true, then Soto's Factor, Luis de Biedma, provides a valuable clue when he calls Soto's inlet Bahía Honda. Moreover, Ranjel-Oviedo informs us that the armada landed "ten leagues to the west of the bay of Juan Ponce," indicating that they knew where they were according to their charts—that is, to the northwesternmost bay of the two the Spaniards knew about on the peninsula. Tampa Bay is considerably farther

from Charlotte then Ranjel-Oviedo's ten leagues, though it's plausible that Soto's secretary (and others in Soto's party) misidentified a small bay below Tampa as Bahía de Juan Ponce. This would be Sarasota Bay, fifteen or twenty miles to the southwest, where Milanich and Hudson believe Soto's fleet first sighted land (Milanich and Hudson, 49–50). Scholars who favor Charlotte Harbor over Tampa Bay insist that Soto's navigators, looking for two bays notched into a peninsula they knew little about, could easily have arrived at Charlotte Harbor and declared it to be Bahía Honda, which would mean that Ranjel-Oviedo was describing San Carlos when he said the Bay of Juan Ponce was ten leagues away—since this more or less accurately describes the actual distance between these two bays.

4) A final piece of evidence came in 1612, seventy-three years after Soto's landing, when the Spanish Governor of Florida in St. Augustine dispatched Juan Rodríguez de Cartaya with twenty soldiers to explore the gulf side of central Florida. Arriving at a large bay at 27.3 degrees latitude—the true location of modern Tampa Bay—they met Indians who told them this was the place where Soto landed. See Milanich and Hudson, 46.

Despite these favorable clues, much about Soto's landing remains murky. For instance, none of the eyewitness accounts provide latitudes and longitudes or other indisputable topographic information. Nor can we call the descriptions given by Soto and other eyewitnesses anything but vague. Consider the following points of confusion:

1) According to eyewitnesses, Soto's bay was situated seventy-five to eighty leagues north of Havana, a measurement that at first glance might seem exact enough to settle the question of which bay—except we have no idea what Soto's chroniclers meant by a "league." This was an era when distances were at best approximations, with the league varying from country to country. For instance, in France, they tended to use the French *lieu commune,* or common land league, measuring 2.76 miles. In Spain there was the *legua común* at 3.46 miles, and in Portugal the "nautical league"—also used by mariners—at 3.67 miles. Which league did Soto's men use—the *legua común,* nautical league, or something else? Did they use a different league on sea than on land? Did Elvas, being Portuguese, use the Portuguese league? Or, most likely of all, are leagues in chronicles simply ballpark figures of distances eyeballed by observers as they traveled or sailed through unexplored territory?

2) One point against Tampa is the description by Elvas and Ranjel-Oviedo of Soto's bay as being so shallow their heavy *navíos* touched bottom as they tried to navigate the main channel. Displacing some eight to fourteen feet of water, these chroniclers say Soto was forced to lighten them by unloading most of the men and horses. This is perplexing since Tampa Bay should have been deep enough to handle Soto's largest *navíos,* even before being dredged in modern times to handle heavy draught vessels. In 1822, *The American Coast Pilot,* long the bible of East Coast navigation, described the virgin Tampa as having two channels—the "West" and "Southwest"—that contained "plenty of water and their bars" for most navigation, even at low tide. "On the first there are 23 feet," says the *Coast Pilot,* "and in the second 18 feet." (Blunt, *The American Coast Pilot,* 279. Quoted from Milanich and Hudson, *Hernando de Soto and the Indians of Florida,* 47.) Predredging records for San Carlos and Charlotte suggest these bays were too shallow for Soto's ships. In 1880, the U.S. Army Corps of Engineers warned that in San Carlos, "no vessels exceeding 5.25 feet in draught can pass from the mouth to Fort Myers at low tide." Even at "high water," says the Corps report, only vessels "drawing from 6 to 7 feet are enabled by taking advantage of tides." (Meigs, Re-

port to Congress, 869. Quoted from Milanich and Hudson, *Hernando de Soto and the Indians of Florida*, 41–42.) *The American Coast Pilot* describes Charlotte as being "only good for vessels of 8 feet draught"—barely deep enough at high tide to accommodate ships with a six-to eight-foot draught. (Meigs, Report to Congress, 869. Quoted from Milanich and Hudson, *Hernando de Soto and the Indians of Florida*, 41–42.)

246 *Joyce Rockwood Hudson:* Joyce Hudson recounts their trip in her book, *Looking for De Soto*. University of Georgia Press (Athens, Georgia, 1993).

247 *sail from Havana:* Ranjel says Añasco planned to sail from Havana to the Dry Tortugas, and then due north to the Bahía de Espíritu Santo. See Ranjel-Oviedo, 254. Evidently, either Añasco's original calculation was slightly off, or Master Pilot Martín erred slightly. In any event, as it turned out, the landfall occurred only a few miles south of Añasco's harbor. Unfortunately, Ranjel does not tell us which island in the Tortugas group the fleet used as its marker to sail north. This might help clear up the mystery of whether the armada landed in Tampa Bay or Charlotte Harbor.

247 *misnamed Cortez Beach:* This scenario of Soto's exploration is suggested by Milanich and Hudson, *Hernando de Soto*, 49–50. See Ranjel-Oviedo, 252–53, for an eyewitness account of these events.

248 *much too small:* See ibid. It should be noted that there is no mention in the chronicles of Soto encountering a barrier island, or passing into a bay hidden by this island.

248 *"to the ships":* Ranjel-Oviedo, 252.

248 *"other small ones":* Ranjel-Oviedo, 253. Cabeza de Vaca says the Narváez *entrada* found *bohíos* in this region large enough to accommodate "more than 300 people" (Cabeza de Vaca, 31). There are several archaeological sites in the Sarasota Bay and southern Tampa Bay area that correspond to the vague description of this village.

248 *"to one another":* Elvas, 57.

248 *"fears of us":* Soto, Letter from Soto to the Magistrates of Santiago de Cuba, July 9, 1539; *The De Soto Chronicles,* I: 375.

248 *torn to shreds:* See Garcilaso, 101, 106.

248 *"rule the army . . .":* Ranjel-Oviedo, 253.

248 *"of the ships":* Ibid.

249 *"was already reconnoitered":* Ibid.

249 *"through the middle":* Ibid.

249 *"concealed and endured":* Ranjel-Oviedo, 254.

249 *suitable landing place:* The shallowness of Soto's Bahía de Honda remains the most viable argument against locating the landing in Tampa Bay, since Tampa easily should have been deep enough to accommodate Soto's ships. (See Meigs, *Examination of Tampa Bay,* 871.) In contrast, an 1822 survey of Florida's harbors describes Charlotte Harbor as being "good for vessels of 8 feet draught," which may have been just deep enough for Soto's *naos*. (See Blunt, The *American Coast Pilot,* 297.) If these were truly the conditions at Charlotte Harbor in 1539, then its depth seems to better fit a harbor where the fleet barely scraped by over sandbars. This speculation does not, however, provide enough counterbalance to other, stronger arguments in favor of Tampa Bay. Quotes are from Milanich and Hudson, 46–47.

249 *and Bishop Harbor:* Milanich and Hudson propose Piney Point as the spot where Soto put ashore for two reasons. First, because the chronicles say after they landed the army crossed

two rivers as they headed north along the bay's shoreline. (Milanich and Hudson identify these as the Little Manatee and the Alafia.) Second, they point out that known archaeological sites in the area tend to correspond to Indian villages visited by the army after they marched inland from the Bay. See Milanich and Hudson, 55–70.

251 *"people they were"*: Ranjel-Oviedo, 254.

251 *"with their masters"*: Elvas, 57. Typically, Garcilaso recounts this story of Soto's first encounter with the Indians with considerable embellishment, saying that a large group of natives "burst on them" with such force they nearly pushed the army into the sea. According to this account, Vasco Porcallo was able to rally the "raw recruits" and chase away the throng of natives. Garcilaso adds a colorful detail that Porcallo's horse was killed during this skirmish, giving us a vivid and quite accurate description of the powerful impact caused by a Floridian's longbow. The arrow, he says, struck, "above the saddle" and passed "through the trappings, saddletree and pads," to penetrate the ribs of the horse "up to the notch." Garcilaso, 99.

251 *bivouac the army:* Elvas says Soto personally led the search for a campsite. Ranjel and Biedma say Vasco Porcallo led this mission.

251 *"its eyes gilded"*: Elvas, 57.

251 *"that they carried"*: Ranjel-Oviedo, 255.

Chapter 21: Ocita

253 *Juan Rodríguez Cabrillo:* Cabrillo, a longtime conquistador in the Indies, was infamous for having used the fat of dead Indians for tallow to seal the hulls of Cortés's ships when the Spaniards attacked the Aztec's island city of Tenochtitlán in 1520. But Cabrillo was not sponsored by Cortés on the California expedition, which sailed in 1542. Instead, he was sent out by Viceroy Antonio de Mendoza, who had finally edged out Cortés in their protracted power struggle, the conqueror of Mexico having returned to Spain in 1540 to voice his grievances to the king. See Weber, 40–41.

253 *long-ago day:* For years, scholars have posed theories about the population of the southeastern United States at the time of initial European contact. John Swanton in 1946 suggested the total number "from the Chesapeake to Texas," was about 171,900. (See Swanton, *The Indians of the Southeastern United States,* 11.) In 1966, Henry Dobyns suggested a number well over a million and a half. (See Dobyns, "An Appraisal of Techniques with a New Hemisphere Estimate," *Current Archaeology* 7:395–416 [1966].) In 1975, Dobyns's influential study of Florida's native population, *Their Numbers Have Thinned,* proposes a population of some 722,000 for the Timucuan of Florida—which suggests the southeast had a population numbering in the millions when Soto came through. (See Dobyns, *Their Numbers Have Thinned,* 293.) Dobyns's numbers for Florida, however, rely heavily on Garcilaso's descriptions of crops, sizes of cities, and so forth—an uncritical dependence on an often inaccurate source that makes it difficult to know if Dobyns's numbers are correct. More recently, deconstructionists such as David Stannard have championed theories putting the native population north of Mexico as high or higher than Dobyns. If true, these numbers would bolster Stannard's thesis in his book *American Holocaust* that vast numbers of American natives died as a result of European conquest and colonization (See Stannard, 266–68). Faced with a debate based largely on speculation, I have suggested a highly tentative num-

ber of about one million people living in the southeastern United States when Soto arrived. For more on this debate, see Ann Ramenofsky, *Vectors of Death: The Archaeology of European Contact,* University of New Mexico Press (Albuquerque, 1987); Marvin T. Smith, *Archaeology of Aboriginal Culture Change in the Interior Southeast: Depopulation During the Historic Period,* University Presses of Florida (Gainesville, 1987); and Daniel T. Reff, *Disease, Depopulation, and Cultural Change in Northwestern New Spain, 1518–1764,* University of Utah Press (Salt Lake City, 1991).

255 *"and great runners":* Quoted in Lawrence, 8.

256 *canebrakes and quickmud:* See Ranjel-Oviedo, 255–57.

256 *"hill . . . artificially built":* Elvas, 57.

256 *other important people:* Usually, important Indians were buried with a cache of native jewelry, pots, baskets, and sometimes exquisite statues of animals and people. As European objects began washing up on shore from shipwrecks, and expeditions began trading trinkets, Timucuans and other Indians in the southeast buried their dead with glass beads, mirrors, knives, coins, rings, and metal cups—items that archaeologists have since dug up. Later, Soto himself would find a Spanish dagger and beads stored in a burial house in the Carolinas; artifacts left behind in 1526 after the survivors of the Ayllón *entrada* escaped back to Hispaniola.

256 *inch by inch:* Another form of burial in Timucuan villages was to collect the bodies in charnel houses on top of mounds until the buildings became filled up with corpses. Then all the bodies were buried *en masse* in the mound, after which the charnel house was ritually burned. The Indians would then "purify" the mound by covering it with another layer of dirt before building another charnel house.

256 *near the bay:* Elvas provides the details of what the Ocita village looked like. See Elvas, 57.

256 *on a "beach":* Ibid.

257 *archaeologist Ripley Bullen:* Other excavations were carried out at this site in 1937, 1939, and 1949. See Hudson and Milanich, 66.

257 *by the evidence:* For scholars trying to recreate Soto's route, there is a strong motivation to make individual sites such as Thomas Mound "fit" into overall theories about where Soto marched. This is because the route is built one site at a time, with successive sites depending on the location of earlier ones. (For instance, if site B is ten leagues from site A, then the location of site B is determined by accurately locating site A.) This means Hudson and others must defend every site along their proposed route, with particular emphasis on Soto's landfall and the early days of the expedition, which sets their entire proposed route in motion. Indeed, if it turns out Soto did not land at Tampa Bay, but Charlotte Harbor, or that Thomas Mound is not Ocita, this casts doubt on the validity of other locales along their proposed route.

257 *Take the sketch:* Penned in 1952, the sketch by Bullen clearly shows a typical Tampa Bay Indian village of the proper period, with one dominant burial mound about 250 feet from the sandy shore of the Little Manatee, another large mound made of sand and shell some 400 feet back from the shore, two more small mounds a few feet from the river, and a nearby shell heap upon which some Timucuan houses were built. Surrounding the village, which was about 500 feet square, Bullen drew in a network of earthen walls and canals. These were either fortifications or trenches used for irrigation. According to Elvas, who offers a detailed

description of Ocita, the village as drawn by Bullen is the right size—i.e., large enough to contain "seven or eight" large houses (Elvas, 57). But Elvas mentions only one mound, which contradicts Bullen's sketch of two big and three small mounds. Elvas also tells us this single mound was "very large," when Bullen's report insists the largest mound was just six feet from top to bottom, and sixty feet in diameter. Would this man-sized mound have seemed "very high" to a chronicler (writing after the fact) who later would see earthen pyramids thirty to forty feet high? Even in the Tampa Bay area, mounds apparently existed as high as fifteen feet—including the Madira Bickel Mound, which still exists near Ruskin, Florida, not far from Thomas Mound. It is twenty feet tall, with a platform on top fifteen or twenty feet wide. And what of the other mounds drawn by Bullen at Thomas? Did Elvas fail to mention them, or was there really only one in Soto's Ocita?

257 *single glass bead:* According to the archaeological record of the Thomas digs, Clarence Moore unearthed 112 bodies from the site's largest mound, some buried with European artifacts that included "a number of blue glass beads and two bits of a looking glass." Some of these items may date from the sixteenth century. (See Clarence Moore, "Certain Antiquities of the Florida West-Coast," *Journal of the Academy of Natural Sciences of Philadelphia,* 11:3:350–94 [1900].) Later archaeologists found more artifacts at Thomas and other sites in the area, some of which may also date from Soto's general era—"200 more glass beads, a triangular piece of sheet copper, measuring three inches on each side, a tubular silver bead, a brass pendant or tablet, and a large silver pendant." (See Ripley Bullen, "Eleven Archaeological Sites in Hillsborough County, Florida," *Florida Geological Survey Report of Investigations,* No. 8, the Florida Geological Survey [Tallahassee, 1952].) Across the river Bullen later recovered "a copper penny, a copper punch, modern iron and brass, lead weights" and "a long glass bead"—all standard European trade items. (Bullen, "Eleven Archaeological Sites in Hillsborough County, Florida," 71–73.) Also see Milanich and Hudson, 68–69.

258 *"the Soto era":* Milanich and Hudson, 69. For information on Nueva Cadiz beads and their relationship to Florida and Soto, see Smith and Good, *Early Sixteenth-Century Glass Beads in the Spanish Colonial Trade,* 27–28; also Deagan, *Artifacts of the Spanish Colonies of Florida and the Caribbean, 1500–1800,* 162–72.

258 *by several centuries:* See Bullen, "Eleven Archaeological Sites in Hillsborough County, Florida," 72–73.

258 *shattered olive jar:* Milanich and Hudson note that an archaeological survey was made of "the Little Manatee River locality" by William Burger, assisted by Arthur Miller, Melanie Hubbard, and students from the New College, University of South Florida. Looking specifically for Soto artifacts, they apparently came up empty-handed. "There is no doubt that such evidence—Spanish artifacts—would have been left at the camp," write Milanich and Hudson. "De Soto's army stayed there for six weeks after the landing, and a hundred men continued to live there until about November 1 of that same year [1539] . . ." (Milanich and Hudson, 69). Milanich and Hudson blame the ravages of time and the destruction of the Thomas Mound in recent years for the nonexistence of Soto artifacts. This may be true, though this argument seems to ignore the fact that the site was extensively excavated before the mound was destroyed sometime after 1952, and turned up little or nothing to suggest Soto was at this site. Despite this negative archaeological proof at Thomas, other evidence—to be presented in this narrative in its proper order—strongly suggests Soto landed somewhere in the vicinity.

258 *as "200 paces"*: Cabeza de Vaca, 42.

259 *"are more hurtful"*: Elvas, 59.

· 259 *"near the river"*: Ibid.

259 *several Indian women*: Ranjel-Oviedo says Lobillo captured only two women, and that nine Indians pursued the Spaniards for two or three leagues, killing one man and wounding "three or four." Ranjel-Oviedo, 256.

259 *of* La Florida: In yet another disastrous foray, Soto sent Juan Añasco in some small boats to investigate an ominous "throng of some 1,000 Indians" gathering on an island in the bay. This led to an intense and bloody skirmish. The Spaniards used cannon and crossbows to kill nine or ten Indians. The natives "shot . . . and wounded" several Spaniards, who were once again unable to capture any locals to use as guides. This fracas on the island must have lasted for many hours, because at one point Añasco sent a desperate message back to the camp asking for reinforcements. These arrived by land just after the battle was over, under the command of Vasco Porcallo.

259 *"bows and arrows"*: Ranjel-Oviedo, 255.

259 *"is Juan Ortiz"*: Ibid., 255.

259 *"me my life"*: Elvas, 59.

259 *to his version*: In this case, as in so many others, Garcilaso de Vega's account follows the basic storyline of the other chronicles. It's possible he read the widely published Elvas before he sat down to write his narrative. He may also have seen Oviedo's version of Ranjel's diaries. Where Garcilaso expands on, or deviates from these eyewitness accounts, one hopes it is because he has received additional information from aging expedition survivors he has interviewed. For this reason, I will continue to quote his version of events, though his tendency to romanticize and exaggerate—with everything always bigger, better, and bolder than the eyewitness accounts—means I will use him sparingly, and always with skepticism. Admittedly, it's hard at times to resist this talented storyteller's lively accounts, particularly given the often dry and unimaginative prose of the chroniclers.

260 *say: "Seville, Seville"*: Garcilaso, 114.

260 *"do any injury"*: Ibid., 115.

260 *"holding a letter"*: Elvas, 60.

260 *"of four stakes"*: Ibid.

260 *"large as half-oranges"*: Garcilaso, 104.

261 *"cut them off"*: Ibid., 106.

261 *very rare occasions*: See Hudson, *The Southeastern Indians*, 255. The question of whether or not the southeastern Indians practiced torture and human sacrifice remains controversial. Some scholars contend that the Indians learned at least some of their techniques of torture from Europeans. (See Hudson, *op. cit.*, 257.) Certainly, if the story of Juan Ortiz is true, the Timucuan in the sixteenth century were familiar with torturing victims over fire. Regardless of who taught whom, there is ample archaeological and historic evidence that the Indians of the southeast could occasionally be cruel—with ritualistic torture and sacrifices—particularly when they sought vengeance against enemies captured in warfare. Elvas suggests that the *cacique* Ocita wanted to sacrifice Juan Ortiz after a rival attacked and burned down an Ocita village, apparently to appease the local gods. See Elvas, 61.

261 *"they can get"*: Elvas, 61.

261 *"know the way.":* Elvas, 61.

261 *helped Juan Ortiz:* This is according to Garcilaso, who relishes telling—or is it inventing?—the story of Mocoso's "ardent desire" for Ocita's daughter, whom Garcilaso says was betrothed to him, until Juan Ortiz arrived in his camp and angered Ocita. Garcilaso adds that Mocoso's friendship with Ortiz also angered another neighboring *cacique,* Urriparacoxi, Mocoso's kinsman, who apparently shared Ocita's loathing of the Spaniards after Narváez's savagery. Garcilaso gushes on and on about the "nobility" and "magnanimity" of Mocoso in treating Ortiz kindly, in the face of losing his betrothed lover and the support of his kinsman. See Garcilaso, 108–11.

261 *"in his hands":* Biedma, 225.

261 *him "with . . . rejoicing":* Elvas, 59.

261 *"gold or silver[?]":* Ibid, 62.

262 *"where he was":* Ibid.

262 *"or the other":* Ibid.

262 *boats, and fortifications:* See ibid., 58, for a description of how the army was organized.

262 *"them by night":* Ibid.

263 *of the Spaniards:* The expedition's priests included Soto's personal confessor, the twenty-three-year-old Francisco de Torres, who routinely heard Soto confess his sins. In 1546, Fray Francisco testified that he was Soto's confessor. See Testimony of Francisco de Torres, May, 1546, Seville; PB I, 19.

263 *"of the Christians":* Ranjel-Oviedo, 255–56.

263 *real Indian chieftain:* Throughout his narrative, Elvas inserts long, verbatim speeches supposedly spoken by Indians. These read more like flowery Spanish oaths and speeches lifted from sixteenth-century romantic novels than words spoken by real Native Americans. In this instance, Elvas has Mocoso speaking for several lines about his love and affection for Soto—a "Very lofty and very mighty Lord"—as this *cacique* offers his fealty as if he were a chivalric knight handing over his services to a king. "The favor of which I ask your Lordship," Mocoso is quoted as saying, after calling Soto a wise, magnificent, and liberal ruler, "is that you consider me as your own, and feel free to command me in whatever I serve you" (Elvas, 59). Mocoso may have said words to this effect. Indeed, the political structure of the Timucua and Mississippians was based on a system of vassal villages and peoples serving more powerful kings and emperors. This suggests that Mocoso, a weak *cacique* who was probably himself a vassal of a strong *cacique* to the east, must have known something about swearing allegiance to a more powerful "ruler."

263 *"against his enemies":* Ranjel-Oviedo, 256.

264 *an Irish greyhound:* An Indian woman during this same period was thrown to the dogs, apparently by Soto, because she told a messenger he should not return from completing an assignment to deliver a message for Soto. See Ranjel-Oviedo, 257.

264 *the same reason:* Garcilaso, 129.

264 *"men to return":* Ibid.

264 *to talk about:* See Ranjel-Oviedo, 258.

264 *"had left behind":* Garcilaso, 129.

265 *"might be true":* Elvas, 64.

265 *"disposition to lie":* Ranjel-Oviedo, 258.

265 *"Governor was scheming"*: Ibid.
266 *"knowing a want"*: Soto, Letter to the Cabildo of Santiago; Smith, 285.
266 *"and many pearls"*: Ibid.
266 *"them their lives"*: Ibid.

Chapter 22: The Swamp of Cale

268 *northeast toward Urriparacoxi:* Biedma writes that the army moved westward from Ocita, not eastward—a point stressed by advocates of Charlotte Harbor, whose theory depends on Soto marching west out of their bay. Most scholars, however, believe the word "west" in Biedma is a printing error, in which *este* (east) was mistakenly written as *ueste* (west). According to the Charlotte Harbor argument, the army landed at Live Oak Point, Florida, and then marched west toward the Gulf coast before swinging northeast into the Florida interior. Some archaeological evidence has been found at Live Oak Point to support this theory. See Schell, *De Soto Didn't Land at Tampa Bay* and Lindsay Williams, "A Charlotte Harbor Perspective," *The Florida Anthropologist,* 42:4 (December 1989).

268 *south of Gainesville:* See Hudson and Milanich, 92–93.

268 *northeastern Tampa Bay:* See ibid., 76–81.

268 *as Maestro Francisco:* See Garcilaso, 152–53. This Maestro Francisco is not mentioned anyplace other than in Garcilaso, though Elvas mentions "a man from Genoa whom it was God's will to preserve . . . who knew how to build ships" (Elvas, 151). In this passage, I have suggested that Soto directly ordered this Francisco to build a bridge across the Alafia. This is a conjecture based on Garcilaso's later statement that Francisco and a team of carpenters built bridges and boats for the *entrada*. Soto's men built this bridge over the "River of Cali," which was probably the Withlacoochee, situated about halfway between Tampa Bay and Gainesville.

270 *"and three muleteers"*: Madariaga, *Hernán Cortés;* quoted in White, 276.

270 *was wearing out:* Testimony of Francisco de Castejón, January, 1547, Mexico City; PB I, 10. Castejón says *"que se ropío bien pronto"*—"it wore out very quickly."

271 *Ranjel looked like:* Rodrigo Ranjel was born into a well-off family of scribes and petty officials in about 1507, in a tiny village called Almendralejo, thirty miles northeast of Soto's hometown of Jerez de Los Caballeros. Though not a *hidalgo,* he was obviously well educated, handling Soto's correspondence, reports, and legal papers, both official and personal. Facts about Ranjel's life come from his chronicle and other official records. On May 13, 1539, he recorded Soto's will in Havana—in which there is a line ordering that "Rodrigo Ranjel, my secretary, be given for the good service he has rendered me, three hundred ducats of my goods" (Soto, *Testamento,* 369). Soto also left three hundred ducats to Alonso Ayala, his majordomo, who remained in Havana, and fifty ducats "to Castro, my carver," who may have been one of the three or four Castros listed in the manifests of the *entrada.* (There is no explanation why this seemingly lowly servant was singled out for inclusion in Soto's will.) Ranjel's sizable inheritance explains why shortly after the rag-tag survivors of the Soto expedition reached Mexico in 1543, he hastened to Havana by ship to deliver news of Soto's death to Isabel de Bobadilla—and to collect his three hundred ducats. As a final duty to his late employer, he signed on as a witness to Isabel de Bobadilla's inventory of Soto's Cuban property on December 6, 1543. Ranjel's inheritance was apparently paid out of the proceeds from selling this property. Afterward, Ranjel took this modest fortune and

settled in Mexico, where he married and became a prominent *vecino* in Mexico City until
his death sometime after 1560. He was a witness to probanzas made by Soto expedition
members, including Gonzalo Méndez de Sotomayor in Mexico City in 1560. (See AGI: Patronato 63, R. 10.) Oviedo tells us that after the survivors of the *La Florida entrada* returned, "Rodrigo Ranjel came to this city of Santo Domingo," where he made a statement
to the royal *Audiencia* "about all these events." Oviedo adds that the magistrates ordered
Ranjel "to write down all he had said and give it to me, so that I, as your Majesty's chronicler of these histories of the Indies, would add to them." According to Oviedo, Ranjel not
only turned over written records of the expedition, but also personally spoke with the historian during a series of interviews. See Ranjel-Oviedo in *The De Soto Chronicles,* I:
251–306. The original of Ranjel-Oviedo's account is in Oviedo, *Historia General,* bk. II,
chap. 22–32.

271 *Gallegos at Urriparacoxi:* Ranjel's personal involvement as messenger between Gallegos
and Soto may explain why he, and not the other chroniclers, knew about Soto's alleged orders to lie about the wealth and promise of Urriparacoxi and the Kingdom of Cale.

271 *the sixteenth century:* See Soto, *Testamento,* 369.

272 *"did not come":* See Ranjel-Oviedo, 259.

273 *U.S. Highway 301:* If Soto came this way, he may have followed an old Indian trail along
U.S. Highway 301. If he did, the Lake of the Rabbits could be today's Lake Thonotosassa,
thirteen miles north of the Little Manatee; and St. Johns would be Lake Pasadena, ten miles
more to the north, near Dade City. Another proposed route swings to the east, where some
scholars have suggested that a large and arid stretch of sandhills and grass northwest of
Lakeland may be the waterless *"sabana"* where Soto's steward died of thirst. The eighteenth-
century naturalist Bernard Romans, traveling though here in 1769, described this region in
much the way Ranjel-Oviedo does his *"sabana,"* saying it had no water or trees, and was
so hot it would likely kill anyone who had not taken "the precaution to carry water." (Romans, *Natural History of East and West Florida,* 36.) The problem with this theory is that
there was no reason for the army to deviate this far east, given that they were headed to
Ocale, which they knew was almost due north from Mocoso. See Milanich and Hudson,
81–87.

273 *hard as stone:* The Spanish word Ranjel-Oviedo uses to describe this plain is *"sabana,"*
which means a grassy plain—either occurring naturally, or created by the Indians as they
burned and cleared land to grow crops, and to make it easier to hunt deer and other game.

273 *and Dade City:* See Milanich and Hudson, 81–87.

273 *fields of maize:* Archaeologists have found numerous sites in this area where Indians lived
in the sixteenth century.

274 *with friendly intentions:* Garcilaso says that a few days after leaving Luca, Soto sent a message to the fleeing *cacique* of Ocale, telling him to "understand and be convinced that they
did not have the intention of injuring anyone, as they had not done in the provinces they had
left behind them, but on the contrary felt a strong friendship for those who had been willing
to receive it." Garcilaso, 133.

274 *"swamp of Cale":* Ranjel-Oviedo, 260.

274 *"the very edge":* Garcilaso, 133.

274 *today's Withlacoochee Swamp:* See Mitchem et al., "Reports on Excavations at the Tatham

Mound, Seasons I, II and III"; Mitchem and Leader, "Early Sixteenth Century Beads from the Tatham Mound"; Mitchem, "Initial Spanish-Indian Contact in West Peninsular Florida," *Columbian Consequences,* vol. 2, 49–59. Tatham was discovered undisturbed in 1984 by Brent Weisman, a University of Florida graduate student, and members of the Withlacoochee River Archaeological Council. Archaeologist Jeffrey Mitchem believes Tatham and other nearby sites were closely related culturally to Ocita and other villages on Tampa Bay. Collectively known as the Safety Harbor Culture—named for sites found in a corner of Tampa Bay called Safety Harbor—these people are linked by their pottery styles, use of burial mounds, and tribal structure. Some also built large platform mounds, probably influenced by the Mississippians to the north. The Safety Harbor people flourished in the mid-sixteenth century, dominating the region from the Withlacoochee Swamp to Charlotte Harbor. Few areas along Soto's probable route contain so much Soto era material. The large caches of Nueva Cadiz beads and other Soto-era "markers" and artifacts at Tatham and other Withlacoochee sites make a strong case that Soto passed through here in 1539.

274 *and well-maintained highway:* Hudson and Milanich believe this broad highway may have been near present-day Inverness, where several small trails converged into a single, heavily-traveled stretch on a strip of high ground between two wetlands. See Milanich and Hudson, 87.

274 *"on the prey":* Ranjel-Oviedo, 259.

275 *"at the Christians":* Garcilaso, 134.

275 *"and wide road":* Garcilaso, 134.

275 *"the Governor had":* Ranjel-Oviedo, 260–61.

275 *bounty of food:* See Elvas, 65 for an account of these events.

275 *"had to carry":* Cabeza de Vaca, 38.

276 *"flying birds fall":* Biedma, 226.

277 *"them off guard":* Garcilaso, 143–44.

277 *"of their country":* Garcilaso, 144.

277 *blade cleaved off:* See Milanich and Hudson, 103–4. Also see Dale Hutchinson, "Post-Contact Native American Health and Adaptation: Assessing the Impact of Introduced Disease in Sixteenth Century Gulf Coast Florida." Ph.D. dissertation, Department of Anthropology, University of Illinois, Urbana.

277 *the Soto* entrada: There is no direct evidence Soto visited Tatham. However, because nearly all the bodies are buried with heaps of Soto-era metal tools, trinkets, and beads—including telltale "plains" beads manufactured in Nueva Cadiz—archaeologists believe Soto was almost certainly in the immediate area. They also suspect he had something to do with the demise of this small village on the Withlacoochee, which was abandoned shortly after this mass burial, forgotten and untouched by human hands until being discovered four and a half centuries after Soto's expedition.

Chapter 23: Onward to Apalachee

278 *"parched and sodden":* Elvas, 65.

278 *"all the land":* Biedma, 226.

278 *"of the people":* Garcilaso, 189.

279 *"from that town":* Biedma, 226.

279 *of North America:* Hudson and Milanich propose two possible routes for Soto as he marched north from Cale, both along old Indian trails—one the Alachua Trail as it runs near the west bank of Orange Lake and Gainesville; the second the Santa Fe Trail as it runs through another set of Indian sites some 15 miles to the west of the Alachua. (See Milanich and Hudson, 134–54.) Archaeologist Kenneth Johnson suggests that Soto followed established Indian trails in the area, since Potano sites he would have visited are not randomly scattered, but located on trails that can be traced on early maps. Johnson notes that both the Santa Fe and Alachua trails intersect north of Gainesville with the east-west running Missionary Trail, which Soto may have taken west toward Tallahassee. See Johnson, *The Utina and Potano Peoples of Northern Florida;* cited in Milanich and Hudson, 148. The Santa Fe and Alachua trails were still in use a generation after Soto's journey, when they became conduits for Spanish missions.

279 *last Ice Age:* When the first humans arrived in the Western Hemisphere remains highly controversial. In 1965, archaeologist Matthew Lively reported that he had found crude stone tools in Alabama possibly dating back 40,000 to 50,000 years—during the ice age that preceded the most recent one, which ended some 10,000 years ago. (See Hudson, *The Southeastern Indians,* 37–38.) Other finds in North and South America suggest that humans may have been in this hemisphere as early as 70,000 B.C. (See Stannard, app. I, 261). Without a doubt, humans had arrived in North America—and in the southeast—by the time the glaciers were receding at the end of the most recent ice age, roughly 10,000 years ago.

279 *Spaniards call Potano:* Archaeologists have found ample evidence that there was a large agricultural population in north central Florida during the Soto era. See Milanich and Hudson, 134–48.

279 *"chance of fortune":* Ranjel-Oviedo, 262.

279 *"bare of maize":* Elvas, 67.

279 *Potano Soto met:* See Milanich and Hudson, 170–77. Excavations of Potano and Utina sites over the years have yielded a few beads and European pottery from several sites in the Alachua County area.

280 *with the Spaniards:* See Luis Gerónimo de Oré, *The Martyrs of Florida (1513–1616),* trans. Maynard Geiger, *Franciscan Studies* 18, Joseph F. Wagner (New York, 1936), 113.

280 *"guard put over":* Elvas, 66.

280 *"through the woods":* Elvas, 66.

282 *"from the Christians":* Elvas, 66.

282 *"Indian was thrown":* Ranjel-Oviedo, 262–63.

282 *or "Bad Peace":* Hudson and Milanich think this village is situated at a large archaeological site near Alachua. No Soto-era artifacts have been found there, but the village was located on the main north-south highway in the region, and its Indian pottery and artifacts prove it was a major town in the area when Soto came through. See Milanich and Hudson, 142–43.

282 *"results were excellent":* Quoted in Bakeless, 28–29.

282 *and venison fat:* See Adin Baber's brief, but informative, article titled "Food Plants of the DeSoto Expedition," in *Tequesta* (1): 34–40 (1942).

282 *other wild game:* Garcilaso, never missing a beat with his hyperbole, describes the wild stag as being the size of "large bulls" in Spain. See Garcilaso, 146.

282 *of the Southeast:* Pollution cannot have been entirely unknown in larger Mississippian towns and cities, where hundreds or thousands of people bathing, washing, and producing waste and garbage must have at least muddied the waters, so to speak.

282 *and major events:* For information on "black drink" see Hudson, *The Southeastern Indians,* 226–29. Also see Bartram, *Observations,* 23. Adair calls this plant *"Yupon, or Cusseena,"* and describes it as "a species of tea that grows spontaneous, and in great plenty, along the seacoast of the two Carolinas, Georgia, and east and west Florida" (Adair, *History of the American Indians,* 48–49). Indians in the interior of the southeast transplanted *Yupon* to use in their black-drink ceremonies.

282 *show and ceremony:* Early British and French settlers learned to stomach black drink as a stimulant, later switching to coffee and tea.

283 *"to be found":* Elvas, 66–67.

283 *"be ready saddled":* Elvas, 67.

283 *O'Leno State Park:* See Milanich and Hudson, 144.

284 *"bridge of pines":* Ranjel-Oviedo, 263. Garcilaso claims the crossing was disputed by 500 Indians.

284 *"by using geometry":* Garcilaso, 152–53.

284 *Moslems at Fez:* See Elvas, 151.

284 *"with heavy ropes":* Garcilaso, 153.

284 *a local chieftain:* See Ranjel-Oviedo, 263.

284 *sixteenth-century Indian settlements:* Aguacaleyquen may be one of the sites in a complex of villages just east of the Ichetucknee River and south of the San Martin Mission site. According to Milanich and Hudson, "the archaeological assemblage associated with these per-mission sites" includes "a faceted chevron bead in a surface collection" which may date from Soto's period. Milanich and Hudson, 156.

284 *of Aguacaleyquen's domicile:* Garcilaso, again confusing names and characters, claims in his narrative that three brothers ruled the region north of the River of Ocali (the Santa Fe?), which he calls the Province of Vitachuco. The oldest brother, Vitachuco, ruled half the province; the second, whose name was "forgotten," ruled three-tenths; the third ruled the rest, with his chief village at Ochile (Aguacaleyquen). Apparently, Vitachuco is a composite of Uzachile, the paramount chief of the area whom Soto never met, and his kinsman, Uriutina, who led several hundred warriors into battle with Soto at the Battle of the Ponds. Garcilaso's *cacique* Ochile apparently refers to the *cacique* Aguacaleyquen. See Garcilaso, 153.

285 *de Bry's imagination:* De Bry never visited the Western Hemisphere. He relied in part on drawings, paintings, and descriptions of travelers who had been there. Given that his ren-derings are frequently inaccurate in matters of dress and custom, and often use European motifs, it is clear de Bry also drew inspiration from his own surroundings—and from his imagination.

285 *a distinctive polity:* See Milanich and Hudson, 170–82; and Laudonnière, 76–91, 119–21. Kenneth Johnson has argued that Soto did not completely destroy Uzachile and his loose al-liance of *caciques.* In 1564, Indians on the St. Johns River told the French about two pow-erful chieftains beyond Potano, called Onatheaqua and Houstaqua. Johnson believes that "Houstagua" is a version of "Yustaga," the Apalachee name for Uzachile. It is also possi-ble that Onatheaqua refers to Aguacaleyquen. The province of "Onatheaqua" is located

about where Aguacaleyquen should be on a French map from the 1560s, between Potano and Apalachee.

285 *"would ally themselves":* Ranjel-Oviedo, 263.

285 *"bare of maize":* Elvas, 67.

285 *riches in Apalachee:* According to Elvas, then with the army at Ocale, even Soto's closest advisors were having serious doubts about the expedition at this time. This included Soto's old Peruvian comrade, Luis de Moscoso, and "many others" who ordered their men to "[bury] iron and other things in Cale" so they wouldn't have to carry these heavy burdens, since they expected Soto to soon give up his quest and order them back to the Bahía de Espíritu Santo, and then to Cuba. See Elvas, 67.

285 *"a large courtyard":* Ranjel-Oviedo, 263, 264.

285 *hundreds of people:* Archaeologists working at the San Luis Mission site in Tallahassee have unearthed the ruins of an Apalachee council house dating from the Spanish Mission era in the late sixteenth and early seventeenth centuries. It measures 118 feet in diameter. The structure was supported by eight massive central posts that held up a sloping roof, which was open in the center. Numerous smaller pine posts supported the exterior walls. Benches were arranged inside in two concentric rows, with small "smudge" pits scattered about where smoldering embers kept away insects. In the center, a large hearth was used for cooking, and to brew and keep warm the Indian's "black drink." See *San Luis Field Notes,* Winter, 1990.

285 *of Muchas-Aguas:* Hudson and Milanich place Uriutina and Many Waters on an unnamed Indian trail that appears on early maps, which connects Alligator Lake to the Suwannee River. They postulate that Uriutina is one of a cluster of village sites near Indian Pond in western Columbia County, west of I-75 and south of I-10. No Soto-era European artifacts have been uncovered here, though the area is rich with Indian artifacts associated with the so-called Weeden Island Culture, which dates to the sixteenth century. (Archaeologists have found Spanish artifacts dating to the seventeenth century, which indicates there may have been a Spanish mission here, possibly the short-lived San Augustín de Urica, established in 1630 and abandoned in the late 1650s.) "Many Waters" may have been another cluster of sites found in the area of Peacock and White Lakes south of U.S. 90, and about five miles east-southeast of Live Oak, Florida. Again, no Soto-era European artifacts have been discovered here. See Milanich and Hudson, 161–62.

285 *city, called Napituca:* Milanich and Hudson place Napituca "just west of present Live Oak." See Milanich and Hudson, 163.

286 *"come in peace":* Elvas, 67.

286 *"with good words":* Ibid., 67.

286 *"a large savanna":* Ranjel-Oviedo, 264.

286 *"he was holding":* Elvas, 67.

287 *profiling this "Vitachuco":* See Garcilaso, 162–80.

287 *"for the birds":* Ibid., 162.

287 *"arm and mount":* Ranjel-Oviedo, 264.

287 *trumpeter, Rodrigo Corona:* According to Elvas, Soto planned to entice Uriutina into his camp at Napituca, where most of his men, including mounted knights, were hidden in the lodges "so that the Indians might not see them." This was a repeat of the same trick Pizarro

used against Atahualpa at Cajamarca. See Elvas, 107. I am not sure if the trumpeter in this case was actually Rodrigo Corona, though he is the only trumpeter listed as such in the expedition records. See Avellaneda, *Los Sobrevivientes,* 25.

287 *"talking with him":* Elvas, 67.

287 *"the infantry separate":* Ibid.

289 *"lancing many Indians":* Ranjel-Oviedo, 265.

289 *"period of time":* Ibid.

289 *"to Juan Ortiz":* Elvas, 68.

289 *"match for them":* Ranjel-Oviedo, 265.

289 *"for their service":* Elvas, 68.

290 *"the common Indians":* Ranjel-Oviedo, 265–66.

290 *"him spit out":* Ibid., 266.

290 *"out" more blood:* According to Elvas, the blow was delivered against Soto's nose, which was the source of the blood.

290 *"by a javelin":* Elvas, 69.

290 *"of the plaza":* Ibid.

290 *is not known:* At first glance, Soto's use of Timucuan auxiliaries to execute Timucuans from another tribe seems odd, when the Spanish seldom showed reticence to perform such grisly tasks themselves—and had every right to under a *Requerimiento* system that vowed to reward any native resistance with instant death and destruction. It's possible the Indians of Urriparacoxi considered their victims to be enemies. Later in his narrative Elvas also makes the point that Indians became loyal and obedient to the Spaniards once they had traveled 150 miles from their own province, and realized they would not be returning home.

291 *it a "massacre":* Elvas, 70.

291 *"are not maltreated":* Ranjel-Oviedo, 266. This passage perhaps reveals more about Oviedo's frame of mind than Soto's or Ranjel's. When he talks about the consciences of the conquerors being more at peace, one suspects he is talking about his own guilt over his role as a conquistador in his youth. His comments praising the Council of the Indies also seem suspect, given that they were then paying his salary as alcalde of Santo Domingo.

291 *probably the Suwannee:* Because we know for certain that Soto wintered in what is now Tallahassee, the closer the *entrada* gets to this modern-day city, the easier it becomes to determine Soto's route, and to locate the places he visited. For instance, all the chronicles talk about a large river to the south that required a bridge to be made, and two more smaller rivers that the army crossed before reaching what is now Tallahassee. A quick glance at a map tells us the big river is the Suwannee, and the other two the Aucilla and the St. Marks.

291 *"perpendicular as walls":* Garcilaso, 148.

291 *Dowling Park, Florida:* See Milanich and Hudson, 163–64.

291 *"ones from Spain":* Ranjel-Oviedo, 266.

292 *"fifty armed cavalrymen":* Garcilaso, 184.

292 *"in Spain romana":* Ibid., 184.

292 *beside Lake Sampala:* Hudson and Milanich hypothesize that Soto followed one of several known Indian highways across Madison County from the Suwannee River, and further suggest that the seventeenth-century mission of San Pedro y San Pablo de Potohiriba, discovered recently by archaeologist Calvin Jones, may have some correlation to the

sixteenth-century Uzachile. Kenneth Johnson and Claudine Payne have conducted limited surveys in the Lake Sampala area, and discovered two small sites. Another larger site in the area was discovered by Keith Terry. These surveys and excavations remain tentative, however, and reveal no direct link to Soto. Nor has there been enough work to prove this area is the heavily populated region Soto's chroniclers describe. See Milanich and Hudson, 165–66.

292 *"beans, and pumpkins":* Elvas, 70.
292 *"[the Lord's] estate":* Garcilaso, 186.
293 *"they could perform":* Elvas, 70.
293 *"they cut it":* Ibid.

Chapter 24: Anhaica

294 *beyond their domain:* See Garcilaso, 189.
294 *unit "without permission":* Ranjel-Oviedo, 266.
294 *"of good persons":* Ibid., 266; see Swanton, 352 for Cadena's full name.
295 *the Aucilla River:* See Milanich and Hudson, 166.
295 *"of them escaped":* Elvas, 70.
295 *Diaz de Herrera:* Ranjel-Oviedo calls this man *"un bachiller, llamado Herrera,"* "a lawyer, named Herrera," without giving a complete name (Ranjel-Oviedo, 266). John Swanton suggests this bachiller Herrera may be the Pedro Diaz de Herrera listed on one of the expedition's registries when they departed Seville. See Swanton, 359.
295 *"have killed him":* Ranjel-Oviedo, 266–67.
295 *"a lustful man":* Ibid.
297 *"and burned them":* Ibid., 267.
297 *many as 100,000:* As always, populations are difficult to ascertain for native polities. Henry Dobyns, in *Their Numbers Become Thinned,* argues that the Calusa, Timucua, and Apalachee together had a population of 919,600 in c. 1517, with about 100,000 of these people Apalachee. This is a high-end estimate based on a highly optimistic analysis of what population the land, based on its fertility, might have supported (Dobyns, 135–44). Milanich and Fairbanks have estimated the Apalachee population to be "at least" 25,000 when Soto came through, adding that disease and other factors had caused it to decline to about 5,000 by the mission period (Milanich and Fairbanks, *Florida Archaeology,* 230). See Hann, *Apalachee,* 160–61, for a detailed analysis of Apalachee population estimates.
298 *crockery to copper:* Garcilaso here is telling the truth, since shells originating in the Apalachee area have shown up in Mississippian tombs as far north as Illinois.
298 *most popular game:* See Father Juan de Paiva, *Origin and Beginning of the Game of Ball;* in Hann, *Apalachee, the Land between the Rivers,* app. 2: 331–53. See also Hann's explanation of the game, 71–95.
298 *"filled with dirt":* Ibid., 333.
298 *"or leg broken":* Ibid.
298 *"a live war":* Ibid.
298 *"stay alive thus?":* Ibid.
299 *before Soto's arrival:* See Milanich and Hudson, 211.
299 *before Soto's entrada:* See Jones, "Southern Cult Manifestations at the Lake Jackson Site,

Leon County, Florida: Salvage Excavation of Mound 3," *Midcontinental Journal of Archaeology,* 7:1, 3–43. Jones says the Lake Jackson site was inhabited from about A.D. 1240 to the 1470s.

299 *the central plaza:* Ibid., 4–5. The exact dimensions of the mound were 11m high and 85m by 95m at the base.

300 *approaching Spanish army:* What exactly the Apalachee were saying and doing on the eve of Soto's invasion is unknown. However, records exist describing how descendants of the Mississippians in the southeast prepared in general for hostilities, acting out rituals undoubtedly originating with their ancestors. For instance, among the Chicasa, there was a ceremony recorded by the French in the eighteenth century where the *cacique* circled the council hut three times. Gathering his warriors together, he would then summon the tribe's aged warriors to stand up and deliver speeches to encourage the young men about to do battle. These speeches were followed by war songs and ceremonies of purification that included purgatives made from herbs. Under strict orders from the elders to abstain from sex and to follow all religious and tribal rules—and thus remain "pure"—the warriors then lathered themselves with red and black paint, colors of conflict and death, armed themselves with clubs and longbows, and lined up behind the standards of their clans and divisions. The Natchez also assigned special warriors to carry square, wooden "arks" filled with holy objects, including fragments of bones and horns supposedly taken from two frightful underworld monsters, Uktena and Water Cougar, whose remains were said to frighten off enemies and prevent wounds. See Hudson, *The Southeastern Indians,* 243.

300 *"a stout wall":* Garcilaso, 189.

300 *"to the waist":* Elvas, 70. For details of this and other battles fought during the Apalachee campaign, we must depend almost exclusively on Garcilaso, who devotes nearly 100 pages of his 643-page narrative to the army's five months in Apalachee. In contrast, our eyewitnesses all gloss over the Apalachee period in just a few lines—a frustrating omission that none explain.

300 *given the topography:* See Milanich and Hudson, 212.

300 *"go along it":* Garcilaso, 189–90.

301 *"deaths and wounds":* Ibid., 190.

301 *"timbers fastened together":* Ibid.

301 *"the other side":* Ranjel-Oviedo, 267.

301 *"take to flight":* Elvas, 70.

301 *"with stray arrows":* Garcilaso, 192.

301 *"attention to them":* Ibid., 193.

302 *"capture or kill":* Ibid.

302 *"as they had":* Ibid., 194.

302 *present-day Lake Iamonia:* Soto's Ivitachuco was probably located at or near the seventeenth-century mission of San Lorenzo de Ivitachuco, which Calvin Jones discovered about a half mile south of Lake Iamonia, and about twenty miles east of Tallahassee. See Milanich and Hudson, 213–14.

302 *"fire to it":* Elvas, 71.

302 *"into the camp":* Garcilaso, 194.

302 *"of a pueblo":* Ibid., 194, 197.

303 *"force of arms":* Ibid., 194.

303 *St. Marks River:* See Milanich and Hudson, 214–15.

303 *"all the others":* Garcilaso, 197.

303 *archaeologist Calvin Jones:* The following information is based on conversations with Calvin Jones, and on Jones, "The Dreamer and the de Soto Site," *The Florida Anthropologist,* 41:3 (September 1988), 403.

304 *"be chain mail":* Jones, "The Dreamer and the de Soto Site," *The Florida Anthropologist,* 41:3 (September 1988), 403.

304 *the mid-sixteenth century:* Narváez didn't get this far north.

304 *"so highly regarded":* Garcilaso, 235.

305 *"through him also":* Ibid.

305 *"ones laid aside":* Ibid., 236.

305 *full-blown excavation:* This was conducted by archaeologist Charles Ewen. See Ewen, "Anhaica: Discovery of Hernando de Soto's 1539–1540 Winter Camp." *First Encounters,* 110–18. Also see Ewen, "Soldier of Fortune: Hernando de Soto in the Territory of the Apalachee, 1539–1540," *The Columbian Consequences,* I, 83–91.

305 *Nueva Cadiz bead:* This same style of Nueva Cadiz bead was discovered at a site in the Withlacoochee Swamp north of Tampa Bay, which Hudson and Milanich believe was the Swamp of Cale, where Soto passed through as he marched north from his landfall. See Ewen, *First Encounters,* 114.

306 *"on all fours":* Garcilaso, 213. As for the litter the Apalachee used to carry their king, this was, in fact, a common prerogative for a High Mississippian king (or queen), whether or not they were fat.

306 *"then or later":* Ibid., 216.

306 *"captains and soldiers":* Ibid.

307 *St. Marks, Florida:* Aute was probably located at or near a dig called the Work Place Site, on the west bank of the Wakulla, where numerous Spanish artifacts were unearthed around 1900 during excavations of a large burial mound near the site, including iron tools, glass beads, and the tiny brass bells Spaniards used to decorate the bridles of their horses. These artifacts might have been left by Soto's men as they came and went from Anhaica to Aute, which became their link with the sea. See Mitchem, "Artifacts of Exploration: Archaeological Evidence from Florida," *First Encounters,* 101. Also see Milanich and Hudson, 219.

307 *palmettos, and palms:* Garcilaso here tells an absurd, if entertaining story about an Indian whom Añasco's party kept trying to kill, but would not die. As this man repeatedly attacked the Spaniards, he survived being beaten, shot, stabbed, and thrown to the dogs. Finally, he was hacked to pieces and died. See Garcilaso, 185–90.

307 *"and spacious bay":* Garcilaso, 203.

307 *"skulls of horses . . .":* Elvas, 72.

307 *"grind the corn":* Ranjel-Oviedo, 267.

307 *"used as mangers":* Elvas, 72.

307 *"in this conviction":* Cabeza de Vaca, 44.

307 *"near the water":* Biedma, 234.

308 *through enemy territory:* See Milanich and Hudson, 221. Their mileage is based on the actual distance from Tampa Bay to Tallahassee, which roughly converts to 93 leagues, using a league of 3.4 miles. This comes close to Biedma's claim that the army had traveled 110

leagues since landing in Florida (see Biedma, 227). As always, distances cited in the chronicles are at best approximations.

308 *just ten days:* To ride the three hundred miles to Tampa Bay in just ten days means the troop averaged an extraordinary thirty miles a day on a route that ranged from wide, open highways to dense swamps.

308 *"distance from habitation":* Elvas, 72.

308 *named Gonzalo Silvestre:* Garcilaso tells us several times in his narrative that he relied on an anonymous source for some of his information, an elderly man who in his youth had participated in the Soto expedition. This was almost certainly Gonzalo Silvestre, who lived near Garcilaso during part of the period the Inca was writing an early draft of his book. See Edward Moore's foreword in *The De Soto Chronicles,* II, 4–5.

308 *"horses and riders":* Ibid., 206.

308 *"by all animals":* Ibid., 220.

309 *"of the night":* Ibid., 207.

309 *"burned and destroyed":* Ibid., 207.

309 *"very infamous punishment":* Ibid., 208.

309 *"on his horse.":* Ibid., 220–27.

310 *"relatives and friends":* Ibid., 227.

310 *Isabel de Bobadilla:* See Elvas, 72.

310 *"toward the west":* Elvas, 73.

310 *"the sea coast":* Biedma, 228.

310 *the more probable:* Elvas says Maldonado traveled sixty leagues, which would place him nearer Pensacola than Mobile. However, a year later, when Maldonado returned to Florida from Cuba to rendezvous with Soto, the chroniclers place him south of Soto's camp at Mabila, in south central Alabama, indicating that Maldonado was in Mobile Bay.

311 *"of those Indians":* Biedma, 228.

311 *"come in peace":* Ranjel-Oviedo, 267.

311 *caused "two thirds":* Elvas, 73.

312 *"the interior country":* Garcilaso, 248.

312 *"gold in abundance":* Elvas, 74.

312 *"asking him about":* Garcilaso, 249.

312 *"to be true":* Ibid.

312 *"many precious pearls":* Ibid., 249.

313 *"of the interior":* Biedma, 228.

313 *"Río Espíritu Santo":* Biedma, 236. For those who still cling to the notion that Soto discovered the Mississippi, Biedma's casual mention of the Mississippi here, is further proof that Soto, his men, and the Spanish world were well acquainted with this river. Biedma indicates that Soto, even at this early date, had the Rio Espíritus Santo in mind as a major geographic feature he expected to run into as he marched west.

Book V: Obsession

Chapter 25: Idylls of Georgia

317 *"during that winter":* Elvas, 74.

318 *"some live oak":* This was Benjamin Hawkins, one of the first U.S. senators from North

Carolina (1789–1795), who negotiated the Treaty of Coleraine with the Creek Confederacy in 1796, and served as the U.S. Agent to the Creeks from 1796–1816. Quoted in Worth, "Mississippian Occupation on the Middle Flint River," Masters thesis (1988), 30.

318 *just one day:* See Ranjel-Oviedo, 269.

318 *full of grain:* It's possible Soto also rode ahead with the vanguard, which would explain why Ranjel, who frequently is seen at the governor's side, says it took three days to reach the Flint, while Elvas and Biedma, traveling with the main army, say it took four or five days.

318 *crossing the Flint:* Biedma says this journey took five days. See Biedma, 228. Hudson and his colleagues Marvin T. Smith and Chester B. DePratter speculate that Soto marched due north from Anhaica-Tallahassee to Cairo, Georgia, where the army might have picked up an old Indian trail, the Hawthorn Trail, taking it to the present-day town of Camilla, twenty six miles to the north. From here, Hudson, et al. suggest that the *entrada* swung northwest along another old trail, Barnard's Path, which roughly followed today's State Highway 37 to Newton, a tiny town situated above the west bank of the Flint. See Hudson et al., "The Hernando de Soto Expedition: From Apalachee to Chiaha," 1984, 67. See also Hudson et al., "Refinements in Hernando de Soto's Route through Georgia and South Carolina," 1990, 98.

320 *"some half drowned":* Ranjel-Oviedo, 269.

320 *"of the horses":* Ibid.

321 *"could not enter":* Elvas, 75.

321 *"or twelve arrows":* Garcilaso, 257–58.

321 *"handles being left":* Ibid. Garcilaso says it took several days for Aguilar to recover his senses. When he did, he told his friends a tale that "amazed" the Spaniards. He insisted that a large group of Indians had moved against them, but only seven had come forward to fight against the seven Spaniards—an action the Spaniards considered an astonishing act of chivalry, according to Garcilaso. For "they had never imagined the Indians were capable of such an . . . action as to desire to fight on equal terms with the Castilians when they could attack them with the advantage [of numbers]."

321 *a different language:* See Elvas, 76.

321 *to the north:* See Hudson et al., "Refinements," 110. The Hudson group believes the main village of Capachequi may have been located at a mound site on the Magnolia Plantation, on the Chicasawatchee Creek five or six miles west of Newton, Georgia, a short distance upstream from where this creek flows into the Flint.

322 *"and native blankets":* Elvas, 75.

322 *"thread from Portugal":* Ranjel-Oviedo, 271.

322 *"the breech clouts":* Elvas, 76.

322 *near Montezuma, Georgia:* Hudson et al. place this crossing at a narrow ford in the river near Montezuma, between two low bluffs. See Hudson, et. al., "Refinements," 111. The chroniclers call their river the River of Toa, suggesting it might be a different river than the one they crossed a few days earlier, called the River of Capachequi. It is probable, however, that the names refer to the Flint, and that Indians of different localities called the same river by different names. In this River of Toa, Ranjel-Oviedo tells us that a horse belonging to Lorenzo Suárez, son of Vasco Porcallo, drowned during a difficult crossing. See Ranjel-Oviedo, 269–70.

322 *"children, and possessions":* Garcilaso, 260.

323 *"some interpreter guides"*: Biedma, 229.

323 *"you fared there"*: Garcilaso, 260.

323 *"his own eyes"*: Ibid., 260.

323 *"under another Captain"*: Ranjel-Oviedo, 270.

323 *"nobles and gentlemen"*: Ibid.

324 *dash to Ichisi*: See Garcilaso, 260.

324 *south of Macon*: Hudson postulates that Soto's eighteen-hour trek took him from the Flint River north of Montezuma along a trail that roughly corresponds to State Highway 127. Here he admits that there are no real candidates for the river Soto crossed that second night, though in this swampy country in the Ocmulgee floodplain, many small rivers and streams feeding the larger river must have come and gone in the past 450 years. Hudson speculates Soto's group camped near Perry, Georgia, near Interstate 75, and some twenty-five miles south of Macon. See Hudson et al., "Refinements," 112.

324 *"are you going?"*: Ranjel-Oviedo, 270.

324 *"other Christian vassals"*: Ibid., 270–71.

325 *"where it dwelt"*: Elvas, 77.

325 *flooded and impassable*: Hudson says this stream was probably Echeconnee Creek. See Hudson et al., "Refinements," 112.

325 *"stewed and raw"*: Ranjel-Oviedo, 271.

325 *subject to Ichisi*: Hudson thinks this is the Cowart's Landing Site. See Hudson et al., "Refinements," 112.

325 *"to carry burdens"*: Ranjel-Oviedo, 271–72.

325 *route, "called Ocute"*: Elvas, 77.

325 *"by the Indians"*: Biedma, 229.

326 *"should reverence it"*: Elvas, 77.

326 *"Ayllón had come"*: Biedma, 229.

327 *"abundance of food"*: Ranjel-Oviedo, 272.

327 *present-day Milledgeville, Georgia*: Hudson and company believe Soto left Ichisi and then followed one of several well-established trading trails identified on early British settlers' maps. Locals in the Milledgeville area believe Soto crossed at a narrow point in the Oconee below the mouths of Reedy Creek and Buck Creek. See Hudson et al., "From Apalachee to Chiaha," 70, and Hudson et al., "Refinements," 101. Altamaha itself may have been located at the Shinholser mound center, south of Milledgeville, which was occupied as early as the mid-sixteenth century. (See Marvin Smith and Stephen Kowalewski, "Tentative Identification of a Prehistoric 'Province' in Piedmont Georgia," *Early Georgia* 8:1–13; also Hudson et al., "From Apalachee to Chiaha," 70.) At this point, the Hudson route begins to deviate significantly from John Swanton's 1939 route, which places Ichisi on the Flint River and Altamaha and Ocute on the Ocmulgee instead of Oconee. This routing thus places the eventual location of Cofitachequi near the Savannah River, far to the south of Hudson's placement near Columbia, South Carolina. But Swanton's route does not take into account recent archaeological data. He also assumes Soto was moving at a considerably slower pace than Hudson says he was capable of—an assessment I agree with, based on Soto's and other's pacing on other similar *entradas*. See Swanton, 172–86. Swanton also did not take into account a later expedition led by the Spanish explorer Juan Pardo, who visited Cofitachequi

in the 1560s, and clearly places it in central South Carolina. See Hudson's *The Juan Pardo Expeditions.*

327 *"command something else":* Ranjel-Oviedo, 272.

328 *"and a feather":* Ibid.

328 *was in Ocute:* Hudson et al. believe that Ocute may be an archaeological locale known as the Shoulderbone Site, near the mouth of Shoulderbone Creek along the Oconee, though because this archaeological site is smaller than it should be based on descriptions in the narrative, this identification remains tentative. See Hudson, et al., "From Apalachee to Chiaha," 70, and Hudson et al., "Revisions," 112.

328 *"populated with Indians":* Biedma, 229.

328 *" 'should not die' ":* Elvas, 77.

328 *"from the paths":* Ibid.

328 *"the Christians do":* Ranjel-Oviedo, 273.

329 *of those Indians:* According to Garcilaso, Soto also left behind a cannon in Ocute, having seen no use for heavy European artillery in *La Florida,* and noting that "it served for nothing except a burden and annoyance." Before he left, however, Soto staged a little demonstration to show the people of Ocute what he was leaving behind. Loading the cannon, he ordered it fired at "a large and very beautiful live-oak tree that was outside the pueblo, and he knocked it down entirely with two shots, at which the *cacique* and his Indians were amazed." See Garcilaso, 264–65.

329 *Ocute, called Cofaqui:* Garcilaso calls this *cacique* Cofachiqui, and claims he is a brother or close kinsman of Ocute (Garcilaso's Cofa). Hudson et al., believe Cofaqui's main village was located at the Dyar Site, near Greensboro, Georgia.

329 *"governed for him":* Ranjel-Oviedo, 273.

329 *local king, Patofa:* The name "Patofa" comes from Elvas. Ranjel-Oviedo calls this *cacique* Tatofa. Garcilaso describes Patofa not as a *cacique,* but as a leading aide to Cofaqui, whom is appointed as captain-general of 4,000 Indian troops the Inca claims accompanied Soto on the march to Cofitachequi.

329 *as twelve hundred:* Garcilaso insists the Indians supplied Soto with 8,000 people—4,000 porters and 4,000 soldiers. This brought the total persons under Soto's command up to 10,000, with 350 horses—an expansive exaggeration, to say the least.

Chapter 26: The Pearls of Cofitachequi

330 *spent time with:* Garcilaso says Perico "went about with the Spaniards as familiarly as if he had been born among them." Garcilaso, 270.

330 *"the rising sun":* Elvas, 80. Biedma says Perico said it was a three day journey to Cofitachequi. See Biedma, 229.

331 *"as if possessed":* Elvas, 80.

331 *"fear the Christians":* Garcilaso, 270–71.

331 *who saved him:* Elvas and Ranjel-Oviedo confirm Perico was baptized.

332 *had abruptly departed:* See Hally et al., "The Protohistoric Period Along the Savannah River"; and Anderson et al., "The Mississippian Occupation of the Savannah River Valley," 47–48.

332 *"were at war":* Biedma, 229.

332 *"war" with them:* Inasmuch as he can be believed, Garcilaso offers us a short speech by Patofa promising "with the aid of these valiant Spaniards to avenge all the injuries, deaths, damages and losses that our ancestors and ourselves have received from the natives of Cofitachequi." The Inca later describes Patofa telling Soto that his people had not waged open battle with Cofitachequi, "one taking an army into the territory of the other," but had fought mostly over hunting grounds. Because "those of Cofitachequi had been superior to his and had always gained many advantages over them in the fights that they had thus had, his Indians . . . [dared] not to go any distance or leave their own boundaries." Garcilaso, 269, 274.

332 *"as they could":* Biedma, 229.

332 *"very large" river:* Ranjel-Oviedo, 274.

332 *probably the Broad:* Soto's precise route through the Wilderness of Ocute has long been a subject of dispute. In 1984, Charles Hudson, Marvin Smith, and Chester DePratter wrote a controversial paper that purported to trace Soto's path through this forest on an almost daily basis. Reading the chronicles with great literalness, and then extrapolating from what little is known archaeologically about this region, they optimistically suggested that the Spaniards left Cofaqui on October 13 and marched along an old Indian path that early British settlers called Hightower Trail, reaching Butler Creek on April 16, and arriving the next day on the banks of the Savannah. Here these scholars postulated that the army crossed at Fort Moore, near Augusta, before heading off toward Columbia, South Carolina. This may be true, though in a later paper Hudson and company conceded that "the evidence cannot sustain such a detailed itinerary, except in a hypothetical way," adding that "drawing a single route across the wilderness can only be done using a very broad line." Indeed, the chronicles are so vague about this march that it's impossible to do much more than speculate about this segment of the route. There is also the question of whether or not the Savannah valley was truly deserted during Soto's visit, as Hudson maintains. This "empty quarter" hypothesis can only be proven when the entire region has been thoroughly and exhaustively investigated, which has not yet happened. See Hudson et al., "Refinements in Hernando de Soto's Route through Georgia and South Carolina," *Columbian Consequences* II, 113.

333 *"to the dogs":* Elvas, 80.

333 *night "greatly disheartened":* Ibid., 80–81.

333 *"he should do":* Ibid., 81.

333 *"should turn back":* Ranjel-Oviedo, 274.

333 *"lacking in maize":* Elvas, 81.

333 *"to go forward":* Ranjel-Oviedo, 274.

333 *"could not escape":* Elvas, 81.

333 *porters and warriors:* Garcilaso says Patofa stayed with Soto for another few days, and describes in considerable detail a series of attacks made later by Patofa's warriors against villages allied with Cofitachequi, in which "they did all the harm and injury they could." For a while, says Garcilaso, they kept these attacks secret from Soto. When the governor discovered what was happening, he ordered the Indians to stop, and dismissed them to go back home—though not before Soto gave Patofa gifts "for the friendliness and good companionship he had shown." These gifts included "silk, and linen, knives, scissors, mirrors, and other things from Spain." None of the eyewitnesses mention these incidents. See Garcilaso, 282–83.

333 *"in the camp"*: Elvas, 81.

333 *from the river*: Garcilaso says these captains were Añasco, the Portuguese Andrés de Vasconcelos, Juan de Guzmán, and Arias Tinoco. See Garcilaso, 276.

333 *"each man daily"*: Elvas, 81. Ranjel-Oviedo says the ration was a pound of pork a day. See
Ranjel-Oviedo, 275. Garcilaso says it was eight ounces a day. See Garcilaso, 277.

333 *"along the streams"*: Garcilaso, 277.

334 *"with considerable trouble"*: Elvas, 81.

334 *game and fish*: See Garcilaso, 277.

334 *"God for mercy"*: Ranjel-Oviedo, 275.

334 *"and a boy"*: Elvas, 81. Biedma says Añasco was gone four days, and that he brought back
three or four Indians. Biedma adds that these Indians were able to communicate not only
with Perico, but with Ortiz, to which Biedma says "this was no little thing for us because of
the great necessity for interpreters that there is in this land." Biedma, 230.

334 *in small numbers*: See Garcilaso, 280; and Crosby, *Ecological Imperialism*, 213.

334 *"most greedy death"*: Elvas, 81.

334 *"strength aided him"*: Ibid.

334 *(five thousand pounds)*: Ranjel-Oviedo says there were two and a half *cahices* of corn, equal
to about three thousand pounds of corn. Ranjel-Oviedo, 275.

334 *"other smaller fruit"*: Biedma, 230.

334 *"delicate and mellow"*: Ranjel-Oviedo, 275.

335 *his sovereign's capital*: Elvas says only one Indian was burned, and that the others told Soto
that Cofitachequi was two days away to the north. See Elvas, 82.

335 *"of her towns"*: Elvas, 82.

335 *"affection and courtesy"*: Elvas, 82.

336 *"to the woods"*: Biedma, 230.

336 *"to her thighs"*: Garcilaso, 285–88.

336 *"very handsome ruby"*: Ibid., 288.

336 *the Mulberry Site*: Also known as the McDowell Site, this site contains two large mounds—
one of which has been reduced by plowing, and the other which has mostly collapsed into the
river—and eight small mounds, seven of which have been leveled by plowing. It is located
two and a half miles south of Camden. It is also possible that Cofitachequi was another of
several contemporaneous sites located within a few miles of one another along this stretch of
the Wateree River. See George Stuart's Ph.D. dissertation, *The Post-Archaic Occupation of
South Carolina* (1975). See also Levy et al., "From Ysa to Joara: Cultural Diversity in the
Catawba Valley," in *Columbian Consequences II*, 153–68, and Hudson, *Juan Pardo*, 68–83.

336 *in North Carolina*: For a review of Cofitachequi's possible boundaries, see Hudson, *Juan
Pardo*, 83; and Levy et al., *Columbian Consequences*, II, 153–68.

337 *"made in Spain"*: Ranjel-Oviedo, 278–80.

337 *"shod and clothed"*: Elvas, 83.

337 *"very good shields"*: Ranjel-Oviedo, 280.

337 *"the hides inland"*: Cañete, 309.

337 *"and beautiful mats"*: Ranjel-Oviedo, 280.

337 *five hundred houses*: If true, this would mean the total population of Talimeco was at least
2,500 people, if one assigns five persons to each house. However, since Mississippian
dwellings tended to house entire clans, the population may have been higher.

338 *"a beautiful sight"*: Garcilaso, 297, 298–99.

338 *"from distant countries"*: Ibid., 305.

338 *"hose, and shoes"*: Elvas, 83.

338 *"had raged there"*: Garcilaso, 306.

338 *"of the provisions"*: Ibid., 286.

339 *"of dry earth"*: Ibid., 294–95.

339 *temple near Cofitachequi:* Both Ranjel-Oviedo and Garcilaso indicate that the Queen of Cofitachequi invited Soto to ransack her temples and take whatever pearls he wanted, though if in fact she did this, my guess is she was hardly enthusiastic. Her assent probably was given because she realized she could not stop the Spaniards, and perhaps hoped to limit their plundering by directing them to specific temples.

339 *"was very delighted"*: Ranjel-Oviedo, 279.

339 *"axes of iron"*: Ibid.

339 *"with the Indians"*: Biedma, 231.

339 *Ayllón's aborted colony:* The discovery of these Spanish artifacts revealed more than the nearby existence of Ayllón's failed settlement. It also provided an explanation for why disease had decimated the Indians. Survivors of the Ayllón fiasco make it clear that one of the chief causes of the debacle was a devastating disease that counted Ayllón himself among its victims.

339 *"leagues from here"*: Biedma, 231.

339 *roughly ninety miles:* In fact, this is roughly the true distance from the Mulberry Site to the Atlantic coast. The location of Ayllón's two attempts at establishing a colony are not known. Most scholars place his initial landfall in or near Winyah Bay and the South Santee River, some sixty miles up the coast from Charleston. Later, he moved south, looking for a more hospitable site, perhaps landing in the Sapelo Sound area on the Georgia coast. Here he may have built the ill-fated town of San Miguel de Gualdape. See Weber, 36–37.

339 *turned them black:* See Garcilaso, 318 for a description of how pearls were opened with fire.

339 *from Indian temples:* Biedma says Soto carted off "seven *arrobas*" of pearls, equal to about 175 pounds. Ranjel-Oviedo says the amount was "eight or nine *arrobas*"; Elvas says six and a half *arrobas*.

340 *earlier, including Cofitachequi:* Pardo's visit to Cofitachequi is one reason we can be reasonably sure about this city's general location near Camden, South Carolina, since Pardo's chronicler, Juan de Bandera, kept far more accurate records than the chroniclers traveling with Soto.

340 *"be worth more"*: Elvas, 84.

340 *the Chesapeake Bay:* Menéndez tried twice to build colonies in the Chesapeake in the 1560s, but both failed, the second one after a massacre of Spanish Jesuits by the Powhatan Indians of Virginia. A few years later these same Indians helped the English establish their settlement at Jamestown.

341 *"port of [Achuse]"*: Elvas, 84, 85.

341 *"determination was learned"*: See ibid., 85.

Chapter 27: Lost Opportunities

342 "tamemes *for carrying"*: Elvas, 85.

342 *"received from her"*: Ranjel-Oviedo, 281.

343 *"André de Vasconcelos"*: The identity or race of this slave is unclear. Garcilaso indicates this slave was African. See Garcilaso, 315.

343 *"husband and wife"*: Elvas, 87.

343 *"so much inconvenience"*: Garcilaso, 285–86. According to Garcilaso, the previous year the plague had forced the Indians to flee their cities and disperse into the savannahs and forests. This meant that since no crops had been planted, grain was in short supply.

344 *long-ago May day*: Garcilaso makes no mention of the queen's imprisonment, indicating that she supplied everything Soto wanted for his upcoming march simply out of her boundless generosity. But remember that one of the Inca's chief reasons for writing his narrative was to encourage the colonization of *La Florida*—an effort that would be made much more attractive if potential settlers believed the Indians to be friendly and accommodating.

344 *"to the other"*: Elvas, 85.

344 *"her slave women"*: Ibid.

344 *to the north*: For information on the archaeology of the area, see Moore, "Archaeological Investigations," 1987, and *Late Prehistoric Aboriginal Settlements in the Upper Catawba Valley,* unpublished Ph.D. thesis, 1990. Also see Levy et al., "From Ysa to Joara," 159–60.

344 *several days later*: Ranjel-Oviedo reports that during this march they stopped to search for the *cacique* of a province called Chalaque. Charles Hudson believes the name Chalaque may have referred to the Muskogean word *cilo-kkitá,* which means "people of a different language." This has led Hudson to surmise that the Chalque may have been Sioux speakers, whose southernmost domain may have bumped up against the northern border of the Muskogean speakers in this general area. See Hudson et. al., "From Apalachee to Chiaha," 73.

345 *Oviedo's paraphrased version*: See Ranjel-Oviedo, 280–81.

345 *"of Spíritu Sancto."*: Ibid.

345 *present-day Asheville*: This is according to Hudson.

346 *seek out mines*: In 1525, Soto was sent to the Olancho Valley in Honduras to investigate reports of fresh mines. In 1528, the city council in León sent him to Juana Mostega, near the Pacific Coast, to "find and discover other mines and to collect a little gold as a sample" (DHN 1, 426).

347 *"through and seen"*: Ranjel-Oviedo, 280–81.

347 *"it was silver"*: Bandera, *The "Short" Relation,* 303.

347 *"be silver ore"*: Bandera, *The "Long" Relation,* 159.

347 *hematite (iron oxide)*: Hudson, *Juan Pardo,* 159.

347 *traces of diamonds*: See Ibid., 159–60.

347 *"more perfect color"*: Elvas, 89.

347 *with great difficulty*: In 1560, Luis de Velasco, Viceroy of New Spain, wrote to Tristán de Luna, founder of a short-lived colony in Pensacola Bay, that the two Spaniards sent by Soto to investigate rumors of copper mines "learned it was true." Velasco may have heard this information from Soto expedition survivors whom the viceroy consulted. See Velasco, Letter to Luna, August 20, 1560, Mexico City; in *The Luna Papers,* 438. None of the Soto chroniclers verify that the men found anything but rugged country, though Garcilaso insists they found "very fine" copper mines and evidence that veins of gold and silver must have been in the area. He also claims that they were entertained lavishly by a *cacique* in a rich province, who provided them with food, sumptuous housing, and "handsome young women to entertain and sleep with them." See Garcilaso, 320.

348 *"to her necessities"*: Elvas, 86–87.

348 *Montanjes, "with deception"*: Ranjel-Oviedo, 281.

348 *does not explain:* Elvas mentions nothing about a deception, saying only that a certain "Alimamos" stayed behind because he was sick with fever, and that when the queen and the three slaves arrived, Alimamos convinced two of the slaves to return to the Spanish camp, presumably with him.

349 *"shrewd black man":* Ranjel-Oviedo, 281. No other chronicler mentions this incident.

349 *east of Knoxville:* This is according to Hudson.

350 *"the same river":* See Ranjel-Oviedo, 281–82.

350 *near Dandridge, Tennessee:* Hudson places Chiaha, where Soto bivouacked for twenty-two days, on Zimmerman's Island in the French Broad, near Dandridge. This island is now submerged under an artificial lake, though archaeologists in the 1940s report at least one large mound on the island and Indian pottery shards that dated to the mid-sixteenth century. Hudson also uses information recorded by chroniclers of the Juan Pardo expedition, which passed through this region in 1566. See Hudson et al., "From Apalachee to Chiaha," 75; and Hudson, *Juan Pardo,* 103–4.

350 *from "bear's grease":* Elvas, 88.

350 *they caused "flatulence":* Ranjel-Oviedo, 282.

350 *"of the land":* Elvas, 88–89.

350 *"them very well":* Ranjel-Oviedo, 282.

351 *"wives and children":* Elvas, 89.

351 *"them to him":* Ibid.

Chapter 28: The Empire of Coosa

352 *some 550 men:* Since landing in *La Florida,* Soto's casualties had been remarkably light for an *entrada* of this era. Based on the battles, skirmishes, and hardships suffered by the Spaniards and reported in the chronicles, I'm guessing he had lost perhaps fifty to a hundred men since making landfall.

353 *corner of Georgia:* This is according to Hudson and his associates. See Hudson et al., "Coosa: A Cheifdom in the Sixteenth Century," *American Antiquity* 52:725–26.

353 *miles a day:* This is based on Charles Hudson's route. He has Soto traveling for an average of about twelve miles a day. The chroniclers also indicate the pace here was comfortable, with no mentions of quick marches or of Soto's usual hard-driving pace.

353 *to build settlements:* For instance, see Testimony of Pedro Carrion; PB I, 9–10, and Testimony of Diego de Tobar; PB I, 24.

354 *"that satisfied him":* Ranjel-Oviedo, 289.

355 *Little Tennessee River:* Hudson et al. place Coste near the juncture of the Little Tennessee and Tennessee Rivers.

355 *from the Indians:* Garcilaso tells a different story about Soto's encounter with the people of Coste. He claims that the Indians initially greeted the Spaniards by deploying fifteen hundred warriors under arms, "decked out with plumes and having their weapons ready . . ." Garcilaso says they behaved belligerently until the next day, when the *cacique* of Chiaha sent a favorable message concerning the Spaniards. This compelled the warriors to put down their arms, and to welcome the Spaniards in friendship, though they insisted Soto pay for the maize he requested—which he did, though we are not told what form of currency was used. See Garcilaso, 321.

355 *"to the plaza":* Ibid.

355 *"carelessly and unarmed"*: Ranjel-Oviedo, 283.

355 *"should anger them"*: Ibid.

356 *"on the Christians"*: Ibid., 283–84.

356 *a familiar friend*: Garcilaso also claims that a message from Chiaha to Coste was responsible for the Coste people receiving the Spaniards in friendship. See Garcilaso, 321.

356 *and so forth*: See Halley et al., "The Archaeological Reality of de Soto's Coosa," *Columbian
Consequences*, II, 121–38.

356 *"going, others coming"*: Elvas, 92.

357 *over "much land"*: Ranjel-Oviedo, 284.

357 *"a hundred leagues"*: Garcilaso, 321.

357 *to break away*: See Priestly, xiii–xiii; "The Luna Papers," I, 226; and Padilla, *Historia de la
fundación*, bk. I, chap. lxiv–lxvi.

357 *speakers near Chiaha*: According to Elvas, the region to the east of Chiaha was uninhabited for a march of five days. (See Elvas, 87.) There was also an uninhabited region to the
north, between Chiaha and the copper city of Chisca.

357 *"the towns palisaded"*: Biedma, 232.

358 *"are very strong"*: Ranjel, 288.

359 *near Gadsden, Alabama*: See Little and Curren, "Conquest Archaeology of Alabama,"
176.

359 *in July, 1540*: Ibid.

360 *Coste at Chattanooga*: Curren seems to hint in places that he leans towards Swanton's
Southern Route, which conveniently places the army where Curren says it should be when
it enters Alabama. However, Curren makes it clear his work has been confined solely to his
own state. See Little and Curren, ibid., 190–91.

360 *"into the trees"*: Elvas, 93.

360 *"canavales in Extremadura"*: Ranjel-Oviedo, 284.

360 *"large and important"*: Garcilaso, 322.

360 *"unite within it"*: Letter of Fray Domingo de la Anunciación to Luis de Velasco, Viceroy
of New Spain, Coosa, August 1, 1560; quoted in Priestly, 241.

361 *with earthen pyramids*: The Sixtoe Fields and Bell Field sites each contain a single mound,
both constructed during the thirteenth and fourteenth centuries. See Kelly, "Explorations at
Bell Field Mound and Village: Seasons 1965, 1966, 1967, 1968." Department of Anthro-
pology, University of Georgia (Athens, 1970); and Kelly et al., "Explorations in Sixtoe
Field, Carters Dam, Murray County, Georgia." Department of Anthropology, University of
Georgia (Athens, 1965).

361 *archaeologist Warren Moorehead*: See Moorehead, "Exploration of the Etowah Site,"
68–105.

361 *"on a height"*: Garcilaso, 322.

361 *the Carters Site*: See Hudson et al., "Coosa: A Chiefdom in the Sixteenth Century," 726.

361 *the mid-sixteenth century*: Ibid., 732.

361 *of Curren's sites*: This might be explained by the fact that some of these sites have not been
thoroughly excavated, or have been robbed by collectors. This includes Little and Curren's
candidate for Coosa itself, the Terrapin Creek Site at Childersburg, where the only evidence
of European goods of the proper date come from the claims of local plunderers, who insist

they dug up sixteenth-century tools there during the 1970s, an assertion that unfortunately cannot be proven.

362 *"playing and singing":* Elvas, 92.

362 *"with great ceremony":* Ranjel-Oviedo, 284.

362 *"to a file":* Garcilaso, 322.

362 *"and polished court":* Ibid., 325.

362 *"in the woods":* Elvas, 93.

362 *"and in chains":* Ranjel-Oviedo, 285. See also Elvas, 93.

364 *"they were carrying":* Elvas, 93.

364 *tens of thousands:* See Kelly et al., "The Archaeological Reality of de Soto's Coosa," 126–27.

364 *Levantine named Feryada:* See Ranjel-Oviedo, 285. Garcilaso calls this man Falco Herrado and says "he was not a Spaniard nor is it known from what province he came; he was a man of the lowest class and thus was not missed until Talisi. Steps were taken to bring him back, for he very shamelessly sent word by the Indians . . . that he wanted to stay with the Indians . . . so that he might not have to see his captain every day, who had quarreled with him and spoken to him abusively." Garcilaso also claims that an African slave named Robles, "who was sick and unable to travel," was left behind at Coosa. See Garcilaso, 326.

364 *"some Indian women":* Ranjel-Oviedo, 285.

365 *"he was unhappy":* Ibid.

365 *"and excellent there":* Elvas, 94.

365 *"reprimanded him severely":* Ranjel-Oviedo, 285.

365 *"lack of maize":* Elvas, 94–95.

365 *with his fleet:* Despite his rush to head south, Soto still felt compelled to halt for six days in a village called Tuasi, though our eyewitnesses provide us with such little information about this march we don't know why he stopped. Possibly, they had heard they were about to enter a lightly inhabited area and wanted to rest up and collect food before plunging into a region where rugged ridges poked up here and there. Here the army ended up camping in the open for two nights, and in an old, abandoned village on the third, without finding any food or Indians.

365 *near Childersburg, Alabama:* Near Childersburg are several Mississippian sites that date to the mid-sixteenth century. Little and Curren, in their reconstruction of the Soto route, identify these sites as the home region of Coosa. Hudson, however, identifies the Childersburg sites as the province of Talisi.

365 *"a big river":* Ranjel-Oviedo, 288.

365 *"in that land":* Ibid.

366 *"in the army":* Garcilaso, 327.

366 *"to make ceremony":* Ranjel-Oviedo, 288.

366 *"and be prepared":* Garcilaso, 327. Garcilaso says the two men were sent out only to investigate the highway from Talisi to Atahachi. They were sent at the request of Tascalusa's son, who asked Soto to have the various roads checked so he could chose the best one.

366 *"from his land":* Ranjel-Oviedo, 288.

366 *the King Site:* See Hudson et al., "Hernando de Soto's Expedition through the Southern United States," in *First Encounters,* 93. See also *The King Site: Continuity and Contact in*

Sixteenth-Century Georgia, ed. Robert L. Blakely, University of Georgia Press (Athens, 1988), for information on the King Site.

367 *least two others:* Three names corresponding to Soto expedition members appear on Luna expedition documents. These are Alvaro Nieto, whom Garcilaso describes as an occasional field captain (see Garcilaso, 524), Juan de Porras, and Juan de Bautista. See Priestly, *The Luna Papers,* 399, 419, 455.

368 *were "little frequented":* Anunciación to Velasco, August 1, 1560, in Priestly, 239.

368 *westward from Cofitachequi:* No strong archaeological or historical evidence exists for the spread of a deadly pathogen west from Cofitachequi. However, Hudson and others have speculated that the disease may have traveled so quickly, there was no time for the affected peoples to formally bury the victims for archaeologists to unearth later. If the Coosa Sauz saw was in a different location than the one seen by Soto, one explanation is that disease forced a relocation.

368 *to the battle:* Garcilaso says Tascalusa organized a force composed of not only his own army but also from surrounding provinces. See Garcilaso, 333.

369 *line in Tennessee:* See Hudson, *Juan Padro,* 34–40.

369 *ashes and fire:* Soto did not pass through Satapo itself, getting only as close as Coste, some thirty miles away. Yet the *cacique* at Satapo boasted to Pardo that he had killed some of Soto's men; something that probably did not happen, unless this *cacique* is referring to Mabila.

369 *"called Cosa [Coosa]":* Hudson, *Juan Pardo,* 272.

Chapter 29: Tascalusa's Fire

370 *"and well built":* Elvas, 96.

370 *size and height:* See Ranjel-Oviedo, 291.

371 *"was a giant":* Biedma, 232.

371 *Soto's larger packhorses:* Spanish horses in this period tended to be small by modern standards.

371 *its immediate vicinity:* See Walthall, 11.

371 *in several sites:* See Charles Hudson, "De Soto in Alabama." *De Soto Working Paper 10,* 12.

371 *a "new town":* Ranjel-Oviedo, 290.

371 *to the Atahachi:* See Garcilaso, 327.

372 *"where he was":* Elvas, 96.

372 *"on a pole":* Ranjel-Oviedo, 291.

372 *"were very perfect":* Elvas, 96. Garcilaso claims this "device" was a banner dyed yellow and streaked with three blue bars, and that it was the same size and shape of a Spanish cavalry standard. See Garcilaso, 328.

372 *"on a mound":* Ranjel-Oviedo, 290.

372 *on high cushions:* Garcilaso says Tascalusa was sitting on a stool about eleven inches high, with a concave seat and without a backrest or arms. See Garcilaso, 328.

372 *"of great authority":* Ranjel-Oviedo, 290.

372 *"and many people":* Elvas, 96.

372 *the entire army:* See Garcilaso, 328.

372 *"on this condition":* Ibid., 333.

373 *"strengthen the stockade":* Elvas, 98.

374 *the Coosa River:* See Hudson, "De Soto in Alabama," 10; also Hudson, "Critique of Caleb Curren's De Soto Route." According to Curren, Soto at this point was traveling away from the Montgomery area, heading west and then southwest along the Alabama River. See Little and Curren, "Conquest Archaeology of Alabama."

374 *of the Alabama:* Garcilaso mentions crossing a "River of Talisi" in rafts and canoes provided by the Indians, though it is unclear what river this might be, since neither Hudson nor Curren believe the army made a major crossing at this town. If Hudson is right, and the army was now following the Coosa River near Montgomery, the army probably crossed the Tallapoosa south of modern Wetumpka, Alabama.

374 *found at Moundville:* See Little and Curren, "Conquest Archaeology in Alabama," 181.

375 *some twenty-five hundred:* See Biedma, 233; Ranjel-Oviedo, 294; Elvas, 104.

375 *"toward the* cacique.*":* Elvas, 96.

375 *"if in disdain":* Ibid.

375 *"with much gravity":* Ranjel-Oviedo, 291.

375 *"peasants of Spain":* Ibid.

375 *"of all this":* Biedma, 232.

375 *"served him before":* Ibid.

375 *"to his liberty":* Ranjel-Oviedo, 291.

376 *"inflicted on us":* Biedma, 232.

376 *"they most desired":* Ranjel-Oviedo, 291.

376 *"a rocky river":* Ibid.

376 *of Soto's guard:* Ranjel-Oviedo says the Indians killed two Spaniards; Biedma says one. Elvas insists the army crossed the river with no fatalities, and that two Spaniards were killed when they went off without permission to search for a woman of theirs who escaped. Garcilaso agrees more or less with Elvas's version, adding that one of those killed was Juan de Villalobos, a foolhardy young horseman who frequently took chances for the sport of it. See Garcilaso, 329.

376 *"killed the Christian":* Biedma, 233.

376 *"in his land":* Elvas, 98.

376 *"pretended to be":* Garcilaso, 329.

376 *"entered the town":* Elvas, 98.

376 *"were so disposed":* Ibid.

377 *"and scattering themselves":* Ranjel-Oviedo, 292.

377 *to be proven:* Luis de Biedma writes as if he, too, accompanied Soto, making him an eyewitness along with Ranjel.

377 *and their retainers:* See Elvas, 100; and Ranjel-Oviedo, 294.

377 *"music and singing":* Elvas, 98.

377 *"strongly palisaded town":* Biedma, 233.

378 *"most important houses":* Garcilaso, 331.

378 *Clark County, Alabama:* See Little and Curren, "Conquest Archaeology of Alabama," *Columbian Consequences,* II, 182–84.

379 *their over-all route:* See Hudson, "De Soto in Alabama," 13–14.

379 *of European artifacts:* See Little and Curren, "Conquest Archaeology in Alabama," 188.

379 *"in all México":* Carmona, quoted in Garcilaso, 333.
379 *"order to dissemble":* Biedma, 233.
379 *"them had come":* Garcilaso, 333–34.
380 *"dominion by force":* Elvas, 99.
380 *"some palm leaves":* Ranjel-Oviedo, 292.
380 *"ready for war":* Biedma, 233.
380 *"Indians came out":* Elvas, 99.
381 *"under his helmet":* Garcilaso, 336.
381 *"we had brought":* Biedma, 235.
382 *"on four sides":* Ibid.
382 *"of the dead":* Elvas, 101.
382 *"again and again":* Ibid.
382 *"he fell dead":* Ranjel-Oviedo, 293.
383 *"burned to death":* Elvas, 104.
383 *"immediately fell dead":* Garcilaso, 335.
383 *"the cavalrymen's lances":* Ibid., 338.
383 *"skill in horsemanship":* Ibid., 339–41.
383 *"than their husbands":* Ibid., 343
384 *"with savage combat":* Ibid.
384 *"of the Spaniards":* Ibid., 342.

Book VI: Madness

Chapter 30: Aftermath

387 *"against the Spaniards":* Garcilaso, 352–53.
387 *"woods, entirely helpless":* Ibid., 351–53.
388 heir *"found lanced":* Ranjel-Oviedo, 294.
388 *"dead or alive":* Ibid.
388 *in the buttocks:* Garcilaso is alone among the narrative writers to report that Soto was wounded, insisting that both of his eyewitness informants, Alonso de Carmona and Juan Coles, confirmed it. See Garcilaso, 351.
389 *eighteen and twenty-five:* Ranjel-Oviedo says twenty-two died at Mabila; Elvas says eighteen; Cañete says twenty-five; Biedma says twenty were killed in the battle itself, and more later. Garcilaso claims eighty-two Spaniards died, which he says was corroborated by his informants, Juan Coles and Alonso de Carmona. More Spaniards died later of their wounds.
389 *Velez of Tordesillas:* In the chronicles, this man is identified only as "Velez." According to recruitment lists, there were two Velezes on the expedition—Juan Velez and Alonso Velez. See Swanton, 370–71.
389 *"died of fright":* Garcilaso, 350.
389 *surviving surgeon-barber:* This is according to Garcilaso, who adds that this surgeon was slow and inept. There also were medical doctors in the army, whom Garcilaso also derides as being ineffective. (See ibid., 349.)
389 *"to make bandages":* Ibid., 349.
389 *"burned that day":* Biedma, 235.

389 *"use as ointment":* Garcilaso, 349.

389 *"sixty arrow wounds":* Biedma, 235.

390 *arrow wounds apiece:* Ranjel-Oviedo says there were 148 men wounded with 688 arrow wounds—a number so exact one wonders if Ranjel counted them and either wrote down the number, or memorized it. Elvas says 150 were wounded, with 700 wounds.

390 *wounded seventy more:* Ranjel-Oviedo says seven horses died; Elvas says twelve died and seventy were wounded; Garcilaso claims forty-five horses died.

390 *pearls of Cofitachequi:* Ranjel-Oviedo says there were 9 *arrobas* of pearls burned, or about 225 pounds. (An *arroba* equals about 25 pounds.) See Ranjel-Oviedo, 294.

390 *"by the Christians":* Elvas, 104.

390 *"for saying mass":* Ranjel-Oviedo, 294.

390 *"from the grape":* Garcilaso, 354.

390 *a "dry mass":* Garcilaso, 353–54.

390 *or four weeks:* Ranjel-Oviedo says the army stayed at Mabila from October 19 to November 13; Elvas says 28 days; Garcilaso says 23–24 days.

391 *to the south:* This fleet was under the command of Francisco Maldonado, Soto's captain. Later, he testified in the *Ponce v. Bobadilla* trial that he was running the coast, looking for the army throughout October and November, 1540. His holds, he said, were filled "with certain men and necessary armaments that [Soto] had wanted." Testimony of Francisco de Maldonado, April 20, 1546, Salamanca; PB I, 17.

391 *"a rich land":* Elvas, 104.

391 *"able to winter":* Biedma, 236.

392 *"as they could":* Garcilaso, 356.

392 *"and miserable country":* Ibid., 357.

392 *"men to rebellion":* Ibid., 356–57.

392 *"his own destruction":* Ibid., 358.

Chapter 31: The Wilderness

393 *"without a scabbard":* Ranjel-Oviedo, 296.

393 *his "sweet talk":* Ibid., 296–97.

393 *on November 17:* See Joyce Hudson, 86–97, for details on her husband's theories regarding this portion of the route.

394 *came this way:* Hudson has speculated that one of the Apafalaya cities Soto visited, called Mozulixa, may have been located at or near ancient Moundville. Hudson also suggests locations for the three other towns Soto visited in this province, placing Talicpacana at a small Mississippian site at Elliott Creek, and the villages of Zabusta and Apafalaya at two sites west of the Black River. See Joyce Hudson, ibid.

394 *"league up stream":* Elvas, 105.

394 *"a large cart":* Ranjel-Oviedo, 296.

394 *where sixty men:* According to Ranjel-Oviedo, ibid. Elvas says thirty men crossed.

395 *"the landing place":* Garcilaso, 364.

395 *so says Garcilaso:* In Garcilaso's version, a hundred Spaniards crossed the river in two Piraguas, which took twelve days to build, and two carts to carry. See Garcilaso, 363–64.

395 *"forbid the crossing":* Elvas, 105.

395 *"landed, they fled"*: Ranjel-Oviedo, 296.

395 *more Apafalaya villages:* Elvas's recollections of town names in Apafalaya and the order in which the Spanish visited them differs from Ranjel-Oviedo. Elvas names only two towns in the province he calls Pafallaya—Taliepataua and Cabusto. He also says that the army passed through other towns "well provided with maize and beans."

395 *"guide and interpreter"*: Ranjel-Oviedo, 296.

395 *"of twenty houses"*: Elvas, 105.

395 *"[French settlers'] ears"*: Adair, 382.

396 *establish a location:* The difficulties of locating where Soto bivouacked that winter has not stopped one particularly innovative anthropologist, Jay Johnson of the University of Mississippi, from searching likely areas with space-age technology. In the early nineties, Johnson talked NASA into experimenting with a low-altitude heat-sensing device flown overhead in a specially outfitted Lear Jet. And what were they looking for? Bits of armor? Swords? Perhaps a few Spanish coins? No—NASA was looking for garbage. Specifically, their technicians were sweeping the area with sensors designed to pick up the heat signatures of potassium, the primary ingredient in ancient Indian trash-heaps composed mostly of shells and bones. So far, neither NASA in the sky nor archaeology teams totting old-fashioned troughs on the ground have uncovered Chicasa.

396 *"-twenty hours together"*: Adair, 383–84.

396 *"than in Castile"*: Biedma, 236.

396 *"or more cold"*: Ranjel-Oviedo, 297.

396 *"could build houses"*: Elvas, 105.

396 *"visit him frequently"*: Ibid., 106.

396 *"pork to eat"*: Ibid.

397 *"to the* cacique*"*: Ibid.

397 *"skins and blankets"*: Elvas, 107.

397 *"the prisoners released"*: Ibid.

398 *"sentinels that night"*: Ranjel-Oviedo, 297–98.

398 *"the whole army"*: Ibid., 298 Elvas says one of these three sentries was Soto's nephew, Diego de Soto, "who until then had been considered a good man." Elvas, 107.

398 *"noticed or seen"*: Biedma, 236.

398 *"from a distance"*: Garcilaso, 367.

398 *"beating their drums"*: Ranjel-Oviedo, 298.

399 *"resisting the Indians"*: Elvas, 108.

399 *"would have escaped"*: Biedma, 237.

399 *"snatch their jerkins"*: Elvas, 108.

399 *"hides of bears"*: Ranjel-Oviedo, 298.

400 *"to do likewise"*: Elvas, 109.

400 *"bright and clear"*: Ibid. Alonso de Carmona says the attack occurred during a downpour, and that the Indians were put at a disadvantage because the rain wet the cords of their bowstrings, making it difficult for them to shoot. He adds that the forges made by Soto were set up "with the two cannons we had brought along." See Carmona in Garcilaso, 373.

400 *be greatly "demoralized"*: Elvas, 109.

401 *"they relinquished it":* Biedma, 237.

401 *"passable on horseback":* Elvas, 111.

401 *modern-day Walls, Mississippi:* See note on p. 429.

401 *fields of maize:* This description comes from archaeologist David Dye, who has excavated and analyzed parts of this site, and has proposed a likely scenario for Soto's route and actions as he approached the Mississippi River. Dye, Interview.

402 *"peace with him":* Elvas, 111.

402 *"to the governor":* Ibid.

402 *"than the Danube":* Ranjel-Oviedo, 300.

404 *"water and current":* Elvas, 113.

404 *river called Aquixo:* Ranjel-Oviedo says the fleet came from Pacaha, a large Mississippian kingdom located about seventy five miles upriver on the opposite bank that Soto would visit later that summer. He mentions a town directly across the river from Quizquiz called Aquijo, which may have been the origin of Elvas's Aquixo. See Ranjel-Oviedo, 300.

404 *"under the canopy":* Ibid., 112–13.

Chapter 32: Last Chance

405 *"along the sides":* Elvas, 118.

405 *hemp and flax:* See ibid., 151. When the Spaniards escaped *La Florida* in 1543, Elvas described the ships as being caulked "with tow from a plant like daffodils," and flax that came from taking apart blankets.

405 *"the camp was":* Ibid., 113.

406 *"offered them again":* Ranjel-Oviedo, 300.

406 *"all of Florida":* Ibid.

406 *West Memphis, Arkansas:* See Dye, "Reconstruction of the de Soto Expedition Route in Arkansas: The Mississippi Alluvial Plain." *The Expedition of Hernando de Soto West of The Mississippi, 1541–1543.,* ed. Gloria A. Young and Michael R. Hoffman, 46.

406 *"there was gold":* Elvas, 114.

406 *"a clear grove":* Ibid.

406 *of Parkin, Arkansas:* Archaeologist Dan Morse says he is "99 percent" sure the Parkin site is Casqui, an assessment most archaeologists agree with. Morse, Personal Communication. See Morse and Morse, *Columbian Consequences,* 201–202; Phyllis A. Morse, in *Soto West of The Mississippi,* 58–67; Dye, in *Soto West of The Mississippi,* 43; Hudson, "De Soto in Arkansas: A Brief Synopsis," 3.

406 *"water around it":* Biedma, 239.

406 *several smaller mounds:* Jeffrey Mitchem, personal communication; also ibid. for details.

406 *"of the hunters":* Ranjel-Oviedo, 300.

408 *knelt to pray:* Garcilaso says this cross was constructed by Maestro Francisco, the boat builder, out of pine. See Garcilaso, 392.

408 *"man from heaven:* Biedma, 115.

408 *"dying of hunger":* Ibid. Juan Coles says it rained fifteen days. See Garcilaso, 393.

408 *present-day Interstate 55:* Dan Morse says he is "70 percent sure" Pacaha is the Bradley site, near Turrell. Morse, personal communication. See also Dye, in *Soto West of The Mississippi,* 48.

408 *from the city:* Garcilaso writes a long account about how Casqui's forces killed their enemies, the Pacahas, and desecrated a temple containing Pacaha's ancestors

408 *"women and children":* Elvas, 119.

408 *almost no people:* See Hoffman, *Soto West of The Mississippi,* 133.

408 *before he came:* Morse, *Columbian Consequences,* 199. Morse speculates the population of northeast Arkansas was 75,000 when Soto came through.

409 *called* 'pexe pereo.' ": Elvas, 118.

409 *"provided with armor":* Ibid., 117.

409 *"wealth for them":* Biedma, 240.

409 *"those of Cofitachequi":* Ranjel-Oviedo, 301.

409 *the "South Sea":* Biedma, 240.

410 *"way through it":* Ibid., 240–41. The grass mentioned is most likely Big Blue Stem. The prairie referred to may be the Grand Prairie in Dunklin County, Missouri. The nomadic Indians may be the Osage. See Dye, in *Soto West of The Mississippi,* 50.

410 *to the west:* Dan Morse, David Dye, and others suggest this may have been the Campbell site, located 95 miles north of the Bradley site (Pacaha). Sixteenth-century brass bells and several chevron beads have been found at Campbell. Dye notes that the closest source of copper and salt is 160 kilometers north of Campbell in the Ste. Francois Mountains. See Dye, *Soto West of the Mississippi,* 49–50.

410 *"and thinly populated":* Garcilaso, 407.

410 *"friend and brother?":* Ranjel-Oviedo, 301–2.

411 *"sin among us":* Ibid., 302–3.

411 *he was older:* Garcilaso says he was then about fifty years old. See Garcilaso, 393.

411 *"ancient in Estate":* Ranjel-Oviedo, 303.

411 *"access to another":* Ibid.

412 *"the other sea":* Biedma, 241.

412 *"than living creatures":* Ibid.

412 *"as they wished":* Elvas, 123.

412 *and Black rivers:* See Dye, *Soto West of the Mississippi,* 52.

412 *"many wild ones":* Ranjel-Oviedo, 304.

412 *some "rugged mountains":* Biedma, 241.

412 *of the Ozarks:* Dan Morse, David Dye, and others speculate that Coligua was located on the Ozark Plateaus where the White River pours into the Western Lowland. The town itself may have been the Magness Site. The mountains they crossed on the way to Calpista were probably the Boston Mountains of the far eastern Ozark Plateaus. See Dye, in *Soto West of the Mississippi,* 52–53.

412 *"until it cakes":* Ranjel-Oviedo, 304.

413 *"a large river":* Ibid.

413 *"river [the Mississippi]":* Biedma, 241.

413 *Cayas's major towns:* Elvas says Tanico was the capital of Cayas. Ranjel-Oviedo says that they were unable to locate the capital of this province.

413 *"quality and delicious":* Ranjel-Oviedo, 305. Soto scholars speculate that these salt works may have been located along the west fork of Point Remove Creek. See Early, Young and Hoffman, 71.

414 *"of the pot"*: Elvas, 124–25.

414 *"fat and throve"*: Ibid., 124.

414 *"populated land was"*: Ibid., 125.

414 *"well-provisioned province"*: Biedma, 242.

414 *as fifty infantry*: Biedma says Soto took twenty horsemen. Ranjel-Oviedo says he took thirteen horsemen and fifty infantry.

414 *"the river made."*: Biedma, 242.

414 *"on three sides"*: Ibid.

414 *"Christians came upon"*: Ranjel-Oviedo, 305.

414 *marshal of Seville*: Saavedra died several days later.

414 *"receive much damage"*: Ranjel-Oviedo, 305. Elvas says that after the battle, most of the Indians escaped, though a few were captured. Soto ordered six of these sent back to the Tula *cacique* with their hands and noses cut off. Eventually, the *cacique* surrendered to the Spaniards, coming into the camp bearing the usual gifts. See Elvas, 126.

415 *south, near Bluffton*: Archaeologists have little to go on in placing Tula. Local experts, including Ann Early, place Tula on the Arkansas River near either Fort Smith or Russellville. Hudson and others have speculated it might have been located near Bluffton, on the Fourche LaFave River. See Early, in *Soto West of The Mississippi*, 71; also, Early, personal communication; and Hudson, in *Soto West of The Mississippi*, 146–47.

415 *the Caddo Indians*: Henri Joutel found Caddo Indians on the Oachita River in 1687. See Hoffman, in *Soto West of The Mississippi*, 133.

415 *understood the Tula*: Garcilaso claims the Tula people deformed the shape of their heads at birth so they were elongated. He says they also pricked their faces and lips with flint needles, and colored them black, "thereby making themselves extremely and abominably ugly." See Garcilaso, 413.

415 *"had no converse"*: Elvas, 125.

415 *visit the Caddo*: See Young and Hoffman, 205.

415 *"rains, and snows"*: Elvas, 127.

416 *"Vaca had gone"*: Ibid.

416 *"named the captains"*: Castañeda, 243. Also see Bolton, 303–4, and 356.

416 *this ever happened*: See Bolton, 356; Weber, *The Spanish Frontier in North America,* 54.

Chapter 33: March of Death

417 *town called Autiamque*: Hudson and his colleagues place Autiamque near Redfield, a small town north of Pine Bluff, on the Arkansas River. See Hudson, "De Soto in Arkansas," 7.

417 *"and dried plums"*: Elvas, 128.

417 *move about "unshackled"*: Ibid., 129.

417 *his loss "deeply"*: Ibid., 130.

417 *"on the words"*: Garcilaso, 384.

417 *"of the Christians"*: Elvas, 130. Unless otherwise indicated, all notes in this chapter are from Elvas, pages 130–39.

418 *v. Bobadilla trial*: For instance, see the testimonies of Juan de Vega, Pedro Calderón, Luis Daza, and many others. PBI, II, 22–23.

418 *"of much value"*: Elvas, 148.

420 *"lying along it":* Ibid., 133.

420 *"land without succor":* Ibid.

420 *"to see him":* Ibid.

420 *"one foot backward":* Ibid.

421 *"rather than force":* Ibid., 134.

421 *"treating them cruelly":* Ibid., 135.

421 *"in that settlement":* Ibid.

421 *"as it happened":* Ibid., 136.

422 *"received from him":* Ibid., 137.

422 *about* La Florida: See PB I, 2–55.

422 *"sickness and died":* Biedma, 243.

422 *"a Catholic Christian":* Garcilaso, 447.

424 *"had been disturbed":* Elvas, 138.

424 *(and heavy sand):* Ibid.

Epilogue

425 *safely to Mexico:* Elvas, 165.

GLOSSARY

adelantado: Marshal, a military and honorific title for a successful commander sent out to conquer a new frontier region.

alcalde: Mayor who serves as administrator and judge.

alguacil: Constable.

arquebus: A small-caliber long rifle operated by a matchlock mechanism, a crude forerunner of a flintlock musket.

audiencia: Judicial council, regional court and judicial authority.

auto-da-fé: Literally an "act of faith," a public or private admission of sin and the assignment of a penitence. Only occasionally did auto-da-fés end in a burning at the stake.

balsa: A raft in Peru, usually made out of reeds.

barbacoa: (1) A grill of branches used to cook meat or to torture a victim with fire; (2) a small Indian hut raised above the ground to store food and supplies.

barco: Dugout canoe.

cabalgada: A raid for plunder.

caballero: Horseman; noble; knight.

cacique: Carribean word for "chief," used throughout the Indies by the Spanish.

campañero: A comrade; a partner in a business enterprise.

capitán: An officer leading a group of men, usually unpaid.

capitán-general: Commander in chief.

capitulación: Royal license to undertake a conquest.

castellano: Unit of Spanish currency, same as a *ducado.*

Castilla del Oro: Spanish name for Panama and Colombia, c. 1514–35.

caudillo: Leader, political boss, dictator.

cédula: A royal edict.

chiefdom: A region dominated by a paramount chieftain, who demanded tribute and fealty from vassal villages.

chieftain: The ruler of a chiefdom, also a paramount religious leader.

Coiba: Indian regional name for west-central Panama, from the Azuero Peninsula to Panama City.

compañia: A company; a business partnership or association; a group of partners in a *cabalgado* or *entrada.*

conquista: The half-century conquest of the Americas by the Spanish following Columbus's discovery in 1492.

contador: Accountant; royal bookkeeper on an expedition.

corregidor: Royal administrator based in a Spanish municipality or royal *encomienda.*

Cueva: Indian regional name for the Darién region of Panama.

ducado (ducat): Unit of Spanish currency, worth 375 *maravedíes*.

encomendero: Holder of an *encomienda.*

encomienda: Territory alloted to the "care" of a Spaniard, who collects tribute and labor from its inhabitants.

entrada: An entry, a first expedition; also refers to the expedition itself.

estanciero: Spanish peasant supervisor living among *encomienda* Indians.

factor: Royal agent in charge of king's supplies and properties.

gold peso: Unit of Spanish currency; 450 *maravedíes* equal a gold peso.

grandee: Noble, courtier.

hidalgo: Spanish gentleman squire; literally "son of someone," the lowest status among the nobility.

Inca: Quecha-speaking tribe originating around Cuzco, and the empire it ruled; also the name and title of the emperor and his family.

La Florida: Southeastern United States.

licenciado: Holder of a university degree equivalent to a master's degree, above a bachelor (B.A.) and below a doctor.

lieutenant general: Second-in-command of an expedition; commandant or military commander of a city or subregion serving under a governor or captain general.

lieutenant governor: Second-in-command, or military governor of a region.

maestro: Teacher.

maestro de campo: Camp master, usually second-in-command of an expedition, responsible for tactics, assignments, and supplies.

mamacona: In Peru among the Incas, a mother, senior chosen woman, virgin consecrated to religious service, often serving in a temple to the sun.

manceba: Concubine or mistress.

marco: Unit of measurement for precious metal, usually for silver, equal to a half pound.

maravedíes: Standard unit of Spanish currency.

mestizo: Mixed-blood, European and Indian.

Mississippian: A river-valley culture that thrived from Minnesota to the Gulf of Mexico from A.D. 600 to A.D. 1550, noted for its sophisticated towns, religion, dress, and political structure.

morrión: Steel helmet, usually open-faced with steep crown and wide, curved brim.

naboría: Cuevan word, means servant indentured for life; another word for slave.

probanza: Legal inquiry or testimonial, often given as a proof of service for a Spaniard petitioning the Crown or other authority for a favor or position.

reconquista: The "reconquest" of Iberia by the Christians against the Moors, lasting from A.D. 711 to 1492.

regidor: Municipal alderman or councillor.

Requerimiento: The document conquistadors were required to read to Indians explaining the church and Crown and demanding they give fealty or face destruction.

repartimiento: Allocation or share, often given as part of the division of spoils after a territory has been conquered; an *encomienda* holding.

residencia: Judicial review of an official's term of office.

serranía: Mountains, mountainous area.

Tierra Firme: "Mainland," early name for the mainland of the Western Hemisphere; later referred to an area roughly consisting of modern Panama and Colombia.

trovador: Troubador.

Santiago: St. James, patron saint of Spain.

tercio: Spanish infantryman.

vecino: Citizen, property owner, respected person.

veedor: Overseer, inspector, supply warden.

CHRONOLOGY

Names of persons important to Hernando de Soto are in boldface; important events in Soto's life are in capital letters.

1500
HERNANDO DE SOTO IS BORN (c. 1500) IN JEREZ DE LOS CABALLEROS
Future **CHARLES V** Born
Juan de la Cosa Produces First Map of the New World
High Renaissance in Italy, Northern Europe

1501
Rodrigo de Bastidas Explores Coast of Panama, Discovers Gulf of Darién; **VASCO NÚÑEZ DE BALBOA** with Expedition
Michelangelo's *David*

1502
Columbus Sails on His Fourth and Final Expedition, Discovers Honduras and Panama

1503
The Casa de Contratación Founded in Seville
Julius II Pope in Rome
Leonardo da Vinci's *Mona Lisa*

1504
Columbus Returns from Final Voyage
Queen Isabel Dies

1506
Columbus Dies

1508
JUAN PONCE DE LEÓN Begins Conquest of Puerto Rico
García Rodríguez de Montalvo's *Amadis of Gaul* Published in Spain

1509

Alonzo de Ojeda *entrada* to Colombia and Panama; **FRANCISCO PIZARRO** in Party

King Henry VIII of England Crowned

1510

BALBOA Stows Away Aboard a Vessel to Panama, Escaping Debts on Hispaniola

1511

Diego de Velázquez Conquers Cuba

1512

Laws of Burgos Enacted, Rules and Regulations for Treatment of Indians, Widely Ignored in Spanish Colonies

Copernicus Asserts that the Earth and Planets Circle the Sun

1513

BALBOA Crosses Isthmus of Panama, Discovers Pacific Ocean, Indians Tell Him About Inca Empire to South

JUAN PONCE DE LEÓN DISCOVERS FLORIDA

Portuguese Reach Canton, China

1514

SOTO PROBABLY SAILS TO PANAMA WITH **PEDRARIAS DÁVILA**

Pineapple Arrives in Europe from the New World

1516

Ferdinand II Dies

1517

SOTO, AGED SEVENTEEN, FORMS PARTNERSHIP WITH **HERNÁN PONCE DE LEÓN** AND **FRANCISCO COMPAÑÓN** IN DARIÉN

SOTO ACCOMPANIES **DIEGO DE TAVIRA** ON EXPLORATION OF ATRATO RIVER IN COLOMBIA

Martin Luther Launches Reformation in Germany

Coffee in Europe for the First Time

1518

SOTO WITH **BALBOA** ON SOUTH SEA EXPEDITION

Juan de Grijalva Explores the Coast of Yucatan and Discovers Mexico

1519

SOTO IS A FIELD CAPTAIN IN **JUAN DE ESPINOSA'S** CONQUEST OF WESTERN PANAMA

BALBOA Beheaded by **PEDRARIAS**
PEDRARIAS Founds Panama City
CHARLES I of Spain Is Crowned Holy Roman Emperor **CHARLES V**
Hernán Cortés Enters Tenochtitlán and Captures Montezuma
Ferdinand Magellan Leaves Europe to Circumnavigate the Globe
Domenico de Pineda Explores Gulf of Mexico from Florida to Vera Cruz

1520

SOTO ACCOMPANIES **ESPINOSA** ON FURTHER CAMPAIGNS IN WEST-ERN PANAMA
CHARLES V Defeats the *Comuneros* Revolt in Spain, Restores Authority of the Crown
Montezuma Is Assassinated by Spanish

1521

SOTO IS A CAPTAIN AND PLANTATION OWNER LIVING IN NATÁ, PANAMA
Magellan Killed in Philippines

1522

GIL GONZÁLEZ DÁVILA Explores in Nicaragua
Pascual de Andagoya Discovers Peru
Guatemala Conquered by Pedro de Alvarado
CHARLES V Names Cortés Governor of Mexico

1524

SOTO IS A BATTALION COMMANDER UNDER **FRANCISCO HERNÁNDEZ DE CÓRDOBA** IN THE CONQUEST OF NICARAGUA
SOTO LEADS EXPLORATION OF EL SALVADOR AND HONDURAS; HE SKIRMISHES WITH **GIL GONZÁLEZ DÁVILA** OVER RIGHTS OF CON-QUEST IN THE REGION
CÓRDOBA ATTEMPTS A REBELLION IN NICARAGUA; **SOTO**, IN OPPO-SITION, IS IMPRISONED, ESCAPES, AND JOURNEYS OVERLAND FROM LEÓN TO PANAMA TO WARN **PEDRARIAS**; **SOTO**, UNDER **PE-DRARIAS**, COMMANDS AN ARMY AGAINST **CÓRDOBA**; **CÓRDOBA** IS CAPTURED AND BEHEADED
PIZARRO Reconnoiters Coast of Colombia and Ecuador in First Attempt to Find Incas
Giovanni da Verrazano Discovers New York Bay

1525

SOTO ELECTED ALCALDE MAYOR OF LEÓN, NICARAGUA; RECEIVES LARGE *ENCOMIENDA* AND SHARES IN A GOLD MINE WITH HIS PART-NERS **PONCE** AND **COMPAÑÓN**; HE IS A MAJOR FIGURE IN NICARAGUA

SOTO AND **SEBASTIÁN DE BENALCÁZAR** EXPLORE LAKE NIC-
ARAGUA AND THE SAN JUAN RIVER
First Use of Muskets by Spanish Infantry in Italy

1526

PIZARRO Reaches Tumbez, Minor Inca City on the Peruvian Coast, on his Second Expedition to Discover Incas
Turks, Under Suleiman, Conquer Most of Hungary

1527

NICARAGUA IN TURMOIL WITH **PEDRARIAS** IN PANAMA; **DIEGO
LÓPEZ DE SALCEDO**, GOVERNOR OF HONDURAS, SEIZES NICA-
RAGUA, WITH SUPPORT OF **SOTO**; **SOTO** PUTS DOWN INDIAN RE-
BELLION IN THE VALLEY OF OLANCHO
SOTO AND **MARTÍN DE ESTETE** OVERTHROW **SALCEDO**, THEY
ATTEMPT, AND FAIL, TO ORGANIZE SPANISH CITIZENS TO FORM
POPULAR GOVERNMENT
PEDRARIAS RETURNS TO NICARAGUA, RESTORES ORDER, PRO-
CLAIMED GOVERNOR OF NICARAGUA BY THE KING
SOTO'S PARTNER, **FRANCISCO COMPAÑÓN**, DIES OF FEVER
CHARLES V Sacks Rome
Huayna Capac, Inca Emperor, Dies of Smallpox; Inca Empire Left to His Son, Huascar

1528

SOTO AMASSING A FORTUNE IN NICARAGUA WITH ESTATES, GOLD
MINES, SLAVE TRADING; OWNS SHIPS AND SHIPPING COMPANY
WITH **HERNÁN PONCE**
PÁNFILO DE NARVÁEZ Lands *Entrada* in Florida; Attempt to Conquer *La
Florida* Fails; Only Four Survive out of Four Hundred Men; Cabeza de Vaca Is
One of Them; He Is Lost in Texas and the Gulf Area for Nine Years
Venezuela Colonized by Spanish

1529

SOTO AND **PONCE** BUILD SHIPS FOR POSSIBLE PERUVIAN EXPEDI-
TION; USE THEM FOR SLAVE TRADING
PIZARRO IN SPAIN, **CHARLES V** AWARDS HIM CONCESSION TO CON-
QUER PERU
ANTONIO DE MENDOZA Appointed First Viceroy of New Spain
Turks Lay Siege to Vienna, European Forces Turn Them Back

1530

SOTO AND **PONCE** SIGN CONTRACT AGREEING TO ASSIST PIZARRO
IN THE CONQUEST OF PERU; **PEDRARIAS** IN NICARAGUA BLOCKS
SOTO'S DEPARTURE

Portuguese Colonize Brazil
Peter Martyr's Book on the New World, *Decades de orbe novo,* Published
Ivan the Terrible Born in Russia

1531

PEDRARIAS DIES AT AGE NINETY
SOTO SAILS WITH ONE HUNDRED MEN FOR PERU, ARRIVES ON PUNÁ
ISLAND TO REINFORCE PIZARRO
PIZARRO'S ARMY OCCUPIES TUMBEZ; SOTO NAMED LIEUTENANT
GOVERNOR AND CAPTAIN OF THE VANGUARD
Henry VIII Breaks with Catholic Church

1532

SOTO EXPLORES IN THE ANDES, DISCOVERS CAJAS; COMMITS THE
RAPE OF CAJAS, ATTACKING SACRED VIRGINS IN THE CAJAS TEM-
PLE OF THE SUN
SOTO AND PIZARRO LEAD *ENTRADA* TO CAJAMARCA. THE SPAN-
IARDS LAUNCH A SURPRISE ATTACK AND CAPTURE ATAHUALPA.
ATAHUALPA RANSOMED FOR 1.5 MILLION GOLD PESOS

1533

DIEGO DE ALMAGRO ARRIVES IN CAJAMARCA WITH REINFORCE-
MENTS
SOTO DISPATCHED TO INVESTIGATE FALSE RUMORS OF A PENDING
INCA ATTACK; ATAHUALPA EXECUTED FOR TREASON IN SOTO'S
ABSENCE
SPANISH ARMY MARCHES TO CUZCO FOLLOWING THE RETREATING
INCA ARMY; SEVERAL ATTACKS LED BY INCA GENERAL
QUIZQUIZ ENSUE BUT ARE UNSUCCESSFUL
SOTO AND A SMALL FORCE ARE NEARLY BEATEN BY THE INCAS AT
VILCACONGA
SPANIARDS CAPTURE CUZCO WITHOUT OPPOSITION
Henry VIII Marries Anne Boleyn and Is Excommunicated; Future Queen Elizabeth Born

1534

SOTO IS DISPATCHED NORTH TO CHASE QUIZQUIZ OUT OF PERU;
QUIZQUIZ RETREATS TO QUITO
PIZARRO NAMES SOTO LIEUTENANT GOVERNOR OF CUZCO; SOTO
RETURNS TO CUZCO TO RESTORE ORDER AND OVERSEE DISTRIBU-
TION OF LAND AND GOLD
INCA PRINCESS, TOCTO CHIMPU, BECOMES SOTO'S MISTRESS AND
TAKES THE NAME LEONOR CURICUILLOR
Jacques Cartier Sights Coast of Labrador
Martin Luther Translates the Bible into German

1535

PIZARRO Founds Lima

ALMAGRO IS NAMED GOVERNOR OF CHILE; HE ATTEMPTS TO ADD CUZCO TO HIS DOMAIN; **PIZARRO** SUPPORTERS THREATEN CIVIL WAR; **SOTO** SIDES WITH ALMAGRO; THE DISPUTE IS SETTLED PEACEFULLY

SOTO RELIEVED OF HIS COMMAND AS LIEUTENANT GOVERNOR

PONCE ARRIVES IN PERU; HE AND **SOTO** RECONFIRM THEIR PART-NERSHIP AND POOL THEIR HOLDINGS, WHICH TOTAL 250,000 PESOS OF GOLD IN GOLD, PROPERTY, AND INDIAN TRIBUTE

SOTO DEPARTS FOR SPAIN WITH 100,000 PESOS OF GOLD

Jacques Cartier Completes Second Voyage to St. Lawrence River, Quebec, and Montreal

Sir Thomas More Executed in England

CHARLES V Conquers Tunis

1536

SOTO ARRIVES TO A HERO'S WELCOME IN SEVILLE, PURCHASES A PALACE, AND ASKS FOR A MEETING WITH THE KING

SOTO MARRIES **ISABEL DE BOBADILLA**

Pedro de Mendoza Founds Buenos Aires

1537

THE KING GRANTS **SOTO** A CONCESSION TO CONQUER *LA FLORIDA,* NAMING HIM GOVERNOR-GENERAL AND ADELANTADO; **SOTO** IS ALSO NAMED GOVERNOR OF CUBA.

SOTO BEGINS PREPARATIONS FOR EXPEDITION

Cabeza de Vaca Returns to Spain, MEETS WITH **SOTO**, BUT TURNS DOWN HIS OFFER TO JOIN IN THE EXPEDITION

1538

SOTO ARMADA DEPARTS SPAIN FOR CUBA, STOPPING BRIEFLY AT GOMERA ISLAND IN THE CANARIES, AND ARRIVING IN SANTIAGO DE CUBA IN JUNE

SOTO ORGANIZES GOVERNMENT IN CUBA AND CONTINUES PREPARATIONS FOR THE EXPEDITION; **VASCO PORCALLO DE FIGUEROA** IS NAMED CAPTAIN GENERAL OF **SOTO'S** ARMY; **JUAN DE AÑASCO** IS DISPATCHED TO FLORIDA TO SE-LECT A LANDING SITE

1539

VICEROY ANTONIO DE MENDOZA LAUNCHES AN EXPEDITION NORTH THREATENING **SOTO'S** CLAIM ON *LA FLORIDA;* **SOTO**

SENDS **ALVARO DE SAN JORGE** TO MEET WITH THE VICEROY; THE VICEROY AGREES TO STAY FAR WEST OF SOTO'S TERRITORY

HERNÁN PONCE ARRIVES IN HAVANA; HE AND **SOTO** REAFFIRM THEIR PARTNERSHIP

SOTO ARMADA DEPARTS FOR FLORIDA ON MAY 18, MAKES LAND-FALL IN THE BAHÍA DE ESPÍRITU SANTO ON MAY 25, WHERE **SOTO** ESTABLISHES A BASE CAMP

SOTO AND THE ARMY LEAVE THE BAY FOR THE FLORIDA INTERIOR, JULY 15; THEY MARCH NORTH UP THE FLORIDA PENINSULA TO THE KINGDOM OF APALACHEE

SOTO WINTERS IN THE APALACHEE CAPITAL OF ANHAICA

1540

IN MARCH, **FRANCISCO MALDONADO** RETURNS TO HAVANA WITH ORDERS TO MEET **SOTO** IN OCTOBER AT MOBILE HARBOR; **SOTO** DOES NOT ARRIVE FOR RENDEZVOUS

SOTO MARCHES NORTH THROUGH GEORGIA AND NORTH CAROLINA, THEN TURNS SOUTH AND MARCHES TO ALABAMA

BATTLE OF MABILA AGAINST THE ATAHACHI ON OCTOBER 18; TWENTY-TWO SPANIARDS KILLED; MOST OF THE ARMY'S EQUIP-MENT DESTROYED IN FIRES

THE ARMY WINTERS AT CHICASA IN MODERN MISSISSIPPI

Coronado Begins Exploration of New Mexico, Texas, Oklahoma, and Eastern Kansas

1541

BATTLE OF CHICASA WITH THE CHICASA INDIANS ON MARCH 4; A DOZEN SPANIARDS DIE; WHAT REMAINS OF THE ARMY'S EQUIP-MENT IS DESTROYED IN ANOTHER FIRE SET BY THE INDIANS

SOTO REACHES THE MISSISSIPPI RIVER ON MAY 8; EXPLORES WEST INTO ARKANSAS, SEARCHING FOR GOLD; TURNS BACK TO THE MISSISSIPPI WHEN HE REACHES THE EDGE OF THE GREAT PLAINS AT THE BORDER WITH OKLAHOMA

THE ARMY WINTERS IN AUTIAMQUE, ON THE ARKANSAS RIVER

Francisco de Orellana Explores Amazon River

1542

THE MASSACRE OF NILCO, MAY; HUNDREDS OF UNARMED INDIANS SLAUGHTERED BY **SOTO** AND HIS ARMY

SOTO BECOMES FEVERISH AND DIES AT GUACHOYA ON THE MISSIS-SIPPI RIVER, MAY 21; BEFORE DYING, **SOTO** NAMES **LUIS DE MOSCOSO** AS ACTING GOVERNOR

MOSCOSO ATTEMPTS TO ESCAPE TO MEXICO BY MARCHING THE ARMY THROUGH TEXAS; HE TURNS BACK WHEN HE REACHES THE DRYLANDS IN CENTRAL TEXAS

MOSCOSO AND THE ARMY WINTER NEAR GUACHOYA ON THE MIS-
SISSIPPI RIVER
Inquisition Reestablished in Rome

1543

MOSCOSO AND THE ARMY ESCAPE *LA FLORIDA* AFTER BUILDING
BOATS AND SAILING DOWN THE MISSISSIPPI TO THE GULF OF MEX-
ICO, AND THEN ON TO MEXICO; 311 SURVIVORS ARRIVE IN PANUCO
ON SEPTEMBER 10.
SOTO'S WIFE RECEIVES WORD OF **SOTO'S** DEATH; SHE AUCTIONS
OFF HIS PROPERTY AND RETURNS TO SPAIN

BIBLIOGRAPHY

Abbreviations and Collections

AGI: *Archivo General de Indias,* Seville. The site where the vast majority of Spanish colonial archival documents are stored. The documents are divided into sixteen sections *(ramos* or *secciones),* of which six are relevant to this book: (1) Patronato (patronage); (2) Contaduría (paymaster); (3) Contratación (commerce); (4) Justicia (justice); (5) Gobierno (government); (6) Escribanía de Cámara de Justicia (actuarial). The documents are tied in dockets *(legajos),* in boxes *(cajas),* and housed in cabinets *(estantes).* Each section is subdivided in different ways, some according to the subject matter of the documents, others (sections 4, 5, and 6) according to colonial capitals, audiencias, and viceroyalties: Santo Domingo, León, Lima, etc. Since 1950, AGI references are listed by section and subdivision, and by the docket number. Before 1950, references were expressed as three numbers, for instance 24-6-1.

AGPS: *El Archivo General de Protocolos de Sevilla.*

BAE: *Biblioteca de autores españoles desde la formación del hasta nuestros días,* ed. Manuel Rivadeneira, 71 vols. (Madrid, 1846–80).

BAE (Cont): *Continuación.* ed. M. Menéndez Pelayo (Madrid, 1905).

BHA: *Biblioteca Hispano Americana,* 6 vols. (Madrid, 1953).

CDH: *Colección de documentos inéditos para la historia de Chile desde el viaje de Magellanes hasta la batalla de Maipo, 1518–1818,* ed. Jose Toribio Medina, 30, vols. (Santiago de Chile, 1888–1902). Second series (Santiago de Chile, 1956–   ).

CDHE: *Colección de documentos inéditos para la historia de España,* ed. M. Fernández Navarrete, M. Salvá, P. Sainz de Baranda. *Continued* by Marqués de Pidal y de Miraflores, Marqués de la Fuensanta del Valle, José Sancho Rayon and Francisco de Zabálburu, 112 vols. (Madrid, 1842–95).

CDHH-A: *Colección de documentos inéditos para la historia de Hispano-América,* 14 vols. (Madrid, 1927–30).

CDI I: *Colección de documentos inéditos relativos al descubrimiento, conquista y colonización de las posesiones españolas en América y Oceanía sacadas en su mayor parte del Real Archivo de Indias,* bajo la dirección de D. Joaquín F. Pacheco, Francisco de Cárdenas, Luis Torres de Mendoza, 42 vols. (Madrid 1864–84). *Continued as CDI II.*

CDI II: *Colección de documentos inéditos relativos al descubrimiento, conquista y organización de las antiguas posesiones españoles de Ultramar,* ed. Angel de

Altolaguirre y Duvale and Adolfo Bonilla y San Martín, 25 vols. (Madrid 1885–1932).

CL: *Libro primero de cabildos de Lima,* ed. Enrique Torres Saldamando with Pablo Patrón and Nicanor Boloña, 3 vols. (Paris and Lima, 1888–1900).

CLDRHP: *Colección de libros y documentos referentes a la historia del Perú,* ed. Carlos A. Romero and Horacio H. Urteaga, 2 series, 22 vols. (1916–25).

CP: *Cartas del Perú, Colección de documentos inéditos para la historia del Perú 3,* ed. Raúl Porras Barrenechea, Edición de la Sociedad de Bibliófilos Peruanos (Lima, 1959).

CPI (1930): *Catálogo de Pasajeros a Indias Durante los Siglos XVI, XVII y XVIII* (Madrid, 1930).

CPI (1940): *Catálogo de Pasajeros a Indias Durante los Siglos XVI, XVII, XVIII* (Seville, 1940–1946).

DHN: *Documentos para la historia de Nicaragua, Colección Somoza,* 17 vols. (Madrid, 1956).

DOP: *El Descubrimiento del Océano Pacífico,* ed. J. T. Medina, 2 vols. Imprenta Universitaria (Santiago de Chile, 1914).

FAAP: *Catálogo de los Fondos Americanos del Archivo de Protocolos de Sevilla,* 5 vols. (Seville, 1937).

Hakluyt: *The Hakluyt Society,* First series, 100 vols. (Cambridge, 1847–98), 2d series (Cambridge, 1899–   ).

Harkness: *The Harkness Collection in the Library of Congress, Calendar of Spanish manuscripts concerning Peru and the Indies* [1431–1641], ed. Stella R. Clemence (Washington, D.C., 1932).

NIW: *New Iberian World: A Documentary History of the Discovery and Settlement of Latin America to the Early 17th Century,* ed. John H. Parry and Robert G. Keith, 5 vols., Times Books (New York, 1984).

PB: Hernán Ponce de León *v.* Isabel de Bobadilla Trial, AGI Justicia 750 A + B, 1546–1550, unpublished archival manuscript.

PB I: Ponce-Bobadilla Trial, Avellaneda, Ignacio: *Notes on the Ponce-Bobadilla Trial.* Unpublished Quotes and Paraphrases from Trial, 1992.

PB II: Ponce-Bobadilla Trial, Avellaneda, Ignacio: *Report on the Ponce-Bobadilla Trial.* Unpublished, 1992.

RGI: *Relaciónes geográficas de Indias,* ed. M. Jiménez de la Espada, 4 vols. (Madrid, 1881); 3 vols. BAE (Cont), 183–5 (1965).

RH: *Revista de Histórica de América.* Instituto Panamericano de Geografía e Historia (Mexico, D.F., 1938).

RI: *Revista de Indias.* Consejo Superior de Investigaciones Científicas (Madrid, 1940).

Solar y Rújula: Solar y Taboada, Antonio del and José de Rújula y de Ochotorena, *El Adelantado Hernando de Soto: Breves Noticias y Nuevos Documentos para su Biografía,* Ediciones Arqueros (Badajoz, 1929).

SF: *Los Sobrevivientes de la Florida,* by Ignacio Avellaneda, ed. Bruce S. Chappell, no. 2, Research Publications of the P. K. Yonge Library of Florida History, University of Florida (Gainesville, 1990).

Swanton: Swanton, John R.: *Final Report of the United States De Soto Expedition Commission* [1939]. Smithsonian Institution Press (Washington, D.C., 1985).

Primary Sources

Archival Manuscripts (unpublished):

The following documents have not been published in any collection.

1. Random Manuscripts (from AGI)

Contaduría, 1825
Contratación 576, F. 164
Justicia 62, no. 2, R. 2
Justicia 719, no. 9
Justicia 750 A + B, 1546–50 (PB: Hernán Ponce de León v. Isabel de Bobadilla Trial)
Justicia 1073
Justicia 1124, no. 3, R. 2; no. 5, R. 3
Patronato 28, R. 55
Patronato 109, R. 4; 185, R. 2
Puná, December 1, 1531

2. "De Soto" Papers

The following manuscripts are collected in the P. K. Yonge Library of Florida History, University of Florida, Gainesville, Florida.
Contratación 3309 F. 60–143: Concession Made by the King of Spain
Contratación 5009: Cedula Real permitting Juan de Añasco to Traffic with the Indians of Florida
Indiferente General 415, F. 37–41
Indiferente General 737, Consejo, 1544
Indiferente General 1205, Daza, 1537
Indiferente General 1962, F. 287–88
Indiferente General 1962, F. 301–2
Indiferente General 1962, F. 331–32
Indiferente General 1963, F. 172
Indiferente General 1963, F. 221–22
Indiferente General 1963, F. 318–18
Mexico 95: Probanza Luis de Moscoso al Rey
Mexico 168: Probanza Camillos, 1557
Mexico 204: Probanza Baltasar de Gallegos
Mexico 207: Probanza Hernán Suárez
Mexico 207: Probanza Gaozales
Patronato 19, R. 2: Probanza Cataño
Patronato 19, R. 3: Probanza Hernando de Soto
Patronato 19, R. 15: (4) copy of agreement of Pedro Menéndez de Aviléz
Patronato 21, no. 2, R. 4: Proceso

Patronato 51, no. 3, R. 1: Probanza García Osorio
Patronato 51, no. 3, R. 2: Probanza Alonso Vázquez
Patronato 57, no. 1, R. 4: Probanza Juan Añasco
Patronato 60, no. 5, R. 7: Probanza Rodrigo Vásquez
Patronato 63, R. 9: Probanza Osorio
Patronato 63, R. 10: Probanza Gonzalo Méndez de Sotomayor
Patronato 69, R. 1: Villegas Prieto de Villegas
Patronato 77, no. 1, R. 1: Grifalón y Suárez
Patronato 90, no. 1, R. 5: Probanza Soto in Peru
Patronato 101, R. 18: Probanza Gonzalo Silvestre
Patronato 105, R. 6: Probanza Juan Cordero
Patronato 109, R. 4: Probanza Leonor de Soto
Patronato 111, R. 7: Probanza Pedro Arias De Canedo
Patronato 150, no. 14, R. 6: Probanza Pedro de Arévalo
Patronato 177, R. 20: Cedula real
Patronato 194, R. 34: Probanza Hernando de Soto in Panama
Patronato 231, no. 7, R. 12: Probanza Hernando de Soto in Peru
Patronato 275, R. 34: Probanza Arias
Patronato 277, no. 4, R. 241: Probanza Sebastián de Villagas
Patronato 281, no. 2, R. 108: Cedula
Patronato 281, no. 2, R. 109: Cedula
Santo Domingo 118, doc. 70
Santo Domingo 118, doc. 72

Archival Manuscripts (published):

The following are miscellaneous documents that have not appeared in a major collection or published extant, but have been published in book appendices, etc.

Expediente of Hernando de Soto for Inclusion in the Order of Santiago, Sección Orderes Militares (Santiago), Expediente 7855 (1538): in Solar y Rújula, 123–55.

Letter of Hernando de Soto at Tampa Bay to the Justice and Board of Magistrates in Santiago de Cuba, in *The De Soto Chronicles: The Expendition of Hernando De Soto to North America in 1539–1543,* ed. Lawrence A. Clayton, Vernon James Knight, Jr., and Edward C. Moore, trans. Buckingham Smith, 375–78.

Letter to Charles V from the Justice and Board of Magistrates of Santiago de Cuba, Giving a Statement of Occurrences on the Island, in *The De Soto Chronicles: The Expedition of Hernando De Soto to North America in 1539–1543,* ed. Lawrence A. Clayton. Vernon James Knight, Jr., and Edward C. Moore, trans. Buckingham Smith, 378–81.

Letter to the King from the Viceroy of New Spain, with Testimony in Behalf of Garcia Osorio, Soliciting the Royal Favour, in Smith and Buckingham, *Narratives of De Soto,* Appendix, 299–300.

Letter to the King of Spain from Officers at Havana in the Army of Soto, sent by Juan de Añasco, and Juan Gaytán and Luis Fernández, in *The De Soto Chronicles: The Expedition of Hernando De Soto to North America in 1539–1543,* ed. Lawrence A.

Clayton, Vernon James Knight, Jr., and Edward C. Moore, trans. Buckingham Smith, 372–74.

List of the Names of Persons Who Came from Florida, Who They Are, and of What Countries Native, in Smith and Buckingham, *Narratives of De Soto,* appendix, 292–99.

Memorial of Alonzo Vázquez (AGI, Patronato 50, no. 3, R. 1), in *Historical Magazine,* vol. 9, no. 9 (September, 1860).

Royal Cedula Permitting Juan de Añasco to Traffic with the Indians of Florida, in *The De Soto Chronicles: The Expedition of Hernando De Soto to North America in 1539–1543,* ed. Lawrence A. Clayton, Vernon James Knight, Jr., and Edward C. Moore, trans. Buckingham Smith, 365–66.

Testimony of Alonso de Argote, trans. Ignacio Avellaneda (AGI, Patronato 77-1-1, Probanza Hernán Suárez de Maruelas, Mexico, 1557). In author's possession.

Will of Hernando de Soto (AGI, Justicia 750A), in *The De Soto Chronicles: The Expedition of Hernando De Soto to North America in 1539–1543,* ed. Lawrence A. Clayton, Vernon James Knight, Jr., and Edward C. Moore, trans. Buckingham Smith, 366–72.

Soto Chronicles

Below are the versions of the chronicles I have used most frequently.

Biedma, Luis Hernández de. *Relation of the Island of Florida by Luis Hernández de Biedma,* trans. John Worth: *The De Soto Chronicles: The Expedition of Hernando de Soto to North America 1539–1543;* vol. d: Lawrence A. Clayton, Vernon Jones Knight, Jr., and Edward C. Moore, pp. 221–46. University of Alabama Press (Tuscaloosa, Ala., 1993).

Biedma, Luis Hernández de. *Relation of the Conquest of Florida presented by Luis Hernández de Biedma. In the year 1544 to the King of Spain in Council,* trans. Buckingham Smith: *Narratives of De Soto in the Conquest of Florida,* pp. 5–203. Palmetto Books (Gainesville, Fla., 1968).

Cañete, Sebastián de. *The Cañete Fragment: Another Narrative of Hernando de Soto.* Eugene Lyon, trans., from *The De Soto Chronicles: The Expedition of Hernando De Soto to North America 1539–1543, vol. 1,* ed. Lawrence A. Clayton, Vernon Jones Knight, Jr., and Edward C. Moore, pp. 307–10. University of Alabama Press (Tuscaloosa, Ala., 1993).

———. *The Cañete Fragment: A Previously Unknown Document Relating Information About the De Soto Expedition,* trans. Eugene Lyon (unpublished). From AGI, "Patronato Real" 19, no. 1, no. 15.

Elvas, Gentleman of. *True Relation of the Hardships Suffered by Governor Don Hernando de Soto and Certain Portuguese Gentleman in the Discovery of the Province of Florida. Now Newly Set Forth by a Gentleman of Elvas,* trans. James Alexander Robertson: *The De Soto Chronicles: The Expedition of Hernando de Soto to North America 1539–1543,* vol. 1, ed. Lawrence A. Clayton, Vernon Jones Knight, Jr., and Edward C. Moore, pp. 47–219. University of Alabama Press (Tuscaloosa, Ala., 1993).

————. *True Relation of the vicissitudes that attended the Governor Don Hernando de Soto and some nobles of Portugal in the Discovery of the Province of Florida. Now just given by Fidalgo or Elvas,* trans. Buckingham Smith: *Narratives of De Soto, in the Conquest of Florida,* pp. 229–61. Palmetto Books (Gainesville, Fla., 1968).

————. *Relacam verdadeira dos trabalbos abo governador do Fernando de Soto e certos fidalgos portugueses . . .* Facsimile of the Original Portuguese of 1557, ed. James Alexander Robertson: *True relation of the Hardships Suffered by the Governor Fernando de Soto . . . ,* vol. 1. The Florida State Historical Society (DeLand, Fla., 1932).

Ranjel-Oviedo: Ranjel, Rodrigo. *Account of the Northern Conquest and Discovery of Hernando de Soto.* From Oviedo, Gonzalo Fernández de: *Historia General y Natural de las Indians,* trans. and ed. John Worth: from *The De Soto Chronicles: Expedition of Hernando de Soto to North America 1539–1543,* vol. 1, ed. Lawrence A. Clayton, Vernon Jones Knight, Jr., and Edward C. Moore, pp. 247–306. Occasionally, the author has made slight changes in this translation based on the Spanish version cited below.

Ranjel, Rodrigo: Account of the Soto expedition taken from Oviedo, Gonzalo Fernández de: *Historia General y Natural de las Indias,* Book XVII, section 1, chap. 1–8.

Early Sources

The date when a manuscript was completed is in brackets after the author and title. Where more than one edition is listed, the first version to appear is the source most often cited in the text. In most cases where I quote one of these texts directly, and a good translation was available, I follow this translation, with occasional modifications of my own.

Andagoya, Pascual de. *Narrative of the Proceeding of Pedrarias Dávila* [1541], ed. and trans. C. R. Markham. Hakluyt Society (London, 1865).

Bandera, Juan de la. *The "Long" Bandera Relation* (AGI: Santo Domingo 224), trans. Paul E. Hoffman. In Charles Hudson, *The Juan Pardo Expeditions: Explorations of the Carolinas and Tennessee 1566–1568,* pp. 205–96. Smithsonian Institution Press (Washington, D.C., 1990).

————. *The "Short" Bandera Relation* (AGI: Patronato 19, R. 20), trans. Paul E. Hoffman. In Charles Hudson, *The Juan Pardo Expeditions: Explorations of the Carolinas and Tennessee 1566–1568,* pp. 297–304. Smithsonian Institution Press (Washington, D.C., 1990).

Cabello de Balboa, Miguel. *Miscelánea Austral,* pt. 3: *Historia del Perú* [1586]; CLDRHP, 2d series, 2. Imprenta y Librería Sanmarti (Lima, 1920).

Cabeza de Vaca, Alvar Núñez. *Adventures in the Unknown Interior of America* [1542], ed. and trans. Cyclone Covey. University of New Mexico Press (Albuquerque, 1988).

————. *The Journey of Alvar Núñez Cabeza de Vaca,* trans. Fanny Bandelier; ed. Adolph Bandelier. A.S. Barnes & Company (New York, 1905).

————. *Relation of Alvar Núñez Cabeza de Vaca,* trans. Buckingham Smith, printed by J. Munsell for H. C. Murphy (New York, 1871).

Cabildos de la Ciudad del Cuzco, Libro Primero de [1534–35], ed. Raúl Rivera Serna. Universidad Nacional Mayor de San Marcos (Lima, 1965).

Castañeda, Pedro de. *The Narrative of the Expedition of Coronado,* from *Spanish Explorers in the Southern United States* [1528–1543], ed. Frederick Hodge. Barnes and Noble (New York, 1984).

Cataño, Pedro. *Relación,* in Probanza for Gil González Dávila [March 5, 1562], quoted in José Antonio del Busto Duthurburu, "Una relación y un estudio sobre la Conquista," RH 27, 280–303 (1964).

Cervantes, Miguel de. *Don Quixote* [1605], trans. John Ormsby; trans. (revised) and ed. Joseph R. Jones and Kenneth Douglas. W. W. Norton and Company (New York, 1981).

Cieza de León, Pedro de. *Parte primera de la chrónica del Perú* (Seville, 1553); many Spanish editions, trans. C. R. Markham, *The Travels of Pedro Cieza de Leon,* Haklyut Society, I series, 68 (1883).

————. *Segunda parte de la chrónica del Perú, que trata del señorió de los Incas Yupanqui (1554),* ed. Manuel González de la Rosa (London, 1873); many later editions, trans. C. R. Markham, *The Travels of Pedro Cieza de Leon,* Haklyut Society, I series, 68 (1883).

————. *Tercera parte* (c. 1554), Descubrimiento y conquista, ed. Rafael Loredo, *Mercurio Peruano; Crónica del Peru Tercera Parte,* ed. Francesca Cantú. Academia Nacional de la Historia (Lima, 1987).

————. *La chrónica del Perú,* Part 4: La Guerra de las Salinas, La Guerra de Chupas, Las guerra de Quito, many Spanish editions, trans. C. R. Markham, *The War of Las Salinas,* Haklyut Society, 2d ser., 54 (1923); *The War of Chupas,* 2d series, 42 (1918), *The War of Quito,* Haklyut Society, 2d ser., 31 (1913).

————. *Descubrimiento y Conquista del Perú* [c. 1554], ed. Carmelo Sáenz de Santa María. Historia 16 (Madrid, 1986).

Cobo, Bernabé. *Historia del Nuevo Mundo* [1653], ed. Luis A. Pardo, 4 vols. (Cuzco, 1956).

Christopher Columbus. *The Four Voyages of Christopher Columbus,* ed. and trans. J. M. Lohen. Penguin Books (Baltimore, 1969).

————. *The Journal of Christopher Columbus* [1474–1566], trans. Cecil Jane. Bonanza Books (New York, 1989).

————. *Four Voyages to the New World, Letters, and Selected Documents,* ed. and trans. R. H. Major. Corinth Books (New York, 1961).

Cortés, Hernán. *Cartas y Documentos,* ed. Mario Hernández Sánchez-Barba (Mexico, 1963).

Cuzco. *Acta de Fundación de Cuzco* [March 23, 1534], in Raúl Porras Barrenechea, *Dos Documentos Essentials Sobre Francisco Pizarro y la Conquista del Peru . . . el Act Prodded de la Fundación del Cuzco.* RH 17, 99–123 (1948); CDHE 26, 221–32.

Dávila Padilla, Fray Augustín. *Historia de la fundacion y discuso de la Provincia de*

544 Bibliography

Santiago de Mexico, de la Orden de Predicadores [1596]. Section translated by John R. Swanton in his *Early History of the Creek Indians and Their Neighbors.* Bureau of American Ethnology, Bulletin 73 (Washington, D.C., 1922), see pp. 231–39.

Estete, Miguel de: *Relación de la Conquista del Perú* [1534]. From *Historia de los Incas y Conquista del Perú.* CDLRHP 8, series 2a. Imprenta y Libería Sanmarti (Lima, 1924).

Garcilaso de la Vega, The Inca. *La Florida,* trans. Charmion Shelby; ed. David Bost: *The De Soto Chronicles: The Expedition of Hernando De Soto to North America 1539–1543, Vol. II,* ed. Lawrence A. Clayton, Vernon Jones Knight, Jr., and Edward C. Moore, pp. 25–562. University of Alabama Press (Tuscaloosa, Ala., 1993).

―――. *The Florida of the Inca: A history of the Adelantado, Hernando de Soto, Governor and Captain General of the kingdom of Florida, and other heroic Spanish and Indian cavaliers, written by The Inca, Garcilaso de la Vega, an officer of His Majesty, and a native of the great city of Cuzco, capital of the realms and provinces of Peru* [1605], ed. and trans. John and Jeannette Varner. University of Texas Press (Austin, Tex., 1988).

―――. *La Florida del Inca,* ed. Sylvia L. Hilton. Historia 16, Información y Revistas (Madrid, 1986).

―――. *Primera Parte de los Comentarios Reales de los Incas* [Lisbon, 1609]; *Segunda Parte de los Comentarios Reales de los Incas* [Córdoba, 1616], trans. Harold Livermore, *Royal Commentaries of the Incas and General History of Peru, Part One.* University of Texas Press (Austin, 1989).

Herrera, Antonio de. *Historia General de los Hechos de los Castellanos en las Islas y Tierrafirme del Mar Océano* [Madrid, 1610–15], trans. Captain John Stevens, *The General History of the Vast Continent and Island of the America, Commonly Called, the West-Indies.* Jeremy Batley (Dove, 1725). Note: Because Stevens's translation is often faulty, I have made extensive corrections using the original Spanish.

Jauja, Cabildo of. *Carta a Su Magestad . . . Con Varias Noticias de Gobierno é Fazienda* [July 20, 1534]. CL 3. Imperie Paul Dupont (Paris, 1900).

Jerez, Francisco. *Verdadera Relación de la Conquista del Perú y Provincia del Cuzco* [Seville, 1577], ed. and trans. C. R. Markham, *The True Account of the Province of Cuzco.* Burt Franklin (New York, 1970).

Las Casas, Bartolomé de. *Historia de las Indias* Vol. I & III [1552–61], ed. Agustín Millares Carlo y. Fondo de Cultura Económica (Mexico, 1951).

―――. *History of the Indies,* ed. and trans. Andrée Collard. Harper and Row (New York, 1971).

―――. *A Selection of His Writings,* ed. and trans. George Sanderlin. Alfred A. Knopf (New York, 1971).

―――. *Brevissima Relación de la Destrucción de las Indias* [Seville, 1552], CDHE, 71 (1842); also in *Nicaragua en los Cronistas de Indians.*

―――. *Obras escogidas,* 5 vols. Biblioteca de Autores Españoles, nos. 95–96, 105–6, 110 (Madrid: Ediciones Atlas, 1957–58).

López de Gómara, Francisco. *Biblioteca de Autores Españoles Desde la Formación del Lenguaje Hasta Nuestros Días* [c. 1550], Ediciones Atlas (Madrid, 1946).

———. *Historia General de las Indias* [Saragossa, 1552], 2 vols. *Los Grandes Viajes Clásicos* (Madrid, 1922).

Laudonniére, René Goulaine de. *Three Voyages* [1565], The University Presses of Florida (Gainesville, Fla., 1975).

Luna, Tristán de. *The Luna Papers: Documents Pertaining to the Expedition of Don Tristán de Luna y Arrello for the Conquest of La Florida in 1559–1561,* ed. and trans. Herbert Ingram Priestley (1928). In *Spanish Borderlands Sourcebooks,* pp. 329–481. Garland Publishing, Inc. (New York, 1991).

Machiavelli, Niccolo. *The Prince,* trans. Edward Dacres, AMS Press (New York, 1905).

Martyr, Peter (Pietro Martire d'Anghiera). *De Orbe Novo* [1555], ed. and trans. F. A. MacNutt. G. P. Putnam's Sons (New York, 1912).

———. *The Decades of the Newe Worlde or West India* [1555] (English Translation). University MicroFilms, Inc. (Ann Arbor, Mich., 1966).

Medina, J. T. *El Descubrimiento Del Océano Pacífico,* vol. 1 & 2. Imprenta Universitaria (Santiago de Chile, 1914).

Mena, Cristóbal de. *La Conquista del Perú,* ed. Raúl Porras Barrenechea, in *Las Relaciones Primitivas de la Conquista del Perú.* Imprimeries Les Presses Modernes (Paris, 1937).

———. *La Conquista del Perú* [Seville, April 1534], trans. Joseph Sinclair, *The Conquest of Peru as Recorded by a Member of the Pizarro Expedition.* New York Public Library (New York, 1929).

Montalvo, García Rodríguez de. *Amadis of Gaul* [14th century], (First Published in Spanish in 1508), trans. Edwin B. Place and Herbert C. Behm, 2 vols. The University Press of Kentucky (Lexington, 1974).

Narváez, Pánfilo de. *Proclamation to the inhabitants of the countries and provinces from Rio de Palmas to the Cape of Florida* [1527], ed. Benjamin F. French. Historical Collections of Louisiana and Florida, pp. 153–58 (New York, 1875).

Oviedo y Valdés, Gonzalo Fernández. *Historia General y Natural de Las Indias, Islas Y Tierra Firme Del Mar Océano* [1526]. Imprenta de la Real Academia de la Historia (Madrid, 1851).

———. *Natural History of the West Indies* [1526], ed. and trans. Sterling A. Stoudemire. University of North Carolina Press (Chapel Hill, N.C., 1959).

———. *Nicaragua en los Cronistas de Indias: Oviedo.* Impreso en los Talleres de Editorial y Litografía (San José, Costa Rica 1976).

———. *The Expedition of Pánfilo de Narváez.* Excerpts from Oviedo's *Historia General in Southwestern Historical Quarterly,* ed. Herbert Davenport. Vol. 27–28 (1924–25).

Pizarro, Pedro. *Relation of the Discovery and Conquest of the Kingdoms of Peru.* Vol I and II [1571], trans. Philip Ainsworth Means. The Cortes Society (New York, 1921).

———. *Relación del Descubrimiento y Conquista del Perú* [1571], ed. Guillermo Lohmann Villena. Fondo Editorial (Peru, 1978).

———. *Relación del Descubrimiento y Conquista del Perú* [1571]. BAE (Cont.) 168: 159–242 (Madrid, 1965).

Poma de Ayala, Felipe Guaman. *Nueva crónica y buen gobierno* [c. 1580–1620], ed. John V. Murra. Historia 16 (Madrid, 1987).

Poema de Mio Cid [c. 1200]. *The Poem of the Cid* (in English and Spanish), trans. Rita Hamilton and Janet Perry. Penguin Books (New York, 1984).

Rojas, Fernando de. *La Celestina* [1499], ed. M. Criado de Val and G. D. Trotter. Espasa-Calpe (Madrid, 1968).

Ruiz de Arce, Juan. *Relación de servicios en Indias de don Juan Ruiz de Arce, Conquistador del Peru* [c. 1545]. *Boletín de la Academia de la Historia,* 102, 327–84. Tipografía de Archivos (Madrid, 1933).

Salinas y Córdova, Fray Buenaventura de. *Memorial de las Historias del Nuevo Mundo Pirv* [1630]. Universidad Nacional Mayor de San Marcos (Lima, 1957).

Sancho, Pedro. *An Account of the Conquest of Peru,* trans. Philip Ainsworth Means. Milford House (Boston, 1972).

———. *Relación de la Conquista del Perú* [c. 1534], ed. Jaoquín García Icazbalceta. Ediciones Jose Porrúa Turanzas (Madrid, 1962).

Trujillo, Diego de. *Relación del Descubrimiento del Reyno del Perú* [1571], ed. Raúl Porras Barrenechea. Escuela de Estudios Hispano-Americanos (Seville, 1948).

Zárate, Agustín de. *Historia del Descubrimiento y Conquista del Perú* [1555], ed. Dorothy McMahon. University of Buenos Aires Facultad de Filosofía y letras (Buenos Aires, 1965).

———. *A History of the Discovery and Conquest of Peru,* trans. Thomas Nicholas. The Penguin Press (London, 1974).

Zuazo, Alonso. *Letter to Monsieur de Xévres,* January 22, 1518. In CDI, I, 247–411.

Recent Sources

Books

Abbott, John. *Ferdinand de Soto, the Discoverer of the Mississippi.* Dodd, Mead & Co. (New York, 1873).

Adair, James. *History of the American Indians,* ed. S. C. Williams. Promontory Press (New York, 1930).

Albornoz, Miguel. *Hernando de Soto: Knight of the Americas,* trans. Bruce Boeglin. Franklin Watts (New York, 1986).

Almodóvar Muñoz, Carmen. *Antología Crítica de la Historiografía Cubana.* Editorial Pueblo y Educación (La Habana, Cuba, 1986).

Altman, Ida. *Emigrants and Society: Extremadura and America in the Sixteenth Century.* University of California Press (Berkeley and Los Angeles, 1989).

Altolaguirre y Duvale, Angel de. *Vasco Núñez de Balboa.* Imprenta del Patronato de Huérfanos de Intendencia é Intervención Militares (Madrid, 1914).

Alvarez Rubiano, Pablo. *Pedrarias Dávila.* Consejo Superior de Investigaciones Científicas Instituto Gonzalo Fernández de Oviedo (Madrid, 1944).

Anderson, C. L. G., *Old Panama and Castilla del Oro.* Page Company (Boston, 1914).

Andrews, Daniel M. *De Soto's Route.* New Era Printing Company (Lancaster, Pa., 1917).

Arciniegas, Germán: *America in Europe: A History of the New World in Reverse,* trans. Gabriela Arciniegas and R. Victoría Arana. Harcourt Brace Jovanovich (New York, 1986).

Arellano, Jorge Eduardo. *Nueva Historia de Nicaragua,* vol. 1. Fondo Editorial CIRA (Managua, 1990).

Ashton, Ray E., Jr. *Identification Manual to the Amphibians and Reptiles of Florida.* Florida State Museum Associates, University of Florida (Gainesville, Fla., 1978).

Atkinson, William C. *History of Spain and Portugal.* Penguin Books (London, 1960).

Avellaneda, Ignacio. *Los Sobrevivientes de la Florida: The Survivors of the De Soto Expedition,* ed. Bruce S. Chappell. No. 2, Research Publications of the P. K. Yonge Library of Florida History, University of Florida Libraries (Gainesville, 1990).

Axtell, James. *The Invasion Within: The Contest of Cultures in Colonial North America.* Oxford University Press (New York, 1986).

Ayon, Tomas. *Historia de Nicaragua.* Banco de America (Managua, 1977).

Bankes, George. *Peru Before Pizarro.* Phaidon Press Limited (Oxford, 1977).

Barber, Richard. *The Knight and Chivalry.* Harper and Row (New York, 1982).

Bartram, William. *Travels of William Bartram* [1791], ed. Mark Van Doren. Dover Publications, Inc. (New York, 1955).

Bell, J. B. *The Hernando de Soto Narrative.* The Committee to Honor de Soto (Hernando, Miss., 1989).

Bishop, Morris. *The Odyssey of Cabeza de Vaca.* Greenwood Press (Westport, Conn., 1971).

Bakeless, John. *America as Seen by Its First Explorers: The Eyes of Discovery.* Dover Publications, Inc. (New York, 1961).

Blakely, Robert L, ed. *The King Site, Continuity and Contact in Sixteenth-Century Georgia.* University of Georgia Press (Athens, Ga., 1988).

Blanco, Castilla F. *Hernando de Soto, El Centauro de las Indias.* Editorial Carrera del Castillo (Madrid, 1955).

Bolton, Herbert E. *Coronado: Knight of the Pueblos and Plains.* Whittlesey House (McGraw-Hill Book Company, Inc.) and University of New Mexico Press (New York, 1949).

Bourne, Edward Gaylord, ed. *Narratives of the Career of Hernando de Soto.* Long Acre (London, 1905).

Brandi, Karl. *The Emperor Charles V: The Growth and Destiny of a Man and of a World Empire,* trans. C. V. Wedgewood. Jonathon Cape (London, 1954).

Braudel, Fernand. *The Mediterranean and the Mediterranean World in the Age of Philip II* [1949], vol. 1 and vol. 2, trans. Siân Reynolds. Harper & Row (New York, 1972).

―――. *The Wheels of Commerce: Civilization & Capitalism 15th–18th Century,* vol. 2 [1979], trans. Siân Reynolds. Harper & Row (New York, 1982).

Brenan, Gerald. *The Literature of the Spanish People from Roman Times to the Present Day.* Cambridge University Press (Cambridge, 1951).

Brose, David S., James A. Brown, and David W. Penney. *Ancient Art of the American Woodland Indians.* Harry Abrams (New York, 1985).

Brown, Lloyd. *The Story of Maps.* Little, Brown, and Company (Boston, 1949).

Brown, Virginia P. *The Gold Disc of Coosa.* Strode Publishers (Huntsville, Ala., 1975).

Bullen, Ripley P. *Eleven Archaeological Sites in Hillsborough County, Florida: Florida Geological Survey Report of Investigations No. 8.* The Florida Geological Survey (Tallahassee, 1952).

Bullock, Alan. *The Humanist Tradition in the West.* W. W. Norton & Company, Inc. (New York, 1985).

Busto Duthurburu, José Antonio del. *Diccionario Histórico Biográfico de los Conquistadores del Peru,* vol. 1 and 2. Libreria Studium Ediciones (Lima, 1987).

Byron, William. *Cervantes: A Biography.* Paragon House Publishers (New York, 1988).

Castañeda, Paulino, Mariano Cuesta, and Pilar Hernández. *Transcripción, Estudio y Notas del "Espejo de Navegantes" de Alonso Cháves.* Instituto de Historia y Cultural Naval (Madrid, 1983).

Chamberlain, Robert S. *The Conquest and Colonization of Honduras, 1502–1550.* Carnegie Institution of Washington (Washington, D.C., 1953).

Chamorro, Víctor. *Historia de Extremadura Tomo II: "Iluminada" (Siglo XVI–XVII).* Editorial Quasimodo (Madrid, 1981).

Clark, Thomas D., ed. *Travels in the Old South: A Bibliography,* vol. 1 and vol. 2. University of Oklahoma Press (Norman, 1956).

Clissold, Stephen. *The Seven Cities of Cibola.* Eyre and Spottiswoode (London, 1961).

Cook, Noble David. *Demographic Collapse: Indian Peru, 1520–1620.* Cambridge University Press (Cambridge, 1981).

Coronado, Francisco R. Blanco. *Fauna Extremeña Protegida* 2.a edición. Juanta de Extremadura (Badajoz, 1988).

Crosby, Alfred W., Jr. *The Columbian Exchange: Biological and Cultural Consequences of 1492.* Greenwood Press (Westport, Conn., 1973).

———. *Ecological Imperialism: The Biological Expansion of Europe, 900–1900.* Cambridge University Press (Cambridge, 1989).

Crow, John A. *Spain: The Root and the Flower: An Interpretation of Spain and the Spanish People.* University of California Press (Berkeley and Los Angeles, 1985).

Cumming, W. P., R. A. Skelton, and D. B. Quinn. *The Discovery of North America.* American Heritage Press (New York, 1972).

Daly, Dominick. *Adventures of Roger L'Estrange, sometime Captain in the Florida Army, of his Excellency the Marquis Hernando de Soto . . . an Autobiography translated from Spanish.* Swan Sonnenschein & Co. (London, 1896).

Davies, Nigel. *The Aztecs, A History.* University of Oklahoma Press (Norman, 1986).

Davies, R. Trevor. *The Golden Century of Spain, 1501–1621.* Mutual Publishing (Honolulu, Ha., 1986).

Day, A. Grove. *Coronado's Quest: The Discovery of the American Southwest.* Greenwood Press (Westport, Conn., 1986).

Deagan, Kathleen. *Artifacts of the Spanish Colonies of Florida and the Caribbean,*

1500–1800. Volume I: Ceramics, Glassware, and Beads. Smithsonian Institution Press (Washington, D.C., 1987).

Defourneaux, Marcelin. *Daily Life in Spain in the Golden Age,* trans. Newton Branch. Stanford University Press (Stanford, Calif., 1990).

Denevan, William M., ed. *The Native Population of the Americas in 1492.* University of Wisconsin Press (Madison, 1976).

Díaz, Bernal. *The Conquest of New Spain,* trans. J. M. Cohen. Penguin Books (New York, 1963).

D'Iberville, LeMoyne Pierre. *Iberville's Gulf Journals* [1698–1702], trans. Richebourg Gaillard McWilliams. University of Alabama Press (Tuscaloosa, 1981).

Dickason, Olive Patricia. *The Myth of the Savage and the Beginnings of French Colonialism in the Americas.* University of Alberta Press (Edmonton, Canada, 1984).

Dobyns, Henry F. *Their Numbers Became Thinned: Native American Population Dynamics in Esatern North America.* University of Tennessee Press (Knoxville, 1983).

Dupuy, R. Ernest and Trevor N. Dupuy. *The Encyclopedia of Military History from 3500 B.C. to the Present.* rev. ed. Harper & Row (New York, 1977).

Durant, Will. *The Story of Civilization: The Reformation.* Simon and Schuster (New York, 1957).

———. *The Story of Civilization: The Renaissance.* Simon and Schuster (New York, 1957).

Elliot, J. H. *Spain and Its World, 1500–1700: Selected Essays.* Yale University Press (New Haven, Conn., 1989).

Erichsen-Brown, Charlotte. *Medicinal and Other Uses of North American Plants: A Historical Survey with Special Reference to the Eastern Tribes.* Dover Publications, Inc. (New York, 1979).

Fields, Rick. *The Code of the Warrior: In History, Myth and Everyday Life.* Harper Perennial (New York, 1991).

Fernández, José B. *Alvar Núñez Cabeza de Vaca: The Forgotten Chronicler.* Ediciónes Universal (Miami, 1975).

Fernández-Armesto, Felipe. *Columbus.* Oxford University Press (New York, 1991).

Ford, Richard I. *An Ethnobiology Source Book: The Uses of Plants and Animals by American Indians.* Garland Publishing (New York, 1985).

Foster, J. W. *The Mississippi Valley: Its Physical Geography, Including Sketches of the Topography, Botany, Climate, Geology and Mineral Resources; and of the Progress of Development in Population and Material Wealth.* S. C. Griggs and Company (Chicago, 1869).

Galloway, Patricia, ed. *Studies in the Historiography of the Hernando de Soto Expeditions.* In Manuscript.

———. *The Southeastern Ceremonial Complex: Artifacts and Analysis.* University of Nebraska Press (Lincoln, 1989).

Gannon, Michael V. *The Cross in the Sand: The Early Catholic Church in Florida, 1513–1870.* University of Florida Press (Gainesville, 1967).

García, Del Cármen Mena. *La Sociedad de Panamá en el Siglo XVI.* EXCMA: Diputación Provincial de Sevilla (Seville, 1984).

Gerbi, Antonello. *Nature in the World: From Christopher Columbus to Gonzalo Fernández de Oviedo,* trans. Jeremy Moyle. University of Pittsburgh Press (Pittsburgh, 1985).

Gibson, Charles. *Spain in America.* Harper Colophon Books (New York, 1966).

———. *The Black Legend: Anti-Spanish Attitudes in the Old World and the New.* Alfred A. Knopf (New York, 1971).

Glazier, Willard. *Headwaters of the Mississippi.* Rand McNally and Company (New York, 1898).

Góngora, Mario. *Los Grupos de Conquistadores En Tierra Firma (1509–1530):* Fisonomia Historico Social de un Tipo de Conquista Universidad de Chile (Santiago, Chile, 1962).

———. *Studies in the Colonial History of Spanish America,* trans. Richard Southern. Cambridge University Press (New York, 1975).

Goza, William and Hugo Ludeña. *Gonzalo Silvestre un Soldado de Extremadura Sobreviviente de la Expedición de Hernando de Soto a la Florida (1539–1543).* (Unpublished manuscript on file at P. K. Yonge Library, University of Florida, Gainesville, 1989).

Graham, R. B. Cunninghame. *Hernando de Soto: Together with an Account of one of his Captains, Gonzalo Silvestre.* W. Heinemann (London, 1903).

———. *The Horses of the Conquest,* ed. Robert Moorman Denhardt. University of Oklahoma Press (Norman, 1949).

Greenblatt, Stephen. *Marvelous Possessions: The Wonder of the New World.* University of Chicago Press (Chicago, 1991).

A Guide to Some of the Common Butterflies of Mississippi. Mississippi Department of Wildlife, Fisheries & Parks (Jackson, 1989).

Hale, J. R. *War and Society in Renaissance Europe, 1450–1620.* Johns Hopkins University Press (Baltimore, 1985).

———. *Renaissance Europe: Individual and Society, 1480–1520.* University of California Press (Berkeley and Los Angeles, 1977).

———. *Age of Exploration.* Great Ages of Man series Time-Life Books (Amsterdam, 1984).

Hallenbeck, Cleve. *Álvar Núñez Cabeza de Vaca: The Journey and Route of the First European to Cross the Continent of North America 1534–1536.* The Arthur H. Clark Company (Glendale, Calif., 1940).

Hanke, Lewis. *The Spanish Struggle for Justice.* Little Brown. (Boston, 1949).

Hann, John H. *Apalachee: The Land between the Rivers.* University Presses of Florida (Gainesville, 1988).

Healy, Paul F. *Archaeology of the Rivas Region, Nicaragua.* Wilfrid Laurier University Press (Waterloo, Ontario, 1975).

Helms, Mary W. *Ancient Panama.* University of Texas Press (Austin, 1979).

Helps, Arthur. *The Life of Las Casas, the "Apostle of the Indies."* Bell & Daldy (London, 1868).

Hemming, John. *The Conquest of the Incas.* Harcourt Brace Jovanovich (New York, 1970).

Herre, Benjamin G. *De Soto's March: A Narrative Poem.* Inquirer Steam Printing (Lancaster, Pa., 1868).

Hodge, Frederick W. and Theodore H. Lewis. *Spanish Explorers in the Southern United States 1528–1543.* Barnes and Noble (New York, 1984).

Hoffman, Paul E. *A New Andalucia and a Way to the Orient.* Louisiana State University Press (Baton Rouge, 1990).

Holder, Trusten H. *Disappearing Wetlands in Eastern Arkansas.* Arkansas Planning Commission (Little Rock, 1970).

Howarth, David. *The Voyage of the Armada: The Spanish Story.* Penguin Books (New York, 1982).

Hudson, Charles. *The Juan Pardo Expeditions: Explorations of the Carolinas and Tennessee, 1566–1568.* Smithsonian Institution Press (Washington, D.C., 1990).

———. *Ethnology of the Southeast Indies: A Source Book.* Garland Publishing (New York, 1985).

———. *The Southeastern Indians.* The University of Tennessee Press (Knoxville, 1976).

Hudson, Charles, and Jerald T. Milanich. *Hernando de Soto and the Indians of Florida.* University Presses of Florida (Gainesville, Fla., 1993).

Hudson, Joyce Rockwood. *Looking for De Soto: A Search Through the South for the Spaniards Trail.* University of Georgia Press (Athens, 1993).

Hulton, Paul. *The Work of Jacques le Moyne de Morgues, Artist.* British Museum Publications (London, 1977).

Humphries, Christopher. *Spotter's Guide to Wild Flowers.* Usborne Publishing Limited (London, 1985).

Incer, Jaime. *Nicaragua: Viajes Rutas y Encuentros, 1502–1838.* Libro Libre (San Jose, 1990).

Innes, Hammond. *The Conquistadors.* Alfred A. Knopf (New York, 1969).

Irving, Theodore. *The Conquest of Florida, under Hernando de Soto,* [1835] 2 vols. Island Press (Fort Myers Beach, Fla., 1973).

Jennings, John Edward. *The Golden Eagle: A Novel Based on the Fabulous Life and Times of the Great Conquistador Hernando de Soto, 1500–1542.* Putnam (New York, 1959).

Johnson, Jay and Goeffrey Olehmann. *Sociopolitical Devolution in Northeast Mississippi and the Timing of the De Soto Entrada.* Paper prepared for the Demographic Collapse in the Spanish Borderlands Symposium. American Association of Physical Anthropologists Annual Meeting (Miami, 1990).

Johnson, Allen W. and Timothy Earle. *The Evolution of Human Societies: From Foraging Group to Agrarian State.* Stanford University Press (Stanford, 1987).

Jones, Charles C. *Hernando de Soto: The Adventures Encountered and the Route Pursued by the Adelantado during his March through the State of Georgia.* J. H. Estill (Savannah, 1880).

Kamen, Henry. *Inquisition and Society in Spain in the Sixteenth and Seventeenth Centuries.* Indiana University Press (Bloomington, 1985).

———. *Spain 1469–1714: A Society of Conflict.* Longman (New York, 1988).

Kann, Robert A. *A History of the Habsburg Empire, 1526–1918.* University of California Press (Berkeley and Los Angeles, 1977).

King, Grace E. *De Soto and His Men in the Land of Florida.* Macmillan (New York, 1898).

Kirkpatrick, F. A. *The Spanish Conquistadores.* Meridian Books, The World Publishing Company (New York, 1968).

Knoop, Faith Y. *Quest of the Cavaliers: De Soto and the Spanish Explorers.* Longmans, Green and Co. (New York and Toronto, 1940).

Knowles, Charles E. *The Quest of Gold: Being a Romance Dealing with the Remarkable Expedition of Ferdinand De Soto and His Cavaliers to Florida in the Year 1539.* John Lane and Company (New York, 1912).

Lacaci, Guillermo Quintana. *Armería Del Palacio Real De Madrid.* Editorial Patrimonio Nacional (Madrid, 1987).

Langstaff, Eleanor DeSelms. *Panama: Bibliography,* ed. Sheila R. Herstein. Clio Press (Oxford, 1982).

Lawrence, Bill. *The Early American Wilderness As the Explorers Saw It.* Paragon House (New York, 1991).

Lawson, John. *A New Voyage to Carolina* [1709], ed. Hugh Talnage Lefler. University of North Carolina Press. (Chapel Hill, 1967).

Lea, Henry Charles. *The Moriscos of Spain: Their Conversion and Explusion.* Haskell House Publishers, Ltd. (New York, 1968).

Litvinoff, Barnet. *Fourteen Ninety Two: The Decline of Medievalism and the Rise of the Modern Age.* Charles Scribner's Sons (New York, 1991).

Lockhart, James M. *The Men of Cajamarca: A Social and Biographical Study of the First Conquerers of Peru.* University of Texas Press (Austin, 1972).

Lovett, A. W. *Early Habsburg Spain, 1517–1598.* Oxford University Press (New York, 1986).

Lyon, Eugene. *The Enterprise of Florida: Pedro Menéndez de Avilés and the Spanish Conquest of 1565–1568.* University Press of Florida (Gainesville, 1976).

McAlister, Lyle N. *Spain and Portugal in the New World, 1492–1700: Europe and the World in the Age of Expansion, Vol. III.* University of Minnesota Press (Minneapolis, 1984).

McDermott, John Francis, ed. *The French in the Mississippi Valley.* University of Illinois Press (Urbana, 1965).

McGimsey, Charles R., III. *Indians of Arkansas.* Arkansas Archaeological Survey (Fayetteville, 1969).

McIntyre, Loren. *The Incredible Incas and Their Timeless Land.* National Geographic Society (Washington, D.C., 1975).

MacNutt, Francis Augustus. *Bartolomé de Las Casas: His Life, His Apostolate, and His Writings.* G. P. Putnam's Sons (New York, 1909).

Malone, Walter. *Hernando de Soto.* G. P. Putnam's Sons (New York and London, 1914).

Mansell, Thomas. *De Soto and Other Poems.* Hugh R. Hildreth Printing Co. (St. Louis, 1879).

Mariéjol, Jean Hippolyte. *The Spain of Ferdinand and Isabella,* ed. and trans. Benjamin Keen. Rutgers University Press (New Brunswick, N.J., 1961).

Markham, Clements Robert. *Cuzco: A Journey to the Ancient Capital of Peru: With an Account of the History, Language, Literature, and Antiquities of the Incas and Lima: A Visit to the Capital and Provinces of Modern Peru: With a Sketch of the Viceregal Government, History of the Republic and a Review of the Literature and Society of Peru.* Kraus Reprint Company (New York, 1973).

———. *Reports on the Discovery of Peru.* Hakluyt Society (London, 1872).

———. *The Travels of Pedro de Cieza de Leon,* A.D. *1532–50.* Hakluyt Society (London, 1864).

Marrero y Artiles, Levi. *Geografía de Cuba.* Ministerio de Educación y la Sociedad Colombista Panamericana (La Habana, 1951).

Marshall, Richard A. *Indians of Mississippi: An Archaeological Perspective.* Cobb Institute of Archaeology (Mississippi State, Miss.).

Marx, Robert. *Shipwrecks in the Americas.* Dover Publications, Inc. (New York, 1987).

Mason, J. Alden. *The Ancient Civilizations of Peru.* Penguin Books (New York, 1988).

Matute y Gavira, Justino. *Noticias relativas a la Historia de Sevilla que no consta en sus Anales.* Rasco (Seville, 1886).

Maynard, Theodore. *De Soto and the Conquistadors.* AMS Press (New York, 1969).

Meléndez, Carlos. *Hernández de Córdoba: Capitán de Conquista en Nicaragua.* Banco de América (Managua, 1976).

Méndez, Eustorgio. *Elementos de la Fauna Panameña.* Derechos Reservados (Panama, 1987).

Métraux, Alfred. *The History of the Incas,* trans. George Ordish. Pantheon (New York, 1969).

Milanich, Jerald T., and Charles H. Fairbanks. *Florida Archaeology.* Academic Press, Inc. (New York, 1980).

Milanich, Jerald T. and Charles Hudson. *Hernando de Soto and the Indians of Florida.* University Presses of Florida (Gainesville, 1993).

Milanich, Jerald T. and Susan Milbrath, ed. *First Encounters: Spanish Explorations in the Caribbean and the United States, 1492–1570.* University Presses of Florida (Gainesville, 1989).

Milanich, Jerald T. and Samuel Proctor. *Tacachale: Essays on the Indians of Florida and Southeastern Georgia during the Historic Period.* The University Presses of Florida (Gainesville, 1978).

Mingo, Milagros del Vas. *Las Capitulaciones de Indias en el Siglo XVI.* Ediciónes Cultura Hispanica, Instituto de Cooperación Iberoamericana (Madrid, 1986).

Mirsky, Jeannette. *The Westward Crossings: Balboa, Mackenzie, Lewis & Clark.* University of Chicago Press (Chicago, 1970).

Mollat, Michael: *The Poor in the Middle Ages: An Essay in Social History.* [1978] Trans. Arthur Goldhammer. Yale University Press (New Haven, 1986).

Monegal, Rodríguez, ed. *The Borzoi Anthology of Latin American Literature, vol. I: From the Time of Columbus to the Twentieth Century.* Alfred A. Knopf (New York, 1988).

Moore, Dwight Munson. *Trees of Arkansas.* Arkansas Forestry Commission (Little Rock, 1989).

Morales Padrón, Francisco. *Historia de Sevilla: La Ciudad del Quinientos.* Editorial Universidad de Sevilla (Seville, 1989).

Morgan, William N. *Prehistoric Architecture in the Eastern United States.* MIT Press (Cambridge, 1980).

Morison, Samuel Eliot. *Admiral of the Ocean Sea: A Life of Christopher Columbus.* Little, Brown, and Company (Boston, 1942).

————. *Christopher Columbus, Mariner.* New American Library (New York, 1983).

————. *The European Discovery of America: The Southern Voyages* A.D. *1492–1616.* Oxford University Press (New York, 1974).

————. *The Great Explorers: The European Discovery of America.* Oxford University Press (New York, 1978).

Morse, Dan F. and Phyllis A. Morse. *Archaeology of the Central Mississippi Valley.* Academic Press, Harcourt Brace Jovanovich (New York, 1983).

Navarrete, Martín Fernández de. *Colección de los viajes y descubrimientos,* 3 vols. Imprenta Real (Madrid, 1825–29).

Newson, Linda A. *Indian Survival in Colonial Nicaragua.* University of Oklahoma Press (Norman, 1987).

————. *The Cost of Conquest: Indian Decline in Honduras Under Spanish Rule.* Westview Press (Boulder, 1986).

Ordax, Salvador Andrés, et al. *Monumentos Artísticos de Extremadura.* Consejería de Educación y Cultura (Merida, 1988).

Pérez-Brignoli, Hector. *A Brief History of Central America* [1985], trans. Ricardo B. Sawrey and Susana Stettri de Sawrey. University of California Press (Berkeley and Los Angeles, 1989).

Pérez-Cabara, José Manuel: *El Capitán Hernando de Soto: Gobernador de la Isla Fernandina de Cuba, Adelantado de la Florida.* Academia de la Historia de Cuba (Havana, 1939).

Pereira, Octavio Méndez. *Núñez de Balboa: El Tesoro de Dabaibe,* 6th ed. Colección Austral (Madrid, 1972).

Peterson, Roger Tory. *A Field Guide to the Birds: A Completely New Guide to All the Birds of Eastern and Central America.* Houghton Mifflin Company (Boston, 1980).

————. *Peterson First Guide to Wildflowers of Northeastern and North-central North America.* Houghton Mifflin Company (Boston, 1986).

Petrides, George A. *A Field Guide to Eastern Trees: Eastern United States and Canada.* Houghton Mifflin Company (Boston, 1988).

Phillips, William D., Jr., *Slavery From Roman Times to the Early Transatlantic Trade.* University of Minnesota Press (Minneapolis, 1985).

Picón-Salas, Mariano. *A Cultural History of Spanish America: From Conquest to Independence,* trans. Irving A. Leonard. Greenwood Press (Westport, Conn., 1982).

Pike, Ruth. *Aristocrats and Traders: Sevillian Society in the Sixteenth Century.* Cornell University Press (Ithaca, N.Y., 1972).

————. *Enterprise and Adventure: The Genoese in Seville and the Opening of the New World.* Cornell University Press (Ithaca, N.Y. 1966).

Porras Barrenechea, Raúl. *Los Cronistas del Perú (1528–1650) y Otros Ensayos,* ed. Franklin Pease. Banco de Crédito del Peru (Lima, 1986).

————. *Las Relaciones Primitivas de la Conquista del Perú.* Cuadernos de Historia del Perú No. 2 (Paris, 1937).

————. *Cartas del Perú, Colección de documentos inéditos para la historia del Perú.* Edición de la Sociedad de Bibliófilos Peruanos. (Lima, 1959).

Powell, Mary Lucas. *Status and Health in Prehistory: A Case Study of the Moundville Chiefdom.* Smithsonian Institution Press (Washington, D.C., 1988).

Prescott, William H. *History of the Conquest of Mexico and History of the Conquest of Peru.* Modern Library, Random House (New York, 1936).

Priestley, Herbert Ingram. *Tristán de Luna Conquistador of the Old South: A Study of Spanish Imperial Strategy.* Porcupine Press (Philadelphia, 1980).

————. *The Luna Papers,* vol. 1. The Florida State Historical Society (Deland, 1920).

Quinn, David, ed. *New American World: A Documentary History of North America to 1612,* 5 vols. Arno Press (New York, 1979).

Reid, George K. *Pond Life: A Guide to Common Plants and Animals of North American Ponds and Lakes.* Golden Press (New York, 1967).

Rice, Eugene F., Jr. *The Foundations of Early Modern Europe, 1460–1559.* W. W. Norton & Company (New York, 1970).

Riley-Smith, Jonathan. *The Crusades: A Short History.* Yale University Press (New Haven, Conn., 1987).

Romoli, Kathleen. *Balboa of Darién: Discoverer of the Pacific.* Doubleday & Company (Garden City, N.Y., 1953).

Rosen, Harry M., ed. *The Golden Conquistadors.* Bobbs-Merrill (Indianapolis, 1960).

Roth, Cecil. *The Spanish Inquisition.* W. W. Norton & Company (New York, 1964).

Sale, Kirkpatrick. *The Conquest of Paradise: Christopher Columbus and the Columbian Legacy.* Alfred A. Knopf (New York, 1990).

Sánchez, Antonio Muñiz. *Todo Extremadura.* Editorial Escudo de Oro, S.A. (Barcelona, 1989).

Sauer, Carl Ortwin. *The Early Spanish Main.* University of California Press (Berkeley and Los Angeles, 1966).

————. *Sixteenth Century North America: The Land and the People as Seen by the Europeans.* University of California Press (Berkeley and Los Angeles, 1971).

Schell, Rolfe F. *De Soto Didn't Land at Tampa Bay.* Island Press (Fort Myers Beach, Fla., 1967).

Serrano y Sanz, Manuel. "Preliminaries del gobierno de Pedrarias Dávila en Castilla del Oro." *Origenes de la dominacón española en America.* Nueva biblioteca de áutores españoles, vol. 25 (Madrid, 1918).

Shaffer, Lynda Norene. *Native Americans Before 1492: The Moundbuilding Centers of the Eastern Woodlands.* M. E. Sharpe (New York, 1992).

Shipp, Barnard. *The History of Hernando De Soto and Florida; or, Record of the Events of Fifty-six Years, from 1512–1568.* Robert M. Lindsay (Philadelphia, 1881).

Smith, Hale G. *The European and the Indian.* Florida Anthropological Society Publications (Gainesville, 1956).

Smith, Marvin T. *Archaeology of Aboriginal Culture Change in the Interior South-*

east: Depopulation During the Early Historic Period. University Presses of Florida (Gainesville, 1987).

Smith, Marvin T. and Mary Elizabeth Good. *Early Sixteenth-Century Glass Beads in the Spanish Colonial Trade.* Cottonlandia Museum (Greenwood, Mo., 1982).

Spence, Lewis. *Spain.* Bracken Books (London, 1985).

Solar y Taboada, Antonio del, and José de Rújula y de Ochotorena. *El Adelantado Hernando de Soto.* Ediciones Arqueros (Badajoz, 1929).

Squier, Ephraim George. *Nicaragua; Its People, Scenery, Monuments, Resources, Condition, and Proposed Canal; with One Hundred Original Maps and Illustrations.* Harper & Brothers (New York, 1860).

———. *Travels in Central America,* 2 vols. D. Appleton & Co. (New York, 1853).

Stamm, James R. *A Short History of Spanish Literature.* New York University Press (New York, 1979).

Stannard, David E.: *American Holocaust: Columbus and the Conquest of the New World.* Oxford University Press (New York, 1992).

Stuart, Gene S. *America's Ancient Cities.* National Geographic Society (Washington, D.C., 1988).

Sutton, Ann and Myron Sutton. *Eastern Forests.* Alfred A. Knopf (New York, 1988).

Swanton, John R. *Final Report of the United States De Soto Expedition Commission.* Smithsonian Institution Press (Washington, D.C., 1985).

———. *The Indians of the Southeastern United States.* Smithsonian Institution Press (Washington, D.C., 1987).

Taviani, Paolo Emilio. *Columbus: The Great Adventure, His Life, His Times, and His Voyages* [1989], trans. Luciano F. Farina and Marc A. Beckwith. Orion Books (New York, 1991).

TePaske, John J., ed. *Research Guide to Andean History.* Duke University Press (Durham, N.C., 1981).

Thatcher, John Boyd. *The Continent of America: Its Discovery and Its Baptism.* Meridian Publishing Co. (Amsterdam, 1971).

Thomas, David Hurst, ed. *Columbian Consequences: Archaeological and Historical Perspectives on the Spanish Borderlands East,* vol. 2. Smithsonian Institution Press (Washington, D.C., 1990).

Tooker, Elisabeth. *Native American Spirituality of the Eastern Woodlands: Sacred Myths, Dreams, Vision, Speeches, Healing Formulas, Rituals and Ceremonials.* Paulist Press (New York, 1979).

Toops, Connie. *The Alligator: Monarch of the Marsh.* Florida National Parks & Monuments Association (Homestead, 1988).

True, David O. *The Narváez and de Soto Landings in Florida.* (Typescript on file at P. K. Yonge Library, University of Florida, Gainesville, 1954).

Tuchman, Barbara. *A Distant Mirror.* Alfred A. Knopf (New York, 1978).

Varner, J. G., and Jeannette Johnson Varner. *Dogs of Conquest.* University of Oklahoma Press (Norman, 1983).

Walthall, John A. *Moundville: An Introduction to the Archaeology of a Mississippian Chiefdom.* Alabama Museum of Natural History, The University of Alabama (Tuscaloosa, 1977).

————. *Prehistoric Indians of the Southeast: Archaeology of Alabama and the Middle South.* University of Alabama Press (1980).

Weatherford, Jack. *Savages and Civilization: Who Will Survive?* Crown (New York, 1994).

Weber, David J. *The Spanish Frontier in North America.* Yale University Press (London, 1992).

Weddle, Robert S. *Spanish Sea: The Gulf of Mexico in North American Discovery, 1500–1685.* Texas A&M University Press (College Station, 1985).

Wilford, John. *The Mapmakers: The Story of the Great Pioneers in Cartography from Antiquity to the Space Age.* Alfred A. Knopf (New York, 1981).

White, Jon Manchip. *Cortés and the Downfall of the Aztec Empire.* Carroll and Graf Publishers, Inc. (New York, 1989).

Wright, Irene Aloha. *The Early History of Cuba, 1492–1586.* Octagon Books (New York, 1970).

Wright, Ronald. *Stolen Continents: The Americas through Indian Eyes since 1492.* Houghton Mifflin Company (New York, 1992).

Yewell, John, Chris Dodge, and Jan DeSirey, ed. *Confronting Columbus: An Anthology.* McFarland and Company, Inc. (Jefferson, N.C., 1992).

Young, Gloria A., and Michael P. Hoffman, ed. *The Expedition of Hernando de Soto West of the Mississippi, 1541–1543: Proceedings of the De Soto Symposia 1988 and 1990.* University of Arkansas Press (Fayetteville, 1993).

Zadra, Dan. *We the People, De Soto: Explorer of the Southeast (1500–1542).* Creative Education (Mankato, Minn., 1988).

Articles, Manuscripts

Anderson, David G., David J. Hally, and James L. Rudolph. "The Mississippian Occupation of the Savannah River Valley." *Southeastern Archaeology,* 5 (1986), 38.

Atkinson, James R. "The De Soto Expedition through North Mississippi in 1540–41." *Mississippi Archaeology* 22 (1):61–73 (December, 1987).

Avellaneda, Ignacio. "Hernando de Soto and His Florida Fantasy." (Unpublished, 1991).

Baber, Adin. "Food Plants of the De Soto Expedition." *Tesquesta: The Journal of the Historical Association of Southern Florida* (1):34–40 (1942).

Blakely, Robert L. "A Coosa Massacre." *Archaeology,* p. 30 (June/July 1989).

Blakely, Robert L., and Bettina Detweiler-Blakely. "The Impact of European Diseases in the Sixteenth-Century Southeast: A Case Study." *Midcontinental Journal of Archaeology* 14:62–89 (1989).

Boyd, C. Clifford, Jr. and Gerald F. Schroedl. "In Search of Coosa." *American Antiquity* 52 (4):840–44.

Boyd, Mark F. "The Arrival of De Soto's Expedition in Florida." *Florida Historical Quarterly* 16:188–220 (1938).

Brain, Jeffrey P. "Artifacts of the Adelantado." *Conference on Historic Site Archaeology Papers* 8:129–38 (1975).

————. "Introduction: Update of de Soto Studies Since the United States de Soto Expedition Commission Report." *Final Report of the United States De Soto Expedition,* by John R. Swanton, pp. xi–lxxii. Smithsonian Institution Press (Washington D.C., 1985).

———. "The Archaeology of the Hernando de Soto Expedition." *Alabama and Its Borderlands from Prehistory to Statehood,* ed. Reid Badger and Lawrence A. Clayton, pp. 96–107. University Alabama Press (Tuscaloosa, Ala., 1985).

Brown, Ian W. "Historic Trade Bells." *Conference on Historic Archaeology Papers* 10:69–82 (1977).

———. "Bells." *Tunica Treasure,* by Jeffrey Brain, pp. 197–205. Papers of the Peabody Museum of Archaeology and Ethnology, vol. 71. Harvard University (Cambridge, 1979).

Bryson, Bill. "The New World of Spain." *National Geographic* 181 (4):3–33 (April 1992).

Bullen, Ripley P.: "De Soto's Ucita and Terra Ceia Site." *Florida Historical Quarterly* 30:317–23 (1952).

Choate, Charles A. "De Soto in Florida." *Gulf States Historical Magazine* 1:342–44 (1903).

Clayton, Lawrence A. "The Spanish Heritage of the Southeast." *Alabama Heritage,* pp. 3–11.

Curren, Caleb B., Jr. "In Search of de Soto's Trail: A Hypothesis of the Alabama Route." *Bulletin of Discovery,* no. 1. Alabama-Tombigbee Commission (Camden, Ala., 1986).

———. "The Route of the de Soto Army through Alabama." *De Soto Working Paper 3.* Alabama De Soto Commission, University of Alabama, State Museum of Natural History (1987).

Davis, T. Frederick. "History of Juan Ponce de Leon's Voyages to Florida." *Florida Historical Quarterly* 14:1–70 (1935).

DePratter, Chester B., and Christopher Amer. "Underwater Archaeology at the Mulberry Site and Adjacent Portions of the Wateree River." Report for South Carolina Institute of Archaeology and Anthropology (November 1988).

DePratter, Chester B., Charles Hudson, and Marvin T. Smith. "The Hernando de Soto Expedition: From Chiaha to Mabila." *Alabama and Its Borderlands from Prehistory to Statehood,* ed. Reid Badger and Lawrence A. Clayton, pp. 108–26. University of Alabama Press (Tuscaloosa, 1985).

———. "The Route of Juan Pardo's Explorations in the Interior Southeast, 1566–1568." *Florida Historical Quarterly* 62: 125–58 (1983).

DePratter, Chester B. "Cofitachequi: Ethnohistorical and Archaeological Evidence." *Studies in South Carolina Archaeology: Essays In Honor of Robert L. Stephenson,* ed. Albert C. Goodyear, III, and Glen T. Hanson, Anthropological Studies 9, Occasional Papers of the South Carolina Institute of Archaeology, The University of South Carolina, pp. 133–56 (Columbia, 1989)

———. "Disease, Death and Disruption: European and Native American Interaction in Colonial South Carolina." Paper presented at the First Encounters in South Carolina Symposium (Columbia, 1990).

Dobyns, Henry F. "Estimating Aboriginal American Population: An Appraisal of Techniques with a New Hemispheric Estimate." *Current Anthropology* 7:395–449 (October, 1966).

Dye, David. "Warfare in the 16th Century Southeast: The De Soto Expedition in the Interior." Paper presented at the 54th annual meeting of the Society for American Archaeology (Atlanta, 1989).

Ewen, Charles R. "Hernando de Soto: The Man and His Times." Paper presented to the XLIX annual meeting of the Arkansas Historical Association (Hot Springs, Ark., 1990).

———. "The De Soto–Apalachee Project: The Martin Site and Beyond." *The Florida Anthropologist* 42: 4: 361–68 (December, 1989).

———. "Apalachee Winter." *Archaeology,* pp. 37–39 (May/June, 1989).

———. "From Spaniard to Creole: The Archaeology of Hispanic American Cultural Formation at Puerto Real, Haiti." Ph.D. dissertation. University of Florida (1987).

———. "The Discovery of de Soto's First Winter Encampment in Florida." *De Soto Working Paper #7.* Alabama de Soto Commission, University of Alabama, State Museum of Natural History (Tuscaloosa, 1987).

Fairbanks, Charles H. "Early Spanish Colonial Beads." *Conference on Historic Site Archaeology* 2:3–21 (1968).

———. "Florida Coin Beads." *Florida Anthropologist* 21:102–5 (1968).

Furguson, Leland, ed. "Archaeological Investigations at the Mulberry Site," in *Notebook* 6 (1):57–122. The Institute of Archaeology and Anthropology, The University of South Carolina (Columbia, 1974).

Gannon, Michael. "Comments on Indian Rights, View in Spain." Conversation (Gainesville, Fla., 4/11/90).

Gibson, Jon L. "The DeSoto Expedition in the Mississippi Valley: Evaluation of the Geographical Potential of the Lower Quachita River Valley with Regard to the DeSoto-Moscos Expedition." *Louisiana Studies:* 203–12 (1968).

Giucciardini, Franscesco. "Relación de España." *Viajes por España,* ed. Antonio María Fabié, pp. 191–229. (Madrid, 1879), trans. Charles Gibson, *The Black Legend* (1971).

Goggin, John M. "Are there de Soto Relics in Florida?" *Florida Historical Quarterly* 32:151–62 (1954).

———. "Spanish Majolica in the New World." *Yale University Publications in Anthropology* 72 (New Haven, 1968).

———. "The Spanish Olive Jar: An Introductory Story." *Yale University Publications in Anthropology* 62 (New Haven, 1960).

Hally, David J., Charles Hudson, Chester B. DePratter, and Marvin T. Smith. "The Protohistoric Period Along the Savannah River." Paper presented at the annual meeting of the Southeastern Archaeology Conference, November 7, 1985 (Birmingham, Ala.).

Hann, John H., "De Soto, Dobyns and Demography in Western Timucua." *Florida Anthropologist* 43 (1): 3–12 (March 1990).

Harrisse, Henry. "Ponce de Leon—First Voyage, Bimini and Florida." *Discovery of North America,* pp. 142–53 and 156–62. (London, 1892).

Hemming, John "Pizarro, Conqueror of the Inca." *National Geographic* 181 (2):90–121 (February, 1992).

Henige, David. "The Context, Content, and Credibility of *La Florida del Inca.*" *The Americas* 43:1–24 (1986).

Hoffman, Paul E. "The Chicora Legend and Franco-Spanish Rivalry." *Florida Historical Quarterly* 62:419–38 (1984).

Hudson, Charles. "An Unknown South: Spanish Explorers and Southeastern Chiefdoms." *Visions and Revisions, Ethnohistoric on Southern Cultures,* ed. George Sabo III and William M. Schneider, pp. 6–24. Southern Anthropological Society Proceedings 20. University of Georgia Press (Athens, 1987).

———. "A Spanish-Coosa Alliance in Sixteenth-Century North Georgia." *The Georgia Historical Quarterly.* LXXII: 4: 599–626 (Winter, 1988).

———. "The Uses of Evidence in Reconstructing the Route of the Hernado de Soto Expedition." *De Soto Working Paper #1.* Alabama De Soto Commission. University of Alabama, State Museum of Natural History (Tuscaloosa, 1987).

———. "Critique of Caleb Curren's De Soto Route." Submitted to the Alabama De Soto Commission. (Tuscaloosa, 1988).

———. "De Soto in Alabama." *De Soto Working Paper #10.* Alabama De Soto Commission. University of Alabama, State Museum of Natural History (Tuscaloosa, 1989).

———. "De Soto in Arkansas: A Brief Synopsis." Field Notes 205 (July/August, 1988).

———. "Juan Pardo's Excursion Beyond Chiaha." *Tennessee Anthropology* 12 (1):76–87 (Spring, 1987).

Hudson, Charles, Chester B. DePratter, and Marvin T. Smith. "The Hernando de Soto Expedition From Apalachee to Chiaha." *Southeastern Archaeology* 3:65–77 (1984).

Hudson, Charles, Marvin T. Smith, David Hally, Richard Polhemus, and Chester DePratter. "Coosa: A Chiefdom in the Sixteenth Century Southeastern United States." *American Antiquity* 50:723–37 (1985).

———. "Reply to Boyd and Schroedl." *American Antiquity* 52 (4):845–56 (1987).

Jones, Calvin. "Southern Cult Manifestations at the Lake Jackson Site, Leon County, Florida: Salvage Excavation of Mound 3," *Midcontinental Journal of Archaeology,* 7 (1):3–43 (1982).

Jones, B. Calvin: "The Dreamer and the de Soto Site." *The Florida Anthropologist* 41 (3): 402–404 (September, 1988).

Milanich, Jerald T. "Hernando de Soto and the Expedition in Florida." Miscellaneous Project Report Series 32. Department of Anthropology, Florida Museum of Natural History (Gainesville, 1988).

———. "Where Did de Soto Land: Identifying Bahia Hondo." *The Florida Anthropologist* 42 (4):295–302 (December, 1989).

———. "Exhibit Includes Shameful Side of Colonization." *Gainesville Sun,* 9 December 1989.

Milanich, Jerald T. and Jeffrey M. Mitchem. "Uncovering de Soto's Route: Bones, Beads, and Armor Point the Way." *Florida State News* 4:3 and 7 (1986).

Milner, George R. "Epidemic Disease in the Postcontact Southeast: An Appraisal." *Midcontinental Journal of Anthropology* 5:39–56 (1980).

Mitchell, Mary L. and B. Calvin Jones. "Hernando de Soto En La Florida." *Revista de Arqueología* pp. 36–51 (November, 1988).

Mitchem, Jeffrey M. and Dale L. Hutchinson. "Interim Report of Archaeological Research at the Tathum Mound, Citrus County, Florida II and III." Miscellaneous Project Reports no. 28 and no. 30. Department of Anthropology, Florida Museum of Natural History (Gainesville, 1988).

Mitchem, Jeffrey M. and Jonathan M. Leader. "Early 16th Century Beads from the Tatham Mound, Citrus County, Florida: Data and Interpretations." *The Florida Anthropologist* 41: 42–60. (1988).

Mitchem, Jeffrey M. and Bonnie G. McEwan. "New Data on Early Bells from Florida." *Southeast Archaeology* 7:39–49 (1988).

Mitchem, Jeffrey M., Brent R. Weisman, et. al. "Preliminary Report on Excavations at the Tatham Mound, Citrus County, Florida: Season I." Miscellaneous Project Report no. 23. Department of Anthropology, Florida Museum of Natural History (Gainesville, 1985).

Moore, Clarence B. "Certain Antiquities of the Florida West-Coast." *Journal of the Academy of Natural Sciences of Philadelphia* (1900), 11 (3):350–94.

Judge, Joseph. "Exploring Our Forgotten Century." *National Geographic* 173 (3):330–63 (March, 1988).

Kelly, Arthur R. "Explorations at Bell Field Mound and Village: Seasons 1965, 1966, 1967, 1968." MS on file, Department of Anthropology, University of Georgia (Athens, 1970).

Kelly, Arthur R., Frank T. Schnell, Donald F. Smith, and Ann L. Schlosser. "Explorations in Sixtoe Field, Carters Dam, Murray County, Georgia." MS on file, Department of Anthropology, University of Georgia (Athens, 1965).

Knight, Vernon James, Jr. "A Summary of Alabama's de Soto Mapping and Project Bibliography." *De Soto Working Paper #9.* Alabama de Soto Commission. University of Alabama, State Museum of Natural History (Tuscaloosa, 1988).

Lange, Frederick W. "Letter from Costa Rica." *Archaeology,* p. 60 (November/December, 1989).

Lanford, George. "A New Look at de Soto's Route through Alabama." *Journal of Alabama Archaeology* 23:11–36 (1977).

Lefevre, Edwin. "The Conquest of Florida." *Museum* 27:130–32 (1836).

Lewis, Theodore H. "The Chronicle of De Soto's Expedition." *Publications of the Mississippi Historical Society* 7:379–97 (1903).

Little, Keith and Caleb B. Curren, Jr. "Site 1Ce308: A Protohistoric Site on the Upper Coosa River, Alabama." *Journal of Alabama Archaeology* 27:117–24 (1981).

Ludeña, Hugo. "Investigación en España Sobre la Expedición de Hernando de Soto á la Florida." *The Soto Trail Project.* Unpublished manuscript on file at P. K. Yonge Library, University of Florida, (Gainesville, 1987).

MacWilliams, Tennant S. "The DeSoto Expedition in the Mississippi Valley II: Armada on the Mississippi." *Louisiana Studies:* 213–27 (1968).

Mashburn, Rick. "A Modern Armor Maker Dresses Men in Knight's Clothing." *Smithsonian Magazine* 20 (9):117–25 (1989).

Moorehead, Warren K. "Exploration of the Etowah Site in Georgia." In *Etowah Papers,* ed. Warren K. Moorehead, pp. 68–105. Yale University Press (New Haven, 1932).

Morse, Dan F. "Scientific Instruments and Early Exploration in the United States." *Florida Anthropologist* 43 (1): 45–47 (March, 1990).

Pereira Iglesias, Jose Luis. "La realidad socioeconómica de Extremadura en la etapa del Descubrimiento." *Alcántara* 17:93–125 (May–August, 1989).

———. "Los Problemas del abastecimiento del pan en Extremadura . . . La Ciudad de Trujillo (1550–1610)." *Studia Historica* 5:159–75 (1987).

———. "Para en estudio las mentalidades religiosas en America: catecismo, sermonanios y crónicas." Paper, X Simposio Internacional de Teología, University of Navarra (March, 1989).

Rackleff, Robert B. "On De Soto's Trail." *Historic Preservation* 41:50–53 (November/December, 1989).

Romero, Carlos Alberto, ed. "Fundación de la Ciudad Incaica." *Revista Histórica Organo del Instituto Historico del Perú,* pp. 98–119 (Lima, 1943).

Scarry, John: "The Apalachee Chiefdom: A Mississippian Society on the Fringe of the Mississippian World." Unpublished paper provided by the author.

Swanton, John R.: "De Soto's First Headquarters in Florida." *The Florida Historical Quarterly* 30 (4): 311–316 (April, 1952).

Temple, Ella Dunbar: "La descencia de Huayna Cápac." *Revista Histórica Organo del Instituto Historico del Perú,* pp. 147–65 (Lima, 1937).

Ward, Rufus. "Reconstructing the Topography of Protohistoric Aboriginal Sites: An Example from Clay County, Mississippi." *Mississippi Archaeology* 22 (2):71–75 (December, 1987).

Weinstien, Richard A.: "Some New Thoughts on the de Soto Expedition through Western Mississippi." *Mississippi Archaeology* 20 (2): 2–24.

Williams, Lindsey. "A Charlotte Harbor Perspective on de Soto's Landing Site." *The Florida Anthropologist* 42 (4):280–94 (December, 1989).

Wolfe, Elizabeth F. "Early Encomienda in Nicaragua." Unpublished Paper presented to Professor B. Nietschmann, University of California, Berkeley (1981).

Worth, John E. "Mississippian Occupation on the Middle Flint River." Masters Thesis, University of Georgia (1988).

INDEX

Abancay River (Peru), 174
Achuse (Indian town), 311, 313
Acla (Panama), 48, 445n., 446n.
Acuera (Timucuan town), 266
Adair, James, 276, 395, 396
Agile (Apalachee village), 295
Aguacaleyquen (Timucuan chief), 284–85, 286, 499n.
Aguero, Diego de, 452n.
Aguilar, Francisco de, 321, 506n.
Alafia River (Florida), 268
Alaminos (Spanish metallurgist), 347, 348
Albítez, Diego, 70, 70n., 89, 446n., 449n.
Alcaldes, 84n.
Alexander VI (pope), 440n.
Alfonso IV (king of León), 4
Aliaga, Geronimo de, 462n.
Almagro, Diego de, 153, 167, 178
    and Atahualpa's execution, 160, 161
    chase after Soto, 174–75
    Chilean concession of, 195–96
    and Quizquiz, 187
    and reinforcements for Pizarro, 156–57
Alonso, Juan, 469n.
Altamaha (Indian kingdom), 327, 507n.
Alvarado, Pedro de, 71, 78, 79, 80–81
    campaign for Quito, 195
    and *La Florida*, 238
    and Mixtón War, 485n.
    and Soto, 451n.
Amaru Cancha (Cuzco), 182–83, 470n.
Amazons (legendary people), 208
Anasazi Indians, 217
Añasco, Juan de, 206, 219, 222, 333, 493n.
    capture of Timucuans, 280
    discovery of Aute, 306–7
    discovery of Himahi, 334
    and Havana, 231, 237
    march to Ocita, 307–9, 310
    reconnoiter of Florida's coast, 239–40, 245, 247, 458n., 485–86n.
    scouting of Mississippi River, 419–20
Andagoya, Pascual de, 36, 55–56, 73–74
    on Atahualpa's execution, 161–62
    in Córdoba, 86
    on Vasco Núñez, 51
Andahuaylas River (Peru), 174–75
Anhaica (Apalachee capital), 296–313
    Indian deaths at, 317
    location of, 303–4
    Spanish deaths at, 311
Antillia Empire (legend), 208
Anunciación, Domingo de la, 360, 367–68
Apafalaya, 394–96
Apalachee Bay (Florida), 216, 307
Apalachee Indians, 278–79, 296–306, 317–18
    atrocities of, 294
    culture of, 297–98
    and Narváez, 216, 278–79, 294
    population, 502n.
    Soto's attempts to pacify, 311
    weaponry, 304–5
Appalachian Mountains, 346–47
Apurímac River (Peru), 175
Aquixo (Indian kingdom), 404, 406
Arawak Indians, 81, 232–33, 235
Arias Dávila, Diego, 73
Arias de Avila, Pedro (Pedrarias Dávila), 15, 22, 96, 111, 454n.
    appointment as governor, 24
    and Balboa, 33–34, 45–47, 52–53
    and Castañeda, 103–6, 113–14
    and Córdoba, 89
    death of, 114–15

departure from Nicaragua, 92
and González Dávila, 68–69
governing style, 27
as governor of Nicaragua, 94
move to Panama City, 54–56
in Natá, 90
Nicaraguan invasion, 71–72
policies of, 47
replacement for, 51–52, 90
and Santa María, 32–34, 35, 44
treatment of own people, 45
Arias, Gomez, 309
Arkansas River valley, 413
Armor, 39–40
Arquebus muskets, 39
Arrows, 258–59
Asiento Viejo (Panama), 57–58
Atahachi Indians, 351, 366, 371, 388
    army, 375
    capital, 374
    warrior class, 372
Atahualpa (Incan emperor), 76, 130, 139, 164, 375
    assassination of royal family members, 467n.
    capture of, 145–49
    and Chalcuchima, 155–56
    execution of, 159–62
    and Incan civil war, 131, 133–34
    ransom offer by, 152–53, 156–59
    Soto's meeting with, 142–44
    Spanish opinion of, 153–54
    surrender of, 150
Atrato River, 29, 37–41
Aucaypata (Cuzco), 181–82
Aucilla River (Florida), 296, 300–1
Audiencia, 84, 89
Aute (Apalachee village), 307, 504n.
Autiamque (Indian town), 417, 523n.
Avellaneda, Ignacio, 431n., 439n.
Ayala, Alonso de, 199, 219, 473n.
    mission back to Peru, 233–34
    in Peru, 193–94
    Soto's legacy to, 495n.
Ayllón, Lucas Vázquez de, 209, 326, 339, 511nn.
Ayora, Juan de, 36, 37
Azetuno, Antonio, 231, 237
Aztec Indians, 67, 76, 80, 110

Badajoz, Gonzalo de, 57, 89, 91–92
Bahía de Espíritu Santo, 240, 245, 247, 487n.
Bahía de Juan Ponce de León, 239, 487n.
Bahía Honda, 239, 487–88n.
Balboa, Vasco Núñez de, 8, 20–21, 24, 30, 442–43n.
    arrest, 52
    boat-building project, 49–50
    colonization policies, 47
    cruelty, 442–43n.
    and Dabaibe legend, 444n.
    description of, 31
    execution of, 52–53
    and Pedrarias, 45–47, 52
    policy toward Indians, 30, 31–32
    South Sea expedition, 48–51
    talent, 31–32
Bandera, Juan de la, 347
Barbacoas, xxxvii, 43n.
Bartram, William, xxxv
Bastidas, Rodrigo de, 29–30
Battle line, 267
Battle of Mabila. *See* Mabila, Battle of
Bayamo (Cuba), 236
Beads, 257, 258

563